Thresholds, Walls, and Bridges

THE WEST SERIES

SERIES EDITOR: George Colpitts

ISSN 1922-6519 (Print) ISSN 1925-587X (Online)

This series focuses on creative nonfiction that explores our sense of place in the West – how we define ourselves as Westerners and what impact we have on the world around us. Essays, biographies, memoirs, and insights into Western Canadian life and experience are highlighted.

No. 1 *Looking Back: Canadian Women's Prairie Memoirs and Intersections of Culture, History, and Identity*
S. Leigh Matthews

No. 2 *Catch the Gleam: Mount Royal, From College to University, 1910–2009*
Donald N. Baker

No. 3 *Always an Adventure: An Autobiography*
Hugh A. Dempsey

No. 4 *Promoters, Planters, and Pioneers: The Course and Context of Belgian Settlement in Western Canada*
Cornelius J. Jaenen

No. 5 *Happyland: A History of the "Dirty Thirties" in Saskatchewan, 1914–1937*
Curtis R. McManus

No. 6 *My Name Is Lola*
Lola Rozsa, as told to and written by Susie Sparks

No. 7 *The Cowboy Legend: Owen Wister's Virginian and the Canadian-American Frontier*
John Jennings

No. 8 *Sharon Pollock: First Woman of Canadian Theatre*
Edited by Donna Coates

No. 9 *Finding Directions West: Readings That Locate and Dislocate Western Canada's Past*
Edited by George Colpitts and Heather Devine

No. 10 *Writing Alberta: Building on a Literary Identity*
Edited by George Melnyk and Donna Coates

No. 11 *Ranching Women in Southern Alberta*
Rachel Herbert

No. 12 *Rocking P Ranch and the Second Cattle Frontier in Western Canada*
Clay Chattaway and Warren Elofson

No. 13 *The American Western in Canadian Literature*
Joel Deshaye

No. 14 *Thresholds, Walls, and Bridges: Journeys Through the Borderlands of History*
Elizabeth Jameson

Thresholds, Walls, and Bridges

Journeys Through the Borderlands of History

ELIZABETH JAMESON

The West Series
ISSN 1922-6519 (Print) ISSN 1925-587X (Online)

© 2025 Elizabeth Jameson

University of Calgary Press
2500 University Drive NW
Calgary, Alberta
Canada T2N 1N4
press.ucalgary.ca

All rights reserved.

This book is available in an Open Access digital format published under a CC-BY-NCND 4.0 Creative Commons license. The publisher should be contacted for any commercial use which falls outside the terms of that license.

Library and Archives Canada Cataloguing in Publication

Title: Thresholds, walls, and bridges : journeys through the borderlands of history / Elizabeth Jameson.
Names: Jameson, Elizabeth, author
Series: West series (Calgary, Alta.) ; 14.
Description: Series statement: West series, ISSN 1922-6519 (print), 1925-587X (ebook) ; no. 14 | Includes bibliographical references and index.
Identifiers: Canadiana (print) 20250244497 | Canadiana (ebook) 20250244535 | ISBN 9781773856612 (hardcover) | ISBN 9781773856629 (softcover) | ISBN 9781773856650 (EPUB) | ISBN 9781773856636 (Open Access PDF) | ISBN 9781773856643 (PDF)
Subjects: LCSH: West (U.S.)—History.
Classification: LCC F591 .J36 2025 | DDC 978—dc23

The University of Calgary Press acknowledges the support of the Government of Alberta through the Alberta Media Fund for our publications. We acknowledge the financial support of the Government of Canada. We acknowledge the financial support of the Canada Council for the Arts for our publishing program.

  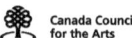 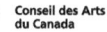 

The manufacturer's authorized representative in the EU for product safety is Mare Nostrum Group B.V., Mauritskade 21D, 1091 GC Amsterdam, The Netherlands. Email: gpsr@mare-nostrum.co.uk

Copyediting by Francine Michaud
Cover photo: Colourbox 15300766
Cover design, page design, and typesetting by Melina Cusano

For Stanley, Spencer, Barbara, and Daniel

And for All the Students—It's Been a Privilege

Contents

List of Illustrations	ix
Acknowledgements	xi
Introduction	1

Thresholds: 2000–2002 — 11

1. Where Have All the Young Men Gone? The Social Legacy of the California Gold Rush — 23
2. Guns to Butter: Reconceiving the American West — 45
3. The Heart of Gold: Working-Class Voices from the Cripple Creek Gold Mining District — 67

Borders: Walls and Bridges: 2003–2007 — 89

4. Telling Differences: The 49th Parallel, the West, and the Histories of Two Nations (with Jeremy Mouat) — 97
5. Dancing on the Rim, Tiptoeing Through the Minefields: Challenges and Promises of the Borderlands — 121
6. God, Santa, and the American Way: The U.S. Alaska Reindeer Project — 145

Bridging: 2008–2011 — 171

7. Race in America: Reflections on the 40th Anniversary of the Kerner Commission Report — 181
8. Remembering Ludlow: The 1913–1914 Coal Strike and the Politics of Public Memory — 205
9. Women Who Crossed a Line: Canadian Single Women Homesteaders in the U.S. West — 229

Bridges: Blocked, Crossed, and Under Construction: 2012–2014   249

10. Are We There Yet? Personal and Historical Reflections on Women in Higher Education   261
11. Seneca Falls, Selma, and Stonewall: Symbolism and Social Change   287
12. "Use My Broken Heart": Making Change Out of Tragedy   311

Approaching the Next Threshold: 2015–2017   335

13. Halfway Across That Line: Gender at the Threshold of History in the North American Wests   343
14. Torches Passed and Present   371

Coda   389
Epilogue: The Times They Are a-Changin'   391
Index   419

List of Illustrations

Figure 2.1	Daniel Boone Escorting Settlers through the Cumberland Gap	47
Figure 2.2	Buffalo Bird Woman in Her Garden	52
Figure 6.1	Map, Northwest Alaska with Reindeer Project Sites	147
Figure 8.1	Ludlow Monument	211
Figure 9.1	Emma Beske and Her Homestead Shack	231
Figure 9.2	Map, Devils Lake Land Office Service Area	233
Figure 9.3	Marital Status at time of Proof	240
Figure 13.1	Ambjør Hagen and Her Homestead Sod Shack	349

Acknowledgments

I first want to thank the donors who established the Imperial Oil-Lincoln McKay Chair in American Studies at the University of Calgary. Their generosity provided the resources to support my research, enabled me to share it, and allowed me to employ gifted graduate research assistants whose work contributed to these essays and other publications. Many thanks to Sean Marchetto, Laurel Halladay, Jamie Warren, Christine Bye, Tim Cole, Amy McKinney, Gretchen Albers, Andrew Varsanyi, Victoria Buckholz, Erin Millions, Stuart White, Celeste Sharp, Kayla Grabia, and Shawn Brackett for all your help. Many of these young colleagues aided with more than one lecture. Shawn Brackett, Andrew Varsanyi, and Amy McKinney continued to help as I prepared this book for publication. Laurel Halladay prepared the Index. It's been a joy to work with all of them.

Deans Stephen Randall, Kevin Quillan, and Richard Sigurdson were gracious in their support of the Chair's Lectures and their post-lecture hospitality. I am grateful for their support. Many thanks as well to the colleagues who provided advice and support over the years. Jeremy Mouat, Sarah Carter, Douglas Francis, Donald Smith, Heather Devine, Michel Hogue, Catherine Cavenaugh, and Sheila McManus were all enormously supportive and generous with their own research as I explored Canadian history. Jewel Spangler, Frank Towers, and Michael Tavel Clarke, fellow Americans and Americanists at the University of Calgary, shared the experience of border crossing and teaching Canadian students about the United States. Jeanne Perrault provided useful comments on an early draft of Chapter Five. Adrienne Kertzer helped me track down documents for Chapter Ten. Dr. Suzzanne Kelley, Editor in Chief of the North Dakota State University Press, provided timely assistance as this book neared publication. Heartfelt thanks to University of Calgary staff members Deborah Isaac, Karen McDermid, Marjorie McLean, Marion McSheffrey, Brenda Oslawsky, Lori Sommers, and Sarah Stevenson who made life in the History Department pleasant and who provided essential staff support for the Chair's Lectures. Thanks as well to Ginger Rodgers and Shauna Selezinka who provided staff support for the Torches Passed and Present conference.

The audiences who attended the Chair's Lectures energized and engaged me with their comments, insights, and stimulating questions. I am grateful to all the colleagues, students and members of the public who attended over the years. I was perpetually surprised by their interest and support, and never more so than on April 10, 2008, when I was scheduled to give my lecture on Race in America. I awoke to a heavy spring snowstorm and slogged to campus through streets clogged with wet snow, certain that I would find almost no one at the lecture when I got there. I learned a lot about Canadian endurance that day. I found a packed room, including my friends Max Foran and Gordon Fairchild who had driven over 50 kilometers from Priddis. I remain grateful and touched by the loyalists who showed up year after year, including Barbara Grant, Temple B'nai Tikvah friends Susan Podlog and Shauna Switzer, and two friends we lost too soon, Jack Switzer and Heather Foran. Don Smith, Nancy Townshend, Gordon Fairchild, and Max Foran also made the trek from Calgary to Corvallis, Oregon for the 2005 conference of the Pacific Coast Branch-American Historical Association, where my 2006 lecture originated as my presidential address. Then they came to hear it again in Calgary. My colleague George Colpitts offered similar support at my presidential address at the 2015 Western History Association conference in Portland, Oregon. I am grateful to everyone who showed up over the years.

My research was supported, as always, by professional archivists. I am indebted to the staffs of the Bancroft Library at the University of California, Berkeley; the California State Historical Society, San Francisco; the Lake Region Heritage Center, Devils Lake, ND; the Minnesota Historical Society; Library and Archives Canada; and the National Archives and Records Administration, Washington, D.C. I owe an enduring debt to the late John Brennan, Director of the Western History Collections at the University of Colorado, Boulder, for trusting me as an undergraduate intern with the archives of the Western Federation of Miners/International Union of Mine, Mill and Smelter Workers. That job launched my research on the Cripple Creek District and western mining labor. When I asked Dr. Brennan why he'd entrusted me with a major collection, he smiled quietly and replied, "That's how we all learn." I'm grateful for his trust and mentorship, and to the WHC staff who made working in their archives a pleasure over the years.

The Chair's Lecture for Chapter One was originally prepared for "The California Gold Rush as a World Event," a lecture series sponsored by the University of California, Sacramento to commemorate the

Sesquicentennial of the California Gold Rush. After my 2000 Chair's Lecture, it was published in Kenneth N. Owens, ed., *Riches for All: The California Gold Rush and the World* (Lincoln: University of Nebraska Press, 2002), copyright 2002 by the Board of Regents of the University of Nebraska, and appears here by permission of the University of Nebraska Press. I am grateful to the *Pacific Historical Review* for granting authors permission to reprint our own work. In this case I thank them for the option to print an earlier version of Elizabeth Jameson and Jeremy Mouat, "Telling Differences: The Forty-Ninth Parallel and Historiographies of the West and Nation," *Pacific Historical Review* 75:2 (May 2006) in Chapter Four and Elizabeth Jameson, "Dancing on the Rim, Tiptoeing through the Minefields: Challenges and Promises of the Borderlands," *Pacific Historical Review* 75:1 (February 2006) in Chapter Five. Thanks as well to Susan Wladaver Morgan, David A. Johnson, and Carl Abbott for their editorial support (and nudges). And special thanks to Jeremy Mouat for allowing me to publish our co-authored work. Chapter Thirteen is a shortened version of my presidential address for the Western History Association conference in 2015. The full version was published as "Halfway Across That Line: Gender at the Threshold of History in the North American West," *Western Historical Quarterly* 47:1 (Spring 2016). I am grateful to Oxford University Press, publisher of the *Quarterly*, which does not require authors to obtain permission to reprint our work. I am also enormously grateful to *WHQ* editor Anne Hyde and former editor David Rich Lewis for all their support, editorial and beyond.

Thanks to the Minnesota Historical Society for permission to reprint "Hidatsa Indian woman hoeing squash with a bone hoe," and to Colin Dunn for his assistance (even on a Saturday morning). Thanks to the Institute for Regional Studies at North Dakota State University, Fargo for permission to reproduce "Emma Beske outside her homestead shack near Streeter, N.D." and "Homestead sod shack of Ambjør Hagen, Grandfield Township, Eddy County, N.D.," and huge thanks to John Hallberg for all his help with those images.

There is one acknowledgment I would like to make but can't. I quoted portions of Carl Sandburg's poem, "For You," in Chapter Fourteen and made every effort to locate the copyright holder for the poem, without success. If I have the opportunity, I will happily acknowledge the rights holder in any future editions of this book.

The University of Calgary Press was the ideal publisher for *Thresholds, Walls, and Bridges*. I am grateful for the early encouragement and enduring patience of Press Director Brian Scrivener. Thanks, too, to Editorial Coordinator and organizational wonder Helen Hajnoczky; Marketing Specialist Alison Cobra, who, among much else, settled the debate about a subtitle; and Graphic Designer and cover designer *extraordinaire* Melina Cusano, for book design, help with the illustrations, and for a cover I love. I couldn't have asked for better professional support.

Much of the transformation of the lectures into the manuscript I submitted to the Press occurred during the COVID-19 pandemic, which created difficulties finding peer reviewers. I am especially grateful to the two thoughtful reviewers for the generous comments they provided while navigating the personal and professional stresses of the pandemic. This volume is better for their insights. Francine Michaud was a delightful colleague in the history department before we both retired and a joy to work with as a copy editor. I am especially grateful for the support of George Colpitts, editor of The West series at the University of Calgary Press, for his longstanding support of my work and of this project.

When he was nine years old, my son Daniel announced in early May, "I am not going to try to talk to you until your finals are over and your grades are in." I was astonished that he was already so aware of the academic calendar, and sad that he had already felt its high-stress periods. I am grateful for his support, understanding, and patience through it all, including joining me in our move to Canada. My family remains my most important anchor and support. Thanks, and love to Alice Caddow, Philip Jameson, Marjorie Cypress, Ariel Caddow, Nicole Caddow, Iran Ramirez, Peter Steward, and Matthew Vinet.

Most of all, I am grateful for Daniel, Barbara, Stanley, and Spencer Lenfest-Jameson. You light my world. This is for you.

Introduction

On a hot Albuquerque summer morning, I hugged my brother and sister-in-law goodbye, piled into my overloaded Toyota with my son Daniel and our cats, Sweetie Pie and Simon, and drove north away from home. It was June 26, 1999. After ten years at the University of New Mexico in the beautiful desert Southwest, I was headed to a new job at the University of Calgary as the Imperial Oil-Lincoln McKay Chair in American Studies. The essays in this book were originally presented as the public Chair's Lectures I offered annually, except when I was on leave. They chart an intellectual, professional, and personal journey that began that hot June day in New Mexico.

Our drive north followed the east slope of the Rocky Mountains, where I have spent most of my adult life and where much of my research as a historian has centered. As I drove through the high plains of Wyoming and Montana the landscape appeared seamless, the changes subtle and gradual. I mused about geography and ecosystems, about barriers like the Shield, the Mississippi River, and the mountain ranges that slice the continent vertically while our borders cut it horizontally into three nations, constructed through political borders and nation-building policies; constructed, too, in popular and historical imaginations.

My musings got interrupted for several hours at the Coutts, Alberta, border station while I dealt with Customs and Immigration Canada—getting the car inspected; producing the legal papers to bring Daniel across the border; showing my work visa, his student visa, and the documents proving I had a job. Daniel dutifully lugged my framed doctoral diploma to demonstrate that I was qualified for my new position. The Immigration Officer was less interested in the certificate I had brought from the U.S. Department of Agriculture, certifying that I had properly cleaned the iris rhizomes in the trunk that I had hopefully dug up and brought from my Albuquerque garden. Nor was he interested in the international vaccination papers I had for the cats. "I can tell you care about your animals," he said. "I don't need to see them."

I figured he was tired. Hauling two reluctant felines in their carriers in the back seat for three days didn't strike *me* as exemplary pet care. The previous night, in fact, Simon had clawed a hole in the bottom of the box springs at our motel in Great Falls and had to be pried forcibly from his hiding place that morning.

We were finally cleared to cross the border, cats, rhizomes, and all, to continue through a landscape a lot like the one we had been travelling. But now the road signs flashed the speed limit and the distance to Calgary in kilometres. The convenience store in Fort Macleod sold Smarties, not M&Ms, and measured my gas in litres, not gallons.

Our brief sojourn in Coutts with Customs and Immigration Canada brought us to the threshold of a new nation, a new community, a new university and junior high—to the threshold of so much that had only been hinted in the highway signs and gas pump. Some of what I had brought with me proved useful; some simply didn't work anymore. The irises didn't make it through their first Alberta winter. Truly traumatized by his confinement in the despised cat carrier, Simon spent a lot of the first six weeks in our new house in the laundry room ceiling, coming out at night to eat and use his litter box, before he slowly re-emerged.

At times I shared his urge to withdraw while I acclimated. I felt uprooted, partly because I didn't know the histories of Calgary, Alberta, or Canada. I hastily read Canadian history texts, though I remained much more secure with the American history I had learned since elementary school.

Some of what I had learned in three decades of teaching remained useful. My University of Calgary students raised new challenges about what it meant to teach American history to Canadians. As I came to view history from north of the 49th Parallel I began to probe national borders, their borderlands, and comparative histories.

Geography and ecology aside, I had not expected Canada to be like the United States. I had gotten a useful caution from my Canadian colleague Jeremy Mouat, who taught me this joke:

Question: What is the difference between a Canadian and an American?

Answer: The Canadian knows there is a difference.

I was, if anything, defensively determined to prove that I knew I was a guest in another country. It was 1999. I am a native Texan. Alberta is oil country, and I grew up across Galveston Bay from the Texas City oil refineries. George W. Bush was clearly gearing up for a presidential campaign.

I did not know how my new neighbors viewed U.S. politics or U.S. investments in Alberta oil, and I did not want my new colleagues to think all Texans are alike. I was overly concerned to prove I was not an ugly American and underprepared to interpret what had and had not crossed our boundaries.

I had been asked at my job interview how I felt about moving across a border. I answered truthfully, but too glibly, "I've been crossing them all my life." Growing up in the *other* U.S. Borderland, crossing the Rio Grande for family vacations in Mexico, living for a decade in New Mexico, I was, like most Americans, more preoccupied with the Mexican border than with Canada, even though my father had lived in Montreal for a few years as a young boy and his father, the grandfather I never knew, was buried there.

As a historian, I had first focused on the Canadian border through the international journeys of miners and their families. I had followed people and social movements across international boundaries but had not focused centrally on the international politics that propelled those journeys or that selectively opened and closed national borders. The historical and human significance of border-crossing had not yet compelled my attention, even though, like all North Americans of non-Indigenous descent, my ancestors had crossed international borders to bring my family to the United States, and even though I grew up with a grandmother who emigrated from London in 1913. Our move to Canada brought new reflections on the process of border-crossing, of transplanting oneself, of learning and adapting to a new culture.

My transnational journey was easier than most. I moved from an English-speaking nation to an Anglophone province. I was an employed professional whose skills were welcomed. To my gratified surprise, the application form for my work visa awarded historians the top possible points for occupation. Along with dentists. As I reflected on my own acculturation process, I remained aware that for most immigrants it was a much more difficult transition, impelled by much more difficult circumstances, and without the economic security and support that brought me to Canada.

Vacations in Mexico notwithstanding, the borders that I had pushed and breached were more socially constructed than national. Boundaries of race, class, and gender marked the social landscape of Galveston, the city on a barrier island in the Gulf of Mexico where I was born and spent my first eighteen years. My mother had crossed the boundaries of gender as she entered medical school there in 1945, and then as she practiced psychiatry until her retirement at age eighty. My father was a veterinarian who violated the tenets of White Southern Manhood by supporting his wife through medical school and then "letting" her practice medicine. First, however, she had to pay the state of Texas $50 to remove her "disabilities as a woman" so she could be licensed to practice medicine and to prescribe narcotics. Dad challenged the boundaries of race in a segregated town as he worked for African American Civil Rights, served as Co-Chair of the County Bi-Racial Commission, ran for the Galveston School Board on a school integration platform, and got elected even though he was a Yankee and had lived on the island for less than two decades. My parents raised us to believe in racial equality. But race remained uncomfortable for me, and worse for African Americans. For Whites in segregated Texas, liberal values were a choice, and White privilege an unescapable fact.

I arrived during my mother's second year in medical school. A blonde Jew with a Scottish name in a Christian culture, born to parents who already defied the racial and gender boundaries of the world I entered, I often viewed that world from the social margins, inescapably aware of my racial and class privilege, of religious difference, and of the ways my mother threatened gender norms. Not quite fitting in, I developed a social radar that continued to serve me as I left the South for college and graduate school, and as I entered a male-dominated profession. Those experiences nourished my interests in social history, the histories of social movements, of women and gender, labor, and people of color. Their histories took me beyond the histories of states and nations, to histories of social relationships, of daily acts and grassroots movements that had changed cultures and made history. I had not confronted how profoundly the histories of place and nation rooted my identity until the histories I knew no longer fit the place I lived.

Since 1999 I've explored borders, both national and social, and the borderlands where social and national differences are clarified and sometimes bridged. The ways I have thought about the United States, Canada, our relationships, our borderlands, and our histories have all changed during my decades in Canada. They changed as my perspective shifted north of the 49th Parallel, and as events changed the ways that the border operated and mattered to us all.

Those unfolding reflections sometimes provided context, sometimes subtext for my Chair's Lectures. One of the gifts of the Imperial Oil-Lincoln McKay Chair was the opportunity it offered for public engagement, and I looked forward each year to meeting audiences that included the Calgary public, undergraduate and graduate students, and colleagues, including Canadian and American historians. With the exceptions of my U.S. history colleagues and some American graduate students, the audiences were predominantly Canadian. I tried to pick topics that would interest both professional historians and the lay public. The lectures covered expanses of time, topics, and geography. Their historical terrain ranged from the gold camps of the California gold rush to northwest Alaska, where the U.S. government tried to "civilize" Alaska Native hunters by turning them into reindeer herders, to Canadian women's North Dakota homesteads, to New Jersey cities rocked by 1960s race riots. They expressed my interests in social movements, the connections of daily lives and private acts to social change and history, and the boundaries that divide people and buttress unequal relationships of power. They were prepared for Canadians unfamiliar with American history and may therefore seem at times to explain the obvious for American readers. They were also prepared to engage public audiences as well as historians and seldom address professional theoretical debates.

My work bridged academic and public audiences and discourses and, increasingly, bridged the histories and professions of two nations. During my years at the University of Calgary I became active in the Canadian Committee on Women's and Gender History and the Canadian Committee on Labour History. I belonged to the Canadian Historical Association, the Organization of American Historians, the Labor and Working Class History Association, Pacific Coast Branch - American Historical Association, and the Western History Association, and served all these organizations in various elected positions, except the American Historical Association. Finding that my Canadian colleagues were much more familiar with U.S. scholarship than Americans were of theirs, I embarked on a mission to introduce American historians to Canadian colleagues and their work. Two conferences I helped organize at the University of Calgary contributed to that effort: Unsettled Pasts: Reconceiving the West through Women's History (June 2002) and Directions West (June 2012). Further opportunities to encourage cross-border conversations came when I was elected President of the Pacific Coast Branch – American Historical Association (PCB-AHA) for 2004–2005 and President of the Western History Association (WHA) for 2014–2015. I appointed the program committees and selected the conference themes for those years. The 2005 PCB-AHA conference program focused on borders and borderlands. Its theme, "Dancing on the Rim," spoke to the challenges and rewards of connecting history across national borders. The theme of the 2015 Western History Association conference, "Thresholds, Walls, and Bridges," was an invitation for participants to address the challenges and possibilities of histories that respect and bridge differences of race, class, gender, and nation, and the limits and possibilities inherent in how we conceive history—how it is made, who makes it, and why it matters.

The three architectural structures of the WHA conference theme were metaphors for historically constructed power, difference, and possibility. Thresholds connoted the complex mixtures of adventure, curiosity, anticipation, and fear that can arise when standing on the brink of entering a new culture or of meeting people different from oneself—standing poised between the known and comfortable and something unknown and new, potentially exciting or dangerous. Walls evoked national borders and social boundaries that have, historically, served both to exclude and protect, that have erected unequal power relationships, and that have also sometimes signalled differences demanding respect. Bridges represented the possibilities for seeing beyond national and social differences, for recognizing humanity and forging productive connections with people on the other sides of "walls," the other sides of social and national divides.

These architectural metaphors also furnished the title of this book. They represent both episodes in a personal journey and my intention as a scholar and a teacher to make humanity visible not only across time, but also across nations and social differences. At the end of my teaching career, they represented some of what I had learned during my years in Calgary as a border-crossing historian and as my historical lens expanded beyond the boundaries of the United States.

As I prepared the essays for this book, I edited the original lectures as little as possible. Mostly I made necessary changes in verb tenses, changing the present tense to past tense as the present from which I had spoken faded into recent history, or changed place references from "here" to "Calgary" or "Canada." A few of the stories and the scholars I quoted appeared in more than one lecture, partly because they had had a formative influence on my thinking, partly because they had proved effective in conveying a concept to a public audience, and partly because the audience changed over the years, and I couldn't be certain that everyone shared the old references. They are also occasionally repeated here to maintain the original lecture material, because readers, as well, may choose not to read every essay, and because these stories chart the ways that formative texts and experiences spoke to me as circumstances and my intellectual perspective changed. The repetitions in chapter 13 were intentional. It was written as my presidential address to the Western History Association, as I stood on the brink of retirement. I delivered it twice during the 2015–2016 academic year, as the capstone of my service to the WHA, which had been my intellectual home for over thirty years, and as my final Chair's Lecture before I retired, the summation of my professional career.[1] I purposely included some material as a kind of shorthand to evoke memories of the intellectual journeys that had charted the trajectory of western women's histories.

I always prefaced my lectures by saying "Since you can't see my footnotes, I like to acknowledge the authors whose work I use; so today I thank . . ." For this volume, I eliminated those opening paragraphs and recreated my reference notes, which reflect the scholarship I used when writing each lecture. I have occasionally added a source published since I spoke, but for the most part have simply documented the sources I used at the time. Following each essay, I have provided brief notes about significant scholarship published since I wrote my lectures, or that I did not use or cite in the lecture. Neither time nor scholarship stand still, however, so these historiographic updates will already be outdated by the time this book goes to press. Consider them invitations to explore further.

I divided the essays into sections that reflect connected themes as my work and my acculturation process both developed. For historians, context is crucial—the contexts of the histories we record, and the contexts that influence our questions, choices of topic, and interpretations. Introductions to each section provide some of those contexts. I wrote in my 2016 lecture: "The historical threshold at which I always stand is the present moment, halfway across the line from the past that shaped my world to the future I want my grandchildren to inherit." Some of these essays responded to such "present moments." They were inspired by contemporary events. Where appropriate, I reflect in hindsight on what happened next.

Because my lectures cover different times and two nations, a note on terminology may be useful. The preferred terms for racial ethnic groups have varied over time and places.[2] In Canada, for instance, the preferred terms for Indigenous people are First Nations or Aboriginal. In the United States, the preferred terms are Native American or American Indian, except in Alaska, where the preferred term is Alaska Native, and Hawaii, where the preferred terms are Native Hawaiian, Indigenous Hawaiian, Kānaka Maoli, Aboriginal Hawaiian, or simply Hawaiian. The preferred term for Americans of African descent has changed during my lifetime from Negro to Black to African American. And there have been many preferred terms for people of Spanish/Mexican/Mestizo descent: Spanish American, Mexican American, Ethnic Mexican, Hispano/a/x, Hispanic, Nuevo Mexicano/a/x, Californio/a/x, Tejano/a/x, Chicano/a/x, and Latino/a/x. I try to use the terms by which people prefer to call themselves as I write, or by which they preferred to call themselves in a particular historic context. I sometimes use Indigenous or Native Peoples to connote all the Indigenous people of North America. I apologize for any mistakes; my intent is respectful. I choose to capitalize all racial ethnic terms, including White, to mark them all equally.

Finally, a note on spelling. I have learned over time to use either Canadian or American spelling, as appropriate. That's more difficult for a book that explicitly crosses the U.S.-Canada border and which I hope will interest readers in both countries. Because the lectures were originally written for Canadian audiences and because the University of Calgary Press is publishing the book, I very carefully used Canadian spelling in the original manuscript. But the press preferred American spelling, perhaps because Canadians are more used to the alternate spellings. So, Canadian readers, please just imagine the "u" in labo(u)r, neighbo(u)r, etc., and know they were there in the original draft.

This book is part scholarship, part memoir. They are inescapably connected. The Women's Liberation Movement insisted that the personal is political. In my experience, the professional is also to some extent personal. I have described history as an ongoing conversation between the past and present, recognizing that the present moment continues to change, and with it the questions we bring to the past. Recognizing the historian's place in this conversation requires honesty, awareness, and caution. I do not think that as historians we can or should abstract ourselves out of our scholarship. Who we are and what we value affects the subjects and questions that engage us. It is more honest to be transparent about those influences than to pretend they don't exist. When I began doing women's history in the early 1970s, for instance, I knew from experience that domestic work was an important topic to explore. I did not, however, assume that domestic work was unchanging or held the same meanings for all women in all times and cultures.[3] Personal experience can help frame questions and conceptual categories, but only evidence should determine conclusions.

I offer my reflections as a border crosser in the same spirit, as those experiences informed my scholarship and the topics I chose to present to Canadian audiences. From the moment I crossed the border at Coutts, I wrestled with the question of national identity and slowly developed an identity and loyalties that span two nations. I became a Canadian Permanent Resident in 2003, but because I held a Chair in American Studies and was often asked to comment on U.S. politics and events, I delayed applying for Canadian citizenship until I retired. I became a dual citizen in 2017.

The journey begun in 1999 brought me to a place where the Bow River meets the Elbow River, a site traditionally known as Moh'kins'tsis to the Blackfoot, Wîchîspa to the Stoney Nakoda, and Guts'ists'i to the Tsuut'ina. In the spirit of reconciliation, I acknowledge that I occupy the traditional territory of the Blackfoot confederacy (the Siksika, Kainai, and Piikani First Nations) as well as the Tsuut'ina First Nation and Îyâxe Nakoda (Chiniki, Bearspaw, and Goodstoney First Nations), a territory that is also home to the Otipemisiwak Métis Government, Regions 5 and 6. As a non-Indigenous newcomer, I acknowledge the difficult histories that enabled my claims to the land I inhabit. I celebrate and respect all those who seek truthfully to examine those histories, to find paths to reconciliation and good ways to live together in this place I have come to call home.

Calgary, Alberta
Treaty Seven Territory

NOTES

1. Although I retired on June 30, 2017, I was on a final research leave during the 2016–2017 academic year, so my 2016 Chair's Lecture was my last. Rather than doing a final lecture in 2017, I hosted a conference, "Torches Passed and Present," featuring some of the graduate students with whom I had worked at the University of New Mexico and the University of Calgary. I discuss that event in Chapter 14 of this volume.

2. I use the term "racial ethnic" because both race and ethnicity are cultural constructs. Who belongs in which category has changed over time and cultures. "Irish" or "Jew," for instance, were at times considered racial categories in the United States. The term "racial ethnic" was coined by Evelyn Nakano Glenn. See Glenn, "Racial Ethnic Women's Labor: The Intersection of Race, Gender and Class Oppression," *Review of Radical Political Economics* 17:3 (1985): 86–108.

3. I discuss how I first came to think about women's domestic histories in my 2012 lecture, "Are We There Yet?: Personal and Historical Reflections on Women in Higher Education."

Thresholds: 2000–2002

The journey to Calgary led to a new job that would challenge and stimulate me in ways I did not yet imagine. I crossed that professional threshold with curiosity, carrying the intellectual baggage of over three decades in U.S. higher education. My expertise consisted largely of U.S. history and culture. I was particularly influenced by the new social histories of the 1960s and 1970s that focused on relationships of race, class, and gender and movements for social change. My scholarship had focused on Rocky Mountain miners and their communities, and women in the U.S. West. I had followed miners and western women across international borders, and was introduced to Canadian mining, labor, and women's histories by colleagues I met through conferences: Jeremy Mouat, a fellow labor and mining historian; historian Catherine Cavanaugh and filmmaker Lorna Rasmussen, who shared the histories of Canadian prairie women. Drs. Mouat and Cavanaugh invited me to write an introduction for their anthology of new Canadian western history, *Making Western Canada*, through which I met future Canadian colleagues and which may have led indirectly to my invitation to apply for the Imperial Oil-Lincoln McKay Chair.[1]

My intellectual baggage also included social theory. I was influenced by historical materialism and feminist theories that helped frame my research questions and topics. My research sometimes led me to re-think or expand those frameworks. In 1975, for example, I had wrestled with evidence that the progressive miners of the Cripple Creek, Colorado, gold mining district were also sexist and racist, and wrote about the overlapping and inseparable identities of class and gender that complicated my analysis of a vibrant labor community.[2] When I arrived in Calgary, I had just completed two book projects that built from that early scholarship: *All That Glitters: Class, Conflict and Community in Cripple Creek* and *Writing the Range: Race, Class, and Culture in the Women's West,* an anthology I co-edited with Susan Armitage.[3] As I began to develop new research projects and new classes, I used my scholarship on the California Gold Rush, Colorado gold miners, and western women for my first lectures, to introduce myself to my new colleagues and community.

Much of my energy was focused on the transition to Calgary and to Canada. My job was the immediate priority—learning more about my students and about the University of Calgary academic programs. In some ways University of Calgary students resembled students at the University of New Mexico. Many undergraduates in both Calgary and Albuquerque worked fulltime while carrying full course loads. But when I taught U.S.

history in the United States, I was teaching my students their own histories. That was particularly powerful when I taught histories of women, or of race, histories to which women students and students of color had had little previous access. In Calgary, I needed to make American history speak to Canadian students.

The University of Calgary graduate program was a bit different from the U.S. programs I knew. It seemed to me to be a cross between the research-based British model and U.S. programs that require more and broader coursework in preparation for teaching. At Calgary we expected students to know their research topics when they entered their graduate programs, though they could change focus as their studies progressed. In the United States, the choice of a dissertation topic often waited until after a student was well into graduate studies, and sometimes until after the comprehensive exams that came just before the final step of researching and writing a dissertation.

There were daily personal adjustments aplenty, some intriguing, some unsettling. I breathed a huge sigh of relief when my son made friends on his first week at Queen Elizabeth II Junior High School. The name of the school was another reminder that I was in another country. The schools he had attended connoted the enormous hemispheric reach I now sought to bridge—he had attended Montezuma Elementary School and Thomas Jefferson Middle School in Albuquerque, so the names of his schools traversed the histories and borderlands of Mexico, the United States, British North America, and Canada.

I noticed that there were five public children's playgrounds within walking distance of my house and commented to my neighbor that no real estate developer in the United States would devote that many residential lots to play space. He looked puzzled and responded, "But children need to play." "How civilized," I thought.

I was, however, shocked the first time I took my son to a doctor's appointment when the physician made me sign a document promising not to sue her before she agreed to examine my child. She explained that she knew Americans were litigious and it was a standard precaution in her practice.

There was a lot to notice and absorb: how long to withhold personal information with new acquaintances, the fact that "progressive conservative" was not an oxymoron in Canada, never to plant my garden or change my snow tires before May Long Weekend, all the nuances of daily social behavior.[4] Each morning I passed three neighborhood schools on the way to work and for some months remained a bit surprised to see the Canadian flag flying over them, not the Stars and Stripes.

I was fascinated with subtle differences between the histories and politics of Canada and the United States. I was astonished with how quickly Canadian political parties and alliances could be formed and dissolved. A Canadian colleague had told me about the notwithstanding clause—Section 33 of the Charter of Rights and Freedoms which gives Parliament and the Provincial legislatures the ability to override portions of the Charter, certain guaranteed rights "notwithstanding."[5] Coming from a country that had rejected its Articles of Confederation after a brief eight-year experiment, it all seemed pretty weird to me. But being forewarned, I could understand a student's question in my first class in the fall of 1999. I had lectured about the 19th amendment to the U.S. constitution, which established woman suffrage, when a young woman raised her hand. "What happened," she asked, "if a state refused to obey the law?" "Some states have ignored federal laws," I admitted, "for instance when they denied African Americans' voting rights. But they were breaking the law. The United States doesn't have a notwithstanding clause."

I enjoyed the enormous multicultural diversity of Calgary, including emigrants from most parts of the British Empire, and enjoyed hearing echoes of my grandmother's British accent. I loved the Canadian concept of a multicultural mosaic, a contrast to the U.S. melting pot. The week we arrived I got my introduction to the distinct migrations that had shaped Calgary's social landscape. I took my car for a required safety inspection at an authorized Toyota dealership. They wanted to keep the car for the day and provided a driver to take me home. He was delighted that I spoke his native Spanish, and we chatted a bit about our separate paths to Canada. In New Mexico I might have assumed he was from Mexico, but he had come to Canada from El Salvador. Many in the small Calgary Latinx community had fled the repressive aftermaths of the failed Sandinista Uprising in Nicaragua and the El Salvador Civil War of 1979–1982. U.S. involvement in his homeland had led my driver to seek refuge in Canada rather than the United States.

Shortly afterwards, a colleague invited me to a lecture about Irish Canadians. As the presenter launched into a discussion of the Orange Order in Canada, I realized with a jolt that of course more Irish Protestants came to Canada. I knew more about the Irish Catholics who chose the United States, including the Irish miners I had studied, who brought the Ancient Order of Hibernians and Knights of Columbus to U.S. mining towns, not the Orange Order that played a large role in Canadian history. The Grand Orange Lodge of Canada, I learned, expanded to include people of non-Irish heritage, and among its members boasted four prime ministers, including Sir John A. MacDonald and John Diefenbaker, and most Toronto Mayors and Council Members from the 19th through the mid-20th centuries.

I soon learned, as well, that different migrations had forged the Jewish communities I had known and to which I now belonged. In Canada, there were proportionately fewer 19th-century German Jewish immigrants, like the ones who had helped found my Reform Jewish congregation in Galveston, and more Eastern European Orthodox Jewish immigrants who fled pogroms in the late-19th and early-20th centuries. Canada admitted proportionately more Jews following the Holocaust, though it, like the United States, had denied entry to Jews fleeing Hitler's Germany. The migrations that shaped the Jewish communities of the Canadian prairies shared some connections with U.S. Jewish agricultural settlements. I had learned about one of those settlements as I wrote an essay to contextualize the memoir of Rachel Calof, a Russian Jew who homesteaded with her husband in a North Dakota Jewish agricultural community from 1894–1917.[6] The history of Jewish settlement in Southern Alberta helped me locate my experience in multicultural Calgary, where Muslims far outnumbered the small Jewish community, and where the members of the Orthodox and Conservative Jewish congregations far outnumbered the Reform congregation my son and I joined in 1999.[7] Some of this history became personal in the summer of 2000 when I met a Calgary family descended from Rachel Calof's brother-in-law. They remain close friends.

While I explored new ground and began new research, I relied on my completed scholarship to introduce my work to Canadians. My first public lecture at the University of Calgary was not a Chair's Lecture, but a talk in November 1999 at the invitation of the English department, based on work I had done on Laura Ingalls Wilder, author of the popular "Little House" children's books. In that talk, "Cinderella Meets Her Manifest Destiny," I discussed how Wilder had tailored and fictionalized her own life, following a narrative that combined the narrative structure of Cinderella with historian Frederick Jackson Turner's frontier thesis that traced American settlement across successive westward-moving frontier lines to claim an ever-receding expanse of "free land."[8] By eliminating periods when her family moved back East and editing out periods of extreme hardship and her own childhood labor, Wilder fit her life into Turner's narrative of frontier progress as pioneers and the nation moved west. Following the Cinderella structure of a long foreground that ends happily-ever-after when the heroine marries her prince, Wilder ended her seven-volume series with her marriage to Almanzo Wilder in 1885. By stopping then, she erased the enormously difficult times that lay ahead for the couple and the Wilders' final move southeast from South Dakota to Missouri. I continued to write about Wilder during my years in Calgary, but this was my only public lecture based on that work.[9]

However, my research on Wilder became part of the University public relations staff's project to introduce me to the community as the new Chairholder. They notified media that on Wilder's birthday, February 7, 2000, I would be available in my office for press interviews about my research on the popular children's author. For most of the day I gave phone interviews, but the *Calgary Herald* sent a photographer who took photos of me holding a Little House book. The next morning, I was asked to come for an early-morning interview about Wilder on the local CBC "Eye Opener" radio program. On the way home, I stopped to buy a *Herald* to see how the story had come out. Below the fold on the front page, I saw the story: "U of C Prof. Says Little House Books a Lie." And then the banner headline—announcing a university tuition hike. By the time I got to my office, my email overflowed with messages from irate Albertans who did not want to pay more to hear their beloved children's books debunked.[10]

That episode introduced me to a new role in the public media. I was surprised, gratified, and challenged to discover how much academic commentary was valued in Canadian political life and public culture. My opinions had not mattered much in the United States, where no public media cared about what I thought at election time. I was a bit startled and unsettled at first when the CBC asked me to comment on American politics. I tried to tread lightly and offer nonpartisan interpretations while I taught at the University, though my values and politics were probably not hard to discern.

My first three Chair's Lectures developed some of the themes I introduced in that first public talk for the English Department. For the decade before my move to Calgary, historians of the U.S. West had debated Frederick Jackson Turner's formative essay, "The Significance of the Frontier in American History," and its enduring influence on history and popular imagination.[11] Academic circles in the 1990s were embroiled in fierce debates about the challenges of a group of New Western Historians, and my lectures reflected the intellectual residue of those debates.[12]

I introduced my Canadian audience to Turner's thesis and interrogated the ways that Americans and Canadians alike had used the frontier narrative to construct a mythic U.S. West. Turner's frontiers continued to influence public imagination long after the 1990s debates over Turner's frontier thesis had left the academic spotlight. Indeed, throughout my teaching career in Calgary, I confronted students' images of a mythic American West that historians of the U.S. West had long contested and complicated.

For my first Chair's Lecture, in the spring of 2000, I used a piece I had prepared for the 1999 Sesquicentennial of the California Gold Rush, tracing the social relationships of gender, class, and race that hopeful gold seekers formed, and contrasting their lived experiences with romantic Gold Rush lore. In 2001 I returned to Turner's frontiers and explored how western women stretched their categories and boundaries, drawing on over two decades researching women's history and helping establish the field of western women's history. That lecture highlighted some of the recurring themes in my work, especially the importance of domestic arenas, families, and private life as sites where social relations are produced and changed, where history-making acts are kindled, and new social institutions imagined.[13] In 2002 I presented work from my research on western hardrock miners. That work began in 1969, when, as an undergraduate history major at Antioch College, I worked as a student intern at the University of Colorado Western History Collections, organizing the archives of the Western Federation of Miners/International Union of Mine, Mill and Smelter Workers. I used the archive to write my senior thesis and later to research my dissertation, moving from a focus on the union itself, to its significance for the miners it represented, their families, and communities. My 2002 Chair's Lecture focused on the story of one extended family in the Cripple Creek, Colorado, gold-mining District, based on oral histories I conducted in the 1970s, and to which I returned in preparation for the centennial of the Cripple Creek strike of 1903–1904, a dramatic chapter in a series of conflicts known as the Colorado Labor Wars. One of those family members, May Wing, had introduced me to the cross-border movements of her father, an Irish immigrant hoist engineer, who she accompanied to the mining community of Rossland, B.C. in the 1890s before returning to Colorado.[14]

Together, these lectures introduced my work and some interests I continued to develop during my tenure as the Imperial Oil-Lincoln McKay Chair of American Studies. They used the tools of social history to explore unequal social relationships of race, ethnicity, class, and gender, as they were constructed and transformed in the American West. Focusing on the daily lives of "ordinary" people, I probed the connections of private lives with public history as they forged social relationships and institutions. I introduced a few scholars and people who deeply influenced my work, and to whom I returned occasionally in subsequent lectures.

In the meanwhile, I tried to learn more about Canada, its history, and the shifting meanings of a border that changed dramatically as I began to focus on what did and did not cross it.

NOTES

1   Elizabeth Jameson, "Introduction," in *Making Western Canada: Essays on European Colonization and Settlement*, eds. Catherine Cavanaugh and Jeremy Mouat (Toronto: Garamond Press, 1996), pp. ix–xix.

2   Elizabeth Jameson, "Imperfect Unions: Class and Gender in Cripple Creek, 1894–1904," *Frontiers* 1:2 (Spring 1976): 89–117; prepared originally for *Class, Sex, and the Woman Worker*, ed. Milton Cantor and Bruce Laurie (Westport, CT: Greenwood Press, 1977), 166–202. In this article, I grappled with the intersections of class and gender as they operated in the Cripple Creek working-class community. My Galveston childhood and subsequent experience had taught me that the intersections of race, class, and gender exponentially disadvantaged working-class women of color, and how these overlapping identities differentiated peoples' experiences and opportunities. I found it painful to confront the fact that miners I admired were also sexist and racist, but I should not have been surprised that gender affected working-class women and men and disadvantaged working-class women. Although I always explored the overlapping intersections of race, class, and gender, I never attempted to develop a theory of intersectionality, as Kimberlé Crenshaw did so elegantly. There were other terms for these intersections before Crenshaw developed the term "intersectionality." I used "co-construction" for awhile. See Kimberlé Crenshaw, "Demarginalizing the Intersection of Race and Sex: A Black Feminist Critique of Antidiscrimination Doctrine, Feminist Theory and Antiracist Politics," *University of Chicago Legal Forum* 140 (1989): 139–67; "Mapping the Margins: Intersectionality, Identity Politics and Violence against Women of Color," *Stanford Law Review* 43:6 (July 1991): 1241–99; *On Intersectionality: Essential Writings of Kimberlé Crenshaw* (New York: The New Press, 2017).

3   Elizabeth Jameson, *All That Glitters: Class, Conflict, and Community in Cripple Creek* (Urbana: University of Illinois Press, 1998); Elizabeth Jameson and Susan Armitage, eds., *Writing the Range: Race, Class, and Culture in the Women's West* (Norman: University of Oklahoma Press, 1997).

4   For U.S. readers: in Canada there are "long weekends," rather than "holiday weekends." The May Long is also known as Victoria Day weekend, in recognition of Queen Victoria's birthday, May 24, 1819. The Monday before May 25 is Victoria Day and comes at the end of the May Long weekend.

5   Section 33 allows legislatures to override Sections 2 and 7–15 of the Charter for five years when enacting new legislation. These sections deal with fundamental freedoms, legal rights, and equality rights, but not democratic rights. The Notwithstanding Clause was intended to address concerns that the Charter would disrupt the balance of powers

between the provinces and the federal government. It was assumed that it would be used only in extraordinary cases.

6   Elizabeth Jameson, "Rachel Bella Calof's Life as Collective History," in *Rachel Calof's Story: Jewish Homesteader on the Northern Plains*, ed. J. Sanford Rikoon (Bloomington: Indiana University Press, 1995), 135–53.

7   On Jewish immigration to Canada, see Gerald Tulchinsky, *Taking Root: The Origins of the Canadian Jewish Community* (Toronto: Lester Publishing, 1992); *Branching Out: The Transformation of the Canadian Jewish Community* (Toronto: Stoddart, 1998), and Irving Abella, *A Coat of Many Colours: Two Centuries of Jewish Life in Canada* (Toronto: Lester & Orpen Dennys, 1990). On World War II era exclusion, see Irving Abella and Harold Troper, *None Is Too Many: Canada and the Jews of Europe, 1933–1948* (Toronto: Lester & Orpen Dennys, 1982). On Jewish settlement in Alberta, and in Calgary, see The Jewish Historical Society of Southern Alberta, *Land of Promise: The Jewish Experience in Southern Alberta* (Calgary: Jewish Historical Society of Southern Alberta, 1996) and *A Joyful Harvest: Celebrating the Jewish Contribution to Southern Alberta Life, 1889–2005* (Calgary: Jewish Historical Society of Southern Alberta, 2007).

8   Frederick Jackson Turner, "The Significance of the Frontier in American History," first presented at the American Historical Association meeting in Chicago, July 12, 1893, coinciding with the World's Columbian Exhibition of 1893, originally printed in *Annual Report of the American Historical Association for the Year 1893* (Washington, DC: Government Printing Office, 1894).

9   My work on Wilder includes "Commentary: Truth, Facts, and Alternative Histories: Views from the Little Houses," *Montana: The Magazine of Western History* 69:2 (Summer 2019), 68–70; "The Myth of Happy Childhood (and Other Myths about Frontiers, Families, and Growing Up)," in *Pioneer Girl Perspectives*, ed. Nancy Tystad Koupal (Pierre, SD: South Dakota Historical Society Press, 2017), 231–63; "Introduction," in *Laura Ingalls Wilder and the American Frontier: Five Perspectives*, ed. Dwight M. Miller (Lanham, MD: University Press of America, Inc., 2002), 1–12; "Unconscious Inheritance and Conscious Striving: Laura Ingalls Wilder and the Frontier Narrative," in Miller, *Laura Ingalls Wilder and the American Frontier*, 69–93; "In Search of the Great Ma," *Journal of the West* 37:2 (April 1998): 42–52; also in Richard W. Etulain, ed., *Myths and the American West* (Manhattan, KS: Sunflower University Press, 1998), 42–52. My 1999 lecture unknowingly influenced a young author in the audience, Hiromi Goto. I was surprised and pleased to read in the acknowledgements of her novel, *Kappa Child* (Calgary: Red Deer Press, 2001) her thanks to me for "the enlightening panel discussion . . . at the University of Calgary on November 17, 1999" that helped her "revisit the Little House books with new eyes." You never know what seeds you're sowing or where they'll sprout.

10 To be clear, I, too, loved the Little House books as a child, and was not "debunking" them as literature, just interrogating their claims as history.

11 Turner, "The Significance of the Frontier in American History."

12 The New Western History encompasses a large body of scholarship and owes a great deal to the new histories of Native Americans, Mexican Americans, women, labor, and new environmental histories of the 1970s and 1980s. Among the leading texts of the New Western History were Patricia Nelson Limerick, *The Legacy of Conquest: The Unbroken Past of the American West* (New York: W.W. Norton, 1987), Patricia Nelson Limerick, Clyde A. Milner II, and Charles E. Rankin, eds., *Trails: Toward a New Western History* (Lawrence: University of Kansas Press, 1991), and Richard White, *"It's Your Misfortune and None of My Own": A New History of the American West* (Norman, OK: University of Oklahoma Press, 1991). For an example of the heated responses to the New Western history, see Gerald D. Nash, "Point of View: One Hundred Years of Western History," *Journal of the West* 33:2 (July 1993): 3–4. My one small contribution to this discourse

was in Susan Armitage, Elizabeth Jameson, and Joan Jensen, "The New Western History: Another Perspective," *Journal of the West* 32:3 (July 1993): 5–6.

13 I served on the organizing committees of the first conference in the field, the Women's West conference in 1983 and the third Women's West conference in 1987, and I co-edited two volumes, Susan Armitage and Elizabeth Jameson, eds., *The Women's West* (Norman, OK: University of Oklahoma Press, 1987) and Jameson and Armitage, *Writing the Range*.

14 Elizabeth Jameson, "The Creatures of Discontent: The Western Federation of Miners and the Radical Labor Movement, 1893–1911" (BA thesis, Antioch College, Department of History, 1970); Elizabeth Ann Jameson, *High Grade and Fissures: A Working-Class History of the Cripple Creek, Colorado, Gold Mining District, 1890–1905* (PhD diss., University of Michigan, 1987); Jameson, *All That Glitters*; Jameson, "Imperfect Unions"; Elizabeth Jameson, "History, Memory, and Commemoration: The Cripple Creek Strike Remembered," in *The Colorado Labor Wars: Cripple Creek 1903–1904*, ed. Tim Blevins, Chris Nichol, and Calvin P. Otto (Colorado Springs, CO: Pikes Peak Library District, 2006), 3–34; and Elizabeth Jameson, "Talking the Walk: The 1903–1904 Strike Centennial in the Cripple Creek District," in Blevins, Nichol, and Otto, *The Colorado Labor Wars*, 101–16. I also co-produced a slide-tape presentation with the support of the Colorado Endowment for the Humanities based on my interviews with residents of the Cripple Creek District, Elizabeth Jameson and David Lenfest, "We Were Never Supposed to be Rich," slide/tape and video, 1979.

1

Where Have All the Young Men Gone? The Social Legacy of the California Gold Rush

April 5, 2000

When 1960s anti-war activists sang, "Where have all the young men gone?" they answered rhetorically, "Gone to soldiers, every one."[1] In many parts of the world in the 1850s, the same question might prompt an equally automatic response: Where have all the young men gone?" "Gone to miners, every one."

The discovery of gold near Sutter's Fort drew a demographically extraordinary influx to the California streambeds—overwhelmingly young, overwhelmingly male, carrying ambitions born from the particular economic and political dislocations that pushed them to California.

Mark Twain indelibly etched the virile masculinity of these gold seekers. They were, he wrote,

> a driving, vigorous, restless population . . . a curious population . . . the only population of the kind that the world has ever seen gathered together, and it is not likely that the world will ever see its like again. For observe, it was an assemblage of two hundred thousand *young* men—not simpering, dainty, kid-gloved weaklings, but stalwart, muscular, dauntless young knaves, brimful of push and energy, and royally endowed with every attribute that goes to make up a peerless and magnificent manhood—the very pick and choice of the world's glorious ones. No women, no children, no gray and stooping veterans—none but erect, bright-eyed, quick-moving, strong-handed young giants—the strangest population,

the finest population, the most gallant host that ever trooped down the startled solitudes of an unpeopled land.

"And," Twain concluded wistfully, "where are they now?"[2]

What legacy remains from the hundreds of thousands of otherwise ordinary men who interrupted their lives for an extraordinary trek to California's rocky streams and slopes?

The social outcome is less apparent than how clearly all those young men touched collective imaginations. Their mythic Gold Rush inspired nostalgic images of youthful adventure and reckless risk-taking—an adolescent fantasyland, free from constraint and responsibility—a place where young men worked hard, played hard, cursed, sweated, spit, whored, and gambled everything on an elusive bonanza and often equally elusive good times.

Twain's Gold Rush, like most good fantasies, bore enough resemblance to reality to fuel generations of romantic histories. It *was* a curious population. And one of its most curious attributes was its ability to reproduce itself in collective memory far beyond its capacity to reproduce itself biologically or socially.

These young men endured as leading actors in a saga of an American West so unreal that historian Susan Armitage dubbed it "Hisland." In this imagined historical terrain:

> . . . under perpetually cloudless western skies, a cast of heroic characters engages in dramatic conflict, sometimes with nature, sometimes with each other. Occupationally, these heroes are diverse; they are mountain men, cowboys, Indians, soldiers, farmers, miners, and desperadoes, but they share one distinguishing characteristic—they are all men. . . . This mythical land is America's most enduring contribution to folklore: the legendary Wild West.

"The problem with Hisland," Armitage continued, "is that many people believe it is history, and some of those people are historians."[3]

In the context of the 1849 Gold Rush, Armitage's critique might sound like so much feminist carping. The Forty-niners were, according to all available evidence, much as Twain painted them: overwhelmingly young, overwhelmingly male. In California, a year after the Gold Rush began, the U.S. census counted twelve men for each woman. The odds were even more skewed in the mining districts—97 percent male. By 1860, three Californians in ten were women, but around the mines, the women were still outnumbered twenty to one.[4]

The early mining booms belonged to young men. But over time placer mining—sifting precious metals from streambeds—gave way to quartz mining as capitalists followed the "leads" underground to mine complex ores that must be milled and refined to yield their precious metals. Wage laborers replaced the exuberant forty-niners, the impermanent placer camps gave way to settled mining communities and supply centers, economic and social institutions became more stable, and increasing numbers of women and children invaded Twain's masculine Eden.

Like most adventurous young men, the Forty-niners grew up, or went home, or settled down. They were seldom as footloose and unattached as the fantasy West painted them. They did not, as Twain would have it, penetrate the virgin territories of their manifest destiny to startle "the solitudes of an unpeopled land." The land was quite "peopled" when they got there, its Indigenous people having already been invaded as a northern frontier of New Spain. To sift history from the mythic West, we must locate the argonauts in their own contexts. Who and what did they leave, and why? What relationships did they build, and with whom? For some youthful gold-seekers, their sojourn in the diggings would represent, as it did for Twain, a brief adventure before they returned East to adult lives very like the ones they left behind. For others, however, the Gold Rush was a step away from the familiar, toward something not yet formed.

The "curious population" of Gold Rush California was part of a much larger international mass migration of people and capital engendered by the worldwide impacts of industrialization, colonial expansion, and the development of market economies.[5] These impelled an extraordinary, but selective, migration to California. The argonauts came more often from the northern U.S. than from the South or the frontiers; from Mexico and Chile, but not from Brazil; from China, but not from India and Afghanistan; from Ireland, Cornwall, and Germany, but not from Portugal or Greece. They left droughts, depressions, crowded farms and unhappy marriages, the chaos of revolutions, and workshops where artisans' skills were being displaced by factory production, hauling their social baggage to the gold fields. Their collective experience recharted how people related to one another as women and men, workers and owners, immigrants and native-born Americans.

It would require more than a single essay to unravel all the strands of their intertwined histories. I focus here on young men from the United States, Great Britain, and China to trace some of the connected relationships of manhood, race, and labor that they forged in the Gold Rush.

Many young men whose hopes drew them to the gold fields came from the Northeastern and Midwestern United States, where factories and wage labor were replacing independent artisans and eroding their skills. The prices craftsmen could command plummeted, and with them the hopes of many Euro-American men of achieving what they called a "competency"—a secure financial future that guaranteed a respected social niche.[6] Many of our most vivid Gold Rush records were penned by men who aspired to such stable middle-class status, who hoped that California opened a route to economic security that seemed increasingly tenuous in New York, Maine, or Massachusetts. Susanna Townsend, who accompanied her husband Emery to his claim on Jackson Creek in Amador County, wrote her family in New York that ". . . if kind Providence smiles upon us Emery thinks he will be able to live the rest of his days without labor. A small capital in this country well invested brings in returns so much greater than in the older states that we could live handsomely on the interest of six thousand dollars while at home it would not be much."[7]

Men with more modest aspirations found that they could do better plying their craft skills in California than in the uncertain gamble of the diggings. New Englander Jotham Varney budgeted two years to improve his fortunes in California. Quickly "discouraged about gold digging" after a brief stint in the summer of 1850, Varney found that it was much more profitable to work in Sacramento as a cooper, making kegs used to haul molasses and liquor to the mines. "A common hand," he wrote his wife, "can make from four to six of them in a day the ten gallons sell for five dollars, and the five gallons sell for a dollar apiece. If I had come out here a little more than a year ago and set up coopering I might have made something handsome them cags they say sold for sixteen dollars apiece."[8] New Yorker James Barnes calculated the value of mining against what he could earn plying his trade as a skilled carpenter, writing from Sacramento in March 1850, that "if work is good here this summer i shall not go to the mines if they get below 12$ a day i shall go to the mines it is thought by some that Carpenter work will be from 12 to 18$ a day all summer. . . ."[9]

Eastern artisans were soon joined by men from all corners of the globe. William Ives Morgan of Bristol, Connecticut, wrote from Amador in 1850 that he: "Worked all day near the road, and saw Yankee, English,

Chinese, German, Scotch, Chileans, Mexicans, Californians, Manilla Men, Indians, Swedes, Norwegians, French men, Kanakas, and don't know how many other Nations pass us."[10] If Twain's curious population included "no women, no children, no gray and stooping veterans," it excluded such international diversity as well. The mythic argonaut was a free White man from the eastern United States, a fitting agent of American national destiny. Many of the first migrants fit that bill. But by 1860 four Californians in ten were immigrants; almost half the people in mining districts came from other lands. Immigrants, particularly people of color, clustered disproportionately in the southern mines, where placer mining continued, while the native-born and northern and western Europeans staked their fortunes to deep-shaft mining further north.[11] Everywhere, class distinctions charted a growing divide between immigrants and Euro-Americans. By 1870 only one working man in four in the industrial mining center, Grass Valley, was a native-born American, four in ten in adjacent Nevada City.[12] International migrations fueled class formation, a process that affected who stayed around the mines and who owned them; who worked underground for wages; who grew food and who sold it; who supported families and who provided the domestic needs of a largely male and increasingly immigrant workforce.

Different dislocations pushed the men who rushed in from distant ports. Irish immigrants fled poverty, the potato famine, and British rule. French argonauts fled the failed Revolution of 1848.[13] Distinct patterns of migration and settlement are suggested in the particular social and economic niches occupied by the Cornish and the Chinese in post-Gold Rush California. By 1870, four Californians in ten were immigrants. One migrant in four was Chinese; one in ten was English, one in four, Irish.[14] Migrations from both England and China were concentrated from areas where specific dislocations and histories sent men to the new gold fields.

The Chinese and English who came to California were only a portion of larger migrations from their homelands, and a tiny fragment of the international migration of labor caused by the global expansion of capitalism.[15] An estimated 2.5 million Chinese left their homeland from 1840–1900, after China lost the Opium Wars and was forced to open to European trade and political domination.[16] Almost all the Chinese who went to California came from the southern Chinese province of Guangdong, close to the ports of Hong Kong and Canton, a land approximately the size of Oregon but so poor and hilly that only 16 percent was cultivated as late as 1955.[17] Much of the cultivated land in the nineteenth century grew commercial crops: sugar cane, fruit, indigo, and tobacco, rather than rice or other staple foodstuffs. Peasants in the Pearl River delta were particularly hard-hit by increased taxes, loss of land, unemployment, and overpopulation. For common people, food was scarce and expensive. From 1787 to 1850 the population of Guangdong grew from 16 million to 28 million. During the 1850s and 1860s, the province was further rocked by the Taiping Rebellion, the Red Turban uprisings, and interethnic warfare. Extreme political, social, and economic dislocations led to reports that "[s]mall families found it difficult to make a living and often drowned their girl babies because of the impossibility of looking after them."[18] Many of the sons emigrated. At least half were married and intended to support a family back home.[19]

Some 75,000 Chinese lived in California in 1880, two years before the Chinese Exclusion Act halted the entry of all but a trickle. The overwhelming majority worked as laborers and miners. In 1868 one-fourth of the Chinese in California labored on the railroad; a third were miners.[20] The proportions remained unchanged from 1860 in Grass Valley, where one U.S. native in four still mined in 1870, and in Nevada City, where the population was still 40 percent native-born Americans. Eighty percent of the British mined in Grass Valley, 80 percent of the Chinese in Nevada City.[21] Compared with native-born Americans, both the Chinese and British were disproportionately working class.

The British miners came from Wales, from the Yorkshire coal fields, and especially from Cornwall, in southwestern England, where generations of Cornish had mined tin, copper, and clay used to manufacture china. In Cornwall, by 1862 some 340 mines employed 50,000 men and women, their lives marked by endless labor and marginal poverty, usually cut short by silicosis and other occupational ailments. The skills and techniques perfected in one of the world's oldest mining regions passed from generation to generation as boys began working at age seven under their fathers' watchful eyes.[22]

Children began work by age six or seven, often working ten hours a day for pennies separating rubbish from the ore. Girls did not work underground but labored on the surface. Older women hammered rude ore with stone mallets and then passed it on to the "bal maidens," adolescent girls who "bucked" it with an iron hammer to the size of half-inch marbles for twelve to eighteen shillings a month. One observer noted that "The use of hammers in dressing ores tends, perhaps, to the production of some fullness of breast, but the sedentary position necessary gives little or no exercise to the lower limbs."[23]

Even the meager living eked from the Cornish mines was threatened by the time of the Gold Rush. An economic depression in the 1840s hastened emigration. By the 1850s high-grade copper was running out at depths of 1,000 feet in Cornish mines. Competition from newly discovered copper deposits in Michigan and Chile led to mine closures and widespread unemployment. By the end of the century, Cornwall lost an estimated third or more of its population: 230,000 left for Australia, Mexico, and Chile, for the Wisconsin lead mining regions, the copper mines of northern Michigan, the gold mines of California, and the hardrock camps that soon dotted western North America.[24] The Cornish brought to the placers their knowledge of alluvial tin-streaming, introducing improved equipment like long toms, cradles, and sluice boxes. John Roberts, who traveled from Cornwall to Wisconsin to Sonora, Mexico to California, wrote that he planned to dig into the quartz veins which were "formed exactly like the copper lodes in Cornwall, only they lie very flat."[25]

Following placer deposits underground to develop quartz mines was a natural step for an experienced Cornish miner. Nevada City and Grass Valley became centers of Cornish settlement, where Cornish men became highly regarded miners, superintendents, managers, and foremen, working as skilled blasters and drillers, and supervising specialized operations like timbering. Cornish shift bosses and foremen would hire newly arrived Cornishmen, in a world where Cornishness, regardless of actual mining experience, came to connote skilled miners.[26]

The Cornish brought their brass bands and Methodist churches and fanned out to take their skills throughout the mining West. The Boise (Idaho) *Owyhee Avalanche* published a common estimate of these immigrants who soon became a common fixture of western hardrock regions:

> The Cornishman is probably the most skillful foreign miner that comes to our shores. For this he deserves no special credit, because it is a calling to what he has been accustomed since his childhood. . . . Generally speaking, he is satisfied to be working for others, but insists on being paid promptly for his services. . . . They are mostly stalwart, good-looking fellows, dress better than any other class of miners, and are very fond of women. They also appear more clannish than any other foreigner and a majority of them are very good singers.[27]

Although Twain did not likely picture the Cornish and Chinese among his "stalwart, muscular, dauntless young knaves," they lived in the company of other men in greater proportions and far longer than the "curious population" of native-born Americans he celebrated. The native-born population, by 1870, was 43 percent female, compared to three immigrants in ten, and only 8 percent of all Chinese.[28]

Cornishmen might be "very fond of women," but they often had to wait to marry them. More Cornish men than women came to California. The instabilities of mining and the excess of men in western mining camps meant that the Cornish, like many skilled working men, delayed marriage until they could support a family, and often until they could send for Cornish sweethearts left behind. For many years Cornishmen shared bachelor cabins, most often with other Cornish miners, or boarded with the few Cornish and American women who provided domestic services for working men in the mining camps.

Ultimately, however, many Cornish miners would marry, settle, and raise families in western mining towns. Generations of California miners traced their roots to the mines of Cornwall, or the Yorkshire coal pits, or Wisconsin lead, or Australian copper. Those who came during the Gold Rush often began a chain migration of family and friends who joined them where mining was stable and jobs available. John and Fred Nettel recalled the story of their father, who began working the mines of Redruth in Cornwall at age twelve. He emigrated to Michigan in 1881, then went to Prescott and Tuscarora before settling in Grass Valley, where his married sister lived. When he had saved enough and had been promoted to foreman at the Ledge mine, he followed the Cornish custom and wrote his sweetheart in Cornwall, asking her to marry him in Grass Valley. She agreed, and in time their sons followed their father into the mines.[29]

Class and race provide social lenses through which to examine the links between wage work and domesticity. Chinese and Cornish men both labored on the mining frontier, but their ability to form families, father children, and form permanent communities diverged sharply.

Cornish miners and their wives reproduced generations of skilled workers, a variation on the pattern whereby generations of Cornish sons followed their fathers underground. Their place in the process of class formation distinguished them from Chinese workers. Although Chinese men worked the placers and built western railroads, neither capital nor labor welcomed Chinese women, who, it was feared, would bear a stable Chinese work force that would demand higher wages and better working conditions. The Chinese were restricted to the placers, allowed to mine underground only in the dangerous quicksilver mines, subjected to a foreign Miners' Tax, and were run out of mining camps throughout the West.[30]

Chinese women were restricted from joining Chinese men in America by patriarchal Chinese tradition, by poverty, and by racist anti-Chinese legislation. The 1882 Chinese Exclusion Act allowed only a few privileged women to emigrate, primarily the wives and daughters of merchants. Most of the Chinese women who were in the country when the doors closed in 1882 were prostitutes, mostly impoverished peasant women imported to serve as sexual companions for Chinese men. Since Chinese could not legally marry people of other races, these few women became virtually the only available marriage partners for single Chinese workingmen. The continued absence of women would separate the Chinese from most other immigrant groups and ensure that only the small Chinese merchant class could legally establish families in California.[31]

Chinese working men generally attended to their own domestic needs, growing vegetables, cooking, and establishing a variety of businesses, from noodle houses to laundries, that served Euro-Americans as well as Chinese. By 1880, almost 8 percent of the Chinese in the Northern Mines were cooks, 12 and 15 percent in the Sacramento and San Joaquin valleys respectively.[32] Some became truck farmers, raising vegetables, hogs, and poultry. By 1860, truck gardeners and laundrymen, who practiced "sedentary occupations that benefited from unpaid family labor," were some of the few Chinese men with wives in California.[33] Farmers, domestic service workers, and the small merchant class represented the very few Chinese in America who could establish families and physically reproduce their communities.

When we know that both Cornish and Chinese lived mostly with other men, the *Owyhee Avalanche*'s insistence that the Cornish were "very fond of women" takes on new meaning. It asserted the masculine and heterosexual identities of men who spent much of their time in homosocial worlds. Chinese men, by contrast, legally *prevented* from cohabiting with women, came to be portrayed as feminized, as less than men. These images had little to do with which Chinese men in fact had wives and families in California, but rather identified an ascribed racial "inferiority" with the lower status of Euro-American women, an association reinforced by images of men who did "women's work" like cooking, gardening, laundry, and domestic service.

Masculinity was thus associated with class and race in social contexts that could be seen alternately as hyper-manly or as lacking women to perform "feminine" and feminizing domestic tasks. Who, after all, were the young men to depend on for food, clothing, sexual companionship, and sociability?

If, indeed, we asked many of Twain's young compatriots about Gold Rush social life, they would have been mystified. "Society" implied women. The absence of women, by extension, defined what was missing in the tents, cabins, and settlements that mushroomed around the placers. James Barnes, who left New York for the gold fields in late 1849, wrote in December 1853 that he had "lived almost 4 years entirely excluded from society" and that "what makes society is females and a party of that kind i have not attended since i have been in the country[.]" "[T]here is very little what we might call society here females are too scarce. [W]hat are here think themselves better than the Angels in heaven." That being the case, Barnes preferred "reading some books" to "a bar room where there is always card playing drinking smoking and swearing such is about all the society there is here but i am here and i intend to make the best of it."[34]

Though there were very few women around the mines, women were never entirely absent, psychically, emotionally, and in the social perceptions of men.[35] In the absence of women, men recharted a social universe using as their compass the gender roles they had left behind. For most middle-class Euro-American men, this meant that things domestic—cooking, cleaning, sewing, doing laundry, making a space a "home" —had been done by women. Women nursed the sick, tended gardens, raised poultry and dairy cows, made butter and bread, championed moral behavior, and were essential for much civilized leisure. In the goldfields, then, men not only had to learn to care for their own domestic needs and amusements. They also had to decide what it meant that they did these things, what their new domestic and recreational arrangements meant for their personal and social identities.

They adapted in various ways, learning to provide for themselves and other men the domestic services that ideally belonged to women. As they did, they walked a fine line. In the social worlds they had left, men had greater status than women. Masculine status was a particularly precarious matter because a crisis in social status prompted many a gold seeker's journeys. They thus hastened to assure the folks back home that they were prospering and living well, while trying at the same time not to appear overly identified with the feminine domestic world. Much of their correspondence connected domestic needs with the pursuit of prosperity: they wrote of food and the cost of provisions, and measured success in terms of health and income. Rodney Odall linked domesticity and finances as he described, for his family back in New York, the division of labor in his all-male household: "Harris makes our bread, Havens cooks in the morning, Fish at noon and I at night. ... Everything looks to me that I shall make some money yet." Food and fortune appear in concert throughout his correspondence: "Wages are 60 dollars per month in this place, eat yourself. The mines are very healthy at present. Smoked salmon 25 cts, beans 38, rice 38, sugar 50, dried apples 50, everything sells by the pound." Six months later he reported from Brown's Bar: "I have been well and healthy; never in my life was I as tough as now. I weigh about 170 pounds." He was, he reported, making $5 some days, some days a dollar.[36]

This connection of food with fortune, or more broadly of domesticity and prosperity, appeared repeatedly in Gold Rush correspondence. James Barnes wrote from San Francisco that it cost him and a group of friends $8 a week to live. "We live first rate we have one cook and baker we have good Oraing [Orange] County butter and potatoes and every thing els that is good."[37] Soon thereafter he wrote from Sacramento: "methinks i hear you say i wonder if he is not home sick far from it i did sometimes think of old daddy table when i was out to sea feeding on salt beef some of it smelt strong enough to knock a Jack ass down our board was moulgy and worms enough in it to cary it of, we have every thing that is good for breakfast something beter for dinner and tea and shortcake for supper that is beter than a seafaring life...."[38] He left the mines both because they didn't pay as well as carpentry and because the food was bad. During his three months in the diggings, he averaged about $3 a day, and "lived on raw pork and sea bisket...."[39]

Over time, food evoked memories of home. Jotham Varney, after almost a year away from his family, wrote his wife "I thought sometimes I should be glad to have a good drink of your buttermilk."[40] As the glamour of the Gold Rush faded, Barnes wrote: "what we live on here . . . is not buckwheat cakes for we do not get them more than once a week but the way we make them suffer even we do get them is a caution."[41] The young men tried to assure home folks they were doing well, but, for many, the homes they had left remained the measure of domestic comfort.

Recreating domestic comfort satisfied both physical and psychic appetites. The few women who joined the migration to the gold fields found their domestic skills in high demand. The domestic desires of thousands of men created a market for domesticity. An unidentified woman wrote from San Francisco in 1850 that California was the only place "where a woman rec'd anything like a just compensation for work." She had been sewing but intended to open a boarding house for thirty to thirty-five boarders, paying a cook $150 a month. "People do not pretend to keep very clean houses here," she wrote. "But if the houses and streets are dirty the money is clean."[42]

In a world so entirely masculine, women found a narrow, if remunerative, set of opportunities. Married or single, respectable or disreputable, rewarded in cash or indirectly through spousal support, they supplied the domestic needs, the heterosexual and heterosocial desires of the overwhelmingly male population. In the paid workforce or in their own households, they cooked, cleaned, sewed, scrubbed, and provided "society" for the male majority. Well paid, at least compared to women's wages further east, their options remained restricted to domestic arenas, in the marketplace, or in the family household.

Their domestic skills could, nonetheless, hold the key to family prosperity. Luzena Stanley Wilson began her road to Gold Rush prosperity when, much to her own amazement, she sold biscuits for $10 to a miner who missed bread baked by a woman. From then on, she cooked for miners and operated hotels in Sacramento, Nevada City, and Vacaville. The day she opened her El Dorado Hotel in Nevada City, on a table she fashioned from two boards, she attracted twenty miners who paid her a dollar a meal and promised to return. "From the first day," she wrote, "it was well patronized, and I shortly after took my husband into partnership."[43]

Emery Townsend, who hoped "to live the rest of his days without labor," found that his wife's dreams led more directly to their security than his endless grubbing in the diggings. Susanna insisted on a garden.[44] The Townsends' security owed as much to Susanna's grubbing after vegetables as to Emery's grubbing for gold in his much-worked diggings. "It is astonishing," she wrote, "how the sale of a few vegetables mounts up."[45] From a half-acre garden, she "cleared twelve hundred dollars." She "felt sure" that they would do better on a small ranch "than mining and not work half so hard." She got her way. By 1853 the Townsends moved to twenty-eight acres near Sutterville.[46] In 1856 Susanna reported that they were growing grapes and had $2400 worth of cabbages in the ground.[47]

Her one lack, Susanna reported in 1857, was female company. There were twelve women in town, but, she wrote, "I have not found one congenial acquaintance. They are all course, low, illiterate women."[48] The reference point for acceptable society remained for Susanna Townsend, as for many middle-class Euro-Americans, the women she had left back East and whose correspondence provided her primary female companionship.

The most significant women in the Gold Rush, however, were not the few exceptional ones like Susanna Townsend and Luzena Wilson who accompanied their husbands West, or the even rarer souls who sought their independent fortunes in Gold Rush California. The men who constituted the "curious" population in California left behind equally "curious" communities, where "Gold Rush widows" managed farms and businesses without male guidance.[49]

Separated couples expressed the gamut of feelings from affection to relief. Jotham Varney wrote before he ever got to California that he "felt the loss of your company more than anything else which I have to regret."[50] But John Bozeman wrote from the gold fields that he would not return to his wife Catharine and their three daughters. "I am a friend to Catharine and always will be, but the way we lived to gether my life was not pleasure to me. We never lived a week to gether without quarling and I doo not think it right for us to live to gether that way." He had been gone long enough, he wrote, for Catharine to divorce him for desertion.[51]

Dearly missed or happily abandoned, the women left behind were often invisible partners in their husbands' adventures. Men who sought to escape debt and downward mobility left women with few resources to support themselves and their children. They relied on "respectable" sources of income like teaching, selling butter and eggs, and keeping boarders. Jotham Varney, like many absent husbands, tried to advise his wife on matters of farm management, like what to do about the tenant who he feared was drinking too much and was violating his agreement to split the hay crop.[52] But he knew his family was essentially on its own. Sending advice for his children, he wrote, "Lincoln, I suppose is to work painting. I hope he will be a good boy and do the best he can. He will be the most of your dependence while I am absent. . . . As things look now," he added, "I shall not be able to send you any money at present."[53]

Women's efforts to sustain families, farms, and businesses while the men were gone remained largely invisible in a world that gauged economic value in the public marketplace. Yet their labor at home represented a very real contribution to the infrastructure of the Gold Rush, an uncalculated sum that supported the men's enterprises.[54] Economics and emotions subtly distinguished the separations of different couples. Chinese women left behind, like those left in New England, worked hard and were often sorely missed. But they had far less independence or leverage than Gold Rush widows in the U.S. A Cantonese folk rhyme captured their dilemma:

> If you have a daughter don't marry her to a Gold
>   Mountain man.
> Out of ten years, he will not be in bed for one.
> The spider will spin webs on top of the bedposts,
> While dust fully covers one side of the bed.[55]

The "grass widows" left behind when Chinese men sought their fortunes at the land they called Gold Mountain faced separations that could last ten years or a lifetime, depending on whether finances allowed a husband to visit or return. An anonymous Chinese miner wrote his "Beloved Wife" from John Day, Oregon: "Because of our destitution I went out to try to make a living. Who could know that the Fate is always opposite to man's design. Because I can get no gold, I am detained in this secluded corner of a strange land. Furthermore, my beauty, you are implicated in an endless misfortune. I wish this paper would console you a little. This is all I can do for now."[56]

The length of separations and what Gold Rush wages gave to the family economy distinguished Chinese couples from their counterparts in the United States. While Chinese men struggled to support families in Guangdong, Gold Rush widows struggled to underwrite American men's enterprises in the gold fields by managing families, farms, and businesses.

The effects of these extended separations are hard to calculate. It would be tempting to hope that men who had done their own domestic chores valued women's work more highly when they returned, that women who had managed on their own became more independent and assertive in their husbands' absences. The men, however, seemed generally all too happy to relinquish domestic tasks to women when they finally reunited. Some women appear to have been more reluctant to relinquish their newfound authority. Abiah Warren Hiller supported her two daughters and her mother in New York by teaching during her husband William's four-year absence in the gold fields. Abiah had to act decisively when her house burned down. She wrote William that she had spent $300 to build a new home, and had finished a kitchen, bedroom, and schoolroom, but had left the rest for him to finish when he returned. "I hope what you have done to your house you have done well so it will be worth finishing when I get home," he replied. "I suppose the roof is too steep to suit you," she wrote in return, "but it suits me."[57]

The personal politics of separation could depend on many factors, including, of course, the previous relationship between husband and wife and the women's assessments of their own work. Abiah Warren was already an independent woman when William Hiller courted her, and she remained an independent woman after he returned. Thirteen years his senior, she had supported herself by teaching for years before they met when he became her student. By contrast, Almira Fay Stearns, who quit her job in a textile factory to marry, remained less able to assert her own needs, though she bore and raised five sons during her husband Daniel's extended absences. Daniel left her and their son in New Hampshire for almost four years, while he packed and sold supplies in the California and Oregon mines. Moving his family west in 1854, he left her behind in Oregon for another eleven years during his extended ventures as packer and merchant in the Oregon and Idaho mines. Finally reunited, she felt unable to oppose his plan to move to their isolated farm, away from women friends and relatives in Roseburg. After years of coping alone, she found herself in almost unendurable isolation and suffered for years from poor health and depression.[58]

The Gold Rush legacy was linked to how race and ethnicity operated in the class system of California mining. Skilled White laborers and the White middle classes were most able to establish families. Merchants and professionals were more able to marry than were miners, and American men moved in disproportionate numbers out of the mines and into middle-class occupations. For the Cornish, marriages were postponed by distance, economic insecurity, and the paucity of single women. Few Chinese men could marry in California, and few wives could join them to raise families in America.

Cornishness nonetheless remained a positive identity in a world where Cornishmen were presumed to be skilled miners, and where Cornish shift bosses and superintendents hired a Cornish workforce. The Cornish remained, in the words of the *Owyhee Avalanche*, remarkably "clannish," though as Protestants and English speakers, they were in a better position than most immigrants to assimilate. Ethnicity became marketable; Cornishness insured the status and wages of highly-skilled working-class men.[59]

Skilled miners could command wages sufficient to support families. White miners increasingly aspired to middle-class Euro-American family norms, which separated the public world of manly labor from female domesticity. Significantly, Cornish sons followed their fathers underground, but Cornish wives and daughters did not join the mining workforce in North America. It became a mark of achievement for western hardrock miners and for their unions, to ensure the wages that kept wives and daughters out of the paid workforce, and their sons in school for an acceptable period.[60] While downwardly-mobile American craftsmen pursued middle-class respectability, immigrant miners from Cornwall, Yorkshire, and Ireland sought wages sufficient to support a family, or at least sufficient to keep married women out of the paid workforce, and sons at school through grade eight.

One of the least-noticed social legacies of the California Gold Rush was its gendered assignment of labor. Domestic work was marked as feminine, regardless of who did it, while mining itself was masculine. Although this division was so commonly assumed it seemed somehow "natural," it was in fact a social invention. Women did perform mining labor in other times and places, and Miwok women in California adapted gold mining to their seasonal round of activities, using tightly woven baskets to pan the California streambeds as they tried to buffer the dislocations wrought by disease and dispossession.[61] Women were restricted from working underground in England only in 1842, when the Mines and Collieries Act forbade the employment of boys under ten and of all females in British mines.[62] Women and girls, as we have seen, continued to perform hard labor for little pay in the surface workings.

Euro-American men worked to establish middle-class homes, marked by wide separations between the public world of masculine commerce and the private domain of female domesticity. For the Cornish the chance to keep women and children out of the mines was a distinct improvement from the worlds of labor they left in Cornwall. The homes of middle-class Chinese immigrants became the sites of social reproduction for a Chinese American community, since only the tiny middle class *could* marry and raise children.

Who did what work, how people of different races and ethnicities stood in relation to one another, what activities were considered manly and which womanly, these were some of their social legacies. We cannot trace their stories from the partial perspectives of Twain's "erect, bright-eyed, quick-moving, strong-handed young giants." They are the stuff of myth and fantasy, but not of history.

It remains important to consider why Twain's fantasy remained for so long imprinted as history. The answer, I think, has to do with the ability of young virile White American men to act in these stories as surrogates for the nation, to represent America's destiny to fill the continent with superior strength, pluck, and energy, to claim the imaginary "unpeopled land." If we stop the action where Twain's restless young giants startle the solitudes of an unpeopled land, then we can fit the Gold Rush into a nostalgic version of the American frontier. But if we widen the focus of our lens to include all the actors, and if we widen our historical perspective to see where they came from and what they did next, Twain's picture becomes fantasy.

Fantasyland is a California cultural creation, and it lies, as I recall, just next door to Frontierland. Frontierland fantasies do not explain adult lives, personal or social, not in 1849, and not now.

Where, then, to return to my rhetorical title, have all those young men gone? With luck, they have forsaken the Wild West, forsaken Frontierland, and left Hisland behind. That leaves historians to trace their complex routes to home and work. In these histories, the young men will not represent the linear movement of the nation across the continent, but the complex and interdependent negotiations of family fortunes. With luck they will enter collective memories not as mythic heroes, but as social ancestors who helped forge the worlds we inherit.

Where did all the real men go? Back to Massachusetts, Maine, and Guangdong; back to a place in Cornwall called Nevada Farm. To fetch their families or rejoin their wives. Underground, to timber the mine shafts. To cook dinner for their cabin mates. They grew up. Into history, every one.

NOTES

This lecture was originally prepared for "The California Gold Rush as A World Event," a lecture series sponsored by the University of California, Sacramento to commemorate the Sesquicentennial of the California Gold Rush. Subsequent to my 2000 Chair's Lecture, it was published in Kenneth N. Owens, ed., *Riches for All: The California Gold Rush and the World* (Lincoln: University of Nebraska Press, 2002) and appears here by permission. I am grateful to the late Ken Owens for the invitation to think about the California Gold Rush, and for his extraordinary hospitality, support, and patience; to the staffs of the Bancroft Library at the University of California, Berkeley and the California State Historical Society, San Francisco, for their assistance and for permission to quote from their collections; and to the historians I cite for the scholarship that makes new interpretations possible.

Additional Sources: One of my sources for this essay was Susan Lee Johnson's doctoral dissertation, "'The gold she gathered': Difference, Domination, and California's Southern Mines" (PhD diss., Yale University, 1993). Shortly after my lecture, her magnificent book based on that work appeared. Susan Lee Johnson, *Roaring Camp: The Social World of the California Gold Rush* (New York and London: W.W. Norton and Company, 2000) remains the most important social history of the California Gold Rush in the southern mines, in the Sierra Nevadas east of Stockton. The southern mines have gotten less attention than the northern diggings, in part because they did not become sites of later industrial mining and in part because of the racial conflict and violence that Johnson probed. Her analyses of race and of negotiating gender identities are unmatched.

1. "Where Have All the Flowers Gone?," words and music by Pete Seeger. Seeger wrote the song in the mid-1950s, sometime after he was indicted for contempt by the House of Representatives on July 26, 1956. David King Dunaway, *How Can I Keep from Singing: Pete Seeger* (New York: McGraw Hill, 1981), 186.
2. Mark Twain, *Roughing It* (Hartford, 1872; repr., New York: Signet Classic, 1980), 307.
3. Susan Armitage, "Through Women's Eyes: A New View of the West," in *The Women's West*, eds. Susan Armitage and Elizabeth Jameson (Norman: University of Oklahoma Press, 1987), 9.
4. Calculated from *Bicentennial Edition, Historical Statistics of the United States, Colonial Time to 1970* (Washington, D.C.: U.S. Department of Commerce, 1970), Series A, 195–209.
5. For European migrations, see for instance Timothy J. Hatton and Jeffrey G. Williamson, *The Age of Mass Migration: Causes and Economic Impact* (New York: Oxford University Press, 1998).
6. For regions of origin, see for instance Ralph Mann, *After the Gold Rush: Society in Grass Valley and Nevada City, California 1849–1870* (Stanford, CA: Stanford University Press, 1982), Table 4, 225.
7. Susanna Townsend to Sister Mary, from Jackson Creek, November 23, 1852, Susanna Roberts Townsend Correspondence, 1838–68, The Bancroft Library, University of California, Berkeley (hereinafter called "Townsend Collection").
8. Jotham Varney to wife from Sacramento, September 8, 1850, and October 27, 1850, Jotham Varney Collection, California Historical Society, San Francisco (hereinafter called "Varney Collection").
9. James S. Barnes, letter from Sacramento, March 21, 1850, in James S. Barnes Collection, Bancroft Library, University of California, Berkeley (hereinafter called "Barnes Collection").
10. William Ives Morgan, journal entry, 53; William Ives Morgan Collection, Bancroft Library, University of California, Berkeley.
11. The following counties were included in each of the mining districts; the date in parenthesis is the first census year in which each appeared. Southern Mines: Amador (1860), Calavaras (1850), El Dorado (1850), Mariposa (1850), Tuolomne (1850); Northern Mines: Butte (1850), Nevada (1852), Placer (1852), Plumas (1860), Sierra (1852), Yuba (1850); Klamath/Shasta/Trinity: Del Norte (1860); Klamath (1852); Shasta (1850); Siskiyou (1852); Trinity (1850). Figures calculated from *Seventh Census of the Unites States: 1850. An Appendix Embracing Notes Upon the Tables of Each of the States, Etc.* (Washington, DC: Robert Armstrong, Public Printer, 1853), 972 (hereinafter called "1850 Census"); "Population and Industry of California, By the State Census for the Year 1852," in 1850 Census, 984 (hereinafter called "1852 Census"). In 1860, in the mining districts, almost half (48 percent) of the residents had come from other lands: 53 percent in the Southern Mines, and 45 percent in the Northern Mines and the Klamath/Trinity/Shasta district. Calculated from *Population of the United States in 1860; Compiled from the Original*

Returns of the Eighth Census (Washington, DC: Government Printing Office, 1864), 33 (hereinafter called "1860 Census").

12 Mann, *After the Gold Rush*, 229.
13 See Susan Lee Johnson, "'The gold she gathered': Difference, Domination, and California's Southern Mines" (PhD diss., Yale University, 1993), 113–15.
14 Overall, some 37 percent of California immigrants were British, 23 percent Chinese. *Ninth Census of the United States: The Tables of Race, Nationality, Sex, Selected Arts and Occupations* (Washington, DC: Government Printing Office, 1872), 336–37 (hereinafter called "1870 Census").
15 See Judy Yung, *Unbound Feet: A Social History of Chinese Women in San Francisco* (Berkeley: University of California Press, 1995), 16.
16 The Opium Wars occurred in 1839–1842 and 1856–1860.
17 The immigrants were particularly concentrated from selected districts. The largest proportions of Chinese emigrants to North America and Australia came from the district of T'oishan, to which an estimated 40–50 percent of the Chinese in America traced their origins. Sucheng Chan, *This Bittersweet Soil: The Chinese in California Agriculture, 1860–1910* (Berkeley: University of California Press, 1986), 17.
18 Shih-shan Henry Tsai, "Chinese Immigration, 1848–1882," in *People of Color in the American West*, ed. Sucheng Chan, Douglas Henry Daniels, Mario T. Garcia, and Terry P. Wilson (Lexington, MA: D.C. Heath and Company, 1994), 110–16, 112; excerpt reprinted from Shih-shan H. Tsai, *China and the Overseas Chinese in the United States 1868–1911* (Fayetteville: University of Arkansas Press, 1983).
19 Tsai, *China and the Overseas*, Table 1, 114; Chan, *This Bittersweet Soil*, 43.
20 Tsai, "Chinese Immigration," 116.
21 Mann, *After the Gold Rush*, 237.
22 Arthur Cecil Todd, *The Cornish Miner in America* (Truro, Cornwall: D. Bradford Barton Ltd. and Glendale, CA: The Arthur Clark Co., 1967), 15.
23 Todd, *The Cornish Miner in America*, 18.
24 Todd, *The Cornish Miner in America*, 19, 21–22; A. L. Rowse, *The Cousin Jacks: The Cornish in America* (New York: Charles Scribner's Sons, 1969), 243.
25 Rowse, *Cousin Jacks*, 245.
26 Rowse, *Cousin Jacks*, 246. On the positive manipulation of Cornish identity in hardrock mining, see Ronald M. James, "Defining the Group: Nineteenth Century Cornish on the North American Mining Frontier," in *Cornish Studies Two*, ed. Philip Payton (Exeter, UK: University of Exeter Press, 1994), 32–47.
27 Quoted in Todd, *Cornish Miner*, 68–69.
28 Calculated from 1870 Census, 606–09.
29 Todd, *Cornish Miner*, 55.
30 See Richard E. Lingenfelter, *The Hardrock Miners* (Berkeley: University of California Press, 1974), 107–27; Sucheng Chan, ed., *Entry Denied* (Philadelphia: Temple University Press, 1991); Alexander Saxton, *The Indispensable Enemy-Labor and the Anti-Chinese Movement in California* (Berkeley: University of California Press, 1971); Roger Daniels, ed., *Anti-Chinese Violence in North America* (New York: Arno Press, 1978); Duane A. Smith, *Rocky Mountain Mining Camps: The Urban Frontier* (Bloomington: Indiana University Press, 1967; paperback ed., Lincoln: University of Nebraska Press, 1974), 29–34.
31 The Chinese Exclusion Act was renewed in 1892 and then renewed indefinitely in 1904, and was not repealed until 1943.

32 Chan, *Bittersweet Soil*, 73; for figures on occupations in 1860, 1870, 1880, and 1900, see Tables 3–6, 54–55, 62–63, 68–69, 73–74.
33 Chan, *Bittersweet Soil*, 86, 103.
34 James Barnes to Sister Mary from Sacramento City, December 31, 1853; from Sac[ramento] July 30, 1854; from Sacramento May 26, 1854; Barnes Collection.
35 Andrew Rotter first explored argonauts' preoccupations with home and family in "'Matilda for Gods Sake Write': Women and Families on the Argonaut Mind," *California Historical Quarterly* 58, no. 2 (Summer 1979): 128–41. See also Malcolm J. Rohrbough, *Days of Gold: The California Gold Rush and the American Nation* (Berkeley: University of California Press, 1997).
36 Letter from Rodney P. Odall, Jr., A Gold Miner in California, to his Parents, from Mariposa, November 25, 1850. Odall to Dear Parents, Brown's Bar, May 18, 1851. Rodney P. Odall, Jr., Collection, Bancroft Library, University of California, Berkeley.
37 James S. Barnes, from San Francisco, February 28, 1850; Barnes Collection.
38 James S. Barnes, from Sacramento, March 21, 1850; Barnes Collection.
39 James S. Barnes, from Sacramento, October 13, 1850; Barnes Collection.
40 Jotham Varney to his wife, from Sacramento, September 8, 1850, Varney Collection.
41 James S. Barnes from Sacramento, January 28, 1851, Barnes Collection.
42 Unsigned letter to Catharine D. Oliver of Boston from a female friend in San Francisco, MS 1596, California Historical Society, San Francisco.
43 Jo Ann Levy, *They Saw the Elephant: Women in the California Gold Rush* (1990; repr., Norman: University of Oklahoma Press, 1992), 91–92, 100–103, 107.
44 Susanna Townsend to sister Fanny, from Jackson Creek, January 19, 1852; Townsend Collection.
45 Susanna Townsend to Skotty, from Secreta Ranch, February 20, 1853; Townsend Collection.
46 Susanna Townsend to Sister Mary, from Sutterville, October 25 and November 13, 1853; Susanna Townsend to Skotty, from Sutterville, December 20, 1853; Susanna Townsend to Skotty, from Scuppernong, October 3–9, 1854; Townsend Collection.
47 Susanna Townsend to Sister Mary, April 25, 1856; Townsend Collection.
48 Susanna Townsend to Skotty, January 23, 1857; Townsend Collection.
49 See Linda Peavy and Ursula Smith, *Women in Waiting in the Westward Movement: Life on the Home Frontier* (Norman: University of Oklahoma Press, 1994); Linda Peavy and Ursula Smith, *The Gold Rush Widows of Little Falls* (St. Paul: Minnesota Historical Society Press, 1990).
50 Jotham Varney to wife, At sea, May 1850; Varney Collection.
51 Peavy and Smith, *Women in Waiting*, 17.
52 Jotham Varney, from Sacramento City, September 18, 1850, October 27, 1850, and November 19, 1850; Varney Collection.
53 Jotham Varney, At Sea, May 1850; Varney Collection.
54 See Peavy and Smith, *Women in Waiting*, 25.
55 Quoted in Yung, *Unbound Feet*, 21.
56 Reproduced in Shannon Applegate and Terence O'Donnell, *Talking on Paper: An Anthology of Oregon Letters and Diaries* (Corvallis: Oregon State University Press, 1994), 215.
57 Peavy and Smith, *Women in Waiting*, 43–88, esp. 43.
58 Peavy and Smith, *Women in Waiting*, 89–131.

59 Peavy and Smith, *Women in Waiting*.
60 See Elizabeth Jameson, *All That Glitters: Class, Conflict, and Community in Cripple Creek* (Urbana: University of Illinois Press, 1998), esp. chaps. 4 and 5.
61 The assumption that women should not mine underground has been breached against considerable resistance in the United States since the 1970s. In other times and places, it has not seemed so self-evident that mining was men's work. See for instance Patricia J. Hulden, "The Rhetoric and Iconography of Reform: Women Coal Miners in Belgium, 1848–1914," *The Historical Journal* 34, no. 2 (June 1991): 411–36; Zoila Hernandez, *El Coraje de las Mineras: Marginalidad Andino-Minera en Canaria* (Lima, Peru: La Asociacion, 1986); Angela V. John, *By the Sweat of Their Brow: Women Workers of Victorian Coal Mines* (London: Croom Helm, Ltd., 1990); Domitila Barrios de Chungara, *Let Me Speak: Testimony of Domitila, a Woman of the Bolivian Mines* (New York: Monthly Review Press, 1978); Lucy Murphy, "Economy, Race, and Gender Along the Fox-Wisconsin and Rock Riverways, 1737–1832" (PhD diss., Northern Illinois University, 1995); Johnson, "'The gold she gathered'," 379–80; Jaclyn J. Gier and Laurie Mercier, eds., *Mining Women: Gender in the Development of a Global Industry, 1670 to 2005* (New York: Palgrave Macmillan, 2006); Albert L. Hurtado, *Indian Survival on the California Frontier* (New Haven, CT: Yale University Press, 1988). In fact, for some British coal miners, the exclusion—or protection—of women from the mines was a distinct achievement they sought to extend to their children.
62 John, *By the Sweat of Their Brow*.

2

Guns to Butter: Reconceiving the American West

March 28, 2001

One of the great pleasures I discovered in Calgary was browsing the second-hand stores in Inglewood. There was an historical object at the Olde Tyme Antique Store to which I returned on every visit. I coveted it, calculating the cost against the frontier history it evoked. I could pass up the branding iron, the saddles, the rodeo posters, and ancient license plates. But I wanted the hand-cranked butter churn.[1] I imagined myself turning the crank with one hand while I read or perhaps savored a prairie sunset. These images, so central to my imagined pioneer past, remain seemingly far removed from the frontiers of history and collective imagination.

Ambrose Bierce once defined history as "an account mostly false, about events mostly unimportant, which are brought about by rulers mostly knaves, and soldiers mostly fools."[2] Substitute sheriffs for rulers, outlaws for knaves, toss in the cavalry, and you could have the "buns and guns" version of the American West. If Bierce's definition resonated for generations of glazed-out school children, it no longer defines all that history can be. A generation of new social histories have taken us some distance from a history bounded by battles, dates, and kings.

In this essay I consider the significance of western women's histories for what we might call History with a capital H—for rethinking a major narrative of American history. Putting women into histories of the American West requires confronting the part that the West has played in American history and American identity. From a Canadian perspective, it may also involve rethinking a mythic American West that has helped define what a mythic Canada is not.

That we can now think about how women and other so-called "ordinary" people made history—that we have the information to do that—is

45

the result of extensive collective labor to recover the stories of a vastly expanded historical cast. My own work has focused on a less heroic cast than the stock characters of our mythic Wests. My faith in their power to reshape the historical narrative was shaken by the literary scholar Carolyn Heilbrun, whose *Writing a Woman's Life* contains a passage I found so troubling that I've been wrestling with it for decades.[3] I read Heilbrun seeking insights about adding women's lives to western history. She suggested that was not enough. "[L]ives," she wrote, "do not serve as models; only stories do that. . . . We can only retell and live by the stories we have read or heard. . . . They may be read, or chanted, or experienced electronically, or come to us, like the murmurings of our mothers, telling us what conventions demand. Whatever their form or medium, these stories are what has formed us all; they are what we must use to make new fictions, new narratives."[4] And new histories.

So I begin with one of the histories that formed America and Americans—the tale of the mythic American frontier. The actors of this essay—hide tanners and translators, gardeners and gatherers, boardinghouse keepers and butter churners—are the female counterparts of a selective cast of men, the protagonists in the most influential essay in American history, Frederick Jackson Turner's "The Significance of the Frontier in American History." American history, Turner announced in 1893, had been "in a large degree the history of the colonization of the Great West. The existence of an area of free land, its continuous recession, and the advance of American settlement westward, explain American development."[5]

Turner opened his story by evoking a popular image of opening the trans-Appalachian West, the artist George Caleb Bingham's painting of Daniel Boone leading pioneers through Cumberland Gap in 1775 (see Figure 2.1). In Turnerian history, a predictable progression of frontiersmen trekked inexorably across the continent. "Stand at Cumberland Gap," he wrote, "and watch the procession of civilization, marching single file— the buffalo following the trail to the salt springs, the Indian, the fur trader and hunter, the cattle raiser, the pioneer farmer—and the frontier has passed them by. Stand at South Pass in the Rockies a century later and see the same procession."[6] In inevitable sequence, generations of pioneers repeated the "trader's frontier, the rancher's frontier, or the miner's frontier, and the farmer's frontier." Men's jobs defined these frontiers. There was no schoolteachers' frontier, no gardeners' frontier, no laundry workers'

Figure 2.1. George Caleb Bingham, Daniel Boone Escorting Settlers through the Cumberland Gap, 1851–52. Oil on canvas, 36 1/2 x 50 1/4". Mildred Lane Kemper Art Museum, Washington University, St. Louis. Gift of Nathaniel Phillips.

frontier, no chicken raisers,' or butter churners' frontier. Turner's frontiers wrote most women out of history, and probably most men as well.

I once thought our job was simply to add the missing players. I no longer think that is true. We have recorded the lives of many western women, but they remain largely separate from mainstream History. Putting new actors into their own histories is harder than recovering their lives. Because, as Heilbrun reminds us, there are two fundamental elements of any story, characters and narrative—people and plots. And there are, I think, three basic stages to reconceiving histories. First, we add the people—this is the stage that feminist historian Gerda Lerner called "add a woman and stir."[7] Next we see how the new actors stretch the limits of inherited histories. And only then can we begin to try to imagine new stories from the perspectives of the expanded cast.

From the perspectives of women and people of color, I think the project is somewhere in the middle of Stage Two. We have added women to history; survey textbooks include women; but only in books about women's history and only in women's history courses do women occupy center stage. Even then they are often simply slotted into inherited plots of westward movement and nation-building or grafted onto popular historical images. Even the newest histories do not cast women as leading actors in a history of all westerners, or all Americans.

To accept this challenge is to grapple with how intricately images of the American West are connected to the history of the nation, and with the stubbornly enduring influence of Dr. Turner, whose frontier thesis excluded women. I revisit Turner not out of any great desire to re-trash his thesis, or out of any disrespect for a man who was, in 1893, a progressive and creative revisionist. I do so because his plot fundamentally shaped the story Americans inherited as the story that "formed us all." It is, in Heilbrun's terms, a necessary starting point for new narratives, new histories.

To add women, we must dissect the plot that excluded them. Turner's subject was not frontiersmen but frontiers, not people but the nation. The frontier separated America from Europe and made Americans American. The story of westward expansion became the story of the country; western frontiers became the crucibles of American individualism and democracy. This, for Turner, was progress.

Three lines defined the forward progress of this history. The first line moved from East to West. As the nation moved west, human society, in an equally linear fashion, improved. The second line moved upward from savagery to civilization, as White Americans conquered the wilderness and the Indigenous people who lived there.[8] History progressed, Turner explained, as "primitive peoples" became "new nations."[9] Like his late-19th-century contemporaries, Turner assumed a ladder of civilization that moved upward in a sequential hierarchy of cultures, with hunters and gatherers at the bottom. The progression through Cumberland Gap charted the onward march of civilization from hunters to herders to pastoral agriculturalists.[10] Americans brought a superior civilization to "savages" whose lives would be improved by adopting nuclear families, private property, agriculture, and Christianity.

Turner's last line of progress wrote women out of history. The third line of progress moved from the inside out; it assumed that public life was more important, historically, than private life. History progressed as people moved from "families into states." "Complex society," Turner wrote, "is precipitated by the wilderness into a kind of primitive organization based on the family."[11] History then progressed as men formed territories and governments, as they established states—the *real* subjects of history.

Family households—those "primitive" social units—buried women in a history of the nation, a history that isolated them behind domestic walls, invisible and unheard. We can see and hear many more women than we could a generation ago. The next step is to try to imagine western history from their perspective, to imagine it, in effect, as the story of the chicken raisers' frontier.

Let's try. Add some women and stir. We begin with a female cast, the counterparts of Turner's Indian, fur trader and hunter, rancher, miner, and pioneer farmer. From women's perspectives, the separate sequence of the Indian, the fur trader, and the hunter become the same frontier. This is because the women of the fur trade frontier *were* Indians. The various fur trades involved exchanges among men from Britain, France, the U.S., and a multitude of Native peoples over a vast time and territory. In 1980, in her pathbreaking book, *Many Tender Ties*, Sylvia Van Kirk showed that the Canadian fur trade *depended* on Aboriginal and Métis women. Aboriginal men served as trappers, guides, and boatmen; Native women trapped smaller animals, particularly the highly prized marten, prepared furs for storage and shipment, made clothing, snowshoes, and moccasins, produced pemmican, an essential staple of the fur trade diet, and served as translators, diplomats, and guides.[12]

For women, the most significant feature of all frontiers was an excess of men. For over a century there were no European women in Western Canada. British and French men married Native women according to the "custom of the country." Native women and their daughters became favored domestic partners who forged a distinct fur trade society.[13]

The smaller U.S. fur trade developed in the early-19th century, conducted largely by men who were themselves trappers. An estimated 80 percent married during their years in the trade; over half married Native American women, a fourth married Hispanic women of the northern Spanish borderlands, and a fourth, European women. About 70 percent of trappers' marriages with Native women lasted until one partner died—fifty-two marriages lasted an average of twenty-six years.[14] White society was often inhospitable to these couples, and husbands more commonly remained with their wives' people. Such was the case when Huntkahitawin (Brule Sioux) married trader James Bordeaux, a union that strengthened her husband's position as trader and her brother's as paramount chief. She and countless other native women literally mothered new peoples throughout the Americas. What that meant for *them* is harder to discern, because most of our sources come from the men. But they suggest that strong emotional bonds linked many couples. Asked, for instance, why he hadn't left his Nez Perce wife behind when he retired and settled in Oregon, Joe Meek put his hand on his chest and said, "I could not do that, it *hurt here*."[15]

Turner's economic categories of trader and hunter become particularly muddy through the story of one Hidatsa woman, known most often as Buffalo Bird Woman, whose name in her own language was Mahidiweash.[16] What we know of her life comes through the filtered translations of Presbyterian minister and anthropologist Gilbert L. Wilson, who worked at the Fort Berthold Indian Reservation in North Dakota for twelve summers, beginning in 1906. He published her story in two volumes, *Buffalo Bird Woman's Garden* (1917), based on a typical seasonal cycle in 1857, when Buffalo Bird Woman was eighteen years old, and *Waheenee: An Indian Girl's Story* (1921).[17]

From 1787–1845, there were three independent Hidatsa villages at the mouth of the Knife River, before the fur trade precipitated enormous changes for the northern Plains tribes.[18] Demand for buffalo hides depleted the herds, intensified women's labor tanning hides, altered the relationships between women and men, and increased conflicts among peoples who competed for buffalo. Horses and guns made it easier for men to kill many buffalo quickly, increasing women's work preparing hides for market. First acquired through raiding, horses entered the tribes as the private property of young and daring men, who were good raiders. Their new prominence elevated youth over age, aggression over cooperation.[19] These changes, however, enter Mahidiweash's account only tangentially, as European trade goods like iron hoes altered women's work. The Hidatsa economy combined hunting and agriculture. The development of agriculture is a central unifying thread in the Hidatsa history Mahidiweash learned from her grandmother, who taught her that the Hidatsa trace their origins to Miniwakan, or Devils Lake, now called Spirit Lake:

> We Hidatsas [she told Wilson] believe that our tribe once lived under the waters of Devils Lake. Some hunters discovered the root of a vine growing downward, and climbing it, they found themselves on the surface of the earth. Others followed them up, until half the tribe had escaped; but the vine broke under

the weight of a pregnant woman, leaving the rest prisoners. A part of the tribe are therefore still beneath the lake. . . .

Those of my people who escaped from the lake built villages nearby. These were of earth lodges, such as my tribe built until very recent years. [20]

The people planted gardens of ground beans and potatoes they brought from their home under the water. Buffalo Bird Woman measured change in gardens, by their size and their crops. The Hidatsa, she said, learned of corn and squashes from the Mandan, who lived at the Missouri River. After the Hidatsa got corn, they joined the Mandan near the mouth of the Heart River. "I think," she said, "this was hundreds of years ago."[21] When firewood grew scarce, they moved to the mouth of the Knife River. "Smallpox was brought to my people here, by the traders. In a single year, more than half my tribe died, and of the Mandans, even more." The worst epidemic, in 1837, killed over half the Hidatsa and perhaps seven-eighths of the neighboring Mandan. Buffalo Bird Woman dated her personal history from that disaster: "I was born in an earth lodge by the mouth of the Knife river, in what is now North Dakota, three years after the smallpox winter."[22]

The survivors moved up the Missouri and "built a village at Like-a-fishhook bend, where they lived together, Hidatsas and Mandans, as one tribe." She continued, "We lived in Like-a-fishhook village about forty years, or until 1885, when the government began to place families on allotments."[23] Whites also, Buffalo Bird Woman said, brought weeds, like thistle and mustard, new seeds for oats, wheat, watermelons, and onions, and for vegetables she considered inferior, like turnips, and big squashes (see Figure 2.2).[24]

Like-a-fishhook village became part of the Fort Berthold Indian Reservation, where missionaries and the U.S. government tried to teach the Native Americans the virtues of Christianity, private property, and patriarchal nuclear families. Buffalo Bird Woman moved from an earth lodge in a village to an isolated square log cabin. But she continued many of her accustomed tasks, particularly gardening.

The history she told Wilson was told to younger women by older women. The historical actors include old women and a pregnant woman as well as hunters and warriors; the important events include exchanges among tribes, the acquisition of crops, and garden technology. The

Figure 2.2. Buffalo Bird Woman in Her Garden. "Hidatsa Indian woman hoeing squash with a bone hoe." Date and photographer unknown. Gilbert L. and Frederick N. Wilson Papers, Minnesota Historical Society, 9448-A. Photo courtesy of the Minnesota Historical Society.

narrative framework places gender and subsistence at the center of the story.

Wilson, however, had her conclude *Waheenee* with words that echo Turner: "I am an old woman now. The buffaloes and black-tail deer are gone, and our Indian ways are almost gone. . . . My little son grew up in the white man's school. He can read books, and he owns cattle and has a farm. . . . Our Indian life, I know, is gone forever."[25] Through Wilson's filters, Buffalo Bird Woman became the unacculturated voice of tradition. Her son, Goodbird, who learned English and converted to Christianity, fit the Turnerian trajectory from savagery to civilization. Goodbird joins mainstream history, while his mother's story lags, unconnected.[26] This was hardly progress for a woman who had not been isolated from other women or separated from her own story.

But the stories she inherited did not shape the story Wilson recorded. *Her* story challenges Turner's. The women of the fur traders' and hunters' frontiers were not only hide dressers and gatherers. They were traders, translators, economic and domestic partners, historians, and agriculturalists—gardeners. The ladder of civilization moved Mahidiweash from collective agriculture and villages where women shared a community and a history, from gardens and lodges owned by women to an isolated farm and nuclear family controlled by men.[27] From her perspective, progress becomes an ambiguous and contested concept.

On Turner's ladder of cultures, mining was a step up from trading, hunting, and gathering. But the women of the mining West rarely found their fortunes sifting precious metals or toiling underground. Their hopes lay in domesticity, in pursuits not so far removed from Buffalo Bird Woman's garden. If you read the previous essay, you encountered Susanna Townsend, who accompanied her husband Emery in the California Gold Rush to a claim on Jackson Creek in Amador County. While Emery worked the diggings, Susanna insisted on a garden. The Townsends' security owed as much to Susanna's grubbing after vegetables as to Emery's grubbing for gold. "It is astonishing," she wrote, "how the sale of a few vegetables mounts up. Our cabbages have been very fine solid heads and we have sold them at a gold shilling per pound and some of them weigh 8–10 and 12 pounds."[28] From a half-acre of cabbages, tomatoes, and other vegetables she "cleared twelve hundred dollars." She had always hoped, she wrote, "to get Emery to settle somehow on a small ranch. I have always felt sure we would do better at it than mining and not work half so hard." By 1853 the Townsends moved to twenty-eight acres near Sutterville. They pinned great hope on a cabbage crop "good for $2000 at least."[29]

If Susanna Townsend followed Turner's progression from the mines to the farmers' frontier, other women violated that trajectory, moving from farming to mining, and inward from the diggings to a domestic marketplace. In the overwhelmingly masculine mining West, women found a narrow set of domestic options. In the paid workforce or in their own households, they cooked, cleaned, sewed, scrubbed, waited tables, and provided "society" for the male majority. Although married White women rarely worked for wages outside their homes, they frequently tended vegetable gardens and small livestock, made clothing, did housework, and provided income by keeping boarders, cooking, or doing laundry at home. Mine shutdowns, strikes, and accidents made women periodically responsible for supporting families. A man's death meant that a woman somehow had to earn money.³⁰ Anne Ellis's husband, for instance, was killed when he drilled into an unexploded dynamite charge in the Vindicator Mine in Victor, Colorado. The mine gave her $600 in exchange for a release from liability. Each man who worked on the Vindicator donated a day's wages. Beyond that, Ellis was on her own with two children to support. At first, she lived by selling baked goods—her landlady promised to "see that all the girls" of the nearby Red Light district bought Ellis's wares. Later she kept boarders.³¹

Four-year-old Beulah Pryor came to Cripple Creek from an Illinois farm when her stepfather was recruited as a strikebreaker during the 1903–1904 miners' strike. He was not only a scab, it turned out, but a wife beater as well. Her mother escaped an oppressive marriage, encouraged by the single miners who lived next door, who promised that they would bring her their laundry and would board with her so she could support her four children. Beulah helped her mother bake the pies that attracted her clientele.³² Anne Ellis and Beulah Pryor's mother might represent one end of an egg and butter frontier. They probably bought their eggs and butter at a local store and then processed them into the bread and pies they sold to support their families.

Their domestic labor intersected the public world of the marketplace. At the same time, women of the mining frontier told the public history of "knaves and soldiers" in terms of private domesticity. Kathleen Chapman, a miner's daughter born in 1895, dated a crucial miners' union victory in family time. "In 1894," she told me, "Tom was born. And that's when the Bull Hill strike was."³³ The story of a key battle between miners and an army of deputy sheriffs became a family story.

> There wasn't too many people up there, you know—and the men went out and they had their wives come along with them. And Mama said she wrapped Tom in a blanket and went along. And the men took their coats off, and their hats, and put them up in a tree and put the guns up in there. And then, of course they were milling around, you know, and oh, they just thought that the *world* was up there, this militia did, when they seen them. . . . boy, they stopped and they turned around and went back to Colorado Springs *on the run!*³⁴

Ten years later, when the militia occupied the Cripple Creek District during a second miners' strike, her mother pointedly kept "two great big butcher knives... razor sharp. And she always said if one of those militia men ever come in her house in the middle of the night, they'd leave with less than they brought in!"[35] When the miners lost that strike, Kathleen Chapman again described the defeat in terms of domestic loss. Asked what difference the strike made for working people, she replied:

> Oh my, it changed it awful!... Well, you should have seen the homes that was up there.... They were beautiful, some of them. They were just gorgeous. Well, people just got up and left, you know, and left their homes like it was, and lots of them never come back to them. People would go in and destroy the homes, and pick up what they wanted, and the houses went to wrack, and they tore them down, and—oh, it just, it just used to make me sick all over.[36]

This history, usually described as a labor war, became a personal and family story of domestic loss.

Ranching was roughly equivalent to mining in Turner's cultural hierarchy. Ranch women, like mining and fur trade women, were outnumbered and often restricted from ranch management or working the cattle. Their relationships with cows involved dairy more than beef. Joan Jensen has documented in some detail how eastern farm women developed butter into a significant cash product and replaced textiles with butter as a primary household industry.[37] Women continued their trade as they moved West—quite literally. Kit Belknap recorded her recipe for making butter on the Oregon Trail in 1848.

> Milk the cows at night and strain the milk in little buckets. Cover them up and set them on the ground under the wagons. In the morning, take off the nice thick cream and put it in the churn. Save the strippings [the last milk drawn from the cow] from... the morning milking and put it in the churn also. After riding all day you have a nice roll of butter as long as you have plenty of grass and water.[38]

We could probably chart a mid-19th-century butter frontier that followed women's ingenuity and the grass and water supply. Nineteenth-century city dwellers like Anne Ellis bought the butter that farm women exchanged for cash or goods at country stores, and women on successive western frontiers supplemented ranch and farm incomes with their butter, eggs, and cream. Guri Olsdatter wrote from her Minnesota farm in 1863 that with her three cows she produced 230 pounds of butter in one summer to earn $66.[39] Montana women by 1910 used their butter money to buy the windmills that made it possible to survive on the arid plains.[40] Elinore Pruitt Stewart wrote in 1913 that her ten cows' butter bought a year's supply of gasoline and flour—two essentials that her Wyoming ranch could not produce.[41] Years later, Mildred Kanipe's dairy herd enabled her to expand her ranch near Oakland, Oregon. She added 700 acres and paid for it by running "a grade-A dairy for eight years. Let me tell you," she said, "don't ever get a dairy unless you want to work yourself to death. Because it don't make any difference. If you died, you'd have to get up and milk those cows. . . . It wouldn't be so bad if you had two people. But I done it alone for eight years."[42]

Ranch women's work was not so far removed from the farmers' frontier, which in turn recharts the meanings of frontier opportunity and frontier individualism. One of the fundamentals of the Turnerian story was the opportunity provided by access to free land. The land may not have been free, or even empty, but the Homestead Act of 1862 offered some women an independent stake in the land for the first time—if they were single or heads of households. Thousands took the chance. Colorado, Wyoming, and North Dakota land records indicate that women constituted anywhere from 5 percent of homesteaders in the 1880s to 20 percent by 1920.[43] In her study of a sample of single women homesteaders, Elaine Lindgren found that 34 percent of women homesteaders in North Dakota were immigrants—24 percent were Norwegian; 5 percent, Canadian.[44] Few women homesteaded as rugged individuals, but often settled near women friends and kin. In Lindgren's sample, only 40 percent stayed on their land much longer than fiver years, the time required to claim it.[45] The sales of homesteads financed numerous dreams. Anna Thingvold and her widowed sister Emma stayed on their homesteads only long enough to gain title, then rented them and used the income to finance a millinery and dressmaking shop in Willow City, North Dakota, to support themselves and Emma's daughter. Theona Carkin's homestead financed her university degree. Maggie O'Connor, from County Cork, filed for land in 1891. She gave the cash from its sale to the Sisters of St. Joseph of Carondelet in St. Paul, the order she joined as Sister Anita.[46] Many women homesteaders married, but later than their contemporaries; many used their homesteads to expand joint marital landholdings.[47]

For the women who remained on the farming frontier, butter and egg income often provided the crucial buffer in family economies. Rosa Ise moved to her western Kansas homestead with her husband Henry in 1873, just before the onset of a four-year depression. "The first butter Rosie sold," that year, her son John later wrote, "brought forty cents a pound, but all prices soon began to decline, and before the end of the summer, butter was worth only ten cents a pound and eggs scarcely worth taking to town. Some of the local politicians talked about a panic and hard times in the country, but Rosie knew only that butter and eggs were cheap."[48] The Ises survived the hard times in part through Rosie's efforts on the local trading frontier as she accumulated butter and egg credits at the store in Cawker City. The welcome arrival of an early spring relieved the successive disasters of grasshoppers, drought, and a hard winter. "When the grass began to turn green in March, Rosie was able to make butter to sell, so that they could buy sugar and real coffee, and material for baby clothes...."[49] During lean times, she gave her friend Mary Bartsch a dressed chicken for Christmas; for her contribution to the local Christmas tree fund Rosie offered her due bills at the store for butter and eggs.[50] Rosie Ise's butter and eggs linked her family to neighbors and the local community. When Anne Ellis bought the butter and eggs that women like Rosie bartered, the butter and egg frontier also linked the mining and farming frontiers.

Equally direct and messy links connected the Indians' and farmers' frontiers. As Buffalo Bird Woman talked to Gilbert Wilson, a young woman homesteader named Rachel Calof journeyed to Buffalo Bird Woman's starting point—a homestead north of Devils Lake, in Ramsay County, where she homesteaded from 1894–1917. Born in 1876, south of Kiev, she came to North Dakota for an arranged marriage to Abraham Calof whose parents, brother, and two cousins had claimed homesteads around a post office called Benzion.[51]

The farmers' frontier hardly seemed the apex of civilization to Rachel, numbed by her mother-in-law's uncaring control and shocked by conditions in the homestead shack she shared with the extended Calof family.[52] Most winters for eighteen years, her parents-in-law and other relatives joined Abe, Rachel, their growing family, and their livestock. During the first winter, their twelve-by-fourteen-foot homestead shanty housed five people, twenty-four chickens, and a calf.[53]

Calof wanted above all to control this domestic space, including the domestic religious ceremonies that established her as a married Jewish woman in her own home. Her first victory came when she fashioned lamps from dried mud and a scrap of rag, fueled by butter. She made more of the lamps "Seeing that the old woman had not even a bit of candle with which to greet and bless the Sabbath ...." Her achievement, she said, won her "status in the household even though I was both young and only a woman."[54]

Soon, pregnant with her first child, she plastered and whitewashed her tiny claim shanty and foraged to augment their meager food supply of "a little flour, some barley, some soured milk, and a little butter." Rachel "found what appeared to be wild garlic.... It tasted wonderful and didn't seem to harm me, so I gathered quite a number of bunches." Since "bread and garlic make a poor meal," she looked further and found wild mushrooms. She hauled water and dry grass to bake bread and fried the mushrooms and garlic in butter. "This meal made in large measure with food gathered from the wild prairie was simply delicious," she recalled over forty years later.[55] Her success as a gatherer became not a step downward on the ladder of civilization, but a rare happy memory on a farmer's frontier.

Pauline Shoemaker journeyed to another site in Buffalo Bird Woman's personal landscape, to teach school on the Knife River where Buffalo Bird woman was born. Shoemaker stayed to homestead. In 1910, a local rancher invited her and some friends to join the annual horse roundup. "Needing some more supplies for the prospective trip," she wrote,

> ... four of us went in the auto to a ranch five miles away to get the butter supply. There was a large sod house at this place and we were invited in and found the interior as cheerful as tho the house were built of the best lumber. The inside was papered and there happened to be a very jolly crowd assembled and they were enjoying music on the piano, cornet, mandolin and phonograph which shows that life is not so dull even in a sod house.

Shoemaker was glad that she had "seized the opportunity" to go on the roundup, she wrote. There would "probably be but one more round up in this section of the country" because a "Reservation [would] be opened up next year."[56]

If Pauline Shoemaker feared that the reservation would end the open range, for Native American women it had long since closed. They experimented with new products to buffer economies endangered by the frontiers that eroded tribal resources. Navajo women wove and Pueblo women sold pottery to buy the items they could no longer produce. Osage women in Oklahoma and Yakima women in Washington turned to butter, producing 24,000 and 20,000 pounds respectively in 1890.[57] They followed a dubious trajectory "from savagery to civilization" as Euro-American gender roles charted new relations of race and power.

While Susanna Townsend sold her cabbages, neighboring Chinese also grew food for California miners. They labored to support themselves, and often their families in China, who were legally prohibited from emigrating to the U.S. after the 1882 Chinese Exclusion Act. To care for the overwhelmingly male Chinese population, Chinese men cooked, did laundry, and labored as domestic servants.[58] Most Chinese farmers specialized in truck farming, but in 1860, one, Ah Sam, churned $200 worth of butter on his Sacramento County farm, a skill he probably learned from a Euro-American woman, since Chinese did not at that time commonly eat butter.[59] Chinese men combined tasks that Euro-Americans separated into men's and women's work. A woman, who signed her name only as "Martha," wrote in the *Stockton Independent* in 1876 that an eighteen-year-old Chinese man helped her care for her family of two boys, an invalid husband, and three hired hands. The young man cooked, washed, ironed, churned, cared for pigs and poultry, butchered, herded stock, and was handy with carpenters' tools—all for $20 a month. She found him "honest," she said, and "with principles that would do credit to a Christian."[60] The delegation of butter making and other domestic tasks to Chinese men marked their subordinate status and identified their race with so-called "women's work."

If butter connects these disparate frontiers, it also moved Euro-American women from private domesticity to public activism to protect their precious cash product. From 1870–1900, an estimated half million farm women joined the Patrons of Husbandry, or the Grange, the Farmers' Alliance, and the Populist Party. Some worked for suffrage, temperance, or other reforms as well. The Grange championed women's political equality, formed consumers' cooperatives that purchased sewing machines for rural women, and fought the manufacture of oleomargarine that threatened women's cash-producing butter. It forced Congress to pass a stiff regulatory law in 1886 that decreased the manufacture of processed oleomargarine for almost a decade.[61]

So we have added all these women to Turner's West along with a hefty dose of butter. If we stir all these ingredients, what do we get?

Even the limited cast of western women glimpsed here demonstrates abundantly how women stretch the boundaries of western history. They make a mess of it. The domestic women of Turner's frontiers make a mess of his neat categories. Their stories do not move neatly from East to West, from savagery to civilization, from family to nation. They come from Russia, Mexico, Canada, China, Ireland, and Norway; they emerge from the waters of Devils Lake. Through their lives, the tidy progression of successive frontiers becomes very messy indeed. The traders' and hunters' frontier becomes the Indians' and farmers' frontier; the miners' frontier becomes the cooks' and gardeners' frontier; the ranchers' frontier becomes an unkosher mess of meat and dairy, where the egg and butter money buys the windmills and grazing land; the farmers' frontier becomes the gatherers'; and in all this complexity there is no simple calculus of progress, civilization, success, or loss. Victories do not always lie in individual triumphs, on western farms; they can lie in towns, to the East, in St. Paul convents, at the sewing machine co-op and the union hall. Rachel Calof might agree with Turner that her household was a primitive social organization, but her life improved, not as it grew more complex, but as it simplified to her nuclear family—as she jettisoned her in-laws. If 160 acres allowed the Calofs and Ises to raise their families and offered single women an economic stake, for Buffalo Bird Woman an isolated square cabin on 160 acres signified no step up the ladder of civilization, but the loss of the community of women who transmitted history and identity with stories told in communal gardens and their mothers' lodges. Turner thought the frontier forged a composite nationality, a single national identity, but his national creation story was not one that Buffalo Bird Woman or Ah Sam could easily or happily claim.

If we combine these scattered stories to imagine a new frontier, a butter makers' frontier, butter making becomes a lens through which to view economic and social needs. It fuels Rachel Calof's lamps, to preserve tradition and claim domestic space. It cooks the garlic and mushrooms she gathered. It funds windmills, flour, gasoline, and baby clothes. It leads to a concert inside a sod house, underwrites a community Christmas celebration, provides the wages to support families in China, the resources to prop up fragile tribal economies. The butter-makers' frontier opens windows on domestic economies, on differences of race and class in the allocation of domestic labor. It connects the private world of domesticity with the public work of activism, and the women of virtually all of Turner's now-not-so-neatly-sequenced frontiers.

The butter makers' West is a complex and messy place. Here we are in the middle of Stage Two, trying to imagine a new history from all these perspectives. How do we tidy up these cluttered histories? Can we combine them all in one neat story, make a different order of this densely populated and multiply chronicled historical landscape? I'm not sure in this case that our mothers tell us to clean up our mess. I'm not sure that I can, or that I want to impose the kind of single linear story told in a single authoritative voice that drives inherited histories of the West or of the nation. Women's stories do, nonetheless, suggest relationships that might link a messy, complicated, and collective history.

They suggest an American West marked not by democratic progress but unequal relationships of gain and loss, a West characterized not by rugged individualism but by interdependence. The staple economies of Turner's frontiers—the economies of fur trading, mining, lumbering, ranching, and farming that produced the staples of Harold Innis's Canadian West[62] as well—these economies, reconceived, would include the domestic and female labor that was an essential part of the frontier infrastructure.

If we cannot divide the West into neat economic categories, women's lives suggest continuities that bridge long-standing debates among western historians. We still argue about the precise boundaries of the region—where somewhere else ends and the West begins. We still debate whether the frontier transformed Americans, or whether settlers brought their culture West with them.[63] This is either/or history: either the frontier changed everything or nothing changed. Women's lives suggest that we move from these "either/or" constructions to more layered "both/and" interpretations. A history that linked private and public experience could embrace both continuity and change, adaptation and tradition, the histories that people share and particular heritages as well.

Turnerian history separated public from private, savagery from civilization, and America from everywhere else. Some of the continuities of women's history cross national boundaries as well, and question the assumption that nations are the main subjects of history. The continuities of ordinary lives may bridge not just Turner's frontiers, but also our separate Wests.

The first crucial step, I think, in reconceiving the West, is to invert Turner's third line of progress that subordinated daily private acts to public events. Most people's lives have revolved around the domestic concerns that Turner casually buried in his primitive organization based on the family. If any aspiration linked women's stories, and the stories of many western men as well, it was the hope of home. Home was where histories were shared, butter was churned, new peoples conceived. Home was a stake in the future, a reason to build schools and churches, a place of resistance. Women's paths to activism often led from home to community to public politics, as they organized concerts and schools, protected union wages and the family butter money. Home for Joe Meek was what it hurt too much to leave.

The West looks different from inside those domestic spaces. If region figures in these stories, it is expressed in the physical dimensions of homes and families—in the water and food supplies, whether there is wood to burn or dried dung, the distance to neighbors or kin, whether there is grass enough for dairy cows. It is in the social relationships that make a place distinct: the mix of peoples, the numbers of women and men.

The common themes that animate women's own words are subsistence, kin, and generations. To claim them as collective histories means turning Turner on his head—to see families not as the most primitive forms of social organization, but the core of human society, those daily private relationships that first transmit culture and that can transform it. From that perspective, women's efforts to preserve traditions—like Buffalo Bird Woman's stories and Rachel Calof's mud-and-butter Sabbath lamps—become significant sources of identity, rather than obstacles to progress that impede a common national character.

The challenge is to connect women's mundane stories of work and kin and domesticity to our vision of what history is: not only the story of the nation, but also the story of people; not only the story of guns, but the story of butter, too.

So, let's return once more to Cumberland Gap. Imagine the untidy procession in no particular order—the buffaloes and hide tanners, the chicken raiser and trader, the teacher and gardener, the gatherer and boardinghouse keeper, the activist and butter churner—your grandmother, your mother. Progress measured not from family to nation, but in iron hoes and millinery shops. The murmurings of our mothers, the family stories, some in uneasy tension with stories learned in school. Imagine all these women at Cumberland Gap. They offer a choice. We can follow Daniel Boone's ghost down the same path west to South Pass, or we can see where the women lead us. We can follow them home.

NOTES

1. I prepared this essay first as a lecture to inaugurate the Research Center on Women at the University of Nevada-Las Vegas, March 30, 2000. I am grateful to Joanne Goodwin, who honored me with the invitation to speak and provided gracious hospitality. This essay rests on the prodigious scholarship on western women's histories generated since the 1970s. I am indebted to this community of historians, whose work enables and enriches my own. I returned to some of the themes in this essay in the last essay in this volume, which also references scholarship published in the interim. Regrettably, the Old Tyme Antique Shop has long since closed its doors. I never got the butter churn.
2. Ambrose Bierce, *The Devil's Dictionary* (Cleveland and New York: The World Publishing Company, 1911), 138.
3. I originally wrote "for over a decade." Now, some twenty years later, Heilbrun continues to speak to me, as chapter 13 attests.
4. Carolyn G. Heilbrun, *Writing a Woman's Life* (New York: Ballantine Books, 1988), 13.
5. Frederick Jackson Turner, "The Significance of the Frontier in American History," first presented at the Historical Congress in Chicago at the World's Columbian Exhibition of 1893, was originally printed in *Annual Report of the American Historical Association for the Year 1893* (Washington, DC: Government Printing Office, 1894). Turner's essay is quoted here from Martin Ridge, ed., *History, Frontier, and Section: Three Essays by Frederick Jackson Turner* (Albuquerque: University of New Mexico Press, 1993), 59.
6. Turner, "Significance of the Frontier," 67.
7. Gerda Lerner, "The Challenge of Women's History," in *The Majority Finds Its Past: Placing Women in History* (New York: Oxford University Press, 1979), 169.
8. The concept of a cultural hierarchy from savagery to civilization was widely accepted in the late-19th century, as expressed, for instance, in the work of Lewis Henry Morgan, *Ancient Society, or Researches in the Lines of Progress from Savagery through Barbarism to Civilization* (New York: World Publishing, 1877).
9. Frederick Jackson Turner, "The Significance of History," in Ridge, *History, Frontier, and Section*, 49. This essay was originally published in the *Wisconsin Journal of Education* in 1891.
10. Turner, "Significance of the Frontier," 67-70.
11. Turner, "Significance of the Frontier," 82; "Significance of History," 55.
12. Sylvia Van Kirk, *Many Tender Ties: Women in Fur Trade Society in Western Canada, 1670-1870* (Winnipeg: Watson & Dwyer; Norman: University of Oklahoma Press, 1980), esp. 53-94.
13. Van Kirk, *Many Tender Ties*, esp. 28-52 and 95-122.
14. William R. Swagerty, "Marriage and Settlement Patterns of Rocky Mountain Trappers and Traders," *Western Historical Quarterly* 11:2 (April 1980): 159-80.
15. Harvey E. Tobie, "Joseph L. Meek," in *The Mountain Men and the Fur Trade of the Far West: Biographical Sketches of the Participants by Scholars of the Subject and with Introductions by the Editor*, ed. Le Roy Reuben Hafen (Glendale, CA: A. H. Clark, 1965), 325. Like many trappers, Meek had sequential marriages with three Native American women. He first married Umentucken (Mountain Lamb), who was killed by enemy Native Americans. His second wife left him because he drank too much. In 1838, he married a Nez Perce woman he called Virginia. They had seven children, and their marriage endured until Meek's death decades later. See *Oregon Encyclopedia: A Project of the Oregon Historical Society*, https://www.oregonencyclopedia.org/articles/meek_joseph_l_1810_1875_/, accessed August 3, 2021.

16 Buffalo Bird Woman's Hidatsa name is commonly spelled Maxidiwiac in anthropological accounts, but Michael W. Stevens, *Biographical Dictionary of the Mandan, Hidatsa, and Arikara* (New Town, ND: Fort Berthold Library, 2003) gives Mahidiweash as the first spelling; it more closely approximates the Hidatsa pronunciation. http://lib.fortbertholdcc.edu/FortBerthold/TATBIO.htm, accessed July 24, 2015.

17 Gilbert L. Wilson in *Buffalo Bird Woman's Garden* (1917; repr., St. Paul: Minnesota Historical Society Press, 1987), 6–7. Originally published as Gilbert Livingstone Wilson, *Agriculture of the Hidatsa Indians: An Indian Interpretation* (PhD diss., University of Minnesota, 1917). Gilbert L. Wilson, *Waheenee: An Indian Girl's Story* (1921; repr., Lincoln: University of Nebraska Press, 1981).

18 Jeffrey R. Hanson, "Introduction to the Reprint Edition," Wilson, *Buffalo Bird Woman's Garden*, xii–xiii.

19 Alan Klein, "The Political Economy of Gender: A 19th Century Plains Indian Case Study," in *The Hidden Half: Plains Indian Women*, eds. Patricia Albers and Beatrice Medicine (Lanham, MD: University Press of America, *1983*), 143–74.

20 Wilson, *Buffalo Bird Woman's Garden*, 6.

21 Wilson, *Buffalo Bird Woman's Garden*, 6–7; see also Wilson, *Waheenee*, 38–39.

22 Wilson, *Buffalo Bird Woman's Garden*, 7; *Waheenee*, 7–9. Hanson, "Introduction," xv, states that the 1837 epidemic reduced the Hidatsa from about 2500 people to 800.

23 Wilson, *Buffalo Bird Women's Garden*, 7–8.

24 Wilson, *Buffalo Bird Woman's Garden*, 119–20.

25 Wilson, *Waheenee*, 176.

26 Wilson, *Waheenee*, 175; Edward Goodbird, as told to Gilbert L. Wilson, *Goodbird the Indian: His Story* (1914; repr., St. Paul: Minnesota Historical Society Press, 1985).

27 Wilson, *Buffalo Bird Woman's Garden*, 10–11; *Waheenee*, 45, 125–26.

28 Susanna Townsend to Skotty, from Secreta Ranch, 20 February 1853; Susanna Roberts Townsend Correspondence, 1838–68, The Bancroft Library, University of California, Berkeley (hereinafter called "Townsend Collection").

29 Susanna Townsend to Sister Mary, from Sutterville, October 25 and November 13, 1853; Susanna Townsend to Skotty, from Sutterville, December 20, 1853; Susanna Townsend to Skotty, from Scuppernong, October 3–9, 1854; Townsend Collection.

30 See Elizabeth Jameson, *All that Glitters: Class, Conflict, and Community in Cripple Creek* (Urbana and Chicago: University of Illinois Press, 1998), chap. 5, 114–39.

31 Anne Ellis, *The Life of an Ordinary Woman* (1929; repr., Lincoln: University of Nebraska Press, 1980), 204–9.

32 Oral history interview with Beulah Pryor, Colorado Springs, Colorado, May 6, 1979.

33 Oral history interview with Kathleen Welch Chapman, Wheat Ridge, Colorado, April 27, 1979.

34 Kathleen Chapman oral history.

35 Oral history interview with May Wing, Victor, Colorado, October 21, 1978. May Wing was Kathleen Chapman's cousin, and told this story about her aunt Hannah Welch, Kathleen Chapman's mother.

36 Kathleen Chapman oral history.

37 Joan M. Jensen, "Butter Making in Mid-Atlantic America from 1750–1850," *Signs* 13:4 (summer 1988): 813–29.

38 Quoted from Belknap's diary in Susan G. Butruille, *Women's Voices from the Oregon Trail* (Boise: Tamarack Books, 1993), 68. For the diary, see Glenda Riley, "Family Life on the Frontier: The Diary of Kitturah Penton Belknap," *Annals of Iowa* XLIV (1977): 31–51.
39 Guri Olsdotter to her family in Norway, December 2, 1866, in Joan M. Jensen, *With These Hands: Women Working on the Land* (Old Westbury, NY: The Feminist Press, 1981), 58–60.
40 Jensen, *With These Hands*, 108.
41 Elinore Pruitt Stewart, *Letters of a Woman Homesteader* (1942; repr., Lincoln: University of Nebraska Press, 1961), excerpt in Jensen, *With These Hands*, 132.
42 Teresa Jordan, *Cowgirls: Women of the American West* (1982; repr., Lincoln and London: University of Nebraska Press, 1992), 120.
43 Sheryll Patterson-Black, "Women Homesteaders on the Great Plains Frontier," *Frontiers: A Journal of Women Studies* 1:2 (spring 1976): 67–88; H. Elaine Lindgren, *Land in Her Own Name: Women as Homesteaders in North Dakota* (Fargo: North Dakota Institute for Regional Studies, 1991).
44 Lindgren, *Land in Her Own Name*, 22.
45 Lindgren, *Land in Her Own Name*, 191.
46 Lindgren, *Land in Her Own Name*, 201–2.
47 Lindgren, *Land in Her Own Name*, 111, 192–93.
48 John Ise, *Sod and Stubble: The Story of a Kansas Homestead* (1936; repr., Lincoln: University of Nebraska Press, 1967), 17.
49 Ise, *Sod and Stubble*, 64.
50 Ise, *Sod and Stubble*, 187.
51 J. Sanford Rikoon, ed., *Rachel Calof's Story: Jewish Homesteader on the Northern Plains* (Bloomington and Indianapolis: University of Indiana Press, 1995). The area that Calof came from was considered part of Russia when she lived there and became the Ukrainian People's Republic in 1917.
52 Rachel Calof had a tense and stressful relationship with her mother-in-law, Charadh Myers Calof, whose "rules" for Rachel and her husband appear cruel or sadistic at times. Charadh Calof presented her rules as Jewish tradition, and it may be that she simply learned or remembered inaccurate folk beliefs rather than Jewish law. Rachel Calof described the flour sack used instead of a veil at her wedding for the actual ceremony and then extended isolation behind a blindfold during the wedding meal and celebration at the insistence of her mother-in-law, so that she could not see the guests, her husband, or the food. She felt isolated and powerless throughout the day. When her first child was born, her mother-in-law refused to clean the baby or feed Rachel because it was the Sabbath and convinced Rachel that she needed to wear a knife and keep a prayer book with the baby to keep away the devils who would try to take the child. She insisted that Rachel's husband Abe, who was working away during the week, could not see her or the baby for almost six weeks because the birth had made Rachel unclean. Rachel's fears of devils consumed her and only the intervention of her husband's cousin, Doba, persuaded her that she was a good person, God was with her, and there were no devils. Calof described her mother-in-law as "a religious fanatic and superstitious beyond imagination." Her dictates were distortions of Jewish law and tradition. For instance, the obligation to care for life supersedes all other laws, including prohibitions on lighting a fire or cooking on the Sabbath. Whether Charadh Calof was ignorant or cruel, the consequence was that Rachel often felt isolated, frightened, and powerless. Rikoon, *Rachel Calof's Story*, 37–39, 46–56.
53 Rikoon, *Rachel Calof's Story*, 38–40, 61–62, 70.
54 Rikoon, *Rachel Calof's Story*, 31–32.

55   Rikoon, *Rachel Calof's Story*, 41–43.
56   Lindgren, *Land in Her Own Name*, 236–37.
57   Joan M. Jensen, "Cloth, Butter, and Boarders: Household Production for the Market," *The Review of Radical Political Economics* 12 (summer 1980): 14–24, reprinted in Joan M. Jensen, *Promise to the Land: Essays on Rural Woman* (Albuquerque: University of New Mexico Press, 1991), 193.
58   Sucheng Chan, *This Bittersweet Soil: The Chinese in California Agriculture, 1860–1910* (Berkeley and Los Angeles: University of California Press, 1986), 52–53; 62–63; 68–69; 74–75.
59   Chan, *This Bittersweet Soil*, 136.
60   Chan, *This Bittersweet Soil*, 364–65.
61   Jensen, *With These Hands*, 145.
62   The book is best known in Canada through the revised edition: Harold A. Innis, *The Fur Trade in Canada: An Introduction to Canadian Economic History* (1930; rev. ed., Toronto: University of Toronto Press, 1956).
63   For a formative essay in this debate, see Earl Pomeroy, "Toward a Reorientation of Western History: Continuity and Environment," *Mississippi Valley Historical Review* V41 (March 1955): 579–600.

3

The Heart of Gold: Working-Class Voices from the Cripple Creek Gold Mining District

April 2, 2002

I am a sucker for historical anniversaries. In 2002, I was already anticipating the centennial of the Colorado Labor Wars, a series of brutal strikes during 1903–1904 that rocked Colorado's coal and hardrock mining industries. The conflicts began as local labor disputes, but became linked through the aggressive responses of mine owners and the state. Governor James H. Peabody repeatedly sent state troops to strike areas to ensure that union miners suffered disastrous defeats throughout Colorado.[1] If this seems an odd anniversary to anticipate, the Labor Wars had preoccupied me for over three decades, since I began researching hardrock miners and their unions. My dissertation was a working-class history of the Cripple Creek, Colorado gold-mining District, where organized labor fought a pivotal battle in these conflicts.[2]

Gold was discovered in Cripple Creek in 1890. Within a decade it was famed as "The World's Greatest Gold Camp," producing over $20 million annually. By 1900, the District's ten towns housed some 30,000 people, most of them miners drawn by the promise of steady work at good pay.[3] Stable mining and steady employment drew married men with families, who organized to protect their jobs and benefits. Bookended by two crucial Western Federation of Miners (WFM) strikes in 1894 and 1903–1904, the District was an organized labor stronghold. The WFM was the keystone of the local labor movement, renowned for its strikes, its endorsements of the Socialist Party, and its leadership in founding the Industrial Workers of the World (IWW). Founded in 1893, the WFM's first major victory was the Cripple Creek strike of 1894, which established the eight-hour day,

$3 minimum daily wage, and the right to organize for District miners.[4] The victorious miners supported other crafts that by 1902 had organized a majority of workers in all trades in some fifty-four local unions.[5]

Organized labor held substantial political, social, and economic power throughout the ten District communities: Cripple Creek, Victor, Goldfield, Independence, Altman, Cameron, Anaconda, Elkton, Lawrence, and Gillet. Unions influenced wages, hours, and working conditions, provided for the health and welfare of their members, organized the local holidays, established libraries and reading rooms, and published a daily newspaper, the *Victor and Cripple Creek Daily Press*, which boasted that it was "The Only Daily Newspaper Owned By Organized Workingmen."

Labor's power ended with "the" Cripple Creek strike of 1903–1904. That conflict began in August 1902, when the WFM organized Colorado City Mill and Smeltermen's Union No. 125. Its members worked in the Standard, Portland, and Telluride Mills in Colorado City that refined Cripple Creek ore, laboring twelve hours for a $1.80 daily wage. The anti-union Standard hired a Pinkerton detective to infiltrate the union. The Pinkerton Detective Agency was an anti-union agency that employers hired to help break unions, either by identifying union members and leaders or by staging illegal acts that could be falsely attributed to union members. The detective who infiltrated Local No. 125 identified forty-two union members to the company, which promptly fired them. The WFM requested their reinstatement, a $2.25 daily minimum wage, and the right to union membership. The Standard refused to negotiate, and the mill workers went on strike.[6]

Between August 1902, when the smeltermen organized, and February 1903, when the Standard refused to bargain, Coloradoans went to the polls to decide a pivotal and hotly contested election. Democrats and Populists won a combined majority of the votes, but Republican James Hamilton Peabody took the Governor's office by a plurality. During his two-year term, major strikes rocked the northern and southern Colorado coal fields, the mills and smelters of Denver and Colorado City, and the hardrock communities of Clear Creek County, Telluride, and the Cripple Creek District. Over the protests of local authorities, Peabody dispatched the National Guard to strikes in Telluride, the southern coal fields, Colorado City, and the Cripple Creek District.[7]

The strike spread from Colorado City to Cripple Creek in March 1903 when the miners refused to work on mines that shipped ore to the unfair plants, attempting to dry up the ore supply to support the mill workers.

The WFM was an industrial union, committed to organizing all the workers in the vertically integrated mining industry into one union to match owners' power. The major District mine owners also owned the mills and smelters, and the railroads that hauled ore from their mines to their refining facilities in Colorado City. Competition among owners who supported and opposed organized labor became a crucial submerged factor in the strike. The president of the Portland Mill, James Burns, had been a plumber before he discovered gold on Battle Mountain above the city of Victor. He did not discriminate against union labor, and his Portland Mine remained open throughout most of the strike, as did other union properties that did not supply non-union mills. The strike became, in part, a struggle for industrial control among pro- and anti-union employers.[8]

The strike dragged on for fifteen months. For much of that time the District was under martial law. Over the objections of local authorities, Governor Peabody sent the National Guard, led by Adjutant General Sherman Bell, a local mine superintendent who announced his intention to destroy "this damned anarchistic federation." Bell took the job only after mine owners agreed to make up the difference between his $1,800 annual salary as Adjutant General and the $5,000 he had earned managing the Moffat mines in the Cripple Creek District. The troops cost over $400,000, which the mine owners advanced in return for certificates of indebtedness from the state at 4 percent interest. The local anti-union Citizens' Alliance was mustered in to help as Company L in the National Guard.[9]

Periodic violence—some major, some minor, some staged—became the justification for the armed force. A carpenter, Thomas Stewart, was beaten as he built a fence around a non-union mine. Someone took spikes from the tracks of the Florence and Cripple Creek railroad; the track walker was tipped off and the incident passed without mishap. On November 21, 1903, an explosion in the non-union Vindicator Mine killed two men. The Vindicator lay within the perimeter of the military encampment and was well guarded at the time. On January 26, 1904, faulty machinery severed the cable hauling miners to the surface of Stratton's Independence mine; one man was thrown clear and fifteen plunged to their deaths. All sides pointed fingers, alternately blaming union miners, Mine Owners' Association (MOA) hirelings, or incompetent non-union labor.[10]

Labor protested the excesses of the militia, which arrested union leaders and held them without charge, suspended the right of habeas corpus, invaded a court room in Cripple Creek with armed troops and trained a Gatling gun on the courthouse rather than obey a court order to surrender imprisoned union leaders, and denied freedom of assembly, freedom of the press, and the right to bear arms. Bell's lieutenant, Thomas McClelland, announced: "To hell with the constitution, we aren't going by the constitution."[11]

The strike ended tragically early on June 6, 1904, when a bomb exploded beneath the platform of the Independence, Colorado train depot, killing thirteen non-union miners coming off shift. Who set the dynamite and who paid them remain fiercely debated.[12] What followed the tragic explosion is clear. Within hours, mine owners and the Citizens' Alliance forced elected officials to resign—they told the Sheriff he could resign or be hanged—and seized control of local governments and the investigation into the explosion. They smashed union halls and four WFM cooperative stores that had provisioned the strikers. The militia deported over 200 union leaders to Kansas and New Mexico; hundreds of others left in fear or were violently driven away by armed masked mobs. The MOA imposed an owners' hiring card and banned union labor from the District.[13]

During the strike many mines that employed union miners were forced to fire them. On June 9, 1904, the militia occupied the largest remaining union property, James Burns' Portland Mine. Accusing Burns of "employing and harboring large numbers of dangerous, lawless men," Bell announced, "I anticipate Mr. Burns will be permanently deposed, and I hope obliterated from that vicinity." On June 19, an anti-union faction deposed Burns as president of the mine he had discovered and the company he had founded.[14] In November, two MOA gun thugs intimidated people from voting by killing two union poll watchers, one of whom was a key witness in the investigation of the Independence Depot explosion.[15]

The strike still sparks arguments about competing versions of events, and particularly about who was most violent. Over a year after the strike's chaotic climax, Harry Orchard, a former member of the Altman WFM local, confessed that he had murdered Frank Steunenberg in Caldwell, Idaho, on December 30, 1905. A sheep rancher in 1905, Steunenberg had been the governor of Idaho during an 1899 WFM strike in the Coeur d'Alenes. Orchard implicated an "inner circle" of the WFM in the Steunenberg murder, particularly WFM President Charles Moyer, Secretary-Treasurer W. D. (Big Bill) Haywood, and George Pettibone, a Denver merchant who had been a WFM activist in the Coeur d'Alenes. The three were abducted to Idaho, imprisoned for over a year and a half, and finally acquitted. In his confession, Orchard also alleged that the "inner circle" had hired him to set the explosives at the Vindicator Mine and the Independence Depot.[16]

Whether Orchard in fact blew up the Depot, whether he acted alone, and who hired him were all hotly contested at the time. These questions remain unresolved.[17]

I was first drawn to this history in 1969 during an undergraduate internship that gave me the extraordinary opportunity to organize the archives of the Western Federation of Miners-International Union of Mine, Mill, and Smelter Workers. I wrote my undergraduate history thesis on the Western Federation of Miners and the Radical Labor Movement.[18] That project left me wondering what difference the union made for the thousands of miners it represented, and for their families, a question that led me to Cripple Creek, and to the period between the two crucial miners' strikes.

One of the challenges of a history that is really about tens of thousands of people is giving it a human face, a human voice. My questions about the human value of the unions and the human consequences of the strikes led me to people who had survived the struggles, and their descendants, who generously shared their stories with a very green young historian. While many histories have focused on organized labor and the lessons it took from its 1904 strike defeats, the survivors I interviewed in the 1970s told more personal stories of the conflict. I developed a particularly close relationship with May McConaghy Wing, from our first interview in 1975 until her death in 1980. Born in 1890, the daughter, wife, and mother of hardrock miners, May Wing lived most of her ninety years in the Cripple Creek District. In our last recorded interview, she voiced the challenge that animates my work. "I lived the history that I can tell," May told me. "And of course, the history today, in books that's written a lot, is not really the true thing, as it was lived."[19]

Writing history as it was lived has been difficult for the best-intentioned historians because sources and memories were among the spoils of the strike. The *Daily Press* folded just as the strike began, after which the Victor *Record* became the only remaining pro-union paper in the District. One night the militia rounded up the *Record*'s workforce and took them to the military bullpen. Emma Langdon, a union printer whose husband was among those arrested, sneaked in, printed the paper, and delivered it to the commanding officer, the ink still wet, its headline blazing, "Slightly Disfigured But Still In the Ring." The *Record* offices were sacked in the aftermath of the strike; after that it abandoned its pro-union stance.[20] Union records were seized or destroyed when mobs poured coal oil on them as they attacked the union halls in the June 6 rioting. Some memories left with the leaders forced from the District. Controlling sources and memories becomes part of the history of the strikes and how they have been interpreted.

The story of Cripple Creek has appeared in multiple versions with multiple leading actors and plots. In none of them would May Wing have played a leading role. Competing versions of the history appeared throughout the strike and immediately afterwards. In 1904, the Colorado Mine Owners' Association published *The Criminal Record of the Western Federation of Miners from Coeur d'Alenes to Cripple Creek*, charging the WFM with virtually every crime committed in the gold and silver camps for a decade. The WFM countered with its *Category of Crimes of the Operators' Association: 851 Murdered in Less Than Four Years*, which blamed all mining-related deaths on owners' negligence. Emma Langdon published her pro-labor history in 1904 and 1905.[21]

The counter-narrative appeared in the first academic history, Benjamin McKie Rastall's *The Labor History of the Cripple Creek District*, published in 1908 from his 1906 University of Wisconsin dissertation.[22] A resident of Colorado Springs, home of many of the major mine owners, Rastall had close ties to local business. He somehow secured some of the few surviving union records, which remain at the Wisconsin State Historical Society. For Rastall, the strike was unreasonable because the miners struck innocent mine owners with whom Rastall maintained they had no grievance. He ignored the vertical integration of mines and smelters. He characterized the District as a "Little Mining Monarchy, shut off from the rest of the world by a high mountain range ... with its own separate political organization, the power in the hands of the miners, the unions controlled by a minority, the strike power in the hands of a clique." It was an "anomaly," "a very recent frontier district, of a highly developed industrial center, which has kept most of its frontier aspects."[23] The mine owners' forcible takeover of the local government and the courts thus "civilized" the frontier.[24]

Rastall insisted that everyone he knew in the District knew that the union had blown up the depot. We clearly talked to different people. Rastall's version dominated local histories, which focused on the entertaining antics of fun-loving, hard-drinking young mine owners, especially those who won control of the District after the strike.[25]

The selective memories and erasures that inscribed different versions of a still-contested history reverberated throughout the centennial commemorations. Commemoration implies a shared understanding of events, a shared set of symbols, a common cast to memorialize. Histories of the

Colorado Labor Wars had established no such common ground. Seeking to explain the WFM's socialist endorsements and the violence of many western miners' strikes, historians have concluded variously that the miners' politics were the product of the frontier[26]; of brutal strike experiences[27]; of the lack of a local middle class[28]; of rapid industrialization[29]; of the dangers of underground work[30]; of loss of control to management[31]; of diminished opportunities for self-employment[32]; of failure to secure an eight-hour law in Colorado[33]; or of the defeats of the Populist Party and the Knights of Labor.[34] For some, the strikes became insignificant because they were not ordinary daily occurrences. As one historian put it, their significance rested in the false assumption that "the WFM's defeat in Cripple Creek was merely the experience of Tincup, Silver City, Lump Gulch, and Tonopah [mining towns] writ large."[35]

Perhaps not. One could argue—and I have—that Cripple Creek was, both materially and symbolically, more significant than Tincup in shaping working-class agendas and in the lived experience of tens of thousands of miners and their families. Violent confrontations did not have to occur in every mining town to influence workers' understandings of their options, because when mine owners broke strong unions, the outcomes shaped relationships throughout the industry.[36]

The lived histories I recorded held this bitter legacy. People told stories about working-class life before 1904 that their children and grandchildren often had not heard. To work in Cripple Creek after the 1904 strike defeat, miners had to hide any hint of union allegiance. By the 1970s, when I interviewed them, most survivors who remembered the union era were elderly women whose fathers had been union miners. Still girls during the strike, they married men who did not begin mining until after the WFM was driven out and so had never belonged to a union. They could still be blacklisted, so it was dangerous to talk about organized labor and the strike. When people agreed to talk to me, the mines were closed, the men had died or retired, and the survivors did not want their memories to die with them.[37] Their narratives varied enormously from both the mine owners' version of the strikes, which blamed the unions for violence, and from labor historians' emphases on the consequences for organized labor and for working-class politics. Few histories said much about what the strikes meant to the strikers and their families.

My work has its place in the longstanding debates about the strike and about who was most responsible for its tragic outcome. But rather than debate the debate further, let's consider what the strike meant for Cripple

Creek "writ small"—not for Tincup or Lump Gulch, but for one miner who could represent many others, and for his extended family.

His name was John Welch. Born in 1864, the son of a Vermont coal miner, he entered the coal mines after his father died in a mining accident on July 4, 1875—hardly an Independence Day for the eleven-year-old who quit school to take his father's place underground. Sometime in the 1880s, John Welch moved to Leadville, Colorado, a silver-mining town, like many coal and lead miners who sought the higher wages and lesser dangers of western hardrock mines. There he met and married Hannah Doran.[38]

Hannah Doran's parents, Edward and Catharine Doran, could represent many immigrant mining families. Born in Ireland in the early 1830s, they married young, probably during the disastrous famine years, 1845–1849. They left Ireland, to settle for a time in Wales; perhaps Edward worked the coal mines there. Catharine began long years of childbearing with the birth of their first son, James, in 1852. Sometime between 1854, when Thomas was born, and 1858, when Mary arrived, the Dorans immigrated to Shullsburg, in Wisconsin's lead-mining region. Edward worked as a lead miner. Catharine cared for their ever-increasing family—she bore twelve children in nineteen years, nine of whom survived. All the Doran children attended school well into adolescence, an important achievement, especially, we might imagine, for Catharine, who could neither read nor write. By the 1880s, lead mining declined, and the new silver mines around Leadville drew many Shullsburg miners, including the Dorans.[39]

Most of the Doran sons mined; the daughters, like Hannah, married miners. Kate Doran married James McConaghy, an Irish immigrant hoist engineer. Their daughter May was born in Leadville November 25, 1890. Three months later Kate died, and in 1893 James took three-year-old May to Victor, in the Cripple Creek District. James' brother John McConaghy moved there, too. So did his brother-in-law Ed Doran, with his wife Mary.[40]

In 1893, John and Hannah Welch followed. John Welch joined the WFM; he and Hannah participated in both Cripple Creek strikes. Their daughter Kathleen dated the first strike in family time with her older brother's birth. "In 1894 Tom was born," she told me, "and that's when the Bull Hill strike was." The strikers, surrounded by an army of sheriff's deputies, entrenched themselves on Bull Hill, the center of union activism. They built a mock fort and pretended to be well armed. Kathleen Welch Chapman recounted her mother's story:

> There wasn't too many people up there, you know—and the men went out and they had their wives come along with them. And Mama said she wrapped Tom in a blanket and went along. And the men took their coats off, and their hats, and put them up in a tree and put the guns up in there. And then, of course they were milling around, you know, and oh, they just thought that the *world* was up there, this militia did, when they seen them.... And when they could look up there and see all them guns shining through with the sun on them, boy, they stopped and they turned around and went back to Colorado Springs *on the run!*[41]

After the first strike, the Welch family moved to a new home they built in Goldfield. Kathleen was born there in 1895, then Edward, Annie, and young John. The Welches' income, welfare, and social life were all connected to John Welch's union membership. Kathleen Chapman remembered the union era for the union men who brought sick benefits when her dad couldn't work, the union Labor Day parades and picnics, and a secure family life. John Welch was, she said, "a great union man. He always believed in that union—for people and among people."[42]

One of the first tasks of local unions was providing for sickness and death. Unions paid sick benefits, cared for widows and orphans, organized funerals, shipped bodies out of the District for burial, and hired doctors and nurses for their members.[43] Kathleen Welch Chapman fondly recalled these union benefits as part of what her father meant when he said that unions were "for people."

> Now, if there was a family that was very hard up or very tight for money, why [the unions would] help them out.... I can remember people in Victor coming to Goldfield when Papa'd maybe have a cold or be sick or couldn't go to work or something. There'd be maybe a half a dozen men come at night to see if he was getting along and if he needed anything.[44]

The unions organized social life as well, hosting balls, socials, picnics, and holidays. The two big local holidays were the Fourth of July and Labor Day. All the Welches took part in the three-day Labor Day celebrations. To little Kathleen Welch, the annual Labor Day picnic at Pinnacle Park was a wonderland of merry-go-rounds, ball games, horseshoes, picnics shared with other union families, speeches by the Governor of Colorado and other "people like that you know, that was really worthwhile."[45] In 1903, the speaker was WFM President Charles Moyer, who lambasted Governor James Peabody for sending the militia to strike areas throughout Colorado.[46]

Labor Day began with a parade. An estimated 3,000 union members marched in the 1899 parade, 5,000 in 1901 and 1903. John Welch marched, though, not with his local union but with his religious fraternal association, the Knights of St. John. He "always wore his uniform," Kathleen Chapman remembered, "and, oh, them were great."[47] She did not remember if her mother belonged to the WFM Women's Auxiliary, but Hannah was, she said, "always quite a church member," and she remembered with great fondness the local priest who sided with the union during the second strike.[48]

Despite the Welches' union allegiance, after the 1894 strike John had generally cordial relations with his employers, the Woods Investment Company. The Woods family were Baptists who believed, apparently, in the stewardship of wealth. Unlike most District mine owners, they invested some of their wealth in the District and were widely perceived as generous and egalitarian for their contributions to working-class social life. The Woods family built Pinnacle Park, the vast picnic ground, zoo, and amusement park that they annually donated for Labor Day.[49]

The Woods Investment Company built a clubhouse for its employees, opposite its Gold Coin Mine in Victor. The two-story building held a library, a large athletic room, a bath room, where men could bathe when they came off shift, a billiard hall and chess tables, and a few bedrooms for company employees. The Club was dedicated with an elaborate party in February 1900. John and Hannah Welch were there. Their daughter remembered the night vividly.

> Papa worked on the Gold Coin there in Victor. . . . And I can remember that night so well. I wasn't very big. Mama and Papa went. I can remember how nice they looked. They got a baby-setter to come in and set with us. . . . We lived in Goldfield, and they went up to Victor to the opening. And . . . they said they had such a good time. Well, they danced and had a big banquet.[50]

Not surprisingly, Kathleen Chapman remembered parades, baby-sitters, and union committees that came to her house when her father was ill, but not what happened at the union hall, or her parents' political affiliations. I don't know, therefore, whether John Welch shared the Populist politics of many District miners in the 1890s, or whether he, like an influential minority of the union leadership, joined the Socialist Party when it was founded in 1901.

In many regards, though, John Welch resembled his co-workers, many of whom shared the heritage of coal mining, who frequently associated with men of other classes in the local lodge halls, saloons, Asian Exclusion campaigns, and political parties. Like John Welch, union leaders and local businessmen alike were likely to belong to at least one lodge or fraternal association, frequently to the same one. They sometimes belonged to the same political parties. Organized labor exerted considerable influence in District politics, and almost a third of the political activists I could identify belonged to unions.

Whatever John Welch's politics, he shared a great deal with the union leadership. They were frequently, like him, married homeowners in their thirties and forties; many lived in the smaller towns, like Goldfield.[51] And like him, they had amicable relations with their employers, provided the employers treated workers with respect. Otherwise, they struck or boycotted businesses unfair to workers in other crafts that sold non-union goods, or that refused to honor labor's demands for wages, hours, and working conditions.[52]

Even the high regard for the Woods Investment Company had its limits. In 1901, the town of Cripple Creek denied the Woods Company a franchise for electric lights. The company retaliated by refusing to employ residents of the town. The Trades Assembly protested the policy as "tyrannical, iniquitous, and totally unjustifiable." The *Press* reported "much ill feeling and indignation" because "the Woods people had acquired all they own in this district right here, by a stroke of good fortune . . . they found it in the ground where God (not the Woods) deposited it; and . . . now they propose to use the power of this wealth to oppress the people—to crush and trample underfoot the liberties of the citizens."[53]

Labor approved and mingled socially only with those owners and managers who supported union labor. Friendly labor-management relationships could always change if employers undermined the local unions. Between the major conflicts in 1894 and 1903–1904, numerous local disputes were settled easily. During 1899–1903, the *Press* reported at least thirty-four minor strikes, primarily over wages and working conditions, most of them quickly negotiated.[54] Workers felt sufficiently powerful to push their demands, and each success increased their faith in collective action.

Strikes were a last resort. Generally, unions simply announced their wages and hours and boycotted businesses that refused to comply. Using the *Press* to publicize banned goods and establishments, organized labor won six o'clock closing for retail clerks, prevented laundries from shipping clothes out of the District to non-union shops, made boarding houses and restaurants hire union help, established the six-day week for cooks and waiters, eliminated non-union products from saloons, groceries, and other retail houses—in short, enforced demands for union recognition, wages, and hours for most District workers.[55]

Boycotts worked for trades that sold consumer goods or services that working-class patrons purchased. But boycotting gold was not an effective labor tactic because few miners could afford to buy the gold for which they risked their lives underground. Instead, WFM organizers often relied on social pressure. One effective tactic was for the secretaries of WFM locals to check miners' union cards as they went on shift and let peer pressure do the rest. John Welch was probably starting his shift at least once when WFM officials checked cards at the Gold Coin shaft house. When Jerry Kelly, financial secretary of Victor Miners WFM local No. 32, checked cards at the Gold Coin in May 1900, only one miner refused to join, saying that he "cared nothing for the Miners' union or its representative." The rest of the miners refused to ride down in the cage with him, creating a stalemate that ended only when the superintendent paid the man's dues.[56]

I don't know if John Welch refused to ride down in the cage with a non-union miner. I don't know his political allegiances, or how he voted. I know that he walked out with other strikers in 1903 and he stayed out. Despite some images of married homeowners as working-class conservatives and despite assumptions that working-class radicals were young single hotheads, that was not the case. Whether they were hotheads or conservatives, single men could more easily simply leave during the strike, which was waged largely by married men with community ties who stayed. The stalwarts during the 1903–1904 strike were, like John Welch, married men and homeowners—those who had the most to risk and the most to lose.[57]

However romantic strikes may seem in history books, they are simply hard in practice. John Welch stuck it out for fifteen months. The Welches made do with union benefits, stretching the union's support to help Hannah's widowed mother, Catharine Doran. The militia considered John Welch important enough to be slated for deportation. He left the District with his brother-in-law Ed Doran, one step ahead of the soldiers.[58]

Kathleen Chapman remembered the strike, and the militia camped on the hill above her home. She stood with other children, waving at trainloads of deportees. She remembered her parents helping a pro-union soldier sneak out of the District, fortified with a lunch Hannah made for him. And she remembered: "Papa had to get ready, him and Uncle Ed, and left, things got so bad. Somebody come and give 'em the word that they were going to get them the next trainload they took out. . . . And so they got ready, and they left in the middle of the night, the two of them. And they went to Leadville and went to work."[59]

After John left, Hannah Welch continued the family's union allegiance. May Wing fondly recalled the strike heroism of her grandmother Catharine Doran and her aunts, Mary Doran and Hannah Welch:

> I did have an uncle that lived in Goldfield. His name was Ed Doran. And Grandma was there, Aunt Mary was expecting. So Uncle Ed, of course, got out. Well, he got word that they were going to raid the house. Of course, the militia had the way of doing, in the middle of the night they'd come after the men and take 'em to the bullpen and then they'd send 'em out. But Uncle Ed got word that they were going to come that night, so he left. Grandma never said just exactly where he went or where he hid. But she was there when they came, and they tore that house to pieces! They even looked in the breadbox. Well, that got Grandma's goat. And she said, "Shure'n he's not little enough to put in the breadbox! Now every God blesset one of you get out of this house and leave this woman alone!" She said, "You can see what condition she's in. Now," she said, "git!"

> Then I had another aunt that lived there. Her name was Hannah Welch. . . . And she had two great big butcher knives, and she kept those knives razor sharp. And she always said if one of those militia men ever come in her house in the middle of the night, they'd leave with less than they brought in![60]

Finally, though, Hannah Welch took the children to join her husband in Leadville, after the militia harassed her son Tom and her nephew, Eddie Bulger, as the boys were going fishing. Kathleen Welch Chapman recounted:

> [T]he militia drove up there and stopped them. And they wanted to know where they were going. They told them, and [the soldiers] said, "Oh, no, you're not. You're hauling out food for the union men someplace." "Oh no," Eddie said, "We're not. We don't have anything, only our lunch." Anyway, they pulled the two kids down off the horse. Eddie was about six years older than Tom. . . . And pulled them down, took their lunch, threw it down on the grass. Took the saddle off the horse and every little nook and corner of that saddle they went through to see if they were taking something. Well, they just put the saddle back on the horse and come back down home. And, you know, that made a wreck out of Tom. He was about, I'd say, ten, eleven years old. . . . And he was just a wreck. He couldn't sleep at night. . . . He'd scream in his sleep, you know. So Mama said, "Well, I can't stand that." So she packed us up and took us to Leadville, where Papa was, until the darned thing would quiet down or get over. And we were up there for over a year and a half. Then we came back to the District.[61]

Hannah Welch and the children stayed in their home in Goldfield. John Welch worked in mines outside the District and visited his family when he could, because "a union man couldn't get a job and he wouldn't work on them scab cards for anything." He came home after being buried in a cave-in that crushed his chest and injured his legs. Unable to mine, he worked as a watchman at a small mine that resisted the Mine Owners' Association. Finally, though, he became too ill to climb the hill to the mine or to do much work. Young Tom Welch left school after grade eight to take his father's place. Just as John Welch entered the workforce when his father died in a Vermont coal mine, Tom Welch, born in a tent during the 1894 strike, became the family breadwinner. In time, Kathleen contributed her wages as a housekeeper and laundry worker. John Welch died of his injuries at age forty-eight. His children remembered the union benefits, the social support, the vibrance and power of the union community their father had helped build. They knew what they had lost.[62]

During the decade of union strength, John Welch could act on his working-class allegiances without significant conflict with his church, lodge, or employer. Union benefits allowed him to get sick without starving; union wages helped him buy a home. John Welch risked his job, his home, his family, his local church, lodge, and community to give other workers the right to organize.

When the unions were smashed, and with them the institutional base for working-class power, miners turned to the fellowship and social support of their lodges and fraternal associations. They turned especially to the families for whom they risked everything, and for whom they stayed. The miners of the Cripple Creek District risked the daily dangers of mining for the things that drive most of us: to support their families, to keep their kids in school, to work in dignity, to go home to a house they owned. Years later, the survivors recalled the strike defeat in terms of domestic loss. Asked what difference the 1904 strike defeat made for working people, Kathleen Chapman replied:

> Oh my, it changed it awful! You've been through Goldfield. Well, you should have seen the homes that was up there in Goldfield. They were beautiful, some of them. Well, people just got up and left, you know, and left their homes like it was, and lots of them never come back to them. People would go in and destroy the homes and pick up what they wanted, and the homes went to wrack, and they tore them down, and—oh,—it just, it just used to make me sick all over.[63]

For Kathleen Chapman, May Wing, and countless others, Cripple Creek was more than the name of a dramatic strike. It was home. Their treasure was not the gold buried beneath the District's slopes, but human relationships and their memories of an empowered working-class community.

The 2003–2004 strike commemoration, like the strikes themselves, was at least partly about who controls history. The story is always in danger of being lost, buried, or trivialized. Though I have published my own version of these events, including circumstantial evidence that might support labor's contention that owners were responsible for the carnage at the Independence Depot, I do not think anyone still living really knows what happened. Perhaps the evidence no longer exists to settle that debate. But whatever else this history is about, it is not, for me, about who was most violent.

Whether or not they staged the fatal accidents at the Vindicator, Stratton's Independence, and the Independence Depot, the Mine Owners' Association, Citizens' Alliance, and the militia fomented the Victor riot that caused two deaths, destroyed union property, arrested and deported people charged with no crimes, deposed elected officials, and at least tacitly approved assaults and the violent mobs that drove men from their homes. They took deportees hundreds of miles from their homes under military guard and left them in the middle of nowhere without food or shelter. If one believes union members staged the bombings, it is still difficult to determine blame as MOA detectives heavily infiltrated the local unions and even the WFM Women's Auxiliary. Even Harry Orchard, whose truthfulness should be subject to doubt, allegedly said that he worked for the Pinkerton Detective Agency during the Cripple Creek strike.[64]

The strike violence magnified a prevalent culture of masculine violence, where prize fights were popular entertainment, and where miners lived with the constant threat of violent death underground. The strike record testifies that men on all sides habitually prepared for violence, and either carried guns or hired them. Even Hannah Welch "kept her knives razor sharp." In terms of the historical outcome, the question of who planted the dynamite at Independence Depot is less important than whose explanation was accepted, and how that justified the consequences.

The casualties of the Colorado Labor Wars went far beyond a destroyed union movement, and far beyond individual lives, to a shared social vision and collective history. Fear of company retaliation was so profound that some people never shared childhood memories and family stories of the strike or union era; many of those memories died with them. Since the employers controlled contemporary press reports and seized union records after the Independence Depot explosion, they controlled not only events, but the history of the conflict as well. The mines closed in the early 1960s, and elderly residents felt free at last to tell their stories.

The history they wished to preserve was not a nostalgic romantic past or a tale of tragic loss. It was about complicated people who lived complex mundane lives. They sought neither romance nor riches, but schools rather than wage work for their children, and a community that they could shape, where work would be honored, and workers dignified. The survivors remembered a world in which union labor won social standing, industrial power, and political influence. Historians may continue to debate the origins of strike violence and how to assign blame. But the most urgent testimony to the importance of the Colorado Labor Wars came from John and Hannah Welch, Kathleen Chapman, May Wing, and countless others, who lived the history that they could tell and told the history they helped to make.

NOTES

I presented a portion of this lecture for the Colorado History Group 25th Autumnal Rendezvous, held in Victor, Colorado, September 12, 1998 in the auditorium of the Victor Elks Hall (Benevolent and Protective Order of Elks). This was the building used as the National Guard Armory during the 1903-1904 strike, from which the attack on the Victor Miners WFM Local No. 32 was launched June 6, 1904. The room where I spoke was the room where Victor Sheriff Henry Robertson was given the choice of resigning his office or being hanged. On June 5, 2004, I presented portions of this talk at the Pike's Peak District Library in Colorado Springs as part of the Centennial Commemoration of the strike and then led a 2 a.m. vigil at the site of the Independence Depot explosion the morning of June 6, 2004, and a walking tour in Victor that day of key strike sites. Those presentations were published as "History, Memory, and Commemoration: The Cripple Creek Strike Remembered," and, "Talking the Walk: The 1903-1904 Strike Centennial in the Cripple Creek District," in *The Colorado Labor Wars: Cripple Creek 1903-1904*, ed. Tim Blevins, Chris Nichol, and Calvin P. Otto (Colorado Springs: Pikes Peak Library District, 2006) and appear here by permission. I am grateful to the staff of the Pikes Peak District Library for hosting the commemoration and to Ed and Cherie Hunter for facilitating the vigil at the Independence Depot site. My greatest debt for this lecture is to the people of the Cripple Creek District who shared their stories and their hospitality with me. For their contributions to this essay, I am enduringly grateful to May McConaghy Wing and Kathleen Welch Chapman, and to the entire extended Wing/Chapman/Pryor family for their hospitality over the years.

1   See George G. Suggs, Jr., *Colorado's War on Militant Unionism: James H. Peabody and the Western Federation of Miners* (Detroit: Wayne State University Press, 1972).

2   Elizabeth Jameson "The Creatures of Discontent: The Western Federation of Miners and the Radical Labor Movement, 1893-1911" (BA thesis, Antioch College, Department of History, 1970); Elizabeth Ann Jameson, High Grade and Fissures: A Working-Class History of the Cripple Creek, Colorado, Gold Mining District, 1890-1905 (PhD diss., University of Michigan, 1987); Elizabeth Jameson, *All That Glitters: Class, Conflict, and Community in Cripple Creek* (Urbana: University of Illinois Press, 1998). This lecture provided some of the groundwork for conference presentations at the Social Science History Association, Western History Association, and the Pikes Peak Regional Library commemorating the strike centennial, and two articles, Elizabeth Jameson, "History, Memory, and Commemoration: The Cripple Creek Strike Remembered," in *The Colorado Labor Wars: Cripple Creek 1903-1904*, ed. Tim Blevins, Chris Nichol, and Calvin P. Otto (Colorado Springs: Pikes Peak Library District, 2006), 3-34; and Elizabeth Jameson, "Talking the Walk: The 1903-1904 Strike Centennial in the Cripple Creek District," in Blevins, Nichol, and Otto, *The Colorado Labor Wars*, 101-16. For the 1903-1904 Cripple Creek strike, see Jameson, *All That Glitters*, 199-225. The city of Cripple Creek was the main commercial center in the Cripple Creek District. In this article I use "Cripple Creek" and "the District" to refer to the Cripple Creek District, not the city.

3   The 1900 U.S. Census enumerated 29,002 people in the District. As with most censuses, this one missed some people. Census takers in 1900 were patronage employees, hired by

the local Postmasters, who were also patronage employees. In 1900 Republicans controlled the White House and federal patronage, and in my reading of the manuscript census, it appeared to me that the local census takers underestimated (or avoided) portions of the smaller towns and neighborhoods that were labor strongholds. Reliable estimates suggest that the population in 1900 was at least 32,000 and likely more.

4   For histories of the Western Federation of Miners (1893–1916), renamed the International Union of Mine, Mill and Smelter Workers (1916–1967), see Vernon H. Jenson, *Heritage of Conflict: Labor Relations in the Nonferrous Metals Industry Up to 1930* (Ithaca, NY: Cornell University Press, 1950), Melvyn Dubofsky, "The Origins of Western Working Class Radicalism, 1890–1905," *Labor History* 7 (Spring 1966): 131–54, and Melvyn Dubofsky, *We Shall Be All: A History of the Industrial Workers of the World* (New York: Quadrangle/The New York Times Book Co., 1969).

5   See Jameson, *All That Glitters*, 62–86, 258–69.

6   *Victor and Cripple Creek Daily Press*, February 15, 1903; February 18, 1903; February 19, 1903; February 20, 1903; February 21, 1903; February 22, 1903; February 26, 1903; March 1, 1903; March 4, 1903; March 6, 1903; March 7, 1903; March 11, 1903 (hereinafter cited as *Press*); U.S. Congress, Senate, Commissioner of Labor, *A Report on Labor Disturbances in the State of Colorado, 1880 to 1904, Inclusive, with Correspondence Relating Thereto*, S. Doc. 122, 58th Cong., 3d Sess. (Washington, DC: Government Printing Office, 1905), 112–16 (hereinafter cited as *Labor Disturbances*); Official *Proceedings of the Eleventh Annual Convention, Western Federation of Miners* (Denver: Western Newspaper Union, 1903), 115–19; Suggs, *Colorado's War*, 44–117, esp. 76–77, 81–83.

7   Suggs, *Colorado's War*, esp. 65–83.

8   Jameson, *All That Glitters*, 54, 199–210, 209, 215, 218, 221, 242, 246–47.

9   *Labor Disturbances*, 165–66, 170–75, 147–48; *Denver Post*, December 9, 1903. Peabody appointed Bell on February 20, 1903, after the Colorado City strike had begun but before the Cripple Creek strike was called; Suggs, *Colorado's War*, 81.

10 *Labor Disturbances*, 189–93, 220–23; Defense Attorney Richardson's notes, affidavits, and related material 1906–1909, State of Idaho vs. Steve Adams, Western Federation of Miners/International Union of Mine, Mill and Smelter Workers Collection, Western History Collections, University of Colorado, Boulder (hereinafter cited as Richardson Notes), 75; "The Situation in Colorado," *Miners' Magazine*, November 26, 1903, 7; *Miners' Magazine*, February 4, 1904, 3–4; "Western Federation Notes," *Miners' Magazine*, February 4, 1904, 9.

11 *Labor Disturbances*, 181–87; *Miners' Magazine*, September 17, 1903, 9; *Pueblo Labor Advocate*, September 18, 1903; "The Governor of Colorado," *Miners' Magazine*, September 24, 1903, 4–5; "The Cripple Creek Situation," *Miners' Magazine*, October 1, 1903, 7; Dubofsky, *We Shall Be All*, 50.

12 See for instance H-Net, Labor History Discussion List, October, 14, October 25, October 27, October 30, and November 3, 2001. See also postings September 11, 1998, and on H-West, October 8, 1996.

13 See Suggs, *Colorado's War*, 110–14; Jameson, *All That Glitters*, 218–25; 243–45; *Labor Disturbances*, 260–68; 274–78, 285–86, 296, 306–8, 313–14.

14 *Labor Disturbances*, 285–86; "The Situation in Colorado," *Miners' Magazine*, June 16, 1904, 10; "The Situation in Colorado," *Miners' Magazine*, June 23, 1904, 9; *Miners' Magazine*, July 21, 1904, 4; "The Situation in Colorado," *Miners' Magazine*, July 28, 1904, 9–10; "The Situation in Colorado," *Miners' Magazine*, February 16, 1905, 11.

15 "The Situation in Colorado," *Miners' Magazine*, November 17, 1904, 10–11; *Denver Clarion Advocate*, November 11, 1904, 1.

16 See Dubofsky, *We Shall Be All*, 97–105; Harry Orchard, *The Confessions of Harry Orchard* (New York: The McClure Company, 1907), esp. 68–109, 129–48.
17 In the five years preceding my 2002 lecture, different interpretations appeared in J. Anthony Lukas, *Big Trouble* (New York: Simon and Schuster, 1997); Bill Albert's charming novel, *Castle Garden* (Sag Harbor, NY: The Permanent Press, 1996); Jameson, *All That Glitters*, 227–33; and a spirited online debate on H-Net, Labor History Discussion List, October 14, October 25, October 27, October 30, and November 3, 2002.
18 Jameson, "The Creatures of Discontent." I remain enormously grateful to the late John A. Brennan, the director of the Western History Collections, who entrusted a valuable collection to an undergraduate history student.
19 Interview with May Wing, Colorado Springs, Colorado, February 16, 1979.
20 *Labor Disturbances*, 261–64.
21 Colorado Mine Owners' Association, *The Criminal Record of the Western Federation of Miners from Coeur d'Alenes to Cripple Creek* (Colorado Springs, 1904); *Category of Crimes of the Operators' Association: 851 Murdered in Less Than Four Years* (Denver: The Miners' Magazine Print, 1904); Langdon, *The Cripple Creek Strike*.
22 Benjamin McKie Rastall, *The Labor History of the Cripple Creek District: A Study in Industrial Evolution*, Bulletin of the University of Wisconsin No. 198, Economic and Political Science Series vol. 3, no. 1 (rpt. Madison, Wisconsin, 1908).
23 Rastall, *Labor History of the Cripple Creek District*, 72–73.
24 Rastall, *Labor History of the Cripple Creek District*, 152.
25 Marshall Sprague, *Money Mountain: The Story of Cripple Creek Gold* (New York: Ballantine Books, 1953).
26 Jenson, *Heritage of Conflict*.
27 Selig Perlman and Philip Taft, *History of Labor in the United States, 1896–1932* (New York: Macmillan, 1935); Dubofsky, We Shall Be All, 49–55.
28 Clark Kerr and Abraham Siegel, "The Interindustry Propensity to Strike," in *Industrial Conflict*, ed. Arthur Kornhauser, Robert Dubin, and Arthur M. Ross (New York: McGraw-Hill, 1954), 189–212.
29 Dubofsky, "Origins of Western Working Class Radicalism"; Dubofsky, *We Shall Be All*; Richard E. Lingenfelter, *The Hardrock Miners: A History of the Mining Labor Movement in the American West, 1863–1893* (Berkeley: University of California Press, 1974), 227–28.
30 Kerr and Siegel, "Interindustry Propensity to Strike"; Ronald C. Brown, *Hard-Rock Miners: The Intermountain West, 1860–1920* (College Station, TX: Texas A&M University Press, 1979).
31 Brown, *Hard-Rock Miners*.
32 John H. M. Laslett, *Labor and the Left: A Study of Socialist and Radical Influences in the American Labor Movement, 1881–1924* (New York: Basic Books, 1970).
33 Mark Wyman, *Hard Rock Epic: Western Miners and the Industrial Revolution, 1860–1910* (Berkeley: University of California Press, 1979).
34 William Preston, "Shall This Be All? U.S. Historians Versus William D. Haywood Et Al," *Labor History* 12 (Summer 1971): 437–38, 442. For analyses that support the trajectory from the Knights and the Populist Party to the Socialist Party and the IWW, see James Edward Wright, *The Politics of Populism: Dissent in Colorado* (New Haven, CT: Yale University Press, 1974); and Jameson, *All That Glitters*.
35 James C. Foster for instance, challenged the assumption that the WFM was a radical union because "the mean number of violent, labor-related outbreaks was only 0.785 incidents in the lifetime of the average local (about seven years)." His argument assumes that all radical

movements are violent, and all violence is radical. From his figures, one could argue that every local stood about an 80 percent chance of a strike every seven years. James C. Foster, "Quantification and the Western Federation," *Historical Methods Newsletter* 10 (Fall 1977): 141–48. See also John Ervin Brinley, Jr., "The Western Federation of Miners" (PhD diss., University of Utah, 1972); Richard H. Peterson, "Conflict and Consensus: Labor Relations in Western Mining," *Journal of the West* 12 (January 1973): 1–17. The quote is from Wyman, *Hard Rock Epic*, 244.

36 Jameson, *All that Glitters*. I most explicitly addressed Wyman's statement in a paper I presented at the Western History Association conference in October 1992, "The Miners of Cripple Creek: Accommodation and Resistance, 1894–1904."

37 Underground mining in the District declined during the 1920s, revived during the 1930s, but was suspended during World War II, as the U.S. government diverted miners to non-precious metals essential to the war effort. It resumed after the war but slowly declined and had all but halted by the time I conducted my interviews. In 1994 deep pit mining was begun, and many of the former townsites, including the union stronghold of Altman, at the top of Bull Hill, no longer exist, having been excavated as the pit expanded.

38 Interview with Kathleen Chapman, Wheat Ridge, Colorado, April 17, 1979.

39 The interconnected Welch, Doran, and McConaghy family histories were provided by John and Hannah Welch's daughter, Kathleen Chapman and James and Kate McConaghy's daughter, May Wing. Chapman interview; May Wing, interviews, Boulder, Colorado, March 6, 1976; Victor, Colorado, October 21, 1978; Colorado Springs, Colorado, February 16, 1979. Further information came from U.S. Manuscript Census, town of Shullsberg, Lafayette County, Wisconsin, 1870; U.S. Manuscript Census, town of Shullsberg, Lafayette County, Wisconsin, 1880; U.S. Manuscript Census, town of Leadville, Lake County, Colorado, 1900; and The (Shullsberg) *Pick and Gad*, June 19, 1884.

40 Wing interview, March 6, 1976.

41 Chapman interview.

42 Chapman interview.

43 In 1896, for instance, the Anna Lee shaft of the Portland Mine caved in, killing eight men. Victor Miners No. 32 buried victim Michael McGuirk and shipped the body of Pat Mee to Denver for burial and the body of Thomas H. Harman to Madison, Wisconsin. *Colorado Springs Gazeete*, January 13, 1896, January 20, 1896; *Ledger, 1894–1903*, Victor Miners' Union No. 32, U.S. mss 14a, Wisconsin State Historical Society, Madison, Wisconsin; *Press*, April 6, 1900, August 1, 1901, October 5, 1902.

44 Chapman interview.

45 Chapman interview.

46 "President Moyer's Address to the Cripple Creek Miners at Pinnacle Park," *Miners' Magazine*, September 3, 1903, 6.

47 *Press*, September 5, 1899, September 5, 1903; William D. Haywood, *Bill Haywood's Book: The Autobiography of William D. Haywood* (New York: International Publishers, 1929; repr., 1974), 133; Chapman interview.

48 Chapman interview.

49 Chapman interview; *Press*, June 27, 1899; January 3, 1900; January 9, 1900.

50 *Press*, June 27, 1899; February 23, 1900; "The Gold Coin Club House," *Miners' Magazine*, July 1900, 13–14; Chapman interview.

51 Jameson, *All That Glitters*, 78–84.

52 Jameson, *All That Glitters*, 68–72.

53 *Press*, October 15, 1901.

54 *Press*, passim; Jameson, *All That Glitters*, 70.
55 Jameson, *All That Glitters*, 70–71.
56 Jameson, *All That Glitters*, 73. See Press May 9, 1900; May 15, 1900. Such tactics were common. The next day Kelly and E. J. Campbell, secretary of Cripple Creek Miners No. 40, visited the Independence Mine. See *Press* May 16, 1900; July 22, 1900.
57 Jameson, *All That Glitters*, 235–39.
58 Chapman interview.
59 Chapman interview. The soldier hid in the Welch's woodpile. John Welch helped hide him and Hannah made the man coffee and sandwiches to take with him as he escaped.
60 Wing interview, October 21, 1978. Kathleen Welch Chapman also knew these stories.
61 Chapman interview.
62 Chapman interview.
63 Chapman interview.
64 *Labor Disturbances*, 189–91; Richardson Notes, 27, 75; Dubofsky, *We Shall Be All*, 98; George E. Dickson, letter to Clarence Darrow, April 25, 1906, in Richardson Notes, 53. Dickson was a Chicago attorney who did investigative work for the defense during the Steunenberg trials of Haywood and WFM member Steve Adams. He got the story from G. L. Brokaw, who was jailed in Spokane for getting money under false pretenses and who said he was with Orchard for ten days before May 26, 1905. See also George E. Dickson to Edmund F. Richardson, May 6, 1906, Richardson Notes, 55.

Borders: Walls and Bridges: 2003–2007

I was editing an article the morning of September 11, 2001, when my telephone rang. Without preface, my American colleague Jewel Spangler asked, "Are you watching TV?"

"No, I'm editing this article," I responded.

"You should turn it on," she said.

"Which channel?"

"It doesn't matter."

I turned on the television to watch a plane slam into the second tower. Numbly watching the Twin Towers crumble, I shakily called my mother in Galveston. "We're under attack," she said. "It's just like Pearl Harbor." I called my cousin in New Jersey to see if her family was safe.

Then, knowing I was being irrational, I called my son's school. "I know this makes no sense," I said, "but I'm American, and I just need to know that my son is alright." A kind woman's voice responded, "I am Canadian, I have children and grandchildren, and all I want to do right now is hug them. So, if you need to see your son, come on to the school."

As I drove through that bright, crisp September morning, I suddenly noticed an unusual number of airplanes heading to the Calgary airport. And for the first time, I began to glimpse how important the border could be. At that moment the 49th Parallel simultaneously provided refuge for the diverted travelers in those planes and erected a wall that barred me from reaching my family.

Needing human contact that afternoon and still stunned from unrelenting news coverage, I drove to my office. My colleague Doug Francis saw me arrive and rushed to hug me. In the coming days, friends and strangers continued to shake my stereotypes of Canadian reserve with their kindness. The Calgary airport remained packed with planes hastily diverted north of the border, while the Calgary Drop-In Centre, erected to house homeless people, sheltered stranded passengers. Helplessly seeking something to do, I chipped in with two American colleagues to send a stack of pizzas to the Drop-In Centre.

The morning of September 10 I had begun a new semester and a new class that my colleague Sarah Carter and I were piloting, "Mild West/Wild West?: Comparative History of the Canadian and U.S. Wests." (The question mark in the title is essential.) The first day of class was September 10, 2001; my first lecture was September 12.

I was supposed to lecture on ways that Americans and Canadians had imagined our borders and our respective Wests. I intended to contrast the place of the U.S. and Canadian Wests in some of the foundational national histories and compare how the Canada-U.S. border had functioned in Canadian and American imaginations.[1] I was going to discuss the work of George F. G. Stanley who drew a line at the border that separated U.S. savagery from Canadian civilization—that separated a mythic U.S. Wild West from a mythic Canadian Mild West.[2] I intended to talk about how Americans, unlike Stanley, thought that Canada was pretty much like the States, but had imagined a racialized southern boundary that separated White Americans from darker poorer Mexicans allegedly clamoring to sneak across the border. I was going to talk about how both these borders were human inventions, and about the part that historians had played in their creation.

The morning of September 12, I was reviewing my lecture notes while CNN droned in the background. Then two newscasters grabbed my attention as they speculated that the flights that leveled the Twin Towers had originated in Maine and Boston because dark people could sneak across the border from Canada. And everything I intended to say that morning shifted beneath my feet.

I somehow got through my lecture that morning. I ended with the CNN newscast and told the students that whatever I thought I knew about our borders was changing as I spoke, and that I hoped that our semester together would help us make sense of the altered realities we were about to confront.

Over two decades later, the events of September 11 still impact American culture and global politics. At the time, they dramatically underscored my nascent understanding of the Canada-U.S. border. I knew that the border, and the nations it separated, had always been historically constructed and contingent. I had not grasped that the ways the 49th Parallel was policed, politicized, and imagined would continue to change after I crossed it. I knew that the border had always been selectively porous, allowing some people and groups to enter Canada while excluding others. I had not yet grasped that at times I would not be able to cross it, as happened immediately after 9/11, and at times during the COVID-19 pandemic. I knew that the border operated symbolically to bridge or to separate the ways Americans and Canadians imagined ourselves and our histories. I had not expected so personally to witness the process of reimagining its significance.

I noticed those changes first at airport security and in my son's heightened anxiety when I traveled to the States. After 9/11, I had to call him every time my plane landed safely. I learned to arrive even earlier to navigate security for crack-of-dawn flights from Calgary to the U.S., to jettison all liquids and take off my shoes to clear security. To my surprise, I often had to endure being singled out for enhanced screening in the United States, in groups that usually consisted of dark young men and me. I think I was there to dispel accusations of racial and gender profiling, as Americans selectively racialized the Canadian border in response to fears of terrorists. I experienced enhanced screening in Calgary as well, but with a difference. For the better part of a year the same Security Officer at the Calgary airport pulled me out of line for enhanced screening. I didn't mind since it got me out of the long screening lines. Finally, I asked her, "How do you decide who to screen?" "Oh," she said, "I just look for people who look nice, who won't yell at me." I didn't know whether to be more flattered or terrified.

The three lectures in this section represent research and thoughts about borders, borderlands, comparative histories, and border crossings that began shortly before my move to Calgary and that responded to daily experience as well as to the dramatic events of 9/11. Collectively, they represent three historical approaches to national borders: comparative, borderlands, and cross-cultural histories.

In April 1999, just before my move to Calgary, Jeremy Mouat and I presented a joint paper at the Organization of American Historians meeting in Toronto, "Frontiers, Staples, and People: State and Society in Western Canada and the American West," the beginning of a joint project comparing the historiographies of western Canada and the U.S. West. That first conference paper eventually mushroomed into a forty-seven-page journal article. During its long gestation we began calling it "The Beast."[3]

Jeremy's generous crash course on the Canadian West provided essential grounding, both personally and professionally. Our collaboration provided much of that first 2001 lecture to "Mild West/Wild West?" It later became the basis of a seminar I developed, "Frontiers, Borders, and Borderlands." Acknowledging Dr. Mouat's shared authorship, I used an early iteration of our work for my 2003 lecture, "Telling Differences: The 49th Parallel, the West, and the Histories of Two Nations."

Canadian colleagues Sarah Carter and Sheila McManus also generously collaborated on comparative projects. Sarah Carter and I developed our undergraduate course, "Mild West/Wild West?" The opportunity to co-teach with Dr. Carter and to learn from her lectures enriched my thinking about our comparative pasts, and I missed our conversations and collaboration when she left the University of Calgary in 2006 to accept the

Henry Marshall Tory Chair at the University of Alberta. I continued to teach "Wild West/Mild West?" until I retired.

I developed new insights into the connected and separate histories of women in the U.S. and Canadian Wests at the Unsettled Pasts conference that Sarah and I collaborated to organize in 2002, and as Sheila McManus and I co-edited *One Step over the Line: Toward a History of Women in the North American Wests* from some of the conference papers.[4] My work on comparative and borderlands histories owes a great deal to those early collaborations with generous colleagues.

During 2004–2005 I served as President of the Pacific Coast Branch-American Historical Association. My presidential address focused on national borders and borderlands. It examined, in part, the ways that the 9/11 attacks affected changing perceptions and policing of the U.S.-Canada border. It served as my 2006 lecture as well.

The gap between my 2003 and 2006 lectures was shorter than the dates might suggest and occurred due to a research leave and a brief medical leave. I gave my 2003 lecture in November 2003, during the 2003–2004 academic year and my 2006 lecture in February 2006, during the 2005–2006 academic year, so there was a gap of only one lecture, during the 2004–2005 academic year.

The final essay in this section began long before 9/11. In 1972, while I was a graduate student at the University of Michigan, I visited a friend serving in the Teacher Corps in Nulato, Alaska, an Athabascan village on the lower Yukon River. I spent that summer studying Alaska history and anthropology at the University of Alaska, Fairbanks. My short time in a Native village and a summer living in a log cabin without running water or indoor plumbing has helped me imagine the isolation and environmental challenges of western homesteaders. Although my trips to Alaska theoretically crossed two U.S.-Canada borders, I did not have to negotiate any international boundaries to fly there from Seattle. Staying in a former missionary's poorly insulated frame house at 40 below (Fahrenheit) and being a White person in an Athabascan village provided instant immersion in the social and environmental boundaries of Native Alaska, a place within U.S. borders yet far removed from the "lower 48." The "Outside" remained remote in pre-pipeline Alaska, even in Fairbanks, where news often arrived on film by plane from Seattle a day after it was broadcast in the lower 48.[5] The pipeline itself was one more reminder of the ways that U.S. economic interests would impact Native people, who once again adapted to changes wrought from the Outside.

During my summer at the University of Alaska, I researched the contacts between newcomers and Indigenous people after European settlers arrived throughout the Americas. For my 2007 Chair's lecture, I returned to that research, which focused on the efforts of missionaries and the U.S. government to "civilize" Alaska Natives by turning hunters into reindeer herders. I explored the diverse ways that Alaska Natives added reindeer to their means of subsistence while adapting with greater complexity to the White newcomers' "civilizing" agendas. My brief sojourn in Alaska and my research into the reindeer project first focused my scholarship on the "cross-cultural contacts" between colonizers and Indigenous people that so centrally shaped the North American Wests I have studied and inhabited. I learned more about the histories of those contacts and their effects on Native Americans as an Anglo newcomer to New Mexico. I taught Latinx and Native American students at the University of New Mexico, where the legacies of Spanish conquest compounded the legacies of U.S. Indian policy.

The legacies of settler colonialism and its devastating impacts on the First Nations were readily apparent in Calgary. The United States had tried to move American Indians far away from Whites and from urban areas to large, mostly remote, reservations in the American West. Albuquerque had been an exception, located near ten of the nineteen New Mexico pueblos.[6] Canada, in contrast, had established numerous smaller First Nations reserves, many of them around urban centers. In Calgary, the nearby reserves of the Siksika, Kainai, Piikani, Tsuut'ina, Chiniki, Bearspaw, and Goodstoney First Nations became a constant reminder of the enduring legacies of European settlement.

I returned to my Alaska research seeking a way to link my work with the history of settler colonialism in prairie Canada. I was reminded, in the process, how much my brief time in Alaska and my research there had influenced how I later approached cultural and social boundaries, the racialized power relations of settler colonialism, the myriad adaptations with which Indigenous people met their radically altered circumstances, and the inescapable connection of that history with my claims to homes in the North American Wests.

NOTES

1. Frederick Jackson Turner, "The Significance of the Frontier in American History," first presented at the American Historical Association meeting in Chicago, July 12, 1893, coinciding with the World's Columbian Exhibition of 1893, originally printed in *Annual Report of the American Historical Association for the Year 1893* (Washington, DC: Government Printing Office, 1894); Harold Adams Innis, *The Fur Trade in Canada: An Introduction to Canadian Economic History* (Toronto: University of Toronto Press, 1930), best known through the revised 1956 and 1999 editions (Toronto: University of Toronto Press), the latter with an introduction by Arthur Ray; Walter Sage, "Some Aspects of the Frontier in Canadian History, in *Canadian Historical Association Annual Report* (Ottawa: Department of Public Archives, 1928).

2. George F. G. Stanley, "Western Canada and the Frontier Thesis," in *Canadian Historical Association Annual Report*, 1940.

3. Elizabeth Jameson and Jeremy Mouat, "Telling Differences: The Forty-Ninth Parallel and Historiographies of the West and Nation," *Pacific Historical Review* 75:2 (May 2006): 183–230.

4. Elizabeth Jameson and Sheila McManus, eds., *One Step Over the Line: Toward a History of Women in the North American Wests* (Athabasca, AB: Athabasca University Press and Edmonton: University of Alberta Press, 2005).

5. In 1972, Alaskans debated the economic and environmental impacts of the proposed North Slope oil pipeline and prepared to implement the Alaska Native Land Claims Settlement Act of 1971 (ANCSA). ANCSA finally resolved the provision of the First Organic Act of 1884, which had guaranteed Alaska Natives' possession of their land, by creating twelve regional profit-making Alaska Native corporations and over 200 villages, groups, and urban corporations to receive what would end up being around 45.5 million acres of land and about $1 billion. A 13th regional corporation headquartered in Seattle was later established for Alaska Natives who lived outside of Alaska; they participated in the cash settlement but did not receive land.

6. Sandia and Isleta Pueblos are closest to Albuquerque; Santo Domingo, San Felipe, and Cochiti Pueblos are between Albuquerque and Santa Fe; and Santa Ana, Jemez, Zia, Laguna, and Acoma Pueblos are all less than 60 miles from the city.

4

Telling Differences: The 49th Parallel, the West, and the Histories of Two Nations

November 4, 2003
With Jeremy Mouat

One of the pleasures of working at the University of Calgary was the opportunity to talk with Canadian colleagues about our respective Wests. Histories that speak across national borders require knowing the histories on both sides, recognizing that different stories, symbols, and social languages connect national identities. My first piece of that ongoing project compared how frontiers, borders, and the West have functioned in the histories and national identities of two nations. This was risky: I was comparing histories of the U.S. West, which I know well enough to know how much I don't know, with Canadian histories that most Canadians knew better than I. Such a comparison requires conversations and collaborations across intellectual and international boundaries.

This essay began with one such conversation when I met my colleague Jeremy Mouat at the 1991 Mining History Association conference and we chatted about our respective work on western gold-mining communities.[1] Dr. Mouat, with typical efficiency and generosity, began sending me articles about western Canada that soon stretched a rapidly expanding file, at first labeled simply "Mouat." Eventually, our conversations led to a joint article from which, with Dr. Mouat's kind permission, my lecture and now this essay were drawn. Portions of this essay were written by each of us, but those portions were not simply assigned by our countries of birth—I wrote some of the sections on Canadian historians and Jeremy wrote some on American historians.

The lecture came while we were still working on the article. It was rapidly getting longer and denser in response to editors' requests, and it benefited from audience responses to my lecture.[2] I focused in 2003 on some histories that might illuminate comparative and transborder Wests. More than defining the debates about frontiers, regions, and identities in both countries, I wanted to suggest their contours and the challenges of the historical borderlands, where the histories of states intersect the histories of people, economies, and ecologies. I began with three images to suggest the challenges and potential of this project.

* * *

Few images better reveal the arbitrary nature of the border between Western Canada and the western United States than those recorded by the survey crews who first marked the 49th Parallel. Both the photographs taken by the British photographer and the paintings of the "Official Artist" assigned to the American survey party show a rough-cut running in an unnaturally straight line through forests and over hills, off into the distance. Nothing but the surveyed boundary separates the land on either side of the border.

We might contrast this image with a scene from John Sayles' film, *Lone Star*, a film that is all about borders, national, social, and personal.[3] At one point, Sheriff Sam Deeds, played by Chris Cooper, crosses the Texas border into Mexico in search of information. He approaches El Rey de las Llantas (the King of the Tires). "You're the sheriff of Rio County, right?" says El Rey. "Un jefe muy respectado" (a very respected leader). El Rey leans over and draws a line in the dirt with a Coke bottle. "Step across this line," he says. "Ay, que milagro!" (ay, what a miracle!) "You're not the sheriff of nothing anymore. Just some Tejano with a lot of questions I don't have to answer. A bird flying south, you think he sees this line? Rattlesnake, javalina, whatever you got. You think halfway across that line they start thinking different? Why should a man?"

The Sheriff replies, "Your government's always been pretty happy to have that line. The question's just been where to draw it."

To which El Rey responds, "My government can go fuck itself. And so can yours. I'm talking about people here. Men."[4]

And a final image: an aerial photograph of the Milk River crossing the 49th Parallel, which illustrates that a bird flying *north* can in fact see the U.S./Canadian border, etched through different patterns of land use and property division in only a bit over a century since the Boundary Commission drew the line across the continent. People rather than nature created the differences on either side of that line. And some of those people were historians.

The 49th Parallel became a border in the 19th century, as the British and American governments divided the territories over which each claimed sovereignty. The agreement following the War of 1812 formally recognized the parallel as a border from the Great Lakes to the Rockies. West of there, the two states simply agreed to a vague "joint occupation." The 1846 Oregon Treaty extended the border along the 49th Parallel to the Pacific, and around the southern tip of Vancouver Island. The border, however, remained dynamic, and for over a decade unmapped, as two emerging nation states sought to assert control over the enormous western territories they claimed.[5]

Authority flowed from east to west, but traffic flowed in all directions. People traveled north or south across the border, seeking asylum or economic opportunity; the line held particular significance for each border crosser. These tensions would be written in competing narratives that emphasized east/west or north/south axes of economies and migration, and, more recently, in comparative and borderlands histories.

The various contested meanings assigned to the border emphasize that neither states nor national identities are fixed or absolute, but are historically constructed, and re-constructed.[6] In Canada and the United States, frontier, region, and a common border have shaped different histories and different identities, as historians participated in that process of telling the differences.

* * *

The Canadian and U.S. Wests share a crucial similarity: the incorporation of western Canada and the American West within transcontinental states during the 19th century was in both cases a deliberate nation-building exercise and was recognized as such. The processes of national expansion differed, however.

The United States gained Britain's land east of the Mississippi River in 1783, at the end of the Revolutionary War. Within seventy years, the new nation stretched to the Pacific Ocean and claimed all the territory that became the forty-eight contiguous states, acquiring this vast area through the Louisiana Purchase in 1803, the annexation of Texas in 1845, the Treaty of Oregon with Britain the following year, the Mexican-American War which secured the northern third of Mexico in 1848, and the Gadsden Purchase in 1853. The purchase of Alaska from Russia followed in 1867, and, finally, the claim to Hawaii in 1898. The phrase "Manifest Destiny" hardly explains this process that imprinted U.S. history and imagination with images of inexorable westward expansion.

Canadian histories followed different trajectories, reflecting both the processes of state formation and of national imagination. The fur trade, for instance, drew Europeans to both Wests long before Canadian Confederation or U.S. independence, but it has figured more prominently in Canadian histories, thus starting the narrative further west from the beginning. The isolated and distinct colonies of British North America did not go through the unifying process of a revolutionary war. Thus, Anglo-Canadians could celebrate the virtues of a civilization transported from Britain to North America, while American historians, represented most formatively by Frederick Jackson Turner, sought to explain what—besides a war—separated the United States from Europe.[7]

* * *

Frontiers, borderlands, regions, and the border itself have been defined differently over time, and across internal and national boundaries. U.S. historians have generally distinguished frontiers from borders. The Canadian border did not fit U.S. understandings of frontiers, formalized in 1893 by Frederick Jackson Turner, for whom a paucity of White people defined frontiers and divided savagery from civilization. In 1892, the U.S. Census Bureau fixed a frontier line of Euro-American density "beyond which the country must be considered as unsettled"; similarly, the Superintendent of the Census declared the frontier closed in 1890 because there was no longer an unbroken line of settlement with two or fewer Euro-Americans per square mile—which is how he defined the frontier. As soon as there was a square mile with three or more Euro-American settlers, by this definition the frontier ceased to exist.[8]

In contrast, frontiers in Canadian historiography have often been defined in the European sense of borders, particularly geographic borders that separate regions as well as nations. Geography in part divided the Canadian West(s) into prairie and British Columbia, a division that avoids the messy debates about the precise borders of the West in U.S. historiography, or efforts to fit the Pacific Northwest into a region that explorers and historians defined by aridity.⁹ Canada's frontiers have been drawn by geography. In the words of J. M. S. Careless: "The unrelenting granite of the Precambrian Shield straddled the midst of the country, not the richly fruitful Mississippi Basin, agrarian heartland of the United States. Agricultural frontiers that loomed so large in Turnerian perspectives were in no way as predominant in the vistas of the north."¹⁰

The border, however, was. The 49th Parallel looms large in Canadian imagination, dividing what is and is not Canadian.¹¹ The border functions much as the frontier did in Turner's history, as the line that divides American cultural savagery from Canadian civilization.¹²

Specific understandings of national origins and colonial relationships led to distinct notions of frontier and region in the two countries. These distinctions are reflected in differences in the historical narratives that are our national creation stories. If a creation story explains, often in mythic terms, how a people come to a place and claim it as their own, then Frederick Jackson Turner's frontier thesis became the creation story of the U.S. nation state, not simply describing its expansion but also providing an ideological basis for it. No precise equivalent exists in Canada, since the frontier never "explained" Canada as Turner claimed it explained the first phase of American history.

Turner's frontier thesis, arguably the most stubbornly influential work of any historian, identified a succession of westward-moving frontiers as the seedbeds of American character and institutions. Americans' ongoing encounters with a series of frontiers made America different from Europe, created individualism and democracy, and forged the crucible in which European immigrants formed not a mosaic but a "composite nationality."¹³ Turner's frontiers marked the progress of Manifest Destiny and justified the conquest of occupied land through late-19th-century assumptions about the nature of progress. These frontiers—the dividing lines between "savagery and civilization"—moved inexorably from east to west, occupied by an equally inexorable sequence of Indian traders, hunters, soldiers, ranchers, miners, and farmers.¹⁴ Turner recognized that this process was colonial, that with each frontier the U.S. claimed the continent. American history, he announced in 1893, was "in a large degree the history of the colonization of the Great West. The existence of an area of free land, its continuous recession, and the advance of American settlement westward, explain American development."¹⁵

Turner considered himself a *U.S.* historian, not a historian of the frontier or the West. He provided an early conceptual road map for American historians, to be challenged, refuted, refined, and re-defined. In Canadian historiography, there is no canonical figure of quite the same stature or confidence, arguing with the same simplicity.

Harold Innis is perhaps the closest Canadian equivalent, largely for *The Fur Trade in Canada*, published in 1930. As the expansion of American investment, American capital, and American culture through radio and motion pictures was of growing concern to many Canadians, Innis attacked the frontier thesis and called for "a philosophy of economic history or an economic theory suited to Canadian needs."[16] *The Fur Trade in Canada* elaborated his staples thesis, which argued that Canada had natural and inevitable borders, and that a logic explained its existence and its growth. The fur trade was one of a series of staple industries, the specific conditions of which dictated the form and character of Canadian development, including its territorial expanse. As Innis summarized, "The present Dominion emerged not in spite of geography but because of it."[17] The Canadian West provided staple raw materials to be developed by eastern and foreign capital. Persistent inequalities, therefore, marked the relationship between the West and central Canada.[18]

Both Innis and Turner located key resources, whether free land or staples, at the heart of national development; each assumed a hierarchy of cultures and races; each saw White men as the principal agents of national progress, although Innis recognized the economic value of Aboriginal and Métis labor. But the frontier thesis wrote innovation from the western margins of an expanding nation. Canadian staples frontiers lay in the North and West, but Innis wrote and imagined Canada from the metropolitan center. He did not, like Turner, separate wilderness and civilization, but rather he saw staples development from a combination of natural bounty, technical skill, and industrial export markets. Transportation fueled the growth and decay of key staples industries—rivers for furs, rails and ships for minerals and agriculture. Each staple generated a particular regional economy and identity, centered on a regional metropole, which in turn was dependent on central Canada, which in turn served the European metropolis.

Harold Innis's West, like Turner's, required fur traders, miners, ranchers, timbermen, fishermen, and farmers to furnish staple resources to the metropolitan center. But they did not function as mythic heroes to forge the wellspring of Canadian national character. Neither frontiers nor staples *explained* Canada.

For Turner, unlike many of his disciples, the closing of the frontier in 1890 marked the end of the first period of American history. By the 1920s, he, too, emphasized resource development, announcing to his Harvard students that: "Failure to use resources will submit people to subordination of a superior type which *does*."[19] Innis's staples thesis, in fact, bears some resemblance to Turner's contemporaneous but less-famous theory of sections. As early as 1914 Turner wrote of "Geographic Influences in American History." In 1925 he published "The Significance of the Section in American History," defining sections, or regions, as changing historical constructs of some combination of environment, culture, and economy. The "West," he wrote:

> wherever found at different years thought of itself and of the nation in different ways from those of the East. It needed capital; it was a debtor region, while the East had the capital and was the creditor section. The West was rural, agricultural, while the East was becoming more and more urban and industrial. . . . [T]he frontier stressed the rights of man, while the statesmen who voiced the interests of the East stressed the rights of property.[20]

In the 1920s, both Turner and Innis discussed how resources mapped regional borders and dependencies. Turner described dependencies between sections, while Innis envisioned a series of unequal relationships among regional and national metropoles and hinterlands. These formative differences influenced debates and shifts in the evolving historiographies. The first of these underscored the differences between how the Mexican and Canadian borders have been represented in U.S. histories. In popular imagination and national historical narratives, from perspectives mostly Euro-American, the Mexican border divides Americans from "others," from darker and mostly poorer people clamoring to come north. The contests for territory that preceded U.S. sovereignty fostered a school of Borderlands history, founded by Herbert Eugene Bolton, whose *The Spanish Borderlands* appeared in 1921. It complicated Turner's emphasis on western frontiers by concentrating instead on cultural conflict and on the north/south frontiers of New Spain and Mexico. Ironically, and to Bolton's considerable discomfort, another north/south axis operated in his book, which was extensively revised and edited by Constance Lindsay Skinner of British Columbia.[21] Both Bolton's borderlands and Innis's northern frontiers superimposed north/south migrations over Turner's westward moving frontiers.

From the 1930s through the 1960s historians' interpretations shifted in response to environmental limits, international expansion, and the cross-border movements of people, capital, and communications. During the 1930s, historians confronted limits imposed by nature and economic depression. As Eden shriveled into the Dust Bowl, Americans revisited their own creation stories to explain human adaptations to difficult landscapes. The key U.S. text was Walter Prescott Webb's *The Great Plains* (1931), which focused on aridity as the environmental factor that defined the region. Webb interpreted regionalism in terms of technological adaptation to this difficult environment. The six-shooter, windmill, and barbed wire became key innovations that enabled settlement on the Plains.[22]

Canadian scholars assessed environmental limits more somberly. In *Settlement and the Forest Frontier in Eastern Canada* (1936) and *The North American Assault on the Canadian Forest* (1938), Arthur M. Lower expressed, according to J. M. S. Careless, "the pejorative view of metropolitanism as inherently subjugating and exploitative, sucking a territory dry because 'business had to go on'."[23] Both Webb and Lower recognized limits. For Webb they were environmental. For Lower they were rooted in capitalism and U.S. exploitation of Canadian resources. Webb optimistically asserted the potential for technical intervention to overcome environmental obstacles. Lower took a less optimistic view, writing of environmental degradation rooted in capitalist exploitation and the greed of the metropole to the south.

Walter Sage also addressed the relationship of U.S. interests for Canadian regionalism in a 1937 essay that argued that Canadian regions—the Maritimes, Quebec, Ontario, the Prairies, and British Columbia—were economically distinct and had closer relations with the adjacent United States than with each other. The focus on separate regions and on north/south economies created nascent tensions for Canadian nationalism and for the place of regions within national histories.[24]

As international attention turned toward war, historians on both sides of the border re-examined the boundaries of national character and national sovereignty. Turner's frontier thesis bore the attack. South of the border, George W. Pierson surveyed professional historians' assessments of the frontier thesis and published their multi-faceted critique in a two-part article in 1941.[25] Fred Shannon and others refuted Turner's concept of the frontier as a safety valve that drained potential class conflict, challenging the frontier thesis for resting in outdated social theory, for its neglect of both continuities and the grimmer side of the frontier experience, and for ignoring important aspects of American development, including the costs of farming free land and farmers' indebtedness to capital.[26] The frontier thesis, if beleaguered, has proved stubbornly resilient. Ray Allen Billington's *Westward Expansion*, for instance, went through six editions from 1949 through 2001. But since the 1940s the Turner thesis has been repeatedly contested, its claims to "explain" American character repeatedly challenged. Alternatively, it has been recognized and dissected more for its mythic appeal than for its historical accuracy.

Canadian historians in the early 1940s delineated the national character at the southern boundary. The 1940 meeting of the Canadian Historical Association focused on the frontier thesis and George F. G. Stanley's rejection of it from a decidedly Anglo-Canadian perspective. If Innis wrote a creation story of Canadian economic development, Stanley wrote the Canadian counter-narrative to Turner's frontier. Stanley emphasized both environmental adaptation in Canadian development and political and cultural continuity. He faulted the emphasis on "one important internal factor," the frontier, to the exclusion of "the many external factors," most notably the French, British, and Spanish heritages that colonial pioneers brought with them.[27] They adapted to "primitive, uncivilized" environments, where they were "obliged to adopt many of the ways of their savage neighbors or to invent new ways and means to meet immediate ends."[28] Thus, Canadian pioneers adopted snowshoes, moccasins, canoes, Red River Carts, new grains, and farming methods. But government, law, religion, and social institutions changed far less than technology.

Stanley emphasized key distinctions between the Canadian and U.S. experiences. The Canadian frontier was still open to the North.[29] The Laurentian shield placed a great barrier between eastern and Western Canada. And in accordance with British tradition, the Canadian government laid great emphasis on law and order. To combat "rampant lawlessness, drunken orgies," "Indian unrest," and American whiskey runners, Canada established the North West Mounted Police, who set out from Manitoba for Alberta in 1874. Law, order, and efficient administration thus predated Anglo-Canadian settlement of Rupert's Land.

> The police were present at the conclusion of the Indian treaties; they shepherded Sitting Bull's Sioux back to the United States; they assisted the Department in gathering the plains

tribes upon the reservations and brought justice to red and white men alike. Doors might henceforth be left unlocked and cattle unguarded; the drunken riots ceased and there was an end to Indian bloodshed.[30]

By contrast, in the U.S.:

... the frontiersman quickly outdistanced effective administration, hence the lawlessness which characterized the history of the American West.... The fighting plainsman of American history, has, however, no counterpart north of the boundary. The Canadian frontier was peopled by peaceful, law-abiding ranchers, farmers, and government-encouraged colonists. Here the settler looked to organized justice and to the Mounted Police for his protection and not to the rifle over his door.[31]

Stanley celebrated the arrival after 1870 of a "racially homogeneous" population, "not infrequently Conservative in politics," that brought "the social and political patterns of Canada and Great Britain."[32] He realistically assessed Anglo-Canadian motives to incorporate Rupert's Land into the nation. Confederation was spurred by fears that Britain might settle convicts in the Hudson's Bay territory, fears of American aggression, and by desires for the resources and agricultural potentials of the western lands.[33]

These conclusions came largely from Stanley's interpretation of the period from 1870 to the completion of the Canadian Pacific Railway in 1885. He left curiously untheorized the next period, which he called the last stage of frontier settlement, a period that brought international settlers to the prairies from the United States, Iceland, Belgium, Ukraine, Sweden, and Hungary, and religious and ethnic minorities like Jews, Mennonites, Doukhobors, and Hutterites. By 1911 the prairies were, he said, "a polyglot mixing bowl" —which sounds less elegant than a mosaic. Apparently, unlike the British, French, and Spaniards, these new immigrants shed much of their traditional baggage at the border. The "polyglot" character of the prairie population might, however, explain militant agrarianism and demands for provincial autonomy. Agrarian movements, though, were the products not of the frontier but of economic conflicts "between producers of primary products selling in an open market and the producers of secondary products selling in a closed market."[34] Stanley thus linked Innis's staples thesis with Anglo culture and Anglo political institutions. The history of the West could be explained by neither alone. Nor did the West explain Canada except in contrast to the United States.

There was, however, dissent from the sharp separation of the two Wests. Walter Sage rebutted Stanley, insisting that "There was one frontier of settlement for the whole of America" and that the American frontier moved into Canada after 1885. He critiqued Stanley for focusing narrowly on prairie agriculture, because Turner's frontiers included ranching and mining, and the B.C. mining frontier was a northward extension of the California gold rush.[35]

The dominant professional opinion in both countries seemed to discredit Turner. But his West continued to define an increasingly mythic American national identity which acted as a foil for Canadian difference, located increasingly in the Canadian North. In *Dominion of the North* (1944) Donald Creighton located the national purpose in Sir John A. MacDonald's National Policy, whereby the railroad, protective tariffs, and recruited prairie settlers established mutual dependencies that revolved around wilderness.[36] In 1946, W. L. Morton challenged both Innis and Creighton from a regional perspective, for casting the West as a mere colony of the imperial center and constructing a false "uniformity of the metropolitan culture throughout the hinterlands . . . ."[37] Morton argued that the West's "few, though great resources," "harsh and hazardous climate," and "inflexible economy" changed "people and institutions greatly from those of the humid forest regions of the east."[38] He, too, emphasized the "open flank to the north. This," he argued, "became a permanent frontier, an enduring demarcation line between wilderness and farmland, between north and south. Ragged, flexible, moving far north in the far northwest," it was an "impenetrable" and permanent frontier that distinguished Canada from the U.S. because it was a force of limitation, not progress, because it necessitated dependence "on one's fellows, on cooperative skills, on communal capital" in contrast to U.S. frontier individualism.[39]

As the Cold War escalated, the differences were drawn increasingly along international borders. In the U.S., the Iron Curtain replaced the frontier as the line between savagery and civilization, while a mythic West came to represent what united Americans. From 1945 through the 1960s, attention shifted to the unifying power of a West inscribed in myths, symbols, and stereotypes. In 1950 Henry Nash Smith published his *Virgin Land: The American West as Symbol and Myth* about a mythic West that entered the cultural mainstream and was transmitted to succeeding generations.[40] It was an apt introduction to a period when Hollywood westerns represented national dramas, from McCarthyism "High Noon," in which Sheriff Will Kane (played by Gary Cooper) faces an outlaw gang alone without the support of his town, to the Cold War "Dakota Incident," in which a politician's support of hostile Indians despite the threat they pose represents Americans' denial of the Soviet threat.[41] Consensus historians emphasized national unity and downplayed internal inequalities and disagreements. Earl Pomeroy challenged the significance of regional environmental differences in 1955, arguing, like Stanley, that there was far greater continuity than innovation in the West, not only of political forms, but of architecture, religion, and other basic institutions as well. The environmental adaptations heralded by Webb and conceded by Stanley became temporary compromises, abandoned as soon as settlers could flee their sod shanties and build frame houses. Pomeroy described what united the West and the nation, but not what made America in the first place, not where the transplanted institutions originated. Like Stanley, his consensus denied racial diversity: he insisted that Spaniards had little influence in the Southwest and ignored other sources of internal difference.[42]

The significance of the frontier remained unsettled in the postwar era but was debated in new terms in new contexts. Historians turned to what Turner might have called "the second phase" of U.S. history, and a regional post-1890 West. Gerald Nash explored the urban 20th- century West, where World War II marked a regional turning point sparked by war industries, military spending, population migrations, and tourism.[43] Nash went further, to insist that the West (or at least California) had become the national trendsetter both economically and culturally. This was ironically true as Hollywood projected one New Old West after another, beaming their images to international audiences, from John Wayne's characteristic frontier rugged individualism to the revisionist vision of a range war in Kevin Costner's "Open Range."[44]

The North's significance as a Canadian symbol entered the political arena in 1958, when Prime Minister John Diefenbaker articulated his "Northern Vision" in the course of a political campaign that focused in part on the role of American investment in Canada, winning a landslide victory as the defender of Canadian nationalism.[45] Ramsay Cook focused on the North in 1971, noting that the frontier had never touched the Canadian imagination as it had in the U.S., but rather "the concept of the North ... provided many imaginative and nationalistic Canadian writers a nature symbol to develop. If the cowboy was the hero of the frontier in the United States, the Royal Canadian Mounted Policeman was the

Canadian symbol—a symbol not only of law and order, but of metropolitan penetration of the frontier."[46]

As frontiers became symbols, a renewed regionalism emerged in the post-frontier era, manifested in Canada in the Prairie School of history to which University of Calgary historians made outstanding contributions. Place and landscape anchored the discourse in new regional historical journals: *BC Studies* (1968); *Acadiensis* (1971); *Prairie Forum* (1976).[47] In the U.S., regionalism led to the founding conference of the Western History Association in 1961, and the *Western Historical Quarterly* in 1970. Yet while historians of the American West continued to assume the significance of their region for national histories, historians of the Canadian West have focused more on regional identities and particularities.

U.S. consensus histories, particularly the Myth and Symbols School, saw the West and western images as sources of national unity and identity. Increasingly, counter-readings of these myths probed what both Turner and Stanley considered the less admirable side of frontier character, dissected for instance in Richard Slotkin's trilogy, *Regeneration Through Violence, The Fatal Environment* and *Gunfighter Nation*.[48]

As the U.S. abandoned isolationism, some historians who believed in the formative influence of the frontier disputed its exceptional influence on the United States. In opposition to the consensus emphasis on the nation, they called for comparative and international histories of global frontiers. Herbert Heaton pleaded with his colleagues in 1946 to abandon "academic isolationism" for a comparative approach to the frontiers of Australia, New Zealand, Canada, South Africa, Latin America, and Siberia. All Wests dealt with common issues: "how to alienate the land, foster manufactures, construct internal improvements, get banks that stayed open, and devise currencies that stayed acceptable."[49]

Heaton saw Canadian development as continuous with the U.S. frontier: settlers moved north as the good land was taken in the U.S.; lumber development followed over-exploitation of U.S. forests; as the U.S. food surplus for export dropped, Canadian wheat found more European markets. He identified, too, a common theme of environmental costs: "The nineteenth century skimmed the cream off the new world; we are now down to the milk, and some of our descendants may have to get their drinks from the faucets."[50]

In a similar vein, Paul Sharp argued in 1950 that the U.S. frontier did not close in 1890, but moved north, as some 1.25 million Americans sought new opportunities in the Canadian West from 1890–1920, as well as Europeans and eastern Canadians. "Affected by a sort of nationalistic astigmatism," he wrote:

> historians have looked only as far as "49 degrees north" for the story of westward movement, of which the settlement of the Canadian West is actually the final chapter in the Anglo-American conquest of the Great Plains. . . . The mass migration into the Canadian West was the last advance in the long march that had begun on the Atlantic seaboard.[51]

Sharp traced the efforts of the Canadian government and the Canadian Pacific Railway to attract these settlers, and the significance of the 1896 U.S. Populist defeat, after which Populists like Henry Wise Wood and John W. Leedy moved north seeking a more promising ideological environment. Many Populists were drawn to prairie provinces that offered hail insurance laws, direct taxes on land values, few taxes on farmers' personal property, and laws discouraging land speculation.[52]

Canadian homesteads attracted religious and ethnic colonies to dot the "polyglot" prairies, like the Mormon migrants to southern Alberta, welcomed by the Ottawa government who reassured uneasy Albertans that "the territory is already organized, and has its laws in regard to property and civil rights and relations, including the subject of marriage."[53] The 49th Parallel, Sharp argued, "became a far more formidable barrier to historians than to the men and movements they sought to describe. The ranchers on the northern plains, for instance, often ignored this boundary in their search for adequate pasturage, and cowboys sought employment with outfits in Alberta as freely as with those in Wyoming and Montana."[54]

As the U.S. expanded its global aspirations, American historians expanded frontier history to encompass the globe and emphasized continuity and similarity throughout the North American Wests. What from the U.S. appeared to be continuously expanding frontiers of culture and development stimulated Canadian resistance to American cultural, political, and economic encroachment.

The historiographies of both countries through the 1960s thus trace narratives that explain the continental claims of both nations and that defend national identities, following separate historical trajectories of colonization and global engagement. Turner's frontier thesis is consistent with the imperial visions of the late-19th and early-20th centuries. Innis's vision was shaped partly by a concern with growing American influence in Canada as well as by his resentment that the U.S. and Britain disparaged Canada's role in World War I. The 1930s debate recognized environmental and economic limits, limits that seemed to some Canadian historians to characterize and inform Canadian interdependence and collectivism, and to some Americans to stimulate further innovation even as they cautioned against the more celebratory interpretations of western opportunity. The Cold War brought from an America discarding isolationism an expansive vision of U.S. frontiers marching northward into Canada, but no parallel recognition of Canadian immigration and influence in the United States. Sharp, for instance, focusing on the northward-moving Populists, omitted an earlier southward migration that brought some of the most outspoken Populist leaders, like Henry Loucks, from Canada to the United States. Canadian historians responded to distinguish the Canadian frontier experience from the United States', to reinscribe historical distinctions at the 49th Parallel, and to locate frontiers of limitation and of potential growth in the Canadian North.

After the 1960s the historiographic terrain shifted yet again. The optimism and exceptionalism of the Old West became hard to maintain through the lenses of 1960s Civil Rights struggles, Vietnam and Bosnia, the atomic Wests of Los Alamos and Hanford, or global warming that threatened the frontiers of the Canadian North. Social historians turned their attention to relationships of unequal power, to social boundaries more than regional or national ones. New ethnic histories rejected the cultural hierarchies of Turner and Stanley and instead documented the high costs of Native peoples' survival.[55] On both sides of the border, historians focused on how previously invisible actors participated in *Making Western Canada*, *The Black West*, *The Women's West*, and so on. Social inequalities prompted U.S. historians to reinterpret western history as *The Legacy of Conquest* or *The Roots of Dependency*. Richard White summed some of these power relationships in the old cowboy song he chose to name his synthesis, *It's Your Misfortune and None of My Own*.[56]

The West as a place dependent on eastern capital, plundered for its resources, and subordinate to the federal government are themes developed in the U.S. by New Western historians.[57] Like Innis in the 1920s and 1930s, William Robbins, for example, emphasized the "broader influence of capitalism on the country's historical development. The failure to reckon with capitalism," he argued, "indicates, in part, an unwillingness to confront significant power and influence in our culture, a tendency that is widespread, especially so in the study of the American West."[58]

Recognitions of limits and conquest undercut some of the celebrated differences between the two Wests. The distinction between the wild and violent U.S. West and the orderly and civilized Canadian West emphasizes that warfare was more commonly used to colonize Native peoples in the U.S. than in Canada. That is true, in part because Canada's First Nations were aware of the carnage to the South and sought to avoid it. Sarah Carter, Hana Samek, and Robin Fisher have all challenged the notion that a more orderly process led to significantly different outcomes for Canada's First Nations than for Native Americans. As Martin Robin quipped, "one cannot excuse a robbery by describing it as orderly."[59]

If New Western histories addressed similar topics on both sides of the border, the New West has generated more heat south of the 49th Parallel, largely, I think, because the stakes are different: the Old West did not shape Canadian national histories. U.S. and Canadian historians have debated with equal fervor the relative merits of social and national political histories, but the contested icon in Canada was a central Canadian housemaid's knee, not Turner's celebrated frontiersmen.[60]

Tensions between political histories and social historians' emphases on difference and on social and geographic mobility led directly to new definitions of frontiers and borders as borderlands where people of different cultures met. Instead of clear lines of separation or the linear trajectories of frontiers and migrations, Howard Lamar and Robin Winks, among others, investigated frontiers in comparative international perspectives.[61] These new frontiers wrote gender, colonialism, race, and power into the categories of comparison. Howard Lamar and Leonard Thompson, in their 1981 anthology *The Frontier in History*, argued that "one of the least persuasive claims of the frontier hypothesis is that American frontiersmen had faith in the equality of all men, an assertion which is contradicted by the fact that the same frontiersmen excluded Indians, Mexicans, and blacks from equal status."[62] Lamar and Thompson reconceived frontiers as multi-racial encounters between indigenous people and intruders, in which "the experience of the indigenous society is as significant as the intrusive one." "We regard a frontier not as a boundary or line," they wrote, "but as a territory or zone of interpenetration between two previously distinct societies."[63]

The new social histories problematized the significance of the constructed boundary at the 49th Parallel by focusing on the people, economies, and physical environments that crossed it. The key categories of frontiers and borderlands were redefined in terms of interactions that negotiated power, difference, and identities. Gloria Anzaldúa, and Sarah Deutsch defined frontiers/*fronteras* as zones of cultural contact, places where intimate but often-unequal exchanges occurred. Sylvia Van Kirk blazed the trail to these borderlands with *Many Tender Ties*, which placed Indigenous and Métis women, and intimate relationships at the center of the staple Canadian fur trade.[64]

It has been harder to maintain the focus on human interactions after the colonial periods, when the subjects of historical narratives became the new nations. The lenses of national history have often filtered the dynamic stories of migrations back and forth across the border.

Recent discussions of borders, frontiers, and borderlands have centered on Jeremy Adelman and Stephen Aron's 1999 article "From Borderlands to Borders," which argued that in the 19th century the "shift from inter-imperial struggle to international co-existence turned borderlands into *bordered* lands." New borderlands historians, including Michel Hogue in publications from his University of Calgary MA thesis, have countered that the borders remained porous, while significant social barriers were erected to separate people of different races within North America's bordered lands.[65]

Viewed through the lenses of race, class, and gender, the border can be re-mapped to chart what Sarah Carter has called "categories and terrains of exclusion" in our respective Wests.[66] Rather than following progressive and linear movements across the continent, these maps follow the back-and-forth movements of people, capital, technology, and markets that illuminate what links and separates our histories. The border has remained selectively and unequally porous. Canada excluded African American singer and activist Paul Robeson and U.S. whiskey runners; the U.S. fears that dark-skinned terrorists might slip through Immigration Canada. The Sioux used the border strategically to escape the U.S. cavalry, just as the Cree and Métis fled south after the 1885 Rebellion, remaining in Montana and North Dakota despite periodic efforts by the U.S. government to deport them. To Sharp's northern homestead frontier, we might add Canadian women who moved south to file for homesteads in their own names as they could not in Canada. Wage working miners, ranch hands, threshers, cannery workers, domestic servants, and lumber workers followed the labor markets back and forth across the 49th Parallel.

As we develop comparative, transnational histories we enter arenas in which all the categories—economy, citizenship, race, ethnicity, and borders themselves—have different, contingent, historically changing and power-laden meanings. Those meanings construct national identities, to be sure, but they intersect personal and local identities as well.

Paul Sharp cautioned historians over a half century ago not to "stop at a line which existed only on a map."[67] Imagine then, the histories that drew westward moving lines across the continent, the line in the dirt at the 49th Parallel. I was drawn across these borders as I followed miners, farmers, and people fleeing racial or religious persecution, and I realized that, as they entered different national histories, no histories linked them to the kin they left behind. I did not think about my own family's transnational migrations until I moved to Canada and pondered the complex identities that linked my father with his English Jewish parents, or me with a grandfather I never knew who is buried in Montreal.

The historical borderlands connect complex webs of territory, privilege, exclusion, and identity. We all cross some borders; we all police some. Most of us also inhabit *some* borderlands where territories are redefined, and identities are constantly renegotiated. History can be one such borderland, crossing state and social boundaries to re-chart the lines that separate and connect people, to re-map the borders that divide and link our histories. It will fall to historians of these borderlands to listen to the silences that remain to be heard there, and to tell the connections and the differences that may bridge their boundaries.

NOTES

I am grateful to Dr. Jeremy Mouat for his partnership in this project, for introducing me to the histories of the Canadian West, and for years of good conversation and friendship. This lecture was part of a larger work in progress when I delivered it in 2003. It benefitted from the critiques of colleagues. I thank Drs. Sarah Carter, R. Douglas Francis, Donald Smith, and Sheila McManus for sharing their expertise in Canadian history and their insights about the comparative histories of the U.S. and Canadian Wests. I also thank the terrific University of Calgary graduate students in western and borderlands histories for all they taught me in our seminars. Finally, thanks to the *Pacific Historical Review* for permission to publish this earlier version of our article, to editors David Johnson and Carl Abbot for their patience and prodding during the long gestation of the finished article, and to Susan Wladaver-Morgan for her keen editorial eye and for shepherding the article through the production process.

Additional Sources: Andrew Varsanyi addressed the lack of attention to Henry Loucks in his MA thesis, "Principle vs. Pragmatism: Henry Loucks and South Dakota Populism 1884–1900" (master's thesis, University of Calgary, 2015).

1. See for instance, Jeremy Mouat, "Mining in the Settler Dominions: A Comparative Study of the Industry from the 1880s to the First World War (PhD diss., University of British

Columbia, 1988); *Roaring Days: Rossland's Mines and the History of British Columbia* (Vancouver, BC: University of British Columbia Press, 1995); and "The Genesis of Western Exceptionalism: British Columbia's Hard Rock Miners: 1895-1903," *Canadian Historical Review* 71:3 (September 1990): 317-45.

2   That article was a work in progress when I delivered my lecture, and it benefitted from comments from colleagues that day. It appeared as Elizabeth Jameson and Jeremy Mouat, "Telling Differences: The Forty-Ninth Parallel and Historiographies of the West and Nation," *Pacific Historical Review* 75:2 (May 2006): 183-230. We were gratified that it received the Louis Knott Koontz Award for the most deserving article to appear in the *Pacific Historical Review* in volume year 2006.

3   *Lone Star*, written and directed by John Sayles (1996; Burbank, CA: Warner Brothers).

4   *Lone Star*.

5   The Northwest Commission began its survey in 1857, but the Northern Boundary Commission did not to begin to survey the boundary across the prairies until 1871.

6   The literature on this topic is large and growing. Important works include Benedict Anderson, *Imagined Communities: Reflections on the Origin and Spread of Nationalism* (London: Verso, 1983); Eric Hobsbawm and Terence Ranger, eds., *The Invention of Tradition* (Cambridge: Cambridge University Press, 1983); Linda Colley, *Britons: Forging the Nation, 1707-1837* (New Haven: Yale University Press, 1992); Geoff Eley and Ronald Grigor Suny, eds., *Becoming National: A Reader* (New York: Oxford University Press, 1996); and Geoffrey Cubitt, ed., *Imagining Nations* (Manchester: Manchester University Press, 1998). Canadian contributions to this growing dialogue include Ian Angus, *A Border Within: National Identity, Cultural Plurality, and Wilderness* (Montreal: McGill-Queens University Press, 1997); Veronica Strong-Boag, Sherrill Grace, Avigail Eisenberg, and Joan Anderson, eds., *Painting the Maple: Essays on Race, Gender, and the Construction of Canada* (Vancouver: UBC Press, 1998); W. H. New, *Borderlands: How We Talk about Canada* (Vancouver: UBC Press, 1998); H. V. Nelles, *The Art of Nation-building: Pageantry and Spectacle at Quebec's Tercentenary* (Toronto: University of Toronto Press, 1999); and Ian McKay, "The Liberal Order Framework: A Prospectus for a Reconnaissance of Canadian History," *Canadian Historical Review* 81 (2000): 617-45.

7   Frederick Jackson Turner, "The Significance of the Frontier in American History," in *History, Frontier, and Section: Three Essays by Frederick Jackson Turner*, ed. Martin Ridge (Albuquerque: University of New Mexico Press, 1993), 62-71. Turner first delivered "The Significance of the Frontier" as a paper at the American Historical Association meeting in Chicago, July 12, 1893, coinciding with the World's Columbian Exposition in that city. *Extra Census Bulletin* 2, April 20, 1892.

8   *Extra Census Bulletin*; John T. Juricek, "American Usage of the Word 'Frontier' from Colonial Times to Frederick Jackson Turner," *Proceedings of the American Philosophical Society* 110 (1966): 33.

9   For the significance of aridity in the U.S. West, see Walter Prescott Webb, *The Great Plains* (Lincoln: University of Nebraska Press, 1931) and Donald Worster, *Rivers of Empire: Water, Aridity, and the Growth of the American West* (New York: Pantheon Books, 1985). For the significance of rivers and water in Canada see, for instance, Donald Creighton, *The Commercial Empire of the St. Lawrence, 1760-1850* (Toronto: University of Toronto Press, 1937); Gerald J. J. Tulchinsky, *The River Barons: Montreal Businessmen and the Growth of Industry and Transportation 1837-53* (Toronto: University of Toronto Press, 1977); and John H. Wadland, "Great Rivers, Small Boats: Landscape and Canadian Historical Culture," in *Changing Parks: The History, Future and Cultural Context of Parks and Heritage Landscapes*, eds. John S. Marsh and Bruce W. Hodgins (Toronto: University of Toronto Press, 1998), 1-33. For debates about mapping the U.S. West, see Donald Worster,

"New West, True West: Interpreting the Region's History," *Western Historical Quarterly* 18 (1987): 141–56; David M. Emmons, "Constructed Province: History and the Making of the Last American West," *Western Historical Quarterly* 25 (1994): 437–59; and, David M. Emmons, "A Roundtable of Responses," *Western Historical Quarterly* 25 (1994), 461–86.

10 J. M. S. Careless, *Frontier and Metropolis: Regions, Cities and Identities in Canada Before 1914* (Toronto: University of Toronto Press, 1989), 54.

11 For example, a manifesto of Canadian left nationalism was entitled *Close the 49th Parallel Etc.*, ed. Ian Lumsden (Toronto: University of Toronto Press, 1970) and Richard Gwyn's reflections on the position of Canada appeared as *The Forty Ninth Paradox: Canada in North America* (Toronto: University of Toronto Press, 1985).

12 Although the point is made satirically, the popular television series "Due South" as well as Rick Mercer's "Talking to Americans" (featured on the Canadian comedy show, "This Hour Has 22 Minutes") both played on this.

13 Turner, "Significance of the Frontier," 75–76.

14 Turner, "Significance of the Frontier," 62–71.

15 Turner, "Significance of the Frontier," 59.

16 Harold Innis, "The Teaching of Economic History in Canada," in Harold Innis, *Essays in Canadian Economic History*, ed. Mary Q. Innis (Toronto: University of Toronto Press, 1956), 3 (originally presented as a paper in May 1929, and published in 1930).

17 Harold A. Innis, *The Fur Trade in Canada* (1931; rev. ed., Toronto: University of Toronto Press, 1956), 393.

18 For example, Innis argued that "Western Canada has paid for the development of Canadian nationality, and it would appear that it must continue to pay. The acquisitiveness of eastern Canada shows little sign of abatement." Harold Adams Innis, *A History of the Canadian Pacific Railway* (1923; rev. ed., Toronto: University of Toronto Press, 1971), 293–94. The book was a revised version of his dissertation, completed at the University of Chicago.

19 John W. Gaus, "Lecture Notes," February-June 1920, Turner Papers, University of Wisconsin Archives, quoted in Allen G. Bogue, "The Significance of the History of the American West: Postscripts and Prospects," *Western Historical Quarterly* 24 (1993): 53.

20 Frederick Jackson Turner, "The Significance of the Section in American History," in Ridge, *History, Frontier, and Section*, 94.

21 A student of Frederick Jackson Turner, Bolton produced extensive borderlands scholarship. See Herbert Eugene Bolton, *Texas in the Middle Eighteenth Century: Studies in Spanish Colonial History and Administration* (Berkeley: University of California Press, 1915); and especially *The Spanish Borderlands: A Chronicle of Old Florida and the Southwest* (New Haven: Yale University Press, 1921). For a more recent Borderlands history, see David J. Weber, *The Spanish Frontier in North America* (New Haven: Yale University Press, 1992). For Skinner's role in editing and revising *The Spanish Borderlands*, see John Francis Bannon, *Herbert Eugene Bolton: The Historian and the Man* (Tucson: University of Arizona Press, 1978), 134–40 and Jean Barman, "Constance Lindsay Skinner and the Marketing of the Western Frontier," in *Canadian Papers in Rural History*, 10, ed. Donald A. Akenson (Gananoque, Ont.: Langdale Press, 1996), 81–116.

22 Webb, *The Great Plains*.

23 H. A. Innis and A. R. M. Lower, eds., *Select Documents in Canadian Economic History, 1783-1885* (Toronto: University of Toronto Press, 1933, two volumes); A. R. M. Lower, *Settlement and the Forest Frontier in Eastern Canada* (Toronto: University of Toronto Press, 1936); *The North American Assault on the Canadian Forest: A History of the Lumber Trade Between Canada and the United States* (Toronto: University of Toronto Press, 1938);

and J. M. S. Careless, *Frontier and Metropolis: Regions, Cities and Identities in Canada Before 1914* (Toronto: University of Toronto Press, 1989), 54.

24 Walter N. Sage, "Some Aspects of the Frontier in Canadian History," Canadian Historical Association, *Annual Report*, 1928; and, "Geographical and Cultural Aspects of the Five Canadas," Canadian Historical Association, *Annual Report*, 1937. The two essays were published together as a pamphlet, Walter Noble Sage, *Canada from Sea to Sea* (Toronto: University of Toronto Press, 1940), which was used as a school text and regularly reprinted up to the 1960s. Chad Reimer provides an excellent overview of Sage's work in "The Making of British Columbia History: Historical Writing and Institutions, 1784–1958" (PhD diss., York University, 1995), 311–62.

25 George Wilson Pierson, "American Historians and the Frontier Hypothesis in 1941 (1)," *Wisconsin Magazine of History* 26 (1942): 36–60, and George Wilson Pierson, "American Historians and the Frontier Hypothesis in 1941 (2)," *Wisconsin Magazine of History* 26 (1942): 170–85.

26 See Fred A. Shannon, "A Post-Mortem on the Labor-Safety-Valve Theory," *Agricultural History* 19 (1945): 31–37; George Rogers Taylor, ed., *The Turner Thesis Concerning the Role of the Frontier in American History* (1949; repr., Lexington, Mass.: Heath, 1971); Richard Hofstadter and Seymour Martin Lipset, eds., *Turner and the Sociology of the Frontier* (New York: Basic Books, 1968); Stanley Elkins and Eric McKittrick, "A Meaning for Turner's Frontier, Part I: Democracy in the Old Northwest," *Political Science Quarterly* 69 (1954): 321–53.

27 George F. G. Stanley, "Western Canada and the Frontier Thesis," Canadian Historical Association, *Report of the Annual Meeting*, 1940, 105. Stanley thus forged a sort of intellectual middle ground, somewhere between the optimism of Webb's environmental adaptations and Earl Pomeroy's later emphasis on institutional and cultural continuity from East to West. See Earl Pomeroy, "Toward a Reorientation of Western History: Continuity and Environment," *Mississippi Valley Historical Review* 41 (1955): 579–600. I am grateful to Donald Smith for his insightful comment at my lecture. Smith pointed out that Stanley spoke in 1940, after Canada had entered World War II, and before the United States entered the conflict. For Stanley, to paraphrase Dr. Smith, Canada had committed to saving western civilization, while the U.S. remained mired in its own savagery.

28 Stanley, "Western Canada and the Frontier Thesis," 106.

29 Stanley, "Western Canada and the Frontier Thesis," 107.

30 Stanley, "Western Canada and the Frontier Thesis," 109.

31 Stanley, "Western Canada and the Frontier Thesis," 109.

32 Stanley, "Western Canada and the Frontier Thesis," 110.

33 Walter N. Sage also emphasized this point in, "Some Aspects of the Frontier."

34 Stanley, "Western Canada and the Frontier Thesis," 114.

35 Sage, "Some Aspects of the Frontier," 115–16.

36 Donald Creighton, *Dominion of the North: A History of Canada* (Toronto: University of Toronto Press, 1944).

37 W. L. Morton, "Clio in Canada: The Interpretation of Canadian History," in *Approaches to Canadian History*, ed. Ramsay Cook et al. (Toronto: University of Toronto Press, 1967), 42–49.

38 Morton, "Clio in Canada," 43.

39 W. L. Morton, "The 'North' in Canadian Historiography," *Transactions of the Royal Society of Canada*, Series 4, 8 (1970): 35, 40. Lyle Dick examined Morton's subsequent role, in the late 1950s, in attempting to forge a canonical history of Canada: "'A Growing *Necessity* for

Canada': W. L. Morton's Centenary Series and the Forms of National History, 1955–80," *Canadian Historical Review* 82 (2001): 223–52.

40   Henry Nash Smith, *Virgin Land: The American West as Symbol and Myth* (Cambridge, Mass.: Harvard University Press, 1950). For the development of this genre, see also Leo Marx, *The Machine in the Garden: Technology and the Pastoral Ideal in America* (New York: Oxford University Press, 1964); Annette Kolodny, *The Land Before Her: Fantasy and Experience of the American Frontiers, 1630–1860* (Chapel Hill: University of North Carolina Press, 1984); Jane Tompkins, *West of Everything: The Inner Life of Westerns* (New York: Oxford University Press, 1992); and Richard Slotkin, *Regeneration Through Violence: The Mythology of the American Frontier, 1600–1860* (Middletown, Conn.: Wesleyan University Press, 1973); *The Fatal Environment: The Myth of the Frontier in the Age of Industrialism, 1800–1890* (New York: Atheneum, 1985); and *Gunfighter Nation: The Myth of the Frontier in Twentieth-Century America* (New York: Atheneum, 1992).

41   Carl Foreman's screenplay for "High Noon" was influenced by his experience when he was forced to testify before the House Un-American Activities Committee (HUAC). Foreman, who had been a member of the Communist Party from 1938–1942, testified that he had belonged to the Communist Party but refused to name other members. That experience reinforced a theme throughout his screenplays of an individual struggling with a hostile society. Because of his refusal to cooperate with HUAC, Foreman was blacklisted by Hollywood after the production of "High Noon." "High Noon," United Artists, Stanley Kramer, producer, 1952; "Dakota Incident," Republic Pictures, Herbert J. Yates and Michael Baird, producers, 1956.

42   Pomeroy, "Toward a Reorientation of Western History."

43   Gerald D. Nash, *The American West in the Twentieth Century: A Short History of an Urban Oasis* (Albuquerque: University of New Mexico Press, 1977); Gerald D. Nash, *The American West Transformed: The Impact of the Second World War* (Bloomington: Indiana University Press, 1985); Gerald D. Nash, *World War II and the West: Reshaping the Economy* (Lincoln: University of Nebraska Press, 1990).

44   "Open Range," Touchstone Pictures, Kevin Costner, producer, director, and actor, 2003.

45   On the origins of Diefenbaker's northern vision and the politics that surrounded it, see Peter C. Newman, *Renegade in Power: The Diefenbaker Years* (Toronto: University of Toronto Press, 1963), 139–41, 196–99. For a summary of the 1958 election campaign, see J. M. Beck, *Pendulum of Power: Canada's Federal Elections* (Scarborough, ON: Prentice-Hall, 1968), 311–28.

46   Ramsay Cook, "Frontier and Metropolis: The Canadian Experience," reprinted in Cook, *The Maple Leaf Forever: Essays on Nationalism and Politics in Canada* (Toronto: University of Toronto Press, 1977), 154–55. For more recent reflections on this point, see the theme issue, "Representing North," *Essays on Canadian Writing*, 59 (1996); Sherrill E. Grace, *Canada and the Idea of the North* (Montreal: McGill-Queen's University Press, 2001); Renée Hulan, *Northern Experience and the Myths of Canadian Culture* (Montreal: McGill-Queen's University Press, 2002), esp. the Introduction, "A Northern Nation?," 3–28; and Janice Cavell, "The Second Frontier: The North in English-Canadian Historical Writing," *Canadian Historical Review* 83 (2002): 364–89.

47   For examples and accounts of the various Prairie historiographical traditions, see R. Douglas Francis and Howard Palmer, eds., *The Prairie West: Historical Readings* (Edmonton: University of Alberta Press, 1992, 2nd ed.), esp. Gerald Friesen, "Historical Writing on the Prairie West," 5–26; J. R. Miller, "Native History," and John Herd Thompson, "The West and the North," in *Canadian History: A Reader's Guide, Vol. 2, Confederation to the Present*, ed. Doug Owram (Toronto: University of Toronto Press, 1994), 179–201, 341–73; Royden Loewen, "On the Margin or In the Lead: Canadian

Prairie Historiography," *Agricultural History* 73 (1999): 27–45; and Robert Wardhaugh, ed., *Toward Defining the Prairies: Region, Culture and History* (Winnipeg: University of Winnipeg Press, 2001), passim.

48 Slotkin, *Regeneration Through Violence, Fatal Environment, and Gunfighter Nation*.
49 Herbert Heaton, "Other Wests Than Ours," *Journal of Economic History* 6, Issue Supplement: The Tasks of Economic History (1946): 51.
50 Heaton, "Other Wests Than Ours," 52, 59.
51 Paul F. Sharp, "When Our West Moved North," *American Historical Review* 55 (1950): 287. See also Paul F. Sharp, "Three Frontiers: Some Comparative Studies of Canadian, American, and Australian Settlements," *Pacific Historical Quarterly* 24 (1955), 369–77. Sharp's dissertation, *The Agrarian Revolt in Western Canada: A Survey Showing American Parallels* (supervised by the Canadian historian A. L. Burt at the University of Minnesota), was published in 1948 (Minneapolis: University of Minnesota Press, 1948).
52 Sharp, "When Our West Moved North," 290. Sharp also quoted Winnipeg's newspaper *The Grain Growers' Guide*, 5 (1 March 1922).
53 Sharp, "When Our West Moved North," 295.
54 Sharp, "When Our West Moved North," 299.
55 One of the challenges of comparative history is culturally sensitive terminology. We attempt to use the terms preferred by the people to whom we refer; hence we use "American Indian" or "Native American" when referring to Native peoples in the United States and "First Nations" for Canada. "Native peoples," as we use it, crosses the national boundaries of North America.
56 William Loren Katz, *The Black West* (Garden City, N.Y.: Anchor Press, 1973); George J. Sanchez, *Becoming Mexican American: Ethnicity, Culture and Identity in Chicano Los Angeles, 1900-1945* (New York: Oxford University Press, 1993); Roger Daniels, *Asian America: Chinese and Japanese in the United States Since 1850* (Seattle: University of Washington Press, 1988); Sucheng Chan, Douglas Henry Daniels, Mario T. Garcia, and Terry P. Wilson, eds., *Peoples of Color in the American West* (Lexington, MA: D.C. Heath and Company, 1994); Susan Armitage and Elizabeth Jameson, eds., *The Women's West* (Norman: University of Oklahoma Press, 1987); Patricia Nelson Limerick, *The Legacy of Conquest: The Unbroken Past of the American West* (New York: W.W. Norton, 1987); Richard White, *The Roots of Dependency: Subsistence, Environment, and Social Change among the Choctaws, Pawnees, and Navajos* (Lincoln: University of Nebraska Press, 1983); Richard White, *"It's Your Misfortune and None of My Own": A New History of the American West* (Norman: University of Oklahoma Press, 1991).
57 See for instance, White, *"It's Your Misfortune"* and William G. Robbins, *Colony and Empire: The Capitalist Transformation of the American West* (Lawrence: University of Kansas Press, 1994).
58 Robbins, *Colony and Empire*, 8.
59 Robin Fisher, *Contact and Conflict: Indian-European Relations in British Columbia, 1774-1890* (Vancouver: UBC Press, 1992, 2nd ed.); Hana Samek, *The Blackfoot Confederacy, 1880-1920: A Comparative Study of Canadian and U.S. Indian Policy* (Albuquerque: University of New Mexico Press, 1987); Sarah Carter, *Lost Harvests: Prairie Indian Reserve Farms and Government Policy* (Montreal: McGill-Queens University Press, 1990); Martin Robin, *The Rush for Spoils: The Company Province 1871-1933* (Toronto: University of Toronto Press 1972), 44.
60 The reference to housemaid's knee is from J. L. Granatstein, *Who Killed Canadian History?* (Toronto: HarperCollins Publishers, 1998), 72–73. To quote Mark Sholdice, "Jack Granatstein's 1998 jeremiad *Who Killed Canadian History?* was the opening shot

of the History Wars, a fierce conflict about the meaning and purpose of our nation's past. Academic historians, he satirically concluded, had abandoned traditional military and political history in order to specialize in topics like 'the history of housemaid's knee in Belleville in the 1890s.'" Mark Sholdice, "The History Wars in Canada," *The Toronto Review of Books* 6 (Spring 2013): 7.

61 Howard R. Lamar, "Comparing Depressions: The Great Plains and the Canadian Prairies Experiences, 1929–1941," in *The Twentieth-Century West: Historical Interpretations*, ed. Gerald D. Nash and Richard W. Etulain (Albuquerque: University of New Mexico Press, 1989), 175–206; Howard R. Lamar, "Coming Into the Mainstream at Last: Comparative Approaches to the History of the American West," *Journal of the West* 35 (1996): 3–5; Howard Lamar and Leonard Thompson, eds., *The Frontier in History: North America and Southern Africa Compared* (New Haven: Yale University Press, 1981); Robin W. Winks, *The Myth of the American Frontier: Its Relevance to America, Canada, and Australia* (Leicester, UK: Leicester University Press, 1971); Robin Winks, "Regionalism in Comparative Perspective," in *Regionalism in the Pacific Northwest*, eds. William G. Robbins, Robert J. Frank, and Richard E. Ross (Corvallis: Oregon State University Press, 1983); Donald Worster, "Two Faces West: The Development Myth in Canada and the United States," in *Terra Pacifica: People and Place in the Northwest States and Western Canada*, ed. Paul W. Hirt (Pullman, WA: Washington State University Press, 1998), 71–92.

62 Thompson and Lamar, "Comparative Frontier History," in Lamar and Thompson, *The Frontier in History*, 4, 7.

63 Thompson and Lamar, "Comparative Frontier History," in Lamar and Thompson, *The Frontier in History*, 7.

64 Sarah Deutsch, *No Separate Refuge: Culture, Class, and Gender on an Anglo-Hispanic Frontier in the American Southwest, 1880-1940* (New York: Oxford University Press, 1987); Gloria Anzaldúa, *Borderlands/La Frontera: The New Mestiza* (San Francisco: aunt lute books, 1987); Sylvia Van Kirk, *Many Tender Ties: Women in Fur Trade Society, 1670-1870* (Norman & Winnipeg: University of Oklahoma Press and Watson & Dwyer, 1980). See also Peggy Pascoe, "Western Women at the Cultural Crossroads," in *Trails: Toward a New Western History*, eds. Patricia Nelson Limerick, Clyde A. Milner II, and Charles E. Rankin (Lawrence: University of Kansas Press, 1991), 40–58; "Editors' Introduction," Elizabeth Jameson and Susan Armitage, eds., *Writing the Range: Race, Class, and Culture in the Women's West* (Norman: University of Oklahoma Press, 1997), 3–16.

65 Jeremy Adelman and Stephen Aron, "From Borderlands to Borders: Empires, Nation States, and the Peoples in Between in North American History," *American Historical Review* 104 (1999): 814–41; John R. Wunder and Pekka Hamalainen, "Of Lethal Places and Lethal Essays," in "Forum Essay: Responses: Borders and Borderlands," *American Historical Review* 104 (1999): 1229–34; see also Jeremy Adelman and Stephen Aron, "Of Lively Exchanges and Larger Perspectives," *American Historical Review* 104 (1999): 1235–39. Michel Hogue, "Disputing the Medicine Line: The Plains Crees and the Canadian-American Border, 1876–1885," *Montana: Magazine of Western History* 53 (2002): 2–7. In this article, Hogue described the Canadian Cree in the late-19th century—a period that Adelman and Aron contend was marked by the creation of "bordered lands"—and argued that, for the Cree, the border remained porous, while significant social barriers were erected to separate people of different races within North America's bordered lands.

66 Sarah Carter, "Categories and Terrains of Exclusion: Constructing the 'Indian Woman' in the Early Settlement Era in Western Canada," *Great Plains Quarterly* 13 (Summer 1993): 147–61.

67 Sharp, "When Our West Moved North," 300.

5

Dancing on the Rim, Tiptoeing through the Minefields: Challenges and Promises of the Borderlands

February 15, 2006

There is a story my father told me, of huddling in the straw beneath a pile of robes in a horse-drawn sleigh, hiding there with his twin brother, two older sisters, and his father, who had paid a farmer to smuggle them across a frozen river to another country. It was sometime in the winter of 1923–1924. Dad was six years old. He and my Uncle David remembered the crisp tart apples they got to keep them quiet crossing the border. They both always loved Granny Smith apples.

They were not fleeing a pogrom, though my mother's grandfather, according to family lore, walked across the Urals to Berlin to avoid serving in the czar's army. He became a rabbi, sailed to New York in 1892, and sent for his fiancée the next year, after a Baltimore congregation hired him.[1] Their journeys, like my Dad's, were part of a worldwide diaspora from 1830 to 1930 when 10 percent of all people moved across national boundaries.[2]

The histories that became U.S. creation stories explained how diverse Europeans forged a common national identity. Frederick Jackson Turner, who authored a formative history, credited the frontier, among other things, with making a "composite nationality" from a nation of immigrants. The Chicago School of sociologists and Oscar Handlin's school of immigration history judged the "uprooted" by how well they assimilated as Americans.[3]

My Dad's story, though, was not of uprooted flight from poverty or persecution. His parents were British descendants of German Jews, merchants whose trade and families crossed and re-crossed the British Channel. One of those ancestors lived awhile in Scotland, where family legend has it, he changed our name from Baruch to Jameson.[4]

My Dad's mother was born Esther Wechsler in London in 1878. She grew up in a comfortable household that included two cousins and thirteen Wechsler children, twelve of whom went to university. Esther became a social worker, worked with sex workers on the London docks, married Jacob Jameson, and, in 1908, bore their eldest daughter, Ena. Jacob left for the United States sometime after that. Esther and Ena joined him in Dayton, Ohio, where my Aunt Babette was born in 1915, and the twins, David and Henry, two years later.[5]

When my Dad was very young, they moved to Montreal and lived for a while with my grandmother's brother Moses and his wife Rae, who had emigrated to Canada, and their children, Margie and Lew, who were born in Canada. Then in 1923 Grandma got a job in Newark as the first director of women's activities in the Young Men's and Young Women's Hebrew Associations.[6] She crossed the border alone, leaving Jacob to follow with the children. The icy river Dad remembered crossing was the St. Lawrence. This raises a question. The three youngest children were U.S. citizens; my grandparents and Ena had already entered the United States. So why the elaborate efforts to evade the border guards? Why was Dad sneaking into the land of his birth?

The answer lies in the changing legal constructions of borders. Grandma and Ena first entered the U.S. in 1913. The family left for Canada after 1917, when the boys were born. That year the 1917 Immigration Act added to the list of people barred from the U.S., among others, "all idiots, imbeciles, feeble-minded persons, epileptics, [and] insane persons" or anyone an "examining surgeon" found to have a "defect" that might "affect the ability of such alien to earn a living. . . ."[7] My Aunt Ena had Down syndrome. Her parents feared that she would be turned back at the U.S. border.

My grandparents knew that nations police their borders. History helps create them. History as a discipline developed with the creation of nation states, assumed to be the proper subjects of histories.[8] In state-centered histories, people were important as citizens—as subjects of states, not of histories. Border-crossing was important only to get them inside the nation. As historians wrote histories of nations, they not only "imagined communities" as Benedict Anderson suggested, but also erected the borders of what Sarah Carter called their "categories and terrains of exclusion."[9] Historians chose the actors and crafted the narratives that told who belonged and who was an outsider, who became part of an imagined collective past and who was marginalized or excluded.

The border, in my father's story, was the line that separates nations, where they assert their sovereignty by determining who and what to admit or exclude. Turner's frontier line served a similar function: it excluded Indigenous peoples and justified conquest as progress from Indigenous "savagery" to the newcomers' "civilization."[10] The popular U.S. image, "a nation of immigrants," excluded lots of people: native North Americans, involuntary immigrants like African Americans, "aliens not eligible for citizenship" like Chinese laborers, and the peoples of northern Mexico, who came into the country involuntarily, through warfare, not immigration.[11] The east-to-west trajectory of the national narrative erased people who arrived at the West Coast from Asia, or north from Mexico, or south from Canada. But it erased them differently. Anglo-Canadians were simply absorbed; Mexicans and Chinese were trivialized and demonized; Native peoples were conquered and then pushed to the margins. That imagined national community erased continental connections and wrote a colonized North American history that began only when White people arrived from the East. The erasures continued within national borders that were supposed to be gateways to the benefits of citizenship. The histories of shared composite nationality detoured around barriers that selectively denied citizenship rights like voting, suing, testifying in court, owning property, or sometimes oneself.

If history helped craft these boundaries, historians have also stretched and breached them as they probed inequalities of race, class, gender, and sexuality, and wrote histories that cross national borders. I am distinguishing borders (lines that separate or divide) from borderlands (zones—sometimes around borders—where diverse people come together or mingle). In this sense, borders and borderlands can be either national or social categories. National borders separate nations: their borderlands are places where social relationships cross those borders. Social borders erect social barriers, like those of race, for instance, while a parallel social borderland might be a zone or place where people of different races meet. Borders and borderlands can have multiple meanings; their significance usually differs for the various people they divide or connect. A border, for instance, can function both to exclude and to protect. A national border can prevent certain people from entering a country; a social border can prevent people of different races or the same sexes from marrying one another. But borders can also function positively, to protect identity—as Canadians have viewed the Canada-U.S. border positively because it separates Canada from the United States.[12] Or as religious institutions—churches, mosques, and synagogues—may exclude people of other religions and at the same time provide safe spaces to share valued common identities and practices.

In recent decades historians have shown increasing interest in transnational, comparative, borderlands, and migration histories that blur the focus on separate national pasts. The *Journal of American History* devoted two issues to transnational histories in 1999. New histories are stretching geographic, social, and temporal boundaries of the borderlands, and are finally exploring the borderlands of Canada and the United States.[13]

The borderlands I want to explore here are the borderlands of national memories, where the histories that move across national and social boundaries clarify their categories and terrains of exclusion. I'll be dancing around the borders of North America and some of their borderlands, especially the ones where I've lived. The tune I danced to as I wrote this essay was Tracy Chapman's "Telling Stories," which refers to the "fiction in the space between" the lines of written memory.[14]

Part of that fiction divides the histories of colonizers and Indigenous peoples, private lore and public history. The family story with which I began is a shorthand into the spaces between personal memories and shared ones, and between shared stories and national ones. Whatever private needs pulled my family across the St. Lawrence, they joined a then-record 200,000 migrants who entered the U.S. from Canada between July 1923 and June 1924, spurred in part by fears that Canada would be included in new U.S. legislation to restrict immigration.[15] Perhaps that fear pushed Grandma to take her job in Newark; I don't know. I do know my family was not that different from many others who crossed and re-crossed North America's boundaries, at least since the first migrants crossed the Bering Land Bridge or emerged from the previous world. We all have such stories. How we connect them to history is something else.

One way to understand my Dad's story was simply that he crossed the border and entered the United States, where his children could claim its history as our own. The reality is messier. My grandparents separated and my grandfather returned to Montreal. One of my grandmother's brothers settled in Toronto; another in Melbourne. I have cousins in (at least) the Netherlands, Australia, England, Israel, and the U.S. Moses and

Rae moved their family to New York. I first met Dad's cousin Margie in the early 1950s when she and her husband George visited us in Texas. They later told me that while Margie stayed to visit, George went on to Mexico to arrange escape routes for American Communists during the McCarthy era. *That* story introduces borders as gateways to sanctuary, as both the Canadian and Mexican borders served for runaway slaves, as the 49th Parallel served for a time for Sitting Bull and Louis Riel, for devout Mormons and Vietnam War draft resisters—as Canada served Chileans fleeing the overthrow of Allende, as it may serve gays and lesbians who wish to marry or women seeking legal abortions.[16]

In 1999, for less dramatic reasons, I moved to Calgary. I was asked at my job interview how I felt about moving across a border. I answered too glibly, "I've been crossing them all my life." I had spent most of my life in the territory that historian Herbert Eugene Bolton called the Spanish Borderlands.[17] My borderlands, though, were social and cultural. They involved race, religion, and gender: being a blonde Jew with a Scottish name; a woman in a male-dominated profession; wrestling with nationalist, androcentric, and Euro-centric histories.

I learned that history in the public schools of Galveston, once a major port of entry that called itself the Ellis Island of Texas. It became an entry to another borderland when, in November 1528, two makeshift boats landed the first Spaniards on its sandy beaches. Karankawa Indians enslaved them, but four survivors—Álvar Núñez Cabeza de Vaca, Alonso del Castillo, Andres Dorantes, and Esteban, his African Moorish slave—began in 1534 to wander westerly across the continent. When Cabeza de Vaca published his reminiscences in 1542, his references to emeralds and towns "of great population and great houses" inspired claims to what became the northern frontiers of New Spain.[18]

I learned Cabeza de Vaca's name but not Esteban's and little else about those complex borderlands in segregated public schools that taught me almost nothing of the history of race that I inherited and *lived* on Galveston island, where boundaries of power separated Euro-Americans, ethnic Mexicans, and African Americans. Before the Civil War, free Blacks had to register with the mayor and weren't allowed on the streets after 10 p.m. Only White men who owned at least $500 in property could vote.[19] Germans were the largest foreign-born group; by 1880 there were also many Italians, Greeks, Belgians, Danes, Mexicans, Portuguese, Poles, Hungarians, Czechs, Spaniards, Swedes, Welsh, and Canadians.[20] Established German Jews and their British-born rabbi founded the

Galveston Movement in 1907 to deal with an influx of eastern European Jews. They met their ships and sent these eastern European Jews to towns that wanted their skills, thus aiding their settlement while keeping them off the island and often isolating them far from any Jewish community.[21] I grew up in a selectively diverse Galveston, attending Greek Easter fairs and Irish Catholic weddings, teen dances at the Episcopal Church but not at the League of United Latin American Citizens (LULAC) Hall, and not the local Juneteenth or Cinco de Mayo celebrations.[22]

The two main industries were the port and the University of Texas Medical School. Married White women did not work outside their homes; African American women were maids. In a town where you were a doctor's kid or a longshoreman's kid, the overlapping inequalities of class, race, and gender were inescapable. My parents crossed those boundaries as Civil Rights advocates, and as my mother graduated from Medical School and practiced medicine, which made us something like the children of cross-dressers in the gender-conscious Galveston of the 1950s.

White children in Galveston attended schools named Alamo, Travis, Crockett, Bowie, Goliad, San Jacinto, and Stephen F. Austin. "Mexican" kids went to the same schools but were seldom tracked into college-bound classes. Black children attended Booker T. Washington and George Washington Carver. We all used the same textbooks in wretched Texas history classes that did not teach us that Stephen F. Austin owned slaves, or that slavery was an issue in what we learned to call the War for Texas Independence. The only character in our textbooks who was not an Anglo man was Antonio López de Santa Anna—and he made it only as the losing general in the battle we pronounced Sayan Djuhssintow (San Jacinto).[23]

Perceptive readers might notice that I have still not really gotten out of U.S. history. Unless you are American, you may have noticed I've been using symbols and stories that exclude you—using Stephen F. Austin, Booker T. Washington, Juneteenth, and Cinco de Mayo, for instance, to represent larger histories. If you are Canadian or Mexican, however, you are more likely to know these references than most Americans would be to recognize the significance of Vimy Ridge, Batoche, Acoma, the Cypress Hills, Obregón, or la Malinche. One huge challenge of the historical borderlands is recognizing the categories and terrains of exclusion within national histories and between them.

I have, in fact, as you have may have perceived, been writing a very American essay: egocentric, self-referential, and self-revealing. That judgment would be very Canadian. Borderlands histories demand that we risk learning how our nations and our comfort zones of behavior appear from the other side of a border.

I began with my Dad's story for several reasons. The first was rhetorical: I used it to claim my family's ties to Canada, though in truth they became important to me only after I began to wrestle with my links to two nations. My identities were learned, not encoded in genetic maps of my ancestors' migrations. The second reason is partly personal: since I crossed the border, I've thought a lot about my grandmother, about what it meant to her to live and work and raise her kids so far from England. I've thought about the subtle processes by which we learn another culture, history, maybe a more multi-valent identity; about how crossing borders changes how we see the past. And I used this story to play with how people and their stories can be connected to histories or separated from them.

My family crossed national borders. So did the people whose histories I recorded in Cripple Creek, like May Wing, whose family odyssey led from Ireland to Wales, to Wisconsin, Colorado, British Columbia, and back to Colorado.[24] So did Rachel Calof, whose memoir has engaged me for some time, who moved from Russia to North Dakota in 1894. Some of the extended Calof clan moved to Winnipeg; I know some of their descendants in Calgary.[25] As they moved, people built movements and institutions. Labor unions, religious organizations, agrarian movements, and fraternal lodges, for instance, all crossed the 49th Parallel. Mutualistas and some of the same labor unions crossed the U.S.-Mexico border.[26]

Yet for much of my life I lost focus at the U.S. border. People moved to the margins of my attention as they left the history I knew. I don't know if this is particular to me, or particularly American. I suspect it may be similar to how some of my colleagues lose focus on women or people of color as their stories cross over the boundaries of place-centered histories or the categories of public and political power those histories privilege. *It is costly not to cross those borders.* Without crossing them, I cannot connect Coxey's Army and the On to Ottawa Band; nor Western Federation of Miners locals in Cripple Creek, Rossland, Cananea, and Nanaimo; nor the Seattle and Winnipeg General Strikes; Ludlow and Mackenzie King; nor Coronado, David Thompson, and Lewis and Clark, much less Sacagawea, Charlotte Thompson, and Malintzin, who played similar roles in three national histories.[27] I can't connect my story with my grandfather's.

If my childhood history classes did not prepare me for the racialized complexities of the social borderlands I inhabited, if they did not prepare me to locate my Latinx or African American neighbors in history (or myself for that matter), they prepared me even less to cross the border into Canada. My childhood taught me about social boundaries that marked inequalities of race or class. These were less apparent to me as I crossed the Canadian border, but other boundaries and differences emerged. Ninety percent of Canadians live within a few hundred miles of the border; the U.S. looms larger here than Canada does in the U.S. Our televisions are saturated with U.S. programming. In Calgary my basic cable package includes the local Spokane and Coeur d'Alene stations. When I asked colleagues who live in the Canada-U.S. borderlands about their television coverage, an interesting—if predictable—pattern emerged. I watch Canadian, U.S., and British newscasts. Susan Armitage, however, whose nightly local newscasts beamed into my living room, did not get Canadian television in Pullman, Washington. According to Chris Friday and Cecilia Danysk, Bellingham, just south of the border, seemed to be a minor exception. Their cable coverage from Seattle did not include Canadian stations, but local radio got Vancouver and Victoria stations that carry English, French, and Cantonese programming. On local TV, without cable, Dr. Friday reported, they "ONLY get Canadian stations and one local station which always gives the weather in BC in centigrade!" Jean Barman reported that in Vancouver, just north of the border, she got ABC, NBC, CBS, and PBS from Seattle; UPN and FOX from Tacoma; the local Bellingham station; and that with cable it was also possible to get Detroit PBS, A&E, CNN, and WTBS from Atlanta. Catherine Cavanaugh reported that Edmonton got the same stations as Calgary, plus Detroit PBS.[28]

If the U.S. airwaves erase Canada, Canadians get a distorted picture of the U.S. according-to-CNN. And if U.S. airwaves regularly cross national borders, U.S. histories do so mostly to cover wars—mostly those in which the U.S. has participated. It has been even easier for American historians to erase Canada than Mexico, perhaps because the Mexican border was secured by warfare and the Canadian border through treaties. The Mexican border became a racialized line that drew differences in skin color and language; the Canadian border became an imagined zone of similarity touted as the longest undefended border in the world. My grandparents' fears notwithstanding, the U.S. did not deploy a Border Patrol along the St. Lawrence in 1924 to keep out an imagined invasion of illegal immigrants as it did along the Mexican border. It did not deport Canadians in the 1930s, as it did Mexicans and their American-born children.[29]

Yet from 1850 through 1970, Canadians outnumbered Mexicans among foreign-born people living in the U.S. Mexican-born migrants did not pass them until 1980.³⁰ My point here is not whose group was bigger, but that size does not matter. Perceptions of threat were economic, racialized, and historically constructed; they had little to do with numbers. Anglo-Canadians, by virtue of skin color and language, "pass" in the U.S. far better than Americans do in Canada. Few in the United States have marked the nationality of Peter Jennings, Morley Safer, John Roberts (the journalist, not the Chief Justice), or Kevin Newman, or feared the foreign slant they might give the news.³¹ Few have feared the cultural imperialism of William Shatner, Mary Pickford, Kiefer Sutherland, Neil Young, Faye Wray, Joni Mitchell, Céline Dion, Dan Ackroyd, Norman Jewison, or Michael J. Fox. But Canadians do notice that the border that was supposed to contain U.S. expansionist designs has been less successful keeping Canadians in. As Charles Dickie, the MP from Nanaimo, moaned in 1928: "we are losing the cream of our population."³² The song for this dance comes from Stan Rogers:

> California! My friends all call you home,
> And if you take away another, I'll be that much more alone . . .
> But can I once taste Northern waters, then forsake them for
>   the South
> To feel California's ashes in my mouth³³

Ashes of another kind stuck in my throat the morning of September 12, 2001, as I scanned my lecture notes for a new class I was co-teaching with Sarah Carter on the Comparative History of the U.S. and Canadian Wests. It was the day after nineteen Al Qaeda terrorists hijacked four commercial airplanes and flew two of them into the Twin Towers of the World Trade Center in New York City and another into the Pentagon in Washington, D.C. A fourth flight, probably intended for the U.S. Capitol, crashed into a field in Pennsylvania after passengers fought back and stormed the cockpit. The attacks killed all nineteen hijackers and 2,996 victims: all 246 passengers and crew on the four planes, 2,606 in the Twin Towers attack, and 125 at the Pentagon.³⁴

In the immediate aftermath, the U.S. Federal Aviation Administration, for the first time ever, grounded all flights over or bound for the continental United States, and guided some 3,300 commercial flights and 1,200 private aircraft to land at airports in Canada or the U.S. As many of them landed at the Calgary airport, I had no idea how long they would be grounded, or how long I would be unable to get to my family in the United States if they needed me.

The next day, still profoundly shaken, I was scheduled to talk about "Mythic Wests and National Histories." I had intended to contrast Turner with his Canadian counterparts like Harold Innis, who located change not on the edges of advancing frontiers, but in distant metropoles that developed staple resources like furs, lumber, minerals, and fish, and with George F. G. Stanley, whose mythic Canadian narrative of western settlement separated a peaceful and orderly Canadian West from the violent individualism of U.S. frontiers. Stanley's kinder, gentler West arrived as the North West Mounted Police marched west from Manitoba in 1874 to protect the prairies from the Métis, First Nations, and lawless U.S. whiskey traders.[35] I intended, too, much as I have here, to talk about how the United States racialized its border with Mexico but imagined whiteness and sameness along the 49th Parallel. As I distractedly reviewed my notes, a CNN newscaster speculated that the planes that leveled the Twin Towers took off from Maine and Massachusetts because dark-skinned terrorists could sneak across the Canadian border. I somehow got through a shaky lecture, ending with the implications of that newscast: borders and borderlands are historically constructed; their meanings change. Whatever I thought I knew about borders and their meanings was shifting around us as I spoke.

The fault lines had long been evident, as a brief perusal of the *Calgary Herald* revealed.[36] For six months before 9/11 and a year afterwards, most border-related stories concerned security and business. Of ninety-five articles that mentioned the U.S.-Canada border, forty-five dealt with border security, twelve with cross-border political protest, and thirty-one with business and trade. The constant lurking subtext pulled tensely between Canadian sovereignty and Canada's economic ties to the U.S. Already, before 9/11, the news began to racialize the border. Pre-9/11 coverage of border security dealt with terrorism, political protest, and immigration. Terrorist coverage focused on Ahmed Ressam, who had been denied Canadian refugee status, and who was arrested in Port Angeles, Washington, on December 14, 1999, trying to smuggle explosives into the United States. Convicted of terrorist conspiracy, Ressam's case resonated even more ominously *after* 9/11.[37]

The threat of illegal immigrants was doubly racialized: in terms of the immigrants themselves *and* of potential points of entry. Amid U.S. charges that illegal aliens were sneaking in through Canada, the RCMP insisted that the traffic worked both ways, that humans "surpassed tobacco and alcohol as the contraband of choice being smuggled into Canada from the United States," and that East Asians preferred the U.S. while most Pakistanis and Middle Easterners chose Canada. The RCMP suggested that the Mohawk reserve spanning Quebec, Ontario, and New York was a prime smuggling site.[38]

The main security issue, however, immediately before 9/11, was protesters from the U.S. bound for the April Summit of the Americas meeting in Quebec. Again, it was feared that "native communities on the Canada-U.S. border support the smuggling of summit protesters," 300 of whom, trying to enter Canada at the Seaway International Bridge in Mohawk territory, met "a gauntlet of more than 100 law enforcement officers."[39] At the Peace Arch crossing south of Vancouver, however, far from Quebec and still racialized as White and open, U.S. and Canadian police closed the border to ensure "the safe movement" of some 2,000 protesters.[40]

In those contexts, U.S. Ambassador Paul Celucci advocated immigration "harmonization" to create a continental security perimeter, a "NAFTA plus" approach to "harmonize trade, immigration, and security policies between Canada and the U.S., and perhaps eventually Mexico."[41] This raised predictable fears, expressed in one op-ed headline: "Erasing borders with U.S. will erase Canada from map." This piece invoked a long history of resistance to U.S. hegemony dating from Confederation, and the defeats of "the Liberal push for commercial union with the U.S. in 1891" and of the "proposed Canada-U.S. free trade agreement in 1911."[42]

As luck would have it, Celucci addressed the Tri-Lateral Business Leaders Conference at the Calgary Chamber of Commerce the night of September 10, 2001. The headline on September 11 announced, "Ambassador urges more open border."[43] The same day, the *Herald's* Ottawa correspondent predicted that:

> Entire forests will fall to document the ramifications of this day on U.S. economic and political relations, but it's clear Canada's interconnected economy will suffer as the U.S. shrinkwraps into an angry, protective shell in response to the attack.
>
> Recent talk of relaxing or eliminating our border suddenly sounds a lot more farfetched.[44]

In the immediate aftermath, the U.S. reported that five terrorists had entered from Quebec and Nova Scotia. North Dakota Senator Byron Dorgan complained that nothing but orange traffic cones stopped people after 10 p.m. at fifteen border crossings into his state. Washington Senator Patty Murray claimed that some of the nineteen terrorists the FBI connected to the attacks entered the U.S. from Canada.[45] Fear and blame reverberated along the 49th Parallel long after the U.S. knew that the terrorists entered through its own borders.

One other pre-9/11 story briefly illuminated the equally racialized borderland that divided the Blackfoot Confederacy into Montana and Alberta tribes when Britain and the United States drew the border in 1818. Claiming that Canadian and U.S. customs officials defiled their sacred bundles, seized sacred objects, and mistook sweetgrass for marijuana, Peigan (Piikani) spokesman Edwin Small Legs said, "We want our own border crossing and our people working there from both sides of the nation." Canada Customs and Revenue replied that officials were trained to respect native religious artifacts "when conducting routine inspections."[46]

As the border was reconstructed, officials struggled to contain a racialized threat but still promote trade. That economic border, too, was only selectively permeable: the U.S. fenced out Canadian softwood lumber, Alberta beef, and PEI potatoes; the Canada Wheat Board prosecuted prairie farmers for selling grain across the border at U.S. prices.[47] As the National Guard patrolled the U.S. side, a spokesman for the U.S. Department of Immigration and Naturalization Services announced: "U.S. border officials are cracking down harder than their Canadian counterparts, but that's because the U.S. has far more enemies than Canada."[48] As I spoke in 2006, latter-day rogue Minutemen patrolled the Arizona desert and were expanding into California, Texas, and New Mexico. The Minutemen predicted that "Historians will write about how a lax America let its unique and coveted form of government and society sink into a quagmire of mutual acrimony among the variant sub-nations that will comprise the new self-destructing America." And the Minuteman Civil Defense Corps announced on its website that: "activated volunteers on the northern border with Canada—Maine, Vermont, Michigan, Minnesota, North Dakota, Idaho, and Washington State" are "creating new operations, this is truly an exciting time for Patriots!"[49] The Mexican newspaper *La Jornada* simply called these "patriots" "la organizacion racista."[50]

I tell this story to suggest the very real challenges of today's borderlands. One urgent pull to imagine transnational histories is that we do not have histories to help us grapple with the transnational present. Terrorists may attack nations, but they are not contained within them.

Nor are greenhouse gasses, the U.S.-Mexico-Canada Trade Agreement (USMCTA), the European Union (EU), capital flight, job outsourcing, avian flu, or AIDS.[51] It is hard to deal with issues that we cannot locate in recognizable frameworks and narratives. Without stories that cross national and social divides, it is hard to recognize humanity across those borders or to imagine a connected future. Histories that patrol national borders serve us no better than my childhood histories that drew racial color lines.

A second reason to pursue transnational histories is to connect ourselves to our pasts, and to futures in which we embody multiple identities. When I travel to the United States, I leave Canada through the U.S. Department of Customs and Border Security; I enter on my U.S. passport. I return to Canada on my permanent resident card. My roots reach to Russia, Poland, Germany, England, and the U.S. I could, if I wished, hold citizenship in the United States, Canada, Israel, and England. The same hungers that drew me to women's histories and the histories of the people I grew up with pull me to the borderlands of the U.S. and Canada and to a history of North America that began long before European empires. A number of historians opened the human meanings of these borderlands for me. Sylvia Van Kirk, Sarah Deutsch, Jennifer Brown, Albert Hurtado, Sarah Carter, and Gloria Anzaldúa, among others, shifted the historical focus to relationships that reveal human agency and its limits, the private arenas where cultures are transformed, the intimate borderlands where new people were born who embodied difference in new ways.[52] It has proved difficult to maintain the focus on agency, intimacy, and human exchange after national borders were drawn and the narratives shifted to state-focused histories. The difference between seeing these borderlands in human terms and nationalizing ones is summed in a brief contrast. Anzaldúa, wrestling with her embodied legacy, wrote:

> To survive in the Borderlands
> you must live *sin fronteras*
> be a crossroads.[53]

Jeremy Adelman and Stephen Aron, in contrast, writing within national and imperial frameworks, projected borderlands that ended in the 19th century with the formation of nation states that turned "borderlands into *bordered* lands." Their borderlands could not bridge colonial and national histories or embrace the post-colonial agency of people born there of brutal and tender intimacies, who, in the borderland-to-nation framework, became one of the "hybrid residuals" of frontier encounters.[54]

My urgent hope is that our borderlands may help us imagine histories to ground more inclusive, egalitarian, and mutually respectful futures. The borders we patrol and the borderlands of national identities are in enormous flux; this moment contains both intense nationalisms and fragile recognitions of interdependent global economies, ecologies, migrations, and politics, of connections to honor and differences to respect.

Richard White once asked rhetorically, "Is There a North American History?"[55] He answered that "It is difficult to write a history of North America if there is no common North American identity" as there is in Europe.[56] To the extent that there is a shared European identity, historians helped construct it. However difficult, the challenge of borderlands histories is not just to find identity and connection, but to explain difference, distrust, and disconnection. There is no particular reason that histories must tell stories of composite identities. They can chronicle relationships of domination and inequality. They can illuminate cataclysmic disconnects like those between the histories of Indigenous North Americans and those of European conquest. Transnational histories will not serve us well if we simply debate whether to draw our borders at the Rio Grande and 49th Parallel, or around the continental perimeter, if they *erase* social and national boundaries rather than illuminate them.

It is challenging to write histories that connect people who know each other so little, challenging both conceptually and practically. States, after all, fund history programs, and the furor over the new social history in both the U.S. and Canada is sobering for the resistance transnational histories will face.[57] *Yet transnational histories are not non-national histories.* As my father's border crossing, the Blackfoot Confederacy's religious objects, and the Minutemen all testify, national histories patrol real borders that construct real power.

So, what may help us on these intriguing journeys? Let me suggest some steps that might help us dance on these rims. We might imagine the dance hall, where lots of people are dancing, but the spotlight has been on one national dance, and only on the folks who lead it. Our task is to refocus, and to imagine dancing in the same space with the Indigenous people to one side, the nations dancing next to us, the women in the corner, the newcomers waiting shyly by themselves—to combine waltzes, fandangos, horas, hip hop, polkas, and jigs without stepping on one another's toes. As a beginning, I offer eight not-so-easy rules for dancing in the borderlands:[58]

1. (As we'd say in Texas): *Dance the first dance with the ones that brung you.* Root yourself in the histories of where you stand. Notice who is not there and whose stories are missing.

2. *Learn the tunes before you dance.* Ground yourself in the histories of all sides of the borders you're crossing.

3. *Dance where they do the dance you want to learn.* To borrow from Matt Garcia's *A World of Its Own*, we might dance at the Rainbow Gardens to learn Latinx dances or go to the El Monte American Legion Dance Hall to learn how a shared teen culture connected Whites, Mexican Americans, Blacks, and Asian Pacific Islanders.[59] The borders we cross and the arenas in which we dance should fit our questions.

4. *Not everyone dances to the national anthem.* Dancing to a bagpipe or the Marine Corps band may not be the best way to approach borderlands where people move to salsa, blues, hip hop, or a sacred Sun Dance.

5. *Evade the chaperones*—the ones who tell you that you'll betray the family if you dance with a stranger, that you can't squander the time to learn a new history, that you can't cross disciplinary boundaries or use non-traditional sources. You know who they are. Give them the slip.

6. *Just because you dance with someone doesn't mean you'll go home with them.* People may work or dance in the borderlands, but few people live there or intermarry. If 10 percent of the world's people crossed national borders between 1830 and 1930, 90 percent did not, and border crossing itself is hard to measure in a century when many borders were drawn, including those of North America. A danger of multicultural histories has been seeing people of color as important only in relationship to White people. Don't repeat the same mistake with people of other nations.

7. *If you usually lead, try following—and vice-versa.* People whose job in the dance is to follow often know all the parts better than those who lead—they have to psych what the leaders are going to do if they don't want to get trampled. To really enter the borderlands is to give up histories based in imperial, national, or public power, in androcentric or racialized categories—to imagine, as Susan Johnson eloquently urged us, a history in which we can disconnect difference from domination.[60]

8. *Dance with a buddy. Better yet, dance with lots of buddies.* It's the only way to learn when your steps are invading someone else's comfort zone, and for those of us trained in national histories, there is too much to

learn to do it alone. The borderlands are about relationships and conversations, some not yet begun. They are best explored collaboratively.[61]

We are dancing into unfamiliar territory. Most of our ancestors did, too, and for similar reasons: so that their children might have better futures. Dance lightly. There are lots of unmined stories in the spaces between our rims, and lots of minefields as well: minefields of national frameworks, national borders that constrict our vision, unexamined assumptions, unfamiliar languages, unequal power, and unshared memories. Let's dance through them. We could learn new ways to move as we dance these rims together.

NOTES

Thanks to Tim Cole for outstanding research assistance; Sean van der Lee for the *La Jornada* story; Doug Francis and Jeanne Perreault for their critiques of an earlier draft; and Jeremy Mouat, Sarah Carter, and my colleagues and students at the Universities of Calgary and New Mexico for helping me think about borderlands. This article was prepared as my 2005 presidential address to the Pacific Coast Branch-American Historical Association. I am grateful to Janet Brodie, then Executive Director of the PCB-AHA, for her support during my presidential year and for her work on conference arrangements. The title of the essay borrows from the theme for the 2005 conference "Dancing on the Rim: Nations, Borderlands, and Identities." I am grateful to Program Committee Co-Chairs Katherine Morrissey and Jose Alamillo, and to Dr. Morrissey for "Dancing on the Rim." I am especially grateful to Calgary friends and colleagues Don Smith, Nancy Townshend, Gordon Fairchild, and Max Foran who made the trek to Corvallis for the conference. My address was published in the *Pacific Historical Review* 75:1 (February 2006). I'm grateful to the journal for granting authors permission to re-publish our own work.

1   My information comes partly from family lore, and partly from an article published by Congregation Shearith Israel in Baltimore, "Rev. Dr. Schepschel Schaffer: Twenty-five Years of Activity in the Cause of Orthodox Judaism, 1893–1918 5653–5678" (Baltimore, January 1918). My copy of the article came from a cousin of my mother. It does not have page numbers or any other publication information. Schepschel Schaffer was born May 4, 1862, in Bausk, in the Province of Courland, Russia; the story of his travels is complicated, and versions of it are not necessarily consistent. In any event, he married Anna Lapidoth, from Rossieny. In Germany, he met my mother's other grandfather, Rabbi Philip Klein, who later served a congregation in New York.

2   Donna R. Gabaccia, "Is Everywhere Nowhere? Nomads, Nations, and the Immigrant Paradigm of United States History," *Journal of American History* 86 (1999): 1120.

3   Frederick Jackson Turner, "The Significance of the Frontier in American History," in *History, Frontier, and Section: Three Essays by Frederick Jackson Turner*, ed. Martin Ridge (Albuquerque: University of New Mexico Press, 1993), 59–91, 75–76. Robert E. Park, Ernest W. Burgess, and Roderick D. McKenzie, *The City* (Chicago: University of Chicago Press, 1925); Oscar Handlin, *Boston's Immigrants, 1790–1865: A Study in Acculturation* (Cambridge, MA: Harvard University Press, 1941) and *The Uprooted: The Epic Story of the Great Migration That Made the American People* (Boston: Little, Brown and Company, 1951).

4   Information on my father's family comes from family oral tradition and from a family tree compiled by Nicholas Landau, "Descendants of David Haenlein Wechsler."
5   My grandmother's father, Joel Barnhardt Wechsler, was born in Schwabach, Bavaria, in 1845 and, like many Schwabach Jews apparently worked in the gold leaf trade. He married Jette (Henrietta) Thalheimer in Rotterdam in 1877. My grandmother was born in 1878, shortly after they moved to London; she was their second child. "Descendants of David Haenlein Wechsler," private communication from Nicholas Landau, and conversations with my grandmother.
6   Moses (Moe) was the ninth child in the family; he married Rachel (Rae) Fleisig, and they emigrated to Montreal sometime before 1916, when Margaret (Margie) was born. "Descendants of David Haenlein Wechsler." My grandmother later became the executive director of the Essex County Council [New Jersey] of Jewish Welfare agencies, a predecessor of the United Jewish Federation (now the United Jewish Communities of MetroWest). She retired and moved to Galveston, Texas, in 1947, shortly after I was born.
7   The law commonly called the 1917 Immigration Act refers to the Act of February 5, 1917, entitled "An Act to regulate the immigration of aliens to, and the residence of aliens in, the United States."
8   Benedict Anderson, *Imagined Communities: Reflections on the Origin and Spread of Nationalism* (London: Verso, 1983); Ian Tyrell, "American Exceptionalism in an Age of International History," *American Historical Review* 96 (1991): 1031–55.
9   Anderson, *Imagined Communities*; Sarah Carter, "Categories and Terrains of Exclusion: Constructing the 'Indian Woman' in the Early Settlement Era in Western Canada," *Great Plains Quarterly* 13 (1993): 147–61.
10 Turner, "The Significance of the Frontier," 60.
11 The term "alien" included any individual who was not a native-born or naturalized citizen of the United States; Chinese were deemed "ineligible to citizenship" under section 14 of the Act entitled "An Act to execute certain treaty stipulations relating to Chinese," approved May 6, 1882, otherwise known as the Chinese Exclusion Act.
12 For how the Canadian-U.S. border has been constructed and functioned differently in the two national histories, see Elizabeth Jameson and Jeremy Mouat, "Telling Differences: The Forty-Ninth Parallel and Historiographies of the West and Nation," *Pacific Historical Review* 75:2 (May 2006): 183–230; Sheila McManus, *The Line Which Separates: Race, Gender, and the Making of the Alberta-Montana Borderlands* (Lincoln: University of Nebraska Press, 2005). For a popular treatment, see Will Ferguson, *Why I Hate Canadians* (Vancouver: Douglas & McIntyre, 1997), esp. 96–113.
13 The *Journal of American History* 86 (1999), special issues on "Rethinking History and the Nation-State: Mexico and the United States as a Case Study," and "The Nation and Beyond: Transnational Perspectives on United States History." For examples of the new migration history, see Marc S. Rodriguez, ed., *Repositioning North American Migration History: New Directions in Modern Continental Migration, Citizenship, and Community* (Rochester, N.Y.: University of Rochester Press, 2004); Samuel Truett and Elliott Young, "Making Transnational History: Nations, Regions, and Borderlands," and Truett and Young, "Conclusion: Borderlands Unbound," in *Continental Crossroads: Remapping U.S.-Mexico Borderlands History*, eds. Samuel Truett and Elliott Young (Durham, N.C.: Duke University Press, 2004), 1–32, 325–28. This scholarship is among the extensive work that developed from the new immigration, ethnic, and social histories; they remain focused on the United States and on the Mexican-U.S. borderland. For the less extensive body of scholarship that addresses the Canadian-U.S. borderland, see Bruno Ramirez, *Crossing the 49th Parallel: Migration from Canada to the United States, 1900–1930* (Ithaca, NY: Cornell University Press, 2000); Randy William Widdis, *With Scarcely a Ripple: Anglo-*

Canadian Migration into the United States and Western Canada, 1880–1920 (Montreal: McGill-Queen's University Press, 1998); McManus, *The Line Which Separates*; Beth LaDow, *The Medicine Line: Life and Death on a North American Borderland* (New York: Routledge, 2002); Theodore Binnema, *Common and Contested Ground: A Human and Environmental History of the Northwestern Plains* (Norman: University of Oklahoma Press, 2001); Paul W. Hirt, ed., *Terra Pacifica: People and Place in the Northwest States and Western Canada* (Pullman, WA: Washington State University Press, 1998); John M. Findlay and Ken S. Coates, eds., *Parallel Destinies: Canadian-American Relations West of the Rockies* (Seattle and Montreal: University of Washington Press and McGill-Queen's University Press, 2002); William G. Robbins, ed., *The Great Northwest: The Search for Regional Identity* (Corvallis, OR: Oregon State University Press, 2001); Carol Higham and Robert Thacker, eds., *One West, Two Myths: Essays on Comparisons* (Calgary: University of Calgary Press, 2005); John J. Bukowczyk, Nora Faires, David R. Smith, and Randy William Widdis, eds., *Permeable Border: The Great Lakes Basin as Transnational Region, 1650-1990* (Pittsburgh and Calgary: University of Pittsburgh Press and University of Calgary Press, 2005); Sterling Evans, ed., *The Borderlands of the American and Canadian Wests* (Lincoln: University of Nebraska Press, 2006); and Michel Hogue, *Metis and the Medicine Line: Creating a Border and Dividing a People* (Chapel Hill and Regina: University of North Carolina Press and University of Regina Press, 2015).

14 I am borrowing this image from the theme of the 2005 PCB-AHA program: "Dancing on the Rim: Nations, Borderlands, and Identities," Ninety-eighth Annual Meeting, Pacific Coast Branch-American Historical Association, Corvallis, Oregon, August 4–7, 2005; Tracy Chapman, "Telling Stories," *Telling Stories*, copyright 1999, Purple Rabbit Music, ASCAP.

15 The figure includes migrants from Newfoundland. Kenneth Lines, *British and Canadian Immigration to the United States Since 1920* (San Francisco: R & E Research Associates, 1978), 58–59, 69.

16 Like many American communists, our cousins abandoned the party as Stalinist realities became known. For the cross-border migrations for sanctuary of Sitting Bull, following the Battle of the Little Bighorn, and of Louis Riel and his followers, after the 1869–1870 Rebellion, see LaDow, *The Medicine Line*, 43–72; Michel Hogue, "Disputing the Medicine Line: The Plains Crees and the Canadian-American Border, 1876–1885," *Montana: The Magazine of Western History* 53 (2002): 2–17; Joseph Kinsey Howard, *Strange Empire: A Narrative of the Northwest* (New York: William Morrow, 1952). The references to gays and lesbians wishing to marry and women seeking legal abortions were located in U.S. legal and political realities in 2005–2006. On June 26, 2015, the United States Supreme Court legalized same-sex marriages throughout the United States. The reference to political assaults on the right to legal abortions remains pertinent in 2025.

17 Herbert Eugene Bolton, *The Spanish Borderlands: A Chronicle of Old Florida and the Southwest* (New Haven, CT: Yale University Press, 1921).

18 David J. Weber, *The Spanish Frontier in North America* (New Haven, CT: Yale University Press, 1992), 43–45.

19 See Susan W. Hardwick, "Galveston: Ellis Island of Texas," *Journal of Cultural Geography* 20 (2003): 76–77.

20 Hardwick, "Galveston: Ellis Island of Texas," 73–75, 77–79.

21 Hardwick, "Galveston: Ellis Island of Texas," 80–82; Natalie Ornish, *Pioneer Jewish Texans: Their Impact on Texas and American History for Four Hundred Years, 1590–1990* (Dallas: Texas Heritage Press, Publishers, 1989), 119–30; Ruthe Weingarten and Cathy Schechter, *Deep in the Heart: The Lives & Legends of Texas Jews: A Photographic History* (Austin: Eakin Press, 1990), 84–85. Funded by New York financier Jacob Schiff, the

Galveston Movement existed largely due to the leadership and commitment of Rabbi Henry Cohen of Galveston's Congregation B'nai Israel. The goal of dispersing the new arrivals was partly humanitarian, to avoid an impoverished urban ghetto, but it also achieved distance between the largely eastern European Orthodox Jewish newcomers and the German Reform Jews of Galveston. Rabbi Cohen arrived in Galveston in 1888 and stayed in Texas until his death in 1952; he was a renowned humanitarian. In the interest of full disclosure, in 1962 I won the annual essay contest that honors his memory. For more on Rabbi Cohen, see Anne Nathan and Harry I. Cohen, *The Man Who Stayed in Texas* (New York: Whittlesey House, McGraw-Hill Book Company, 1941); *Henry Cohen: Messenger of the Lord*, compiled by A. Stanley Dreyfus (New York: Bloch Publishing Co., 1963); and Jimmy Kessler, *Temple B'nai Israel: The Story of a BOI* (Austin: Nortex Press, 2004), 42–47.

22 Juneteenth, which commemorates the emancipation of Texas slaves, has particular resonance for the Galveston African American community. On June 19, 1865, Union troops landed at Galveston and Major General Gordon Granger issued General Order No.3, which enforced the January 1, 1863, Emancipation Proclamation in Texas and ended slavery in the state. See Quintard Taylor, *In Search of the Racial Frontier: African Americans in the American West* (New York: W. W. Norton & Company, 1997), 61. As a child, I noticed gatherings of African Americans along the Galveston beachfront each June, but I was an adult before I had any idea why they had gathered or what they were celebrating.

23 The Battle of San Jacinto was the final battle in Texas's successful war for independence from Mexico.

24 See Elizabeth Jameson, *All That Glitters: Class, Conflict, and Community in Cripple Creek* (Urbana: University of Illinois Press, 1998), 26–27, 33–34.

25 J. Sanford Rikoon, ed., *Rachel Calof's Story: Jewish Homesteader on the Northern Plains* (Bloomington: University of Indiana Press, 1995); Maier Calof, *Miracles of the Lives of Maier and Doba Calof* (n.p., 1941).

26 Which organizations and associations do and do not cross borders is a subtle matter. For instance, the Western Federation of Miners (1893–1916), later the International Union of Mine, Mill and Smelter Workers (1916–1967) had local unions in Mexico, the United States, and Canada, but different ethnic groups were admitted to or excluded from local unions in different localities. The Ancient Order of Hibernians and the Knights of Columbus were more common sites of Irish association in the United States, while the Orange Order was more common in Canada. As in Ireland, the Orange Order is primarily Protestant.

27 This is an admittedly idiosyncratic set of examples, rooted in my own research interests. It is clear that people and ideas crossed borders to connect the social movements and strikes listed. William Lyon Mackenzie King, later the Prime Minister of Canada, advised John D. Rockefeller and helped devise the plan for company unions Rockefeller implemented after the Ludlow, Colorado, coal miners' strike. Sacagawea, who guided Lewis and Clark on their westward journey, Charlotte Thompson, wife of explorer David Thompson, and Malintzin, Hernán Cortes's interpreter and the mother of his son, all occupy similar places in their respective national histories as Native women who assisted European/European American explorers and ultimately helped them claim Native territory.

28 Quote from Chris Friday, private communication. Thanks to historians Sheila McManus (Lethbridge, Alberta), Catherine Cavanaugh (Edmonton, Alberta), Jean Barman (Vancouver, British Columbia), Cecilia Danysk and Chris Friday (Bellingham, Washington), Susan Armitage (Pullman, Washington), and Howard Shorr (Portland, Oregon) for private communications regarding their respective local TV stations. Based on this limited sample, it appeared that U.S. viewers got Canadian television only if they

lived within range of Canadian stations, a relatively rare situation, but Canadian cable packages regularly include U.S. networks. Thanks to Brian Scrivener for the additional information that the Bellingham station was started by Canadian interests to serve the Vancouver market at a time when CBC had a monopoly. Private ownership of TV stations was not allowed until 1958.

29 Jameson and Mouat, "Telling Differences"; Alexandra Minna Stern, "Nationalism on the Line: Masculinity, Race, and the Creation of the U.S. Border Patrol, 1910–1940," in Truett and Young, *Continental Crossroads*, 299–323; Camille Guérin-Gonzales, *Mexican Workers and American Dreams: Immigration, Repatriation, and California Farm Labor, 1900–1939* (New Brunswick, NJ: Rutgers University Press, 1994); Guérin-Gonzales, "Repatriacion de familias immigrantes durante la Gran Depresion," *Historia Mexicana* 138 (1985): 241–74; Mae M. Ngai, *Impossible Subjects: Illegal Aliens and the Making of Modern America* (Princeton, NJ: Princeton University Press, 2004); Raymond Rodríguez, *Decade of Betrayal: Mexican Repatriation in the 1930s* (Albuquerque: University of New Mexico Press, 1995).

30 Canada's rank among sources of the foreign-born population in the United States as reported on the decennial U.S. census varied between third and fourth from 1850–1980; Mexico ranked roughly seventh or eighth numerically until 1970, when it moved to fourth (Canada was third); in 1980 Mexico moved to first place and stayed there through 2000. Canada's third-fourth place ranking held until 2000, when an influx of Chinese, Filipinos, Indians, Cubans, Vietnamese, El Salvadorans, Koreans, and Dominicans reconfigured the foreign-born population and dropped Canada to tenth place. The "Mexican" ranking among the foreign-born, however, from 1850 through much of the 19th century, discounts many ethnic Mexicans born in Mexico, whose birthplaces became "United States" after the Mexican-American War. See "Countries of Birth of the Foreign-Born Population, 1850–2000 (resident population)", http://infoplease.com/ipa/A0900547.html, accessed July 20, 2005.

31 See Anthony Wilson-Smith, "Canadians Invade U.S. News," *Maclean's*, June 22, 1998.

32 Lines, *British and Canadian Immigration to the United States*, 57–69.

33 Stan Rogers, "California," copyright 1981, Fogarty's Cove Music, used by permission. I am grateful to Ariel Rogers for her gracious response to my request to quote these lyrics.

34 Passengers and crew aboard the fourth hijacked aircraft learned from friends and family about the attacks in New York and Washington. As they attempted to retake the plane, the hijackers deliberately crashed it into a field in Somerset County, Pennsylvania. The death figures are from Patrick Jackson, BBC News, "September 11 Attacks: What Happened on 9/11?," BBC, https://www.bbc.com/news/world-us-canada-57698668, accessed August 3, 2021.

35 Harold A. Innis, *The Fur Trade in Canada* (Toronto: University of Toronto Press, 1930), best known in Canada through the revised edition. Harold A. Innis, *The Fur Trade in Canada: An Introduction to Canadian Economic History* (Toronto: University of Toronto Press, 1956) or through the 1999 edition (Toronto: University of Toronto Press, 1999), with a new introduction by Arthur Ray; George F. G. Stanley, "Western Canada and the Frontier Thesis," Canadian Historical Association, *Report of the Annual Meeting* (1940), 105–14.

36 This discussion is based on ninety-five articles in the *Calgary Herald* from March 11, 2001, through September 11, 2002, that mentioned the U.S.-Canada border. I am grateful to Timothy J. G. Cole for assistance with the newspaper research.

37 "Ressam guilty of terrorism: Millennium celebrations targeted," *Calgary Herald*, April 7, 2001; Tim Naumetz, "Entry to US shows leaks: 11,000 illegals caught last year," *Calgary*

Herald, November 7, 2001; Kari Shannon, "Al-Qaeda links land terror suspect in Jail," *Calgary Herald*, September 4, 2002.

38   Rick Mofina, "Feds mum on border-crossing threat," *Calgary Herald*, March 16, 2001; Dene Moore, "Most illegal human cargo heading south of border," *Calgary Herald*, May 28, 2001.

39   Rick Mofina, "Feds mum on border-crossing threat"; Dene Moore, "Most illegal human cargo heading south of border."

40   "Border crossing closed for march," *Calgary Herald*, April 22, 2001.

41   Mike Trickey, "U.S. ambassador favours closer links with Canada: Celucci urges immigration 'harmonization'," *Calgary Herald*, June 30, 2001; Mike Trickey, "Border blues cost billions," *Calgary Herald*, August 7, 2001.

42   David Orchard, "Erasing borders with U.S. will erase Canada from map," *Calgary Herald*, August 20, 2001. See also Charles Mandel, "National identity just a memory after NAFTA," *Calgary Herald*, June 30, 2001; James Baxter, "Security over sovereignty, Canada told," *Calgary Herald*, September 19, 2001; Mike Trickey, "US plans a worry to Ottawa," *Calgary Herald*, December 12, 2001; Trickey, "Sovereignty weighs heavily on 'smart border' plan," *Calgary Herald*, December 13, 2001; Norma Greenway and Tim Naumetz, "Proposed security pact draws criticism," *Calgary Herald*, August 29, 2002.

43   Kerry Williamson, "Ambassador urges more open border," *Calgary Herald*, September 11, 2001.

44   Don Martin, "Eerie quiet falls on Ottawa," *Calgary Herald*, September 11, 2001.

45   Paul Cherry and William Marsden, "Canada linked to suspects: Five terrorists entered U.S. from N.S. and Quebec," *Calgary Herald*, September 13, 2001; Jonathan Peterson, "Congress plans tougher security: Orange cones only deterrent at some crossings," *Calgary Herald*, October 3, 2001; Norma Greenway and Mike Trickey, "Traffic cones only deterrent at border; U.S. senator calls for humans at checkpoints after dark," *Calgary Herald*, October 4, 2001. See also David Pugliese, "Canada called a weak link: Report critical of border security," *Calgary Herald*, September 13, 2001; "Stand on guard: Much will depend upon who Canada lets in, and how," *Calgary Herald*, September 14, 2001; Wayne Winters, "We're sorry," *Calgary Herald*, September 13, 2001; Helen Branswell, "U.S. vows to beef up 'porous' border," *Calgary Herald*, September 26, 2001; James F. Smith and Maggie Farley, "What Americans are saying about us: Two articles in major U.S. papers raise questions about Canada and its security," *Calgary Herald*, September 29, 2001; Rod Love, "Leaky borders are a threat to everyone," *Calgary Herald*, September 30, 2001; Robert Russo, "Ashcroft backs off on border criticism," *Calgary Herald*, October 3, 2001; Juliet O'Neill, "Manley tackles Clinton over border allegations: Minister fights perception of lax security," *Calgary Herald*, October 25, 2001; Joe Laurie, "Manley irked by rumours: Border weakness called unfounded," *Calgary Herald*, November 6, 2001; Matthew Sekeres, "Manley denies Canada a hotbed for terrorists," *Calgary Herald*, April 26, 2002.

46   Mark Reid, "Sacred bundles 'defiled' by border guards: Blackfoot want own border crossing," *Calgary Herald*, June 8, 2001.

47   See James Baxter and Hilary MacKenzie, "US fires first salvo in softwood lumber war," *Calgary Herald*, April 3, 2001; Juliet O'Neill, "US lumber tariff 'dead wrong': Energy minister heats up trade battle," *Calgary Herald*, August 23, 2001; Graham Thomson and Ed Struzik, "Alberta bristles at trade threat," *Calgary Herald*, March 27, 2002; "Ottawa sours on U.S. tactics: Manley says Americans are 'irresponsible'," *Calgary Herald*, May 15, 2002; James Baxter, "Ottawa plans softwood lumber attack: Feds to spend 20 million to promote Canada's cause," *Calgary Herald*, May 28, 2002; Lisa Schmidt and Chris Varcoe, "Trade spats can be resolved, says Bush," *Calgary Herald*, June 26, 2002; James Baxter, "WTO ruling favours Canada: Moral win declared in softwood tiff," *Calgary*

Herald, July 27, 2002; Linda Slobdian, "Making public aware of a lonely fight," *Calgary Herald*, June 15, 2002; Slobdian, "Farmers stand their ground: Trio risks jail rather than pay fine," *Calgary Herald*, July 15, 2002.

48 Mark Reid, "Border delays sink town's economy: Lineups keep Canadians at home; Series; G8 summit; Kananaskis," *Calgary Herald*, May 12, 2002.

49 "U.S. Border Control: The Minuteman Project," The Minuteman Project, http://www.usbc.org/minuteman1.html, accessed July 22, 2005; "Minuteman Civil Defense Corps: Minuteman Corps New Mexico," The Official Minuteman Civil Defense Corps, http://www.minutemanhq.com/nm/, accessed July 22, 2005; "MinuteManHQ On Patrol: In Four States All Month In October," The Minuteman Project, http://www.minutemanhq.com/project/, accessed July 22, 2005.

50 Cristobal Garcia Bernal Enviado, "La SG refuerza su vigilancia en la frontera norte ... con 8 agentes Beta," *La Jornada*, April 3, 2005. See also Sergio Lagarde Moguel, "Reclutan en EU a niños y ancianos para cazar immigrantes," *La Cronica*, March 29, 2005; Leslie Gómez, "La SRE condena a caza immigrantes y exigo\e a Estados Unidos detenerios," *La Cronica*, March 30, 2005. Thanks to Sean van der Lee who directed me to these sources.

51 In 2021, I would add COVID-19.

52 Sylvia Van Kirk, "'Women in Between'": Women in Fur Trade Society in Western Canada," Canadian Historical Association, *Historical Papers* (1977), 31–46, and *Many Tender Ties: Women in Fur-Trade Society, 1670-1870* (Norman & Winnipeg: University of Oklahoma Press and Watson & Dwyer, 1980); Sarah Deutsch, *No Separate Refuge: Culture, Class, and Gender on an Anglo-Hispanic Frontier in the American Southwest, 1880-1940* (New York: Oxford University Press, 1987); Peggy Pascoe, "Western Women at the Cultural Crossroads," in *Trails: Toward a New Western History*, eds. Patricia Nelson Limerick, Clyde A. Milner II, and Charles E. Rankin (Lawrence: University of Kansas Press, 1991); Albert L. Hurtado, *Intimate Frontiers: Sex, Gender, and Culture in Old California* (Albuquerque: University of New Mexico Press, 1999), 40–58; Sarah Carter, *Capturing Women: The Manipulation of Cultural Imagery in Canada's Prairie World* (Montreal: McGill-Queen's University Press, 1997); Gloria Anzaldúa, *Borderlands/La Frontera: The New Mestiza* (San Francisco: aunt lute book, 1987).

53 Gloria Anzaldúa, "To live in the Borderlands means you," in Anzaldúa, *Borderlands/La Frontera*, 216.

54 Jeremy Adelman and Stephen Aron, "From Borderlands to Borders: Empires, Nation-States, and the Peoples in Between in North American History," *American Historical Review* 104 (1999): 814–41, esp. 815–16. For critiques, see "Forum Essay: Responses: Borders and Borderlands," *American Historical Review* 104 (1999): 1229–34; see also Adelman and Aron, "Of Lively Exchanges and Larger Perspectives," *American Historical Review* 104 (1999): 1235–39.

55 Richard White, "Is There a North American History?," *Revue française d'études américaines* 79 (1999): 8–28.

56 White, "Is There a North American History?," 24.

57 For Canada, see Michael Bliss, "Privatizing the Mind: The Sundering of Canadian History, the Sundering of Canada," *Journal of Canadian Studies* 26 (1991–1992): 5–17; J. L. Granatstein, *Who Killed Canadian History?* (Toronto: HarperCollins Publishers, 1998). For the United States, see Alan Bloom, *The Closing of the American Mind* (New York: Simon & Schuster, 1987); William J. Bennett, *The De-valuing of America: The Fight for Our Culture and Our Children* (New York: Summit Books, 1994); Lynne V. Cheney, *Telling the Truth: Why Our Culture and Our Country Have Stopped Making Sense—and What We Can Do About It* (New York: Simon & Schuster, 1995).

58 I borrowed the reference from the then-popular TV sitcom "8 Simple Rules for Dating My Teenage Daughter," starring John Ritter and Katey Sagal and co-starring Kaley Cuoco, Amy Davidson and Martin Spanjers. The series ran on ABC from September 17, 2002, to April 15, 2005.

59 Matt Garcia, *A World of Its Own: Race, Labor, and Citrus in the Making of Greater Los Angeles, 1900-1970* (Chapel Hill: University of North Carolina Press, 2001), esp. chap. 6, "Memories of El Monte: Dance Halls and Youth Culture in Greater Los Angeles, 1950-1974," 189-214.

60 Susan Lee Johnson, *Roaring Camp: The Social World of the California Gold Rush* (New York: W.W. Norton, 2000), esp. 19, 342-44.

61 I have learned the value of collaborative work from some class collaborators. I thank the Learned Society of Calgary for making the dance fun; and Sheila McManus, Sarah Carter, Sue Armitage, and Jeremy Mouat for being great dance partners.

6

God, Santa, and the American Way: The U.S. Alaska Reindeer Project

April 10, 2007

The first reindeer I ever saw was hitched to a parking meter in Anchorage. It was March 17, 1972. The reindeer was decked out for the St. Patrick's Day parade with green ribbons strung through its antlers. A reindeer hitched to a parking meter is not common, even in Alaska, yet for me, a newcomer from "the lower 48," it seemed no stranger than much else in pre-pipeline Alaska. What else would you do with a reindeer in Anchorage?

How the reindeer's forebears came to Alaska is a more interesting story. Though wild caribou are native to Alaska, domesticated reindeer are not. They were imported in the 1890s to help Native people whom U.S. officials mistakenly thought were starving, and to help "civilize" village-based hunters and gatherers by turning them into nomadic herders.[1] That policy was the brainchild of the Reverend Sheldon Jackson, from 1872 to 1885 superintendent of Presbyterian missions for the Rocky Mountain Territories, and, from 1885 to 1908 General Agent for Education in Alaska.[2]

The United States bought Alaska from Russia in 1867, but Alaska did not become a Territory until 1905 and had no government structure until the First Organic Act of 1884, which, among other things, guaranteed the Native peoples' possession of their lands and appropriated $25,000 for the Secretary of the Interior to educate school-age children—a task he delegated to the Commissioner of Education, who delegated it to Jackson.[3] Jackson was responsible for all Alaska Natives: Haida, Tlingit, Aleut, Tsimshian Athabaskan, and Eskimo (Inupiaq, St. Lawrence Island Yupik, Yup'ik, and Cup'ik). The reindeer were primarily for the Inupiaq, St. Lawrence Island Yupik, and Yup'ik.[4]

Alaska Natives were resourceful and maximized their food sources in a challenging environment. They accepted reindeer as an additional potential food source. But reindeer were only one component of Jackson's civilizing mission, which consisted of five "Rs": reading, 'riting, 'rithmetic, religion, and reindeer.[5] Each Native village adapted reindeer as a new resource in its own way, while selectively accepting, rejecting, or adapting the other "civilizing" intentions of the missionaries and the U.S. government.

To understand the reindeer project requires some background on everyone involved: the Alaska Natives, the Whites who brought the reindeer and managed them, and the situation in Alaska when they met. These provide the background and contexts for an analysis of Native reindeer owners and how they selectively incorporated reindeer into Native subsistence and culture.

Unlike Canadian Inupiaq, Alaska Natives have continued to use the term "Eskimo," a name conferred by neighboring groups that means "raw flesh eaters." In the 1890s, they might say they were "Inuit" or "Yuit," which mean "the people," and add, "I am Kingikmiut," "I am Kuskowagmiut," "Taremiut," "Tigaramiut," "Utkiavmiut," or "Sivokakmete"[6]—"I am from Kinegan, the Kuskokwim, the coast, Tigara, Utkeavie, or Sivokak"—places Whites called Cape Prince of Wales, the Kuskokwim River, the Arctic Coast, Point Hope, Point Barrow, and Gambell (see Figure 6.1). People traveled from their village base throughout a territory that supported seasonal hunting and gathering rounds, a pattern that led anthropologist Margaret Lantis to call them "excursionists."[7] Identification with a village implied identification with this territory as well and with the subsistence activities it supported.

In most northwestern Alaska villages from 1890 to 1920, there were one or two White Americans. They would not have introduced themselves saying "I am from Kansas," or "I am a real person," or even, "I am a White American." They would say "I am a Christian missionary." Their identities and support came from Christian service, which infused the version of American culture they represented. Their primary ties were to other missionaries, the government, and sometimes, over time, to the people they came to serve.

Eskimo culture was neither monolithic nor unchanging. There is a split at about the present-day village of Unalakleet: the Yup'ik live south of there and speak the Yup'ik dialect; the Inupiaq, who speak Inup'ik, live North of there and along the Arctic coast. The people of St. Lawrence Island are related to Siberian Eskimos, speak a Yupik dialect, and had little

Figure 6.1 Northwest Alaska with Reindeer Project Sites. Map by Jennifer Arthur.

contact with the Alaska mainland. There was considerable local diversity in social organization, family, kinship systems, and local foodways, but much that was common, too.[8]

I could at one time recite the kinship systems and annual hunting and gathering cycles, village by village that I learned in my Alaska Anthropology class at the University of Alaska, Fairbanks, in the summer of 1972. I can't do that anymore but focus here on the subsistence practices that the reindeer project was intended to change.

Almost all able-bodied men hunted; what they hunted and with whom depended on local environment and practice. Each village had a food the people considered particularly "theirs"—walrus for St. Lawrence Island, salmon on the lower Yukon and Kuskokwim Rivers, whale and seal at Point Hope and Point Barrow, and caribou inland. The dogs ate the foods considered "inferior" that humans avoided, except in emergencies. The inland Nunamiut hunted their prized caribou communally. Walrus and whale hunting were crew activities, similar in organization and importance for the villagers who valued them.

No area depended on a single food source. That would be a foolish survival strategy in a climate that could affect the migration routes of game and otherwise deplete a food source for a time. The Sivokakmete of St. Lawrence Island hunted walrus from November through March, as well as seals, fish, and birds. The whales ran there in April and May. From June through October, when the pack ice left the island, they might hunt spotted seal, fish, and birds, and gather roots, greens, berries, seaweed, and bird eggs.[9] Point Hope, Cape Prince of Wales, and Point Barrow depended on whales, which ran in early spring; they got a second chance in the fall, when the whales migrated south again, except at Point Barrow, where the whales turned to return south and which had only one annual whale run. Before U.S. whalers came, people as far north as Point Hope could catch walrus in late spring. In summer and fall, they hunted caribou, salmon, sea trout, beluga whales, ducks, and eggs; by late October or November, the shore ice would be firm enough to hunt seal; after December, women and old people might "jig" for tomcod through the ice.[10]

Salmon ran on the lower Kuskokwim and Yukon Rivers in late spring and summer. In fall and winter, riverine Yu'pik hunted caribou, moose, or fish and trapped inland. They hunted caribou and birds at spring camps, trapped, fished, and gathered berries. On the coast of the Seward Peninsula, the main foods were walrus, seal, whales, and ducks. By the 1890s, the caribou had left, creating a niche for the reindeer.[11]

The inland caribou hunters had intensive, communal caribou drives in late spring, when the caribou migrated through the Brooks Range. The Nunamiut also hunted foxes, wolves, wolverines, Grizzly and Polar bears, and a variety of seals.[12]

Women, girls, and older people also had specific gathering tasks in each locality, fishing and gathering plants and berries. In the spring, families might travel to fish or hunt. In the summers they met to trade with other groups. Everyone needed seal and walrus skins for boat covers, waterproof clothing, and boots. Everyone needed caribou skins for clothes and bedding, and seal and whale oil for fuel and for fat. Coastal mammal hunters traded with inland caribou hunters; St. Lawrence Island traded with Siberians for caribou skins and fat.

These diets were very high in protein. Seal and whale oil are rich in vitamins and minerals and are polyunsaturated to boot. Survival depended on all available food sources and a flexible toolbox of skills. Adult men and sled dogs could eat seven or eight pounds of meat a day, particularly while doing hard work in winter. A family of ten with eight dogs would need 125 pounds of meat daily.[13] The labor required to get so much food varied by task and by place. Communal walrus hunting at Gambell on St. Lawrence Island, whaling at Barrow and Point Hope, and caribou drives in the Brooks Range were important socially and religiously as well as for pooling skills and labor.

Social status was achieved through wealth in food, skins, and other needed goods, but only if that wealth was distributed generously. Acquiring the food to share required the support and cooperation of kin, so family, wealth, status, and generosity were all intertwined. The word "kamookbrook," which means "flesh," connoted both food and close kin.[14] The word for orphan was the same as the word for poor—to be without kin was to be poor. Sharing food with kin was a fundamental obligation, generosity a basic value.[15] The word for "rich and powerful person" was "oomalik," which literally meant "boat owner." An oomalik had to command the loyalty of a crew composed largely of kin, support his kin and crew, distribute his first catch throughout the village, and give food to anyone who asked for it.[16] Cooperation and group survival were more important than individual achievement.

A lot about Alaska Native life might have perplexed Sheldon Jackson. Survival required diverse skills, not specialization. Kin, skill, and community relations determined identity and social standing, not one's profession. There were no full-time religious specialists or priests. Marriage was easily contracted and easily dissolved. Sex was natural, carried no special moral implications, and might be involved in long-term trading partnerships.[17] In some villages, men spent most of their time in a men's house, or kashigi, and households consisted of women, and boys under age twelve.[18] There was no school, no church, no state.

Jackson found much of this barbarous. His mission, he said, was:

> [T]o establish English among a people the larger part of whom do not speak or understand the English language. . . . to instruct a people, the greater portion of whom are uncivilized, who need to be taught sanitary regulations, the laws of health, improvement of dwellings, better methods of housekeeping, cooking, and dressing, better methods of labor, honesty, chastity, the sacredness of the marriage relation, and everything that elevates man. So that, side by side with the usual school drill in reading, writing, and arithmetic, there is the need of instruction for the girls in housekeeping, cooking, and gardening, in cutting, sewing, and mending, and for the boys in carpentering, and other forms of wood working, boot and shoe making, and the various tasks of civilization.[19]

The civilizing influence of the schools, Jackson believed, would instill desires for American material goods and technologies. New industries must be established, because: "The income that was sufficient when the family ate off the ground without dishes, cooked over a fire without a chimney, and slept on the floor under skins of wild beasts, is not sufficient to purchase cook stoves, dishes, tables, chairs, bedsteads, &c." The schools were "not only to teach reading, writing, and arithmetic, but also how to live better, and how to utilize the resources of the country in order to make more money."[20] There should be instruction in forestry, agriculture, and commercial fishing; girls should learn how to be housewives.[21]

Of all Jackson's "civilizing" educational agenda, only housewifery might have worked in northwest Alaska, a place hardly hospitable to forests, agriculture, or sustainable commercial fisheries. Jackson found the solution in 1889, on an inspection tour of Native settlements on the U.S. Revenue Cutter *Bear*. He and the Captain, Michael Healy, observed that the Natives in Siberia herded reindeer, but Alaska Eskimos only hunted them. Domesticated reindeer herding was clearly higher on the ladder of civilization according to the late-19th-century ideology that informed

Jackson's worldview, in which people became more civilized as they progressed from hunting and gathering, to herding, to farming.[22] Reindeer herding, Jackson said, was "the only industry that can live and thrive in that region, and take a barbarous people on the verge of starvation, lift them up to a comfortable support and civilization, and turn them from consumers into producers of natural wealth."[23]

He raised over $2,000 through appeals in religious newspapers, and in July 1892, imported fifty-three Siberian reindeer and four Siberian herders to establish the first Alaska reindeer herd.[24] The next year Congress appropriated $6,000 to fund the venture.[25] Between 1892 and 1905, 1,280 reindeer were imported from Siberia, which, with natural increase, numbered 10,241 by 1905. Seventy-eight Alaska Natives were apprenticed as herders at fourteen reindeer stations and earned reindeer each year of their apprenticeships.[26] Deciding that the four Siberian herders were themselves "uncivilized," Jackson arranged in 1894 to hire six Christian Saami from Norway as reindeer instructors. In 1898, another sixty-seven Saami, Finn, and Norwegian families came as contract employees. Eighty-six of the reindeer instructors remained in Alaska, but many became miners, and only eight remained in government service as herders.[27]

Under Jackson, and even later, there was virtually no distinction among church, state, school, and industrial training. Jackson's own salary was augmented by mission contributions until 1907.[28] Jackson sought teachers who offered examples of Christian home life, and preferred married couples to "unmarried ladies." In some places, the official missionary and the government teacher were the same person. When a husband and wife worked together as a team, one might officially be the government teacher and the other officially a missionary. More often, when not in the classroom, teachers performed church services and sought converts. They came to teach and convert heathens and didn't care whether their pay came from the church or the state.

Jackson placed missionaries from only one denomination in each village, a policy that avoided inter-denominational rivalry and led to a religious mosaic of Alaska villages.[29] Point Barrow and St. Lawrence Island became Presbyterian; Point Hope, Episcopalian; Cape Prince of Wales, Congregational; Kotzebue, Quaker; Teller, Norwegian Evangelical Lutheran; Golovin, Swedish Evangelical Lutheran; Bethel, Moravian, and so on. Until 1907, the missions supervised the reindeer enterprise: the local missionary was also the local Reindeer Superintendent. Jackson considered the missionaries "the most intelligent and disinterested friends of the Natives," and believed "that the Natives who most completely come under the mission influence, civilization, and education are the coming men of affairs among their own people, and therefore are also the best men to lead in a new movement."[30] The reindeer, he thought, would attract Alaska Natives to the villages and give the missionaries a way to reward "those families that give evidence of being teachable, advancing in civilization, attentive to the instruction of the mission and exemplary in their lives by establishing them in the reindeer industry."[31]

After Jackson retired in 1908, responsibility for the reindeer was transferred to the teachers, but that didn't change much, since if the teacher and missionary were not actually the same person, they shared similar values and goals. Missionaries and teachers came as representatives of the U.S. government, and of God and Santa Claus, as well.[32] The Gambell mission herd actually had two reindeer named Donder and Blixen.[33]

The government and missionaries imported the "5 R's" to a place already reeling from change. There were many more sea mammals before White men hunted the walrus for ivory, seals for pelts, and whales for oil and baleen. It is estimated that the Pacific walrus population fell from some 200,000 in the 17th and 18th centuries to at most 45,000 by 1920. The decline most affected villages on the fringes of walrus migration, but it did not seriously affect the Bering Sea islands, where walrus was a crucial food.[34] The number of whales plummeted, and it was reported in 1897 that no whales were taken at Point Hope, where they were a primary food.[35] Whalers operated in Alaska waters from the 1840s through 1908. They established whaling and trading stations along the arctic coast, brought new goods, like guns and whaling tools, and traded for caribou, disrupting trade between the coastal and inland Inupiaq.[36] Still no area suffered a significant depletion of *all* its game, and it does not appear that starvation was in fact imminent. But the whalers also brought alcohol and diseases that affected the ability to hunt more than any shortage of game.

The diseases devastated Alaska: smallpox, chicken pox, whooping cough, influenza, tuberculosis, measles, and syphilis claimed a third of the population between 1850 and 1900.[37] Inupiaq have lived at Point Hope for at least a thousand years; archaeologists uncovered 500 houses in one site there. From 1880 through 1970 the population hovered between only 200 and 300 people, the devastating result of diseases the whalers brought.[38] A measles epidemic in 1900 took at least half the Native population of the northern Pacific, Bering Sea, and Arctic regions. In 1902 alone, Point Hope lost 12 percent of its population when a whaler brought measles to the area. Whole villages died on the lower Kuskokwim River. By 1911, 90 percent of the Alaska Natives on the lower Yukon River had tuberculosis. Then came the 1918 influenza epidemic.[39] It is difficult to imagine the pain and devastation the survivors endured.

To all this turmoil, add gold rushes to the Klondike in 1896 and Fairbanks in 1902; add 40,000 prospectors who swarmed to Nome beginning in 1899. Short-lived booms brought more social turmoil while they created temporary markets for reindeer meat and freight reindeer.[40]

Wallace Olsen, my Alaska anthropology professor, reminded his students repeatedly that "Cultures do not meet; people do." American culture did not meet Alaska Native cultures; specific Americans met specific Alaska Natives. The available sources offer only glimpses into the human beings who were connected through the reindeer enterprise. There's a bit more personal information about the missionaries in government reports, enough to show that though they shared some common goals, they were personally a diverse lot. There was no "typical missionary." A few brief biographies suggest the diversity of those who devoted their careers to the "civilizing projects" of religion, education, and reindeer herding.

The missionaries were as culturally diverse as the Alaska Natives. They included John Henry Kilbuck, a Delaware Indian converted and educated by a Moravian missionary. Kilbuck married the missionary's daughter, Edith, and the Kilbucks helped found the Moravian mission in 1885 at a new town on the Lower Kuskokwim they called Bethel. Kilbuck served in Alaska as a missionary, teacher, and Superintendent of Education for the Western District until he died of typhoid in 1922.[41]

The Reverend Tollef Brevig, a Norwegian Evangelical Lutheran missionary at the Teller reindeer station, was himself an immigrant to the United States. Born in Norway, Brevig came to the United States at age ten. He graduated from Luther College and from Theological Seminary, married Julia Johnson, and in 1894 was hired as minister for the Saami herders at Teller. He became the government teacher there, and manager of the Teller reindeer herd in 1897, then returned to the U.S. where he lectured on behalf of the Alaska mission most of the time until the spring of 1900. The Brevigs returned to Teller amid the flu and measles epidemics and immediately opened an orphanage at the station. After that, the Eskimos called Reverend Brevig "Apaurak," "the Father of All," and Mrs. Brevig "Amarora," "the Mother of All."

Through most of 1903–1904 the Brevigs and two of the orphans lived at their farm in Stanwood, Washington. They returned to Teller in July

1905. Brevig's journals are peppered with concern about his wife's illnesses and those of their children, two of whom died in Alaska. Mrs. Brevig died in 1908, no doubt in part from the rigors of managing a household in the Arctic for over thirty orphans and her immediate family, while bearing seven children and burying two. Brevig took his five surviving children back to the Washington farm, then returned to Teller in 1913, with his daughter Dagny, who taught while the Norwegian Evangelical Board of Missions paid Brevig. They left for good in 1917.[42]

The local community adopted Brevig. He was allowed in the kashigi to see ceremonies not ordinarily open to Whites.[43] His opinions of his neighbors, though, were not entirely positive. He found the stench in Native homes unbearable. He consciously worked at not acting superior and sought Natives' confidence to help him win their souls. A much beloved representative of the U.S. government, Brevig was not a native-born citizen. He preached that World War I violated the spirit of the Gospel and was punishment for sin.[44]

The teachers at Cape Prince of Wales, Harrison Thornton and Thomas Lopp, suggest the importance of personality in establishing trust among the Natives they came to serve.[45] The two men applied independently to establish a contract school and founded the Congregational mission at Cape Prince of Wales in 1890. Thornton left for eight months in 1891–1892 and returned with a wife and with a new teacher, Ellen Kittredge, who married Lopp in August 1892. In an "improved and extended" curriculum, "the two ladies organized classes of Eskimo girls to receive instruction in the domestic arts."[46]

Lopp, who rivaled Jackson's influence on the reindeer project, was remembered as a quiet, peaceful man, called "Tom Gorrah," or "Tom, the Good Man." He initiated the plan to train apprentices in reindeer herding and to distribute reindeer to them. Lopp learned to speak the Native languages, and the Natives' regard for him helps explain the success of the reindeer experiment at Wales. Though Lopp represented the Congregational Church, he was not a minister and often relied on Reverend Brevig in some religious matters, though they represented different denominations.

Except for an occasional year-long furlough, Lopp worked in Alaska until 1925. He served as a missionary at Wales until 1905, except for a year when he supervised the U.S. reindeer station at Teller. From 1904 to 1909, he was superintendent of the government schools and supervisor of the reindeer stations in the Northern District. Then, from 1909 until 1925 he was Superintendent of the Alaska Division of the U.S. Bureau of

Education, with authority over all the schools and reindeer herds. He established the United States Reindeer Service and secularized the reindeer project, moving control from the mission schoolteachers to school superintendents employed by the Bureau of Education. He broke up the larger government herds and transferred some reindeer to more remote villages to get more reindeer into native hands. Lopp left Alaska in 1925 and worked for two years for the Hudson's Bay Company as reindeer expert for Baffin-Land and Norway, before he retired in 1927.[47]

Thornton's service did not last as long, nor did Thornton himself, who was much less popular than Lopp. In 1893 he won the dubious distinction of being the only missionary who Alaska Natives killed. No sources I have found explain why three Native men killed Thornton. The murder was reportedly mourned in the village, and the murderers were executed by their next of kin, following the obligation to take responsibility for the actions of their kin.[48]

Finally, Dr. Edgar Omer Campbell, who from 1901 to 1911 was the government teacher at Gambell on St. Lawrence Island. Campbell found his calling in 1892 when he attended a YMCA convention where he met "the picked young men of the West—strong, manly, vigorous, both mentally and physically, the future lawyers, doctors, merchants, ministers, manufacturers, and leading men wherever they should make their homes." He became convinced of "the manliness and need of an out-and-out life work for the Lord Jesus Christ."[49] Campbell earned his MD and spent a year at the Moody Bible Institute in Chicago before Sheldon Jackson recruited him to St. Lawrence Island in 1901. On the way to the Island, Campbell and his wife visited the Brevigs at Teller to observe the reindeer and their management.[50]

Arriving at Gambell, they rang the school bell to summon the clan leaders. "We told them," Campbell wrote, "we had come to stay with them, to live for them, and to help them in every way we could."[51] It isn't clear in what language Campbell made this introduction, or how it was received. Although officially a government teacher, and never paid by a missionary society, Campbell's chief aim was to civilize and convert heathens. He wrote: "The $1,200 offered me as a teacher to a lonely, isolated village of 250 dirty, greasy, polygamous Eskimos in Bering Sea, with only one mail a year and no companion but my wife, would never have induced me to leave the practice of my profession" but for "the opportunity to do missionary work."

Without, as far as I know, infringing upon the duties devolving upon me through my commission by the Bureau of Education, I have, as missionary and representative of the Presbyterian Board of Home Missions, treated the sick (using my own instruments, medicines, and hospital supplies), conducted an orphanage with four inmates in my own rooms, married those who were inclined, baptized the believing, buried the dead, cherished the faint, comforted the sorrowing, and preached the Gospel of Jesus Christ to all who would listen.[52]

The Campbells made the school and mission central village institutions and helped the villagers start a cooperative store in 1910. After they left in 1911, no missionaries stayed long, and many converts returned to their Native religions. By the 1920s, only one or two men were still practicing Christians. Some returned to the Church after a few men requested a missionary. By 1940 the village was about evenly split between people who practiced the old ceremonies and those who didn't.[53]

The missionaries as a group were both diverse and incredibly similar. Representing an impressive variety of backgrounds, ethnicities, educations, and denominations, they shared a common sense of mission. They believed in good works, not the Social Gospel. Some believed in a kind of reform Darwinism; most advocated individual effort and evangelical Christianity. They were certain it was their Christian duty to change the Alaska Natives, to teach that their ceremonies, marriage customs, and many subsistence and living habits were sinful and repugnant. They were certain that salvation was necessary and directed their religious teachings to rebirth after death.

To some extent they, too, changed. They adopted some Native survival practices; they were all touched by the solitude of Arctic villages. They had to learn to live there, to get wood and water, drive dog teams, hunt, fish, and run households on limited goods and inspiration. If their yearly shipments didn't make it, they, like all Arctic dwellers, had to rely on the environment and on their neighbors for material assistance, companionship, and help in emergencies. Their children grew up influenced by Native playmates, speaking Native languages. Some took up their parents' callings, like missionary daughters Ruth Kilbuck and Dagny Alaska Brevig. Some developed profound respect for Native peoples, but that did not extend to approving of Native morality, family practices, or religion.

They tried, at considerable sacrifice, to help people they thought needed them, physically, morally, and spiritually.[54]

Just as the missionaries accepted some local customs and rejected others, Alaska Natives took what they needed from the missionaries and left the rest. Which brings us, finally, back to our reindeer, last seen in 1892 on their way from Siberia to save Alaska Natives and turn them into self-sufficient nomadic herders, a nation of civilized, converted, specialized, and self-sufficient Christians. The reindeer, it turned out, were much less effective than the missionaries.

Before 1909, two major policies and rationales supported Native ownership. The reindeer were first intended as a major new subsistence source to help a starving population in an area with depleted game. After gold was discovered in Nome and elsewhere in the late 1890s, the emphasis shifted. Eskimos were not to be self-sufficient herders. Rather, they became important but subservient assistants to White development. Jackson wrote, "the Eskimo, trained as a herder or teamster, will prove valuable to the white man, and the white man, in turn, as director and employer, will be valuable to the native."[55]

That policy worked best on the Seward Peninsula, with local markets but few caribou, site of the first reindeer industrial school at Teller, and of some of the first herds loaned to missions. Apprentices were supported at the stations for two to five years, and then got a small number of reindeer and were loaned additional reindeer to start their own herds.[56] By 1904, thirty-nine Alaska Natives had completed apprenticeships; they employed sixty-one apprentices in their own herds. The government estimated, incorrectly, that at least 400 Native herders, apprentices, and their families got support from reindeer.[57] After 1908, when Jackson retired, to be replaced by Lopp in 1909, government policy emphasized greater proportionate ownership of reindeer by Eskimos, rather than the government or missions. The program control became more secular; control of reindeer passed from the missionaries to teachers, but in practice this was a distinction without a difference. Natives were not allowed to sell female reindeer to non-Natives, to prevent their herds from reproducing and growing large enough to become competitors.[58] After 1909 Natives could buy reindeer without serving apprenticeships, and Lopp emphasized more extensive Native ownership, because he feared the control of a few powerful Native families. By 1916, almost 1,300 Alaska Natives owned reindeer.[59]

In 1909 the Reindeer Service arranged for the export of reindeer meat, hides, and horns, and in 1911 the first reindeer meat left Nome for Seattle.[60]

Lopp and the Barrow teacher, Walter Shields, decided that outside markets required White interest and capital. That opportunity attracted Carl Lomen, who had come to Nome with his father Gudbrand Lomen in 1900 to take advantage of the Nome gold rush. Gudbrand Lomen, a Norwegian immigrant, had, coincidentally, attended college with Tollef Brevig. Shields helped Carl Lomen buy out a Saami herder whose contract ended in 1914. Unlike Alaska Natives, the Saami could sell female reindeer to Whites. By 1929, the Lomens had bought over 14,000 reindeer from Saami and from the Golovin and Teller missions.[61]

The Lomens quickly worked to dominate the commercial reindeer market, building cold storage facilities and working to generate markets for reindeer meat and bi-products in the Lower 48. Within two years, Carl Lomen had organized Lomen Reindeer and Trading Company, which owned 40,000 reindeer and had over $1.5 million in stock. The Lomens hired some Natives to work with their herds and promised to focus on the export market, leaving the local markets for Native owners. By then, the gold excitement had passed and there was virtually no local market to exploit.[62]

The Lomens' commercial control of the reindeer markets may have influenced Thomas Lopp by the 1920s to change the emphasis on Native ownership of small herds and instead to encourage the consolidation of native reindeer into cooperatively managed or "corporate" herds.[63] By then, both the Native owners and their reindeer were adjusting to yet more difficult challenges. The 1918–1919 influenza epidemic had again devastated the Native populations, the local market for reindeer had virtually evaporated, and the reindeer themselves were running out of range to graze as their numbers increased.

The highest estimates placed 640,000 reindeer in Alaska in 1930; that number was probably inflated. Only 250,000 were counted in 1940, which plummeted to 2,500 in 1950. By 2003 there was a modest recovery to 15,000.[64] Many reasons are posited for the decline: overstocked ranges, lack of close-herding, predators, and wholesale losses to migrating caribou.

Part of the answer can be found in changing patterns of ownership. I focused on the individual herds Eskimos owned through 1911, especially herds established by 1905, when the government published brief biographies of some of the herders and apprentices. I combined herd histories with all I could learn about their owners: how they managed their herds; relationships with family, mission, and home village; their responses to American religion and education. This information is incomplete, and suggestive at best. There was no information for some apprentices in 1905, nor for many owners after that. Each official reported different information and probably over-represented the herders most influenced by the missionaries. With these caveats, what I could learn about fifty-four Native owners provided a window into different strategies employed to manage the reindeer and incorporate them into Native subsistence and economies.

Because the data are incomplete, each figure about the fifty-four herders should be preceded by "at least." At least twenty-three of the fifty-four (43 percent) were involved in a family reindeer operation; at least fifteen (28 percent) had other people managing their herds at least part of the time; six (11 percent) were fairly certainly oomaliks; three (6 percent) were children of oomaliks. At least twenty-three (43 percent) were married; eleven (20 percent) had living children; fifteen (28 percent) supported immediate family; nineteen (35 percent) supported extended families. In a period marked by disastrous epidemics, seven (13 percent) inherited their reindeer from a parent; three (6 percent) from husbands. At least eighteen (33 percent) performed some money-making activity; at least eight (15 percent) engaged in subsistence activities like hunting or fishing; thirteen (24 percent) worked for the government or a mission. At least five (9 percent) were Christians; two (4 percent) were definitely not Christians; two (4 percent) were orphans for whom the missionaries had cared; and three (6 percent) were married women for whom they had cared. Five (9 percent) died before 1905. Forty (74 percent) stayed in the reindeer business after 1905; four (7 percent) may have had family connected with reindeer after 1945.

These incomplete figures suggest that reindeer were incorporated into the Native Alaska economy much as other subsistence animals had been—through enterprises comprised of extended kin, often headed by an oomalik already established by skill, kin support, and generosity. I found at least nine discernible extended family herding groups who kept and owned reindeer together, and groups of wealthy men who owned reindeer and supported non-kin as apprentices for their herds. These groups involved thirty-six, or two-thirds of the fifty-four owners.[65]

It is likely that all owners were also involved in traditional subsistence. It does not take very sophisticated math to know that other food sources were needed. An adult reindeer weighs at most 250 pounds, much of which is bone.[66] A man accustomed to eating over five pounds of meat a day would eat at least ten to twenty adult reindeer a year. If he were supporting a family, he might have to kill most of his herd to feed them, too. Most estimates suggest that it would take from 1,000 to 2,000 reindeer to support a family, but that would not allow for supplying village needs, an essential obligation in Native villages.[67] In 1905 the largest herds had fewer than 400 reindeer; most people owned fewer than fifty.[68] Only one herd in 1911 exceeded 1,000 reindeer.[69] Clearly, if reindeer owners were supporting entire extended families, they weren't doing it on reindeer alone. They all needed some other form of support: traditional foods; wages earned as a government or mission herder, teamster, or mail carrier; independent commercial activity like freighting or selling meat and hides; support from kin; or partial support from a reindeer station during apprenticeship.

The herd sample suggests four broad patterns of reindeer involvement: owners who used reindeer as one resource to buttress their leadership positions; those who herded reindeer as their contribution to supporting extended kin; orphans dependent on the missionaries who supervised the reindeer enterprises; and owners who became government employees and remained primarily tied to the reindeer enterprise.

The first group used their reindeer as oomaliks used other resources: to extend wealth and to offer greater generosity to kin and community. Oomaliks' statuses were more secure the greater their sources of wealth. Their reindeer helped consolidate their positions of leadership. But reindeer alone could not make an oomalik. Far from making specialized herders of Eskimos, reindeer became one more resource for Native leaders. Two men, Takpuk and Charlie Antisarlook, exemplified this pattern.

To dispel doubts among Natives that they would ever get their own reindeer, in 1895 the government loaned a herd of about 100 reindeer to Charlie Antisarlook, who was well respected from Wales to Cape Nome, and who joined the Teller herd in 1894.[70] Antisarlook died in the 1900 measles epidemic, and his widow, Mary Antisarlook, inherited 379 reindeer. Known as "Reindeer Mary," her 404 reindeer constituted one of the largest herds in 1911.[71] The Antisarlook herd extended through a wide network of kin. In 1900 six kin, including the widow of Charlie's brother, kept reindeer with Mary Antisarlook's herd. Charlie Antisarlook's nephews, Sagoonick and Anikravinik, herded for her. In 1911 the family herd included Simon Sagoonick's sixty-seven reindeer, Fred Anikravinik's 101, Charlie's brother Angolook's 132, and 106 that belonged to another brother.[72] Mary Antisarlook eventually remarried but managed her herd and shared its benefits widely with family and friends. Though childless, she raised at least ten children. In January 1939, inflated records numbered her reindeer at 5,000; in 1945 she owned only 234, but still owned reindeer in 1951.[73] She earned some profits selling sled reindeer to Nome miners.[74] Sagoonick carried the mail between Unalakleet and Kaltag for a time.[75] Koktoak, Charlie Antisarlook's younger brother, freighted awhile for miners, but the herd was never the sole means of support for any of the family.[76] They prospected at Nome, went sealing and whaling, and various apprentices and Lapp herders cared for the herd at times.[77] A final fact about Charlie Antisarlook. Not only was he an oomalik helping a large extended family; he was a shaman as well. Brevig reported in the Teller station log, "The leading shaman had a confab with the spirits to-night.... Four new doctors were with him, guarding the fires; Charley was one of them."[78] Charlie Antisarlook, like an unknown number of the apprentices, never converted to Christianity. It would be consistent with Yup'ik and Inupiaq values of non-aggression and conflict avoidance not to disagree openly with a missionary, but simply to do what was necessary to live at a reindeer station, without relinquishing traditional values and spiritual practices.

Takpuk, the second successful oomalik owner, began his apprenticeship at Barrow in 1898. By 1911 he owned 161 reindeer. He combined his herd with that of his adopted son, Panigeo, who cared for his own reindeer, his father's, and the reindeer that belonged to James Brower, the son of local trader Charles Brower and his Inupiaq wife. "Tommy Brower" owned an estimated 1,250 reindeer at Point Barrow in 1948.[79] Takpuk owned a frame house, supported his family, a large whaling crew, and a workforce of men who trapped for him. He helped the Barrow missionary supervise the local reindeer. In 1909 the Barrow teacher reported that one of his most promising students married the daughter of "our richest Native, Takpuk, who has somewhere around $14,000 worth of whalebone in the storehouse this year, and is our biggest reindeer owner." Of the thirteen whales caught at Barrow that year, Takpuk's crew caught four.[80] Perhaps Takpuk wanted reindeer to increase his sources of wealth; perhaps he accepted them and helped the Barrow missionary and trader because they could provide access to other resources useful to his village and kin.[81]

The second group of owners were people who herded to contribute to the support of an extended family group, who received help from kin for taking that responsibility, and who might be relieved from time to time to do other things. Takpuk's son, Panigeo, and the apprentices who cared for Mary Antisarlook's herd, exemplify this pattern. At Cape Prince of Wales and on St. Lawrence Island, families enrolled young boys in the apprenticeship program, planning for them to contribute support to their family, or, on St. Lawrence Island, their clan. Those two herds were among the most successful and most integral to their village economies, so this herding strategy seems significant, especially since the two villages were dissimilar in other respects.[82]

The third group consisted of orphans who came under strong mission influence, and who were most dependent on the missionaries for education, identity, and support. This pattern was most common where kin support was least dependable, as was the case in the new settlements at Teller and Bethel, and places especially hard hit by the 1900 measles epidemic. Several of the Teller herders had close ties to the Brevig family, especially Ablikak, son of an apprentice who died in the 1900 epidemic, leaving seventy-five reindeer. His widow gave Brevig her twelve-year-old son to raise, and the reindeer as well. Ablikak lived with the Brevigs, accompanied them to Washington for two years, then returned to Washington in 1905 to attend parochial school. His herd increased steadily, though he did little to manage it. In 1911, when he was twenty-three years old, he owned 420 reindeer, one of the largest herds in Alaska.[83] Mission support and the chance to earn reindeer offered extraordinary assistance and access to a comfortable living for youngsters who had no kin and were therefore poor.

The final group consisted of government employees hired to supervise herds, who remained tied to the reindeer enterprise. There is much less personal information available about them or how the reindeer affected them. Their fortunes changed considerably after 1909, when herd supervisors began being paid in reindeer rather than in cash or supplies. The number of apprentices fell then, and it is likely that the supervisors' herds were not large enough to support apprentices.

Before 1910, a few Alaska Natives got most of their support from work with reindeer. After herd supervisors began receiving pay in reindeer rather than currency, fewer people wanted the jobs, and there was less opportunity for government work than when the industry was new.[84] This pattern emphasizes that a specialist in the Arctic needed to be tied to an outside agency for support. There weren't many jobs for reindeer specialists, nor many ways to subsist on reindeer alone.

Instead of becoming reindeer specialists, the Native owners used reindeer to supplement and stabilize existing food supplies, following a basic rule of Arctic survival: never depend on a single food source. Reindeer themselves were subject to unpredictable disease and problems of winter pasturage. Few people could devote all their energy to a supplementary activity, so herd owners needed the support of kin or an outside agency. Mission and government personnel complained that the herders wouldn't spend all their time with the herd and consider it their home. Most remained excursionists with strong ties to villages and kin. Reindeer herding did not necessarily, or usually, change fundamental Native values and practices. The major exceptions were orphans raised at missions, who in a sense followed the tradition of respecting those who extended generosity and cared for them.

The reindeer never became a primary food, but were rather a new source of necessary goods, especially hides. As the inland caribou hunters moved to the northern coast, and as the Seward Peninsula caribou disappeared, reindeer became a new source of caribou products. The St. Lawrence Island herd allowed the Natives there to stop trading with the Siberians, whom they greatly feared.

St. Lawrence, too, illustrates a final point: success with reindeer usually operated separately from the other cornerstones of Jackson's civilization plan. As elsewhere in the 1920s, ownership changed in 1923 from individuals to a communal joint stock company. A chief herder supervised the operation. Teenage boys worked as replacement herders and remembered the camps as "lot of fun." The three annual reindeer roundups were major social events. The Reindeer Company merged with the Gambell and Savoonga stores on the Island to form a single cooperative; in 1925 there were 4,629 shares of reindeer stock, and shareholders could claim a ten percent annual dividend, or one reindeer for each ten shares. As elsewhere, the herd began to decline by the 1940s. There was no herding for at least five years: the range was overgrazed, and the animals starved. St. Lawrence Island, unlike the mainland, had no ready access to markets, and no caribou, so its herds didn't run off with wild reindeer. And, despite Jackson's dreams for his "5 R's", the period of greatest reindeer success came in the 1920s and 1930s, after most of the Natives had left the Church.[85]

The 1920s were also a turning point on the mainland. Many established owners died in the 1918 flu epidemic. Mining declined, most Whites left, and the local markets shrank. Because the Lomens controlled the export trade, they began buying reindeer at their trading posts on the Seward Peninsula, which functioned like company stores. By 1933, reindeer owners owed the Lomens $45,000, and the Lomens began offering $2 a reindeer to liquidate the debts.[86] By the 1930s, fur trapping was more profitable than reindeer, and more compatible with seasonal subsistence rounds. The reindeer exceeded the carrying capacity of the range, and

Natives began using them for trap bait. In 1937, when the Reindeer Act restricted ownership of domestic reindeer to Alaska Natives, it became clear that there had been large losses or wildly inflated herd estimates on the books of the Native ownership associations.[87]

The reindeer could be incorporated into traditional subsistence arrangements but could not easily transform them. They succeeded best when they were incorporated into extended kin operations and declined after the decision to undermine the powerful reindeer families. As part of a kin network, a herder could leave the reindeer and participate in village life and other activities. After the responsibility passed to hired herders with no other stake in the animals, the herders sometimes abandoned the herds, which was when large losses occurred.

Success in herding, as in all else, required kin support and generosity. Oomaliks did a better job with reindeer than the joint stock companies did. Most of the Native owners remained Yup'ik or Inupiaq first, responsible to kin and the village community. Most of the missionaries left Alaska. The reindeer owners maintained their herds only so long as they served their basic obligations to village and kin. Many reindeer became good Alaskans—they followed the pull of kinship to join their wild caribou cousins.

NOTES

I spent several weeks during 1972 in Nulato, an Athabascan village on the lower Yukon River, visiting a friend who served there in the Teacher Corps. I am grateful to the people of Nulato for their hospitality and for the opportunity briefly to experience winter in a bush village. This essay is excerpted from a much longer, 210–page study submitted in fulfillment of a degree requirement for the University of Michigan Program in American Culture. I did the primary research during the summer of 1972, when I studied Alaska anthropology and history at the University of Alaska, Fairbanks. It owes a great deal to my anthropology professor, Dr. Wallace Olsen, and to Dr. Herman Slotnick, my professor in History of Alaska. I was fortunate, as well, to learn from Alaska Native students at the U of A, and from members of the distinguished Anthropology Department at the University of Michigan, particularly Mick Taussig, my Social Anthropology professor, who supported my sojourn in Nulato in the middle of his course, and Joseph Jorgenson, who read my paper and offered comments. I'm grateful to all, none of whom are responsible for my work. I'm grateful, too, to John Heaton, who invited me to speak at the University of Alaska, Fairbanks in 2019, for the opportunity to revisit Fairbanks and for his gracious hospitality.

Additional Sources: Most of the literature on Alaska reindeer concerns the reindeer themselves. Much less has addressed the social agenda that brought them to Alaska or the human and social outcomes of the reindeer project. A good example is David R. Klein, "The Introduction, Increase, and Crash of Reindeer on St. Matthew Island," *The Journal of*

Wildlife Management 32:2 (April 1968): 350-67. The most important recent contribution to that literature was published just months before my 2007 lecture: Roxanne Willis, "A New Game in the North: Alaska Native Reindeer Herding, 1890-1940," *Western Historical Quarterly* 37:3 (Autumn 2006): 277-301. I cite it in this article but do not highlight Willis's analysis of the increasing economic power of the Lomen family in the marketing and capitalist control of the reindeer. Sveta Yamin-Pasternak and Igor Pasternak, "Cooking and Commensality Along the Bering Food Bridge," *Études Inuit Studies* 45:1-2 (2021), 259-82, records a story from Savoonga, Alaska, on St. Lawrence Island, that indicates that reindeer fat and reindeer meat remain a part of the local diet. Apparently, there are still reindeer on the Island, and they remain a part of the diet there (260-61). The article does not address how the reindeer are owned or managed.

1   The preferred term for the indigenous people of Alaska is Alaska Native, or simply Native.
2   For more on Jackson's career, see John Thomson Faris, *The Alaskan Pathfinder: The Story of Sheldon Jackson* (New York: F. H. Revell, 1926); Robert Stewart, *Sheldon Jackson: Pathfinder and Prospector of the Missionary Vanguard in the Rocky Mountains and Alaska* (New York: Fleming H. Revell Company, 2nd ed. 1908); J. Arthur Lazell, *Alaskan Apostle: The Life Story of Sheldon Jackson* (New York: Harper, 1960); Norman J. Bender, *Winning the West for Christ: Sheldon Jackson and Presbyterianism on the Rocky Mountain Frontier, 1869-1880* (Albuquerque: University of New Mexico Press, 1996); Karl Ward and Karl Wood, "A Study of the Introduction of Reindeer into Alaska," *Journal of the Presbyterian Historical Society* 33:4 (December 1955): 229-37; Karl Ward, "A Study of the Introduction of Reindeer into Alaska—II," *Journal of the Presbyterian Historical Society* 34:4 (December 1956): 245-56.
3   The Organic Act of 1884 provided for an appointed governor and a U.S. federal district court. Class notes, History 341, Alaskan History, Professor Herman Slotnick, University of Alaska, Fairbanks, summer, 1972; Claus M. Naske and Herman E. Slotnick, eds., *Alaska: A History of the 49th State* (Norman: University of Oklahoma Press, 1987), 73; Stephen W. Haycox and Mary Childers Mangusso, eds., *Alaska Anthology: Interpreting the Past* (Seattle: University of Washington Press, 1996), xxii. In 1905, Alaska became a territory and gained a Congressional Delegate; the 1912 Second Organic Act created a territorial legislature with sharply restricted power. For a readable introduction to these periods of Alaska history, see Ernest Gruening, *The State of Alaska* (New York: Random House, 1957), chaps. 2 through 5.
4   Preferred ethnic terms change historically. When I was in Alaska in 1972, the preferred terms were Inuit and Yuit; Eskimo was not considered a racial insult, as it is in Canada. In my 2007 lecture, I used Yuit and Inuit. In 1977, delegates to the Inuit Circumpolar Conference officially rejected the term "Eskimo" and adopted "Inupiaq" as their preferred designation. Unlike the Arctic Peoples of Canada and Greenland, Alaskan Natives have continued to use "Eskimo" rather than "Inupiaq," in both written and oral language. Here I have used the terms preferred on the website of the Alaska Federation of Natives, https://www.nativefederation.org/, accessed August 9, 2021. I also sometimes use Natives or Alaska Natives to connote, in this case, Yup'ik, Inupiaq, and Yupik. I use Eskimo at times to connote all three groups and because it was a term in common use in the period of this study. It was the common form of self-reference in 1972, when I was in Alaska, and continues in common usage.
5   In American slang, the "Three R's," which constitute the building blocks of education, are reading, 'riting, and 'rithmetic. Add religion and reindeer, and you have the Five R's.
6   The suffix "miut" or "mete" means "of" or "from" some place.
7   Margaret Lantis, "Introduction of Reindeer Herding to the Natives of Alaska," in *Human Problems in Technological Change*, ed. Edward H. Spicer (New York: Russell Sage Foundation, 1952), 127-48.

8   Wendell H. Oswalt, *Alaskan Eskimos* (San Francisco: Chandler Publishing Company, 1967), xii; Charles Campbell Hughes, *An Eskimo Village in the Modern World* (Ithaca: Cornell University Press, 1960), 1.

9   See Hughes, *An Eskimo Village*, 102-7, 115-17, 131; James W. Vanstone, *Point Hope: An Eskimo Village in Transition* (Seattle: University of Washington Press, 1962), 40-57; Robert F. Spencer, *The North Alaskan Eskimo: A Study in Ecology and Society* (Washington, DC: Government Printing Office, 1959), 177-82.

10 Vanstone, *Point Hope*, 28-64; Spencer, *The North Alaskan Eskimo*, 26; Sheldon Jackson, *Thirteenth Annual Report on the Introduction of Domestic Reindeer into Alaska* (Washington: Government Printing Office, 1904), 112-13. (This report and all others will, after the first citation, be called by the year of the report, i.e., "1904 Report"; when that year differs from the publication year, the reference is to the year the report was submitted).

11 Wendell Oswalt, *Mission of Change in Alaska* (San Bernardino, CA: The Huntington Library, 1963), 117-27.

12 Spencer, *The North Alaskan Eskimo*, 33.

13 Spencer, *The North Alaskan Eskimo*, 142-43; Vanstone, *Point Hope*, 69.

14 Charles D. Brower, *Fifty Years Below Zero* (London: Robert Hale, 1942), 184.

15 Spencer, *The North Alaskan Eskimo*, 38.

16 Spencer, *The North Alaskan Eskimo*, 147-58, 171-81; Hughes, *An Eskimo Village*, 103-6; Vanstone, *Point Hope*, 38-58.

17 For marriage practices, see Spencer, *The North Alaskan Eskimo*, 44, 77-79, 84-85, 87; Hughes, *An Eskimo Village*, 38, 245; Vanstone, *Point Hope*, 77; Oswalt, *Mission of Change*, 139; Harrison Robertson Thornton, *Among the Eskimos of Wales, Alaska, 1890-93*; edited and annotated by Neda S. Thornton and William H. Thornton, Jr. (Baltimore: The Johns Hopkins University Press, 1931), 100, 107.

18 Throughout most Alaskan Inupiaq and Yu'pik communities, but not on St. Lawrence Island, the men's house was an important village institution, variously called kashim, kaszgi, kashigi, karigi, etc., depending on the locality. These were centers of male activity, where boys learned skills and were initiated into male roles. On the lower Kuskokwim, the men lived in the kashigi, moving in when they were about twelve years old; an orphan might move in earlier. Men might visit their wives and children during the day and might leave the kashigi late at night to sleep with their wives, returning in early morning. A household usually consisted of a maternal line of women and male children under twelve. See Spencer, *The North Alaskan Eskimo*, 44 and Oswalt, *Mission of Change*, 51-58, 135-39.

19 Sheldon Jackson, *Report on Education in Alaska* (Washington, DC: Government Printing Office, 1886), 22-23.

20 Sheldon Jackson, *Report on Education in Alaska*, 30.

21 Sheldon Jackson, *Report on Education in Alaska*, 30-31.

22 Sheldon Jackson, *Introduction of Reindeer Into Alaska: Preliminary Report of the General Agent of Education for Alaska to the Commissioner of Education, 1890* (Washington, DC: Government Printing Office, 1891), 9-10, 13-14 (hereinafter "1890 Report"). For press support of the project based on Darwinian theory and the ladder of civilization model, see Ward, "Introduction of Reindeer into Alaska—II", 250.

23 Sheldon Jackson, *Introduction of Domestic Reindeer Into Alaska 1893* (Washington, D.C.: Government Printing Office, 1893), 16.

24 1890 Report, 6, 27.

25 Sheldon Jackson, *Report on Introduction of Domestic Reindeer Into Alaska 1895* (Washington, DC: Government Printing Office, 1896), 13.
26 Sheldon Jackson, *Fifteenth Annual Report on Introduction of Domestic Reindeer into Alaska, 1905* (Washington, DC: Government Printing Office, 1906), 8, 10–11.
27 Sheldon Jackson, *Report on Introduction of Domestic Reindeer into Alaska, 1897* (Washington, DC: Government Printing Office, 1898), 10; *Report on Introduction of Domestic Reindeer into Alaska, 1898* (Washington, D.C.: Government Printing Office, 1898), 14; *Report on Introduction of Domestic Reindeer into Alaska, 1899* (Washington, DC: Government Printing Office, 1900), 11; Dean F. Olson, *Alaska Reindeer Herdsmen: A Study of Native Management in Transition* (College, AK: Institute of Social, Economic and Government Research, University of Alaska, 1969), 10–11.
28 1886 Report, 30.
29 1886 Report, 34.
30 Sheldon Jackson, *Report on Introduction of Domestic Reindeer into Alaska, 1894* (Washington, DC: Government Printing Office, 1895), 14.
31 Sheldon Jackson, *Twelfth Annual Report on Introduction of Domestic Reindeer into Alaska, 1902* (Washington, DC: Government Printing Office, 1903), 24.
32 There is a North Pole, Alaska, a small community in the Fairbanks North Star Borough.
33 1902 Report, 13.
34 Hughes, *An Eskimo Village*, 143.
35 1898 Report, 95.
36 Class Notes, Wallace Olsen, Anthropology 341, University of Alaska, Fairbanks, August 1, 1972; Vanstone, *Point Hope*, 21. Baleen imports into San Francisco for selected years were: 1885, 441,400 pounds; 1887, 561,694 pounds; 1889, 291,400 pounds; 1901, 76,550 pounds; 1904, 102,000 pounds; 1905, 38,200 pounds; Vanstone, *Point Hope*, 24.
37 Spencer, *The North Alaskan Eskimo*, 18.
38 Vanstone, *Point Hope*, 18.
39 Vanstone, *Point Hope*, 24; Brower, *Fifty Years Below Zero*, 187–88; Oswalt, *Mission of Change*, 48, 83–84; Sheldon Jackson, *Tenth Annual Report on Introduction of Domestic Reindeer into Alaska 1900* (Washington, DC: Government Printing Office, 1901), 9–10. For accounts of other epidemics, see United States Bureau of Education Alaska School Service, *Report on Education of the Natives of Alaska and the Reindeer Service, 1910–11* (Washington, DC: Government Printing Office, 1912), 10; 1904 Report, 103; Thornton, *Among the Eskimos of Wales, Alaska*, 25.
40 See for instance Spencer, *The North Alaskan Eskimo*, 26, 38, 71.
41 Oswalt, *Mission of Change*, 22, 37, 85; 1904 Report, 17; United States Department of Education, *Report on Education in Alaska, 1908–1909* (Washington, DC: Government Printing Office, 1910), 1348.
42 Dr. J. Walter Johnshoy, *Apaurak in Alaska: Social Pioneering Among the Eskimos* (translated and compiled from the records of Reverend Tollef L. Brevig, "Pioneer Missionary to the Eskimos of Alaska from 1894–17") (Philadelphia: Dorrance & Company, 1944), 62, 97, 323–34.
43 Dr. J. Walter Johnshoy, *Apaurak in Alaska*, 69.
44 Dr. J. Walter Johnshoy, *Apaurak in Alaska*, 76, 79, 82, 108–9, 122, 128, 143, 205, 293; 1903 Report, 45.
45 William Thomas Lopp was called Tom or Thomas during his time in Alaska. He sometimes submitted reports as W. T. Lopp. I have chosen to call him Thomas Lopp, as he was known by the Natives he served, and in recognition of their name for him, "Tom

Gorrah—Tom, the Good Man." Roxanne Willis refers to Lopp as William Lopp in, "A New Game in the North: Alaska Native Reindeer Herding, 1890-1940," *Western Historical Quarterly* 37:3 (Autumn 2006): 277-301. They are the same person.

46   Johnshoy, *Apaurak in Alaska*, 45; Thornton, *Among the Eskimos of Wales, Alaska*, vii–xiv, xi, xvii–xix.
47   1906 Report, 56-8; Thornton, *Among the Eskimos of Wales, Alaska*, xix–xx.
48   Johnshoy, *Apaurak in Alaska*, 45, 48; Thornton, *Among the Eskimos of Wales, Alaska*, xxv.
49   "Annual Report of Gambell Reindeer Station," in 1902 Report, 67–87.
50   "Annual Report of Gambell Reindeer Station," 68; 1903 Report, 77; "Annual Report of Gambell Reindeer Station," in 1902 Report, 173.
51   "Annual Report of Gambell Reindeer Station," 173.
52   1906 Report, 64.
53   Hughes, *An Eskimo Village*, 312–13, 323–24.
54   1908-1909 Report, x–xi; 1903 Report, 98, letter dated October 5, 1903; Johnshoy, *Apaurak in Alaska*, 126; 1903 Report 112, 114, and 119; 1896 Report, 47; Report of J. C. Widstead, Superintendent, Teller Reindeer Station, June 30, 1896, in 1896 Report.
55   1903 Report, 21; see also statement of Sheldon Jackson in 1904 Report, 14–15.
56   1895 Report, 67.
57   1904 Report, 16.
58   See 1906 Report, 14–41, 76; Report of W.T. Lopp on "Education of Natives of Alaska, United States Bureau of Education," *Report of the Commissioner of Education for the Year Ended June 13, 1913* (Washington, DC: Government Printing Office, 1914), 632–42.
59   1908–09 Report, 1322–26; United States Bureau of Education, *Report on the Work of the Bureau of Education for the Natives of Alaska, 1915-1916* (Washington, DC: Government Printing Office, 1917), 18.
60   United States Bureau of Education, *Report on Education of Natives of Alaska and the Reindeer Service, 1910–11* (Washington, DC: Government Printing Office, 1912), 24.
61   See Carl J. Lomen, *Fifty Years in Alaska* (New York: David McKay Company, 1954), 24; Olson, *Alaska Reindeer Herdsmen*, 13.
62   Lomen, *Fifty Years in Alaska*, 90. For more on the Lomens' control of the reindeer industry, see Willis, "A New Game in the North," esp. 293-99.
63   For more, see Willis, "A New Game in the North," 295.
64   Olson, *Alaska Reindeer Herdsmen*, v, 14–16.
65   Compiled from Sheldon Jackson, *Fifteenth Annual Report on Introduction of Domestic Reindeer into Alaska, 1905* (Washington, DC: U.S. Government Printing Office, 1906), 12, 20–34.
66   1903 Report, 53.
67   Olson, *Alaska Reindeer Herdsmen*, 119–21.
68   Compiled from Herd Records, 1905 Report, 20–22.
69   Compiled from Herd Records, 1910–1911 Report, 81–91.
70   1894 Report, 14–15, 46, 67; 1896 Report, 14.
71   Olson, *Alaska Reindeer Herdsmen*, 23.
72   Note the missionary influence on names, using a person's Native birth name for a surname, and assigning an English name for a first name.
73   1905 Report, 25.
74   1903 Report, 29.

75 1905 Report, 32.
76 1905 Report, 29.
77 1905 Report, 29, Brower, *Fifty Years Below Zero*, 177; 1895 Report, 120, 123–24; 1896 Report, 54–55.
78 1895 Report, 111.
79 Olson, *Alaska Reindeer Herdsmen*, 70.
80 1903 Report, 58; 1908–1909 Report, III–IV.
81 I am grateful to Dr. Josephine Smart who made this observation in the discussion following my lecture.
82 For the St. Lawrence Island herd, see 1900 Report, 17, 37; 1905 Report, 28, 32; 1902 Report, 80, 131; 1903 Report, 731; 1904 Report, 88; for Cape Prince of Wales, see 1905 Report, 27–29, 31, 33; 1908–1909, LIX; Olson, *Alaska Reindeer Herdsmen*, 71–73; 1902 Report, 61; 1896 Report, 100; 1899 Report, 109; 1903 Report, 65.
83 Johnshoy, *Apaurak in Alaska*, 152–53, 226; 1900 Report, 144; 1905 Report, 24.
84 Spencer, *The North Alaskan Eskimo*, 252–55, 299–306, 310–13; Hughes, *An Eskimo Village*, 65–70.
85 Oswalt, *Mission of Change*, 25–29, 35–36, 65–70, 75–77.
86 Oswalt, *Mission of Change*, 20–22, 24, 37.
87 Olson, *Alaska Reindeer Herdsmen*, 48–49, 65, 88.

Bridging: 2008–2011

The lectures from 2008–2011 covered a wide swath of history—1960s urban race riots, a coal miners' strike, and single women homesteaders in late-19th-century North Dakota. Together, they represented the key social relationships of race, class, and gender. In distinct ways, they bridged into new territories for my lectures—the history of race and contemporary racism, public history, and gender in transnational history.

My 2008 lecture focused on the race riots that erupted in cities throughout the United States during the summer of 1967. In more than one sense it covered old ground. In 1967 I had worked as a research assistant at the National Advisory Commission on Civil Disorders, popularly called the Kerner Commission for the Commission Chairman, Illinois Governor Otto Kerner. Established by President Lyndon B. Johnson to investigate the riots, the Commission released its report in March 1968, famously suggesting that racial inequality created the conditions for the riots. The fortieth anniversary of the Commission report invited a retrospective reflection on the riots and their interpretation. The more immediate powerful context was then-Senator Barack Obama's campaign for the Democratic presidential nomination, the first presidential bid by an African American that appeared to have substantial chance of success. Inevitably, race was an issue in the Obama campaign, sometimes overt, always an unspoken subtext that continued throughout his presidency. I had found that Canadians were sometimes unsure how to ask me about the underlying racial politics of the election, for fear it might be a difficult subject. The lecture allowed me to address some unvoiced questions.

My 2009 lecture bridged a different divide, between academic scholarship and public history. I spoke again about a Colorado miners' strike. This one occurred a decade after the Cripple Creek strike of 1903–1904 that I discussed in 2002, and it involved coal miners, not the gold miners of my own research. In 1913–1914 coal miners struck three large coal companies in southern Colorado and were evicted from their company housing. They established tent colonies on land that their union, the United Mine Workers of America (UMWA), had leased, anticipating the evictions. The strike is best known for its horrific climax, when the Colorado National Guard shot into the Ludlow tent colony and then set it on fire, killing women and children as well as striking miners, an event known as the Ludlow Massacre. The UMWA bought the tent colony site and erected a monument to the dead, represented by statues of a miner and a woman holding a baby.

I knew the history of the Ludlow Massacre but became personally involved with it after May 2003, when someone vandalized the monument, decapitating the male figure and severing the woman's arm. The UMWA vowed to restore the monument, and the Labor and Working Class History Association (LAWCHA) promised to seek National Historic Landmark (NHL) status for the Ludlow site. At the time, I served on the LAWCHA board of directors. In January 2004, LAWCHA President James Green asked me to co-chair a committee to secure NHL designation for the Ludlow site. My 2009 lecture covered the strike itself, and the five-year odyssey working to win the NHL designation. I lectured that year shortly before I spoke at the official NHL plaquing ceremony at the annual Ludlow Memorial Commemoration.

Winning National Historic Landmark designation had required extensive coordination, negotiation, and translation among a committee of labor historians, the UMWA leadership, Colorado politicians, local stakeholders, U.S. Park Service personnel who would interpret the site, and the U.S. Department of the Interior and its site selection criteria. A challenging and rewarding project, it required diplomacy as well as scholarship and provided a textbook introduction to bridging academic, political, and public interests.

Another research leave in 2009–2010 created a one-year pause in my lectures. Having dealt with race and class in my two previous presentations, it seemed appropriate in 2011 to consider gender. Race, class, and gender operate together in most social relationships, in concert with other perceived social differences—religion, age, sexuality, and many others. These three lectures provided lenses into the intersections of race, class, and gender in three historical contexts, extending the focus on those intersections I had begun with my Cripple Creek research in the 1970s. In 2011, I was happy to turn from race riots and violent strikes to women homesteaders, to remember that most Americans are not violent and lead prosaic, even dull, daily lives. I spoke from a work in progress that probed what difference the 49th Parallel had meant for women, focusing on single Canadian, American, and Norwegian women who claimed North Dakota homesteads. The project followed 121 women whose lives bridged the boundaries of nations and gender to claim homesteads near the Canada-U.S. border. My lecture was based on the homestead claim files of every woman who won title to her own land during the first decade that the Devils Lake, North Dakota, Land Office operated, from 1883–1893.[1] That project has so far expanded to include 773 women who gained title to their claims by 1903; a portion of that research appears in my 2016 lecture.

That "to be continued" aspect of ongoing research leads back to my 2008 lecture, which more than any other demands a postscript.

* * *

One of the challenges of an ongoing conversation between past and present is that it is ongoing. I chose, for the most part, to maintain my 2008 perspective as I prepared my lecture for this volume. But the long history of racial injustice in the United States predated 1967 and did not end then, or in 2008, or as I revised my lecture for publication, or the moment I sent it off to be published. By the fiftieth anniversary of the Kerner Commission report in 2018, the racism and poverty that the Commission named as chief causes of the 1967 riots remained pervasive problems according to "Healing our Divided Society," a report released by the Milton S. Eisenhower Foundation, which has continued to study, fund, and advocate for efforts cited in the Kerner report. Its 2018 report acknowledged progress in closing economic, social, and political gaps among U.S. racial groups, and significant growth of African American and Hispanic middle classes. And, of course, the United States had twice elected Barack Obama president. But, the report continued, since the 1960s an increasing proportion of American children lived in poverty, income inequality and the wealth gap among classes had widened, and residential and school segregation had again increased.[2]

I concluded my lecture in 2008 by noting that despite continued poverty, racism, and widening class inequality, no one was rioting that year. It was a special moment, as the nation witnessed the ultimately successful Obama presidential campaign. The Obama presidency fueled African American hope and rising aspirations. It also energized a White backlash. Protests, demonstrations, and some riots have occurred since 2008, often sparked, like those in 1967, by excessive police force. A list of only a few of the better-known assaults and deaths since 2008 includes: Oscar Grant, killed in Oakland, California, by a Bay Area Rapid Transit police officer New Years Day, 2009; Eric Garner, choked to death by a New York City police officer July 17, 2014; Michael Brown, fatally shot by a Ferguson, Missouri, police officer August 9, 2014; Laquan McDonald, dead in a Chicago police shooting October 20, 2014; Tamir Rice, age 12, shot to death by Cleveland police November 22, 2014, who mistook his toy gun for a real one; Freddie Gray, killed by Baltimore police April 12, 2015; Sandra Bland, hanged in a Waller County, Texas, jail cell July 13, 2015, three days after her arrest on the pretext of a traffic violation; Philando Castile, fatally shot during a traffic stop in a Saint Paul, Minnesota suburb, July 6, 2016; Stephon Clark, killed March 18, 2018, by Sacramento police who mistook his cell phone for a gun; Anton Black who died September 15, 2018, under the weight of three Greensboro, Maryland, police officers; Atatiana Jefferson, killed October 12, 2019, by Fort Worth police officers who shot through her window after a neighbor reported that her door was open; Breonna Taylor, killed March 13, 2020 when police broke into her Louisville apartment; George Floyd, suffocated May 25, 2020 by Minneapolis police officer Derek Chauvin; Daunte Wright, fatally shot April 11, 2021 by a Brooklyn Center, Minnesota, police officer during a traffic stop. At least twenty-three more unarmed African Americans were shot and killed by police officers in the remainder of 2021 after Duante Wright died, including three-month-old La'Mello Parker, killed May 3, 2021 in a gun fight between Biloxi, Mississippi police and the infant's father. At least thirty-five were killed in 2022; thirty-three in 2023; twenty in 2024; and another four died in the first three months of 2025.[3] This list will, sadly, be outdated long before this volume goes to press.[4]

Since 2008 we have witnessed a continuous litany of murdered African Americans, many dead at the hands of the police, many documented by courageous witnesses who used their cell phones to record history in the making. The realities of vigilante racism and police brutality that African Americans had always known became undeniably real for sympathetic Whites. As the hopes for the Obama presidency collided with the painful realities of yet another death, African American youths founded the Black Lives Matter movement. The violence and death generated protests throughout the nation and internationally, in hotspots reaching from Atlanta, to Seattle, Ferguson, Washington, D.C., Portland, Kenosha, Tulsa, Tahlequah, and beyond.

These protests were more focused than most of the 1967 riots; they were multi-racial; they were not always peaceful, nor was the violence confined to the protestors. A Princeton University study of some 10,600 demonstrations during four months in 2020 surrounding the George Floyd murder found that 93 percent were non-violent. Peaceful protests were reported in 2,400 U.S. communities, while demonstrations in 220 communities turned violent.[5] As in 1967, these protests were ignited when rising expectations collided with internalized and systemic racism.

I responded to some of this unfolding history in my 2013 and 2014 lectures, and in my classroom teaching. In the fall of 2009, I introduced a graduate seminar, "Race in American History," and two years later, an undergraduate course, "Race, Film, and History," that examined the history of race relations in the United States through the lens of movies. The first time I taught "Race in American History," the course description began: "As the 2008 U.S. presidential election amply demonstrated, race has been central to American history and American identities."

I edited my 2008 lecture for this volume during the 2021 trial of former Minneapolis police officer Derek Chauvin, accused of murdering George Floyd by pressing his knee into Floyd's neck for 9 minutes and 29 seconds, a brutal death I witnessed because a courageous teenager, Darnella Frazier, recorded it on her cellphone and broadcast it on Facebook.[6] During the Chauvin trial, my thoughts inescapably went to Emmett Till, whose brutal murder and mutilation in 1955 had indelibly etched the human face of racist brutality in my child's mind. I thought of Marquette Frye and John Smith, whose arrests and beatings sparked the 1965 Watts riot and the 1967 Newark riot. I pictured the photos of lynchings, of the "strange fruit" hanging from southern trees I had used in classes about the violent aftermath of post-Civil War Reconstruction. I pictured the televised images of police brutality against Civil Rights activists, of "Bloody Sunday" in Selma, Alabama. I thought of the daily humiliations of African Americans I witnessed as a child.

I completed the last footnote for my 2008 lecture, "Race in America," on April 20, 2021, an hour before the jury found Derek Chauvin guilty of two counts of murder and one count of manslaughter. Philonise Floyd immediately connected his brother's death to the longer history of racist violence, referring to Emmett Till as the "first George Floyd." Speaking shortly after the jury rendered its verdict, Minnesota Attorney General Keith Ellison put George Floyd's murder in the explicit context of the Kerner Commission:

> This verdict reminds us *how hard* it is to make enduring change. In 1968 [sic], the Kerner Commission was formed to investigate the causes of uprisings in cities across America. Dr. Kenneth Clark—the famous African American psychologist who, along with his equally accomplished psychologist wife Mamie, contributed compelling research to the *Brown v.*

Board of Education case—testified at the Kerner Commission. He said:

"I read that report ... of the 1919 riot in Chicago, and it is as if I were reading the report of the investigating committee on the Harlem riot of '35, the report of the investigating committee on the Harlem riot of '43, the report of the McCone Commission on the Watts riot....

"I must again in candor say to you members of this Commission—it is a kind of Alice in Wonderland—with the same moving picture re-shown over and over again, the same analysis, the same recommendations, and the same inaction."

"Here we are in 2021," Ellison continued, "still addressing the same problem. ... It did not need to get to this point. There are far too many *more* names. Each is painful to name. This verdict reminds us that we *must* make enduring change."[7]

Documenting the history of racism does not make enduring change. When I taught Canadian students the history of American racism, I also taught the histories of African American resistance and of the abolitionist and Civil Rights Movements in which White allies had joined. I did not want to inflate the history of White anti-racism, but I did want to complicate students' understandings of American racism and the ongoing historical resistance to it. There are some bridges between past and present that cannot remain unchallenged. I offered these histories in the hope that we might someday disconnect the legacy of the racist past from yet another painful present.

NOTES

1. Dakota Territory was established in 1861 and was carved into the separate states of North Dakota and South Dakota in 1889. I use "North Dakota" for convenience here, though the land office was located in Dakota Territory until 1889.
2. Vanessa Williams, "Fifty years after the Kerner Commission, a new report cites some of the same concerns about race and poverty," *Washington Post*, February 26, 2018.
3. "List of unarmed African Americans killed by law enforcement officers in the United States," a copiously footnoted but probably still incomplete list, Wikipedia, https://en.wikipedia.org/wiki/List_of_unarmed_African_Americans_killed_by_law_enforcement_officers_in_the_United_States, accessed May 26, 2025.

4   This grim litany is hardly exhaustive, nor does it represent African Americans killed by armed civilians. I do not mean to imply that all, or most, police officers exert excessive force against people of color, but I do mean to demonstrate a pervasive and repeating reality that fuels African American fears, inspires the Black Lives Matter movement, and that has engendered renewed protests and demonstrations.

5   "Demonstrations and Political Violence in America: New Data for Summer 2020," U.S. Crisis Project, a joint effort by the Armed Conflict Location & Event Data Project and the Bridging Divides Initiative at Princeton University, September 2020, https://acleddata.com/acleddatanew/wp-content/uploads/2020/09/ACLED_USDataReview_Sum2020_SeptWebPDF.pdf, accessed September 2, 2021.

6   In 2021 the Pulitzer Prize committee awarded Darnella Frazier a special citation for the video. She testified that it has haunted her ever since. See Jonathan Allen, "Pulitzers honor Darnella Frazier for cellphone video of George Floyd Murder," *New York Times*, June 11, 2021.

7   "Accountability ... is the first step to justice," Attorney General Ellison's remarks after the verdict in *State v. Derek Chauvin*, Saint Paul, April 20, 2021.

7

Race in America: Reflections on the 40th Anniversary of the Kerner Commission Report

April 10, 2008

On March 18, 2008, Senator Barack Obama announced with blunt understatement, "[R]ace is an issue that I believe this nation cannot afford to ignore right now."[1] The United States has always ignored race only at enduring peril to its founding principles. During the 2008 presidential primaries, the first serious Latinx, African American, and woman presidential contenders drew attention to historic changes since the U.S. Civil Rights and Women's Liberation Movements challenged racial and gender inequality. Then, in March and April 2008, reports about Obama's pastor, Reverend Jeremiah Wright, redirected the focus to race as an issue in electoral politics. Rev. Wright, had, among many statements in his long career, called the United States "racist."[2]

As both major parties conducted presidential primaries, in March and April the U.S. media also focused on two landmark anniversaries in the U.S. Civil Rights Movement. March 1, 2008 marked forty years since the publication of the report of the National Advisory Commission on Civil Disorders; April 4, the fortieth anniversary of the assassination of Dr. Martin Luther King, Jr.[3] Journalists focused particularly on Dr. King's leadership in the southern Civil Rights movement, culminating with the passage of the Civil Rights Act of 1964 and the 1965 Voting Rights Act. Both were major victories for African Americans, and for President Lyndon Johnson, who invited Dr. King to the White House signing ceremonies.

Then, from 1964–1968, the focus of Black discontent seemed to shift, and tactics moved away from the South and from nonviolent civil disobedience. As so-called "ghetto riots" erupted in one city after another,

Blacks seized control from the police and property from local merchants.[4] The search for causes and meaning began after the 1965 riot in the Watts section of Los Angeles and peaked in the half-year scramble for a "theory" of riot causation by the commission President Johnson appointed to investigate 165 riots that rocked the nation in the summer of 1967.

President Johnson addressed a stunned nation the night of July 27, 1967. Detroit smoldered under U.S. army occupation in the final hours of a riot that had erupted four days earlier. Seven northern New Jersey communities were reeling from disturbances that began July 12 in Newark and ended in Englewood July 26. Officials in the small Maryland shore community of Cambridge charged that H. Rap Brown, national chairman of the Student Nonviolent Coordinating Committee, had instigated a riot there the night of July 24. Mayors and police chiefs throughout the country braced for impending violence as the President announced plans to appoint a special commission.[5] On July 29, he signed Executive Order 11365, Establishing a National Advisory Commission on Civil Disorders, charged to investigate and make recommendations with respect to:

> (1) The origins of the recent major civil disorders in our cities, including the basic causes and factors leading to such disorders and the influence, if any, of organizations or individuals dedicated to the incitement or encouragement of violence; (2) The development of methods and techniques for averting or controlling such disorders. . . .; (3) The appropriate role of the local, state, and Federal authorities in dealing with civil disorders; and (4) Such other matters as the President may place before [it].[6]

Critics charged that Johnson had the answers on July 27. "The only genuine, long-range solution," he said, was an "attack—mounted at every level—upon the conditions that breed despair and violence. All of us know what these conditions are: ignorance, discrimination, slums, poverty, disease, not enough jobs."[7] Gordon Lightfoot voiced his cynical reaction to the official response in his song about the 1967 Detroit riot, "Black Day in July": "In the mansion of the governor/ There's nothing that is known for sure/. . . And they wonder how it happened/ And they really know the reason/ And it wasn't just the temperature/ And it wasn't just the season."[8]

The Commission operated in an enormously charged political arena, with a President who wanted answers that fit his assumptions, and critics who assumed its report would be a whitewash. Chaired by Illinois Governor Otto Kerner, sometimes known as the Kerner Commission, its members were the Vice-Chair, New York Mayor John Lindsay; Oklahoma Senator Fred Harris; Massachusetts Senator Edward Brooke; California Congressman James Corman; Ohio Congressman William McCulloch; United Steelworkers of America President I. W. Abel; Litton Industries Founder and Chairman Charles B. "Tex" Thornton; NAACP Executive Director Roy Wilkins; Kentucky Commissioner of Commerce Katherine Graham Peden; and Atlanta Police Chief Herbert Jenkins. Kerner, Harris, and Corman were Democrats; McColloch, Brooke, and Lindsay, Republicans.[9] Most were moderate to liberal. Lindsay and Brooke (the first African American elected to the Senate since Reconstruction) were liberal Republicans. They existed back then.

The Kerner Commission Report surprised almost everyone and totally pleased very few. It concluded famously, "Our nation is moving toward two societies, one black, one white—separate and unequal," and issued the first official acknowledgment that White racism engendered the conditions that bred Black discontent.[10]

From September-December 1967, I worked as a research assistant on the Kerner Commission staff. I treasure the hardbound copy of the report that each staff member received, our names embossed on the cover. My status may be hinted by the fact that my name is misspelled. I treasure it nonetheless.[11]

Four decades later, the 2008 historic context invited reflection on the legacies of those tumultuous years. It could be easy to succumb to self-indulgent nostalgia, and I am not certain I escaped that urge as I returned to the days between when the Commission was appointed and when it released its report, as I pondered what that history might offer to the contemporary discourse about race and the politics of memory.

The riots, the Report, and my reflections all require some context. The urban disorders of the 1960s were not the first race riots in U.S. history. African American history originated in violence, and Black resistance erupted periodically in urban confrontations, especially around wartimes, fueled by the contradiction between inequality at home as Black and Latinx soldiers fought for democratic rights abroad. Three hundred and fifty thousand African Americans served in segregated units during World War I, 42,000 of them in combat. In 1917, there were "race riots" in Philadelphia and Chester, Pennsylvania. Thirty-nine Blacks and nine Whites died when Whites rioted and destroyed 300 buildings in the Black section of East St. Louis, Illinois. Two years later, thirty people died in a Chicago riot, and there were similar disorders in Omaha, Charleston, and Washington, D.C. The horrific Tulsa riot of 1921 killed over thirty people and destroyed a square mile of the Black section of Tulsa known as "the Black Wall Street."[12]

Again, during World War II, the races clashed in Mobile, Los Angeles, Beaumont, Harlem, St. Louis, Youngstown, Cicero, and Chicago. Federal troops were called out to put down the 1943 Detroit riot that killed twenty-five Blacks and nine Whites and destroyed over $200 million in property.[13]

World War II began to transform the urban social landscape that set the stage for the civil disorders of the 1960s, as African Americans moved north and west for jobs in wartime factories. An estimated 1.5 million left the South during the 1940s; another 1.1 million the following decade, seeking jobs and better opportunities. They found a North as residentially segregated as the South they left, and fewer good jobs than they had hoped. Many cities underwent an unsettling demographic shift: Black in-migration, White flight as large numbers of White European Americans fled racially diverse urban areas for more racially homogenous suburbs, thereby eroding urban tax bases.[14]

As James Gregory demonstrated in *The Southern Diaspora*, the migrations of Black and White southerners cannot be understood in isolation from one another. The separate but connected histories of White and Black southerners wove through my childhood. I grew up in Galveston, Texas, raised by civil rights advocates in the segregated South. The connected inequalities of race were as clear as the differences between my mother and the Black housekeepers who made it possible for her to practice medicine. I didn't know until I read Gregory that I left Galveston as part of a migration of 5.6 million Whites who left the South in the postwar decades. "In the 1950s and 1960s," he wrote, "as civil rights struggles dominated regional politics, new cohorts of southerners left the South for political reasons. Especially this was an option for young people, college-bound or recent graduates, both young African Americans and young Whites of liberal ideals, including quite a few among the region's small Jewish population."[15]

Including me. I left in June of 1965 to attend Antioch College in Yellow Springs, Ohio. Founded by abolitionists in 1853, Antioch was the second U.S. college to admit women and African Americans, and Yellow Springs was an underground railway stop for escaped slaves heading to Canada. Many Antioch students worked in the southern Civil Rights movement;

the brothers of two civil rights workers slain in 1963, David Goodman and Steve Schwerner, both attended Antioch. So did Coretta Scott King.

Idealism and naivete drew me North, where I thought I would find equality and brotherhood. That lasted three months. Antioch had a work-study program. For five years students alternated quarters studying on campus with work quarters at co-op jobs throughout the country. My first job, in the fall of 1965, was at the National Opinion Research Center in Chicago, on the edge of Woodlawn, an impoverished African American neighborhood.[16] If my fantasy of racial equality faded abruptly in Chicago, imagine the impact of northern realities on my African American counterparts. I carried that tension between hope and racial realities with me to Washington in the fall of 1967.

The Commissioners were already hard at work. From August through November, they held twenty days of closed hearings, interviewed 130 witnesses, and, in groups of two or three, visited eight of the riot areas, meeting with Black residents, militants, and public officials.[17]

The President appointed a trusted adviser, Washington attorney David Ginsburg, as executive director of the Commission. His deputy, Victor Palmieri, recruited over ninety consultants and professional staff—many detailed to the Commission from federal agencies—to document and analyze what caused the riots. The deputy assistant director for research was Dr. Robert Shellow, a social psychologist who was seconded from the National Institute of Mental Health. "A number of social scientists wouldn't touch the commission with a 10-foot pole," he later remembered. "They were concerned about their reputations. They thought the report would be something that would pervert social science."[18] Shellow regularly hired Antioch interns at NIMH, so he called the College for three student research assistants (at least that is what I was told at the time).[19] The core staff consisted of three young research associates, David Boesel, Louis Goldberg, and Gary Marx, and the three students, Jesse Epstein, Oliver "Lock" Holmes, and me. Derek Roemer and Elliot Liebow from NIMH helped with some of our case studies.[20]

Dr. Shellow believed that our "social science input" could shape the report's ideological basis; he encouraged his staff to let the evidence shape the analysis. With that promise, he attracted star consultants like Nathan Caplan and Jeffrey Paige of the University of Michigan, Ralph Turner of UCLA, and Neil Smelser from the University of California, Berkeley. Everyone was vetted for security: the White House rejected Herbert Gans for his anti-war activism.[21] Late one night Jesse Epstein and I decided to read our security clearances and got a sobering lesson in what the FBI knew about our short political histories.

We were all swallowed up in the urgency of the research agenda, and the impending deadlines for an interim report by March 1, 1968, and a final report by August. Facing urgent timelines and an enormous task, the staff ranked disturbances in over 150 cities by the degree of violence and damage, the duration of the violence, the number of active participants, and the level of law enforcement response. A sample of twenty-three cities was selected from this list, including nine cities that had "serious disturbances," three with disorders in university settings, a chain of six New Jersey cities surrounding Newark, and five cities that experienced lesser degrees of violence.[22] For each city, staff collected and reviewed reports from the FBI, Department of Justice, and other government agencies, and newspaper accounts. Then, over several months, six-person investigative teams went to twenty cities—the three university towns got contracted out. The larger six-person teams divided themselves into pairs to interview people from the official sector, the private sector, and residents and leaders of community groups in the riot area; they interviewed more than 1,200 people in all. After interviewing in each area, they returned to Washington to dictate reports and to be debriefed by Commission staff. Their data were augmented by interviews with samples of Detroit and Newark residents, and socioeconomic profiles of all twenty-three cities. From these sources, the research staff prepared analyses of causal factors, collective behavior, leadership structures, and the bargaining processes during the disorders.[23]

I was assigned to assist David Boesel with what we called the "New Jersey string": Newark, Elizabeth, Englewood, Jersey City, New Brunswick, Paterson, and Plainfield.[24] I had worked during the winter quarter of 1967 as a student intern for Senator Clifford P. Case of New Jersey. Every morning for three months I clipped New Jersey newspapers—it turned out to be time well spent. I attended the debriefings with the interview teams and wrote chronologies of the "disturbances" in each city, noting participants' backgrounds, precipitating factors, grievances, duration of violence, official response, and the resolution and aftermath. As we digested the data, the research associates wrote preliminary analyses, city by city. Aiming for a draft analysis by late November, they churned out a thirty-page analysis of each riot every three days. Dr. Shellow brought in cots. At times we worked virtually around the clock, seven days a week.[25]

The office was under tight security. One Sunday, as Jesse, Lock, and I were typing away, dressed in grubby weekend clothes, a strange guy wandered in. We told him that he had entered a secure area and offered to help him find his way out. "Perhaps I should introduce myself," he said. "My name is Otto Kerner." That is the only visit I remember from a member of the Commission, but Senator Harris and Representative Corman assigned staff to drop in and check on us.

The New Jersey string was included in the research sample to investigate how violence spread from Newark to the surrounding communities. Cambridge, Maryland, was included as well to examine possible outside influence. One of Executive Director David Ginsberg's top priorities, as he later put it, was "the idea that these riots were a result of a conspiracy, communist or otherwise. It was our objective first to determine whether it was true, and if it was false, to kill it."[26] The conspiracy theory had many powerful adherents, including the President.[27] The Commissioners addressed the conspiracy question on August 1, with FBI Director J. Edgar Hoover. Hoover testified that he had no "intelligence" to indicate a conspiracy. "Outside agitators," he said, had played a role in the riots, though he had no evidence to link the riots in one city to those in another.[28]

And so, we turned to New Jersey. We found common links there: poverty, longstanding grievances with White-dominated local power structures, and a triggering incident, usually involving the police. After that it depended—on whether there were clearly articulated grievances and demands, on whether local Black leadership emerged, and on the official response. These differences were obscured by the official language of civil unrest. We were not supposed to use the word "riot," the forbidden four-letter word for all Commission discourse. The "civil disorders" ranged from Newark, which cost twenty-three lives and over $10 million in damage, to several very minor "outbreaks." Newark, Plainfield, and New Brunswick illustrate the range.

Newark had all the classic preconditions. Between 1960 and 1967, it lost 70,000 White residents, and went, in six years, from 65 percent White to 52 percent Black and 10 percent Latinx. Whites lived elsewhere, worked in Newark, and paid no taxes for city services. Property taxes rose, by 1967, to $661.70 for a $10,000 house; 74 percent of Whites and 87 percent of Blacks rented. Newark spent much less per capita on education than surrounding communities. Twenty thousand children went to overcrowded schools that operated on "double sessions," with two groups of students that each got only a half-day of school. Almost half the Blacks between ages sixteen and nineteen were not in school; most Black adults had less than a grade eight education.[29]

Whites held seven of nine seats on the City Council and Board of Education. Blacks were politically disillusioned by losing battles against converting over 150 acres in the Black Central Ward to a medical school and appointing a less-qualified White as Secretary of the Board of Education rather than the city's African American Budget Director, who had a master's degree in accounting. With a police force proportionately larger than any other major city, the crime rate was among the highest in the nation. There was longstanding antagonism between African Americans and the largely Italian American police force. Twelve percent of Blacks were unemployed, plus 20,000 teenagers with no jobs or summer recreation programs.[30]

On the evening of July 12, Newark police arrested a Black cabdriver named John Smith who they said was tailgating them and who was driving without a license. Smith, who either could not or would not walk, was dragged out of a police car into the Fourth Precinct Police Station in full view of a high-rise housing project. Rumors flew, a crowd gathered, as well as Black community leaders Oliver Loftus, Timothy Still, and Robert Curvin, and Inspector Kenneth Melchior, the senior police administrator on the night watch. Melchior sent the injured Smith to hospital; doctors found that he'd been beaten and suffered broken ribs. A line of police in front of the station "exchanged volleys of profanity" with Blacks across the street. Loftus persuaded the crowd to begin a march to City Hall, which disintegrated as youngsters began throwing rocks. A line of cabs drove to City Hall to protest, leading to rumors of an organized disturbance. The night passed with only minor property damage.[31]

The next day Black leaders met with Mayor Hugh Addonizio, who took the two officers who arrested Smith off active duty and agreed to promote a Black police lieutenant. That night picketers protested police brutality in front of the Fourth Precinct until a barrage of rocks and bottles shattered windows at the precinct and set off a wave of looting and vandalism.[32]

At 2:20 a.m. Mayor Addonizio asked Governor Richard Hughes for help, and Hughes activated the State Police and National Guard. By Saturday, July 15, the Guard and State Police patrolled a fourteen-mile perimeter that sealed the riot area. Looting and sniping resumed that night. Many residents testified that the National Guard, mostly young, scared, and inexperienced, deliberately shot into businesses that displayed "Soul Brother" signs, and targeted peaceful Black residents. The violence tapered off by Sunday, leaving twenty-three people dead, including a

White detective, a White firefighter and twenty-one Blacks, among them a 73-year-old man, six women, and two children.[33]

Newark was the classic "bad riot" in a major urban center with Black poverty and unemployment, little access to power, a growing core of militant leaders, a precipitating incident involving the police, high levels of violence, and one or more deaths.

Plainfield, a bedroom community next door, shared similar characteristics. A post-World War II influx raised the city's Black population to 30 percent, concentrated on the city's west side. The West End was impoverished, but not as depressed as Newark's Central Ward. Blacks had a median 7.9 years of education, Whites, 11.7. Only two city council members out of eleven were African American. The National Association for the Advancement of Colored People (NAACP) was so frustrated that it had tacked a list of complaints and demands on City Hall in February; none were acknowledged. There were widespread complaints of police brutality and racism.[34]

Plainfield's riot began July 14, when two Black youngsters got into a fight at a local teenage hangout. An off-duty police officer, recently accused of brutality, who was working as a private guard, refused to intervene and one youth was taken to hospital. The other teenagers gathered at a nearby housing project to protest. As the two Black city council members, Henry Judkins and Everett Lattimer, addressed them, about fifty angry youths split off to break windows in Plainfield's business district. The police turned them back.[35]

Shortly after midnight, Judkins, Lattimer, and a young Black news reporter, David Hardy, met with the group to discuss their grievances. They arranged a meeting with Mayor George Hetfield, scheduled for that afternoon at the Teen Center. Police heard that Black youths were making firebombs at a filling station, ran them off and found about a dozen badly made Molotov cocktails. The meeting with the mayor was postponed until 7–9 p.m., when Hetfield met with fifty to one hundred Black youths, Judkins, Lattimer, and Hardy. The young people voiced complaints about police behavior and about recreational facilities, including a long-standing demand for a swimming pool that had been promised the year before. Instead, the city was busing children to the county pool three days a week, and charging twenty-five cents, a considerable burden for poor families. The mayor was not impressed; the meeting disintegrated. Eight fires were set that night, none of which destroyed buildings. Quiet returned.[36]

On July 16, following some rock throwing, the mayor called in the State Police and National Guard. Two to three hundred Black youths met on Plainfield Avenue. David Sullivan, the only Black member of the Plainfield Human Relations Commission, persuaded them to move to a local park. The orderly meeting elected ten representatives and was drawing up a list of grievances. Then the police broke it up because there was no permit to use the park.[37]

As looting and window-breaking resumed, the State Police sealed the area. That night, a White police officer, John Gleason, pursued a Black youth into the riot area and shot him, but not fatally. Angry Blacks stomped Gleason to death. Forty-six carbines were stolen from a local manufacturer and distributed in apparent preparation for police retaliation. The next day, July 17, State Community Relations Director Paul Ylsivaker and the Attorney General met with adult African American representatives. They agreed that the state police would maintain the perimeter and Blacks would patrol their own area. Ylsivaker and Hardy met with fifty youths at the Teen Center. The youths chose ten representatives to present their grievances to city officials. These included the promised swimming pool, police brutality, and housing and rental practices. The mayor, the two state officials, and the State Police Commander went to the African American neighborhood and addressed a crowd of three-to-four-hundred people. Later that night a deal was struck to release twelve people arrested during the riot if Black leaders would try to recover the carbines.[38]

Sporadic shots were fired during the night. On July 18, Black residents started cleaning the streets while the Department of Community Relations distributed food and milk in the riot area. On July 19, Officer Gleason was buried, and a State Police search found only three guns, none of them carbines. Cleanup continued July 20; the State Police and National Guard left.[39]

Considering Plainfield's population, about 50,000, its riot was among the most severe. The leadership nucleus appeared to be a small group of militant Black youths. Without realizing it, young people had been becoming a powerful political force. In the period leading up to the riot, there had been a growing conflict between Black race-consciousness and an inflexible White social and political power structure. That conflict included the youths' demands for the swimming pool. It had taken strikes and boycotts to achieve school integration, and then "tracking" students into separate academic cohorts kept Black students segregated from White students in separate "tracks." Black junior high students boycotted the cafeteria to protest discrimination. Finally, the youngsters opposed an anti-loitering amendment the City Council was considering because they thought it was directed at them and would fuel police harassment.[40]

The research staff concluded that in Plainfield, "rebellion" was a better descriptive term than "riot" because there had been:

> ... a well-documented set of political and racial problems in Plainfield to which the use of violence by young Blacks was a definite and connected response. There was a deliberate alternation in the response between the use of violence and steps to negotiate with city authorities. There were social developments within the ghetto from the precipitating incident to the terminal action which gave rise to a loosely structured Black leadership and to the establishment, partly by default, of physical control of the ghetto itself by armed youths. And there was the emergence of a high degree of racial-communal solidarity which continued after the riot and which provided the base for the development of new, politically conscious organizations.[41]

Grievances were quickly articulated, and the inclination to meet and talk rather than immediately starting to riot indicated an unusual degree of collective deliberation and rationality. The riot was a political event—not an anomic spasm in response to admittedly bad living conditions, but a response to the unequal distribution of social power.[42]

New Brunswick defined a different pattern and spectrum of violence. Ten miles from Plainfield, about the same size, a commercial center and home of Rutgers University, the population in 1960 was 16 percent Black with no discernible African American neighborhood. Black median income was 71 percent of Whites'; three Blacks in ten had a family income under $3,000; 30 percent owned homes.[43]

During the Plainfield rebellion, rumors flew that New Brunswick was "really going to blow."[44] Staff members of the local antipoverty agency met with the city council, and with Mayor Patricia Sheehan, who had been elected two months earlier on a reform platform. Sheehan appointed a Black community relations officer and sent Black plainclothes police to the streets to fight rumors. The police were told to act with restraint. The radio station decided to play down rumors and news of any disturbance. The antipoverty agency set up a multiracial task force to cool the situation. Then, the night of July 17, a group of youngsters began breaking windows.

The youths, including twelve- and thirteen-year-olds, chose their targets and looted an odd assortment of goods, including bubble gum and witch hazel. Tuesday morning the mayor invoked a curfew and recorded a radio appeal for order. The antipoverty agency, which had just received funding for its summer program, began hiring teenagers as recreational aides. So many applied that they cut the stipends in half and hired twice as many youths. The mayor and city commissioners met with thirty-five teenagers who "poured out their souls to the mayor" and agreed to draw up a statement attacking discrimination, inferior education and employment opportunities, police harassment, and poor housing. Four of the youths broadcast appeals on the radio urging their "soul brothers and sisters" to "cool it, because you will only get hurt and the mayor has talked with us and is going to do something for us."[45]

That evening there was a confrontation at a housing project between the police and a crowd angered by a large squad of police in riot dress. The mayor ordered the police to withdraw, then grabbed a bullhorn and addressed the crowd, asking for a chance to correct conditions. Finally, they decided: "She's new! Give her a chance!" The crowd demanded and got the right to inspect the jail to ensure that everyone arrested the night before had been released.[46]

The Commission report emphasized the proactive official acts, not the disorder. The youngsters had learned what Boesel called coercive protest. They targeted selected stores, issued their demand to meet with the mayor, and stopped the violence when they got a response.[47]

The events in Plainfield, New Brunswick, and the rest of the New Jersey string were clearly part of a "spillover effect" from Newark. Many African Americans had moved out of Newark but had family and friends in the Central Ward. The behaviors on all sides became increasingly stylized and deliberate as the disturbances progressed. The participants got younger, the lists of demands more clearly articulated, the official responses either more proactive, as in New Brunswick, or more repressive, as in Jersey City where the mayor promised to "meet force with force."[48]

We found no evidence of conspiracy or of outside agitators. Rather we found poor living conditions, real local grievances, inflammatory media reports, and ties of family and friendship that bound the African Americans of northern New Jersey.[49] David Boesel requested records of the northern New Jersey telephone activity beginning with the Newark riot. Finding huge increases in calls among Black neighborhoods, he concluded that riots spread by word of mouth among African Americans who were literally and psychically brothers. In Cambridge, where Rap Brown did make a militant speech, the staff report concluded: "It may be emotionally satisfying to think that Brown came to Cambridge and that therefore a riot followed; it may be simpler for the public to grasp. But the facts are more complex and quite different."[50]

Those complex facts challenged key assumptions about who rioted and why. In Newark and Detroit, rioters were not immiserated southern migrants. The "typical" rioter in 1967 was an unmarried Black man between age 15 and 24, born and raised where the riot occurred. His economic situation did not differ markedly from his neighbors who did not riot. He was not likely to be a high school graduate but was better educated than most inner-city Blacks. If he had a job, it was menial, low status part-time work as an unskilled laborer, interrupted by frequent unemployment. He felt he deserved and was qualified for a better job but was barred by employer discrimination. He was proud to be Black and felt equal hostility toward most Whites and middle-class Blacks.[51] He was, in short, a slightly upwardly mobile person who found his aspirations blocked by institutionalized racism and who interpreted his situation through the lens of Black activism.

Nothing that we learned could predict riots. Correlation is not causality. The same underlying conditions existed in cities that did not riot, the same daily brutality, the same reservoir of Black anger and frustrated hopes.

The research team began in November to write its preliminary report, "The Harvest of American Racism," using the case studies to analyze riot processes, and the political, economic, and educational structures that maintained Black inequality. Written during the last two weeks of November, before the city analyses were completed, it was a 176-page preliminary draft, written in the belief that there would be time to revise and expand until June. Most of it never made it into the Commission's Report.[52] I've used parts of it here, especially in the section on Plainfield, working partly from memory, and partly from later publications by Boesel, Goldberg, and Marx.[53] I first read their 1971 article on Plainfield in 2008, as I wrote my lecture, and discovered that they had given me my first published acknowledgement for scholarship, for my Plainfield riot chronology.

"Harvest" was hardly a polished document or one that a government agency was likely to embrace. None of us fully understood that the senior staff expected us to support the President's political agenda based in the causal importance of "ignorance, discrimination, slums, poverty, disease, not enough jobs." "Harvest" combined liberal assumptions that the President embraced with analyses of structural racism and African American responses that he would reject, especially in the final section, "America on the Brink: White Racism and Black Rebellion." The Kerner Report diverged from "The Harvest of American Racism" in its analysis of White racism, which The Kerner Report treated as an individual attitude, whereas "Harvest" pointed to an analysis of the institutions that reinforced racism and the systems of power that maintained Black subordination. As Gary Marx observed regarding the characterization of racism as individual prejudice, "Because it accuses everyone, it accuses no one."[54]

Palmieri and Ginsberg were appalled. "Harvest" was no more poorly done than much of the final report, but it challenged too many assumptions and was not what they wanted from the "social science input." Palmieri fired Shellow and excluded him from then on.[55]

Ginsburg had apparently long since decided to issue the final report March 1. He told the Commission on December 8 that there would be no interim report, and then 120 investigators and social scientists were "released," purportedly because it was time for a small team to write the final document. Palmieri turned "Harvest" over to Deputy Director Stephen Kurzman, who used some of our work minus the more difficult analyses.[56]

In the wake of these disillusioning events, some of the commissioners threw a party for the departing staff. Amidst a lot of smoke and alcohol, Senator Harris cornered some of us and said, "I hear there's a report we're not seeing." Someone—either Harris or a Congressional staffer—said, "You know, I'd be surprised in the current circumstances if some researchers weren't xeroxing a lot late at night." Harris somehow got his copy of "Harvest," and Boesel, Marx, and Goldberg preserved enough to publish from our drafts and data.

Within the Commission, there was a struggle over content. Lindsay, Harris, and Roy Wilkins insisted that the report could not ignore racism. But the "White racism" for which the report is noted is mentioned only briefly in the summary. The causal analysis rested on individual race prejudice, the formation of racial ghettos and their living conditions, unemployment, family structure, and social disorganization. The Report proposed policies to handle disorders, hire Black journalists, and adopt a national agenda to increase opportunities in jobs, housing, and education and "remove the frustration of powerlessness."[57]

The Report opened to mixed reviews March 1, 1968.[58] President Johnson faced an election year as his domestic War on Poverty was threatened by the mounting costs of Vietnam. He was angry with Dr. King, who blamed the War for eviscerating the Poverty programs and for sending Black soldiers "to guarantee liberties in Southeast Asia which they had not found in southwest Georgia and East Harlem."[59] Johnson did not, as was common, invite the Commission to the White House for the unveiling.[60] Then, on March 31, he announced that he would neither seek nor accept nomination for another term. Four days later, the Rev. Martin Luther King, Jr., was assassinated in Memphis, and the cities exploded yet again. Gordon Lightfoot released "Black Day in July" that April. It was immediately banned by U.S. top-40 radio stations, for fear, they said, that Lightfoot's lyrics might incite racial violence.[61] So much for causal analysis.

The Report became a runaway best seller. Over two million copies were sold.[62] Most big city mayors embraced its findings. Future President Richard Nixon, campaigning for the Republican presidential nomination, said the report "blames everybody for the riots except the perpetrators," and put "undue emphasis on the idea that we are in effect a racist society, White racists versus Black racists."[63]

Forty years later, when I gave my lecture, what had changed? What might this small chapter add to the long history of race in America? The riots of the mid-1960s differed from earlier riots, which had been direct clashes between Blacks and Whites, not between African Americans and the police or the military. They were different from the southern Civil Rights Movement but not separate, as Dr. King and other leaders turned their attention after 1965 from legal change to poverty and structural racism. Though they took the focus off the segregated South, they were not confined to northern cities; our sample of twenty-three riots included Atlanta, Houston, Tampa, and Jackson, Mississippi. Urban grievances did not lend themselves to immediate legal solutions, and they could not rely on the well-developed leadership that the southern Black church had provided. The riots gave leadership training, in fact, to some young African Americans born just before the Supreme Court ordered school integration in 1954, just before Emmett Till was murdered and Rosa Parks began the Montgomery bus boycott the following year, who came of age with rising expectations that were not fulfilled in their daily lives.[64]

For African Americans, there have been mixed responses to the conditions the Kerner Commission targeted. The two surviving Commissioners in 2008, former Senators Fred Harris and Edward Brooke, both emphasized the unfinished agenda. Fred Harris quit the Senate and in 1976 joined the Political Science department at the University of New Mexico. In March 2008 he told an Albuquerque journalist, "A lot of people think we solved all that, but we didn't. We did a lot of things back then that worked, but we aren't doing those things now. We have 37 million people living in poverty today. We have 47 million people without health insurance. And it's shameful that America ranks 22nd in the world in infant mortality"[65] Edward Brooke wrote in the *Washington Post* April 3, 2008, that "despite the visibility of accomplished African Americans and Hispanics and the progress in race relations that ha[d] been made" in the past forty years:

> for America's poor—those who don't know what health care is, because for them it doesn't exist, those for whom prison is a more likely prospect than college, those who have been abandoned in the worst of decaying, crime-ridden urban centers because of the flight of middle-class Blacks, Whites and Hispanics—the future may be as bleak as it was for their counterparts in the 1960s.[66]

Harris and Brooke based their sober assessments on the February 2008 report of the Eisenhower Foundation, which they had helped found and which periodically assesses the progress toward the Kerner Commission's policy objectives of reducing poverty, inequality, racial injustice, and crime. In 2008, the mutually reinforcing inequalities of race, class, and gender still characterized the experiences of most African Americans. The Eisenhower Foundation found, for instance, that the 2006 poverty rate was almost 44 percent in households headed by African Americans women with children under age eighteen. Black unemployment had been consistently twice as high as White unemployment from 1968 to 2008. The class divide had widened; over those forty years the U.S. experienced the most rapid growth in wage inequality in the industrial world. Among full-time workers, Whites earned over 22 percent more than equivalent Black workers and almost 34 percent more than Latinx workers. Residential segregation remained high and was highest for Blacks. African American men aged twenty-five to twenty-nine were seven times more likely to be imprisoned than their White counterparts.[67]

All the cities in the New Jersey string were proportionately more African American and more Latinx in 2000 than in 1967, but there were significant class differences between those who lived in Newark and the smaller suburban cities. Plainfield, by 2000, was 64 percent Black and a quarter Latinx; three-fourths of the population had at least a high school education. Its poverty was less than the national average: 12 percent of all families, and 20 percent of female-headed households lived below the poverty line.[68] In Newark, half the population hadn't finished high school, and twice as many families were impoverished: 25 percent overall, and 40 percent of female-headed households.[69] New Brunswick fell somewhere in between: a quarter Black, 40 percent Latinx; 36 percent had not graduated high school; 17 percent of all families and 29 percent of female-headed households fell below the poverty line.[70]

There is no evidence that these differences were related to the riots of 1967. The striking changes included the growth of an African American middle class, the increase in Black elected officials, including big city mayors like Kenneth Gibson of Newark, elected shortly after the riot, and Cory Booker, the mayor in 2008, who was born in 1969. Booker was elected to the U.S. Senate in 2012, following Obama's historic election as the first African American U.S. President in 2008.

It was easy in 2008 to see similarities to 1967 in the racial class divide and an increasingly unpopular war in which people of color again fought and died in disproportionate numbers. Yet among the striking differences was this: no one was rioting in protest. No one rioted at the Super Dome in New Orleans which housed so many people of color during Hurricane Katrina in 2005, though the connections of race and poverty and inability to flee the hurricane could not have been starker. The few major riots since the early 1970s were ignited, as in 1967, by police brutality.[71] I can only speculate about why this was.

The residents of riot areas lived with the ruins for years, while White America and the Black middle class moved on, taking their rising expectations with them. Middle-class African Americans, of course, continued to experience racism. Like many other White Americans who did not directly experience the violence, I could choose when and how to engage with racist realities. The spring of 1968 brought the assassinations of Reverend King on April 4, 1968, and Senator Robert Kennedy on June 6. Fearing another summer of violence, I took my savings from the Kerner Commission to hitchhike and hostel through Europe with a friend, which is how I came to be picking peaches in an international work camp in Hungary as the Soviet Union invaded Czechoslovakia.[72]

I lived with these memories in early 2008, in the midst of the furor over the Rev. Wright's comments and Senator Obama's eloquent March 18 speech on race in America. Obama characterized his differences with Rev. Wright as generational; he described Wright as one of the generations who came of age in the late 1950s and early 1960s, "when segregation was the law of the land and opportunity was systematically constricted. What's remarkable is not how many failed in the face of discrimination, but rather how many men and women overcame the odds; how many were able to make a way out of no way for those like me who would come after them." Those who did not make it, Obama said, passed on a "legacy of defeat."[73]

That legacy underscores differences of class as well as generations. Of all the candidates for the 2008 Democratic presidential nomination, John Edwards most clearly addressed the enduring poverty of working-class Blacks. Both he and Rev. Wright took criticism from the media for being angry. The discomfort with their anger reminded me of Carolyn Heilbrun's observation in *Writing a Woman's Life*, that women's stories are limited by forbidden emotions, particularly "anger, together with the open admission of the desire for power and control over one's life."[74] Part of the legacy of Rev. Wright's generation, including, I suspect, the youngsters in New Brunswick and Plainfield, was the change they made in themselves by voicing anger, and by articulating the desire for power and control over their lives. The 1967 riots illuminated that anger, and the high cost of repressing it, of hopes deferred. They illuminated, too, the audaciously enduring hope, planted sometimes in anger in infertile soil, for power and control. Hope fueled the anger that erupted so tragically in the summer of 1967, and hope remains, against huge odds, part of the complex harvest of American racism.

NOTES

I am grateful to Amy McKinney for her unfailingly meticulous research assistance, and to then-Dean Kevin Quillan and the University of Calgary Institute for U.S. Policy Research (now sadly defunct) and its Director Stephen Randall for sponsoring the 2008 Chair's Lecture.

Additional Sources: The Report itself has been reprinted several times with introductions by respected scholars. See United States National Advisory Commission on Civil Disorders, *The Kerner report / the National Advisory Commission on Civil Disorders*, with an introduction by Julian E. Zelizer (Princeton, NJ: Princeton University Press, 2016); Jelani Cobb and Matthew Guariglia, eds., *The Essential Kerner Commission Report* (New York: Liveright Publishing Corporation, 2021) is a condensed version of the report with annotations and an introduction by Jelani Cobb. Cobb argues that the Report was prescient in its examination of race, economic inequality, and policing.

In 2018 the Russell Sage Foundation devoted an issue of its journal to the 50th anniversary of the Kerner Commission report. The issue contains ten articles that provide critiques of the report and assess the state of African Americans and race relations in the intervening fifty years. The articles that focus on the Kerner Commission Report itself include Susan T. Gooden and Samuel L. Myers Jr., "The Kerner Commission Report Fifty Years Later: Revisiting the American Dream," *RSF: The Russell Sage Foundation Journal of the Social Sciences* 4:6 (September 2018): 1–17; Keisha L. Bentley-Edwards, Malik Chaka Edwards, Cynthia Neal Spence, William A. Darity Jr., Darrick Hamilton, and Jasson Perez, "How Does It Feel to Be a Problem? The Missing Kerner Commission Report," 20–40; Matthew W. Hughey, "Whither Whiteness? The Racial Logics of the Kerner Report and Modern White Space," 73–98; and Rick Loessberg and John Koskinen, "Measuring the Distance: The Legacy of the Kerner Report," 99–119. The remaining articles examine changes in policing civil disorders, the status of African American students in higher education since 1968, changes in Black neighborhoods, in distribution of wealth, etc.

The most important addition to the literature on the Kerner Commission was the 2018 publication of the long-buried report of the Commission research staff, discovered in an archive at the LBJ School of Public Affairs at the University of Texas, Austin, with the word "Destroy" stamped on the cover page. Robert Shellow, ed., *The Harvest of American Racism: The Political Meaning of Violence in the Summer of 1967* (Ann Arbor: University of Michigan Press, 2018) contains the original suppressed report, a foreword by Michael C. Dawson, the introduction by Robert Shellow, recollections of the history and development of the Harvest Report by Robert Shellow, David Boesel, Gary T. Marx, and David O. Sears, and two appendices: "Appendix A: A Calendar of Disturbances in 1967, Showing Intensity and Duration," 149–56, and "Appendix B: Paul F. Lazersfeld and Martin Jaeckel, "The Commission's Report in Two Guises: The Role of Politics," 157–63. The essays by David Boesel and Gary Marx also describe their efforts after the staff was fired to continue publishing analyses of the riots. The volume is a valuable addition to the history of the Kerner Commission and of political responses to racism in the 1960s.

1 "A More Perfect Union," speech delivered by Senator Barack Obama in Philadelphia, March 18, 2008. The full text of Senator Obama's historic speech is widely available on the internet. I accessed the transcript from *The Wall Street Journal*, March 18, 2008.

2 The three candidates were New Mexico Governor Bill Richardson, Senator Obama, and Senator Hillary Clinton. After reports of Rev. Wright's angry rhetoric created problems for the Obama campaign, Senator Obama responded with his "A More Perfect Union" speech about race in America. Then, following televised appearances in which Rev. Wright suggested that the U.S. had been attacked on 9/11 because it had engaged in terrorism abroad and that the U.S. government was culpable for the AIDS epidemic, on April 30 Senator Obama announced his resignation from Rev. Wright's church. See Barack Obama, *A Promised Land* (New York: Crown, 2020), 140–48.

3 For examples of the numerous reflections on the anniversaries of the Kerner Commission Report and of Dr. King's assassination, see R. B. Jones, "Forty Years after the Kerner Commission Report," *Baltimore Times*, March 7, 2008; Jim Belshaw, "Eyes Still on the Prize That's Out of Reach," *Albuquerque Journal*, March 28, 2008 and (former Senator) Edward F. Brooke, "King and Kerner: An Unfinished Agenda," *Washington Post*, April 3, 2008. Thanks to Kevin Quillan for the Edward Brooke article.

4 The use of "ghetto" is problematic today, when African American neighborhood would be a preferred terminology. I use "ghetto" only as the National Advisory Commission on Civil Disorders did in its official documents, and when it accurately reflected the ways African Americans described their living conditions in racially segregated and impoverished neighborhoods.

5   For a summary of riots from 1963 through the summer of 1967, see Chapter 1, "Profiles of Disorder," *Report of the National Advisory Commission on Civil Disorders* (Washington, DC: U.S. Government Printing Office, 1968), 19–61 (hereinafter *Kerner Report*). For excerpts of President Johnson's July 27, 1967 address, *see Kerner Report*, 297–98.

6   Executive Order 11365, Establishing a National Advisory Commission on Civil Disorders, July 9, 1967, *Kerner Report*, Appendix A, 295–96, Remarks of the President upon Issuing an Executive Order Establishing a National Advisory Commission on Civil Disorders, July 29, 1967, *Kerner Report*, Appendix B, 296–97.

7   Lyndon Baines Johnson, Address to the Nation, July 27, 1967; excerpts from the *Kerner Report*, Appendix C, 297, and quotes as Epigraph to the *Kerner Report*.

8   Gordon Lightfoot, "Black Day in July," Warner Brothers, Inc. For contemporary coverage of the Detroit riot, see for instance "Detroit is Swept by Rioting and Fires; Romney Calls in Guard; 700 Arrested," *New York Times*, July 25, 1967; Jerry M. Flint, "Detroit Negroes Call Police Slow," *New York Times*, July 25, 1967; M.S. Handler, "Detroit Riots Reported Curbed after Tanks Battle Day Snipers; 4 Negro Leaders Call for Order," *New York Times*, July 27, 1967; "Troops Battle Detroit Snipers, Firing Machine Guns from Tanks; Lindsay Appeals to East Harlem," *New York Times*, July 26, 1967; "Detroit Police Chief Finds No Riot Conspiracy," *New York Times*, July 28, 1967; "Bystanders of the Detroit Riot Line Up for Food where Stores Lie in Ruins," *Washington Post*, July 27, 1967.

9   See Appendix D, "Biographical Material on Commission," *Kerner Report*, 298–99.

10 See *Kerner Report*, especially the summary, which announced on page 1, "This is our basic conclusion: Our nation is moving toward two societies, one black, one white—separate and unequal."

11 It is spelled "Elizabeth Jamison" on the cover.

12 See *Kerner Report*, Chapter 5, "Rejection and Protest: An Historical Sketch," 95–113, esp. 101–2; Fred R. Harris and Roger W. Wilkins, eds., *"Quiet Riots"* (New York: Pantheon Books, 1988), 5–15, esp. 6–7; Richard C. Wade, "The Riots in History," in *Cities Under Siege: An Anatomy of the Ghetto Riots, 1064–1968*, eds. David Boesel and Peter H. Rossi (New York: Basic Books, Inc., Publishers, 1971), 277–96, esp. 287–89. For police behavior during the riots in historical perspective, see Gary T. Marx, "Civil Disorder and the Agents of Social Control," in Boesel and Rossi, *Cities Under Siege*, 157–84, esp. 158–66.

13 *Kerner Report*, 103–4; Wade, "Riots in History," esp. 289–90; Harris, "The 1967 Riots," 7.

14 James N. Gregory, *The Southern Diaspora: How the Great Migrations of Black and White Southerners Transformed America* (Chapel Hill: University of North Carolina Press, 2005), 13–15, 82–86, 95–98; *Kerner Report*, Chapter 6, "The Formation of Racial Ghettos," 115–21.

15 Gregory, *The Southern Diaspora*, 36.

16 The National Opinion Research Center and University of Chicago are in the Hyde Park neighborhood where the Obama family later lived; President Obama had taught Constitutional Law at the University.

17 *Kerner Report*, 16; for a list of witnesses who testified before the Commission, 300–302.

18 Andrew Kopkind, "White on Black: The Riot Commission and the Rhetoric of Reform," in Boesel and Rossi, *Cities Under Siege*, 226–59, 232–36.

19 Dorothy Scott, the Co-op Advisor who placed me in my job at the Kerner Commission, told me that this was why Dr. Shellow asked the college to send him three research assistants.

20 See Kopkind, "White on Black," 239, 245–46. The account here of the staff and its work in the office of the Deputy Assistant Director for Research draws as well from my personal memories. Ten years after my 2008 lecture, Dr. Shellow remembered staff hirings

differently in his "Recollections—Robert Shellow," in *The Harvest of American Racism: The Political Meaning of Violence in the Summer of 1967*, ed. Robert Shellow (Ann Arbor: University of Michigan Press, 2018), 115.

> In short order I began to meet and interview candidates for the team, mostly young social scientists referred by their doctoral professor or senior faculty colleagues. The other members no doubt know better than I the reasons behind these referrals, but I suspect that several of the leading scientists who had avoided the spot I was in nonetheless wanted to have one of their own close to the action. In any case, I was particularly grateful to whoever it was that suggested three Antioch college co-op students, seniors Elizabeth "Betsy" Jameson, Oliver "Lock" Holmes, and Jesse Epstein, who provided invaluable support to their elder team members. We eagerly sought their opinions, and their energy and enthusiasm was unbounded.

I don't know whether Dr. Shellow's memory or mine is the more accurate, nor does it matter greatly. It's a useful reminder that minor details may be mis-reported in retrospect, including one in Dr. Shellow's account. None of us were seniors. Jesse and I were third-year students; Lock was in his fourth year of Antioch's five-year undergraduate program. Such details aside, I was moved by Dr. Shellow's words.

21 Kopkind, "White on Black," 237.
22 The twenty-three "civil disorders" selected for the research sample were: Atlanta, Georgia (June 17-21); Bridgeton, New Jersey (July 18-23); Cambridge, Maryland (June 24-27); Cincinnati, Ohio (June 12-17); Dayton, Ohio (June 14-18); Dayton, Ohio (September 19-20); Detroit, Michigan (July 23-28); Elizabeth, New Jersey (July 17-20); Englewood, New Jersey (July 17-20); Grand Rapids, Michigan (July 24-27); Houston, Texas (May 16-27); Jackson, Mississippi (May 10-12); Jersey City, New Jersey (July 17-19); Milwaukee, Wisconsin (July 30-August 6); Nashville, Tennessee (April 8-11); New Brunswick, New Jersey (July 17-18); New Haven, Connecticut (August 19-24); Newark, New Jersey (July 12-17); Paterson, New Jersey (July 15-20); Plainfield, New Jersey (July 14-19); Rockford, Illinois (July 28-31); Tampa, Florida (June 11-15); Tucson, Arizona (July 23-25). For graphic representations of the levels of violence in each city, see *Kerner Report*, "Charts on Levels of Violence and Negotiations," 359-407.
23 *Kerner Report*, 16, 61; Appendix K, "A Statement on Methodology," 319-22.
24 The chronology of these disorders was Newark (July 12-17); Plainfield (July 14-19); Paterson (July 15-20); New Brunswick (July 17-18); Jersey City (July 17-19); Elizabeth (July 17-20); Englewood (July 17-20). Although Bridgeton also experienced a disorder, July 17-23, it was excluded from the New Jersey "string" because it was located outside the Newark metropolitan area.
25 See Kopkind, "White on Black," 247-48.
26 Kopkind, "White on Black," 231.
27 Former Senator Fred Harris, a member of the Kerner Commission, wrote: "President Johnson, like a lot of people at that time, thought that there had been some kind of conspiracy behind the disorders; he told me so himself." Harris, "The 1967 Riots," 12.
28 Roy Reed, "Hoover Discerns No Plot in Riots," *New York Times*, August 2, 1967; Roy Reed, "Riot 'Agitators' Cited by Hoover: But Outsiders Played Minor Role, He Told U.S. Panel," *New York Times*, August 3, 1967.
29 *Kerner Report*, 30-31. For another official analysis of the Newark riot, see The New Jersey Governor's Select Commission on Civil Disorders, 'The Newark Riot," in Boesel and Rossi, *Cities Under Siege*, 22-66.
30 *Kerner Report*, 30-32.
31 *Kerner Report*, 32-34.

32   *Kerner Report*, 34.
33   *Kerner Report*, 35–38.
34   For the *Kerner Report* summary of the Plainfield riot, *Kerner Report*, 41–47, 75–77. As I wrote this portion of my 2008 lecture, I discovered David Boesel, Louis Goldberg, and Gary Marx, "Rebellion in Plainfield," in Boesel and Rossi, 67–83, on which I base this description. The authors graciously acknowledged me "for preparing an earlier version of the chronology; the basis of the present one." Boesel, Goldberg, and Marx, "Rebellion in Plainfield," 67.
35   Boesel, Goldberg, and Marx, "Rebellion in Plainfield," 67–68.
36   Boesel, Goldberg, and Marx, "Rebellion in Plainfield," 68–69.
37   Boesel, Goldberg, and Marx, "Rebellion in Plainfield," 69.
38   Boesel, Goldberg, and Marx, "Rebellion in Plainfield," 69–71.
39   Boesel, Goldberg, and Marx, "Rebellion in Plainfield," 71.
40   Boesel, Goldberg, and Marx, "Rebellion in Plainfield," 75–77.
41   Boesel, Goldberg, and Marx, "Rebellion in Plainfield," 77–78.
42   Boesel, Goldberg, and Marx, "Rebellion in Plainfield," 78. See also David Boesel, "An Analysis of the Ghetto Riots," in Boesel and Rossi, *Cities Under Siege*, 338.
43   *Kerner Report*, 354.
44   *Kerner Report*, 46. This summary of the New Brunswick riot is based on the *Kerner Report*, 46–47, and on my memory.
45   *Kerner Report*, 46.
46   *Kerner Report*, 46–47.
47   Boesel, "Analysis of the Ghetto Riots," 335.
48   *Kerner Report*, 39.
49   For the official conclusions regarding conspiracy and the causes of the 1967 riots, see Kerner Report, 89, 91–93. The Kerner Commission would ultimately conclude that "the urban disorders of the summer of 1967 were not caused by, nor were they the consequence of, any organized plan or 'conspiracy.' Specifically, the Commission has found no evidence that all or any of the disorders or the incidents that led to them were planned or directed by any organization or group—international, national, or local." *Kerner Report*, 89.
50   The quote is from the unpublished report prepared by our staff. See Gail Bensinger and Maurice McLaughlin, "Report Says Rap Brown Didn't Cause Md. Riot," *The Washington Post, Times Herald*, March 5, 1968. See also David Boesel and Louis Goldberg, with a chronology by Jesse Epstein, "Crisis in Cambridge," in Boesel and Rossi, *Cities Under Siege*, 110–29; Louis C. Goldberg, "Ghetto Riots and Others: The Faces of Civil Disorders in 1967," in Boesel and Rossi, *Cities Under Siege*, 149–51. For contemporary coverage of Brown and the Cambridge riot, see Ben A. Franklin, "S.N.C.C. Chief Shot In Cambridge, Md.," *New York Times*, July 25, 1967; Ben A. Franklin, "Leader of S.N.C.C. Seized in Virginia," *New York Times*, July 17, 1967; Leon Dash, "Cambridge Riot Beautiful, Brown Says," *The Washington Post, Times Herald*, July 27, 1967.
51   See *Kerner Report*, 73–77; Dr. Robert M. Fogelson and Dr. Robert B. Hill, "Who Riots? A Study of Participation in the 1967 Riots," in *Supplemental Studies: The National Advisory Commission on Civil Disorders* (Washington, DC: U.S. Government Printing Office, 1968), 217–43, esp. 233–40; Nathan Caplan, "The New Ghetto Man: A Review of Recent Empirical Studies," in Boesel and Rossi, *Cities Under Siege*, 343–59; and Clark McPhail, "Civil Disorder Participants: A Critical Examination of Recent Research," *American Sociological Review* 36:6 (December 1971): 1058–73.
52   Personal memory and Kopkind, "White on Black," 247–48.

53 Boesel and Rossi, eds., *Cities Under Siege*; Boesel, Goldberg and Marx, "Rebellion in Plainfield"; Boesel, "Analysis of the Ghetto Riots"; Boesel and Goldberg with Epstein, "Crisis in Cambridge"; Goldberg, "Ghetto Riots and Others"; Gary T. Marx, "Civil Disorders and Agents of Social Control," in Boesel and Rossi, *Cities Under Siege*, 157–84; David Boesel, Richard Berk, W. Eugene Groves, Bettye K. Edison, and Peter H. Rossi, "White Institutions and Black Rage," in Boesel and Rossi, *Cities Under Siege*, 309–24; Gary T. Marx, *Racial Conflict: Tension and Change in American Society* (Boston: Little, Brown and Company, 1971); Gary T. Marx, "Issueless Riots," *Annals of the American Academy of Political and Social Sciences* 391 (September 1970): 21–33.
54 Kopkind, "White on Black," 248; Gary Marx, quoted in Kopkind, "White on Black," 256.
55 Although Palmieri "fired" Dr. Shellow immediately, the actual separation process was drawn out over some months and appeared more ambiguous at the time. Kopkind, "White on Black," 249, and personal memory.
56 Kopkind, "White on Black," 252. Most staff in our office suspected at the time that the 120 staff were "let go" in reaction to our report, and we feared a cover up. For a personal "inside chronicle" of the tumultuous events of late November and early December 1967, see a letter that Lou Goldberg wrote to Commission Vice-Chair John Lindsay, but never sent, in Kopkind, "White on Black," 249–51.
57 Kopkind, "White on Black," 252–56.
58 Kerner had anticipated some negative response in advance, and press reports that anticipated the Commission findings foreshadowed the mixed responses. See Robert B. Semple, Jr., "Kerner Says U.S. Riots Report May Appear Abrasive to Some," *New York Times*, January 11, 1968; John Hebers, "Riot Study Is Said to Express Alarm," *New York Times*, February 18, 1968. For coverage of the *Kerner Report* when it was released, see "Panel on Civil Disorders Calls for Drastic Action to Avoid 2-Society Nation," *New York Times*, March 1, 1968; John Hebers, "Riot Panel Fears U.S. May Develop 'Urban Apartheid,'" *New York Times*, March 3, 1968; "Negroes and Rights: New Controversy in Wake of Kerner Report," *New York Times*, March 10, 1968.
59 Martin Luther King, Jr., "Beyond Vietnam: A Time to Break Silence," a speech to Clergy and Laymen Concerned about Vietnam," Riverside Church, New York City, April 4, 1967.
60 Because the Kerner Commission Report essentially confirmed President Johnson's own analysis of the riots, there is considerable speculation about why he distanced himself from the report and snubbed the Commission when it was released. Senator Harris believed that Johnson was erroneously informed that the report would criticize his civil rights policies and his War on Poverty. Others thought that the political agenda had shifted to the Vietnam War, and Dr. King's anti-war activism only highlighted the widening break between the President and African American leaders. See Brooke, "King and Kerner" and Harris, "The Riots and the Commission," 12–13.
61 See "Lightfoot banned in the U.S.A.," CBC radio broadcast, Reporter Alan Milar, interview with Gordon Lightfoot, CBC Digital Archives, http://archives.cbc.ca, accessed April 7, 2008.
62 Bantam Books sold 740,000 copies of a 708-page paperback version of the Report within the first eleven days. See Henry Raymont, "Riot Report Book Big Best Seller," *New York Times*, March 14, 2008; Stephan Thernstrom, Fred Siegel and Robert Woodson, Sr., "The Kerner Commission Report and the Failed Legacy of Liberal Social Policy," Heritage Lecture #619, The Heritage Foundation, March 13, 1998, http://www.heritage.org/Research/PoliticalPhilosophy/hl619.cfm.
63 "Negroes and Rights: New Controversy in the Wake of the Kerner Report," *New York Times*, March 10, 1968. Nixon's Democratic rival for the presidency in 1968, Vice-President Hubert Humphrey, was also cool on the report. *New York Times*, March 10,

1968. Carl Bernstein, "After Criticizing Riot Report, HHH Writes Laudatory Letters," *The Washington Post/Times Herald*, March 27, 1968; John Herbers, "The Kerner Report: A Journalist's View," in Harris and Wilkins, *Quiet Riots*, 21.

64 For an analysis of the riots as part of a continuous Black revolt, see Boesel, "An Analysis of the Ghetto Riots." As I prepare this essay for publication over half a century since the *Kerner Report* was published, and since the development of the Black Lives Matter movement, Boesel's analysis seems even more insightful.

65 Belshaw, "Eyes Still on the Prize That's Out of Reach."

66 Brooke, "King and Kerner: An Unfinished Agenda."

67 The Eisenhower Foundation is "the private sector continuation of the Kerner Riot Commission (and the National Violence Commission)." It periodically updated the Kerner Commission. In February 2008 the Foundation released a forty-year update on the Kerner Commission. I consulted the Executive Summary of the Foundation's preliminary findings, http://www.eisenhowerfoundation.org/kerner.php. The report was subsequently published. See The Eisenhower Foundation, *What Together We Can Do: A Forty Year Update on the National Advisory Commission on Civil Disorders Preliminary Findings* (Washington, D.C.: The Eisenhower Foundation, 2008). The twenty-five-year update, "In Commemoration of the Twenty-Fifth Anniversary of the National Advisory Commission on Civil Disorders," is available at the organization's website, first accessed March 28, 2008. A return visit to the site in April 2021 did not show any subsequent updates, though the organization continues to publish on race, inequality, poverty, and violence and to advocate for public policy.

68 U.S. Census Bureau, Census 2000, Table DP-1, Profile of General Demographic Characteristics: 2000, Geographic area, Plainfield city, New Jersey; Profile of Selected Social Characteristics; 2000, Geographic area, Plainfield city, New Jersey; Table DP-3, Profile of Selected Economic Characteristics: 2000, Geographic area, Plainfield city, New Jersey. For racial compositions of the rest of the New Jersey "string," see U.S. Census Bureau, Census 2000, Table DP-1, Profile of General Demographic Characteristics, 2000, Geographic areas, Elizabeth city, New Jersey; Jersey City, New Jersey; Englewood city, New Jersey; Paterson City, New Jersey.

69 U.S. Census Bureau, Census 2000, Table DP-1, Profile of General Demographic Characteristics: 2000, Geographic area, Newark city, New Jersey; Table DP-2, Profile of Selected Social Characteristics: 2000, Geographic area, Newark city, New Jersey; Table DP-3, Profile of Selected Economic Characteristics: 2000, Geographic area, Newark city, New Jersey.

70 U.S. Census Bureau, Census 2000, Table DP-1, Profile of General Demographic Characteristics: 2000, Geographic area, New Brunswick city, New Jersey; Table DP-2, Profile of Selected Social Characteristics: 2000, Geographic area, New Brunswick city, New Jersey; Table DP-3, Profile of Selected Economic Characteristics: 2000, Geographic area, New Brunswick city, New Jersey.

71 The period of few riots did not last long after 2008; as before, many confrontations were sparked by police actions.

72 The year 1968 was a time of enormous upheaval in many parts of the world. It marked a turn from Civil Rights to Black Power in the United States, increased mobilization against the Vietnam War following the Tet Offensive, student uprisings in France and Germany, and the violence at the 1968 Democratic convention in Chicago. I learned about the events in Chicago only after I left Hungary, where news from the West was not available following the Soviet invasion of Czechoslovakia.

73 Obama, "A More Perfect Union."

74 Carolyn G. Heilbrun, *Writing a Woman's Life* (New York: Ballantine Books, 1988), 25.

8

Remembering Ludlow: The 1913–1914 Coal Strike and the Politics of Public Memory

April 7, 2009

On May 30, 1918, 3,000 people gathered in a field just north of the Ludlow, Colorado, train depot. The United Mine Workers of America had leased this land in 1913 for the largest of eight tent colonies it erected to house miners and their families evicted from company housing when they struck three coal companies in southern Colorado. The crowd came in 1918 to dedicate a granite memorial to seventeen people who died during the strike, which climaxed on April 20, 1914, in an event known as the Ludlow Massacre.[1]

As in other Colorado miners' strikes, the coal operators requested state troops quickly after the strike was called in September, 1913. On October 28, 1913, Democratic Governor Elias Ammons sent the Colorado National Guard.[2] As the strike wore on, company guards and hired guns were mustered in as soldiers. On April 20, some of them shot and killed UMWA organizer Louis Tikas and two other strikers. Then they poured machine gun fire into the Ludlow tent colony, killing two more union men and eleven-year-old Frank Snyder. Witnesses said the guardsmen shot at anything that moved, set fire to tents, and looted families' possessions. The miners fought back with rifles they had hidden in case of attack. Some of the women and children ran for shelter in nearby arroyos; some hid in a well; some huddled in underground pits the strikers had dug under the tents in case of just such violence. When the fires burned out the next morning, camp residents discovered the bodies of two women and eleven children who suffocated and died in one pit: Patricia Valdez and her four children, the pregnant Cedilano Costa and her two children, the three

Petrucci children, and Cloriva and Roderlo Pedregon, ages four and six. Altogether, twenty people died on April 20, including one militia man, Private Albert J. Martin, whose body appeared to have been subsequently mutilated, although official reports differed regarding the nature of his injuries and the alleged mutilations.[3]

Union officials wired UMWA national headquarters that "all hell is loose in this state" and issued a "Call to Rebellion" for miners to organize into military-like companies. One thousand furious strikers armed with carbines mounted "a coordinated attack" on the National Guard. Fighting raged over a fifty-mile front until May 1, when the U.S. army arrived to intervene on President Woodrow Wilson's orders.[4]

The full death toll remains unknown: different sources report wildly different figures. The number of battle casualties was never clear, and the total depends on when one starts counting, because the violence started long before April 20, 1914. On September 23, 1913, miners walked off their jobs in the coal towns that stretched south along the front range of the Rockies. Of 11,000 miners in the southern fields, 9,000 left the mines at the Rocky Mountain and Victor American Fuel Companies, and at the largest company, Colorado Fuel and Iron, or CF&I, controlled by the Rockefeller family.[5] Before the strike began, though, on August 16, two Baldwin-Felts detectives who worked for the coal operators shot and killed UMWA organizer Gerald Lippiati on the street in Trinidad, Colorado.[6] On September 24, Bob Lee, a hated mine guard widely regarded as a rapist, was killed in the Segundo camp, probably by a Greek striker, as Lee charged strikers on horseback and drew his rifle. The *Rocky Mountain News* considered his death "the first flame of outlawry which sprang from the smoldering fires of class hatred in the southern coal field."[7] On October 7, two strikers and a guard were killed at Ludlow. Another union man was killed two days later. On October 17, the CF&I Death Special, a car equipped with armored plating and an armored machine gun, shot into the UMWA tent colony at Forbes, killing one striker, shooting a young girl in the face, and hitting a boy nine times in the legs.[8]

Nor was Ludlow unique in a long history of brutal strikes that had rocked Colorado coal and metal mining communities for decades, strikes waged over the same demands for which the coal miners struck in 1913.[9] They wanted union recognition, an eight-hour day, and a 10 percent increase in tonnage rates. They wanted pay for all "dead work"—work that did not directly produce coal and was therefore unpaid labor for miners paid by the ton, not the day. Dead work included breaking rock, timbering mine shafts to prevent cave-ins, and removing rock falls. Short weights also cut their pay, so the miners demanded "a check-weighman at all mines to be elected by the miners, without any interference by the company officials in said elections." They continued: "We demand the right to trade in any store we please, and the right to choose our own boarding place and own doctor." "We demand the enforcement of the Colorado mining laws and the abolition of the notorious and criminal guard system which has prevailed in the mining camps of Colorado for many years"—guards who identified union supporters to be fired and blacklisted.[10]

Four of these demands were Colorado state law, enacted through past struggles. Union recognition was a demand in 1903–1904, when a strike wave rocked the northern and southern Colorado coal fields, Idaho Springs, the Cripple Creek District, Telluride, and Colorado City. Some of those strikes were waged for an eight-hour day, after the state legislature ignored a statewide referendum that approved an eight-hour law for mines and smelters.[11]

Colorado coal and hardrock communities shared this strike history, but a different union, the Western Federation of Miners, organized the hardrock miners, who mined precious metals and who were more native born, more northern and western European than the coal miners. Unionized hardrock miners drove out Mexicans, Chinese, and southern and eastern Europeans to maintain what they called "White man's camps."[12] The hardrock unions were virtually destroyed in the disastrous 1903–1904 strike wave, when the same National Guard general who commanded the troops ten years later at Ludlow, General John Chase, invaded a federal district courtroom in Cripple Creek rather than turn over union leaders as mandated by a writ of habeas corpus. Chase was court marshaled for defying Governor James Peabody, who was himself fiercely anti-union, and who reinstated Chase after his conviction for disobeying orders.[13]

Industrial conflict was nothing new in the northern Colorado lignite fields, nor in the rich bituminous fields of southern Colorado. The coal camps grew along with the railroads, beginning in the 1870s, when the Kansas Pacific; Atcheson, Topeka and Santa Fe; and Denver and Rio Grande laid their tracks across treeless prairies to Colorado. Coal miners organized the Knights of Labor in the 1880s and then joined the UMWA after it was founded in 1890.[14] The Ludlow strikers identified with at least twenty-seven ethnic groups and spoke as many languages. The largest group among the southern Colorado coal miners was the Italians. Next came Hispanos and Mexican immigrants (16 percent), who coal operators considered ignorant and subhuman "foreigners," though their ancestors had established Santa Fe in 1598. They entered the mines as Anglos took their communal Spanish land grants, leaving homes in northern New Mexico and Colorado's San Luis Valley for wage work underground. The rest of the workforce consisted of eastern Europeans (15 percent), Anglo-Americans (13 percent), Austrians—including Serbs and Slavs—(11 percent), African Americans (7 percent), Greeks (6 percent), and a few Japanese, Germans, Scandinavians, Scotch, Irish, English, French, Spanish, and Canadians.[15]

The 1913 strike, like earlier ones, challenged social and economic relations in the coal camps, where miners had to live in company housing, trade at company stores, pray in company churches with ministers the company hired, and send their children to company schools—at least until they entered the mines themselves. If sick or injured, they had to go to a company doctor, who was not likely to testify against the company in cases of workplace injury.[16]

The miners, in fact, would argue that the strike violence began with the dangers they faced daily underground. Between 1884 and 1912, over 1,700 miners died in Colorado mines. Dust explosions were common in the dry climate, and the mine operators blatantly ignored the coal mining safety laws. Colorado's death rate was two to three times the national average. In 1912, the Colorado death rate among miners was 6.81 per thousand; the national average was 3.12, not counting occupational deaths from diseases like black lung.[17]

Violence was neither new to western coal miners nor unique in the contested history of industrial America. But Ludlow wrote a pivotal chapter in that history, in part because of how it affected American public opinion and entered public memory. No industrial conflict shocked the nation, or troubled its collective conscience, more than the Ludlow massacre. Workers had been evicted and deported in previous strikes, and had died in previous labor struggles, but those deaths, especially those of immigrant men, aroused little public outcry. Children had even died, as in the 1913 Calumet miners' strike, when someone yelled "fire" into a union Christmas party, and seventy-three people, mostly children, were crushed to death in the ensuing panic.[18] But not before Ludlow had the actions of the state so clearly led to the deaths of women and children. Their deaths won some moderates to side with labor and mobilized journalists and political activists to support the strikers.

The tide of public outrage found a target. At the 1918 dedication ceremony, UMWA President Frank Hayes read his poem, "On Ludlow Field":

> But alas! There came a day.
> Greed demanded: "Stalk your prey,
> Fire the tents and shoot to slay!"
>   Here on Ludlow Field.
>
> In the embers grey and red,
> Here we found them where they bled,
> Here we found them stark and dead,
>   Here on Ludlow Field.[19]

Hayes' audience knew *whose* greed had caused the tragedy: the mine owners and especially John D. Rockefeller, Jr., of CF&I. After the massacre, novelist Upton Sinclair organized mourning pickets outside the Rockefeller offices and residences. Sinclair then wrote two novels inspired by Ludlow, *King Coal*, published in 1917 and *The Coal War*, which wasn't published until 1976 because it was so transparently about Ludlow.[20]

Even before the first shot was fired, Rockefeller knew he had a public relations problem—one born in large part of his own belligerence. On April 6, 1914, a Congressional Committee asked him if he would insist on maintaining the open shop at CF&I's coal camps even "if it costs all your property and kills all your employees?" "It is a great principle," Rockefeller replied.[21] To battle the negative publicity, he hired a publicist, Ivy Lee, and future Canadian Prime Minister Mackenzie King, who drew up the Rockefeller Industrial Plan for a company union. This compromise led to some reform in labor-management relations without conceding any power to labor.[22]

As the U.S. Commission on Industrial Relations probed the Ludlow Massacre in 1915, it became clear that Rockefeller deserved much of the blame. The Commission called Rockefeller to testify and found that, contrary to his public testimony, Rockefeller was in constant touch with CF&I management during the strike, supported his managers' uncompromising refusal to bargain with the union, and was, to quote United States Commission on Industrial Relations Chairman Frank Walsh, "the directing mind throughout the struggle."[23] Rockefeller did not order the massacre, but he knew massive violence was a distinct possibility.

Incredibly, then, he tried to attend the dedication of the Ludlow monument and to address the crowd. On May 30, 1918, Rockefeller and his wife arrived in a chauffeur-driven car, along with Mackenzie King. King got out, spoke with union leaders, and returned to warn Rockefeller that he was not wanted. Though it is often reported that Rockefeller attended the dedication, according to King, the Rockefellers drove off without ever leaving their vehicle.[24] Their departure signaled one of the most interesting outcomes of a failed strike. Labor lost the battle but seized the crucial terrain of memory.

The United Mine Workers bought the land in 1917 and dedicated the granite monument next to the site of the lethal pit. The stone cenotaph represented a coal miner, sleeves rolled up, and a woman holding a child in her arms. The names of seventeen union dead are inscribed on the monument—those shot by soldiers on April 20, 1914, and those who died in the pit (see Figure 8.1).[25] Every year since 1918, the UMWA has held a memorial ceremony at the massacre site. It later preserved the pit with cement walls and ceiling and built a picnic structure for the annual services. Visitors record their comments in a register that has generated an archive of memories. For instance:

> September 18, 1993: We came with our family Tanya age 9 and Sergei, age 8. I told them this was a memorial for children killed in the struggle for human rights and dignity. Rosemary Zibort, Santa Fe, NM.
>
> October 12, 1991: . . . I'm passing through—just went to my father's funeral in California. He was Wesley J. Thompson who was born in Ludlow in 1907. He was 7 years old when the massacre happened. He saw it while he and family were in a wagon being shot at. He described the puffs of dirt popping up around the wagon from the bullets being shot at them.
>
> July 3, 1994: I Frank Luchetta am related to Charles Costa. His brother Nicolas Costa was my Grandfather. He spoke of his Bro. Charles often. I'm 65 years old & this experience will last forever. May they rest in God's peace.[26]

The militia shot and killed UMWA organizer Charles Costa on April 14. His wife Cedi and their children, Lucy and Onofrio, died in the death pit.

Figure 8.1. Ludlow Monument, photo by M. K. Walker, CC BY 2.0, uploaded on April 28, 2005, https://flickr.com/photos/84132439@N00/11360031.

For many years the Ludlow monument drew visitors who passed by or who came because they knew the story. Until the mid-1990s the only direction to the site just off Interstate 25 was a rusty sign the union had erected. Today there's a highway marker at the Ludlow exit. Ludlow remained vivid for the miners' descendants, for some union members, and for the American left, its memory preserved by organized labor and oral tradition. During the strike, Frank Hayes wrote "We're Coming, Colorado!" to be sung to the tune of the Battle Hymn of the Republic, verses that were adapted to later labor struggles.[27]

Labor honored its strike heroes: Mother Jones, the feisty octogenarian who worked the southern Colorado fields for much of the strike, and the victims of the Ludlow massacre, like the slain Louis Tikas, who had organized the Greek miners. The UMWA had brilliantly overcome ethnic divisions that employers had exploited by hiring ethnic organizers, like Tikas and Costa. A musical poetic homage emphasized that Tikas was a "knight of humanity... more than American or Greek."[28] Yet in Ludlow's aftermath the union emphasized gender and downplayed ethnicity, focusing on the innocent women and children who died but seldom mentioning the slain men, and almost never the names of the victims that would call attention to their Hispanic, Italian, or Greek ancestry.

The songs and verses created selective memories. In the early 1940s, Woody Guthrie wrote his moving but inaccurate Ludlow ballad:

> That very night your soldiers waited,
> Until all us miners were asleep,
> You snuck around our little tent town, Soaked our tents with your kerosene.
> You struck a match and in the blaze that started,
> You pulled the triggers of your gatling guns,
> I made a run for the children but the fire wall stopped me.
> Thirteen children died from your guns.[29]

The soldiers began firing the morning of April 20, not at night. One child died from gunfire, eleven suffocated. Yet more Americans learned the story of Ludlow from Guthrie than from Frank Hayes or the U.S. Commission on Industrial Relations. The story increasingly narrowed to focus on the thirteen innocent victims in the pit. In 1990, the Trinidad, Colorado, UMWA Auxiliary concluded its history of the strike with Frank Hayes' poem, "On Ludlow Field." But it omitted the first two finger-pointing verses, and kept only three more heart-rending stanzas:

> Ah, we knew them every one,
> Father, Mother, Daughter, Son,
> Ere the course of life was run,
> Here on Ludlow Field.
>
> Here today we dedicate,
> Here today we consecrate,
> A monument to their Estate,
> Here on Ludlow Field.

> Lo! the goal of Justice nears,
> And we vision through our tears,
> Freedom's martyred volunteers,
> Here on Ludlow Field.

Moral outrage fueled these memories. Guthrie used the accusatory tone and directly addressed the soldiers and mine owners. John D. Rockefeller as villain grabbed public attention. Today, most U.S. history texts mention the Ludlow Massacre and link it to Rockefeller. In one text, *Out of Many*, Rockefeller's name appears only in connection with Ludlow.[30]

Still, Ludlow was hardly a household word. It was mostly remembered locally, or by organized labor and historians. A new campaign to inscribe it in national memory began on May 8, 2003, when the union caretaker drove to the Ludlow site to clean it up for the annual memorial gathering. He found, to his horror, that the head of the male figure on the memorial had been severed from the torsos along with the left arm of the female figure. The image of the disfigured monument galvanized labor supporters, who called the monument "Our Twin Towers."[31] The *Denver Post* called the desecration an "outrageous act." "Those who died at the site of the miners' tent camp on April 20, 1914, sanctified this patch of southern Colorado as hallowed ground for the American labor movement," the *Post* editorialized. "For Coloradoans, the tears shed over Ludlow have never quite dried and they never should."[32] News of the vandalism went out on the history listserv H-LABOR. I saw it and sent a contribution to the Trinidad UMWA local for the fund to restore the monument. Local unions offered a $5,000 reward for information leading to the arrest of the perpetrators, who still have not been found.

The 2003 gathering revived an event that had long drawn only the faithful few. The Labor and Working Class History Association (LAWCHA) offered to send Julie Greene, a labor history professor at the University of Colorado-Boulder. Julie reported that half an hour before the service was to begin, about a hundred striking steelworkers arrived from Pueblo chanting "Remember! Ludlow!" The main speaker, UMWA President Cecil Roberts, had the audience on its feet as he declared: "This is our Vietnam Veterans Memorial, our Tomb of the Unknown Soldier, our Lincoln Memorial. There is no question whatsoever that ... this monument will be restored." Julie Greene drew loud applause with LAWCHA's offer to help make the site a National Historic Landmark.[33]

And so began the work of getting National Historic Landmark (NHL) status for the Ludlow site. Landmarks are historic places designated by the Secretary of the Interior because they are exceptional in illustrating or interpreting the heritage of the United States. Landmark status is not easily achieved: fewer than 2,500 sites had made it through the daunting nomination process, and only a handful were labor history sites. According to historian John Bodnar, the class backgrounds of Park Service professionals reinforced the practice of promoting "progress and patriotism" as dominant themes. The few labor landmarks include the well-preserved homes of national leaders like Terence Powderly, Samuel Gompers, Eugene Debs, and Frances Perkins. By 2003, only three, the Passaic textile strike headquarters, the Triangle Shirtwaist factory, and the Haymarket Martyrs Monument at Waldheim Cemetery were associated with labor conflicts.[34]

Incoming LAWCHA President James Green asked the Board to approve a project to seek landmark status for Ludlow, and in January 2004, he appointed me and fellow Board member Zaragosa Vargas as co-chairs of the Ad Hoc Committee on Labor History Landmarks (otherwise known as "the Ludlow Committee"). Dr. Vargas was unable to take an active leadership role after the first few months, and so I found myself chairing a committee of scholars who stretched from Penn State to Wisconsin to Binghampton, New York, South Florida, and Santa Barbara with backgrounds as diverse as their geography. Alan Derickson of Penn State and I had both worked on the Western Federation of Miners; "Z" Vargas and the late Camille Guérin-Gonzales were experts in Latinx labor history; Guérin-Gonzales had written on women in coal mining communities, including southern Colorado, and on international labor migrations. Anthony DeStefanis had researched the use of troops in mining strikes; Jonathan Rees, who taught at Colorado State University, Pueblo, was well informed on local developments; Randall McGuire was one of three archaeologists who had directed the Colorado Coalfield Project which excavated parts of the Ludlow site. We got help from Holly Syrakkos of the AFL-CIO; Martin Blatt, from the National Park Service; Tobias Higbie, Newberry Library; UMWA Regional Representative Bob Butero; and Mike Romero, President of the Trinidad, Colorado UMWA local.

On February 3, I called Lysa Wegman-French, a National Park Service historian I knew because we were for years the only women active in the Mining History Association. It turned out that she coordinated National Historic Landmarks in Colorado and was "delighted" that LAWCHA was "interested in pursuing NHL designation for the Ludlow site." She warned all-too-accurately that the NHL process could be difficult, and that some successful nominations took "years and years of on-again off-again work."[35]

The case for the historical importance of the Ludlow massacre seemed self-evident to labor historians and unionists, but NHL guidelines require that sites retain their historical integrity and meet National Park Service criteria of "national significance." There are six primary criteria for determining "significance." Sites are significant if they were "associated with events that have made a significant contribution to and are identified with ... the broad patterns of United States history" or that are associated with "nationally significant" persons or that "represent some great idea or ideal of the American people" or that "embody characteristics of an architectural-type specimen exceptionally valuable for the study of a period," and so on. Some sites are "ordinarily not eligible" for designation: cemeteries, birthplaces, graves of historical figures, and religious buildings.[36]

Louis Tikas is buried at Ludlow, but it is not a cemetery. It qualified under landmarks criteria as a memorial. The tent colony site retained integrity because the ground on which it rested had not been seriously disturbed since the strike. And though the monument had been damaged, it retained integrity as a site of memory, as did the disturbing death pit. It qualified, too, because some archaeological sites can be landmarks. The tent colony area qualified because it had been investigated by the Colorado Coalfield War Archeological Project, funded by the Colorado Historical Society, State Historical Fund. The archeological exploration was directed by Dean Saitta, University of Denver; Philip Duke, Fort Lewis College; and Randall McGuire, Binghampton University, who was a member of the LAWCHA Ludlow Committee.[37]

The Ludlow Committee negotiated the competing imperatives of our professional assessments of Ludlow's history, the practical demands of the nomination process, and the particular urgencies of supportive politicians, of Park Service requirements and deadlines, and of the union itself. The UMWA wanted to know that it would retain ownership of the Ludlow site, and that it could withdraw from the landmark designation if it had qualms about government interpretations of its history. It was challenging to coordinate, by email and conference calls, a team of academics, all with day jobs, each with a particular interpretation of Ludlow that sometimes had to be reconciled with the significance criteria, and with the politics of achieving NHL designation.

Once completed, the extensive nomination materials had to be reviewed by NHL staff in Denver and Santa Fe, as well as the Park Service in Washington, all of whom suggested revisions. Elected officials and site owners had to be notified and their comments invited. Once revised, the nomination could go to the National Park Service Advisory Board at one of its two annual meetings; it had to be on the agenda six months in advance. The Advisory Board reviews nominations and recommends to the Secretary of the Interior, who makes the final decision.

We first had to decide what site to nominate: the tent colony itself or the whole Ludlow battleground. The UMWA owns forty acres that includes most of the tent colony site, but a small part of the site belongs to another owner. We were told that more territory could be added after a site received Landmark status and decided to begin with the union's forty acres.

The more fundamental challenge was to meet the criteria for historical significance without losing the story. Some of the strategies that had preserved the memory of the Ludlow Massacre were not likely to succeed with the Department of the Interior during the George W. Bush administration. Blaming John D. Rockefeller, Jr., for instance, was likely a losing strategy. While maintaining historical honesty, we needed to emphasize points that fit the criteria and we had to write a focused narrative that could communicate easily to the lay public. Some Committee members felt strongly that we should not write a "battles, dates, and outcomes" history of industrial conflict, but that we should include the processes of class formation, and how the tent colony had functioned as a multi-ethnic community that included women and families.

Meanwhile, the more tangible landmark was being restored. By early 2004, $80,000 in donations had come from all over the world and the damaged statues were removed for repair at Griswold Conservation Associates in Beverly Hills, California. The Memorial was re-dedicated in 2005, when 400 people gathered at the annual commemoration. The entire UMWA Executive Board attended, and the charismatic Cecil Roberts addressed the crowd. Jim Green spoke about LAWCHA's work to make the site a National Historic Landmark. Representatives of Colorado U.S. Senator Ken Salazar and his brother, Congressman John Salazar from the Pueblo district, promised any support we needed in Washington. Someone—no one would tell me who—promised that the site would have Landmark status within a year, an impossible goal that complicated my life as I explained endlessly why we couldn't do it.

By July 2005 the Committee summarized four themes to establish Ludlow's historical significance. The first addressed Ludlow as the apex of a long series of western mining strikes that pitted employers, workers, and the state against one another. The Ludlow Massacre provided the impetus for checks on state force, and, from the perspectives of employers and the state, for finding new ways to manage industrial relations and contain unions.

The second topic concerned Ludlow's influence on industrial and social policy. One major outcome, the company union, was later outlawed under the 1935 National Labor Relations Act, and some historians argue that the Industrial Relations Commission investigation ultimately led to New Deal reforms.

Third, Committee members underlined the significance of the strike itself, and its importance as an organized response to the dangers, low pay, community-focused social control, and ethnic discrimination in coal mining. The union's strategy was unique: the UMWA leased the tent colony sites for their evicted members; the strike organization included leaders from all the ethnic groups, who spoke all the miners' languages. Tent colony governance included the women and addressed domestic arrangements, community needs, and union strategy.

Finally, the Committee emphasized the cultural significance of the site as a catalyst for memory and identification among contemporary workers and Mexican Americans in particular, and the wider cultural influence of Ludlow, through contemporary newspaper coverage, "muckraking" reports, and Upton Sinclair's novels.[38]

Randall McGuire summarized the archaeological significance of the site and its future research potential:

> In many ways the Ludlow Massacre site is the perfect archaeological site, a short-term occupation destroyed by fire. The catastrophic abandonment of the tent colony and subsequent burning create a "Pompeii"-like situation. Objects that would normally have been taken with a family when they moved were left behind in the rush to escape the violence and fire.[39]

The latrine pits, trash pits, and tent cellars filled with artifacts recorded families' lives and customs and offered a highly unusual view of the everyday lives of early-20th-century working-class families.[40]

As we discussed significance, the National Park Service weighed in, deciding that since the Ludlow Massacre site had such an important archaeological character it would be best to have an archeologist be our Park Service contact person. So Charles Haecker, the archaeologist for the National Historic Landmarks Program, intermountain region, replaced Lysa Wegman-French as point person for the project.[41] Haecker and Wegman-French jointly decided in August 2005 that two of the six criteria "of national significance" would best serve the Ludlow nomination: Criterion 1 (sites "associated with events that have made a significant contribution to, and are identified with, or that outstandingly represent, the broad national pattern of United States history and from which an understanding and appreciation of those patterns may be gained") and Criterion 6 (sites that "have yielded or may be likely to yield information of major scientific importance by revealing new cultures, or by shedding light upon periods of occupation of large areas of the United States. Such sites are those which have yielded, or which may reasonable be expected to yield, data affecting theories, concepts, and ideas to a major degree").[42] Their advice provided focus, though it frustrated some members who argued for the importance of other criteria.

In November 2005, Haecker suggested that since we all had academic responsibilities, it might be useful to get help from someone experienced with NHL nominations. The Park Service hired Tom and Laurie Simmons to prepare the nomination but guaranteed that the Ludlow Committee would complete its "professional responsibility of reviewing the nomination since your names will be on it—and you all have a personal interest that the presented information gets your ideas, interpretations across."[43]

Meanwhile, I got a new job: handling supportive politicians and stakeholders who were frustrated with the lengthy nomination process, particularly after the unrealistic promise of a one-year completion. As the impossible deadline approached, Senator Salazar decided to introduce a bill to legislate landmark status for Ludlow, and the Park Service asked me to intervene. The UMWA invited me to speak at the annual Ludlow commemoration on June 11, 2006, which gave me the opportunity to meet with the stakeholders: Bob Butero, Mike Romero, and Dan Kane of the UMWA; Pam DiFatta, representing Congressman John Salazar; John Rodriquez, representing Senator Ken Salazar; and Charlie Haecker, and Tom and Laurie Simmons from the Park Service, who helped me explain the nomination process. Later in June, I met with Matt Lee-Ashley, of Senator Salazar's staff, to explain Park Service concerns about the proposed bill, which they feared could make Landmarks into political footballs, and could designate Landmarks without appropriate historical documentation. Lee-Ashley wrote his BA thesis on the 1903–1904 southern Colorado coal strike and knew his Ludlow history.[44] He agreed to convey these concerns to the Senator, who agreed not to submit his bill until the nomination was completed.

The final nomination totaled over sixty pages single-spaced, plus maps, figures, and photographs. Committee members offered comments and corrections on the draft document and answered queries throughout the review process.[45] The nomination was finally submitted on December 12, 2007, and the stakeholders sent support letters. Senator Salazar wrote:

> I strongly believe that the Ludlow Tent Colony should be designated a National Historic Landmark and that the National Park Service should play a greater role in assisting with the protection and interpretation of this vital chapter in our nation's history. I stand ready to assist in the landmark designation, which is strongly supported in the local communities, by championing legislation in the U.S. Senate to create the Ludlow National Historic Landmark.[46]

In January, while working at the National Archives, I met again with Matt Lee-Ashley and later helped draft the bill.

On April 18, 2008, in commemoration of the ninety-fourth anniversary of the Ludlow Massacre, Senator Salazar submitted, for himself and Senator Jay Rockefeller of West Virginia, "A Bill To Designate the Ludlow Massacre National Historic Landmark in the State of Colorado." Salazar stated:

> The events that occurred during the Ludlow Massacre, and the site that memorializes the conflict, are central to our nation's story. The history is still significant to the Coloradoans who live and work in the region. Residents of Las Animas, Huerfano and Pueblo counties, along with many people across America, rightly see the 1913–14 coal strike and the Ludlow Massacre as a defining moment in our shared history and integral to the region's identity. I am proud to introduce the bill in the Senate and will continue to work to ensure it is designated as a national landmark, so that we can better

remember the struggles and sacrifices our nation endured on the path to safer and fairer labor conditions.[47]

Senator Salazar's statements resonated powerfully for members of the Ludlow Committee, particularly because Salazar's family was from the San Luis Valley and had lived the history of class and ethnic relations in southern Colorado. Senator Rockefeller's co-sponsorship powerfully evoked his family's involvement. Together, Salazar and Rockefeller symbolically affirmed Ludlow's significance for all its descendants.

But their bill never got a committee hearing. The nomination was presented at the October 28–29, 2008, meeting of the National Park Service Advisory Board. LAWCHA and the United Mine Workers sent support letters. I wrote for the Ludlow Committee that:

> Ludlow was pivotal in the history of U.S. industrial relations as a dramatic example of the limits of the use of force in industrial struggles, and of the need to find new accommodations between labor and management. It was also unusual in the organization of the strike, and in the effectiveness of the strikers in forging a multi-ethnic community that worked cooperatively across barriers of culture and language. It was particularly significant for the effective organization of domestic life, and the involvement of miners' wives and children in the daily functioning of the strikers' community. The tragic end of the strike dramatized their involvement, and the archaeological remains of their community allow us to link the daily lives of working families with the more dramatic public events of strikes and industrial conflict that are more commonly represented in history books. Most simply, the site links what the strikers were sacrificing for with the public events of industrial conflict.[48]

On November 3, Charles Haecker phoned the good news: the NPS Advisory Board unanimously and enthusiastically recommended that the Ludlow site be designated a National Historic Landmark. On December 17, President-elect Barack Obama seemed to seal the deal when he nominated Senator Ken Salazar to be Secretary of the Interior. But in the final days of the Bush administration, on January 16, 2009, Secretary of the

Interior Dirk Kempthorne officially designated the Ludlow Tent Colony site a National Historic Landmark.

A coalition of the United Mine Workers of America, elected officials, local union members, Colorado residents, Park Service personnel, and historians worked together for this recognition of Ludlow's significance in American history. Inevitably, each of us left a bit of our own interpretations on the cutting room floor. My 2009 lecture gave me another chance to share some reflections.

When I began the landmarking project, I had been visiting the Ludlow memorial for over thirty years. Each time was different—I was different, the context was different, and I knew it would be different again when I returned in June for the plaquing ceremony. That is the nature of memory and of the ongoing project of making sense of history. The annual Ludlow Memorial Service, the comments of the visitors who sign the registry, and even the violently disfigured statues all testify to the power of historical memory: there is no need to attack monuments that don't inspire living memories. The outcry in 2003, and the determined effort to repair the statues, testified to the enduring significance of Ludlow for many people.

Ludlow's significance has been contested since it happened. It remains a place to question which events and whose histories weave a collective past. We will continue to debate its legacy, as we should continue to debate all history that matters. But for too long, I think, we have told the story as one of victims and villains, debating who was most violent, who was most innocent. Mother Jones, who used to counsel miners to "Pray for the dead and fight like hell for the living," suggested that no one cared about the miners' conditions until women and children died. "Little children roasted alive make a front page story," she said. "Dying by inches . . . does not."[49]

It would be easy to romanticize Ludlow and lose the grubby daily details of what the fight was about and what it cost on all sides. Ludlow put a human face on industrial America. When I visit Ludlow, I don't think about John D. Rockefeller, or Mackenzie King, or Upton Sinclair, or even Mother Jones. I think about Louis Tikas, Charles and Cedi Costa, and especially about Mary Petrucci. Mary Petrucci, age 24, born in a coal mining family in the shadow of the Victor-American mine tipple at Hastings, raised in a company house, educated at a company school, married at sixteen to a man who loaded boxcars for the coal company in Walsenburg. The morning of April 20, 1914, Mary Petrucci was doing the laundry when her tent in the Southeast corner, front row, of the tent colony seemed to her to be the first tent set on fire. She ran with her children to the Pedregones' tent and got them all safely inside the pit. When she regained consciousness, she was holding her dead infant, surrounded by the corpses of her friends, their children, and her own. She was found the morning of April 21, wandering in a daze, unclear about where her children were, or how she got out of the pit where she had hidden, or where the pit was.[50]

Mary Petrucci chose to be at Ludlow. She was not simply a powerless victim, but neither was she an all-powerful agent who controlled her life or her options. She joined three other activists, Pearl Jolly, Mary Thomas, and Margaret Dominiske, who traveled to Chicago, Washington, D.C., and New York to speak at rallies and give interviews. But Mary Petrucci broke down during the trip and returned to Colorado. She explained her decision to reporter Lucy Huffaker of the *New York Tribune*:

> Perhaps it seems strange to you that I want to go back home. But I do. My man is there and my children are buried there, and I don't believe I could ever live anywhere else. I have been so happy there. . . . I used to sing around my work and playing with my babies. Well, I don't sing any more. And my husband doesn't laugh as he used to do. I'm twenty-four years old and I suppose I'll live a long time, but I don't see how I can ever be happy again, but I try to be cheerful on account of my husband. It is so hard for him when he comes home from work to find only me in the house, and none of the children.

Nonetheless, she told Huffaker "not to think that we could do any differently another time. . . . We are working people—my husband and I—and we're stronger for the union than we were before the strike. . . . I can't have my babies back," she concluded. "But perhaps when everybody knows about them, something will be done to make the world a better place for all babies."[51]

Ludlow connects the larger stories of industrial America and national significance with the individual people who waged the fight, risked the cost, and made the history. Remembering Ludlow, I think, begins with their names. Those who died in the cellar were:

Patricia (or Patria or Petra) Valdez, 37
Eulalia Valdez, 8
Mary Valdez, 7
Elvira Valdez, 3 months

Rudolph Valdez, 9
Joe Petrucci, 4 1/2
Lucy Petrucci, 2 1/2
Frank Petrucci, 6 months
Roderlo Pedregon, 6
Cloriva Pedregon, 4
Cedilano Costa, 27
Onafrio Costa, 6
Lucy Costa, 4

Dead from gunshots April 20:

Primero Laresse, 18
Louis Tikas, 30
James Filer, 43
John Bartolotti, 45
Charles Costa, 31
Frank Snyder, Jr., 11
Private Albert Martin, 21[52]

NOTES

I am grateful to James Green for appointing the LAWCHA Ad Hoc Committee on Labor History Landmarks and asking me to co-chair; to the members of that committee, Alan Derickson, Jonathan Rees, Randall McGuire, Anthony DeStefanis, and especially the late Camille Guérin-Gonzales; to Marty Blatt and Holly Syrrakos for their help; to Lysa Wegman-French and Charles Haecker of the National Park Service; to Bob Butero of the UMWA, to Mike and Yolanda Romero for keeping the Ludlow visitors' books and sharing them and for their hospitality, and to the members of the Trinidad UMWA local who have maintained the site and the memories.

Additional Sources: The 2014 centennial of the Ludlow Massacre engendered commemorations, exhibits, publications revisiting the 1913–1914 strike and its legacy, and a Centennial Commemoration at the Ludlow site hosted by the United Mine Workers of America, at which I was honored to speak. Fawn-Amber Montoya, ed., *Making an American Workforce: The Rockefellers and the Legacy of Ludlow* (Boulder: University Press of Colorado, 2014), an anthology of eight essays published in conjunction with the 2014 strike centennial, probes the legacy of Ludlow at the Rockefeller-controlled Colorado Fuel and Iron Company (CF&I) and John D. Rockefeller, Jr.'s influence on welfare capitalism, particularly the company union and "sociological" programs intended to "Americanize" an ethnically diverse workforce through the YMCA, sports, and other community programs. Fawn-Amber Montoya and Karin Larkin, eds., *Communities of Ludlow: Collaborative Stewardship and the Ludlow Centennial Commemoration Commission* (Louisville, CO: University Press of Colorado, 2022) includes nine articles that examine how the history of Ludlow is remembered and taught, and two oral histories with Trinidad

UMWA memory keeper Yolanda Romero and UMWA official Robert (Bob) Butero who have done much to preserve the history of Ludlow. The book is based in the work of the members of the Ludlow Centennial Commemoration Commission: Thomas Andrews, Robert (Bob) Butero, William Convery, Dawn DiPrince, Victoria Miller, Adam Morgan, Jonathan Rees, Dean Saitta, Maria Sanchez-Tucker, and Josephine Jones, and explores the contributions of anthropologists, historians, and the union itself in preserving memory. I have an article in the volume, "Remembering Ludlow."

1. The sculpture on the monument dedicated in 1918 is inventoried in the Save Outdoor Sculpture project of the Smithsonian. Save Outdoor Sculpture, Colorado survey, 1994; National Park Service, American Monuments and Outdoor Sculpture Database, CO0001, 1989; *Monumental News*, October 1918, 451–52; *Denver Post*, 15 May 1918, 5. The best account of the Ludlow strike and the massacre remains the late Senator George S. McGovern's doctoral dissertation, "The Colorado Coal Strike, 1913-1914" (PhD diss., Northwestern University, 1953). For a description of the field with a detailed account of the events that led to the massacre, see also George S. McGovern and Leonard F. Guttridge, *The Great Coal Field War* (Boston: Houghton Mifflin, 1972). Other superb accounts of the Colorado coal wars can be found in Priscilla Long, *Where the Sun Never Shines: A History of America's Bloody Coal Industry* (New York: Paragon House, 1989); Howard Zinn, "The Colorado Coal Strike, 1913-14," in *Three Strikes: Miners, Musicians, Salesgirls and the Fighting Spirit of Labor's Last Century*, eds. Howard Zinn, Dana Frank, and Robin D.G. Kelley (Boston: Beacon Press, 2001), 5–55; and John Graham, "Introduction," Upton Sinclair, *The Coal War* (Boulder, CO: Colorado Associated University Press, 1986), vi–xcii. The most recent books are Scott Matelle, *Blood Passion: The Ludlow Massacre and Class War in the American West* (New Brunswick, NJ: Rutgers University Press, 2007) and Thomas G. Andrews, *Killing for Coal: America's Deadliest Labor War* (Cambridge: Harvard University Press, 2008) which places the events in the very broad context of environmental history.

   The names of the victims were sometimes reported with different spellings; many were taken from coroners' reports. Dead from gunshots the first day were: Primero Laresse, 18; Frank Snyder, 11; Louis Tikas, 30; James Filer, 43; John Bartolootti, 45; Charles Costa, 31; Albert Marin, 21 (militia man). Those who died in the cellar were: Patricia (or Patria or Petra) Valdez, 37; Eulalia Valdez, 8; Mary Valdez, 7; Elvira Valdez, 3 months; Rudolph Valdez, 9; Joe Petrucci, 4 1/2; Lucy Petrucci, 2 1/2; Frank Petrucci, 6 months; Rogerio (or Roderlo or Rodgerio) Pedregone, 6; Cloriva (or Gloria or Clovine) Pedregone, 4; Cedilano (or Cardelima or Fedelina) Costa, 27; Onafrio (or Oragio) Costa, 6; and Lucy Costa, 4.

2. McGovern and Guttridge, *The Great Coalfield War*, 134.
3. McGovern and Guttridge, *The Great Coalfield War*, 210–31. For disagreements about Martin's injuries, see 222.
4. McGovern and Guttridge, *The Great Coalfield War*, 232–33, 239–68.
5. McGovern and Guttridge, *The Great Coalfield War*, 100–6; Graham, ed. "Introduction" *The Coal War*, xxxiii–xxxv.
6. McGovern and Guttridge, *The Great Coalfield War*, 110.
7. McGovern and Guttridge, *The Great Coalfield War*, 109–10; Long, *Where the Sun Never Shines*, 264, 278.
8. McGovern and Guttridge, *The Great Coalfield War*, 122–23; Long, *Where the Sun Never Shines*, 278.
9. For the long history of strikes in hardrock mining, see Vernon H. Jenson, *Heritage of Conflict: Labor Relations in the Nonferrous Metals Industry Up to 1930* (Ithaca, NY: Cornell University Press, 1950); Melvyn Dubofsky, *We Shall Be All: A History of the Industrial Workers of the World* (New York: Quadrangle/New York Times Book Co., 1969), 19–87; George G. Suggs, Jr., *Colorado's War on Militant Unionism: James H. Peabody*

and the Western Federation of Miners (Detroit: Wayne State University Press, 1972), 84–117; Elizabeth Jameson, *All That Glitters: Class, Conflict, and Community in Cripple Creek* (Urbana: University of Illinois Press, 1998); Richard E. Lingenfelter, *The Hardrock Miners: A History of the Mining Labor Movement in the American West, 1863–1893* (Berkeley: University of California Press, 1974); Ronald C. Brown, *Hard-Rock Miners: The Intermountain West, 1860–1920* (College Station, Texas: Texas A&M University Press, 1979); Mark Wyman, *Hard Rock Epic: Western Miners and the Industrial Revolution, 1860–1910* (Berkeley: University of California Press, 1979). For coal, see Long, *Where the Sun Never Shines*, 167–271; McGovern and Guttridge, *The Great Coalfield War*, 1–91.

10 McGovern and Guttridge, *The Great Coalfield War*, 102.

11 See Suggs, *Colorado's War on Industrial Unionism*; Jameson, *All That Glitters*, 199, 224; Long, *Where the Sun Never Shines*, 217–41.

12 See Jameson, *All That Glitters*, 140–60.

13 Jameson, *All That Glitters*, 199–252; Suggs, *Colorado's War on Militant Unionism*; McGovern and Guttridge, *The Great Coalfield War*, 38–44, 141; Dubofsky, *We Shall Be All*, 42–56.

14 Long, *Where the Sun Never Shines*, 169–216.

15 McGovern and Guttridge, *The Great Coalfield War*, 51–52; Dean J. Saitta, Randall McGuire, and Philip Duke, Paper presented in the symposium "Communities Defined by Work: Life in Western Work Camps and Towns," chaired by T. Van Bueren and M. Maniery, Society for Historical Archaeology Meeting, Salt Lake City, 1999; Sarah Deutsch, *No Separate Refuge: Culture, Class and Gender on an Anglo-Hispanic Frontier in the American Southwest, 1880–1940* (New York: Oxford University Press, 1987), 87–106. The figures are from *Report Upon the Possible Service of the Young Men's Christian Association the Mining Communities of the Colorado Fuel and Iron Company, 1915*, cited in a superb unpublished essay that Camille Guérin-Gonzales prepared as a member of the LAWCHA Ludlow Committee, "Ludlow Monument NHL Nomination Narrative Draft," 5, in author's possession.

16 There is an extensive literature on company coal towns. See for instance Deutsch, *No Separate Refuge*, 87–106; Fawn-Amber Montoya, ed., *Making an American Workforce: The Rockefellers and the Legacy of Ludlow* (Boulder: University Press of Colorado, 2014); Long, *Where the Sun Never Shines*.

17 James Brian Whiteside, "Protecting the Life and Limb of Our Workmen: Work, Death and Regulation in the Rocky Mountain Coal Mining Industry" (PhD diss., University of Colorado, 1986), 134, as cited in Guérin-Gonzales, "Narrative Draft," 7.

18 See Aaron Goings and Gary Kaunonen, *Community in Conflict: A Working-Class History of the 1913–14 Michigan Copper Strike and the Italian Hall Tragedy* (Lansing: Michigan State University Press, 2013). The 1913 Calumet strike and Ludlow are discussed further in Chapter 12.

19 Frank J. Hayes, "On Ludlow Field," *United Mine Workers Journal* 29 (June 6, 1918): 4.

20 *King Coal* was first published in 1917. A sequel, *The Coal War* was not published until 1976, by the Associated University Press of Colorado, through the efforts of Professor John Graham, University of Colorado, Boulder. See Graham, "Introduction," xlviii, lvi–xcii.

21 Testimony April 6, 1914 in response to questioning by Congressman Martin Foster, Washington, D.C., quoted in McGovern and Guttridge, *The Coalfield War*, 197–201; Graham, "Introduction," xl–xlii.

22 McGovern and Guttridge, *The Coalfield War*, 282, 284, 289–92, 293–307, 335–42.

23 *New York Herald*, April 24, 1915. For the U.S. Industrial Relations Commission's investigation of Ludlow, and its Chairman, Frank Walsh's analysis of Rockefeller's role, see

McGovern and Guttridge, *The Coalfield War*, 312–32; Long, *Where the Sun Never Shines*, 314, 316–17; Graham, "Introduction," liii.

24 Jonathan Rees, "The Ludlow Memorial: Inspiration, Solidarity and Historical Memory," paper presented at the annual conference of the Organization of American Historians, Washington, D.C., 2006, in author's possession.

25 *Denver Post*, May 15, 1918. Hugh Sullivan designed the monument. The granite was quarried in Barre, Vermont; the fabricator was the Jones Brothers Co. There is a Granite Cutters International Association insignia on the monument. In the early 1900s, Italian anarchists and socialists came to Barre to cut stone and built an active labor culture. Holly Syrakkos of the AFL-CIO reported that "[t]here is some speculation that the monument was in part a gesture of solidarity from the Italian and Scottish workers who formed the union." Holly Syrrakos, e-mail to Elizabeth Jameson, May 17, 2005.

26 The registers were preserved and kept by Trinidad United Mine Workers of America local union President Mike Romero. I read and copied them during a lovely afternoon at the home of Mike and Yolanda Romero in Trinidad, following the June 11, 2006 annual memorial gathering at Ludlow.

27 McGovern and Guttridge, *The Great Coalfield War*, 106.

28 Lyrics reproduced in George Korson, *Coal Dust on the Fiddle: Songs and Stories of the Bituminous Industry* (Philadelphia: University of Pennsylvania Press, 1943), 390–91. For more on Tikas, see Zeese Papanikolas, *Buried Unsung: Louis Tikas and the Ludlow Massacre* (Lincoln: University of Nebraska Press, 1991).

29 Woody Guthrie, "Ludlow Massacre," Liner Notes by Moses Asch," *Struggle* by Woody Guthrie (New York City: Folkways Records, 1976).

30 John Mack Faragher, Mari Jo Buhle, Daniel Czitrom, and Susan H. Armitage, *Out of Many: A History of the American People, Combined Edition* (Englewood Cliffs, NJ: Prentice-Hall, Inc.), 668.

31 This account is based on telephone interviews by James Green with UMWA Regional Representative Bob Butero on June 10 and September 5, 2003 and with Mike Romero on September 8, 2003. See Jim Green, "Crime Against Memory at Ludlow," *Labor: Studies of Working Class History in the Americas* 1 (Spring 2004): 3–10; Gary Cox, "Ludlow-Our Twin Towers-Beheaded." Posted by Holly Syrrakos of the Inventory of Labor Landmarks on H-LABOR, June 12, 2003. For more about the attack on the monument and efforts to achieve National Historic Landmark status for the Ludlow site, see James Green and Elizabeth Jameson, "Marking Labor History on the National Landscape: The Restored Ludlow Memorial and Its Significance," *International Labor and Working-Class History* 76:1 (September 2009): 6–25.

32 "Restore Ludlow Monument," *Denver Post*, May 31, 2003.

33 Julie Greene, "Ludlow Massacre Memorial," H-LABOR, July 1. 2003.

34 John Bodnar, *Remaking America: Public Memory and Patriotism in the Twentieth Century* (Princeton, NJ: Princeton University Press, 1992), 14.

35 E-mails from Elizabeth Jameson to Lysa Wegman-French, February 3, 2004; from Lysa Wegman-French to Elizabeth Jameson, February 10, 2004.

36 For National Landmarks Program nomination criteria, see U.S. Department of the Interior, National Park Service, *National Register Bulletin: How to Prepare National Historic Landmark Nominations* (Washington, DC: U.S. Department of the Interior, 1999), 11.

37 For the Colorado Coal Field War Project, including the Ludlow camp site archeological dig, see http://www.du.edu/anthro/ludlow.html.

38 E-mail from Elizabeth Jameson to Alan Derickson, Anthony DeStefanis, Camille Guérin-Gonzales, Holly Syrakkos, Jonathan Rees, Zaragosa Vargas, Randall McGuire, Tobias Higbie, Marty Blatt, Jim Green, Julie Greene, Lysa Wegman-French, and Charles Haecker, July 15, 2005. Summarized from e-mails to Elizabeth Jameson from Alan Derickson, May 17, 2005; Camille Guérin-Gonzales, June 4, 2005; Jonathan Rees, May 27, 2005; Holly Syrrakos, May 17, 2005; Zaragosa Vargas, June 8, 2005; and Anthony DeStefanis May 25, 2005.
39 E-mail from Randall McGuire to Elizabeth Jameson, July 15, 2005.
40 E-mail from Randall McGuire to Elizabeth Jameson, July 15, 2005.
41 E-mails from Lysa Wegman-French to Elizabeth Jameson, and from Elizabeth Jameson to Lysa Wegman-French, May 27, 2005; from Charles Haecker to Elizabeth Jameson and the Committee, and from Elizabeth Jameson to Charles Haecker May 31, 2005.
42 E-mail from Charles Haecker to Elizabeth Jameson, August 25, 2005. *How to Prepare National Historic Landmark Nominations*, 11.
43 The Park Service paid for the Simmons' work. E-mails from Charles Haecker to Elizabeth Jameson, November 29, 2005; January 20, 2006; January 23, 2006; March 9, 2006; March 10, 2006; e-mails from Elizabeth Jameson to Charles Haecker, January 20, 2006, March 9, 2006.
44 Matthew Lee-Ashley, "*Carbone e Potere*: The 1903–1904 Coal Strike and the Origins of Corporate Hegemony in Southern Colorado" (BA thesis, Pomona College, 2004).
45 Haecker sent the draft nomination to me on May 14, 2007; I circulated it electronically to the Committee members, who sent responses to me. I compiled the responses and sent them to the Simmonses and Haecker. E-mails, Charles Haecker to Elizabeth Jameson, and Elizabeth Jameson to Charles Haecker, July 10, 2007.
46 "Senator Salazar Vows to Help Make Ludlow Tent Colony Site a National Historic Landmark," news release, January 23, 2008, http://salazar.senate.gov/news/releases/080123ludlow.htm.
47 "Sen. Salazar Commemorates the 94th Ludlow Massacre Anniversary/Introduced Bill to Make Ludlow Site National Historic Landmark," news release, U.S. Senator Ken Salazar, April 18, 2008; email communications, Matt Lee-Ashley to Elizabeth Jameson April 18, 2008.
48 Letter from Elizabeth Jameson to J. Paul Loether, Chief, National Register of Historic Places and National Historic Landmarks Program, October 22, 2008.
49 Mary Field Parton, ed., *The Autobiography of Mother Jones* (Chicago: Charles H. Kerr & Co., 1925), 191.
50 McGovern and Guttridge, *The Great Coalfield War*, 227–28, 231, 234; Long, *Where the Sun Never Shines*, 291–94.
51 Lucy Huffaker, "WOMAN'S VARIED INTERESTS: That the Sacrifice of Her Three Children's Lives May Count for Workers' Betterment, Mary Petrucci Goes About Telling Ludlow's Story," *New York Tribune*, February 4, 1915.
52 See note 1 above for the spelling of victims' names.

9

Women Who Crossed a Line: Canadian Single Women Homesteaders in the U.S. West

April 12, 2011

My 2011 lecture approached a question that had preoccupied me for a very long time: what on earth do place and gender have to do with one another? Does region or nation matter differently in the lived experiences of women and men? I had thought about place and gender for over thirty years, since I began to research western women's histories. I had focused more recently on the difference national borders make, since I crossed one myself, and began thinking more about my grandmother and all the other women who left their homelands hoping for something better for themselves or their families.

History has usually dealt with public life and public events, while most women have lived their lives in private and domestic arenas and so have seen their own lives as historically insignificant. This too-simple separation of private life and public history posed a simple question: Why did the women cross the line?

That simple question was rooted in a body of scholarship on single women homesteaders in the United States. The Homestead Act of 1862 allowed single women to claim 160 acres of public land for homesteads in their own names, a policy that drew large numbers of women to the American West. Some of those women were Canadians.

***

Sometime in the spring of 1884 a young woman named Mary J. Rushton left her parents' home in Nova Scotia and traveled west to Manitoba.

229

She turned south in May to cross the 49th Parallel at Bottineau, Dakota Territory, and on June 16 declared her intention "to renounce forever all allegiance and fidelity" to "The Queen of England" and to become a citizen of the United States. In early 1885 she moved onto 160 acres in Bottineau County; almost three years later she filed a Homestead Application for her land. Swearing that she was a single woman "over the age of 21 years of age and have declared my intention to become a citizen of the United States," she was, she said, already "residing on the land I desire to enter" and had "made a bona fide improvement and settlement thereon" that "commenced January 27th 1885." (In her final proof application, she would say she took up residence in April.) She had taken possession of a frame house and barn, for which she paid $150, had sunk a well, and had broken approximately ten acres; she estimated the total value of these improvements at $200. Two weeks later, on November 7, she paid her $14 filing fee on the northwest quarter section 28' in Township 161 of Range 73, Bottineau County, under Section No. 2290, Revised Statutes of the United States.[1]

Mary Rushton became a U.S. citizen on August 9, 1889. A year later, to the day, she filed her final proof statement to gain title to her land. She had, by then, claimed a second quarter section under the provisions of the Timber Culture Act of 1873, a statute that allowed homesteaders to claim a second 160 acres in the naive faith of the U.S. Congress that they could change the climate by planting at least forty of those acres in trees.[2]

Mary Rushton was putting down roots. She had, she said, lived on her claim continuously, in her two-room frame house. She had a sod and pole barn and had raised wheat and oats for four years on her ten acres of broken land, letting two to three acres lie fallow each summer; raised a garden each year and had dug a second well. She estimated that her homestead had grown in value to $235. Mary Rushton owned a horse, bed, bedding, table, chairs, stove, and cooking utensils. She had not been regularly employed, she reported, but "would help a neighbour occasionally" who lived three-fourths of a mile from her home. Exercising her new citizenship, she had voted once, she said, in the "last school election." (North Dakota women won the right to vote in school elections in 1883 but did not exercise the full franchise until 1920.)[3] Such are the barest facts of six years in the life of Mary Rushton, recorded in her homestead claim file, stored at the U.S. National Archives, together with those of all successful homesteaders.

Folded into thirds, slim yellowed sheets of flaking records, often fastened with rusty straight pins, have been fading largely untouched

Figure 9.1. "Emma Beske outside her homestead shack near Streeter, N.D.," 1906. H. Elaine Lindgren Photograph Collection, 2008.116.15. Photo courtesy of the Institute for Regional Studies, NDSU, Fargo.

since some clerk filed them over a century ago. They include the files of thousands of women whose spare official forms offer glimpses into the hopes and labor they invested to claim homesteads in the U.S. West. Mary Rushton's file was one of 121 women's that I found in the records of the Devils Lake, North Dakota, Land Office, filed during the first decade it operated from 1883–1893.[4]

A frame house, 160 acres of semi-arid North Dakota land, a horse, two wells, some household furnishings. It might seem like a small gain for so much time living alone on the northern Plains. To this, Mary Rushton might have replied that if her home were modest, it was hers alone. The promise of land in their own names drew thousands of women to the U.S. West.[5] They crossed international borders and social boundaries to pursue whatever dreams the land might promise. Unequal access to land forged gendered international borders that pulled and pushed women to a country they thought might offer them more than the nations they left. Among them were many thousands of Canadian women, for whom crossing the line to the United States meant that they could file for homesteads if they, like Rushton, were over 21, single or the head of a household, and willing to become naturalized citizens of the United States.

Countless women staked their time, energy, and scant resources in a wager with the United States government, which, as Senator William Borah famously quipped, bet homesteaders "160 acres against the entry fee of $14 that the settler can't live on the land for five years without starving to death."[6] By some estimates, fewer than half of all homesteaders won that bet; more recent estimates suggest a 37–45 percent failure rate before 1900.[7] Among those who made it for five years to win title to their land, a sizeable number were women, who, some studies suggest, were more successful than men in making final proof and winning title to their claims.

Since 1976, when Sheryll Patterson-Black published her pioneering article "Women Homesteaders on the Great Plains Frontier," historians have found women constituting from 5–20 percent of homestead entrants in various times and places. They appear to have been fewest in the earliest years of homesteading, and to account for one homestead entrant in five later, through the 1920s. Patterson-Black processed data from the Lamar, Colorado, land office in 1887 and 1907, and from the Douglas, Wyoming, land office in 1891, 1907, and 1908. She found that 11.9 percent of the homestead entrants were women, and that 42.4 percent succeeded in getting final title to their land, compared to 37 percent of the men.[8]

H. Elaine Lindgren, whose book *Land in Her Own Name* was based on case studies of 306 North Dakota women homesteaders, found that many, like Mary Rushton, were young, and most—83 percent in her sample—were single when they filed their claims; 15 percent were widows. Lindgren generated her 306 case studies through a public appeal, supplemented by land office data from nine counties. Of her 306 women, 5 percent were Canadian. Two of her nine counties, Pembina and Burke, abutted the 49th Parallel. The predominant ethnic groups among the Burke homesteaders were Norwegians, Swedes, and Danes; in Pembina County it was Anglo Canadians. Though ethnic Europeans did not settle the surrounding counties until the late 1870s and 1880s, a fur trading post was established in Pembina in 1797; the community was built by Pembina Chippewa and Métis settlers. Part of the Red River Settlement, it was thought, until 1823, to lie north of the 49th Parallel. The Pembina Land Office operated from 1870–1874; some original Red River Colony settlers filed for homesteads there. Lindgren found that women constituted only 6 percent of all Pembina County independent homesteaders, a fairly typical figure for the first years that a Land Office operated.[9]

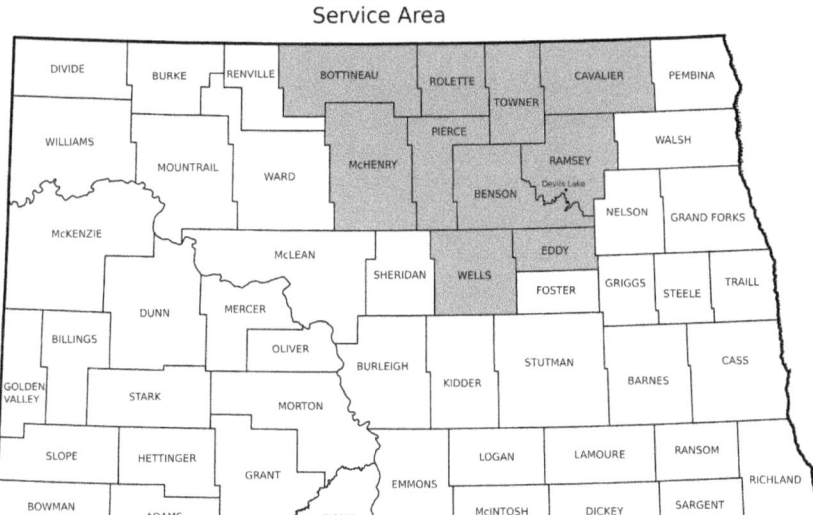

Figure 9.2. Devils Lake Land Office Service Area. Map by Jennifer Arthur.

The Devils Lake Land Office records offer some contrasting data, based on the first decade of final proof statements after the Devils Lake office opened on August 21, 1883. Devils Lake handled claims for north central Dakota Territory, an area that became North Dakota after statehood was achieved in 1889. It covered Ramsey Country, where the Land Office was located, and Eddy, Wells, Benson, Pierce, McHenry, Bottineau, Rolette, Towner, and Cavalier counties—a territory with only sparse non-Indigenous settlement before the 1880s (see Figure 9.2).

Land opened for settlement there as American Indians were first pushed onto reservations, and then as their land was progressively alienated under the terms of the 1887 Dawes Act. Following the same assumptions that underlay the Homestead Act, the Dawes Act envisioned American Indians farming as patriarchal nuclear families on privately owned parcels of land. As tribal land became family farms, much reservation land was offered for homesteads or for sale. North Dakota contained all or part of five reservations, two of which lay within the territory of the Devils Lake Land Office: the Turtle Mountain Reservation in Rolette

County, established in 1882, and the Devils Lake Sioux Reservation, now called the Spirit Lake Sioux Reservation, established in 1867, in Benson and Eddy Counties. As land around and in the reservations opened for homesteading in the 1880s, homesteaders rushed to the Devils Lake Land Office to stake their claims.

I did not determine how many people filed for homesteads without gaining title to their land, but 1,229 succeeded and filed their final proof statements in the Devils Lake office between 1883 and 1893. Among these were 121 women, or 9.7 percent, who achieved final title to their claims—the highest proportion of women I have seen during an early settlement period. And of these 121 women, 23, or one in five, were Canadian, four times the proportion in Lindgren's sample. Another 25 were Norwegian; fewer than half—only 48—were native-born U.S. citizens.[10]

Collectively, American, Norwegian, and Canadian women predominated. The differences among the three nationalities suggest some of what pushed and pulled them to North Dakota homesteads. Proof statements are frustratingly short on personal information; they offer more clues than conclusions. Still, the statistical portrait that emerges provides some insight into the circumstances that drew at least twenty-three women to cross a gendered international border that separated their opportunities in the Canadian and U.S. Wests. I say "at least" because of twelve women, whose place of birth was not given, several, like Mary Rushton, renounced "allegiance and fidelity" to the Queen of England, but whether they were born in Canada, England, or another Commonwealth nation was not stated.[11]

In most respects, the land policies of Canada and the United States were similar. Both surveyed and allocated public land using the grid system established in the U.S. Land Ordinance of 1785, dividing their western territories into townships six miles square. Each 36 square-mile section was, in turn, divided into half sections, and then into quarter sections of 160 acres, each identified by range, township, and section numbers. In both countries, two sections in each township were dedicated to supporting public education. The uniform grids took no account of terrain, climate, tree cover, water, or other essentials, but the system established a basic land survey, which could precede settlement, and insure verifiable property lines.

Both countries required homesteaders to live on the land and improve it. Both charged a filing fee—$14 in the United States, $10 in Canada. Under the terms of the U.S. Homestead Act of 1862, settlers could purchase the land for $1.25 an acre after they lived on it for six months, or they could "prove up" their claims if they lived on them at least seven months a year for five years, and improved them by building a house, planting crops, or otherwise putting the land to productive use. The Canadian Dominion Lands Act of 1872 differed in a few particulars. Seeking to attract settlers, it required only three years residence before a settler could claim final title to the land and initially allowed a settler to pre-empt a second adjacent quarter section.

There were two significant differences between these national land policies. The United States did not permit group settlements, but after 1886 Canada allowed agricultural colonies in some circumstances, a provision that made it possible for Ukrainians, Doukhobors, Mennonites, Hutterites, and Jews to found separate communities on the Canadian prairies. The second difference involved the definition of persons. In the United States, homesteads were offered to "any person who is the head of a family, or who has arrived at the age of twenty-one years, and is a citizen of the United States, or who shall have filed his declaration intention to become such . . . , and who has never borne arms against the United States Government or given aid and comfort to its enemies." Personhood and the rights of citizenship remained contested in the United States as in Canada, but the Homestead Act clearly counted women among those persons who could claim land. The second section clarified in unusually gender-inclusive language: "That the person applying for the benefit of this act shall, upon application to the register of the land office in which *he or she* is about to make such entry, make affidavit before the said register or receiver that *he or she* is the head of a family, or is twenty-one year or more of age," etc., "that such application is made for *his or her* exclusive use and benefit. . . ." (italics added)

The Dominion Lands Act of 1872 stipulated more simply that homesteads were open to "any person who is the head of a family or has attained the age of twenty-one years." In practice, however, such persons included virtually no women. Single women were excluded. A woman could homestead only if she were widowed, divorced, deserted, or separated, and then only if she had a minor child living with her who was solely dependent on her for support. Not until the 1930s, when there was almost no land left, did women finally win the right to Canadian homesteads. The law was so strictly applied, and women candidates so scrupulously screened, that in 1916 only twenty-one women operated their own homesteads in western Canada, compared to thousands in the United States.[12] South of the border, women had only to swear that they were not married when they filed their claims, or, if married, that they were the sole support of their families, that they were "over 21 years of age," and that they were or had declared their "intention to become" citizens of the United States.

By 1893, twenty-three Canadian women went to the Devils Lake Land Office and so swore. They resembled in many ways women homesteaders from other countries drawn to the same patch of earth. There were subtle differences as well, as fine as the small distinctions in two homestead laws that defined their rights to public land on either side of the 49th Parallel. There were differences, too, among some Canadians and their individual paths to North Dakota homesteads.

At least part of what drew all the women was clear: they wanted to own land. What pushed them might in part be equally clear: it was harder, where they came from, for a single woman to become propertied.

Two of the Norwegian women had lived in North Dakota, two in Minnesota before claiming land, but most were recent immigrants.[13] Forty-one percent of all Norwegians who came to the United States in the 19th and 20th centuries were women. Population growth in Norway pushed thousands of peasants off the land. Thousands of young women left rural communities for cities that offered them only low-paid work as domestic servants, in the needle trades, or as sex workers. Women were the most impoverished Norwegians throughout the 19th century: in 1860 two-thirds of the poor in Kristiania (as Oslo was known at the time) were women, many of them single mothers. Prostitution was widespread. After 1905 Norwegian immigrants were canvassed about why they left. Two-thirds of the women said they were leaving either to make more money or because they had no income; the remaining third said they were going to relatives. Land ownership was a powerful draw for women with such narrow options, and for families forced from the Norwegian countryside.[14]

Similar circumstances may have drawn the American and Canadian women, who would have had little hope of inheriting family farms, and whose job possibilities were limited and poorly paid. The American women, like most U.S. homesteaders, came predominantly from nearby agricultural states; over half had lived in Minnesota, Iowa, Wisconsin, or North Dakota. Although few gave their previous occupations, five of the nine who did said they had been farming before filing for their land.[15] We might guess that the land they farmed was poorer, or that they had worked on family farms as daughters or sisters.

What drew the Canadian women to stake their claims south of the border is also, for most, a matter of guesswork and inference. Among the twenty-three Canadians, four had French surnames; several were Métis. Sparse statistics and a few brief portraits suggest their collective stories and particularities. Six (26 percent) were still under thirty when they gained title to their land; over half were under forty. Eight—over a third— were over fifty. Although proportionately fewer American or Norwegian women filed for land in their early twenties, more made final proof in their thirties, and the Norwegian women included many fewer women over fifty, suggesting that they fit the pattern of young women pushed out of the Norwegian countryside, who perhaps spent a few years working before they could leave. The Canadians' age distribution separated the majority who came to the United States expressly to claim land and a smaller group who seized the option after living awhile south of the border. When they filed for land, they fell roughly into three groups: very young single women, middle aged single women, and widows.[16]

Mary Rushton was the youngest; she filed for her homestead at the earliest opportunity, shortly after her twenty-first birthday. Margaret Belgarde (or Margaret Belgairde or Marguerite Belgard) was easily the oldest. Born Marguerite Dufort in Red River Colony in 1794, she married Alexis Joseph Belgarde from Quebec in 1814. The Belgardes had some thirteen children before immigrating to the United States; they entered through Pembina in 1844 and apparently stayed there. Alexis was listed on the 1850 Pembina census but died two years later. A census taker found Margaret there in 1880, but she moved to a farm in Rolette County—perhaps one of her children's—before filing her intention to become a U.S. citizen in 1884 and moving onto her claim. Her final proof papers, filed in August 1889, listed her age as 106, but she was likely only a youthful 95, living in a log house with her daughter on her farm in Bottineau County. She was able to enjoy her claim for four years before she died at Turtle Mountain February 12, 1893, at age 99.[17]

Most of the Canadian women seem, like Mary Rushton, to have come to the United States expressly to claim land for themselves. I don't know much about their lives before that: at least one came from Manitoba, one from New Brunswick, one from Quebec, one from Nova Scotia, one from Ontario. Their entry points may indicate their origins: two entered the United States in New York, one in Boston, nine came through Michigan, suggesting that about half had roots in the Maritimes or central Canada. Another nine entered through Pembina, or just across the Red River in St. Vincent, Minnesota, or Bottineau, Turtle Mountain, or St. John in north central North Dakota. Six had entered the United States before 1880, but most came after 1881, likely with the intention of homesteading.[18] Their trajectories support historian Walter Sage, who argued in 1928 that there was a North American frontier of settlement that crossed and recrossed national borders, but their movements do not fit Sage's continuous east-to-west wave-like pattern of cross-border settlement.[19] Four entered through New York or Michigan before 1880; then, from 1879–1885 thirteen entered through North Dakota, Minnesota, or Michigan; the last four entered through Detroit, Port Huron, or Boston in 1886–1887 and headed straight west to stake their claims. These complex trajectories illustrate myriad patterns of cross-border migrations, in search of what we can only guess.

Only a few specified where they lived prior to filing their claims, but most came directly from Canada. Only six, including Margaret Belgarde, said that they had lived in the United States before filing for land. Three of these early migrants appear to have been either French Canadian or Métis; two had lived in North Dakota, one in Minnesota, one in Michigan, and one, Eulalie Gauthier, had worked in a New Hampshire factory before emigrating to North Dakota with her husband Arcade and their two sons. Arcade located a quarter section of land, built a house and stable, and the family moved onto the claim in 1883. Arcade became a citizen, voted, and filed a tree claim before he died in 1888. As his heir, Eulalie filed her final proof statement in 1889, though her title was delayed until she became a naturalized citizen in 1891.[20]

Mary Boyd, too, was widowed and had lived in the United States for some years before filing for her land, having emigrated from Quebec in 1865. Her husband died three years later, leaving her, at age 35, alone with four children. It is not clear how she supported them; she said that before she moved to her homestead in 1883 she had been "living with my income" in Michigan. Though she considered herself a head of family, none of her children lived with her; three were married and they all had homes of their own. She had no trade, she said, but worked "for myself only," making her claim "[her] home and farm for [her] exclusive use and benefit."[21]

Frizine Sayer, a 32-year-old unmarried woman, entered the United States at the port of St. John, Turtle Mountain, in June 1879 and apparently lived briefly in Minnesota before moving onto her homestead claim in 1883.[22] Forty-year-old Ida Williams was single when she filed her proof statement in 1889. She had, she said, worked as a servant in Canada and for two years in Dakota Territory before moving onto her homestead claim in Eddy County.[23] Belgarde, Williams, Gauthier, Sayer, and Boyd all moved onto their land as soon as the Devils Lake office opened in 1883. Two were widowed; two were single women moving quickly to grab the land that offered them a chance to make a home. The Gauthiers' homestead offered a chance to leave the New Hampshire factories.

Jennie Draper Garver, the remaining Canadian with prior U.S. residence, was much younger and, more than any other Canadian-born woman, most clearly resembled the single American women homesteaders. Jennie Draper entered the United States with her family in 1870 when she was only eight years old. She filed for her homestead in November 1884. A month later she married and had one child before gaining title to her land.[24] Like her, about a third of the U.S. women married before filing their proof statements, many of them shortly after filing their homestead claims. For a significant minority, their claims allowed them to bring land to a marriage or to increase total family holdings. Whether that changed their status in their marriages we can only guess.

But while 35 percent (17) of the American-born women and 32 percent (8) of the Norwegians married between when they filed their claims and when they gained title, that was less the pattern for the Canadian women. As their ages might suggest, most were either single or widows. Eight—almost 35 percent—were still single when they got title to their land; five had married between filing their claims and gaining title. Another eight were widows; the marital status of one woman was not recorded. Sarah Boyd's husband had deserted her and their three-year-old child in December 1885, ten months after he filed for their Rolette County homestead. She achieved final proof in her own name in November 1891. More native-born Americans (35.4 percent) and Norwegian immigrants (32 percent)—about a third of both—married before they made proof; more Norwegians (48 percent) and fewer Americans (19 percent) were still single; and fewer Norwegians (20 percent) were widows (see Figure 9.3).

Fourteen of the twenty-three Canadians said they had families at the time they made final proof; twelve had children, including seven of the eight widows, three of five married women, one single woman, and the deserted wife, Sarah Boyd. In other words, the Norwegian women were younger, and more were single when they came to the United States, reflecting the demographic and economic pressures that pushed them from their native land.

All evidence suggests that the Canadians diverged from the practice of some women who came West with their fiancés, waiting to marry until both partners had filed for land in order to double the family land holdings. This appears to have been the case for up to a third of the American and

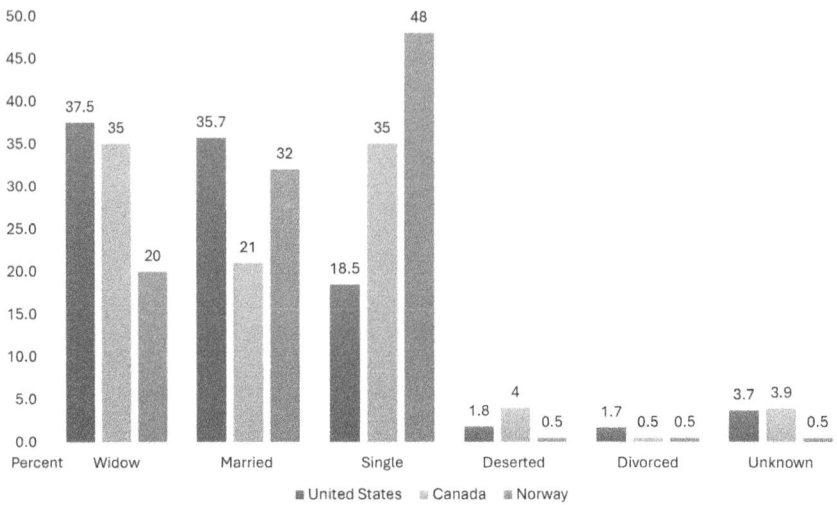

Figure. 9.3. Graph by Amy McKinney.

Norwegian women but was not evident among the Canadian immigrants. Two widows and one deserted wife inherited their husbands' homestead claims, and of the single women, only Jennie Draper married soon after filing. Most of the widows, in fact, filed their claims after their husbands died. And even those who married before gaining title came to Dakota Territory on their own, long before any married. Marion Beaton, for instance, was 24 when she entered the U.S. through Detroit. Three years later she filed for her homestead in Bottineau County. At age 31 she made final proof on her claim as Marion Cleveland, stating that she lived alone on her claim until she married and had lived there with her husband ever since. She had raised crops for four seasons and had worked hard to establish the farm. She had, she stated, lived on her land continuously except "for 6 terms of School at Devils Lake ND. I was on the claim at different times while teaching as my work would allow and spent my Vacation on the Claim and had the land cultivated all the time." Her witnesses, Robert Lyon and Archibald McArthur, put it bluntly: She resided on her claim continuously, they said, "All but the time she was teaching School as she was a single woman and had to work for her living."[25] Similarly, Frizine Sayer Lavallee made final proof on an 80-acre homestead near Rolla, North

Dakota, in 1892, thirteen years after she emigrated to Dakota Territory. She had lived on the land since 1883; it was, she said, heavily wooded and "most valuable for timber." She had cleared six acres and raised a garden for eight years. She married her husband only a month before making final proof. He was probably a widower; he and his two children were living in her home.[26] It is not likely that forty-three-year-old Frizine Lavallee had lived on her land for nine years waiting to establish a home for a man who was probably with the mother of his children when she arrived.

At least some of the Canadian women followed the pattern documented by other historians of settling near friends or family. The majority (60 percent) stated that they had families. And there are other scattered clues. Azilda Beaudoin filed final proof certificate No. 434 on her Rolette County homestead; certificate number 431 was filed by Louis Beaudoin, relationship uncertain. Ida L. Williams was away from her claim when she was "employed in Grand Forks from Nov. 1st '83 until May 1st 1884, doing housework for different persons. . . . I also," she stated, "worked for my sister in Arvilla, Dak from Nov. 1st '84 to May 1st 1885 doing housework. . . ."[27]

It is hard to know for certain what the land represented to the women who staked considerable time and labor to claim it. Somehow, they scraped together enough money to file on their land, improve it, and develop it for five years of uncertain crops and weather. It has been estimated that it cost an average $1,000–$1,500 to develop a homestead, and even if these women did it more cheaply, they needed some capital to survive on their claims.[28] Where, we might ask, for instance, did Mary Rushton get the $150 to buy her house and barn before she filed? Some, like Rushton, Ida Williams, and Marion Beaton worked for neighbors or away from their claims to support themselves and their homesteads. Ann Hockney obtained a leave of absence from her claim from May 1890–May 1891. She was, she wrote, "compelled to be away at work to earn her living and make improvements." She had filed her claim in November 1888, had "85 acres under cultivation. A good well. A Frame house. . . . a Frame Barn that will hold 18 head of stock." She swore, however, "That on account of the drought her crop last year 1889 was a failure that she seeded the whole 85 acres and on account of such failure she has been obliged to seek employment elsewhere." To support her application for a leave, two neighbors, Thomas McDonald and Maggie Kennedy, swore that they knew her and believed that her statements were true.[29] Hockney, like many women homesteaders, likely managed her land and hired labor or traded for someone to work her farm. And, like many others, she found neighbors to support her. Thomas McDonald and Maggie Kennedy were not her kin but were part of a local community that recognized the challenges that women homesteaders faced in common with all who tried to farm the northern plains, and those they faced particularly as women.

If Canadian women followed the pattern of other women homesteaders—indeed of all homesteaders—only a minority would continue to live on their land and farm it for very long after gaining title. Lindgren found data about what women did with their land for 237 of the 306 women in her study. Sixty percent stayed on their homesteads only a bit longer than the time they needed to prove up, five years or less; 18 percent stayed 6–24 years; about one in five (22 percent) stayed 25 years or more. Her sample is skewed for persistence, both because she omitted women for whom she had no information, and because she gathered information about these 306 women by advertising in North Dakota.[30] And yet, those who left their land should not be deemed failures. For some women land represented an investment of time and labor to gain equity that they could trade for a business, an education, a house in town, or some other goal.

These 121 women from the Devils Lake Land Office may seem a small number, and yet they are not a sample—they are the complete universe of all women who succeeded as homesteaders and gained title to their land in that time and place. It is harder, though, to determine their subsequent life trajectories and what they did with their land once they owned it. In part, there is the perennial problem for women's historians of the fact that women's last names change. By 2011, I had been able to trace a few. In 1900, the widow Mary Boyd was listed on the U.S. census living in Williston, Williams County, North Dakota. Perhaps she sold her land; perhaps she rented it; perhaps one of her four children farmed it for her. Perhaps it bought her a business, or perhaps she was, once again, "living with her income."

I have, with Andrew Varsanyi's help, pieced together the most information for Elizabeth Winkler Gailfus. Born in St. Jacobs, Woolwich Parish, Ontario, in 1840, she married Blasius Gailfus in 1858, who was, like her parents a Bavarian immigrant. They had five children. After Blasius died in 1880, she and her children walked to Clearwater, Manitoba, herding cattle ahead of them. Elizabeth Gailfus wrote on her homestead proof statement that she entered the United States in June 1884, at Turtle Mountain, Dakota Territory. Four years later she filed her intention to become a U.S. citizen and filed her homestead claim near Picton in Towner Country. She built a house and moved in that June; in October two of her three surviving children joined her there and were still living with her. Her third son, Hugo, later said that the family squatted on Elizabeth's future homestead in 1883; the land wasn't surveyed so they plowed a furrow around the land they wanted. He also built a log shack which cost $8.00, and then the family went back to Clearwater for the winter, returning in the summer of 1884. The first house was a shack with a sod roof that leaked when it rained. The first summer, Hugo said, he broke four- or five-acre patches with their oxen, to raise only forty bushels of wheat. Elizabeth said in 1888 that she had cultivated fifteen acres and used sixty acres for pasture; she estimated the value of her farm at $700. In 1900, at age 60, she was still living on her land, though the U.S. census predictably listed Hugo (or Hugh) as the head of the family. Elizabeth remarried in 1901, but her land stayed in the family. Hugo had returned to Canada before 1891, where he worked as a laborer. He moved back and forth across the border for over a decade. He married Lillah Bower in 1901, who died the following year giving birth to their son Clarence; Elizabeth raised the boy. She had, in the meanwhile, returned to Woolwich to marry John Wideman in October 1901; she died there ten years later. In 1904, Hugo married Mary Hilgardner in the Gailfus hometown of Ayton. They had six children. In about 1906, Hugo and Mary returned to North Dakota and took over the family farm. They built a home and lived there until Hugo's death in 1964 at the age of 101. Hugo Gailfus was the Grand Marshal of the Rolla town celebration at the age of 100.[31] Elizabeth Gailfus's U.S. citizenship signified a transient allegiance, but her land enabled her to support herself and her children for almost two decades, and gave her a legacy to leave her son.

It is easiest to trace women who did not marry after making final proof, or whose land stayed in the hands of male descendants. While proving up, they had cultivated as little as one acre and as much as 125. Most had planted crops, principally wheat and oats; most had some livestock. At the time of proof, they valued their holdings at anywhere from $200 to $1,200, with a median value of $500 ($534 average value). Whether or not they stayed on the land, they had won their bets with the U.S. government and gained an economic stake for themselves.

The Canadian women who gained their homesteads during the Devils Lake Land Office's first decade shared a great deal with women homesteaders from other nations. But there is one intriguing detail that might have accounted for their high proportions among the Devils Lake homesteaders, and that is where they chose to settle. They claimed homesteads as close as they could to the border. Of course, I looked at a land office that served an area that abutted the border, which was arguably why I found Canadian women close to the international boundary. But most of the Canadian women (eighteen of twenty-three) filed in Bottineau, Rolette, Towner, and Cavalier counties—the four counties west of Pembina County just below the 49th Parallel. Two settled in McHenry County, one in Benson County, two in Eddy County. The nine who had entered the United States in Minnesota or North Dakota never went very far after they got across the line, though some, like Mary Rushton of Nova Scotia, had traveled quite a distance before turning south. The twelve who came through Michigan, New York, and Boston likewise headed for northern North Dakota, though there was plenty of land available in places that might seem more attractive by virtue of climate or proximity to rail lines. Yet they clustered near the boundary they had crossed to claim land in their own names.

Fifteen of the twenty-three in fact settled in two counties: Bottineau and Rolette. And there may have been more. Two of the Rolette County settlers whose birthplaces are unknown came from somewhere in the British Commonwealth. So why these two counties? Rolette County was named for a Métis fur trader "Jolly Joe" Rolette, and Bottineau County for Pierre Bottineau (1817–1895), a Métis pioneer, hunter, and trapper who became a successful land speculator. Both counties were formally organized in 1884, the year after the Land Office opened. Settlers began moving to Rolette County in 1883, the year after the Turtle Mountain Chippewa Reservation was established there. The ancestors of the Pembina Chippewas migrated to the Pembina area from the Great Lakes in the 1400s. Many worked in the fur trade as trappers, voyageurs, and guides. The Pembina Chippewa developed lasting relationships with the Cree and French, and the area remains a center of settlement for them and their Métis descendants. The populations of the two counties had diverged sharply by 2000, when fewer than 2 percent of all Bottineau County residents claimed Native American ancestry, and only 5.4 percent French; one in four was of Norwegian descent. Rolette County, in contrast, was 73 percent Native American; a bit over 3 percent of the residents listed Ojibway, Cree, or French Cree as their first languages.[32]

For the minority of the Canadian women homesteaders who were likely French Canadian or Métis, the draw to this area might have been ties of history or kinship. Two French-surnamed women, Azilda Beaudoin and Frizine Sayer Lavallee, settled in Rolette County. Margaret Belgarde lived there for a time and died there. She and Eulalie Gauthier settled in

Bottineau County, and the presence of French speakers, kin, or the historic ties to the Canadian fur trade may have drawn some of the women to these two counties. But the names of the remaining Rolette and Bottineau County settlers don't, on the face of it, suggest that this was the case: Elliott, Boyd, Robertson, Rushton, White, Garver, Beaton, and Murta. Some, like Mary Ann Finlayson, might have had ties to Red River or the fur trade. Perhaps it was simply that land opened in Rolette and Bottineau Counties when these women sought to homestead. Perhaps some had kin in Manitoba. Perhaps the climate and farming conditions were familiar, or timber more available. Perhaps we may find equal proportions of Canadian women filing elsewhere. Perhaps, for these few early Canadian homesteading women, it felt good to be close to home. I don't know.

But from what the data from one land office in its first decade can tell us, here is how I would respond to the question, "Why did the women cross the line?" The women crossed the line because that seemed their best option. The lives they chose were not easy and promised no great wealth— often not even modest security. They might have fled limited options or abusive families; they might have been drawn by adventure or the urge to provide better for themselves or their families. Some of them were single women, some were widows, likely with few resources. Although a few married soon after immigrating, only one seems to have planned to marry before she chose to homestead. Some, like most western homesteaders, joined friends or family; some forged new communities of neighbors who, like them, wagered the government that they could survive in a difficult land. For some, U.S. citizenship was a necessary expedient; for others and their descendants the United States truly became home.

The 49th Parallel, which separated their options in two countries, bridged the artificial distance between public politics and private lives, as national policies made a gendered difference in the daily lives of ordinary women. That twenty-three women had to cross that international boundary line to stake their claims was surely Canada's loss, Dakota's gain. It remains eloquent testimony to the ways an unevenly porous border filtered the promise of western opportunity for different people, depending at times on race, on their circumstances in their countries of birth, depending on their family status, and on their gender.

And whatever the cost—separation from friends, family, and homeland; loss of Canadian citizenship; long winters in sod houses and frame shanties; working hard to break the land or to earn money to hire it done— whatever the cost, it clearly seemed worth the effort to Mary Rushton,

Margaret Belgarde, Marion Beaton, Ann Hockney, Sarah Boyd, Azilda Beaudoin, Frizine Sayer Lavallee, Elizabeth Gailfus, and many more.

NOTES

Dedicated to the memory of Maggie Osler, who crossed many lines, and in so doing enriched her friends, colleagues, and the history of science.

I thank the donors who established the Imperial Oil-Lincoln McKay Chair in American Studies, who made the research for this essay possible, and whose generosity enabled me to have the help of an extraordinary group of graduate students: Gretchen Albers, Amy McKinney, and Andrew Varsanyi.

Additional Sources: Elizabeth Jameson, "Halfway Across That Line: Gender at the Threshold of History in the North American West," *Western Historical Quarterly* 47:1 (Spring 2016): 1-26, contains some information from the expanded sample of women homesteaders from the first two decades the Devils Lake Land Office operated; a shorter version of that article appears as chapter 13 in this volume. Sarah Carter, *Imperial Plots: Women, Land and the Spadework of British Colonialism on the Canadian Prairies* (Winnipeg: University of Manitoba Press, 2016) examines the largely failed efforts to achieve women's access to land in the Canadian West and is the most important analysis of the relationships of women, gender, and North American settler colonialism.

1. Mary J. Rushton Homestead Claim File, National Archives and Records Administration (NARA), Records of North Dakota Land Offices, Records of the Bureau of Land Management, 1685–1993, Record Group 49, Washington, DC (hereinafter cited as Homestead File and name of entrant).
2. Mary J. Rushton Homestead File. The Timber Culture Act of 1873 required 40 acres of trees; as amended in 1878, it required 10 acres.
3. Rushton Homestead File.
4. It became the Devils Lake Office November 7, 1884, when the town of Creelsburg was renamed Devils Lake.
5. Histories of women homesteaders began with Sheryll Patterson-Black's pathbreaking article, "Women Homesteaders on the Great Plains Frontier," *Frontiers: A Journal of Women Studies* 1 (Spring 1976): 67–88. For an excellent study of North Dakota women homesteaders, see H. Elaine Lindgren, *Land in Her Own Name: Women as Homesteaders in North Dakota* (1991; repr., Norman: University of Oklahoma Press, 1996). See also Katherine Benton-Cohen, "Common Purposes, Worlds Apart: Mexican-American, Mormon and Midwestern Women Homesteaders in Cochise County, Arizona," *Western Historical Quarterly* 36 (Winter 2005): 429–52; Dee Garceau, "Single Women Homesteaders and the Meanings of Independence: Places on the Map, Places in the Mind," *Frontiers: A Journal of Women Studies* 15 (Spring 1995): 1–26; and Sherry L. Smith, "Single Women Homesteaders: The Perplexing Case of Elinore Pruitt Stewart," *Western Historical Quarterly* 22 (May 1991): 163–83.
6. Roy M. Robbins, *Our Landed Heritage: The Public Domain, 1776-1936* (Lincoln: University of Nebraska Press, 1962), 375.
7. In 2011, like most historians at that time, I used the more than 50 percent failure rate estimated by Fred A. Shannon, "The Homestead Act and the Labor Surplus," *American Historical Review* 41, no. 4 (1936): 637–51 and *The Farmer's Last Frontier: Agriculture,*

1860-1897 (New York: Farrar & Rinehart 1945). Shannon's figures have since been challenged by Richard Edwards, Jacob K. Friefeld, and Rebecca S. Wingo, *Homesteading the Plains: Toward a New History* (Lincoln: University of Nebraska Press, 2017), chap. 2, "Recalculating Homesteading's Reach and Success," 25–40, who offer the 37–45 percent correction. The precise proportion of homestead filings that resulted in achieving title to the land remains uncalculated for all times and regions, but a significant proportion of people who filed for homesteads failed to gain title to their claims.

8 Patterson-Black, "Women Homesteaders on the Great Plains Frontier," 68. See also Lindgren, *Land in her Own Name*.
9 Lindgren, *Land in Her Own Name*, xiii, 19–22.
10 All demographic data were calculated from the Homestead Claim records of the 121 women who achieved title to their claims in the Devils Lake Land Office from 1883–1893, Records of the Devils Lake Land Office (1884–1893), Records of North Dakota Land Offices, Records of the Bureau of Land Management, 1685–1993, Record Group 49, NARA (hereinafter cited as Homestead Files).
11 Record Group 49, NARA.
12 Sarah Carter, "'Daughters of British Blood' Or 'Hordes of Men of Alien Race': The Homesteads-For-Women Campaign in Western Canada," *Great Plains Quarterly* 29 (Fall 2009): 269–70. For other examples, see Sarah Carter, "Transnational Perspectives on the History of Great Plains Women: Gender, Race, Nations, and the Forty-Ninth Parallel," *American Review of Canadian Studies* 33 (Winter 2003): 565–96.
13 Homestead Files.
14 Odd S. Lovoll, "Norwegian Immigration and Women," in *Norwegian American Women: Migration, Communities, and Identities*, eds. Betty A. Bergland and Lori Ann Lahlum (St. Paul: Minnesota Historical Society Press, 2011), 51–73.
15 Homestead Files.
16 Homestead Files.
17 Margaret Belgairde Homestead File (Belgarde claim); U.S. Bureau of the Census, *Seventh Census of the United States–1850, Minnesota Territory*, Population Schedules for Pembina County, Minnesota Territory, microfilm, reel 367, M432, Records of the Bureau of the Census, RG 29, NARA (hereinafter census records); and U.S. Bureau of the Census, *Tenth Census of the United States–1880, Dakota Territory*, Population Schedules for Pembina County, Dakota Territory, microfilm, reel 114, T9, census records. Margaret Belgarde died February 12, 1893 and was buried in Pembina. Belgarde's given name on her homestead claim file was Margaret; it appears as Margaret or Marguerite on different documents.
18 Homestead Files.
19 Walter Sage, "Some Aspects of the Frontier in Canadian History," in Canadian Historical Association, *Annual Report*, 1928. Sage spent his career at the University of British Columbia, described in Chad Reimer, "The Making of British Columbia History: Historical Writing and Institutions, 1784–1958" (PhD diss., York University, 1995), 311–62.
20 Eulalie Gauthier, Final Proof Statement, Eulalie Gauthier Homestead File.
21 Mary A. Boyd, Final Proof Statement, Mary A. Boyd Homestead File.
22 Frizine Sayer Lavallee, Testimony of Claimant, Frizine Sayer Lavallee Homestead File.
23 Ida P. Williams Homestead File.
24 Jennie Draper Garver Homestead File.
25 Marion Beaton Cleveland Homestead File.
26 Frizine Sayer Lavallee Homestead File.

27 Ida L. Williams Homestead File, Final Proof Statement.
28 Estimate in Shannon, "The Homestead Act."
29 Ann Hackney Ketcham Homestead File.
30 Lindgren, *Land in Their Own Name*, 191.
31 Elizabeth Gailfus Homestead File; 1885 Census of Dakota Territory; 1915 Census of Picton Township, Towner County, North Dakota; 1925 Census of Picton Township, Towner County, North Dakota; 1920 and 1930 U.S. Censuses of Picton Township, Towner County, North Dakota; Hugo Gailfus entry in *History of Towner County 1883-1989*; 1861, 1871, 1881, 1891 Censuses of Canada; 1851, 1861, 1871, and 1911 Censuses of Woolwich, Waterloo, Ontario.
32 In 2011, I relied on on-line sites for some of the history of the Pembina and Wood Mountain Chippewa and Métis communities. I also received wise counsel from colleagues Heather Devine and Michel Hogue, who helped me place Métis women homesteaders in their own contexts. I am very grateful. Since I wrote my lecture, Michel Hogue's masterful history of Métis and the border that divided them has appeared, and I include appropriate references from his book that I couldn't use in 2011, but which could expand readers' understanding of Métis history and help locate women like Margueriste Belgarde and Azilda Beaudoin in their historical and community contexts, as well as provide information on Métis migrations to the United States after the Métis Rebellions of 1870 and 1885. I list the references I used in 2011 first: Reference Desk, "Bottineau County, North Dakota," https://www.ereferencedesk.com/resources/counties/north-dakota/bottineau.html; Reference Desk, "Rolette County, North Dakota," https://www.ereferencedesk.com/resources/counties/north-dakota/rolette.html;North Dakota; County History, https://www.nd.gov/government/state-government/county-history,"Bottineau County, North Dakota," https://en.wikipedia.org/wiki/Bottineau_County,_North_Dakota;

"Pierre Bottineau. (1816-1895)," compiled by Lawrence Barkwell, Coordinator of Métis Heritage and History Research, Louis Riel Institute, https://www.metismuseum.ca/media/document.php/07413.Pierre%20Bottineau.pdf; "Rolette County, North Dakota," https://en.wikipedia.org/wiki/Rolette_County,_North_Dakota; "ROLETTE (Rollette), JOSEPH," *Dictionary of Canadian Biography*, Vol. X, https://www.biographi.ca/en/bio/rolette_joseph_10E.html; all online articles accessed April 6, 2011; Michel Hogue, *Metis and the Medicine Line: Creating a Border and Dividing a People* (Regina: University of Regina Press and Chapel Hill: University of North Carolina Press, 2015), 13, 23-35, 40-41, 48-51, 60-61, 64-65, 69, 88-90, 101, 105, 143, 171,180, 230, 257n50.

Bridges: Blocked, Crossed, and Under Construction: 2012–2014

The lectures in this section focused on American social movements. In 2012 and 2013, I addressed movements for women's rights, voting rights, racial equity, and LGBTQ2S+ liberation. Each lecture, either implicitly or explicitly, addressed issues of law: organized efforts to secure rights through legislation or through the enforcement of existing laws, challenges to laws that limited rights or liberties, and the power and limits of the law to achieve change or retard it.

I had explored the historical roots of contemporary social issues in previous lectures, trying to be transparent about the concerns that fueled my historical questions. My process shifted subtly in these lectures. I had previously begun by thinking about the anniversaries of historic events, like the publication of the Kerner Commission Report or the centennial of the Colorado Labor Wars, and had reflected on the contemporary relevance of their histories. Beginning in 2012, my talks responded to immediate events that pushed me to return to precedents and historical roots. I had become more comfortable addressing U.S. issues with Canadian audiences and had become secure enough to tackle Canadian issues as well.

In 2012, I addressed gender bias in Canadian and U.S. higher education as I explored the progress toward gender equity in higher education following the passage of Title IX of the U.S. Educational Amendments of 1972 and the adoption of the Canadian Charter of Rights and Freedoms in 1982. Both legal documents forbade discrimination based on sex. Both had supported positive change. But achieving equity required more than the law, and remained then, as now, an unfinished project.

Inspired by one line in President Barack Obama's Second Inaugural Address, in 2013, I compared the histories of Seneca Falls, Selma, and Stonewall, three pivotal events in the struggles for women's, African American, and LGBTQ2S+ rights. By the time President Obama spoke, Seneca Falls, Selma, and Stonewall had become mythic symbols of the three liberation movements in the United States.[1]

The long struggle for woman suffrage in the United States is usually dated from the first U.S. Women's Rights Convention in Seneca Falls, New York, in 1848. U.S. women won the vote in some states and territories beginning with Wyoming Territory in 1869, but did not win the vote nationally until the adoption of the Nineteenth Amendment to the U.S. Constitution in 1920.[2] African American men were theoretically enfranchised in 1868, when the Fourteenth Amendment to the U.S. Constitution guaranteed the rights of citizenship to former slaves and the right to vote to all male citizens. In 1870 the Fifteenth Amendment to the Constitution guaranteed that "The right of citizens of the United States to vote shall not be denied or abridged by the United States or by any State on account of race, color, or previous condition of servitude." That promise remained unfulfilled for many African Americans, and the U.S. Congress had still not passed legislation to enforce voting rights for African Americans by March 9, 1965, when non-violent voting rights activists in Selma, Alabama, tried to cross the Edmund Pettus bridge and march to the state capital in Montgomery. They marched to protest the murder of voting rights activist Jimmie Lee Jackson by an Alabama State trooper. But Dallas County sheriff's deputies and those same State troopers blocked them, and the nation witnessed that "Bloody Sunday" as the law officers beat, clubbed, and tear gassed non-violent demonstrators. More than fifty were hospitalized, among them John Lewis, then the Chairman of the Student Non-Violent Coordinating Committee (SNCC) and from 1987 until his death in 2020 U.S. Representative from Georgia's Fifth District. That brutal spectacle prompted President Lyndon Johnson to introduce the Voting Rights Act of 1965, which Congress passed, and the President signed into law on August 6, 1965.

The Fourteenth Amendment, one of the most litigated portions of the U.S. Constitution, also provided the basis for Supreme Court decisions guaranteeing women's reproductive rights in *Roe v. Wade* (1972) and the rights of same-sex couples to marry in *Obergefell v. Hodges* (2015). The modern movement for LGBTQ2S+ rights is often dated from a 1969 event known as Stonewall, when gays, lesbians, and transgender people rioted against police who raided the Stonewall Inn in New York City and threatened its gay and transgender patrons. The Stonewall protesters did not immediately demand legal change, but the movement they energized went on to demand full citizenship rights regardless of sexuality or gender, including the rights to non-discrimination in employment, housing, military service, and marriage.

My 2014 lecture focused on children murdered because of their race, ethnicity, and class, and on responses to those tragic losses. Although most of my work and many of my lectures addressed the history of social inequality, my 2014 lecture, more than any other, responded to contemporary events: the murders of two African American youths, Jordan Davis and Trayvon Martin, by armed individuals claiming the right to self-defence against unarmed teenagers because they "felt threatened," and therefore justified under the Florida "stand your ground" law. I examined the youths' deaths, and their parents' anguished responses. When the boys were murdered, I had been thinking about the centennials of the 1914 Ludlow Massacre (which I addressed in my 2009 lecture), and the 1913 Calumet, Michigan, copper miners' strike, two labor conflicts in which children died. My lecture explored these unconnected tragedies, and the historical constructions of race that linked and separated the murders of African American youths and those of miners' children a century earlier.

One of the minor editorial changes I made to these lectures was to substitute the past tense for the present tense when I had referred to then-current events. And yet, for each of the issues raised in these lectures, the present tense remains in some sense accurate. The stubborn persistence of prejudice and discrimination after legal change had been achieved recurred disturbingly throughout these lectures. I was troubled by parallels between the successful efforts to undermine African American rights theoretically guaranteed in the Thirteenth, Fourteenth, and Fifteenth Amendments to the Constitution following the Civil War, and the efforts to undercut the hard-won legislative achievements of the Civil Rights Movement.

In neither the United States nor Canada have we eradicated inequalities of race, class, gender, or sexuality. In the United States, the legal protections of *Roe v. Wade* that guaranteed the right to reproductive choice, including the right to abortions, were eroded in numerous states through legal restrictions on the clinics that provided reproductive health services. Then, on June 24, 2022, the United States Supreme Court ruled in *Dobbs v. Jackson Women's Health Organization*. A Court dominated by anti-choice jurists, three of whom had been nominated by President Donald Trump, voted 6–3 to overturn the 1972 *Roe v. Wade* decision that had legalized abortion in the United States for half a century. At the same time, nativist tropes used a century ago to combat union labor were revived, as they have been periodically throughout American history, to resist racialized immigrants from Central America, Haiti, and the Middle East, represented dramatically in President Trump's attempt to ban Muslim immigrants during his first days in office.[3]

Some of the great achievements of the African American Civil Rights Movement have been eroded and remain under threat. On June 25, 2013, the Supreme Court decision in *Shelby County v. Holder* overturned the key oversight provisions in the 1965 Voting Rights Act: Section 5, which required certain states and local governments to obtain federal preclearance before implementing any changes to their voting laws or practices; and subsection (b) of Section 4, which specified the formula that determined which jurisdictions were subject to preclearance based on their histories of racial discrimination in voting.[4] Removing the oversight provisions rendered the Act largely unenforceable and opened the way to voter suppression. Writing for the majority in the narrow 5–4 decision, Chief Justice John Roberts justified the move, asserting "that the conditions that originally justified these measures no longer characterize voting in the covered jurisdictions," although, as Roberts admitted, "voting discrimination still exists; no one doubts that." To which Justice Ruth Bader Ginsburg, writing for the minority, responded, "But the Court today terminates the remedy that proved to be best suited to block that discrimination." Citing numerous continuing cases of racial discrimination in access to voting, Ginsburg concluded: "The sad irony of today's decision lies in its utter failure to grasp why the VRA has proven effective. The Court appears to believe that the VRA's success in eliminating the specific devices extant in 1965 means that preclearance is no longer needed. ... With that belief, and the argument derived from it, history repeats itself." And indeed, it has, through restrictive identification requirements, limiting the numbers and locations of polling places, and restricting early voting options.[5] In the eleven years since the *Shelby* decision, states have passed over a hundred laws restricting access to the vote, laws that have disproportionately affected people of color. Many of the new laws were enacted in states that had a history of racial discrimination in voting.

Racism and gun violence have not been eradicated. African American youths continue to die from the deadly combination of institutionalized racism, internalized racist assumptions, and easy access to guns. In 2018 the National Council on Family Relations published a report, "Gun Violence and the Minority Experience," by Yolanda T. Mitchell and Tiffany L. Bromfield, who found that the frequent gun violence in poor racial ethnic urban communities received much less media attention than mass violence affecting White Americans. Mass shootings in largely White schools, like the tragic mass murders at Sandy Hook elementary school in Connecticut on December 14, 2012; Marjorie Stoneman Douglas High School in Parkland, Florida, on February 14, 2018; and Robb Elementary School in Uvalde, Texas on May 24, 2022, captured widespread media coverage and public sympathy. Nonetheless, students of color remained disproportionately the victims of gun violence on school grounds.[6] In 2017, almost 3,000 children were shot and killed in the United States annually, claiming the lives of ten times more Black children than White children.[7] Yet gun violence that killed Whites was viewed as a social problem, while gun violence that claimed Black lives was viewed as "a separate, individualized matter." As Mitchell and Bromfield argued:

> Movements born from gun violence help to expand the picture. Students from Parkland have organized rallies, and the news media covers the "march" and fortitude of the young survivors who have taken to the streets of our nation's capital. When communities like Ferguson, Missouri, organize, though, they are labeled "protesters" and "rioters"; they are met with the National Guard, army tanks, and tear gas.[8]

The racially inflected responses to murdered children thus link the histories of urban riots, excessive police force, and the murders of Black youths by individual civilians that I discussed in 2008 and 2014.

These facts pain me personally and as a citizen. As an historian, I am pulled to examine them for historical patterns and examples of effective change. The importance of laws to guarantee rights or abrogate them seems both evident and inadequate. Laws must be enforced to make a difference, and they can be overturned. But the ongoing tolls of internalized racism, sexism, nativism, and homophobia, of religious and class prejudices, also caution that legal change alone is insufficient without the longer processes of attitudinal and cultural change. No meaningful change occurs without courageous change-makers, and without daily individual acts outside the public limelight that change attitudes, behaviors, and social practices.

I have studied social movements because I feel for the victims of discrimination and am drawn to the courageous activists who resist inequity and work for justice, whose resistance, individually and collectively, is as enduring as the inequities themselves. I remain drawn to the historic actors, well-known and celebrated, private and obscure, who have sought to stop human suffering, who have supported marginalized communities and fostered pride among subordinated people. Which brings me back to the unhappy histories of my 2014 lecture.

I was drawn to my topic in 2014 not only by the painful horror of young lives lost, but even more by the courage of parents determined to make change out of unimaginable personal tragedy. As I prepared this book, I have similarly grieved the lost Indigenous children buried in the unmarked graves historians have known must have existed somewhere, and the strength of Indigenous parents to endure unimaginable grief. These histories bridge time in the unhappy persistence of discrimination and suffering. They can also bridge the experiences of people who have been privileged or subordinated by virtue of race, ethnicity, sexuality, class, or gender, by making visible the lived experience of marginalized and subordinated people, their endurance and resistance.

For those of us privileged not to have experienced overt discrimination, to have been spared demeaning and dangerous attacks, these stories open windows on enormous suffering and awesome resilience, dignity, and courage. On International Women's Day, March 8, 2021, I joined the audience as U.S. Representative Lucy McBath hosted an on-line gathering with Sybrina Fulton to reflect on their shared journeys as mothers of murdered children. Fulton, the mother of slain teen Trayvon Martin, joined her ex-husband Tracy Martin, to establish the Trayvon Martin Foundation to "provide both emotional and financial support to families who have lost a child to gun violence." She went on to found the Circle of Mothers, who support mothers who have lost children to violence.[9] McBath, the mother of murdered teen Jordan Davis, left a thirty-year career as a Delta Airlines flight attendant to run for Congress, winning election in 2018 and re-election in 2020 and 2024, from Georgia's Sixth Congressional District, the first Democrat since 1979 to win the seat formerly held by Republican Newt Gingrich.[10] From 2023-2025 she represented the neighboring Seventh Congressional District. She had shepherded two pieces of gun control legislation through the House of Representatives and in 2021 was trying to win Republican Senators' support for both bills "not as a Member of Congress, but as a mother, as Jordan's mother."

McBath decided to run for office after the Parkland tragedy, and after the federal government again did nothing to curb gun violence. She acted, as well, from a sense of history, both public and personal. She wrote during Black History Month, 2020:

> I didn't have to look much further than the dinner table for civil rights heroes growing up during the 1960's.
>
> When I was growing up, my father Lucien Holman was a dentist by trade, but he was also active in the civil rights movement.
>
> His position as an NAACP chapter president in Illinois afforded me the opportunity at a very young age to attend marches, rallies, and protests alongside civil rights heroes like Dr. Martin Luther King Jr.

Dr. Holman was invited to the White House to witness President Johnson signing the Civil Rights Act of 1964. Lucy McBath traced her own activist roots to her father and their family table:

> All these years later, I never imagined I'd also become an advocate after Jordan's death. *But those moments watching my father and his friends organizing around the dinner table helped me form the foundational values and strategies I bring to our gun safety movement today.*
>
> So before Black History Month is over, I wanted to honor civil rights heroes like my father and the folks that gathered around our kitchen table, as well as my good friend and colleague Rep. John Lewis who just turned 80 years old.
>
> I'm honored to follow in their footsteps and work beside so many of them who are still alive today in our continued fight for justice for all.[11]

Sybrina Fulton also turned to politics, losing her 2020 race for Miami-Dade County Commissioner by only 333 votes. McBath encouraged her to try again, calling Fulton "the mother of the movement for her generation." In 2021 Sybrina Fulton said she took hope even in the context of George Floyd's murder by Minneapolis police May 5, 2020, in part because the image of George Floyd dying was undeniable because it was captured on a cell phone video and could not be erased from memories. Most people who protested her son's murder in 2012 were Black, she said. More people became involved after Floyd was killed, both Black and White. She placed great faith "in the young people to make positive change." [12]

Trayvon Martin and Jordan Davis guide their mothers' activism. McBath has become a leading Congressional voice for gun control. Constituents and supporters receive her pained but determined email messages after each new mass shooting, on her son's birthday, and as she introduces gun control legislation in the House of Representatives. She has shared the letters she writes to her son each year on his birthday and the anniversary of his murder, and her reflections on Mother's Day, for her "one of the hardest days of the year."[13] McBath has insisted on wresting some meaning from her loss, writing to her dead son: "I know that change hasn't happened as fast as we may have hoped, but there is a light in the future. I know that you were not taken from us in vain eight years ago today. It cannot be that way. … [M]y promise to you is that I will continue to fight for you and your legacy. To make this world a better place, a safer place for families like ours."[14]

Trayvon Martin and Jordan Davis remain present for their mothers, enduring losses and enduring sources of inspiration. Their sons' photos were visible in the background of each woman during the on-line gathering; Sybrina Fulton brushed away tears throughout the 45-minute program. Both women have been painfully public about their losses and their activist responses. Lucy McBath is eloquently transparent about the tragedy that sent her to Congress, about the activist histories and personal ties that motivate her efforts for change. "I cried, I prayed, and I decided to fight for justice for my son. And to make sure that no other mother had to feel the pain I did," she wrote. "Even though he's gone, I'm still mothering Jordan through this work."

The tragedies that impelled Sybrina Fulton and Lucy McBath on their paths of public activism made them the vocal representatives of many less-visible social change activists, who have committed long years of hard work to make a better world for other people, other families, other children. They make explicit what has linked the personal and the political in movements for historic change.

NOTES

1 On the making of these myths see, for instance Lisa Tetrault, *The Myth of Seneca Falls: Memory and the Women's Suffrage Movement, 1848-1898* (Chapel Hill: University of North Carolina Press, 2014); Elizabeth A. Armstrong and Susanna M. Crage, "Movements and Memory: The Making of the Stonewall Myth," *American Sociological Review* 71:5 (October 2006): 724-51; Joe Street and Henry Knight Lozano, eds., *The Shadow of Selma* (Gainesville: University Press of Florida, 2018), esp. Aniko Bodroghkozy, "Mediating Selma," 133-49; Mark Walmsley, "'They Just Couldn't Write It the Way it Wasn't Anymore': Mainstream Media Narratives and the 1965 Selma Campaign," 150-70; George Lewis, "Sidelining Selma's Segregationists: Memory, Strategy, Ideology and Agency," 170-95; and Megan Hunt, "'Men of God and Goodwill Everywhere': *Selma* and the Role of Religion in Civil Rights Drama," 196-214.

2 By 1919, women had gained the full franchise in fifteen states, starting with Wyoming Territory in 1869, but women in all states did not achieve full suffrage until 1920.

3 Seven days after taking office in his first term, President Trump signed Executive Order 13769, "Protecting the Nation from Foreign Terrorist Entry into the United States," known popularly as the "Muslim ban" or the "Trump Muslim Travel Ban." It was suspended by a number of courts until March 6, 2017, when it was superseded by Executive Order 13780, again titled "Protecting the Nation from Foreign Terrorist Entry into the United States." Executive Order 13769 cut to 50,000 the number of refugees who could enter the country in 2017, suspended the United States Refugee Admittance Program (USRAP) for 120 days, indefinitely suspended the entry of Syrian refugees, and suspended the entry of

people from Iran, Libya, Somalia, Sudan, Syria, and Yemen. Iraq was also briefly included. More than 700 travelers were detained, and up to 60,000 visas were "provisionally revoked." The order met immediate opposition because it equated all people from these predominantly Muslim countries with terrorists, and hurt many, like the Syrian refugees, who were fleeing violence in their countries. Enforcement of the order was suspended by a temporary restraining order issued February 3, 2017 in *Washington v. Trump* and was upheld by the U.S. Court of Appeals. Later, Trump signed Executive Order 13780 and Presidential Proclamation 9645, which superseded Executive Order 13769. On June 26, 2018, the U.S. Supreme Court, in a 5–4 decision, upheld the third Executive Order (Presidential Proclamation 9645) and its accompanying travel ban. The day he took office, on January 20, 2021, President Joe Biden revoked the Trump Muslim Travel Bans with Presidential Proclamation 10141.

4   The covered jurisdictions had been regularly updated based on the preclearance provisions. The Voting Rights Act thus allowed for changes in historic patterns of racial discrimination in voting.

5   Examples of these restrictions include requiring drivers' licenses for identification, thus disadvantaging people who can't afford cars, or, in Texas, not accepting student photo IDs but allowing gun registrations as identification, which do not have photographs. Other strategies have included placing polling places where they are not accessible by public transportation, eliminating Sunday voting, and limiting the numbers and locations of drop boxes to deposit advance ballots. As well, legislatures in some states have drawn the lines of districts for Congress and state legislatures to divide and dilute the votes of people of color or of opposition political parties.

6   Yolanda P. Mitchell, PhD and Tiffany L. Bromfield, MA, "Gun Violence and the Minority Experience," National Council on Family Relations, https://www.ncfr.org/ncfr-report/winter-2018/gun-violence-and-minority-experience, accessed June 7, 2021.

7   Katherine A. Fowler, Linda L. Dahlberg, Tadesse Haileyesus, Carmen Gutierrez and Sarah Bacon, "Childhood Firearm Injuries in the United States," *Pediatrics* 141:1 (July 2017): 1–11.

8   Mitchell and Bromfield, "Gun Violence and the Minority Experience."

9   Online Gathering, hosted by Representative Lucy McBath with Sybrina Fulton, International Women's Day, March 8, 2021.

10 The Republican Georgia state legislature has twice redrawn the lines of Rep. McBath's congressional district, trying to include enough Republicans to defeat her at the polls. After the legislature redrew the boundaries of District 6 in 2022 to include significantly more Republicans, McBath won election in the newly redrawn 7th Congressional District. Again in 2024, Republican legislators redrew the lines of the 7th District to make it difficult for a Democrat to win, whereupon Ms. McBath announced she would run for election in 2024 in the again re-drawn 6th District and was re-elected to Congress from her original district. Both districts, in their various configurations, are in suburban Atlanta.

11 Representative Lucy McBath, "My Father," email to supporters, February 22, 2020. Representative John Lewis died July 17, 2020, months after Rep. McBath penned this letter. He was a revered Civil Rights leader, who had participated in formative acts of civil disobedience in the 1960s, including the 1960 Nashville sit-ins and the Freedom Rides to integrate seating on interstate busses. He served as chairman of the Student Nonviolent Coordinating Committee (SNCC) from 1963 to 1966, and was part of the leadership in organizing the 1963 March on Washington. In 1965 Lewis led the first of three Selma to Montgomery marches across the Edmund Pettus Bridge and suffered a brutal attack on that Bloody Sunday that required hospitalization. The image of his being bludgeoned on the head was part of what moved President Johnson to introduce the Voting Rights Act.

He was elected to the United States House of Representatives in 1986 and represented the Atlanta, Georgia 5th congressional district from 1987 until his death.

12   Representative McBath's Online Gathering.

13   For examples, Lucy McBath, emails to supporters: "Boulder," March 22, 2021; "one of the hardest days of the year," May 9, 2021; "My letter to Jordan on the eighth anniversary of his murder," November 23, 2020; "Our movement prevailed," November 4, 2020; "Today is Jordan's 29th Birthday," February 16, 2024; "A Letter to Jordan," November 23, 2024.

14   McBath, "My letter to Jordan."

10

Are We There Yet? Personal and Historical Reflections on Women in Higher Education

April 9, 2012

As I've previously confessed, I'm a sucker for historical anniversaries—especially fortieth anniversaries. The number forty in the Bible always signals massive transformations: there were forty days of Noah's flood; the children of Israel wandered for forty years in the wilderness before reaching the Promised Land; Moses spent forty days on Mount Sinai receiving the Ten Commandments. Scholars speculate that this is related to forty weeks of pregnancy.

In 2012, I was drawn to the fortieth anniversary of Title IX of the United States Educational Amendments of 1972. Title IX banned sex discrimination in U.S. education, mandating that "No person in the United States shall, on the basis of sex, be excluded from participation in, be denied the benefits of, or be subjected to discrimination under any education program or activity receiving Federal financial assistance."[1] People concerned with efforts to achieve educational equity in the United States know that landmark legislation; it was, understandably, less familiar to Canadians.

Title IX did not, of course, cover higher education in Canada. But Canada, too, celebrated a landmark anniversary in 2012: the thirtieth anniversary of the Charter of Rights and Freedoms. The Charter enshrined the principle of gender equality in employment, public life, and education in Part I, section 15: "Every individual is equal before and under the law and has the right to the equal protection and equal benefit of the law without discrimination and, in particular, without discrimination based on race, national or ethnic origin, color, religion, sex, age or mental or physical disability." From the standpoints of either anniversary, the challenges to achieving gender equity had been substantial and the changes by 2012 were notable.

Title IX covered discrimination in both academics and athletics. When it became law in 1972, virtually no women got athletic scholarships, and science and math were overwhelmingly male bastions. Women earned 9 percent of all U.S. medical degrees, 7 percent of all law degrees, and 16 percent of all U.S. PhDs.[2]

I have been part of a very fortunate academic generation. I graduated from college and entered graduate school in 1970, the year that the first women's studies program in the United States was established at Cornell University. In 1972, I was assisting the first women's history course offered at the University of Michigan. Although I have never taken a women's history class, I was the teaching assistant for some of the first ones, and I was in the first cohort of graduate students to study women and gender, to get to help invent the field of women's history. At Michigan, I got to work with some gifted, often isolated, feminist scholars with whom graduate students began to research women as subjects and employ gender as a category of analysis. We began a collective project to increase women's participation and status in the university, and to include women's experiences in the curriculum. It has been an extraordinary journey, sometimes exhilarating, sometimes frustrating, occasionally depressing. So, when I reflect on the status of women in higher education, my benchmarks are personal, professional, and, since 1999, bi-national.

My lecture in 2012 moved back and forth across the border and offered personal, structural, and historical measures of change. Forty years after Title IX, thirty years after the Charter of Rights and Freedoms, I asked the questions my students asked me. How far had we come? Were we there yet? The answers depend on where you think we started, who "we" are, and what measures "there" represents. Are we talking about gender equity among undergraduate students, graduate students, academic staff, support staff? About how women students are treated in classrooms and how they are advised on their career paths? How we handle sexual harassment and pay discrimination? How women, genders, and gender as a category of analysis are represented in the curriculum? All of the above? By any of these measures we were not there in 2012. We still aren't there in 2025. I can only hope that gender inequities will indeed be history sometime in the future when someone may read this essay. However, despite persistent inequities, it was also true that by most measures there had been substantial positive change in the forty years since Title IX became law.

Despite the fortieth anniversary benchmark, I had not intended to speak on this topic in 2012. I was drawn to it by three events. Two concerned students. I was sobered and angered in February 2012 by the experience of Sandra Fluke, President of Georgetown Law Students for Reproductive Justice, when Republican members of the House Oversight and Government Reform Committee refused to allow her to testify at the Committee's hearing on contraception. Then radio talk-show host Rush Limbaugh called Fluke a slut and a prostitute because she wanted student health insurance to cover contraception.[3] That spectacle unfolded a few months after I had attended a Brainstorming Session hosted by the American Historical Association's Committee on Women Historians at the 2012 annual meeting of the AHA. A young woman graduate student asked the professors there for advice. "I have been told," she said, "not to wear my wedding ring to job interviews. What do I say if I am asked whether I'm married?" When I told this story to a senior woman colleague at the University of Calgary, she replied, "I didn't wear *my* wedding ring to job interviews." Both events evoked issues I thought we had settled in the 1970s. I want younger colleagues and students to find new challenges of their own, not grapple with my generation's. But it seems, as with many things, the past is rarely entirely past.

The third impetus for my reflections came on August 30 and 31, 2011, when I got calls from the *Calgary Herald* newspaper and the CBC's "Eye Opener" radio program, asking me to comment on a Statistics Canada report that the University of Calgary had the largest gender wage discrepancy among twenty-nine Canadian universities. During the 2010–2011 academic year, male professors at the University of Calgary earned, on average, $20,168 more than female professors.[4] The reporters asked me to comment because I had served on the committee that prepared a Faculty Salary Equity Report in 2005 that analyzed the gender difference in faculty salaries that existed in 2004, when the difference was $16,179.[5] The gap had grown by almost $4,000 in seven years. On the face of it these figures did not look good. I returned to our findings from 2005 seeking clues to sources of persistent inequities.

All three events represented the residue of past discrimination and gendered social expectations. They were evidence of continuing inequities, but they could also obscure considerable progress. Sometimes I return to the past to remind myself how far we've come.

I entered kindergarten in 1952. By 2012 I had spent six decades in educational institutions in the United States and Canada and for each of those sixty years gender had mattered. I knew in my gut the answer to "Are we there yet?" "No, but we have come light years from my years as a student." My high school physics teacher asked me and the only other girl in his class to drop the course so he could discuss the subject "with greater frankness." We stayed and endured his repertoire of lame sexist jokes. My statistics professor in graduate school announced that he didn't expect any women to pass the course and tried to ensure that outcome by making every question on the first exam about football.[6]

When I entered graduate school at the University of Michigan, there was only one woman in the history department, Sylvia Thrupp, a medievalist. She was there because someone had endowed a chair for a woman, the Alice Freeman Palmer Chair, named for the founding president of Wellesley College who was a Michigan alumna. Dr. Thrupp was hired in 1961 only after the department tried and failed to break the terms of the bequest so it could hire a man. This would not have surprised Sylvia Thrupp, who earned her BA at the University of British Columbia in 1925, her MA there in 1928, and her doctorate in medieval history at the University of London in 1931, but who found it hard to find work in Canada. She wrote Walter Sage, her mentor at UBC, that she was somewhat discouraged in her job search by the "anti-feminist feeling in the eastern universities." "At McGill," she wrote, "they once had a woman in history whom they didn't like and have never taken the risk again and never will while the present staff lives." Chester Martin, head of the University of Toronto department, "also made it clear," she wrote, that "he would appoint only men." Thrupp worked as a non-tenure-track instructor at UBC from 1935-1944 and taught a year as a special lecturer at U of T before getting hired as an assistant professor at the University of Chicago in 1945, fourteen years after she earned her PhD. She was a distinguished scholar, the founder and editor of *Comparative Studies in Society and History,* whose books and articles on guilds and on demography broke new ground in medieval social history. When she died, her University of Michigan colleague Raymond Grew wrote that "Thrupp had made her way in a scholarly world reluctant to grant women permanent positions, battling without bitterness for ideas more than status." I have no idea whether she battled without bitterness; I do know that in 1970 some of her male colleagues felt she was hired *only* because she was a woman. I know she did not make full professor for almost three decades after earning her last degree; that she did not marry until age eighty-three.[7]

Dr. Thrupp, like many Canadian women of her generation, left Canada for graduate study and employment. The situation was slightly better in the United States because Alice Freeman Palmer and other women founded women's colleges which, by the late-19th century, employed women faculty. Most of these women were single, though "singleness" at that time covered a spectrum of intimate realities. At a time when women were virtually required to choose career or marriage, they chose career, but not necessarily as a choice over marriage to a man. Some of these educational pioneers had intimate partnerships with other women, and they all had access to the support of feminist colleagues and communities.

Although the wedding ring question that prompted my lecture concerned a heterosexual woman's marriage, by 1972 the "marriage issue" was even more fraught for lesbian academics, who could not marry their partners. Canada did not legalize same-sex marriage nationally until 2005; the United States did not legalize it until 2016, when the Supreme Court struck down all laws banning same-sex marriage. Some provinces and states legalized same-sex marriages before the landmark national policies,[8] but for lesbian and non-binary academics, decisions to discuss their partnerships or to come out to their students were infinitely more difficult than straight women's very real dilemmas about how much personal information to share with potential employers. In an interview situation, even after same-sex marriage was legal, there were no reliably safe answers to questions about intimate partnerships. The unspoken questions for all women concerned institutional fears about partner hires and pregnancy, adoption, and maternity leaves, as well as sexist and homophobic biases.

After the 1920s, as women faculty retired, they were most often replaced by men, even at the Seven Sisters colleges that pioneered U.S. women's higher education. I attended Antioch College, founded by abolitionists in 1853, the second college in the United States to admit both African Americans and women. When I arrived there in 1965, there were fewer than five women among the fulltime tenure-stream faculty.

There were enormous changes after my years in college and graduate school in the numbers of women earning degrees and entering the faculty ranks. In both Canada and the United States, women gained access to higher education in increasing numbers and became a majority of undergraduate students. In the United States, women of all racial ethnic groups earned the majority of degrees in 2008–2009: 62 percent of associate's degrees, 57 percent of bachelor's degrees, 60 percent of masters, and 52 percent of doctorates. The figures were higher among African American students, among whom women earned 68 percent of associate's degrees, 66 percent of bachelor's degrees, 72 percent of master's degrees, 62 percent of first-professional degrees, and 67 percent of PhDs. Among Hispanic students, women earned 62 percent of associate's degrees, 61 percent of bachelor's degrees, 64 percent of master's degrees, 53 percent of first-professional degrees, and 57 percent of doctoral degrees. White females earned more degrees than White males at each degree level except first-professional degrees, of which they earned 46 percent.[9] This was enormous progress since 1972, when women were outnumbered at all levels.

In Canada and at the University of Calgary, the gains were also impressive. Among Canadian university students in 2010, 58.1 percent of undergraduates were women, 54.1 percent of master's students, and 46.4 percent of doctoral students.[10] At the University of Calgary, the figures were somewhat lower but still good: 53 percent of undergraduates and 51 percent of graduate students.[11]

Yet increased access to higher education did not mean economic or social equity for women after they graduated. In March 2011, the White House released the first comprehensive report on the status of American Women since 1963 when President Kennedy's Commission on the Status of Women published its findings. The 2011 report found that women were a majority of American undergraduates, that younger women were more likely than younger men to earn university or graduate degrees, and that the proportions of women and men in the workforce had nearly equalized. Women's wages constituted a significant share of household income.[12] In both Canada and the United States, women's incomes maintained the middle-class status of many two-income households. But the White House report found that women's wages still lagged significantly behind those of men with comparable educations and that "gains in education and labor force involvement have not yet translated into wage and income equity." At all levels of education, women earned about 75 percent of what their male counterparts earned in 2009—still an improvement over the 59 percent when the U.S. Equal Pay Act was signed in 1963.[13] Women were more likely than men to live in poverty, in part because of these lower earnings and in part because unpartnered and divorced women usually raise and support their children. These economic inequities were even more acute for women of color.[14]

In neither the United States nor Canada had the gains in educational attainment translated to women's representation in the professoriate, nor to gender equity in hiring, promotion, tenure, or salaries. In 2003, Canada ranked below Australia, New Zealand, the United Kingdom, and the United States for women among full-time faculty.[15] By 2010, women comprised 20 percent of Canadian full professors, 31.4 percent of associate professors, 42.9 percent of assistant professors, and 15.4 percent of university presidents—a figure that rose to 23 percent with the appointment of Dr. Elizabeth Cannon as the first woman president of the University of Calgary in 2010.[16] South of the border, women earned doctorates at record rates, but our position in the academy had not kept pace. Despite enormous gains, women remained more likely than men to be part time, not tenure track, or in colleges and community colleges rather than in graduate research universities. In 1972 women were 27 percent of all faculty; in 2009, women's representation had increased to 42 percent of full-time faculty. Women were only 9 percent of full professors in 1972, 28 percent in 2009. Given these trends, it was estimated in 2006 that it would take almost sixty years for women to be half of the full-time faculty.[17]

Yet as women entered the profession, the numbers of full-time faculty began to shrink, and women remained over-represented in the growing ranks of part-timers and sessional instructors. By the fall of 2009, three-fourths of all U.S. teaching faculty were in contingent positions, including full- and part-time non-tenure-track faculty and graduate students.[18] As more women joined the professoriate, the status and job security of those positions declined. And there were scattered signs, too early to be considered trends, that bore watching as indicators of slowed or reversing progress. In 1980, women comprised just 14 percent of all U.S. history faculty; by 2008, women approached 31 percent of historians compared with 42.5 percent representation throughout all fields, and the rate of growth had slowed. The cohort who entered the discipline in the 1980s and 1990s was advancing to the higher ranks, but the numbers of women entering the field as assistant professors had dropped by about a fourth, and far fewer women, proportionately, were entering the profession than were earning doctorates. In 2003, 32.8 percent of assistant professors were women, compared to 41 percent of recent history PhDs.[19]

Women earned less in every rank than our male colleagues, in all types of institutions. The salary disadvantage in all U.S. institutions was about 7 percent for assistant and associate professors in 2011, 12 percent for full professors. Because women remained over-represented in the lowest ranks, in less lucrative fields, and in less prestigious institutions, faculty women's salaries had remained about 80 percent of men's since the 1970s.[20] Which brought me back to the still unsolved issue of pay equity.

The report I co-authored in 2005 was not the first to address the gender gap in pay at the University of Calgary. In 1979, Wayne Kelly of the Office of Institutional Analysis conducted a "Faculty Salary Study." In 1996 Dr. Jim Frideres prepared "Income Distribution for Males and Females at the University of Calgary, 1966–1995." The *Status of Women at the University of Calgary, 2001* recommended regular reviews and listed pay equity as one of the top five priorities to improve the status of women in the university.[21] In 2003, the Academic Women's Association conducted a Faculty Salary Equity Study with support from then-President's Adviser on Women's Affairs, Dr. Hermina Joldersma, to determine if much had changed since the Frideres study. In 2004, we found that full-time women faculty earned approximately 82 percent of men's salaries, a 2 percent gain since 1996.[22] In 2011, despite the larger dollar difference in average salaries, rising faculty pay scales meant that the gap had narrowed proportionately while the dollar amount had increased; women's salaries were 84.6 percent of men's.[23]

For the 2005 study, Dr. Jean Wallace conducted a multiple regression analysis to account for variables that might affect earnings. She found that men were more concentrated in the upper ranks and had worked on average 6.6 years more since their last degree. However, even taking into account differences in rank, education, work history, and years since the last degree, we could not explain $2,643 of the difference between men's and women's salaries.[24] It should be noted as well that none of these figures included honoraria, research supplements, and market supplements (that is, salary increases to make some fields competitive with what scholars could earn outside the university). Market supplements in particular tend to be concentrated in faculties with proportionately more men.[25]

There were other troubling indicators. Part of the wage discrepancies began at hire: there was a significant $2,898 gap in starting salaries for women assistant professors, and women were disproportionately concentrated at the assistant and associate ranks at hire. Three times more men than women were hired in as associate and full professors.[26] Part of the difference was related to the gendered representation in fields and faculties. Women earn more doctorates in the Humanities, Arts, and Education, and have made the biggest gains in admission to the ranks of these faculties. At the University of Calgary, in some largely female faculties like nursing and social work, fewer faculty have doctorates. Also troubling was the fact that all faculty with "prior work history at the University of Calgary," earned on average $732 less annually than faculty without prior work experience there.[27] While years since the last degree can result in some salary differences, it did not explain why men earned on average $1,233 per year for each year since their last degree, but women only $758, or 61 percent of the annual increase for men.[28]

Factors such as maternity leaves and dislocation due to partner moves did not explain this difference. There were, however, gendered differences related to family and life cycle. Significantly more women than men had taken leaves in the prior five years. There had been only thirty-six adoption, maternity, and parental leaves, and men took only three of them. The fact that men don't take maternity leave and that parental leaves are unpaid explains some of this difference. But three women in ten under age forty took a family leave, although 83 percent of male faculty were married compared to 65 percent of the women.[29]

These patterns are not unique to the University of Calgary, and considerable research has sought to explain continuing gender differences. A number of studies, including one at the University of Calgary, have found that women faculty in particular and shorter people with higher voices in general tend to get lower student evaluations.[30] The ranking of journals in some fields assigns lesser value to journals devoted specifically to gender research, or to knowledge directed at practical application more than theory. Studies over several decades have found that women spend more time teaching on average than men, and specifically on undergraduate teaching and advising. Hermina Joldersma's survey of 67 faculty from Science, Engineering, and Kinesiology for her 2005 *Next Steps* report found that women spent on average 55.74 hours a week on work compared to 51.42 for men, and 14.53 hours on childcare or other caring work—over twice the 7.22 for men.[31] A 2011 study found that disproportionate time spent in teaching and service presented a significant obstacle to promotion for women associate professors. All associate professors worked an average of 64 hours a week, but men spent seven and a half hours a week more on their research. The women spent an hour a week more teaching, mentored an additional two hours a week, and spent five hours more on service.[32] The need to have women represented on committees—a goal that I endorse—has meant a disproportionate service load for women throughout my years in the academy, particularly at the higher ranks.

So far, I have presented a lot of numbers that follow a pattern almost as predictable as salary equity reports. The reason the numbers matter is the people behind the averages, and the clues the numbers offer to the history and the lives they represent. I interpret the numbers at least partly through the lens of my own experience. So, in the interests of transparency and to suggest some patterns and changes, I leave the seemingly concrete world of statistics for the more suspect terrain of the personal.

I began thinking about some of what I shared in this lecture in 2004, during a health crisis—thankfully long resolved. For two months, as I recovered from surgery, I had time to think. I had always accepted that it would be a long struggle to achieve gender equity. But I realized that somewhere in the ahistorical recesses of my mind I had assumed that we would reach equity in the academy before I retired, or at least before I died. The equity I imagine includes equity in education, hiring, promotion, and pay, for starters. I also hoped that some of the particularities of women's professional life cycles might influence the rules and culture of the profession. And I hoped that we would not just add women to the curriculum, but that we would rethink it from the perspectives of women, people of color, people of all classes and genders, and so on. I wanted not simply to add women to existing structures and textbook narratives, but also to achieve equity of knowledge production.

I had to confront that my timeline, if not my hopes, represented an ahistorical fantasy— that a lot would remain to be done long after I would be part of the effort. I began thinking about what I needed to do to nurture my hopes toward fruition. I had somehow gotten to be a senior member of the profession, and it seemed time to tell the stories I had not been telling for fear of seeming to make excuses or of being pigeonholed as an "abrasive woman." Mine is only one life; all women have their own stories. But I think that those of us who have lived through changes in higher education need to tell our stories, as benchmarks of how far women have come and as a caution about where, without continued vigilance, we could return.

I thought again about the troubled connections of the personal and the professional on January 7, 2012, at the American Historical Association conference when I attended the annual breakfast meeting of the Committee on Women Historians. The speaker, Barbara Young Welke, who holds a dual appointment in law and history at the University of Minnesota, moved many to tears with her paper, "Telling Stories: A Meditation on Love, Loss, History, and Who We Are." With clarity, grace, and an extraordinary balance of openness and restraint, Welke structured her talk around the letters she had written daily for a year and half to her daughter Frances, who died suddenly from a cerebral hemorrhage just after her eighteenth birthday. Welke periodically interrupted the words that maintain her daughter's presence, to ruminate on how her personal tragedy influenced her scholarship, which deals with how flammable fabrics have devastated children who suffered disabling and fatal burns. Acknowledging her empathy for burn victims' parents while recognizing what separates their losses from her own, Welke urged historians not to drown out the emotions that draw us to our subjects, not to leach the humanity from our subjects to get at larger theoretical or historiographic principles. She did not ask us to abandon general conclusions, just not to forget the people behind them. My statistics matter. So do the life experiences they suggest.

Welke, from the vantage of an intensely personal loss, asked how we should account for personal factors in professional contexts. How should we record such catastrophic interruptions as the loss of a child on a curriculum vita? Curriculum vitae. The words mean the record of a life. And yet women have for good reason erased from our vitas personal details like marital or partnership status and children. The normative male faculty member when I entered college had a wife who did the household chores and primary parenting. Being married helped men's careers. Families were assumed to be liabilities for women, and those assumptions limited women's access to degrees and to academic careers. It was very important for my generation to separate the personal from the professional—to insist that our minds and our work mattered, but not our intimate partners or children, not our biology or our reproductive systems, not our personal lives. And yet I became convinced that to make sense of the numbers and to safeguard the gains made since 1972 we must address what connects the personal and the professional. The marginal notes that don't appear on my CV record the not-so-hidden assumptions I encountered in the 1970s. I use them to return to the subtexts of the statistics: the impacts of family on careers, the assessment of women's teaching and scholarship, the value assigned to different kinds of knowledge, and the continuing projects of equity in education, in professional advancement, and in knowledge production.

Family. Mine was extraordinary. Both of my grandmothers earned university degrees, one of them before 1900, at a time when gender and Jewish quotas at many universities made their achievements doubly extraordinary. My parents married in 1943, when my mother was 18. My Dad put her through her last two years of university and then through medical school. She earned her MD, practiced psychiatry until she retired at age 80, and had four kids without stopping. My parents joked that I made it half-way through the second year of medical school before I dropped out. There was never any question that I would go to college, only where I would go and what I would study. My Mom showed me I could do anything—and that it would be hard. Although she pioneered in child and adolescent psychiatry, she spent decades longer than her peers as an associate professor and earned far less.

When I got to college, I encountered conflicted messages about being smart and being female. Some of those messages came from me. During my third year, I suddenly had trouble reading. I could read, but I couldn't tell you what I had read. At some deep level I was trying to become a dumb blonde, certain that that was the only way to attract a man. I was blessed with a perceptive faculty adviser, a philosopher named Jim Green. At the beginning of the next quarter Jim told me "There's a great class on the European Enlightenment. You should take it. There were some great thinkers then. You'll love it." The professor was Hannah Goldberg, a large, vibrant, brilliant woman who taught part time because her husband was in the English department, and who had a young daughter. Hannah was a galvanizing teacher and an even more important model. Sometime during that class, I began to be able to read again. When I accused Jim of deliberate manipulation, he just shrugged and said, "You wouldn't be able to hear anything I could say—you had to see what you can be."

Hannah was an exceptional mentor, but she did not get hired full-time until her husband suddenly died. She and several male professors encouraged me to think about graduate school, but the chair of the history department encouraged me to consider high school teaching the same day he advised my friend Steve to go on for a doctorate.

Antioch students alternated quarters working off campus with quarters studying on campus, and I had to decide whether to apply to graduate school during the fall of 1969, while I was in Boulder working at the Western History Collections at the University of Colorado. So, I sought advice from a senior western historian in the University of Colorado history department. He told me I should not go to graduate school because I would just get married, and I would be taking a slot that should go to a man. I got mad enough to send in my applications.

I faced similar messages when it came to funding. In the spring of 1970, I was interviewed at Ohio State University by a selection committee for Woodrow Wilson Graduate Fellowships. There were four senior historians on the committee, three men and one woman. The woman looked down and doodled except when she asked me a question. Most of the interview was predictable—questions about the Gilded Age, my research interests, Andrew Carnegie's attitudes about inheritance, and so on. And then, after forty-five minutes, the Chair of the Committee suddenly said, "And now, Miss Jameson, I must ask you—are there any young men in your life?" I was lucky. The woman looked up, smashed her fist on the table and said, "That is an inappropriate question. I will not allow her to answer it. Don't you open your mouth." I stayed obediently silent, and was, I think, the only woman or one of very few who made it through the selection process at OSU that year.

That woman, Mary Young, was one of the rare women, like Sylvia Thrupp and Hannah Goldberg, hired in U.S. history departments after World War II, who made an enormous difference for my generation. I did not want to study medieval history, and Dr. Thrupp was the only woman in the University of Michigan history department when I got there. But over in the Residential College, the University of Michigan honors college, there were some magnificent women professors, including Marilyn Blatt Young and Kathryn Kish Sklar, who were there because they were married to men in the history department and nepotism rules forbade hiring spouses.[33] The catch was that history graduate students were not allowed to work with them because they weren't history department faculty. But I was in an interdisciplinary program in American Culture, and my program chair sensibly said that they were perfectly qualified scholars, and I should go work with them. They taught me much more than history. Marilyn told me that it was perfectly possible to combine career and family if I accepted that my family did not have to be able to eat off every surface in my house. One would suffice. I got lessons in teaching as well. Although I've never taken a women's history course, because there weren't any, I did readings in women's history with Kitty Sklar and assisted the first women's history class she taught.

I hadn't intended to study women. During my first year of graduate school I resented being assigned what I called the "women and" papers— about Margaret Fuller, the leading U.S. intellectual of the 19th century, and Kate Chopin, whose literature was just being rediscovered. Then I got engrossed. One day, standing in the History department, I told a friend I was really getting into women's history. An eminent historian stuck his head out his office door and intoned: "Women's history? Why, that's just the history of dishwashing!"

My first reaction was anger. He meant, of course, that women had always done the same trivial things and were therefore unchanging, ahistorical. Women, I fumed, had done the same things men had: they had thought great thoughts, fought political battles, worked professionally. But the remark rankled. After fuming for several months, I decided he was right: women's history *is* in large measure the history of dishwashing, if by "dishwashing" we mean domestic labor, physically and socially reproducing human beings, and reinforcing or changing human cultures through daily acts.

When I assisted Kitty Sklar's women's history class, she assigned me two lectures, one on women and work in colonial America, and one on women and work in the 19th and 20th centuries. So, I headed off to the graduate library in search of sources. For the first lecture, I found Alice Morse Earle's classic *Colonial Dames and Good Wives*, published in 1895. I had to cut the pages—the book had not once been opened since the library acquired it. The assumption that women were private and trivial, men public and consequential had left Earle unopened on the library shelf for seventy-seven years. I cribbed my first lectures from books like Earle's and Edith Abbot's *Women in Industry* and the publications of the U.S. Women's Bureau of the Department of Labor—all legacies of the first generations of university-educated feminists.[34]

So began the unfinished project of recovering women's lives and women's stories. A generation of feminist scholarship has spanned academic discourses, the personal and the political, private lore and public history. It has always been a collective endeavor. During 1972–1973, a group of women professors and graduate students collectively taught the first Introduction to Women's Studies class at the University of Michigan. It was an extraordinary group. The faculty included Kathryn Sklar from History, Judith Bardwick from Psychology, Norma Diamond from Anthropology, and Linda Nochlin from Art History. My graduate student colleagues included names now familiar in many disciplines: Gayle Rubin and Rayna Rapp in Anthropology, Nancy Faires Conklin in Linguistics, and Lee Chambers Schiller in History. I am astounded now at the company I got to keep. The first semester we organized the course by discipline—women and history, women and psychology, women and art, and so one. The second semester we rethought our conceptual framework and organized it in three parts: Myths about Women, Socialization to the

Myths, and Resistance. We worked as volunteers, got over two hundred students a term, then refused to work for free anymore, and organized to establish a Women's Studies program, a journal, and a university day care center.

We had learned the importance of breaking isolation, and the extraordinary empowerment of beginning to see women as subjects of our own lives and authors of our own histories.

I was taken a bit aback, then, when I hit the job market. At my first job interview I was asked what form of birth control I used. Knowing there was no correct answer, and the job was lost, I replied, "Why are you asking me that question? Are you asking every candidate?" Sandra Fluke's experience reminded me of that moment, and of the combination of prurient interest and neglect with which the academy treated women's sexuality. When I assisted Robin Jacoby's first women's history class in the University of Michigan History department, the first student who came to my office didn't come to talk about history. She wanted advice and support about an unplanned pregnancy. She was not the last student who came to me simply because I was a woman. The university health services were not prepared to provide contraception or advice. The health service at Antioch would prescribe contraception only if a student had a note from her parents. For many years I gathered the names of professionals better prepared than I to counsel students and did my best, sharing publications from women's self-help collectives. My favorite pamphlet was from the University of Toronto: *How to Have Intercourse Without Getting Screwed.*

My ill-fated first job interview notwithstanding, I did get a job at the University of Virginia, which had admitted African American students under court order in 1969 and women under court order in 1970. It was still highly gendered and racialized terrain when I was hired in 1976. Every year there was a lottery to select graduate students who got to live in the original slave quarters, which still lacked running water and were heated with wood stoves. I joined over sixty colleagues in the History department, a faculty that included one other White woman and one African American man, both untenured assistant professors. My office was on the first floor, where two White secretaries shared one office, two African American secretaries another office across the hall. We had an understanding. If they had news for me, they would signal me to meet them in the women's room, where no suspicious colleagues could hear us. That is where they told me that the African American woman who cleaned our offices had just had her electricity cut off because she couldn't pay her bill on her University of Virginia pay. They wanted me to help pay her bill and to help hit up colleagues likely to contribute.

When I went to my first (obligatory) faculty cocktail party, a well-meaning senior colleague refreshed my drink for me, then turned red, and stammered, "Well, uh, mah deah, uh, well—have you managed to find a good gynecologist in Charlottesville yet?" He wanted to welcome me but simply didn't know how to think about or talk to a woman colleague. During my first year at Virginia, the other woman in my department, Susan Hirsch, came up for tenure. She, and three other equally well-qualified women in other departments, were all denied tenure, all for allegedly inadequate scholarship. Sue's tenure book, *Roots of the American Working Class: The Industrialization of Crafts in Newark, 1800–1860*, published by University of Pennsylvania Press, was one of the first histories of pre-Civil War class formation.[35] The day after her tenure denial, my department chair came to my office, discreetly closed the door, sat down, and said, "Don't worry my dear. We know you're a good one."

I left Virginia and took a less prestigious job at Loretto Heights College in Denver, directing its Research Center on Women and Women's Studies Program. The Sisters of Loretto founded Loretto Heights as a women's college. By the time I got there, they had left the convent, admitted male students, and turned the college over to lay trustees. It is, however, the only predominantly female institution in which I have worked, and I might be there still except that the trustees wearied of negotiating with a faculty union dominated by radical nuns. As they prepared to close the college and sell it to the local Jesuit men's school, they abolished my job and the profit-making childcare center. They did offer me $4,000 a year to continue teaching. When I turned them down, the President asked me what my husband did for a living that I couldn't accept their offer.[36]

This brings me to an awkward period on my own CV. During 1984–1987 I taught as an adjunct at Denver-area universities and community colleges, consulted with the Colorado Department of Education, and worked as an independent contract historian for the Colorado State Council of Carpenters. I had no full-time appointment. During that time, I published eight articles and two books. I was fortunate finally to find Dean Julius Erlenbach at the University of Wisconsin – La Crosse who looked at my CV and said, "Well, you've done it in unusual order, but you've earned your rank," and hired me as an associate professor and chair of the new Women's Studies Department. But when I joined the faculty of the University of New Mexico, the History department there made me agree in advance not to receive credit toward tenure for my two previous books, because they were completed before I entered the tenure stream, and later refused to credit them toward promotion to full professor.

I tell these stories to think about how far we have come in a generation and to think about the challenges ahead. Although some people may still *think* some of the sexist remarks I heard as a young historian, we've pretty much learned that it's gauche to say them. We can gauge some of the progress and some of the remaining inequities through numbers—numbers of women undergraduate and graduate students, numbers of women earning doctorates and winning teaching positions, numbers of women in each academic rank and in university administration, numbers of women in the indexes of survey texts and on syllabi, and—yes—the numbers on men's and women's paychecks. But numbers alone provide neither the analysis of how gender operates in higher education nor the roadmaps to achieving greater equity.

The numbers of women in higher education matter because education should help women achieve better lives for themselves and their families. Numbers matter because it is hard to work in isolation. I remember sitting in a department meeting at the University of New Mexico in the early 1990s and realizing that I had six women colleagues, that we were a fourth of the department. I thought, "Oh wow—I can sneeze and they can't say 'All Women Get the Flu'." Because the pressure of being the only woman carried with it the pressure to represent *all* women. It was an enormous luxury to be able to be as idiosyncratically myself as any male colleague.

Increased numbers and increased diversity in the professoriate bring new perspectives and new experiences to scholarship. When I began to consider the history of dishwashing, I did not expect to find women in other times and cultures doing what I did, but I did use my experience to ask new questions about the histories of housework and childrearing and reproduction. Shortly after my angry reaction to "dishwashing," Juliet Mitchell visited the University of Michigan. Dr. Sklar had used Mitchell's article, "Women the Longest Revolution" in her Women's History class, and I had read Mitchell's *Woman's Estate* shortly before her visit. I was influenced by her model for analyzing women's histories by considering women's relationships to production, reproduction, sexuality, and the socialization of children.[37] Those analytical categories offered ways to think about histories of domesticity and how, for instance, household production or the socialization of children might be linked to industrial production and the children's views of their own adult options. Mitchell's categories informed the questions I asked miners' wives in oral histories I recorded a few years later, and how I taught women's history. The early 1970s were a heady time as scholars in many fields began to think about how to put women at the center of our scholarship, and how to forge more inclusive curricula.

Certainly, we've come a long distance toward adding women to the curriculum in many fields. At the same time, we have not yet re-evaluated all canonical standards from the diverse perspectives of an expanded cast. History remains largely framed by the nation or the region and inevitably privileges the public arenas of war and politics from which most women have been excluded for most history. I once turned down a job because my primary responsibility would have been teaching great books to engineering students, and it would have been my responsibility to add women to a great books curriculum that at that point included only one woman, Jane Austen. By the Great Books criteria most books by and about workers, women, or people of color would be excluded. To some extent, the unexplained gaps in women's salaries represent assumptions about what is canonical, what scholarship is most valuable, which journals are top tier.

The data on salary differentials with which I began mirror similar data in similar studies for many institutions. The numbers explain large portions of salary inequities but leave significant amounts unexplained. I am concerned, as I was in 2004, not only by what the numbers say but also by the models we use to generate them and how we interpret them. They leave unaddressed, untheorized, and unremediated the persistent differences. But equally concerning is the tendency not to interrogate the explanations that we *can* account for: last degree, years in rank, publications, work experience, employing institution, and so on. Think, for instance, about the $4,000 salary loss at hire for those with prior experience working at the University of Calgary. What it says essentially is that after working as a sessional for low pay and with little time to publish, a colleague earns less at entry, a deficit that compounds throughout a career. I think about this in the context of Sylvia Thrupp's fourteen years as an adjunct after her last degree, of my three "lost" years teaching and writing between 1984 and 1987, as I watch women graduate students decide whether to apply for jobs because they might not be compatible with a partner's career. Our colleagues lose money; we risk losing the benefit of their experience.

Equally problematic, many of the gendered differences are often explained as the consequences of women's individual choices. Women, this argument goes, "choose" disciplines that pay less, choose (sometimes) to have children, choose to spend more time caregiving rather than taking full-time tenure-track jobs, and just don't choose to put in the time and effort to advance professionally. We do not expect most men to choose between career and family. Women's choices are constrained by our options, by gendered jobs at home and at work, by implicit biases against women, by caregiving and service, by stereotypes about female competence, by the physiology of human reproduction, by socially constructed gendered expectations, and are compounded by race, gender, sexuality, and other marginalizing factors. Part of the issue is the female academic life cycle, which may include more years in part-time employment before ever getting into tenure-track position and which may involve, for some of us, a different productivity cycle.

So, I offer a final story and a few modest proposals. In 1988 I found myself with a two-year-old, a new job where I chaired a department and taught three classes a term, and an embarrassment of success. I had applied to present papers at five conferences, thinking I'd get accepted at two or three. But I scored all five, to the profound irritation of my husband, and to my exhaustion. At the fifth conference in six weeks, I found myself rooming with Louise Tilly, who I knew only slightly but admired enormously for her pioneering work in European women's history. When I'd been at Michigan, her husband, Charles Tilly, had been a senior member of the Sociology department. Louise had earned her BA and MA by 1955. She taught part-time at the University of Michigan-Flint, Michigan State University, and the University of Michigan while raising four children and earning a PhD in 1973 from the University of Toronto. Finally, the University of Michigan hired her as the first Chair of the new Women's Studies Program. Her pathbreaking co-authored *Women, Work and Family* followed in 1978, and after nearly a decade at Michigan, the New School for Social Research wisely offered her and Charles Tilly positions founding a new graduate program in historical studies.[38] In 1992 Louise Tilly was elected President of the American Historical Association. In 1988 I poured out my doubts to her: "I have a young child, I have an intensive teaching schedule, I'm in my early 40s, I'm tired, and I just don't know if I can make it in this profession." She calmly replied, "You are measuring yourself against a male model, dear. Don't worry. We do our best work in our 50s and 60s." Louise Tilly's model is not every woman's, but it helped me stop measuring my productivity and potential against a professional model generated by elite men with substantial domestic support.

Professional life cycles, like everything else, are historically constructed, changing, and changeable. Many of us, especially younger colleagues, have different assumptions about how to combine personal and professional lives, and those of their partners, and we have new policies to support childbearing and adoption, to address sexual harassment, and to enable spousal hires. Still, it is not easy, and the fact that women bear children and men earn more often means that women's careers are delayed or compromised to other goals. After years of part-time work, we may be so grateful to get a job that we don't bargain very hard over starting salaries.

I don't have answers for the hard questions and hard choices behind these numbers and lived realities. To destabilize and disrupt them, I think we need to interrogate how the normative academic career path was constructed, and how those normative expectations have devalued and penalized women. I offer a few immodest proposals, not as carefully formulated solutions, but as invitations to the conversations that may lead us there. For starters, I suggest that we cannot achieve equity or diversity if we measure achievement against a single standard, or a fixed hierarchy of value. Anthropologists have long since abandoned the 19th-century model of a hierarchy of cultures that progressed from hunters and gatherers to herders to farmers. Even the categories contained gender biases, based as they were on men's jobs. Now we grapple with cultural relativism, and the complex and contested nature of relationships in any culture. What if we apply this concept more broadly, to the ways we assess academic achievement? What if there were not a single measure of what made a good novel, or a good history? What if there were not a single standard for what constitutes a top-tier journal? What if we rewarded meritorious service and teaching as we do scholarship? What if there were not a single normative academic career path?

And I suggest, with some unease, that we cannot assume a clear separation of the personal and the professional. One step toward gender equity might be crediting more generously at hire the experiences of colleagues who have previously worked in public sectors or as sessional instructors. Most of Sylvia Thrupp's female classmates worked in public history if they found jobs at all, as did most women who earned graduate degrees in history before the 1980s and a growing number since then. They built archives and museums and did research for government agencies. Like my own work from 1984–1987, their labor could have brought new perspectives to any faculty that hired them, but they were likely to be paid as newly minted PhDs. Part of the unexplained difference in what women and men earn for each year since our last degrees may lie in measures of productivity that do not account for the diversity of our professional experience and what we produce and contribute. The gender difference in faculty salaries is better than income differences in the population as a whole, and it has improved light years since the 1960s, when women in the U.S. earned 59 cents for each dollar a man took home. But the $7,000 annual difference in University of Calgary faculty salaries adds up over a lifetime, to lower pensions and greater stress juggling finances, family, and work. We may continue to make progress, but until we read the data about gender inequality to fix it rather than explain it, we won't get to equity.

I make these suggestions with trepidation. It is comforting to think that quantitative measures are fair, that student evaluations and numbers of articles are fair and objective standards, and there are huge dangers in opening up multiple criteria and subjective assessments. Yet the objective measures are not addressing the unexplained differences, and they can flatten out the richness that diverse perspectives bring to teaching and learning. I have told my own stories to illustrate both what has changed and the challenges we face, but I tell them with misgivings. I do not wish to appear either egocentric or representative—I do not presume to speak for all women, or for all White middle-class women. I fear reinforcing the stereotype of the self-involved and self-referential American. And I feel uncomfortably vulnerable. Linda Hall, an eminent Mexican historian, and my colleague at the University of New Mexico, once said "I think every woman in this business secretly thinks she's an imposter." For my lecture, I chose to wear a brown and white houndstooth jacket with leather-covered buttons and brown elbow patches that reminded me of the uniforms many men wore when I was in graduate school—corduroy or tweed jackets with leather buttons and elbow patches. And pipes. I was delighted when I found a feminine version, but I knew it was female academic drag. Showing my vita is dangerous because you may figure out that beneath the drag I'm really an imposter. Until we can confront the historical residues and normative expectations that fuel that fear, we can't achieve equity.

And I risk sharing my stories because I still hope. As I told the "Eye Opener" and the *Herald*, I am hopeful about the potential for progress at the University. Sandra Fluke gave me hope. Rush Limbaugh tried to intimidate her and sparked a much bigger reaction than he bargained for.

Feminists in the 1970s would say, "The personal is the political." The personal is also the professional and the institutional. Breaking silence and sharing our stories can establish common ground, can help us analyze when differences are rooted in institutional constraints, and when we need to acknowledge individual shortcomings. The changes I have lived through were won collectively, with the support of other women and of many supportive men. Forty years after Title IX we hadn't reached the Promised Land, but we were no longer in the wilderness. We hadn't achieved equity, and I no longer expected to before I left higher education. I hope that my experiences may become an amusing story about how it used to be. There are plenty of challenges for the future. Full-time faculty are shrinking, particularly in the "softer" disciplines gendered feminine because they are about caregiving or art or beauty or non-utilitarian knowledge. In this context, gender equity is not a women's issue; it matters for anyone who cares about the arts and humanities. Universities remain, despite increasing numbers of women, profoundly gendered spaces, where women are concentrated in specific disciplines, most support staff are women, and immigrant women clean our offices. In 2011–2012 the University of Virginia students struck to increase custodians' pay. I take enormous strength and pride from how far we have come. It has been a lot of fun, in no small part because I've had great companions on the journey, like those who came to hear my talk. And I take heart from Louise Tilly: our best work does not come in the first forty years. It lies before us in the decades ahead.

NOTES

The issues addressed in this article remain pertinent. See my concluding remarks in chapter 14. I am grateful for the help of wonderful research assistants, Amy McKinney and Andrew Varsanyi; thanks, too, to Shawn Brackett for his assistance as I prepared the essay for publication.

Additional Sources: I based my comments on discrimination against LBTG+ faculty on my own observations and conversations with colleagues. In 2014 a study based on interviews with ten lesbian and queer women faculty at Calgary institutions of higher education was published, documenting their decisions about whether and how to disclose their sexuality in the classroom. See Elly-Jean Nielsen and Kevin G. Alderson, "Lesbian and Queer Women Professors Disclosing in the Classroom: An Act of Authenticity," *The Counseling Psychologist* 42:8 (2014): 1084–107. See also Christi R. McGeorge, Thomas Stone Carlson, and Candice A. Maier "Are We There yet? Faculty Members' Beliefs and Teaching Practices Related to the Ethical Treatment of Lesbian, Gay, and Bisexual Clients," *Journal of Marital and Family Therapy* 43:2 (2017): 322–37 and Darcy Hango, "Harassment and Discrimination among Faculty and Researchers in Canada's Postsecondary Institutions," Statistics Canada, *Insights on Canadian Society*, Release Date July 16, 2021, concludes that women, sexual minority groups, and persons with disabilities are disproportionately likely to experience harassment and discrimination. https://www150.statcan.gc.ca/n1/pub/75-006-x/2021001/article/00006-eng.htm, accessed January 17, 2024.

1   Title IX of Public Law No. 92318, 86 Stat. 235 (June 23, 1972), codified at 20 U.S.C. §§ 1681–1688.
2   "About Title IX," Bailiwick Library, University of Iowa, http://bailiwick.lib.uiowa.edu/ge/aboutRE.html, last accessed May 6, 2021.
3   Sandra Fluke and her conflicts with Committee member Darell Issa and conservative talk-show personality Rush Limbaugh were well known in 2012. For contemporary coverage, see for instance Tom Shine, "Rep. Darrell Issa Bars Minority Witness, a Woman, on Contraception," ABC News, February 16, 2012, https://abcnews.go.com/blogs/politics/2012/02/rep-darrell-issa-bars-minority-witness-a-woman-on-contraception-2, accessed May 6, 2021; "Sandra Fluke Finally Testifies before Congress," Press Release, House Committee on Oversight and Reform, February 23, 2012, https://oversight.house.gov/news/press-releases/sandra-fluke-finally-testifies-before-congress, accessed May 6, 2021; Maggie Fazeli Fard, "Sandra Fluke, Georgetown student called a 'slut' by Rush Limbaugh, speaks out," *Washington Post*, March 2, 2012.
4   See "uCalgary to review gender gap in faculty salaries," academica group, September 1, 2011, https://www.academica.ca/top-ten/ucalgary-review-gender-gap-faculty-salaries, accessed May 6, 2021.
5   *Faculty Salary Equity Report*, prepared by Dr. Jean E. Wallace for the Academic Women's Association through the Office of Dr. Hermina Joldersma, President's Advisor on Women's Issues, University of Calgary, May 2005. The report is archived at http://contentdm.ucalgary.ca/digital/collection/ucpub/id/81843/, accessed May 6, 2021.
6   Having grown up in Texas, where football is the state religion, I knew enough about the game to hold a workshop for other women in the class before the next exam.
7   Caroline M. Barron, "Sylvia Thrupp: The Making of an Early Social Historian," *Medieval Feminist Forum: A Journal of Gender and Sexuality* 41, no. 1 (2006): 18–26; Raymond Grew, "In Memoriam: Sylvia Thrupp (1903–97)," *Perspectives on History*, March 2000.
8   Ontario was the first province to legalize same-sex marriage, in 2003. When the Civil Marriage Act was passed on July 20, 2005, only Alberta, New Brunswick, and the Northwest Territories still prohibited same-sex marriage. Massachusetts became the first state to legalize same-sex marriage, in 2004. Before the Obergefel decision in 2015, the following states and territories had also liberalized their marriage laws to include same-sex marriage: Alaska, Arizona, California, Colorado, Connecticut, Delaware, District of Columbia, Florida, Guam, Hawaii, Idaho, Illinois, Indiana, Iowa, Maine, Maryland, Minnesota, Montana, Nevada, New Hampshire, New Jersey, New Mexico, New York, North Carolina, Oklahoma, Oregon, Pennsylvania, Rhode Island, South Carolina, Utah, Vermont, Virginia, Washington, West Virginia, Wisconsin, and Wyoming.
9   L.G. Knapp, J.E. Kelly-Reid, and S.A. Ginder. *Enrollment in Postsecondary Institutions, Fall 2009; Graduation Rates, 2003 & 2006 Cohorts; and Financial Statistics, Fiscal Year 2009* (NCES 2011–230) (Washington, DC : U.S. Department of Education, National Center for Education Statistics, 2011), retrieved March 25, 2012 from http://nces.ed.gov/pubsear. See also Thomas D. Snyder and Sally A. Dillow, *Digest of Education Statistics* 2010, NCES 2011-015 (Washington, D.C.: U.S. Department of Education, Institute of Education Sciences, National Center for Education Statistics, April 2011), esp. tables 295–303.
10 *Postsecondary Pyramid Equity Audit 2010, Canadian Federation for the Humanities and Social Sciences*, http://www.unb.ca/PAR-L/Pyramid2010.pdf, accessed March 7, 2012.
11 *Office of Institutional Analysis Fact Book 2009-2010*, http://oia.ucalgary.ca/system/files/2009-2010FB.pdf, accessed March 7, 2012.
12 Office of the Press Secretary, The White House, "White House Releases First Comprehensive Federal Report on the Status of American Women in Almost 50 Years," March 1, 2011, https://affirmact.blogspot.com/2011/03/white-house-releases-first.html,

accessed May 6, 2021; White House Council on Women and Girls, *Women in America: Indicators of Social and Economic Well Being* (Washington, DC: U.S. Department of Commerce and Executive Office of the President, March 2011), 17–23; for updates see, Office of the White House Press Secretary, "White House Releases Report on Women and the Economy," April 6, 2012; The White House Council on Women and Girls, *Keeping America's Women Moving Forward: The Key to an America Built to Last* (Washington, DC: The White House, April 2012).

13 Office of the Press Secretary, The White House, "White House Releases First Comprehensive Federal Report on the Status of American Women in Almost 50 Years"; *Keeping America's Women Moving Forward*, 1, 4.

14 White House Council on Women and Girls, *Women in America*, 14, 34.

15 David Robinson, *The Status of Higher Education Teaching Personnel in Australia, Canada, New Zealand, the United Kingdom, and the United States* (Ottawa: Canadian Association of University Teachers, 2006), 7.

16 *Postsecondary Pyramid Equity Audit 2010.*

17 Martha S. West and John W. Curtis, *AAUP Faculty Gender Equity Indicators 2006* (Washington, DC: American Association of University Professors, 2006), 5–7.

18 John W. Curtis, "Persistent Inequality: Gender and Academic Employment," prepared for "New Voices in Pay Equity," an event for Equal Pay Day, April 11, 2011. Curtis was the Director of Research and Public Policy, American Association of University Professors.

19 Robert B. Townsend, "The Status of Women and Minorities in the History Profession, 2008," *Perspectives on History*, September 1, 2008.

20 John W. Curtis, "Persistent Inequality," 4.

21 *Faculty Salary Equity Report*, 1.

22 *Faculty Salary Equity Report*, tables 4 and 9.

23 "uCalgary to review gender gap in faculty salaries."

24 *Faculty Salary Equity Report*, a.

25 See Christine Doucet, Claire Durand, and Michael Smith, "Who gets Market Supplements?: Gender Differences within a Large Canadian University," *Canadian Journal of Higher Education/ Revue canadienne d'enseignement supérieur* 38:1 (2008): 67–103.

26 *Faculty Salary Equity Report*, b, tables 9 and 10, 12–13.

27 *Faculty Salary Equity Report*, 8, tables 2 and 18, 18.8. The report contains the following summary statement, on page c:

> The gendered correlation between field and salary: The salary gap between Faculties (Appendix A) is much more significant than between genders. However, the lowest-paid Faculties are also those with the highest proportion of women. That in some of these latter Faculties proportionately fewer PhDs are held (e.g. NU, SW) can partly explain this, but not e.g. the $10,750 difference between Humanities and Kinesiology (note that market supplements were not included in this study). This appears to confirm studies elsewhere showing that fields perceived as "masculine" receive higher status and rewards than those perceived as 'feminine'.

28 *Faculty Salary Equity Report*, tables 18 and 20.

29 *Faculty Salary Equity Report*, b, d, 7, 15, 16.

30 For a sample of this literature, see Dr. Hermina Joldersma, President's Advisor on Women's Issues, *Next Steps: Report of the Gender Equity Project, University of Calgary*, June 2005, 43–47, 147–54; Minutes, "Women in Academia," Meeting of the Action Group on Next Steps in Gender Equity, University of Calgary, July 4, 2005; F. Costin, W.T. Greenough, and R.J. Menges, "Student Ratings of College Teaching: Reliability, Validity, and Usefulness," *Review of Educational Research* 41, no. 5 (1971): 511–35; D. Wilson and K.

O. Doyle, "Student Ratings of Instruction: Student and Instructor Sex Interactions," *The Journal of Higher Education* 47, no. 4 (1976): 465–70; S.K. Bennett. "Student Perceptions of and Expectations for Male and Female Instructors: Evidence Relating to the Question of Gender Bias in Teaching Evaluation," *Journal of Educational Psychology* 74, no. 2 (1982): 170–79; S. Basow and N. Silberg, "Student Evaluations of College Professors," *Journal of Educational Psychology* 798, no. 3 (1987): 308–14; D. Kierstead, P. D'Agostino, and H. Dill, "Sex Role Stereotyping of College Professors: Bias in Students' Ratings of Instructors," *Journal of Educational Psychology* 80, no. 3 (1988): 342–44; K. A. Feldman, "College Students' Views of Male and Female College Teachers: Part I, Evidence From the Social Laboratory and Experiments," *Research in Higher Education* 33, no. 3 (1992): 317–75; K. A. Feldman, "College Students' Views of Male and Female College Teachers: Part II, Evidence From Students' Evaluations of Their Classroom Teachers," *Research in Higher Education* 34, no. 2 (1993): 151–211; S. A. Basow, "Student Evaluations of College Professors: When Gender Matters," *Journal of Educational Psychology* 87, no. 4 (1995): 656–65; K. Andersen and E.D. Miller, "Gender and Student Evaluations of Teaching," *PS-Political Science and Politics* 30, no. 2 (1997): 216–19; Therese A. Huston, "Race and Gender Bias in Higher Education: Could Faculty Course Evaluations Impede Further Progress Toward Parity?," *Seattle Journal for Social Justice* 4:2 (2006): 591-611; Kerry Chávez and Kristina M.W. Mitchell, "Exploring Bias in Student Evaluations: Gender, Race, and Ethnicity," *Political Science and Politics* 53:2 (April 2020): 270–74.

31 Joldersma, *Next Steps*, 17–26, 95, 112, tables 13 and 112.

32 Joya Misra, Jennifer Hickes Lundquist, Elissa Holmes, and Stephanie Agiomavritis, "The Ivory Ceiling of Service Work," *Academe* 97:1 (January-February 2011): 22–26. For University of Calgary data, see Joldersma, *Next Steps*, 1, 7, 10, 21, 39, 47–51, 72, 82, 84, 88, 92, 93, 95–97, 102, 108–11, 117–19, 155–57.

33 Mary Young, Kathryn Sklar, and Marilyn Young, who so influenced my career, had not yet been accorded the professional stature they had earned. Interested readers might Google them. Here are a few of their accomplishments by the time I first encountered them: Mary Elizabeth Young, *Redskins, Ruffleshirts and Rednecks: Indian Allotments in Alabama and Mississippi, 1800-1860* (Norman: University of Oklahoma Press, 1961); when I assisted her, Kathryn Kish Sklar was writing *Catherine Beecher: A Study in American Domesticity* (New York: W.W. Norton, 1976); Marilyn Blatt Young, *American Expansionism: The Critical Issues* (Boston: Little Brown, 1973): *Women in China: Studies in Social Change and Feminism* (Ann Arbor: Center for Chinese Studies, University of Michigan, 1973): *The Rhetoric of Empire: American China Policy, 1895-1901* (Cambridge, MA: Harvard University Press, 1969).

34 Alice Earl Morse, *Colonial Dames and Good Wives* (Boston: Houghton Mifflin, 1895); Elisabeth Anthony Dexter, *Colonial Women of Affairs: Women in Business and the Professions in America before 1776* (Boston: Houghton Mifflin, 1924); Edith Abbott, *Women in Industry* (New York: Appleton, 1910); *1969 Handbook on Women Workers*, Women's Bureau Bulletin 294 (Washington, DC: Wage and Labor Standards Division, Department of Labor, 1969).

35 Susan E. Hirsch, *Roots of the American Working Class: The Industrialization of Crafts in Newark, 1800-1860* (Philadelphia: University of Pennsylvania Press, 1978).

36 See Elizabeth Jameson, "Reflections on the Backlash," *Frontiers* 8:3 (1986): 79–82.

37 Juliet Mitchell, "Women: The Longest Revolution," *New Left Review* no. 40, December 1966; *Woman's Estate* (New York: Random House, 1971), 101.

38 Louise A. Tilly and Joan W. Scott, *Women, Work, and Family* (New York: Holt, Rinehart & Winston, 1978).

11

Seneca Falls, Selma, and Stonewall: Symbolism and Social Change

April 10, 2013

After the 2008 presidential election, U.S. Senator Jeff Bingaman (D-New Mexico) held a lottery for his quota of tickets to Barack Obama's presidential inauguration, and I got lucky. So, the morning of January 20, 2009, I walked from Washington's Union Station to my assigned gate near the House of Representatives, surrounded by thousands eager to share that momentous transfer of power to the first African American President. We passed the east entrance of the Supreme Court on 2nd Street NE, and, across the street, the place I'd lived in 1967 when I worked as an intern in the U.S. Senate. The current tenants appeared to be anti-abortion-rights activists, judging from the enormous signs on their porch. That brief personal dissonance notwithstanding, the crowd of strangers seemed to share a sense of history—particularly people my age and older who remembered the Civil Rights Movement. One African American woman from Indiana smiled at me. "I thought this day would never come," she said. "Me, too," I replied. "I grew up in the segregated South and I never thought I'd see an integrated classroom." "I was one of those kids who integrated your classrooms," she said. The morning was full of such shorthand exchanges about histories shared—but shared differently. Standing in line at my gate, I met an African American Baptist minister from Los Angeles and his wife, who were there, they said, "Because you have to be."

The sense of connection kept building, but everything else ground to a halt. Thousands stood immobile as the security personnel assigned to screen us proved totally inadequate for the crowd. They closed the gate before the inauguration, with thousands of disappointed ticketholders still outside. One woman managed to get Obama's inaugural address on her cell phone, and a small group of us huddled around her to listen—so near, but still outside the fence.[1]

Four years later I watched President Obama's second inauguration from the warmth and privacy of my Calgary living room—far from Washington but closer to the event. As the President repeatedly intoned the first words of the Declaration of Independence, "We, the people," I remembered the people who had stood with me four years earlier, and all those whose long decades of collective action brought us to that historic day. Then came the passage, paraphrasing the Declaration's "self-evident truth" that "all men are created equal," that evoked three social movements dedicated to the promise of that founding document: "We, the people," the President repeated, "We, the people, declare today that the most evident of truths—that all of us are created equal—is the star that guides us still; just as it guided our forebears through Seneca Falls, and Selma, and Stonewall."[2] It was the sentence of a lifetime for a historian of social change.

Seneca Falls, Selma, and Stonewall—three places rich with connotation for the rights of American women, African Americans, and LGBTQ2S+ Americans. Yet I pondered why—alliteration aside—the President chose those particular sites for his evocative imagery. Seneca Falls, New York: site of the first U.S. women's rights convention in 1848. Selma, Alabama: where police violence against Civil Rights activists at the Edmund Pettus Bridge moved Congress to pass the historic 1965 Voting Rights Act. And the Stonewall Inn in New York City's Greenwich Village: where, on June 27, 1969, gay and transgender patrons resisted a routine police raid and ignited the Gay Liberation Movement.

There were obvious political reasons for the President to choose these images. He owed his re-election to women, people of color, and LGBTQ2S+ voters. He had won 55 percent of women's votes, seven in ten Latinxs', three-quarters of Asian American ballots, 93 percent of African Americans'. He had scored more than a three-to-one edge in exit polls among the 5 percent of voters who identified themselves as gay, lesbian, or bisexual.[3] So Seneca Falls, Selma, and Stonewall rhetorically acknowledged his base, commitments honored, and the work to come. The President continued:

> It is now our generation's task to carry on what those pioneers began. For our journey is not complete until our wives, our

mothers, and daughters can earn a living equal to their efforts. Our journey is not complete until our gay brothers and sisters are treated like anyone else under the law—for if we are truly created equal, then surely the love we commit to one another must be equal as well. Our journey is not complete until no citizen is forced to wait for hours to exercise the right to vote.[4]

Thus, the President connected Seneca Falls to the first law he signed, the Lilly Ledbetter Fair Pay Act, and Stonewall to his personal "evolution" to support gay marriage equality and to allow gays and lesbians to serve openly in the U.S. military. He challenged efforts to undermine the historic victory won at Selma, as many states enacted new voter ID regulations and public officials shortened polling hours to discourage African American voters; he honored those who stood for hours in long lines to resist disenfranchisement yet again.[5]

Selma and Stonewall spoke as well to issues that were before the U.S. Supreme Court, which was considering the constitutionality of key portions of the 1965 Voting Rights Act, of the Defense of Marriage Act which defined marriage as between one man and one woman, and of California's Proposition 8, which outlawed gay marriage and was found unconstitutional by a U.S. Court of Appeals.[6] In these contexts, Seneca Falls, Selma, and Stonewall connoted long and hard-won journeys to electoral power, inspiring hope while providing benchmarks against which to gauge new challenges and to underscore a political agenda that addressed unfulfilled promises of civic equality.

The President's *political* intentions for invoking Seneca Falls, Selma, and Stonewall fit the contexts of his re-election victory. But historians and politicians approach history differently, and his juxtaposition of three symbolic events caught my imagination. What really linked Seneca Falls, Selma, and Stonewall and the movements they represented—what linked them historically and in 2013? Selma and Stonewall involved violent confrontations between protesters and the police; Seneca Falls was a peaceful assembly that began decades of organizing before women finally won the vote in 1920.[7] Seneca Falls and Stonewall are popularly considered important "firsts"—the events that ignited the Women's Rights and Gay Rights Movements. Historians quibble about the significance of such "firsts," about what preceded and enabled them. But Selma is considered a culmination—one of the bitter final struggles in the southern Civil

Rights Movement that won a signal victory, ending a century of *de facto* African American disenfranchisement through poll taxes, literacy tests, grandfather clauses, and economic and physical violence.[8] Seneca Falls, Selma, and Stonewall were not exactly parallel chapters in the history of U.S. social change. I was particularly intrigued by Obama's inclusion of Stonewall, a name known to most LGBTQ2S+ activists, but not to most Americans.

I am intrigued with how particular places and events enter collective memory to connote shared identities, struggles, and aspirations. Those who came to witness President Obama's first inauguration understood it as an historic moment, whatever individual paths led us there. We imply shared histories when we ask, "Where were you when Kennedy or King was killed?" "Where were you when the Berlin Wall fell, or the Twin Towers?" I don't know that Stonewall or Seneca Falls or even Selma evokes similarly shared histories. In the polarized American political climate, they are likely to prompt deeply divided responses if they are known at all.

The President's choice of images led me to revisit these three historic events—to think about their lessons for how the local, personal, and particular have inspired collective aspirations and acts, about how they enter collective consciousness and histories.

I begin with the histories of each event to get us all on the same page, starting, chronologically, with Seneca Falls. Like most historic events, the 1848 Seneca Falls Convention for women's rights began much earlier. We could begin with the moment a participant came to oppose slavery, attended a Quaker meeting where women spoke, or witnessed spousal abuse. The story is often begun at the 1840 World Anti-Slavery Convention in London, which deemed women "constitutionally unfit for public and business meetings," and relegated them to the balcony. Two of those segregated delegates, American abolitionists Lucretia Mott and Elizabeth Cady Stanton, visited the British Museum, where they first discussed the idea of a mass meeting for women's rights. As abolitionists, they embraced human equality and extended it to full human rights for women. Stanton, a newlywed in London on her honeymoon, had refused to promise to "obey" when she married abolitionist Henry Stanton.[9] But she was quickly immersed in domestic duties and bearing the first of her seven children. The women's rights convention waited eight years until Mott visited her sister in Seneca Falls, New York, where the Stantons lived. Abolitionist Jane Hunt held a tea for Mott at her home in nearby Waterloo on July 13, and invited Stanton, Martha Coffin Wright, and Mary Ann

McClintock. Stanton later wrote that, unhappy with her life as a housewife, she "poured out the torrent of my long-accumulating discontent with such vehemence and indignation that I stirred myself, as well as the rest of the party." The women revived the conference idea and the next day announced in the *Seneca County Courier*: "A Convention to discuss the social, civil and religious condition and rights of woman, will be held in the Wesleyan Chapel, at Seneca Falls, N.Y., on Wednesday and Thursday, the 19th and 20th of July."[10] They wrote eleven resolutions and a Declaration of Sentiments. Paraphrasing the Declaration of Independence, it began: "We hold these truths to be self-evident; that all men and women are created equal" and then detailed a history of "repeated injuries and usurpations on the part of man toward woman."

> He has never permitted her to exercise her inalienable right to the elective franchise.
> He has compelled her to submit to laws, in the formation of which she had no voice.
> He has withheld from her rights which are given to the most ignorant and degraded men—both natives and foreigners....
> He has made her, if married, in the eye of the law, civilly dead.
> He has taken from her all right in property, even to the wages she earns.

The women opposed husbands' power "to administer chastisement," and, in the event of divorce, to get custody of children. The Declaration continued:

> ... [I]f single and the owner of property he has taxed her to support a government which recognizes her only when her property can be made profitable to it.
> He has monopolized nearly all the profitable employments, and from those she is permitted to follow, she receives but a scanty remuneration....
> He has denied her the facilities for obtaining a thorough education—all colleges being closed against her....
> He has endeavored, in every way that he could to destroy her confidence in her own powers, to lessen her self-respect, and to make her willing to lead a dependent and abject life.

The women demanded "immediate admission to all the rights and privileges which belong to them as citizens of these United States."[11] Yet they chose not to chair the meeting but instead recruited Lucretia Mott's husband James Mott. Only Stanton wanted to include the right to vote. "Ah, Lizzie," Lucretia Mott told her friend, "thee will make fools of us all." Henry Stanton left town.[12]

But more than three hundred people showed up, including forty men, among them Frederick Douglass, ex-slave, abolitionist, and newspaper owner. The first day, participants discussed and amended the Declaration of Sentiments. Lucretia Mott and Elizabeth Cady Stanton spoke in the afternoon.[13] Stanton tried to deflect anticipated ridicule with humor:

> We do not propose to petition the legislature to make our husbands just, generous, and courteous, to seat every man at the head of a cradle, and to clothe every woman in male attire. . . . [W]e still admire the graceful folds, and consider our costume far more artistic than theirs. Many of the nobler sex seem to agree with us . . . , for the bishops, priests, judges, barristers, and lord mayors of the first nation on the globe, and the Pope of Rome, with his cardinals, too, all wear the loose flowing robes . . .[14]

The eleven resolutions came up for discussion and votes the second day. Ten passed unanimously, but many feared that the suffrage resolution would undermine other demands. An impassioned speech by Frederick Douglass won over a slim majority. Sixty-eight women and thirty-two men signed the Declaration of Sentiments.[15]

Two weeks later, on August 2, 1848, the women hosted another women's rights convention in Rochester, New York. This time a woman, Abigail Bush, presided, the suffrage resolution passed by a wider margin, and plans began for women's rights conventions in other states.[16] Women held women's rights conventions most years during the 1850s. Susan B. Anthony, who was not at Seneca Falls, joined the movement in 1851, beginning her lifelong collaboration with Stanton. Anthony, who was single, shared childcare at times to give Stanton time to write. Stanton once wrote her friend, "Come here and I will do what I can to help you with your address, if you will hold the baby and make the pudding."[17]

Women's rights advocates temporarily shelved their movement during the Civil War, turning their energy to working for a Union victory and an end to slavery. After the war, the movement split over support for the Fourteenth and Fifteenth Amendments to the Constitution, which guaranteed that no right, including the vote, could be denied because of color or previous condition of servitude. In often racist tones, Stanton and Anthony opposed the amendments because they did not include women and because they inserted the word "male" into the Constitution for the first time. The opposing sides formed two organizations: the National Women's Suffrage Association and the American Women's Suffrage Association. The rift was not healed until 1890, when opposing camps merged to form the National American Women's Suffrage Association.[18]

Beginning with Wyoming in 1869, states and territories began to enfranchise women, but women did not win the vote nationally until 1920, with the Nineteenth Amendment to the Constitution. Of all the women who signed the Declaration of Sentiments at Seneca Falls only Rhoda Palmer lived to cast her ballot for the first time at age 102.[19] It took another sixty years—until 1980—for gender to become a recognized factor influencing votes in presidential elections, and only in recent elections have women's *issues* affected election outcomes.[20]

African American men, in theory, got the vote long before women, when the Fifteenth Amendment was ratified in 1870, but that right was denied in most southern states until after Selma, when Congress passed legislation to enforce the Amendment.[21] Selma, of course, was not the opening chapter of the African American Civil Rights Movement, which might be dated from the 1954 Supreme Court decision in *Brown v. Board of Education* that outlawed school segregation, the Montgomery bus boycott of 1955, the March on Washington Movement that persuaded President Roosevelt to create the Fair Employment Practices Committee in 1941, or from the first slave ship bound for the Americas.[22] Unlike Seneca Falls, Selma signified not a beginning, but a pivotal moment in the long struggle for African American voting rights. Accounts of Selma usually focus on January to March 1965, but the local voting rights movement began two years earlier when local African Americans formed the Dallas County Voters League and organizers from the Student Non-Violent Coordinating Committee (SNCC) began a voter registration campaign.[23] Dallas County sheriff Jim Clark and the local White Citizens' Council retaliated with arrests, violence, and economic intimidation. By late 1964 SNCC was exhausted, nearly broke, and fewer than 1 percent of Selma's Black majority could vote. Shortly after the Reverend Martin Luther King, Jr. received the Nobel Peace Prize in December 1964, his Southern Christian Leadership

Conference (SCLC) joined the Selma campaign. On January 18, SNCC and the SCLC began daily marches to the Dallas County Courthouse, hoping for media attention as Sheriff Clark responded with characteristic unrestraint. Black teachers marched in protest after Clark pushed and arrested local activist Amelia Boynton. On February 18, at a night march in nearby Marion, angry Whites sprayed the television cameras with black paint and clubbed NBC reporter Richard Valeriani. An Alabama State Trooper fired point blank at Jimmie Lee Jackson as he tried to protect his mother from a similar attack; Jackson died eight days later. To channel the grief and outrage at Jackson's murder, on Sunday, March 7 SNCC Chairman John Lewis and the SCLC's Rev. Hosea Williams began leading some 600 protesters to the state capitol in Montgomery. They got only as far as the Edmund Pettus Bridge, where some 150 Alabama State Troopers and Clark's posse met them with horses, billy clubs, and tear gas. Television networks interrupted their Sunday night programming to broadcast the violence. Amelia Boynton, beaten and gassed nearly to death, appeared on the front page of newspapers around the world. John Lewis suffered a fractured skull; he and sixteen others were hospitalized.[24]

In response to Bloody Sunday, SCLC called for people of good will to come to Selma for a second march. Despite a federal restraining order, on Tuesday, March 9 Dr. King led two thousand marchers to the Edmund Pettus Bridge, among them 450 White ministers, nuns, and rabbis. Troopers again blocked them. The marchers stopped, prayed, and turned around. King asked the clergy to stay if they could. That night a White mob followed three White ministers and clubbed Rev. James Reeb in the head. Reeb died two days later.[25]

Protests erupted in sympathy throughout the country. On Monday night, March 15, President Johnson made a televised address to a joint session of Congress to ask for a voting rights act. His opening words established Selma's place in U.S. history: "At times history and fate meet at a single time in a single place to shape a turning point in man's unending search for freedom. So it was at Lexington and Concord. So it was a century ago at Appomattox. So it was last week in Selma, Alabama." He continued:

> The real hero of this struggle is the American Negro. His actions and protests, his courage to risk safety, and even to risk his life, have awakened the conscience of the nation. His demonstrations have been designed to call attention to

injustice, designed to provoke change, designed to stir reform.
... This cause must be our cause too. It is not just Negroes, but
all of us, who must overcome the crippling legacy of bigotry
and injustice. And we *shall* overcome.[26]

That night Johnson federalized the Alabama National Guard to protect marchers for the fifty-seven miles from Selma to Montgomery. The next day, Judge Frank Johnson affirmed that the First Amendment to the U.S. Constitution guaranteed the rights to free speech, the right to assemble, and the right to petition the government for redress of grievances. Finally, on March 21, 3,200 marchers crossed the Edmund Pettus Bridge. Their ranks swelled to 25,000 by March 25 when they entered Montgomery, joined by celebrities like Harry Belafonte and Joan Baez, and by ordinary White supporters like Michigan housewife Viola Liuzzo. The Ku Klux Klan murdered Liuzzo that night, as she drove marchers back to Selma.[27]

Five months later, on August 26, 1965, President Johnson signed the Voting Rights Act, which outlawed literacy tests, poll taxes, and other obstacles to voting, and provided for federal enforcement of voting rights. The impact was dramatic. By late 1966, a majority of African Americans were registered to vote in most southern states. In 1964, 22 percent of all Blacks could vote in Alabama; by 1968, 57 percent had registered.[28] African American votes would elect the SCLC's Andrew Young to Congress from Georgia's 5th district, the first African American to represent Georgia in Congress since Reconstruction. Then they elected him to two terms as Mayor of Atlanta. Former SNCC leader John Lewis would also represent Georgia's 5th Congressional District from 1987 until his death July 17, 2020.[29]

The story could end there, a victory for democratic rights won with blood and courage. But it can also be told as the end of the fragile coalition that upheld non-violent civil disobedience. Below the surface in Selma there were rifts between the SCLC and some SNCC activists who resented moderate middle-class ministers who could attract the funds and media attention to capitalize on two years in the trenches for SNCC and the local activists. On the way to Montgomery, SNCC's Stokely Carmichael began organizing impoverished Blacks in Lowndes County, planting the seeds of the Black Panther Party. Five days after President Johnson signed the Voting Rights Act, the Watts section of Los Angeles erupted in a massive race riot protesting police beating Marquette Frye.[30]

Four years later, Stonewall, too, erupted in public resistance to a closeted underground existence, as young gay, lesbian, and transgender individuals battled police who raided the Stonewall Inn in New York's Greenwich Village for operating without a license. Although homosexuality was legal in New York, the State Liquor Authority refused to license gay bars, claiming they were "disorderly houses" where "unlawful practices are habitually carried on by the public."[31] Manhattan police conducted a routine raid the night of June 27, 1969, seizing alcohol and arresting thirteen people. But the patrons didn't follow the script. Men refused to show their IDs; transvestites refused to go with female officers to confirm their gender. Those not arrested joined a crowd outside the bar that grew to over 2,000 people. As police tried to haul prisoners away, the crowd heaved coins, beer bottles, cobblestones, and trash cans. Shouting "Gay power," they rammed the Stonewall's door with an uprooted parking meter, smashed its windows, and threw a firebomb into the bar. Four police officers were injured. The rest had their hands full for six days. The Stonewall Rebellion took many forms. LGBTQS2+ protesters fought the police; got drenched with fire hoses; chanted bawdy songs; performed in-your-face Rockette-style kick lines; yelled "occupy—take over, take over," "Fag power," "Liberate the bar!," and "We're the pink panthers!"; and sang a high camp version of "We Shall Overcome."[32]

Stonewall galvanized the Gay Liberation Movement. As one activist put it, "Every movement arrives at a moment when people say, 'Enough is enough.' That was the Stonewall riots for the gay rights movement."[33] Within weeks gay men and lesbians in New York formed the Gay Liberation Front; similar groups formed throughout the country, and gay pride banners appeared at anti-war demonstrations.[34] Stonewall signaled a collective coming out that won the support of many straight Americans as they discovered that they had LGBTQ2S+ friends and family. The first Gay Pride March was organized in Manhattan to celebrate the first anniversary of the Stonewall Rebellion.[35] Since 1970, Stonewall has been celebrated with an annual gay pride parade down Fifth Avenue. The Stonewall Bar at 53 Christopher Street, the site of the Stonewall Inn uprising of June 27–29, was recognized on the National Register of Historic Places in June 1999 and was named a National Historic Landmark in June 2015. The Stonewall Veterans' Association still met monthly in 2025.[36]

Stonewall did not erupt in a vacuum. Some historians trace its roots to World War II, when gay men and lesbians met in sex-segregated military units and war industries.[37] In 1950 gay men founded the first homosexual rights organization, the Mattachine Society, followed five years later by the Daughters of Bilitis, a "Woman's Organization for the purpose of Promoting the Integration of the Homosexual into Society." Called homophiles, these activists mirrored the militant middle-class respectability of the 1950s Civil Rights Movement, contesting Cold War stereotypes and employment discrimination. Homophiles opened dialogues with Protestant clergy and the American Civil Liberties Union in the 1960s and lobbied the American Medical Association to stop classifying homosexuality as a mental disorder. New York Mattachines staged the first public protest in 1964, picketing a lower Manhattan Induction Center to protest banning gays from the military and releasing draft records to employers. Despite misgivings about the Vietnam War, in 1966 the first National Planning Conference of Homophile Organizations made military service its top priority.[38]

But for draft-age gay men the last question on the medical surveys they had to answer at their draft physicals forced a difficult choice—how to check the last box: "Have you ever had or do you now have . . . homosexual tendencies?" If they checked "yes" they avoided the draft but risked employment discrimination. If they lied and checked "no" they risked federal prosecution, fines, and prison. As one man put it, "[I]t was the first time I had to take total responsibility for my life and accept the consequences. . . . In order to come to terms with the draft ... I had to come to terms with [being] gay."[39]

Even before Stonewall, the anti-war, women's, and student movements and the new counterculture created rifts between homophile liberals and gay youth, who turned from fighting for acceptance to combating the Vietnam War, and to concerns about LGBTQ2S+ poverty, addiction, and homelessness. The LGBTQ2S+ community was no more monolithic than any other. Stonewall was a police target in part because it served patrons not welcome at many gay bars—drag queens, transgender individuals, and homeless gay youth who could buy shelter and community for the $3 cover charge.[40]

It is common to divide gay history into two epochs, before and after Stonewall.[41] Stonewall becomes the catalytic event that transformed homophile activism to the more radical Gay Liberation Movement, signaled in part by dropping the demand for integration into the armed forces. This linear narrative obscures more complex and contested shifts before and after Stonewall, as do stories that move sequentially from Civil Rights to Black Power, or from liberal to radical feminism. There were voter registration drives before Selma, feminist orators before Seneca Falls, marches and protests for women's equality long before women won the vote and the Women's Liberation Movement inherited unrealized dreams from Seneca Falls.

These were not entirely separate movements: each confronted multiple and connected inequalities. Just as the anti-war movement led some men to gay liberation, the abolitionist and Civil Rights movements broke women's isolation and planted the egalitarian philosophies that led to Seneca Falls and Women's Liberation. The arguments against allowing gays to serve in the military mirrored earlier ones against racially integrated units. The cases for marriage equality that were before the Supreme Court as I spoke in 2013 built from the historic 1967 *Loving v. Virginia* decision that legalized interracial marriage. Lesbians and transgender individuals contest their marginalization in histories of Stonewall; African American women challenge their marginalization in histories of feminist and civil rights activism.[42] Histories of Selma that record the tensions between the male leaders of SNCC and SCLC still subordinate the importance of grass roots women leaders like Amelia Boynton and the teachers who risked their jobs to march for her. But more complex and accurate histories do not communicate or inspire as easily as dramatic events do, which brings us back to the questions of collective memory and symbolic resonance.

It is not surprising that Seneca Falls, Selma, and Stonewall have entered collective consciousness to different extents in different ways. Events are more easily embedded in public memory if they are dramatic, if large-scale violence attracts news coverage, and if they remain politically relevant. By such measures, Selma had the edge over Seneca Falls and Stonewall. National media etched Selma indelibly for those who witnessed it on the nightly news. As NBC's Richard Valeriani put it, "The standard answer ... to the question of how much of a role did the camera play in shaping events is 'There were no cameras at the Boston Tea Party.' ... [T]elevision helped accelerate the progress of a movement whose time had come."[43] The Voting Rights Act established Selma's place in history; dramatic images, historic sites, and annual commemorations established its symbolic resonance. Today the National Voting Rights Museum and Institute proudly claims that it is "Located in the Historic District of Selma, Alabama at the foot of the famous Edmund Pettus Bridge, the scene of 'Bloody Sunday'," its mission to chronicle and preserve "the historic journey for the right to vote that began when the 'Founding Fathers' first planted the seeds of democracy in 1776."[44] Annual commemorative marches draw movement veterans and political allies. Barack Obama and Hillary Clinton both marched in 2007 as they vied for the Democratic presidential nomination. In 2012 the Rev. Al Sharpton led the annual trek to Montgomery along with Valerie Jarrett, senior advisor to President Obama, Congressman John Lewis, Ethel Kennedy, the Rev. Jesse Jackson, Alabama Congresswoman Terri Sewell, and Martin Luther King, III. Media coverage, the Voting Rights Act, historical sites, and the annual commemorative march established Selma's place in the Civil Rights Movement.

More the product of Gay Liberation than its opening shot, Stonewall came to represent Gay Pride in part through the political skill of Stonewall Veterans, who skillfully transformed the Rebellion into a potent symbol for their movement. Gays had battled police raids over a dozen times before Stonewall. There were well-documented confrontations at a 1965 San Francisco New Year's Ball and two years later in Los Angeles, when four hundred demonstrators, including "Negroes, Mexican Americans, and Sunset Strip Youths," protested police brutality during a raid at the Black Cat Bar. In August, 1966, patrons rioted after police raided Compton's Cafeteria, an all-hours coffee shop in San Francisco's Tenderloin popular with "gay hustlers, 'hair fairies,' queens, and street kids."[45] Yet these events are largely forgotten. Stonewall gained mythic stature in part because New York Mattachines got the mainstream media and growing gay press to cover it. They distributed flyers on Sunday June 29, while the Rebellion still raged, that claimed Stonewall would "go down in history as the first time that thousands of Homosexual men and women went out into the streets to protest."[46] Gay organizers insured Stonewall's place in history as they mobilized to commemorate it. Beginning in 1965, East Coast Homophile Organizations had demonstrated each July 4 at Philadelphia's Independence Hall, an "Annual Reminder" that they were still denied "basic rights to life, liberty and the pursuit of happiness." After Stonewall, activists tired of respectable protest passed a hard-fought resolution at the Eastern Regional Conference of Homophile Organizations. To "be more relevant, reach a greater number of people, and encompass the ideas and ideals of the larger struggle in which we are engaged—that of our fundamental human rights [,]" they changed the Annual Reminder to "a demonstration be held annually on the last Saturday in June in New York City to commemorate the 1969 spontaneous demonstrations on Christopher Street." There were to be no age or dress regulations, and Homophile Groups throughout the country were asked to hold demonstrations the same day. They thus transformed a low-turnout event with an abstract message on a day already claimed for all Americans to one that mobilized gay pride and activism. New York, Chicago, and Los Angeles launched annual parades in 1970; the next year Dallas, Boston, Milwaukee, and San Jose joined them, followed in 1972 by Ann Arbor, Atlanta, Buffalo, Detroit, Washington, D.C., Miami, and Philadelphia. Ten years after Stonewall, a quarter million turned out for San Francisco's Gay Pride celebration. Seeking to include "radical as well as conservative Gay organizations and all of those in between," San Francisco organizers subordinated politics to a celebration for "all Gay persons to re-affirm their various lifestyles and take pride in their homosexuality." Stonewall came to symbolize and spread a diffuse culture of gay pride that resonated far beyond the homophile and Gay Liberation communities of the 1960s.[47]

Seneca Falls was at a distinct disadvantage compared to Selma and Stonewall—no violence, no cameras, its cause far from popular, even among women, and over seventy years removed from the distant suffrage victory. From the outset, women's rights leaders understood the historic significance of their movement and sought to establish it in historical memory. Elizabeth Cady Stanton complained in 1870 that ". . . history is silent concerning the part woman performed. . . ." Angered at women's exclusion from the historical record, she refused to donate to buy George Washington's Mount Vernon estate and opposed a federal appropriation to build Grant's Tomb. "If we must keep on continually building monuments to great men," she wrote, "they should be handsome blocks of comfortable homes for the poor. . . . Surely sanitary homes and schoolhouses for the living would be more appropriate monuments . . ."[48] Believing that knowing their history would support women's struggles for equal rights, Stanton, Anthony, and Mathilda Joslyn Gage wrote their massive *History of Woman Suffrage* that irritated some feminists in the American Woman Suffrage Movement by emphasizing Seneca Falls.[49] But Seneca Falls did not make it into survey texts or national consciousness until long after its centennial. The fiftieth anniversary of women's suffrage passed in 1970 with only a single march in New York City.[50] Women's history was not widely known nor had women yet used the ballot for feminist goals. When I assisted the first women's history course at the University of Michigan in 1971–1972, we assigned one of the first texts to focus on Seneca Falls, Eleanor Flexner's *Century of Struggle,* published in 1959.[51] The Women's Liberation Movement organized to recover women's history, a campaign that led back to Seneca Falls, where the National Park Service established Women's Rights National Historic Park in 1980. The Park includes a visitor center and an education and cultural center, the restored Wesleyan Chapel, where the Convention was held, the Elizabeth Cady Stanton House, and the homes of Mary Ann McClintock and Jane Hunt. [52] This park was won with feminist political organizing, with pressure carefully mobilized to establish the park and gain legislation and funding to buy the houses and excavate the Wesleyan Chapel.

In 1998, as part of the year-long observance of Seneca Falls' 150th anniversary, the Park Service and the Organization of American Historians held a conference there. First Lady Hillary Clinton gave the keynote. She began where all movements start, at the grass roots:

> Imagine if you will that you are Charlotte Woodward, a nineteen-year-old glove maker working and living in Waterloo. Every day you sit for hours sewing gloves together, working for small wages you cannot even keep, with no hope of going on in school or owning property, knowing that if you marry, your children and even the clothes on your body will belong to your husband. But then one day in July, 1848, you hear about a women's rights convention to be held in nearby Seneca Falls . . . . You run from house to house and you find other women who have heard the same news. Some are excited, others are amused or even shocked, and a few agree to come with you, for at least the first day. When that day comes, July 19, 1848, you leave early in the morning in your horse-drawn wagon. You fear that no one else will come; and at first, the road is empty, except for you and your neighbors. But suddenly, as you reach a crossroads, you see a few more wagons and carriages, then more and more all going towards Wesleyan Chapel.
>
> Eventually you join the others to form one long procession on the road to equality. . . .[53]

Charlotte Woodward reminds me that whatever the tensions between SNCC and Dr. King, Selma inspired Viola Liuzzo; that although the Homophiles preceded Stonewall, the Stonewall Rebellion reached lots of scared and closeted LGBTQ2S+ youth who had never heard of the Daughters of Bilitis.

Seneca Falls was for Hillary Clinton a reminder "that the rights and opportunities that we enjoy as women today were . . . fought for, agonized over, marched for, jailed for and even died for by brave and persistent women and men who came before us." She ended with Seneca Falls' challenge for the future: "If we are to finish the work begun here—then no American should ever again face discrimination on the basis of gender, race or sexual orientation anywhere in our country."[54]

In that sentence Clinton linked the legacies of Seneca Falls, Selma, and Stonewall—which brings me back to President Obama's inaugural, to the question no historian should try to answer about what these sites symbolize now and how widely they speak to deeply divided Americans. If they remain powerful symbols, it is partly because they have been written as touchstones into histories of social change, and partly because they have been effectively preserved as sites to inspire memory. Their evocative power varies for each person, depending on what they connote. For me, as for Hillary Clinton, Seneca Falls evokes Charlotte Woodward as well as Stanton and Mott, but we are likely a minority. Selma, and to a lesser extent Stonewall, had the advantage of film to etch powerful visual images, and of commemorative events to carry their messages to subsequent generations. Memory is fragile, though, and historic sites and annual commemorations alone do not insure the potency of political symbols. The ongoing conversation between the past and present urgencies reframes history; it constantly resurrects symbols, erases them, or rewrites their meanings. The President's mention of Stonewall provoked curiosity for many people who hadn't heard of it, and necessitated explanations from mainstream media.[55]

The symbolic value of Seneca Falls, Selma, and Stonewall rests with how they speak to enduring inequalities. When I first taught women's history, fully employed American women earned 59 cents for every dollar a man earned; by 2013 it was 77 cents—and had risen only a penny since the Seneca Falls sesquicentennial in 1998. The Seneca Falls grievance that women "receive but a scanty remuneration" still spoke then and still speaks in 2025 as I prepare this volume. Husbands no longer "chastise" wives with legal impunity, but spousal abuse is still with us.

One grievance articulated at Seneca Falls remains a troubling touchstone—the third one, that women were denied "rights which are given to the most ignorant and degraded men—both natives and foreigners." The nativism of 1848 still speaks to contemporary anti-immigrant prejudice. At the 2012 Selma to Montgomery March, Janet Murguia, president of the

National Council of La Raza, urged African Americans and Latinos to push back together against voter suppression and anti-immigration laws. Representative John Lewis told an estimated 3,500 listeners: "We march today for what we did 47 years ago—for what is fair, what is right and for what is just."[56]

In 2013 more than 5,000 people followed Lewis and Vice President Joe Biden across the Edmund Pettus Bridge. Biden, the first sitting vice president to take part, said that Selma "broke the back of the forces of evil," but that voting rights remained threatened by bans on early voting and new voter ID laws. The week he spoke, the Supreme Court accepted a case from Shelby County, Alabama, seeking to overturn the section of the Voting Rights Act that required states with histories of racial discrimination to get Justice Department approval before implementing any changes in election laws.[57] On June 25, 2013, the Court ruled in *Shelby County v. Holder* and by a narrow 5–4 vote overturned the oversight provision, opening the door to increasing voter restrictions.

Seneca Falls and Selma may still inspire those who support gender and racial equality, yet as President Obama spoke, their movements fought defensive battles to preserve rights won decades before. Only Stonewall seemed to represent a movement making affirmative gains, as a majority of Senators and of the American public moved with surprising speed to support marriage equality—an issue, like voter suppression, then before the Supreme Court. The outcome, unlike the *Shelby County v. Holder* decision, was positive. On June 26, 2015, in another 5–4 decision in *Obergefell v. Hodges*, the Supreme Court ruled that same-sex couples had the right to marry throughout the United States.

Interestingly, President Obama linked Seneca Falls to pay equity, but not to reproductive choice, although that issue swung close Senate races in Arkansas and Indiana, and although reproductive rights were threatened by legislative attacks on Planned Parenthood, and by state regulations that had closed all abortion clinics in Mississippi and threatened to do so in Alabama and North Dakota. If these issues did not appear in the Seneca Falls Declaration, it was perhaps because there was no reliable birth control in 1848 and abortion was legal in most states.[58]

Rather than address a divisive issue that mobilized many women voters, the President chose instead to attach his symbols to more seemingly "respectable" issues—to pay equity, the democratic right to vote, and the right to marry. Recent LGBTQ2S+ victories owe more to the goals of the Homophile movement than to the radical resistance at Stonewall.

However controversial gay marriage may be for many Americans, and however important the right to serve openly in the military, the rights to marry and to serve in the armed forces fit the respectable agendas of the Mattachine Society and Daughters of Bilitis, not the rage and exuberant counterculture of Stonewall. Nor do marriage equality and military service address urgent needs for many of Stonewall's descendants. Transgender individuals remain at high risk for violence. LGBTQ2S+ youth, according to a 2012 study, constitute 40 percent of clients served by youth service agencies, most of them homeless because their families rejected them for their sexual orientations or gender identities.[59]

I don't know what Stonewall, Selma, and Seneca Falls mean to people battling such inequalities. The President spoke powerfully to me as an historian when he invoked Seneca Falls, Selma, and Stonewall because no President had ever linked them, and because by invoking them he moved their causes to the center of American political discourse. Their meanings may be diluted or revised and are certainly contested, but they became nonetheless symbols for the entire nation. That does not mean that everyone knows them, likes them, or embraces the movements they represent. Maybe someday they will function as symbols of national unity, but that day has not yet come. Rather, they occupy the cultural space that James Clifford defined: culture as a site of contestation, not consensus.[60]

I was startled by responses I found online to a news story about the 2013 Selma March, most of which I could not repeat in a public lecture. A small sample illustrated the depth of Selma's contested meaning. Redfish 52 wrote: "We get it . . . all white people should be ashamed now for something that happened 50 years ago . . . Bla . . . bla . . . bla . . ." Joe the Patriot wrote: "It's 2013 and they're still telling blacks that 'whiteys don't want you to vote'. . . . When are they going to give it a rest? I'm sick of the race card, I'm sick of the victim card. I'm sick of barry [Obama] dividing this country. . . ." The Big Mick was more hopeful: "Very soon now the ONLY people with DIRECT EXPERIENCE with 'segregation' are going to be either in the Graveyard or the Nursing Home in Diapers. So WITHOUT these 'reenactments' very soon they won't be able to keep the Myth of America the Still Racist alive." Catty wrote simply: "Celebrating history is so stupid." But I was heartened by one brave soul, Jessenc, who answered her: "So you disagree with historical memory in principle? I suppose we should not have holidays such as Veteran's Day or Memorial Day? I suppose Jewish people are wrong for remembering the Holocaust? Your comment is very strange. I think we should all remember our past."

Seneca Falls, Selma, and Stonewall may inspire controversy. But then they always did. Jim Clark and John Lewis never saw Selma the same way. Many conservative homophiles distanced themselves from Stonewall. Henry Stanton left town before the Seneca Falls convention. The contested values these events evoke, the rights hard-won and still besieged, the difficult and divisive histories they connote—that is precisely their national meaning. Equal rights remain a compass for U.S. social change, toward destinations still contested and not yet reached—and for that historical legacy Seneca Falls, Selma, and Stonewall remain eloquent symbols.

NOTES

    Additional Sources: Lisa Tetrault, *The Myth of Seneca Falls: Memory and the Women's Suffrage Movement, 1848-1898* (Chapel Hill: University of North Carolina Press, 2014) examines the construction of Seneca Falls as a symbol of the feminist movement. Following the release in 2014 of the historical drama *Selma*, written by Paul Webb and directed by Ava DuVernay, and the 50th anniversary of Selma in 2015, the University Press of Florida published Joe Street and Henry Knight Lozano's edited anthology, *The Shadow of Selma* (Gainesville: University Press of Florida, 2018), which examines how Selma entered public consciousness and the various ways it has been represented and interpreted. When I wrote this lecture, I had not yet read Melissa Harris-Perry's article, "From Seneca Falls to Selma to Stonewall," in *The Nation*, February 11, 2013, 10. It is not surprising that Harris-Perry, like many social scientists and historians, recognized the symbolic significance of the three events. She contended, however, that Obama's evocation of Seneca Falls, Selma, and Stonewall was important not because they evoked collective significance for all Americans, but for what each event signified for the people it represented. It told women, African Americans, and LGBTQ2S+ individuals that the President saw them and recognized their importance for national history. "Being seen was part of the struggle," she wrote. "Being seen is still part of the struggle. President Obama's inaugural address is yet another step in the long march toward fairness."

1   I described this in a blog for the University of Calgary website, Betsy Jameson, "Dispatches from Washington: Waiting for History at the Blue Gate," January 21, 2009.

2   "President Obama's second inaugural address (Transcript)," *Washington Post*, January 21, 2013.

3   "Election 2012, Presidential Election Polls," *New York Times*, https://www.nytimes.com/elections/2012/results/president/exit-polls.html, accessed May 12, 2021.

4   President Obama's Second Inaugural Address.

5   The Lilly Ledbetter Fair Pay Act of 2009, Public Law No: 111-12 (01/29/2009): was the first bill that President Obama signed into law, on January 29, 2009. Its long title is An Act to amend title VII of the Civil Rights Act of 1964 and the Age Discrimination in Employment Act of 1967, and to modify the operation of the Americans with Disabilities Act of 1990 and the Rehabilitation Act of 1973, to clarify that a discriminatory compensation decision or other practice that is unlawful under such Acts occurs each time compensation is paid pursuant to the discriminatory compensation decision or other practice, and for other purposes. For Obama's "evolution" on gay rights and his policies as president, see Barack Obama, *A Promised Land* (New York: Crown, 2020), 603, 609-14;

"Obama's 'evolution' about gay rights," https://gayandlove.com/obamas-evolution-about-gay-rights/, accessed May 12, 2021.

6   On June 25, 2013, in a narrow 5–4 decision in *Shelby County v. Holder*, the U.S. Supreme Court struck down section 4(b) of the Voting Rights Act, which had provided for federal oversight of voting requirements in states with histories of racial discrimination. That decision opened the door for states to pass restrictive laws, limiting access to the vote by identification requirements (Texas, for instance, accepted gun permits, which have no photographs, but not student photo IDs), by restricting numbers of voting places or voting hours or restricting access to advance voting options. Those efforts continue. On June 26, 2015, in another 5–4 decision in *Obergefell v. Hodges*, the Supreme Court ruled that same-sex couples had the right to marry in the United States.

7   The 19th Amendment to the U.S. Constitution, certified on August 26, 1920, prohibited the United States or any state from denying the right to vote based on sex. Women first won the right to vote in Wyoming Territory in 1869 and had won the full franchise in fifteen states and Alaska Territory prior to the passage of the 19th amendment. All but two—New York and Michigan—were west of the Mississippi River.

8   Urban race riots, police violence, and attacks on voting rights would qualify the sense of victory that the 1964 Civil Rights Act and 1965 Voting Rights Act signaled in the mid-1960s, but Selma remains a culminating event in a significant chapter of the long struggle for African American rights in the United States.

9   Frederick B. Tolles, ed., *Slavery and "The Woman Question": Lucretia Mott's Diary of Her Visit to Great Britain to Attend the World Anti-Slavery Convention of 1840*, Supplement no. 23 to the *Journal of the Friends' Historical Society* (Haverford, PA: Friends' Historical Association and Friends' Historical Society, 1952); Judith Wellman, *The Road to Seneca Falls: Elizabeth Cady Stanton and the First Woman's Rights Convention* (Urbana and Chicago: University of Illinois Press, 2004), 44, 59–64; Constance Rynder, "'All Men and Women Are Created Equal'-Cover Page: April '99 American History Feature," HistoryNet, https://www.historynet.com/all-men-women-are-created-equal-cover-page-april-99-american-history-feature.htm, accessed May 20, 2021; Eleanor Flexner's pioneering work, *Century of Struggle: The Woman's Rights Movement in the United States* (Cambridge, MA: Belknap Press of Harvard University Press, 1959), 71–77, esp. 71–73; Sally G. McMillen, *Seneca Falls and the Origins of the Women's Rights Movement* (Oxford: Oxford University Press, 2008), 72–77; and Ellen Carol Dubois, *Woman Suffrage and Women's Rights* (New York: New York University Press, 1998).

10 Flexner, *Century of Struggle*, 74.

11 Flexner, *Century of Struggle*, 74–75; Wellman, *The Road to Seneca Falls*, 98–100. For the full text of the Declaration of Rights and Sentiments and of the Resolutions passed at Seneca Falls, see McMillen, *Seneca Falls*, Appendix A, 237–41.

12 Flexner, *Century of Struggle*, 75; Jean H. Baker, "Getting Right with Women's Suffrage," *The Journal of the Gilded Age and Progressive Era* 5:1 (January 2006): 7–17; 15; Wellman, *The Road to Seneca Falls*, 193, 195.

13 Rynder, "'All Men and Women Are Created Equal'"; Wellman, *The Road to Seneca Falls*, 195–96; McMillen, *Seneca Falls*, 90.

14 Elizabeth Cady Stanton: Seneca Falls Keynote Address Delivered July 19, 1848, Seneca Falls, New York, https://susanbanthonyhouse.org/blog/wp-content/uploads/2017/07/Elizabeth-Cady-Stanton-Seneca-Falls-1848.pdf, accessed May 13, 2021.

15 Jennifer Chapin Harris, "Celebrating Women's Herstory: The Story of Seneca Falls," *Off Our Backs* 28:7 (July 1998): 9, Stable URL: http://www.jstor.org/stable/20836139, accessed February 17, 2013; McMillen, *Seneca Falls*, 93–94.

16 Harris, "Celebrating Women's Herstory"; Flexner, *Century of Struggle*, 80; McMillen, *Seneca Falls*, 95–97.

17 McMillen, *Seneca Falls*, 104–48; Flexner, *Century of Struggle*, 78–102; Reva B. Siegel, "Home As Work: The First Woman's Rights Claims Concerning Wives' Household Labor, 1850–1880," *The Yale Law Journal* 103: 5 (March 1994): 1090–91, Stable URL: http://www.jstor.org/stable/797118, accessed February 17, 2013.

18 Siegel, "Home As Work," 1048–1050; Flexner, *Century of Struggle*, 148–50, 226. Stanton and Anthony led the National Women's Suffrage Association, Lucy Stone Blackwell and Henry Blackwell, the American Women's Suffrage Association. The two groups merged in 1890.

19 Wellman, *The Road to Seneca Falls*, 231; Judith Wellman "Rhoda Palmer," Women's Rights National Historic Site website, National Park Service, U.S. Department of the Interior, https://www.nps.gov/wori/learn/historyculture/rhoda-palmer.htm, accessed February 13, 2013.

20 Although there had been some gender differences in votes in previous elections, the 8 percent gender gap in the 1980 presidential election brought gender differences in politics to public attention. See Jo Freeman, "Gender Gaps in Presidential Elections," letter to the editor of *P.S.: Political Science and Politics* 32:2 (June 1999): 191–92.

21 The Fifteenth Amendment to the U.S. Constitution reads: "Section 1. The right of citizens of the United States to vote shall not be denied or abridged by the United States or by any state on account of race, color, or previous condition of servitude. Section 2. The Congress shall have power to enforce this article by appropriate legislation." Congress did not pass such "appropriate legislation" until 1965, following the events in Selma, when it passed the Voting Rights Act.

22 For a discussion of periodizing the Civil Rights Movement, see for instance Jacquelyn Dowd Hall, "The Long Civil Rights Movement and the Political Uses of the Past," *The Journal of American History* 91:4 (March 2005): 1233–63.

23 Good sources for the history of the Selma civil rights campaign include Harvard Sitkoff, *The Struggle for Black Equality* (1981; 24th Anniversary Edition, New York: Hill and Wang, 2008): esp. 174–82; David J. Garrow, *Protest at Selma: Martin Luther King, Jr., and the Voting Rights Act of 1965* (New Haven: Yale University Press, 1978); Clayborne Carson, ed., chap. 26 "Selma," *The Autobiography of Martin Luther King, Jr.* (New York: Warner Books, 1998), 270-89; John Lewis and Michael D'Orso, *Walking with the Wind: A Memoir of the Movement* (New York: Simon and Schuster, 1998); *Eyes on the Prize*, Episode 6 "Bridge to Freedom (1965)" (series produced for PBS by Blackside, Inc., Henry Hampton producer) (hereinafter EOTP 6). Much of Selma's impact was visual. *Eyes on the Prize* used contemporary news footage; see also *Selma 1965: The Photographs of Spider Martin* (Austin: University of Texas Press, 2015).

24 Sitkoff, *Struggle for Black Equality*, 174–76; R. Bruce Brassell, "From Evidentiary Presentation to Artful Re-Presentation: Media Images, Civil Rights Documentaries, and the Audiovisual Writing of History," *Journal of Film and Video* 56:1 (Spring 2004): 3–16; John Lewis, "The Voting Rights Act: Ensuring Dignity and Democracy," *Human Rights* 32: 2 (Spring 2005): 2–3, 7; EOTP 6.

25 Sitkoff, *Struggle for Black Equality*, 177–79; Carson, ed., *Autobiography of Martin Luther King, Jr.*, 179–83; EOTP 6.

26 Sitkoff, *Struggle for Black Equality*, 179–80; EOTP 6; President Lyndon Johnson's Speech to Congress on Voting Rights, March 15, 1965, RG 46, Records of the United States Senate, National Archives, U.S. National Archives and Records Administration, https://www.archives.gov/legislative/features/voting-rights-1965/johnson.html, accessed May 14, 2021.

27 Sitkoff, *Struggle for Black Equality*, 179–82; EOTP 6; Carson, ed., *Autobiography of Martin Luther King, Jr.*, 183–89.
28 Sitkoff, *Struggle for Black Equality*, 182; Lewis, "The Voting Rights Act."
29 Calvin Woodward and Desiree Seals, "John Lewis, Lion of Civil Rights and Congress, Dies at 80," *The Washington Post*, July 17, 2020; Andrew Young, Jr., *Biography*, https://www.biography.com/activist/andrew-young-jr, accessed May 14, 2020.
30 Vincent Harding, Robin D.G. Kelley, and Earl Lewis, "We Changed the World, 1945–1970," in *A History of African Americans*, eds. Robin D.G. Kelley and Earl Lewis (New York: Oxford University Press, 2000), 516–19; Sitkoff, *Struggle for Black Equality*, 185.
31 "Why Did the Mafia Own the Bar?," *American Experience*, PBS, https://www.pbs.org/wgbh/americanexperience/features/stonewall-why-did-mafia-own-bar/, accessed February 16, 2013. Useful sources for the Stonewall riots include Martin Duberman, *Stonewall* (New York: Penguin, 1993); David Carter, *Stonewall: The Riots that Sparked the Gay Revolution* (New York: St. Martin's Press, 2004); and, published after I gave my 2013 lecture, Marc Stein, *The Stonewall Riots: A Documentary History* (New York: New York University Press, 2019).
32 Garance Franke-Ruta, "An Amazing Account of the Stonewall Uprising," *The Atlantic*, January 24, 2013, anecdotes based on "An Analytical Collation of Accounts and Documents Recorded in the Year 1969 Concerning the Stonewall Riots," compiled by historian David Carter, author of *Stonewall: The Riots That Sparked the Gay Revolution*. See also Duberman, *Stonewall*, 194–292 for events of the first night;192–211 for events through July 4.
33 Michael Adams, executive director of Services and Advocacy for Gay, Lesbian, Bisexual and Transgender Elders, or SAGE, quoted in Dave Singleton, "40 Years Later: A Look Back at the Turning Point for Gay Rights," *AARP Bulletin*, June 2009, https://www.aarp.org/politics-society/rights/info-06-2009/stonewall_riots_40_years_later_.html, accessed February 17, 2013.
34 John D'Emilio and Estelle B. Freedman, *Intimate Matters: A History of Sexuality in America* (New York: Harper and Row, Publishers, 1988), 319; Simon Hall, "Protest Movements in the 1970s: The Long 1960s," *Journal of Contemporary History* 43: 4 (October 2008): 657, 660, http://www.jstor.org/stable/40543228, accessed February 17, 2013; Stein, *The Stonewal Riots*, 238.
35 S. Hall, "Protest Movements," 660.
36 William Rubenstein, "The Stonewall Anniversary: 25 Years of Gay Rights," *Human Rights* 21:3 (Summer 1994): 18–23, http://www.jstor.org/stable/27879846, accessed: February 17, 2013; https://www.nycpride.org/, accessed May 15, 2021; "Stonewall Inn," NYC LGBT Historic Sites Project, https://www.nyclgbtsites.org/site/stonewall-inn-christopher-park/, accessed May 15, 2021; http://www.stonewallvets.org/, accessed May 15, 2021.
37 Allan Berube, *Coming Out under Fire: The History of Gay Men and Women in World War Two* (New York: Free Press, 1990); John D'Emilio, "It Didn't Start with Stonewall," (Boston) *Gay Community News*, June 23, 1979; John D'Emilio, *Sexual Politics, Sexual Communities: The Making of a Homosexual Community in the United States, 1940-1970* (Chicago: University of Chicago Press, 1983); Peter Boag, "'Does Portland Need a Homophile Society?': Gay Culture and Activism in the Rose City between World War II and Stonewall," *Oregon Historical Quarterly* 105:1 (Spring 2004): 6–39.
38 Jonathan Katz, *Gay American History: Lesbians and Gay Men in the U.S.A.* (New York: Crowell, 1976), 411–33; Duberman, *Stonewall*, 78–77, 110–17; Justin David Suran, "Coming Out Against the War: Antimilitarism and the Politicization of Homosexuality in the Era of Vietnam," *American Quarterly* 53:3 (September 2001): 453, 456–61.

39 Suran, "Coming Out Against the War," 460–63.
40 Suran, "Coming Out Against the War," 460–63; D'Emilio and Friedman, *Intimate Matters*, 320–22; Duberman, *Stonewall*, 199; Duberman, "The Night They Raided Stonewall"; Franke-Ruta, "An Amazing Account of the Stonewall Uprising."
41 See for instance the structure of Duberman, *Stonewall*, which is divided into three sections: "Before Stonewall," "Stonewall," and "After Stonewall."
42 See for instance Amy C. Branner, Laura Butterbaugh and April Jackson, "There Was A Dyke March?," *Off Our Backs* 24:8 (August/September 1994): 1–2, 16–17, 20, http://www.jstor.org/stable/20834872, accessed February 17, 2013 and Gloria T. Hull, Patricia Bell Scott, and Barbara Smith, *All the Women Are White, All the Blacks Are Men, But Some of Us Are Brave: Black Women's Studies* (Old Westbury, NY: The Feminist Press, 1982).
43 Interview with Richard Valeriani, December 10, 1985, Eyes on the Prize Interviews, Henry Hampton Collection, Washington University Film and Media Archive, http://digital.wustl.edu/cgi/t/text/text-idx?c=eop;cc=eop;rgn=main;view=text;idno=val0015.0857.101, accessed February 20, 2013.
44 National Voting Rights Museum and Institute website, http://nvrmi.com/, accessed February 17, 2013.
45 Elizabeth A. Armstrong and Suzanna M. Crage, "Movements and Memory: The Making of the Stonewall Myth," *American Sociological Review* 71: 5 (October 2006): 724–51; D'Emilio, "It Didn't Start with Stonewall"; Brett Beemyn, "The Silence Is Broken: A History of the First Lesbian, Gay, and Bisexual College Student Groups," in "Sexuality and Politics Since 1945," special Issue, *Journal of the History of Sexuality* 12:2 (April 2003): 205–23.
46 Armstrong and Crage, "Movements and Memory," 738.
47 Armstrong and Crage, "Movements and Memory," 738–43; Duberman, *Stonewall*, 226–29.
48 Vivien Ellen Rose, "From the Editor: 'Men Make No Mention of Her Heroism': Natural and Cultural Resources and Women's Past," *OAH Magazine of History* 12:1, *The Stuff of Women's History: Artifacts, Landscapes, and Built Environments* (Fall 1997): 3–4; 3.
49 The work grew to six volumes, published between 1881 and 1922; the trio were joined by Ida Husted Harper as the project progressed. Elizabeth Cady Stanton, Susan B. Anthony, Matilda Joslyn Gage, and Ida Husted Harper, *History of Woman Suffrage*. The six volumes, available through Project Gutenberg, Google Books, and Internet Archive, as well as in research libraries, are: *History of Woman Suffrage, Volume I* (1848–1861), *Volume II* (1861–1876), *Volume III* (1876–1885), *Volume IV* (1883–1900), *Volume V* (1900–1920), and *Volume VI* (1900–1920). For resistance to this founding narrative, see Tetrault, *The Myth of Seneca Falls*, esp. chap. 5.
50 Ellen Carol DuBois, "Seneca Falls Goes Public, "*The Public Historian* 21: 2 (Spring 1999): 42.
51 Flexner, *Century of Struggle*.
52 Heather Lee Miller, Emily Greenwald, and Dawn Vogel, *Women's Rights National Historical Park: Ethnographic Overview and Assessment* (Boston: Northeast Region Ethnology Program, National Park Service, 2009); Women's Rights National Historic Park website, https://www.nps.gov/wori/index.htm, accessed February 5, 2013.
53 Remarks by the First Lady Hillary Rodham Clinton, 150th Anniversary of the First Women's Rights Convention, Seneca Falls, New York, July 16, 1998, https://clintonwhitehouse4.archives.gov/textonly/WH/EOP/First_Lady/html/generalspeeches/1998/19980804-3206.html, accessed February 13, 2013.
54 Remarks by H. Clinton, 150th Anniversary of the First Women's Rights Convention.

55 See for instance Liz Halloran, "Stonewall? Explaining Obama's Historic Gay-Rights Reference," National Public Radio, It's All Politics: Political News from NPR, January 22, 2013, https://www.npr.org/sections/itsallpolitics/2013/01/22/169984209/stonewall-explaining-obamas-historic-gay-rights-reference, accessed February 16, 2013.

56 Sam Fulwood, III, "Selma to Montgomery, Then and Now," Center for American Progress, March 6, 2012, https://www.americanprogress.org/issues/race/news/2012/03/06/11199/race-and-beyond-selma-to-montgomery-then-and-now/, accessed May 18, 2021; Salvador Guerrero, "Latino group joins re-enactment of Selma to Montgomery March," Scripps Howard Foundation Wire, March 7, 2012, https://www.shfwire.com/latino-group-joins-re-enactment-selma-montgomery-march/, accessed May 18, 2021; Charles J. Dean, "Selma march to Alabama capital relaunched with new spirit, purpose (slideshow)," March 5, 2012, https://www.al.com/spotnews/2012/03/selma_march_to_alabama_capital.html, accessed May 20, 2021.

57 Philip Rawls, "Biden: Selma beatings shaped him, nation," AP, March 3, 2013, https://news.yahoo.com/biden-selma-beatings-shaped-him-nation-184906535.html, accessed May 20, 2013.

58 See James C. Mohr, *Abortion in America: The Origins and Evolution of National Policy* (New York: Oxford University Press, 1979).

59 Laura E. Durso and Gary J. Gates, "Serving Our Youth: Findings from a National Survey of Services Providers Working with Lesbian, Gay, Bisexual and Transgender Youth Who Are Homeless or At Risk of Becoming Homeless," The Williams Institute, UCLA, 2012, https://escholarship.org/uc/item/80x75033, accessed February 22, 2013.

60 James Clifford, *The Predicament of Culture* (Cambridge, MA: Harvard University Press, 1988).

12

"Use My Broken Heart": Making Change Out of Tragedy

April 8, 2014

On Friday, July 26, 2013, Sybrina Fulton rose to speak to assembled African American advocates at the National Urban League meeting in Philadelphia. It had been a bit over seventeen months since February 26, 2012, when her seventeen-year-old son, Trayvon Martin, was shot and killed in Sanford, Florida, walking home from a convenience store, carrying a bag of Skittles and an iced tea. It took forty-four days and considerable public outcry before neighborhood watch volunteer George Zimmerman was charged with second-degree murder in her son's death, though Zimmerman admitted killing the boy after calling 911. The call recorded: "Hey, we've had some break-ins in my neighborhood and there's a real suspicious guy." "This guy looks like he's up to no good or he's on drugs or something." "These [expletive], they always get away." Then, against police orders, Zimmerman left his car to pursue the youth. He claimed that he shot Trayvon Martin only after the teen punched him repeatedly, and the Sanford police said that Florida's 2005 Stand Your Ground defense law allowed the use of deadly force if a person fears death or bodily harm, as Zimmerman claimed he did. Only mounting public outrage led to Zimmerman's finally being charged with second-degree murder on April 11.[1]

These events fed a spirited public conversation about racial profiling and gun control in America. Still, race remained at most an unspoken subtext in Zimmerman's trial. Sybrina Fulton addressed the Urban League just thirteen days after a Sanford jury acquitted George Zimmerman of manslaughter and second-degree murder in her son's death.[2] With the almost unbearable grace that has characterized her public persona, Fulton sought words to transform the unendurable. "My message to you," she told the assembled activists, "is, please use my story, please use my tragedy, please use my broken heart to say to yourself, 'We cannot let this happen to anybody else's child'."[3]

Other children clearly remain at risk. In another highly reported case, on November 23, 2012, Michael Dunn shot and killed another seventeen-year-old unarmed African American high school student, Jordan Davis, in a Jacksonville, Florida, gas station parking lot after Davis and three friends refused to turn down the music in their car that Dunn considered "thug music" and "rap crap." Dunn grabbed a gun from his own car and fired into the teens' vehicle because, he said, he felt threatened and thought the unarmed Davis had a gun. On February 15, 2014, Dunn was convicted on three charges of attempted murder for shooting at the three surviving teens but was acquitted of killing Davis under the Stand Your Ground defense because he said he felt threatened.[4]

Trayvon Martin and Jordan Davis represent countless equally wrenching stories. Their deaths have generated a wide range of responses to the appalling numbers of children lost to gun violence in the United States, and heated debates about the so-called "stand your ground" laws that many, including the parents of Trayvon Martin and Jordan Davis, consider at least partly responsible for their deaths. According to the Children's Defense Fund in 2012, gun violence was eclipsed only by car accidents as the leading cause of death among all American children ages nineteen and younger. In all, 2,694 children died of gun shots in the United States in 2010. Two-thirds of those deaths were homicides. American children were seventeen times more likely to be killed by guns than their peers in other high-income countries.[5]

Appalling as these figures are, the situation is far worse for children of color. In 2010, White children were nearly three times more likely to die in a car accident than from firearms, but gun violence was the leading cause of death for African American children and adolescents. "Black children and teens were twice as likely to be killed by a gun" than in a car accident in 2010.[6]

These figures are sobering, the losses they represent horrific. Still, I might, as a historian, have spared you this topic were it not for connections to other children's deaths that tugged and troubled me as I witnessed the determined grace of four bereft parents seeking through social activism some redemptive justice for their slain children. Jordan Davis's mother, Lucia McBath, became a national spokesperson for Moms Demand Action for Gun Sense in America.[7] Sybrina Fulton and Tracy Martin founded the non-profit Trayvon Martin Foundation in March 2012 "to create awareness of how violent crime impacts the families of the victims and to provide support and advocacy for those families in response to the murder of Trayvon Martin." The Foundation's mission includes increasing public awareness of all forms of racial, ethnic and gender profiling, and "educat[ing] youth on conflict resolution techniques," to "reduce the incidences where confrontations between strangers turn deadly."[8]

The desire of grieving parents to change laws and combat prejudices that contributed to their children's deaths is understandable; it is laudable; it evokes empathy. For me these events also evoked unsettling histories of children lost in two labor struggles over a century ago, and of other children whose deaths have fueled more recent battles for racial equity. My 2014 lecture developed as I wrestled with what might link the legacies of these lost young lives besides the fact that these children occupied the tangled terrains of my memory.

"[P]lease use my broken heart to say to yourself, 'We cannot let this happen to anybody else's child'." Sybrina Fulton's words evoked those of another mother, Mary Petrucci, whom I introduced in my 2009 lecture. Mary Petrucci lost her children on April 20, 1914, in the brutal climax of a strike, an event known as the Ludlow Massacre. The Petruccis joined 9,000 coal miners who went on strike on September 23, 1913 against three southern Colorado coal companies, the largest of which, the Colorado Fuel and Iron Company (CF&I) was controlled by the Rockefellers.[9] The miners averaged $1.68 a day, paid in company scrip; their death rate was double to triple the national average.[10] They struck for recognition of their union, the United Mine Workers of America (UMWA), an eight-hour day, and a 10 percent increase in tonnage rates. They wanted pay for all so-called dead work, like timbering; a check-weighman elected by the miners to ensure fair weights for their coal; the right to trade in any store, to live where they pleased and to choose their own doctor, rather than submit to the social and economic control of their company towns. They sought enforcement of Colorado mining laws and an end to the company guard system. Four of their demands were Colorado state law, won in past struggles.[11]

Knowing that their striking members would be evicted from their company housing, the UMWA leased land and erected eight tent colonies to house the miners and their families.[12] The Petruccis lived in the largest tent colony, near the Ludlow, Colorado train depot.

As in other Colorado miners' strikes, the coal operators asked for state troops, and on October 28, Democratic Governor Elias Ammons sent the Colorado National Guard. As the strike wore on, company guards and hired guns were mustered in as soldiers.[13] On April 20, 1914 some of them shot and killed UMWA organizer Louis Tikas and two other strikers. Then they poured machine gun fire into the Ludlow tent colony, killing two more union men and eleven-year-old Frank Snyder. The miners fought back with rifles they had hidden in case of attack. Some of the women and children ran for shelter in nearby arroyos; some hid in a well; some huddled in underground pits the strikers had dug under the tents in case of violence.[14]

The morning of April 20, Mary Petrucci was doing the laundry when her tent in the southeast corner, front row, was set on fire. She ran with her three children to a neighboring tent and got them safely inside the pit beneath its floor. When she regained consciousness, she was holding her dead infant, surrounded by the corpses of her friends, their children, and her own. The dead included two women and eleven children—Patricia Valdez and her four children, the pregnant Cedilano Costa and her two children, the three Petrucci children, and Cloriva and Rodgerlo Pedregon, ages four and six.[15]

Like Sybrina Fulton and Lucia McBath, Mary Petrucci went public, joining three other women survivors who traveled to Chicago, Washington, D.C., and New York to tell the story of Ludlow and the union cause. Just weeks after losing her children, Mary Petrucci told a reporter:

> I used to sing around my work and playing with my babies.... I'm 24 years old and I suppose I'll live a long time, but I don't see how I can ever be happy again.... But you're not to think we could do it any differently another time. We are working people—my husband and I—and we're stronger for the union than before the strike.... I can't have my babies back. But perhaps when everybody knows about them, something will be done to make the world a better place for all babies.[16]

Mary Petrucci might have spoken as well for other parents who had lost their children just four months before, when an event known as the Italian Hall Disaster climaxed a strike of copper miners in Michigan's Keweenaw Peninsula. The Michigan strike involved copper miners, not coal, and a different union—the Western Federation of Miners (WFM) which focused on hardrock metal miners, while the UMWA organized coal miners. By summer 1913 the WFM had enough members in Michigan copper mines to make seemingly modest requests of their employers, the largest of which was the Calumet and Hecla mining company. On April 23, 1913, they asked the Mass Mines company for a full dinner hour without having to sort "drills, tools, etc. at dinner hour as we have to do at present," and to "kindly issue orders to the hoisting engineers not to run the hoist so fast while the men are riding on the skip." The company responded by firing all union men.[17]

In early June, mass union meetings drew up to 3000 miners. Management hired spies to infiltrate the unions and braced for a strike. The strike came on July 23, 1913, when members of the Western Federation of Miners struck for a $3 day, better working conditions, and the elimination of the new one-man drill that cut jobs and left miners working alone underground without a partner in case of accidents. Most of all they struck for what no employer would grant: recognition of the WFM as the miners' representative and acceptance of collective bargaining.[18]

As at Ludlow and as had been common practice in miners' strikes for half a century, the companies hired private detectives to infiltrate the unions, local businessmen organized an anti-union Citizens' Alliance, and the mine owners got Michigan Governor Woodbridge Ferris to send the National Guard to keep order, sparking confrontations between the strikers and soldiers.[19] The use of state troops and of detectives hired to break unions, and the contexts of employer paternalism and social control characterized both strikes.

In both, too, largely Anglo-American owners faced well-organized multi-ethnic workers. The striking coal miners identified with at least twenty-seven ethnicities and spoke as many languages. Italians formed the largest group, followed by Latinxs (16 percent), who coal operators considered "foreigners," though their ancestors had settled Santa Fe in 1598. The rest, in order, were eastern Europeans (15 percent), Anglo-Americans (13 percent), Austrians (including Serbs and Slavs) (11 percent), African Americans (7 percent), Greeks (6 percent), and a few Japanese, Germans, Scandinavians, Scotch, Irish, English, French, Spanish, and Canadians.[20] The striking copper miners included large numbers of Finns, Croatians, Slovenians, Italians, Russians, and Poles, as well as Cornish, Irish, and Americans. In 1913–1914, many White Americans racialized some of these ethnic groups—Latinx, Serbs, Slavs, Italians, Greeks, and even Finns—and considered them people of color. The Calumet strikers maintained community spirit and solidarity with frequent parades.[21] As in the coal miners' tent colonies, women played central roles—they paraded, picketed, taunted strikebreakers, and, in Michigan, formed broom brigades, dipping their brooms in outhouses before using them to poke strikebreakers.[22]

Both strikes were violent at times. Union men beat strikebreakers. In Colorado, CF&I detectives shot into the Forbes tent colony, killing one miner, shooting a young girl in the face, and riddling a boy's legs with machine gun bullets. Two detectives who worked for the coal operators shot and killed UMWA organizer Gerald Lippiati on August 16, 1913, before the strike began.[23] The next day, August 17, in Michigan, the miners buried two strikers, Steve Putrich and Alois Tijan, slain in their boardinghouse in Seeberville by four operatives of the Waddell-Mahon Detective Agency acting as Sheriff's Deputies, because two other men in the same boardinghouse had walked on company property.[24] Then on Labor Day, September 1, there was a clash between the sheriff's deputies, strikers, and women picketers, in which the deputies yelled at the women that they should be at home cooking and the women called the deputies scabs. The deputies opened fire, and fourteen-year-old Margaret Fazekas was shot in the back of the head as she ran away. Margaret Fazekas survived, and later explained that the doctor who treated her "said some of my brain came out, but he put it back in again, and he took a bone out of it—a small bone."[25]

Prominent labor leaders came to support both strikes, among them the feisty octogenarian Mother Jones.[26] Anarchist Carlo Tresca, a leader of the Industrial Workers of the World, spoke to the copper strikers at Calumet's Italian Hall.[27] Built in 1908, Italian Hall was a three-story showpiece for the local Italian community. In the minds of employers and mine managers, it was associated with foreigners and radicals who they considered synonymous with the WFM.[28]

Italian Hall boasted brick walls, a fireproof roof, iron fire escapes, and a 40x70 foot auditorium on the second floor, where, on Christmas Eve, 1913, the Calumet WFM Women's Auxiliary held a Christmas party for strikers' children.[29] Gifts poured in from outside to help brighten Christmas for striking families facing a Michigan winter. The Chicago Women's Trade Union League sent "little wooly hoods, stout shoes, warm flannels and coats."[30] Four-to-five hundred people crowded into the hall, mostly children eagerly awaiting Santa Claus and the promised oranges, candy, and other scarce treats. Eyewitness reports of what happened next differed, but most agreed that as the children moved toward the stage to receive gifts, a man entered the hall and yelled "Fire" several times. There was no fire—the Women's Auxiliary had not used candles on the Christmas tree for fear that the children might get hurt—but in the ensuing panic, people crowded down the stairs to escape. Apparently, someone tripped toward the bottom of the stairs. Chaos ensued as bodies piled upon one another, filling the stairwell with crushed and suffocating humanity. In the ensuing days, lists of the dead appeared in union and ethnic newspapers. These lists, combined with the Houghton county coroner's inquest, produce a frustratingly vague accounting of seventy-two dead listed in various papers to seventy-five bodies in the morgue. These imprecise figures may be incomplete, as some families took their dead home rather than to the morgue. Of the dead, at least fifty were children younger than thirteen; two were infants. Among the children were five groups of siblings: three Heikkenen brothers, three Klarich girls, three Mihelchich children, three or four Montanen children, and two Myllykangas boys. Twenty-nine mothers died with their children in the stairwell. Like the strikers overall, the dead represented many ethnicities, but Finns suffered the greatest toll, with forty-nine lost.[31]

The man who yelled "Fire" got away. Some witnesses insisted that he wore a badge of the anti-union Citizens' Alliance. Others said they were prevented from rescuing some of the victims by members of the Citizens' Alliance and Houghton County deputies who pushed them away, blocked the entrance to the hall, and kept them from untangling the bodies at the foot of the stairs.[32]

The national president of the WFM, Charles Moyer, was in the district. He told his members that the union would provide for the dead and their families, and to reject offers of money from all but union members, a policy aimed at the Citizens' Alliance, but that excluded and alienated other local citizens. Nonetheless, Moyer's position could not justify what happened next. Two days after the tragedy, some thirty members of the Citizens' Alliance led by Calumet and Hecla attorney Albert Petermann broke into Moyer's hotel room in Hancock, beat Moyer, shot him, and forced him and a bodyguard on a train for Chicago.[33]

Funerals for the victims were held December 28, 1913, at three Catholic Churches and the Finnish Apostolic and Finnish Synod Lutheran churches. Some 5,000 mourners paraded past an estimated 20,000 supporters in solemn procession to Lake View cemetery. The caskets of the adult victims were transported in horse-drawn carriages. Miners carried the children to their graves.[34]

We still don't know who yelled "Fire" in Italian Hall. A coroner's jury quickly rejected charges that a Citizens' Alliance member caused the panic. It also refused to allow translators for witnesses who could not testify in English, thus eliminating a number who claimed they could identify the culprit. No one was ever prosecuted for the tragedy, but on December 27 the editor and four staff of the Finnish Tyomies Publishing Company were arrested for printing detailed sworn statements that accused the Citizens' Alliance and sheriff's deputies of fostering the Italian Hall disaster.[35] Regardless of who yelled "Fire," there would have been no Christmas party, and no inflamed tensions in Copper Country without the strike, and the aftermath would have been different without mine management's considerable power over local officials and the local press.

One common thread in all these unhappy histories is the lack of legal justice for the victims. Neither of the self-confessed killers of Trayvon Martin or Jordan Davis was convicted for their murders. Both dead youths were in effect tried posthumously for behaving like teenagers.[36] No one was convicted for the carnage at Ludlow or for the Italian Hall tragedy. Six men were charged with murder in the Seeberville shootings; four were convicted of manslaughter; one accused detective fled to New York where he continued to work for Calumet and Hecla. But strikers were arrested in the Copper Strike by the hundreds for everything ranging from indecent language to assault with intent to murder. Eighty-eight were charged with intimidation, eighty with "rioting," sixty-one with assault and battery, fifty-eight with carrying concealed weapons, thirty-six with assault with intent to murder. Key union organizers were arrested up to seven times.[37]

Both strikes failed. John D. Rockefeller, Jr., realizing that he faced a public relations disaster, hired publicist Ivy Lee and William Lyon Mackenzie King as a labor consultant. King invented the company union as a solution for Rockefeller's labor issues.[38] In Copper Country, Italian Hall sucked any remaining energy out of the strike. Union organizers left or were forced out, and the WFM, which had spent over $800,000 on the strike, called it off after the members voted to end their struggle on April 13, 1914, just a week before the Ludlow Massacre.[39]

As the strikes ended in defeat and the courts failed the victims, the unions and bereaved parents turned to the court of public opinion. The WFM hired a film company to record the Italian Hall victims' funeral on December 28 and distributed it nationally.[40] The UMWA reached sympathizers through the four women's speaking tour. Author Upton Sinclair led a picket of the Rockefeller offices in New York and ultimately wrote two novels about Ludlow.[41] Scholars of organized labor and American progressive reform have squeezed some indirect victories from Ludlow and Italian Hall. Many Keweenaw copper mines adopted an eight-hour day, and the two strikes may have influenced national legislation to limit the hours of labor and ban child labor.[42] Italian Hall may have informed Justice Oliver Wendell Holmes' 1919 Supreme Court Decision in *Schenck v. United States* that limited the First Amendment's protection of free speech to exclude dangerous speech like "falsely shouting fire in a theater and causing a panic." Certainly, employers learned that it was very bad press to kill children, so found other methods to obstruct organized labor. These mines remained unorganized until the 1930s; the company union was ruled illegal in 1935.

Could such gradual gains satisfy Mary Petrucci and her hope that "something [might] be done to make the world a better place for all babies"? It was those words that I heard echoed in Sybrina Fulton's plea: "Use my broken heart to say to yourself, 'We cannot let this happen to anybody else's child'." Because the world is not yet safe for all babies. Mary Petrucci's deceptively simple hope, it seems to me, presents a two-part challenge. The first part is to hear and remember: "Perhaps when everyone knows about them." The next part: "something will be done," invokes the imperative to act.

Memory first. The UMWA was more successful than the WFM in seizing the terrain of memory, in part because it was able to own the literal terrain of struggle. In 1915 it bought the land the Ludlow tent colony had occupied and in 1918 dedicated a monument there to the union dead, where it has held an annual memorial commemoration ever since. The copper miners were not evicted from the company towns of the Keweenaw, but most union loyalists chose to leave or were forced out because the mines would rehire only those who renounced the union. Historian James Foster once quipped, "history is written by the literate and the sedentary."[43] The forced mobility of union miners erased their story from much local lore—at least from versions that could be safely shared. Locals still debate who was responsible for the Italian Hall tragedy, but the Hall was torn down in 1984, too-raw a reminder of a painful past. Only the arch around the front door was saved as a small memorial, now a Michigan State Historic Site.[44]

Both strikes entered cultural memory of sorts through two ballads that legendary American folk singer Woody Guthrie recorded on his 1946 album *Struggle*: "Ludlow Massacre" and "1913 Massacre." Guthrie got his inspiration from activist Ella Reeve Bloor's autobiography, *We Are Many*,[45] ghostwritten when Bloor was in her late seventies. Bloor emerges as something like the Forrest Gump of the American Left, claiming first-hand knowledge of most major labor struggles, though she played minor roles if any at Ludlow and Italian Hall. Guthrie's songs are not accurate in all details, but they kept the memories before historians cared.

These memories still inspire the union faithful. Historian Gary Kaunonen reported that he was:

> ... giving walking tours of downtown Calumet in 2006, and one of the stops was of course the Italian Hall Memorial. I was there giving the talk and at the end one of the guys in the tour said, "Okay that makes sense now." He went on to say that he was in the Michigan Corrections Officers union and just before they were taking a key vote the delegates from the Baraga and Marquette locals yelled from the back of the room, "remember Italian Hall."
>
> Almost 100 years later it had significance to those union members.[46]

Collective memory is something else, and these histories have only recently begun to enter the mainstream. During the 2013–2014 strike centennials, the governments that once vilified union labor and the local communities once torn by these conflicts took a much more proactive role in preserving their troubled pasts. The National Park Service has created a Keweenaw National Historic Park, which in June 2013 hosted a commemoration of the 1913 Italian Hall tragedy at the memorial in Calumet.[47] Michigan Technological University got federal and state humanities funding for an exhibit about the Copper Strike that travelled through the Keweenaw for the centennial year. Houghton hosted "Retrospection & Respect: Michigan's 1913–1914 Mining/Labor Strike Symposium."[48]

Colorado Governor John Hickenlooper established the Ludlow Centennial Commemoration Commission, a historic truth and reconciliation commission of sorts that included representatives from Colorado universities, History Colorado, Colorado Humanities, the Colorado National Guard, and the United Mine Workers of America.[49] The Commission and local communities hosted commemorative activities from September

2013 to December 2014, including an exhibit, "Children of Ludlow: Life in a Battle Zone, 1913–1914," at the Pueblo museum.[50] The UMWA hosted a Ludlow Centennial Remembrance Ceremony on May 18, 2014, at the Ludlow Massacre site.

The centennials drew me back to these chapters of my own work as well. The Ludlow Massacre site was designated a National Historic Landmark in 2009, an effort spearheaded by a committee I chaired for the Labor and Working Class History Association that I discussed in my 2009 lecture (see chapter 8). I also consulted with the U.S. Park Service as it developed an interpretive plan for the Keweenaw National Historic Park Visitors Center in 2009–2010. As I sat glued to the George Zimmerman trial, I was consulting with filmmakers who produced a PBS documentary "Red Metal" about the Michigan Copper Strike. As I wrote my 2014 lecture, I consulted with other filmmakers working on a documentary about Ludlow and I prepared to speak at the 100th Anniversary Commemorative Service at the Ludlow National Historic Landmark site. The personal and idiosyncratic ways that these events connect for me made me curious about their links, but cautious, too. I resisted this topic, but it wouldn't let go as I struggled to trace those connections, and my compulsion to find some meaning there.

What links and separates these troubled tales? They all involve children who died tragically and whose losses inspired someone—a parent, a union, a movement—to use their memories for positive change. The circumstances of their deaths differed. The children at Ludlow and Italian Hall suffocated; only Frank Snyder, shot by the militia at Ludlow, died of gunshot wounds. They died in grown-ups' labor disputes that affected the quality of their young lives, and that might have shaped their adult options, but they did not share a common risk of death by suffocation with most other working-class children. They died in collective struggles. Trayvon Martin and Jordan Davis, seeming victims of individual violence, nonetheless shared such risks with other Black youth. Miners' children in 1913–1914 did not wake up each morning afraid they'd be suffocated that day. A century later, African American children in the United States still face the threat of potential random armed violence.

Italian Hall and Ludlow entered popular memory as forcefully as they did because children died in both tragedies, yet the focus on child victims often obscured the larger history of industrial conflicts in which they were embedded. Children participated in the strike parades and pickets; perhaps they threw rocks and taunts at scabs, as children had in other labor conflicts.⁵¹ But children had not died in strikes before, at least not so many, so dramatically. Their fathers, though, died in large numbers, underground and of occupational diseases like silicosis. Mother Jones suggested that no one cared about the miners' conditions until women and children died. "Little children roasted alive make a front page story," she said. "Dying by inches... does not." She also famously urged the faithful to "Pray for the dead, and fight like hell for the living." ⁵² That, in more genteel language, is Sybrina Fulton's message. It was Mary Petrucci's, too.

So how might a history of tragic losses speak to the present? At the memorial ceremony in Calumet in June 2013, Calumet village President Dave Geisler called Italian Hall a "senseless act of violence" and connected it to then-recent mass shootings in an Aurora, Colorado, movie theater; the Sandy Hook, Connecticut, elementary school; and the Boston Marathon bombing. Drawing parallels between Italian Hall and these tragedies, he said, "Such violence continues today."⁵³ It does—but I think Calumet and Ludlow are more accurately linked to the deaths of Trayvon Martin and Jordan Davis, which also occurred in contexts of contested social power and which might be seen as symptoms of mass phenomena, if not as mass murders. Historian Robin D. G. Kelley contrasted the deaths of twenty school children at Sandy Hook and the murder of Trayvon Martin, writing that "In the aftermath of the Sandy Hook Elementary School massacre," the National Rifle Association and its supporters insisted "that had the teachers and administrators been armed, those twenty little kids . . . would be alive today," but that they had not "argued that had Trayvon Martin been armed, he would be alive today."⁵⁴

Trayvon Martin may evoke historical links to Ludlow and Italian Hall only for me and a handful of labor historians. He has more often evoked comparisons with other African American youths who carried the burdens of racial profiling and struggles for Black equality in past decades. Oprah Winfrey unintentionally provoked a heated argument with Fox News pundit Glenn Beck when she compared Trayvon Martin to Emmett Till, who was fourteen in August 1955 when he went from his home in Chicago to visit relatives in Mississippi and violated local norms by saying, "Bye, baby," to a White woman at a store. Kidnapped four days later by her husband and brother-in-law, Till's body was fished out of the Tallahatchie River a few days later, bound to a cotton gin fan, a bullet in his skull, his eye gouged out and one side of his forehead crushed. His mother, Mamie Till-Mobley, insisted on an open casket to "let the world see what they did to my boy," and this picture was burned into the memory of an

American generation, especially young African Americans. Till's killers were acquitted by an all-White jury. They then sold their story of his murder to *Look* magazine for $4000. Beck found it "offensive" for Winfrey to compare Till and Martin. He "call[ed] it evil to compare these events" because, he said, Zimmerman acted in self-defense but Till was brutally murdered by racists.[55]

The Winfrey-Beck debate captured a national discourse across a racial divide that cannot be bridged until we examine law in the sometimes unconscious but nonetheless structured racial contexts within which it operates. The dead children at Ludlow and Italian Hall, like Emmett Till and like too many twenty-first-century American youngsters, died then and are dying now in part because they were and are devalued as racialized "others." The names of the Italian Hall victims were not publicized at the time, at least partly because their names marked them as "others"—mostly Croatians, Serbs, and Finns—therefore foreign, maybe socialists. Until quite recently the United Mine Workers invoked the tragic loss of women and children at Ludlow but rarely used their names, because in 1914 names like Pedregone, Costa, and Petrucci marked them as dark, foreign, outsiders. When Mary Petrucci testified before the U.S. Industrial Relations Commission investigating the Ludlow Massacre, the *New York Times* reported that the audience was in tears. It went on to say that Petrucci was born in Colorado "of Italian parents twenty-four years ago and married when but 16. She spoke good English," it marveled, "and impressed the audience as a woman of refinement above her station."[56] *Above her station.* Unexamined racist assumptions suffused all these lost young lives. But a century later, the risk of racial violence had receded for Italian youth.

The charge of racial profiling sparked heated controversy about the Trayvon Martin and Jordan Davis murders, and these exchanges recorded personal histories of racism. On March 15, 2012 *Washington Post* columnist Jonathan Capehart wrote: "One of the burdens of being a black male is carrying the heavy weight of other people's suspicions. One minute you're going about your life, the next you could be pleading for it, if you're lucky. And far too many aren't." Capehart listed the lessons his mother taught him to survive: "**'Don't run in public.'** Lest someone think you're suspicious. **'Don't run while carrying anything in your hands.'** Lest someone think you stole something. **'Don't talk back to the police.'** Lest you give them a reason to take you to jail or worse."[57]

Other pundits echoed Capehart, climaxing on July 15, after the Zimmerman acquittal. Bracing for the "impossibly heartbreaking conversation" he could not bring himself to have with his children, *New York Times* columnist Charles Blow asked, "'Now, what do I tell my boys?' We used to say not to run in public because that might be seen as suspicious, like they'd stolen something. But according to Zimmerman, Martin drew his suspicion at least in part because he was walking too slowly. So what do I tell my boys now? At what precise pace should a black man walk to avoid suspicion? And can they ever stop walking away, or running away, and simply stand their ground?"[58] The *Washington Post*'s Eugene Robinson wrote:

> Our society considers young black men to be dangerous, interchangeable, expendable, guilty until proven innocent. This is the conversation about race that we desperately need to have—but probably, as in the past, will try our best to avoid.... I don't know if the jury, which included no African Americans, consciously or unconsciously bought into this racist way of thinking—there's really no other word. But it hardly matters, because police and prosecutors initially did. The assumption underlying their ho-hum approach to the case was that Zimmerman had the right to self-defense but Martin—young, male, black—did not. The assumption was that Zimmerman would fear for his life in a hand-to-hand struggle but Martin—young, male, black—would not.... The conversation we need to have is about how black men, even black boys, are denied the right to be young, to be vulnerable, to make mistakes.[59]

The kids weighed in, too. Throughout the United States, demonstrators dressed in hoodies—as Martin was when he was killed—rallied to protest the verdict, to raise issues of racial profiling, and to contest Stand Your Ground laws. Howard University students posted a video on YouTube of students wearing hoodies asking if they, like Martin, should be presumed suspicious.[60] Florida students organized The Dream Defenders, who occupied Governor Rick Scott's office for a month, trying to get him to call a special legislative session to consider their "Trayvon Martin Act," to address racial profiling, "Stand Your Ground" laws, and school-to-prison pipeline issues. They failed to convince Scott or to get their special session, but they did get Florida House Speaker Will Weatherford to hold a hearing on Stand Your Ground.[61] On March 10, 2014, Rev. Al Sharpton led a march of protestors, including Tracy Martin and Sybrina Fulton, to the Florida state capitol. Calling Florida "ground zero" in the movement against Stand Your Ground laws, Sharpton said that "laws that tell people that they can shoot first and then ask questions later" violate "civil rights. . . . The law in effect says . . . if you imagine I'm a threat—you have the right to kill me."[62]

A majority of states have some version of Stand Your Ground. Texas A&M economists found in 2012 that their adoption correlated with a statistically significant 8 percent increase in murders and manslaughters.[63] Just as the children killed at Ludlow and Italian Hall were casualties of larger class and ethnic inequalities, it is not just African American children who die disproportionately from guns. According to the Center for Disease Control and Prevention (CDC), 11,078 Americans were murdered by firearms in 2010. That year homicide dropped below the top ten causes of death nationally for the first time since 1965, but not for people of color. CDC data indicated that a White person was five times as likely to commit suicide with a gun as to be shot with one, but an African American was five times more likely to be killed by someone else with a gun than to use one for suicide.[64] Stand Your Ground law enforcement reflects racial bias as well. According to one study using FBI data on homicides from 2005 to 2009, "White people who kill Black people in 'Stand Your Ground' states" were over three and a half times more likely than Blacks to be cleared of murder.[65] Not surprisingly, then, African Americans favor stricter gun control almost four to one, while Whites are about evenly split.[66]

Although President Obama weighed in for gun control, his direct comments on race focused less on law and politics, and more on the difficult conversation about deeply held racist assumptions. In a powerful speech during the 2008 presidential campaign, he spoke of his White grandmother, "a woman," he said, "who helped raise me, a woman who sacrificed again and again for me, a woman who loves me as much as she loves anything in this world, but a woman who once confessed her fear of black men who passed by her on the street."[67]

After the Zimmerman verdict, on July 19, the President shared his own experience:

> . . . when Trayvon Martin was first shot I said that this could have been my son. Another way of saying that is Trayvon

> Martin could have been me 35 years ago. . . . There are very few African American men in this country who haven't had the experience of being followed when they were shopping in a department store. That includes me. There are very few African American men who haven't had the experience of walking across the street and hearing the locks click on the doors of cars. That happens to me. . . . There are very few African Americans who haven't had the experience of getting on an elevator and a woman clutching her purse nervously and holding her breath until she had a chance to get off. That happens often.

". . . [T]hose sets of experiences inform how the African American community interprets what happened one night in Florida," he went on. The President suggested that a conversation on race could happen most honestly outside the political arena, in "families and churches and workplaces," and challenged Americans to "ask . . . am I wringing as much bias out of myself as I can? Am I judging people as much as I can, based on not the color of their skin, but the content of their character? That would be an appropriate exercise in the wake of this tragedy." He wanted Americans to recognize that African Americans experienced "a lot of pain around what happened" because, he said, "the African American community is looking at this issue through a set of experiences and a history that doesn't go away."[68]

History that doesn't go away becomes painfully vivid through the repeated deaths of children, through the burdens some children have shouldered to make change. It may not matter which pieces of a tangled past speak directly to the present predicament—it could be Italian Hall and Ludlow, or Birmingham and Selma, or residential schools, or Emmett Till's Money, Mississippi. Mamie Till-Mobley said in a 1996 interview that "People really didn't know that things this horrible could take place. And the fact that it happened to a child, that ma[d]e all the difference in the world."[69]

Sybrina Fulton has staked her efforts for change in the hope that her son's death might "make all the difference in the world."

> Trayvon was my son, but Trayvon is also your son. I just ask you, as a mother, as a grandmother, as an aunt, an uncle, a grandfather, to wrap your mind around what has happened. . . .

Wrap your mind around no prom for Trayvon. . . . No college for Trayvon. No grandkids coming from Trayvon. All because of a law, a law that has prevented the person who shot and killed my son to be held accountable and to pay for this awful crime.[70]

Sybrina Fulton suggested that George Zimmerman might not have killed her son if there had been no Stand Your Ground law in Florida to protect him from being held accountable for murder. Perhaps not; perhaps a White jury would have acquitted him anyway. President Obama did not directly address Stand Your Ground; he did invite Trayvon Martin's and Jordan Davis's parents to the White House February 27, 2014, when he announced his My Brother's Keeper Initiative to provide support and opportunities for Black boys and men. And he invoked the same claim of common kinship as Sybrina Fulton, asking that we remember "that we may have different stories, but we hold common hopes; that we may not look the same and we may not have come from the same place, but we all want to move in the same direction—towards a better future for our children and our grandchildren."[71]

These murdered children compel me, but so do the poignant hopes that Mamie Till-Mobley and Sybrina Fulton and Mary Petrucci have each tried to wring from their murdered children. In 2009 I was honored to speak at the dedication of the Ludlow National Historic Landmark, and I planned to conclude with Mary Petrucci's story. During the ten-minute ride from my hotel in Trinidad to the Ludlow site, I learned that a ninety-year-old man named Frank Petrucci would be there. Five years after the Ludlow massacre, Mary and Thomas Petrucci began having babies again. They named the first three after the children who died at Ludlow; Frank was named for the six-month-old infant who died in his mother's arms. Before the program, I introduced myself and asked Mr. Petrucci if it was okay for me to speak about his mother. Then, in the most extraordinary experience I have had as an historian, as I spoke I could see nothing but Frank Petrucci's face—that held at that moment the legacy of the tragic past and of parents who dared to bring more babies into a still-imperfect world.

Mary Petrucci, according to her son and granddaughter, never sang again, but she risked enough hope to love more children.[72] My first eagerly awaited grandchild was due the month after my 2014 lecture. As I spoke, I knew he would be born into a world not yet secure for all children. That reality certainly drew me to these stories, and I had to acknowledge that personal and presentist frame. I feared, as well, that these histories might only reinforce Canadian images of a violent and racist America. Still, I was pulled to these challenging stories for the difficult lessons they can wring from histories we'd rather avoid—the painful lessons of "a history that doesn't go away." History that doesn't go away continues to wreak human consequences. It demands difficult questions and choices. If I remember Ludlow and Italian Hall, Emmett Till and Trayvon Martin, then what am I doing to confront my own bias, what acts can I choose to make a better world for all babies? Or at least for some. Histories that don't go away may break our hearts. How we use them might, in some small ways, make history.

NOTES

Thanks to Victoria Buckholz for her research assistance.

1. For accounts of Trayvon Martin's death and public reaction, see Hasan Kwame Jeffries, "Justice Denied: The Killing of Trayvon Martin in Historical Perspective," *Origins: Current Events in Historical Perspective* 7:2 (November 2013), https://origins.osu.edu/article/justice-denied-killing-trayvon-martin-historical-perspective/page/0/1, accessed March 2, 2014; Jonathan Capehart, "Under 'suspicion': The Killing of Trayvon Martin," *Washington Post*, March 18, 2012; Greg Botelho, CNN, "What happened the night Trayvon Martin died," May 23, 2012, https://www.cnn.com/2012/05/18/justice/florida-teen-shooting-details/index.html, accessed May 27, 2021; Julia Dahl, CBS News, "Trayvon Martin Shooting: A Timeline of Events," July 12, 2013, https://www.cbsnews.com/news/trayvon-martin-shooting-a-timeline-of-events/, accessed May 27, 2021.

2. I watched most of the trial, which was televised. See also *Washington Post* Editorial Board, "Mr. Zimmerman goes free, but tragedy remains," *Washington Post*, July 14, 2013; Jeffries, "Justice Denied."

3. Sybrina Fulton's address can be viewed on-line via YouTube, https://www.youtube.com/watch?v=kxWs-YtYa4E, as well as on several news links.

4. Michael Dunn was found guilty of attempted murder of the three surviving teens in the car; he had not been found guilty of Jordan Davis's murder when I delivered my 2014 lecture but was convicted of Davis' murder in a second trial on October 1, 2014 and was sentenced to life in prison plus 90 years. His appeal was denied. See Samuel Momodu, "Jordan Russell Davis (1995–2012)," *Black Past*, October 6, 2017, https://www.blackpast.org/african-american-history/davis-jordan-russell-1995-2012/, accessed May 26, 2017; Associated Press, "Loud music shooting: Michael Dunn guilty of attempted murder," February 15, 2014; Derek Kinner, "Michael Dunn Verdict: Florida Man Found Guilty Of Attempted Murder In Loud-Music Trial," *Huffington Post*, February 15, 2014; Julia Dahl, CBS News, "'Loud music' shooter Michael Dunn gets life in prison," October 17, 2014, https://www.cbsnews.com/news/michael-dunn-loud-music-shooter-gets-life-in-prison/, accessed May 26, 2021.

5. Katy Hall, Jan Diehm, and Alissa Scheller, "The Horrific Risk Of Gun Violence For Black Kids In America, In 4 Charts," *Huffington Post*, August 19, 2014, https://www.huffpost.

com/entry/black-children-gun-deaths_n_5692423, accessed May 28, 2021; Children's Defense Fund, "Protect Children, Not Guns 2012" (Washington, DC: Children's Defense Fund, 2012). According to Everytown Research and Policy, by 2024, more than 4,300 children and teens (ages 0 to 19) were shot and killed annually and more than 17,000 were shot and wounded. An estimated three million children witnessed a shooting each year. Gun violence continued to affect children of color disproportionately. Black children and teens in the United States were more than eighteen times more likely than White children to die by gun homicide, and thirteen times more likely to be hospitalized for a firearm assault than White children. Latinx children and teens were more than three times more likely to die by gun homicide than White children, https://everytownresearch.org/report/the-impact-of-gun-violence-on-children-and-teens/, accessed June 2, 2025.

6   Hall, Diehm, and Scheller, "The Horrific Risk of Gun Violence." In 2022, the Johns Hopkins University Bloomberg School of Public Health reported that for three straight years gun violence was the leading cause of death among children and teens, outstripping both cancer and automobile crashes. Black children continued to suffer disproportionately. In 2022, in the 1 to 17 age group, Black children and teens had a gun death rate 18 times higher than that of White children. See "New Report Highlights U.S. 2022 Gun-Related Deaths: Firearms Remain Leading Cause of Death for Children and Teens, and Disproportionately Affect People of Color," September 12, 2024, https://publichealth.jhu.edu/2024/guns-remain-leading-cause-of-death-for-children-and-teens, accessed June 2, 2025.

7   Lucy McBath left a thirty-year career as a Delta Airlines flight attendant to run for Congress to further her fight for gun control. She became the first Democrat since 1979 to win election from Georgia's 6th Congressional District in 2018, a seat formerly held by Republicans Newt Gingrich and Johnny Isakson. She was re-elected in 2020, 2022, and 2024.

8   The Trayvon Martin Foundation, https://www.trayvonmartinfoundation.org/, accessed March 28, 2014. The mission was subsequently reworded: "The Trayvon Martin Foundation was established by Sybrina Fulton & Tracy Martin in March of 2012. We are a non-profit organization whose main purpose is to provide both emotional and financial support to families who have lost a child to gun violence. Our goal is to shift the conversation from intervention to reform. Our programs are strengthening families through leadership, support, guidance, and counseling. The Foundation is supported by a network of individuals and companies who share a unified vision of a world free of senseless killings. Our core mission is to gain fellowship toward personal restoration and ultimately community building." Accessed May 29, 2021.

9   The most comprehensive published history of the 1913–1914 UMWA Ludlow strike is George S. McGovern and Leonard F. Guttridge, *The Great Coal Field War* (Boston: Houghton Mifflin, 1972). Other superb accounts of the Colorado coal wars can be found in Priscilla Long, *Where the Sun Never Shines: A History of America's Bloody Coal Industry* (New York: Paragon House, 1989); Howard Zinn, "The Colorado Coal Strike, 1913–14," in *Three Strikes: Miners, Musicians, Salesgirls and the Fighting Spirit of Labor's Last Century*, eds. Howard Zinn, Dana Frank, and Robin D. G. Kelley (Boston: Beacon Press, 2001), 5–55; and John Graham, "Introduction" to Upton Sinclair, *The Coal War* (Boulder, CO: Colorado Associated University Press, 1976), vi–xcii. The most recent books are Scott Matelle, *Blood Passion: The Ludlow Massacre and Class War in the American West* (New Brunswick, NJ: Rutgers University Press, 2007) and Thomas G. Andrews, *Killing for Coal: America's Deadliest Labor War* (Cambridge, MA: Harvard University Press, 2008), which places the events in the very broad context of environmental history.

10 McGovern and Guttridge, *The Great Coalfield War*, 22. Between 1887–1897 the national average was 2.56 deaths per thousand coal miners; in Colorado the rate was much higher, 4.64 per thousand. Between 1884–1912, Colorado's rate jumped to 6.81, while the national average

was 3.12. James Brian Whiteside, "Protecting the Life and Limb of our Workmen: Work, Death, and Regulation in the Rocky Mountain Coal Mining Industry" (PhD diss., University of Colorado, 1986), 134.

11 McGovern and Guttridge, *The Great Coalfield War*, 102; Graham, "Introduction," xxvi. This section repeats material in Chapter 8, where I discuss the Ludlow strike and the efforts to achieve National Historic Landmark status for the Ludlow Massacre site.

12 Long, *Where the Sun Never Shines*, 273; Graham, "Introduction," xxxiv.

13 McGovern and Guttridge, *The Great Coalfield War*, 134, 146, 169.

14 McGovern and Guttridge, *The Great Coalfield War*, 210-31.

15 McGovern and Guttridge, *The Great Coalfield War*, 227-28, 231, 234-35; Long, *Where the Sun Never Shines*, 291-93; "Two Women Depict Battle of Ludlow," *New York Times*, February 4, 1915.

16 "Mary Petrucci Remembers Her Four Little Children," *New York Tribune*, February 4, 1915, https://weneverforget.org/hellraisers-journal-mrs-mary-petrucci-of-ludlow-there-is-sorrow-in-our-hearts-but-there-is-no-dishonor/#more-5985, accessed May 28, 2021; quoted in Long, *Where the Sun Never Shines*, 300.

17 Gary Kaunonen and Aaron Goings, *Community in Conflict: A Working-Class History of the 1913–1914 Michigan Copper Strike and the Italian Hall Tragedy* (East Lansing: Michigan State University Press, 2013). See also Vernon H. Jenson, *Heritage of Conflict: Labor Relations in the Nonferrous Metals Industry Up to 1930* (Ithaca: Cornell University Press, 1950), 272-88, and Larry D. Lankton, *Cradle to Grave: Life, and Work and Death at the Lake Superior Copper Mines* (New York: Oxford University Press, 1991).

18 Lankton, *Cradle to Grave*, 100-04; Aaron Goings, "100 Years Later: Michigan's 1913–14 Copper Country Strike," *Labor Online*, Labor and Working Class History Association website, July 21, 2013, https://www.lawcha.org/2013/07/25/100-years-later-michigans-1913-14-copper-country-strike/, accessed March 30, 2014.

19 Kaunonen and Goings, *Community in Conflict*, 149-65; Goings, "100 Years Later"; Jenson, *Heritage of Conflict*, esp. 277.

20 McGovern and Guttridge, 51-52. The figures are from *Report Upon the Possible Service of the Young Men's Christian Association the Mining Communities of the Colorado Fuel and Iron Company, 1915*, cited in a superb unpublished essay that Camille Guérin-Gonzales prepared as a member of the Labor and Working Class History Association Ludlow Committee, "Ludlow Monument NHL Nomination Narrative Draft," 5, in author's possession.

21 Kaunonen and Goings, *Community in Conflict*, 45-65, 117-19.

22 Kaunonen and Goings, *Community in Conflict*, 119-21; 150.

23 Kaunonen and Goings, *Community in Conflict*, 131-33; McGovern and Guttridge, *The Coalfield War*, 90, 122-23; Long, *Where the Sun Never Shines*, 267, 278.

24 Kaunonen and Goings, *Community in Conflict*, 149, 153-54.

25 Kaunonen and Goings, *Community in Conflict*, 153, 155-56; Margaret Fazekas Testimony, "Conditions in the Copper Mines of Michigan: Hearings Before a Subcommittee of the Committee on Mines and Mining, House of Representatives, Sixty-third Congress, Second Session, Pursuant to H. Res. 387, a Resolution Authorizing and Directing the Committee on Mines and Mining to Make an Investigation of the Conditions in the Copper Mines of Michigan" (Washington, DC: U.S. Government Printing Office, 1914).

26 Kaunonen and Goings, *Community in Conflict*, 116, 124-25; McGovern and Guttridge, *The Coalfield War*, 114-15, 171-72, 189-92.

27 Kaunonen and Goings, *Community in Conflict*, 176-77.

28 Kaunonen and Goings, *Community in Conflict*, 176–77, 167–73; Historic American Buildings Survey, Italian Hall (Societa Mutua Beneficenza Italiana), HABS No. MI-425, Calumet, Houghton County Michigan, Written Historical and Descriptive Data, National Park Service, U.S. Department of the Interior, Washington, D.C., https://web.archive.org/web/20170223052714/https://cdn.loc.gov/master/pnp/habshaer/mi/mi0600/mi0643/data/mi0643data.pdf, accessed May 30, 2021.

29 For contemporary coverage of the Italian Hall Tragedy, see *New York Times*, "Xmas Tree Panic Costs 80 Lives," December 25, 1913; "Wants U.S. Inquiry in Calumet Horror," *New York Times*, December 26, 2013; "Calumet Inquiry Urged on Congress," *New York Times*, December 29, 2013. The best published account is Kaunonen and Goings, *Community in Conflict*, 167–98; see also Goings, "100 Years Later."

30 *Miners' Bulletin*, December 24, 1913, quoted in Kaunonen and Goings, *Community in Conflict*, 180.

31 Most sources say seventy-three died at Italian Hall, but the exact figure may be obscured by conflicting accounts of the dead. See Kaunonen and Goings, *Community in Conflict*, 168, 181–87, 190–92.

32 Kaunonen and Goings, *Community in Conflict*, 186–89, 199–219.

33 Kaunonen and Goings, *Community in Conflict*, 192, 222–27.

34 Kaunonen and Goings, *Community in Conflict*, 194–95; "Calumet Buries Dead," *Washington Post*, December 29, 1913.

35 Kaunonen and Goings, *Community in Conflict*, 186, 190–94, 200–201, 203; "Acquit Union's Foes of Calumet Panic," *New York Times*, January 1, 2014.

36 See note 4 above.

37 Kaunonen and Goings, *Community in Conflict*, 149–51, 153–56, 194.

38 McGovern and Guttridge, *The Great Coalfield War*, 282–84, 289–92, 295–96, 302, 304, 329–31, 335; Long, *Where the Sun Never Shines*, 312–13.

39 Kaunonen and Goings, *Community in Conflict*, 229, 232–33, 240–41.

40 Kaunonen and Goings, *Community in Conflict*, 195–97.

41 Graham, "Introduction," lvi–lxii. Sinclair's Ludlow novels were *King Coal* (1917) and *The Coal War* (1976). *King Coal* is the better known. The *Coal War*, billed as a sequel, could not find a publisher because it was so clearly based on Ludlow, and was finally published in 1976 through the efforts of Sinclair scholar John Graham.

42 Goings, "100 Years Later."

43 James Foster, "The Ten Day Tramps," *Labor History* 23:4 (Autumn 1982): 608–23.

44 Lucy Hough, "100 Year Ago, The Italian Hall Disaster," https://upsupply.co/journal/italian-hall-disaster-1913, accessed May 30, 2021.

45 Ella Reeve Bloor, *We Are Many* (New York: International Publishers, 1940), 118–38.

46 Quoted in an e-mail from Aaron Goings to author, March 28, 2014.

47 Kurt Hauglie, "Ceremony conducted at Italian Hall site," *The Daily Mining Gazette*, June 21, 2013.

48 "Archives Premiers New Exhibit about 1913 Strike," Michigan Tech Archives Blog, October 28, 2012, Calumet/Archives%20Premiers%20New…%20_%20Michigan%20Tech%20Michigan%20Tech%20Archives%20Blog.htm, accessed February 26, 2014; "Registration for UP History Conference Extended through Monday," Michigan Copper Miners' Strike 2013–2014 Centennial, June 21, 2013, Calumet/Registration%20for%20UP%20History%20Conference%20Extended%20Through%20Monday%20_.htm, accessed February 26, 2014.

49 Members of the commission were: scholars Thomas Andrews (University of Colorado), Karin Larkin (University of Colorado, Colorado Springs), Fawn-Amber Montoya (Colorado State University-Pueblo), Jonathan Rees (Colorado State University-Pueblo), and Dean Saitta (University of Denver); Robert Butero (United Mine Workers of America); public historians William Convery (History Colorado), Dawn DiPrince (Pueblo History Museum, History Colorado), and Victoria Miller (Bessemer Historical Society); Josephine Jones (Colorado Humanities); and Adam Morgan (Colorado National Guard). "Commemoration Commission, Ludlow 100 website, https://ludlow100.wordpress.com/commission/, accessed June 7, 2021.

50 "Children of Ludlow: Life in a Battle Zone," History Colorado website, https://www.historycolorado.org/exhibit/children-ludlow, accessed June 7, 2021.

51 Kathleen Welch Chapman, oral history interview, Wheat Ridge, Colorado, April 27, 1979.

52 Mary Field Parton, ed., Mary Harris Jones, *The Autobiography of Mother Jones* (Chicago: Charles H. Kerr, 1925), 19, 40–41.

53 Hauglie, "Ceremony conducted at Italian Hall site." Twelve people were killed and seventy injured in a mass shooting June 20, 2012, at the Century 16 movie theater in Aurora, Colorado. Twenty-six people were murdered, twenty of them children, in a mass shooting at the Sandy Hook Elementary School, Newtown, Connecticut, December 14, 2012. On April 13, 2013, two terrorists detonated two homemade bombs at the running of the Boston Marathon, killing three people and injuring hundreds others, seventeen of whom lost limbs.

54 Robin D. G. Kelley, "The U.S. V. Trayvon Martin: How the System Worked," *Huffington Post*, July 15, 2013, also posted on UCLA Newsroom, July 16, 2013, https://newsroom.ucla.edu/stories/the-u-s-v-trayvon-martin-how-the-247451, accessed July 25, 2013.

55 "Glenn Beck: Oprah's Trayvon Martin Comment 'Offensive,' 'Evil' (VIDEO)," HuffPost, August 7, 2013, https://www.huffpost.com/entry/glenn-beck-oprah-trayvon-martin_n_3719560, accessed February 17, 2014. For Emmett Till's murder, see Stephen J. Whitfield, *A Death in the Delta: The Story of Emmett Till* (Baltimore: The Johns Hopkins University Press, 1991) and *Eyes on the Prize*, Episode 1 "Awakenings (1954–1956)" (series produced for PBS by Blackside, Inc., Henry Hampton producer). "The Shocking Story of Approved Killing in Mississippi," *Look*, January 24, 1956, published the confessions of J.W. Milam and Roy Bryant, two White men who had been acquitted in the 1955 kidnapping and murder of Emmett Till.

56 "TWO WOMEN DEPICT BATTLE OF LUDLOW: Audience in Tears as Miner's Wife Tells of Smothering of Three Children," *New York Times*, February 4, 1915.

57 Jonathan Capehart, "Under 'suspicion': The killing of Trayvon Martin," *Washington Post*, March 18, 2012.

58 Charles M. Blow, "The Whole System Failed Trayvon Martin," *New York Times*, July 15, 2013.

59 Eugene Robinson, "Black boys denied the right to be young," *Washington Post*, July 15, 2013.

60 Howard University Trayvon Martin "Am I Suspicious?" Campaign Video, YouTube, posted March 25, 2012, https://www.youtube.com/watch?v=rH5bB8HUWFs, accessed July 17, 1913.

61 "The Dream Defenders' occupation to end racial profiling and repeal Stand Your Ground laws in Florida, 2013," Global Nonviolent Action Database, https://nvdatabase.swarthmore.edu/content/dream-defenders-occupation-end-racial-profiling-and-repeal-stand-your-ground-laws-florida-20, accessed June 2, 2021.

62 Associated Press, "Al Sharpton leads protests against Florida's stand-you-ground law," *The Guardian*, March 10, 2014.
63 "Texas A&M Study Says Castle-Doctrine Laws Increase Homicides, Don't Deter Crime," *Dallas Observer*, June 12, 2012.
64 Sherry L. Murphy, B. Jiaquan Xu, and Kenneth D. Kochanek, "Deaths: Final Data for 2010," Division of Vital Statistics, Centers for Disease Control, *National Vital Statistics Report* 61:4 (May 8, 2013). By 2024 deaths from firearms were declining, the result of some gun control laws and declining gun sales. Deaths from firearms peaked during the pandemic at over 21,000 in 2021. The figure for 2023 was almost 19,000; in 2024, there were 16,576 U.S. firearms deaths, excluding suicide; 5151 children and teenagers were shot in 2024, of whom 1403 died. "Gun Violence by the Numbers in 2024," *The Trace*, https://www.thetrace.org/2024/12/data-gun-violence-shooting-stats-america/, accessed June 3, 2025.
65 Jill Reilly, "White people who kill black people in 'Stand Your Ground' states are 354% more likely to be cleared of murder," *Daily Mail*, July 15, 2013, https://www.dailymail.co.uk/news/article-2363939/White-people-kill-black-people-Stand-Your-Ground-states-354-likely-cleared-murder-Fresh-questions-self-defence-law-wake-Zimmerman-verdict.html, accessed July 18, 2013.
66 ABC News/Washington Post Poll: Hot-Button Issues, April 30, 2009, https://abcnews.go.com/images/PollingUnit/1089a6HotButtonIssues.pdf, accessed June 3, 2021.
67 "A More Perfect Union," speech delivered by Senator Barack Obama in Philadelphia, March 18, 2008. The full text of Senator Obama's historic speech is widely available on the internet. I accessed the transcript from *The Wall Street Journal*, March 18, 2008.
68 "Remarks by the President on Trayvon Martin," The White House, Office of the Press Secretary, July 19, 2013, https://obamawhitehouse.archives.gov/the-press-office/2013/07/19/remarks-president-trayvon-martin, accessed June 7, 2013.
69 Mamie Till Mosley in an interview in December, 1996 with Devery S. Anderson, author of *Emmett Till: The Murder That Shocked the World and Propelled the Civil Rights Movement* (Jackson: University Press of Mississippi, 2015).
70 Sybrina Fulton to National Urban League, Philadelphia, Friday, July 26, 2013, YouTube https://www.youtube.com/watch?v=kxWs-YtYa4E.
71 "Transcript: Obama announces 'My Brother's Keeper'," CNN, February 27, 2014, https://www.cnn.com/2014/02/27/politics/obama-brothers-keeper-transcript/index.html, accessed March 22, 2014.
72 Interview with Mary Elaine Petrucci, Frank Petrucci, and Mary Rose, Denver, August 8, 2013.

Approaching the Next Threshold:
2015–2017

In 2014–2015 I was honored to serve as President of the Western History Association (WHA), my primary professional organization since 1986. That honor brought with it the opportunity to appoint the program committee, to help shape the 2015 annual conference program, and to offer a presidential address. The 2015 WHA conference marked a high point and culmination of my career as a historian of the North American Wests. The 2015–2016 academic year was my last year in the classroom. After a final research leave in 2016–2017, I retired from the University of Calgary.

For my presidential address, I chose to reflect on the scholarship in western women's history that engaged me throughout my career. I had served on the Steering Committee for the 1983 Women's West conference, the first conference devoted to western women's history.[1] One of the products of that conference was an organization, the Coalition for Western Women's History, which still meets annually at the WHA conference and supports scholarship on women, gender, and sexuality in the North American Wests. I assessed the progress toward integrating women and gender into western history in my 2015 WHA presidential address, "Halfway Across that Line: Gender at the Threshold of History in the North American West."[2] In February, 2016, I presented it as my last Chair's Lecture.

I returned to some themes of earlier lectures: borders and borderlands; differences of race, class, gender, and nation and how to bridge them; categories of inclusion and exclusion in the ways we imagine history and community; connections and disconnects between public and private acts in history and historical narratives. I brought new research to the themes and subjects of earlier lectures. Mahidiweash—Buffalo Bird Woman—appeared in my 2001 lecture. In the interim I had worked with the field notes of anthropologist Gilbert Wilson, who recorded her story, and was able to compare his records of what she said with the versions he published in *Buffalo Bird Woman's Garden* and *Waheenee*, the texts through which historians had learned her history.[3] I returned to the international cast of border-crossing women homesteaders, the subjects of my 2011 lecture. By 2015 I had extended the study to cover all the women who succeeded in gaining title to their claims in the first two decades the Devils Lake Land Office operated. My case studies had swelled from 121 women who won their claims in the first decade, who I discussed in 2011, to 773 women who succeeded in the first two decades. With the help of historians Heather Devine and Michel Hogue I had located Métis women homesteaders more clearly in their historical contexts and communities.

337

Some of the people and scholars in earlier lectures appeared again because they had formatively influenced my work. May Wing, who I first interviewed in 1976, continued to inspire my efforts to write history as "ordinary people" experienced and made it. Carolyn Heilbrun's *Writing a Woman's Life* continued to influence my thinking about the importance of historical narratives.[4] I began, as I had in 2003, with a key scene in John Sayles' movie *Lone Star*, because it so vividly summarized the political and cultural processes of bridging borders. And, to be honest, because *Lone Star* remains my favorite movie, and so clearly challenges the boring and biased Texas history classes of my childhood.

Having had the opportunity to draw together so much of my scholarship in my presidential address, I chose a different way to close my teaching career as I prepared to retire from the University of Calgary in 2017. Instead of attempting a final Chair's Lecture, I hosted a conference featuring some of the graduate students with whom I had worked at the University of New Mexico and the University of Calgary. The "Torches Passed and Present" conference highlighted their diverse work and career paths and allowed me to celebrate the graduate teaching that was one of the great pleasures of my professional life. Here, I present an essay that combines my introduction to the conference and my closing remarks.

Retirement, I have found, is not so much an event as a process. Part of that process is letting go and trusting others to carry on the work in their own ways. As my friends and family will attest, I have a few control issues, and I didn't expect letting go to be easy. The "Torches Passed" conference became an opportunity to share professional space with former students who had become valued colleagues and who would continue their careers as I ended mine. It was a useful ritual along the path of retirement.

This book has been another useful part of that journey, a way to reflect on recurring themes in my work, and on my border-crossing journey. "Halfway Across That Line" comes from Chucho Montoya, the fictional character in *Lone Star*, who draws a line in the sand and issues the challenge for any border crosser: "Bird flying south—you think he sees that line? Rattlesnake, javelina—whatever you got—halfway across that line they don't start thinking different. So why should a man?"[5] Or a woman.

Chucho Montoya was right. Crossing the 49th Parallel did not immediately change how I thought. But over time the change did jar my thinking and expanded the perspectives from which I viewed my work and my world.

My border crossing adventure was far easier than most. I was not a refugee from famine, war, poverty, pogrom, or other violence. I arrived with a job; I spoke the language. The experience was, nonetheless, profound. I was over fifty when I arrived in Canada. I was formed in the United States and had chosen professional and personal paths that responded directly to American history and U.S. social concerns. I remain in fundamental ways American, even as I have developed Canadian roots and loyalties, and as my identity has subtly included Canada as well.

But there are differences, rooted in part in childhood and in my formative school years. I spoke English when I got here and have learned to be deliberate about how I spell it for different contexts and audiences. I usually remember when to use lab*our*, neighb*our*, fav*our*, flav*our*, and col*our*, but they still look odd to me. I carefully used Canadian spellings in my book manuscript, only to be overruled by my editor, so all those carefully inserted "u's" came back out. I can recite the American presidents in order, but not the British monarchs. In a habit probably rooted as much in generation as culture, I still think in miles and Fahrenheit, but I now automatically translate from kilometers and Centigrade. Years of traveling back and forth from Canada to the United States and navigating changing exchange rates have taught me that money is an abstraction. Having spent considerable time mentally converting Canadian dollars into U.S. dollars and back again or trying to translate kilometers per liter into miles per gallon, I finally realized that it doesn't matter how much a quart or liter of milk costs on either side of the border if I have enough money to pay for it.

I have often been surprised with realizations of my growing bi-national identification. One of the earliest occurred during the women's hockey championship game at the 2002 Winter Olympics. In retrospect, the fact that I was engrossed with women's hockey at all was one sign that I'd been in Canada for more than one winter. In the final game between the Canadian and U.S. women's hockey teams I found myself reflexively cheering for Canada and crying tears of joy when the Canadian women triumphed. I am no longer surprised by such moments, though they still pop up occasionally at odd times.

Acculturation has been a two-way process. As I became more at home in Canada, I developed a new capacity to view the United States with curiosity from the outside. I can be surprised that American drivers don't stop for me as I wait on a curb. In Calgary, traffic would grind to a halt if I put so much as a toenail into the street. I cringe now when I hear an American tourist exclaim, "Canadians are just like us," and assume it's a compliment. I remain distressed by all the social ills that led me to study American social movements and provided the subjects of some of my lectures. And I have become rooted enough in Canada to feel comfortable being similarly distressed by Canadian quirks and social ills. It's part of feeling at home and being committed to home. Some people have summer cottages. I have two countries.

Part of belonging to two countries is remaining engaged with events in both. It has often been frustrating to witness events in the United States from the Canadian side of the border, to not fully share celebratory moments or to helplessly witness distressing ones. I've witnessed both U.S. tragedy and triumph in the quarter century since I left, from 9/11 through Barack Obama's election as president to the COVID-19 pandemic and the political polarization of the 2020s. The country I left in 1999 is not the country to which I return in 2025.

Neither is Canada, of course. Some of the changes in both countries have been connected: I've taught Canadian students just returned from military tours in Afghanistan and known colleagues who lost children there. Some are purely Canadian. I've become more accustomed to a political landscape with more than two major parties; I've seen the Progressive Conservatives merge with the Canadian Alliance and become the Conservative Party. I've seen the New Democratic Party win control of the Alberta government in 2015 and lose it again four years later. I've heard the wrenching testimony to the Truth and Reconciliation Commission and engaged in debates about how to reckon with the long-dead leaders' complicity in residential schools. But most changes, lived daily, have been less stark, and more immediate.

Unsettling as the process of culturally transplanting myself has been at times, I have come to regard being unsettled as a gift. My greatest growth has never happened when I was most comfortable; often it has come when I was most distressed. The move to Canada challenged my American-centric perspective and my personal comfort zones. I've learned to let friendships unfold at their own pace, without immediately sharing all my personal history. I've been pushed to view history differently, to question older "self evident truths," including the assumption that all history is national history. It's been well worth the journey.

The most difficult times have occurred when I was viewing painful U.S. events from the Canadian side of the border, especially the terrorist attacks of September 11, 2001, and the more recent political events surrounding the Trump presidency and re-election. I have been selfishly very grateful that I retired in 2017 and avoided daily questions about American politics. History has been for me, among much else, a form of engagement with the present, and in that sense an act of faith. The essays in this final section represent both professional culminations and the thresholds to all that comes next.

NOTES

1 The conference, held in Sun Valley, Idaho, was sponsored by the Institute of the American West. Other members of the Steering Committee were Susan Armitage and Melissa Hield. Patricia Albers and Paula Petrik chaired the Program Committee.
2 A longer version of my address was published as Elizabeth Jameson, "Halfway Across That Line: Gender at the Threshold of History in the North American West," *Western History Quarterly* 47:1 (Spring 2016): 1–26, and appears here with the permission of Oxford University Press, which grants ownership of articles to their authors.
3 Gilbert L. Wilson, *Buffalo Bird Woman's Garden* (1917; repr., St. Paul: Minnesota Historical Society Press, 1987) and *Waheenee: An Indian Girl's Story* (1921; repr., Lincoln: University of Nebraska Press, 1981).
4 Carolyn G. Heilbrun, *Writing a Woman's Life* (New York: Ballantine Books, 1988).
5 *Lone Star*, written and directed by John Sayles (Burbank, CA: Warner Brothers, 1996).

13

Halfway Across That Line: Gender at the Threshold of History in the North American Wests

February 9, 2016

There is a scene in my favorite movie, *Lone Star*, which compresses the social and spatial boundary lines of western history. *Lone Star*, according to writer/director John Sayles, is "a story about borders." "In a metaphorical sense," Sayles elaborated, a border "can be any of the symbols that we erect between one another—sex, class, race, age."[1] Eagle Pass, Texas, where *Lone Star* was filmed, becomes the fictional town of Frontera—"frontier," in the sense of border. The Anglo minority there has long dominated the ethnic Mexican majority and the smaller African American community. Borders there both exclude and protect—the international border, the racial neighborhoods and cafes, the intimate boundaries of sex, the narrative lines of contested histories, of personal lives and public stories.

At one point in the film, Sheriff Sam Deeds drives across the bridge to Mexico to speak to Chucho Montoya, "El Rey de las Llantas" (The King of the Tires), who, he has heard, witnessed a long-buried murder. As they chat at one of "El Rey's" tire lots, Deeds broaches the murder. Montoya responds: "You the sheriff of Rio County, right? Un jefe muy respetado." He bends down and draws a line on the ground with a Coke bottle, mimicking the line in the sand that William Travis reportedly drew at the Alamo. "Step over this line," he says. Sam obliges. "Ay, que milagro!" Montoya exclaims. "You're not the Sheriff of nothing anymore—just some Tejano with a lot of questions I don't have to answer. Bird flying south—you think he sees that line? Rattlesnake, javelina—whatever you got—halfway across that line they don't start thinking different. So why should a man?"

Sam responds, "Your government's always been pretty happy to have that line. The question's just been where to draw it."

"My government can go fuck itself," retorts Chucho. "And so can yours. I'm talking about people here—men. Mi amigo Eladio Cruz is giving some friends of his a lift in his camion one day...."

And the scene fades to a day some decades past, as young Chucho Montoya crouched beside a bridge and watched then-sheriff Charlie Wade shoot Eladio Cruz, who was changing a tire in the middle of the bridge while smuggling friends across the border.[2] The bridge that might have been the threshold to another country became a wall for his friends, and a dead end for Eladio Cruz.

Halfway across that bridge, did Chucho Montoya start thinking differently? Perhaps he glimpsed the value of a tire.

"The symbols that we erect between one another"

The visual metaphors in *Lone Star* mirror the structural metaphors of this book and of the 2015 Western History Association conference theme, "Thresholds, Walls, and Bridges." The bridge evokes for me Cherrie Moraga and Gloria Anzaldúa's pathbreaking anthology, *This Bridge Called My Back*, about the exclusionary terrains of race and gender, and the personal costs of bridging them.[3] Sayles, Anzaldúa, and feminist literary scholar Carolyn Heilbrun led me to the metaphor of the threshold. Anzaldúa suggested in *This Bridge We Call Home* that bridging led to an uncertain threshold. "To step across the threshold," she wrote, "is to be stripped of the illusion of safety because it moves us into unfamiliar territory and does not grant us safe passage. To bridge is to attempt community, and for that we must risk...."[4] Heilbrun insisted in *Writing a Woman's Life* that narrative in any story is more important than actors, and that narrative conventions constrained how women could tell their lives.[5] A decade later, she wrote in *Women's Lives* that the feminist movement had taken women's narratives to a liminal threshold, "poised upon uncertain ground" akin to "leaving one country or condition or self and entering upon another."[6]

"Leaving one country" does not lead directly to a new self, or a new history. As Chucho Montoya insisted, patterns of thought don't change as people cross borders. It is harder to bridge nations' histories than their borders, and harder still to connect the histories of nations or regions with the stories of people. Even after new actors cross into histories, it takes a while to change the story.

This is a reflection about adding women to history and changing the story—about what has changed and what hasn't since women began crossing the lines of western history, and about what might come next.

"I'm talking about people here—men."

When Chucho Montoya said, "I'm talking about people here—men," he could have been talking about the history books of my Texas childhood. I got a pretty good education in the Galveston public schools in the 1950s and 1960s, but my required Texas history classes sat far removed from where I lived. I learned linear tales of battles, dates, and politics, with a limited cast of generals and governors. In grade seven we memorized the governors' names, so I met Miriam "Ma" Ferguson, then the only woman who had served as governor, who famously promised that if elected she would take the advice of her recently impeached husband, thus giving Texans "two governors for the price of one."[7] Ma Ferguson knew her place.

The Galveston of my childhood believed in a place for everyone—African Americans in the back of the bus and in separate schools named Booker T. Washington and George Washington Carver; Mexican Americans in informally semi-segregated classrooms in schools named for battles and heroes in the Texas War for Independence from Mexico: Alamo, Travis, San Jacinto, Sam Houston, Bowie, Crockett, and Stephen F. Austin. Men in the history books, women—at least White women—at home.[8] It unsettled folks when people were not where they were supposed to be, doing what they were supposed to do. My mother's career as a doctor unsettled other women, who told me my Mom was "unnatural." Yet the history classes of my childhood seemed natural to me—history was about states, about ancient Rome, the United States, and Texas; it was made by powerful people, mostly White, mostly men.

Except for Mr. Bell in grade eight, all my history teachers were women. I don't know if they wondered why there were no women in our textbooks. I didn't.

Nor did I plan to study women's history. My first year of graduate school I resented being assigned what I called the "women" papers—about Margaret Fuller, brilliant transcendentalist and feminist, and Kate Chopin, whose literature was being rediscovered. Then a weird thing happened—I began to feel connected to my work in some indefinable new way. One day in the University of Michigan History Department, I told a friend I was really getting into women's history. A senior historian stuck his head out his office door and intoned: "Women's history? That's just the history of dishwashing!"

I had run into the analytic wall separating the private domestic space gendered female, and therefore trivial and ahistorical, from the public arenas of consequential acts gendered male. The histories preserved in female spaces became "individual memory," "family stories," or "lore"; those told in masculine public arenas became "collective memory" or "history." The wall that separated dishwashing from history erected what Sarah Carter has called "categories and terrains of exclusion."[9] Social histories have unsettled the lines between histories of places and histories of people, creating tense connections between histories *of* the West and histories of people and social relationships *in* the West. The challenge remains, from the thresholds between private and public, people and states, to imagine new categories and terrains of inclusion.

Gender has been most successfully incorporated at the centers of western history in studies of the fur trade, but that focus has been harder to maintain once nations claimed the spotlight.[10] Some four decades of scholarship on western women and gender occupies center stage in women's history and gender history classrooms, but rarely in western history.[11]

Still, we've made progress. Lots of women have invaded the androcentric mythic West that my generation inherited. Most western historians acknowledge women in western history; most of us have added some women to our courses and textbooks. We began by adding women to the histories we knew, the Wests of national expansion and frontier opportunity. To Lewis and Clark, we could add Sacagawea; to David Thompson, add Charlotte Small. To frontier opportunity, add the first woman suffrage victories, in Wyoming in 1869, Utah in 1870, and the three Prairie Provinces in 1916. This was the stage in reconceiving history often caricatured as "add a woman and stir."[12] When we stirred, we found that it took decades of women's work to gain the hard-won ballot. Stirring again, we asked if votes alone defined opportunity, and what most women did when they weren't fighting for suffrage. One more stir took us beyond the frontiers of national expansion to the Indigenous people on the other side of frontier lines, presumably enduring what Elliott West called their "long centuries of boredom waiting for invaders from the East to show up."[13] *They* took us to new conceptual frameworks like conquest and settler colonialism, and to Indigenous and settler women's distinct roles bridging cultures or erecting racial differences.[14] Yet, as Heilbrun cautioned, adding actors did not automatically change the story.

Several years ago, I did some crude measures of women's representation in six textbooks: two Western history texts, two U.S. surveys, and two Canadian.[15] Senior feminist scholars co-authored three of them. All six texts had added women, but they remained vastly outnumbered, especially in the western histories, where the populations resembled the skewed sex ratios of cattle drives or gold camps: only 7–9 percent of the people in the indexes were women. Adding the pages that clearly contained content in gender or women's history, women's representation ranged from a low of 6 percent to the high teens.[16] These figures are imprecise; they are skewed by different indexing systems, page duplications, and counting as whole pages any page on which a woman appeared. I am not impugning the authors, who I respect and who worked to include women—in one case with my clearly imperfect advice. But adding women to histories of nations or the West does not in itself change the narratives, and imagining inclusive narratives is much harder than adding women to history. The limits of inclusion highlight the categories and frameworks that privilege specific arenas, actors, and acts.

"Step over this line."

I've been wrestling with these challenges for some time, in a project that follows an unruly cast of women through the Dakota-Manitoba borderlands and tries to bring place and gender into common focus. A few stories from one small place and time in the West illustrate the ways that women strain western and national histories and suggest some possible categories of inclusion.

Sometime in the spring of 1884, Mary J. Rushton left her parents' home in Nova Scotia and traveled west to Manitoba. Turning south, she crossed the line into Dakota Territory, and on June 16 declared her intention "to renounce forever all allegiance and fidelity" to "The Queen of England" and become a U.S. citizen. In early 1885 she moved onto 160 acres in Bottineau County and filed her Homestead Application, swearing that she was "over the age of 21" and a single woman. She had paid $150 for a frame house and barn, had sunk a well, and had broken approximately ten acres. She valued these improvements at $200.[17]

Mary Rushton became a U.S. citizen on August 9, 1889. Exactly one year later she filed her final proof statement to gain title to her land. She had, by then, claimed a second quarter section under the Timber Culture Act, which required her to plant ten acres in trees.[18] She had, she said, lived continuously in her two-room frame house, had raised wheat and oats for four years, cultivated a garden, and dug a second well. She owned a horse, bed, bedding, table, chairs, stove, and cooking utensils. She had not been regularly employed, she wrote, but "would help a neighbor occasionally" who lived three-fourths of a mile away. Exercising her new citizenship, she had voted in the "last school election." Such are the bare facts of six years of her life that Mary Rushton recorded in her homestead claim file.[19]

Rushton was one of 773 women who filed final proofs for their North Dakota homesteads within two decades after the Devils Lake Land Office opened on August 21, 1883.[20] Devils Lake handled claims for north central North Dakota: for Ramsey Country, where the Land Office was located, and Eddy, Wells, Benson, Pierce, McHenry, Bottineau, Rolette, Towner, and Cavalier counties (see Chapter 9, Figure 9.2, page 233). Land opened for settlement as Indigenous people were pushed onto the Devils Lake (now Spirit Lake) Sioux Reservation, established in 1867, and the Turtle Mountain Chippewa Reservation, established in 1882. More land became available as these reservations were carved into privately owned allotments under the 1887 Dawes Act. Within twenty years, 7,548 people had filed their final proof statements in the Devils Lake Land Office. One in ten (773) were women—almost two-thirds of whom were naturalized citizens.[21] At least 123 (16 percent) were Canadian, 145 (19 percent) were Norwegian, and 273 (35 percent) were native-born Americans.[22]

For many Canadian women, the lure lay in subtle differences between Canadian and U.S. land policies. The 1862 U.S. Homestead Act and the 1872 Canadian Dominion Lands Act were similar in most respects. Both offered homesteaders 160 acres; both charged a small filing fee, required claimants to live on their land part of the year and put it to productive use. Both appeared surprisingly egalitarian. Section Two of the Homestead Act clarified in unusually gender-inclusive language: "That the *person* applying for the benefit of this act shall, upon application to the register of the land office in which *he or she* is about to make such entry, make affidavit before the said register or receiver that *he or she* is the head of a family, or is twenty-one years or more of age," and "that such application is made for *his or her* exclusive use and benefit. . . ." (italics added). Beyond this, women had only to swear that they were unmarried when they filed their claims, or, if married, that they were the sole support of their families, and that they were or had declared their "intention to become" U.S. citizens.

Figure 13.1. "Homestead sod shack of Ambjør Hagen, Grandfield Township, Eddy County, N.D.," [189-?]. S. A. Olsness Photograph Collection, Mss 220.4.7. Photo courtesy of the Institute for Regional Studies, NDSU, Fargo. Ambjør Hagen, a Norwegian immigrant, filed the final proof for her homestead on April 10, 1896 at age 61; she received the title to her land on May 2, 1896. Ambjør Hagen Homestead Claim File, file 1672, box 642, Records of the Devils Lake Land Office (1884–1913), Records of North Dakota Land Offices, Records of the Bureau of Land Management, 1685–1993, Record Group 49, National Archives and Records Administration (Washington, DC).

Canada, too, initially offered homesteads to "any *person* who is the head of a family or has attained the age of twenty-one years who is a subject of Her Majesty by birth or naturalization." But in 1876, the law was changed to restrict homesteads to "[a]ny *person*, male or female, who is the sole head of a family, or any *male* who has attained the age of eighteen years."[23] (italics added). Until 1930, a Canadian woman could homestead independently only if widowed, divorced, deserted, or separated, and then only if she also had a minor child living with her and solely dependent on her for support. From 1876–1930, a gendered border divided unmarried women's access to homesteads in Canada and the United States.[24]

It would be a mistake, though, to overstate the differences between the nations on either side of that border. Both offered homesteads and restricted Indigenous Peoples to reservations and reserves to serve their nation-building aspirations. The Homestead Act, Dominion Lands Act, and Dawes Act all inscribed the values of private property, patriarchy, and monogamous nuclear families.[25] All presumed that the head of a family was male, unless no man were present. Both Canada and the U.S. wanted White women to bring their civilizing influence to their Wests. Both recruited homesteading *families*; they chose different means to attract *unmarried* women. The United States offered homesteads; Canada recruited domestic servants from Britain and Scandinavia.[26] Both hoped that the women who came would marry, bear children, and help build western farms and communities. Three in ten women (225) in the Devils Lake cohort did just that, marrying before gaining title to their land. About as many, 228, remained single; 274 (35 percent) were widows.[27]

Although the 49th Parallel served as the threshold to land for single Canadian women, the border they crossed and the land they claimed meant different things to women who shared Canadian "nationality." British North America became the Dominion of Canada only sixteen years before the Devils Lake Land Office opened. "Canadian" women had diverse identities and reasons to claim U.S. citizenship. Mary Rushton was among the youngest, claiming land just after her twenty-first birthday. The oldest, Margaret Belgarde, had crossed the border four decades before. Born in the Red River settlement in 1794, Marguerite Dufort married Alexis Belgarde in 1814. The Belgardes moved south across an indistinct border to Pembina in 1844, twenty-three years before Confederation and twenty-eight years before the 49th Parallel was surveyed between Manitoba and Dakota Territory.[28]

The North West Company had established a trading post in 1797 at the junction of the Red and Pembina Rivers, and, later, a second post at Pembina that Alexander Henry ran from 1801 to 1805.[29] Métis descendants of British and French fur traders and Indigenous mothers, and their Ojibwe, Cree, and Assiniboine maternal kin staged buffalo hunts from there to provision the fur trade.[30] The Pembina post closed in 1823. Norman Kittson opened a new fur trade post on the site in 1844, perhaps inspiring the Belgardes' move that year.[31]

Six years later the census listed Alexis as a carpenter; he died in 1852. Marguerite lived in Pembina County with her son's family until the early 1880s. Then, in 1884 she filed her intention to become a U.S. citizen and moved onto her own homestead in Bottineau County. Her final proof papers, filed in August 1889, listed her age as 106, but she was likely only 95, living in a log house on her homestead with her daughter. She died four years later.[32]

Colonial settler societies were mapped in gendered and racialized spaces. Marguerite Belgarde did not support dependent minor children; she could not claim land in Canada. Her homestead reflected gendered access to land, and the contested categories of race and citizenship in the U.S.-Canada borderlands. Over half the Canadian women located their homesteads in two counties just south of the 49th Parallel: in Rolette County, site of the Turtle Mountain Chippewa Reservation, or in Bottineau County.[33] Most appear to have been Anglo Canadians, but a combination of factors drew Belgarde and other Métis, as the buffalo trade collapsed, and the failed armed resistance of 1885 cemented Anglo Canadian authority north of the border. I cannot determine how many of the 773 women were Métis, but Marguerite Belgarde was not alone. Many Métis moved to the Turtle Mountain area in Rolette County in 1883, when the Land Office opened, the year after the Turtle Mountain Chippewa Reservation was established. By 1884, over 1,200 Métis lived around Turtle Mountain.[34]

More Rolette County homesteads became available after the U.S. government cut the Turtle Mountain Reservation from twenty-two townships to two while limiting access to Chippewa "full bloods."[35] Barred in Canada from receiving Métis scrip because they were "U.S. Indians" and hindered from settling on the Turtle Mountain Reservation because they were not "full-blood Chippewas," some Métis adapted to the new racial and national boundaries by claiming homesteads in an area where they had long hunted, trapped, and traded, and where they could live among Métis and Indigenous kin.[36]

The citizenship requirement that Canadian women satisfied to claim their land skirted the complex racial ethnic categories of two nations and more subtle identities that linked and separated the incoming settlers, Indigenous people already there, like the Pembina Chippewas, whose ancestors had migrated to the area in the 1400s, and newcomers like the Dakotas, pushed west by European Americans.[37] The U.S. was challenged to fit Métis into binary racial categories. In 1870 the Secretary of the Interior appointed C. W. McIntyre to "investigate allegations of the fraudulent issue of scrip under the 1863 treaty" with the Pembina Band of Chippewa. Only "mixed bloods residing with the Red Lake and Pembina Indians at the date of the treaty who were connected with them by blood" were supposed to receive scrip; "all such as were foreign born" were to be "excluded."[38] Though she was "foreign born," Marguerite (Dufort) Belgarde "was on the 1868 annuity list" for the Pembina band. Four of her children and her son-in-law also claimed annuities and were deemed Pembina Chippewa. But three Belgarde sons, Joseph, Theodore, and Augustin were denied scrip as "Assiniboine/Sioux living in the Turtle Mountains." So was one son-in-law, whom McIntyre found to be "Sioux ½ breed—not good," although his mother was Pembina Métis.[39] Such slippery racial categories skirted longstanding ties among Métis and their mothers' Indigenous kin.

The international boundary and U.S. law allowed unmarried Métis women to claim homesteads. For the women themselves, Métis identity was likely more important than national citizenship. Months before the Devils Lake Land Office opened, on April 15, 1883, a sixty-year-old "American born" widow, Marguerite Azure, moved onto a homestead claim in Rolette County. A brief comment on her homestead application linked the modest plot to rapidly constricting Indigenous space. Azure swore on May 22, 1890, that the land she claimed was "not improved, occupied or claimed by Native born Indian or half Breeds of the United States," [sic]— an ironic claim, since Azure was Pembina Métis.[40] Her homestead claim, like Belgarde's, evaded preoccupations with blood quantum, birthplace, citizenship, and national residence that determined what the Canadian and U.S. governments considered they owed Indigenous peoples or "half breeds."[41]

As they crossed the property lines of their homesteads, Azure, Belgarde, and other Métis homesteaders claimed more than private property: they gained proximity to kin and to a Métis community that had spanned the northern Plains long before the 49th Parallel bisected it. They used U.S. law to claim homesteads, but I doubt that their chief goals were new national identities. Marguerite Azure spoke for many homesteading women. "I make this entry," she said simply, "for my own benefit & children."[42]

Many Rolette County children knew another woman who further complicates what private property meant for homesteaders and their Indigenous neighbors. On June 25, 1888, Rose M. Sheridan claimed a quarter section in Rolette County; she filed her final proof statement on November 23, 1893. Born in Ireland, Sheridan immigrated to the United States with her family at age two. Her homestead prospered: she farmed 120 acres and valued her land, log house, and stable at $660. Perhaps land drew Rose Sheridan to Rolette County; perhaps she came for the job that helped support her claim. She lived on her homestead, she wrote, except "when my duties called me away as Superintendent and teacher at the mission school of the Turtle Mountain reservation. . . ."[43]

Whichever came first—Sheridan's job or her homestead—their combined significance mattered enormously. The national policies that supported family farms and nuclear families generated different options for women who homesteaded independently or as wives; for Norwegian or Anglo Canadian settlers; for Métis, for whom "settling" meant making the best of constricting options; and for their Indigenous neighbors, whose allotments tied them to vastly shrinking territories. Government employees and missionaries worked to reverse Indigenous divisions of labor by giving Indigenous men agricultural equipment, stock, seeds, and legal title to family farms. Sheridan's job at the Turtle Mountain mission school likely included teaching her pupils the values of private property, Christianity, monogamy, and patriarchal nuclear families. She would seek to change Indigenous concepts of kinship, marriage, and divorce, to eliminate concepts of third genders, to inculcate binary heterosexual roles and sexualities. The girls would learn "proper" housework, the boys, farming—though Rose Sheridan was single and managed her own farm, and though many Indigenous women farmed.[44]

One of the best-known accounts of Indigenous women's agriculture came from a Hidatsa woman named Mahidiweash (or Maxidiwiac), known in English as Buffalo Bird Woman, who traced Hidatsa origins to Miniwakan, or Spirit Lake, next to the Devils Lake Land Office.[45] Born in 1839 or 1840 at the mouth of the Knife River "three years after the smallpox winter" killed over half the Hidatsa and perhaps seven-eighths of the Mandan, her people moved with the surviving Mandans to a new village at Like-a-fishhook bend. They lived there until 1885, "when," she said, "the government began to place families on allotments" at the Fort Berthold Indian Reservation.[46] Presbyterian minister and anthropologist Gilbert L. Wilson recorded her history at Fort Berthold from 1906–1918 and published it in two volumes, *Buffalo Bird Woman's Garden* and *Waheenee: An Indian Girl's Story*.[47]

For Wilson, Mahidiweash represented the "old ways" being replaced by Christianity and "civilized" gender roles. Her assessment was more nuanced. As Hidatsa men learned to farm, Mahidiweash told Wilson that "White men knew nothing about our gardens. We knew all this I tell you, since the world began." Whites, she said, brought new seeds for oats, wheat, watermelons, and onions, but also weeds, like thistle and mustard, and vegetables she considered inferior, like turnips and big squashes.[48] Wilson's field notes recorded her views of the changes brought by missionaries, government personnel, and traders:

> In old times, and even when I was young, it was hard for us to get tools; and house-building of any kind was hard work. Now we can build a house of any shape we wish, and tools are easy to get. In this respect our new way of living is better than the old.
> On the otherhand [sic], we had plenty to eat and wear then, abundance of meat and fur robes and tanned skins. We did not have to buy food with money, and the new food that white men have brought us, and their diseases, cause our people to die. In olden days we did not thus die.
> Neither do I like white men's laws. I do not understand them nor know how to make them rule my life.
> I think also that it is a very hard thing for us to have to let our children be taken from us and sent away to school where we cannot see them.[49]

This complex judgment appeared in neither of Wilson's published volumes. It did not support the path to assimilation that Wilson assumed and for which Rose Sheridan labored.

Mary Rushton, Margaret Belgarde, Marguerite Azure, Rose Sheridan, and Mahidiweash—five women in one place and time in the North American West, separated by distinct gender systems, nationalities, racial ethnic cultures, classes, spiritual practices, ages, and much more. That they lived in proximity was, for some, the consequence of birth; for some, the intimate legacy of the fur trade; for some, the limits of their options elsewhere coupled with the policies of settler colonialism and national expansion. The fact that they were unmarried women shaped their options, inscribed in national land policies, borders, and survey lines. We can fit them into the history of westward expansion, but that narrative can't hold their diversity. They challenge us to imagine narratives that respect and link their diverse stories—to add women to western history and then go further, to explore the distinct ways they experienced history and made it.

Guns to Butter

Most women have not made it into history, even interesting women like Rushton, Belgarde, Azure, and Sheridan on the standard homesteading frontier. They owe their absences, in part, to gendered assumptions about where history was made, whose acts were important, whose stories worth saving, and to gendered historical categories.

In 1986 William Cronon, Howard Lamar, Katherine Morrissey, and Jay Gitlin identified frameworks and categories of western history that excluded women. Chief among these was the frontier, defined by masculine economies: the fur trade, mining, ranching, and farming.[50] There was no gardeners' frontier, no hide tanners' frontier, no missionaries' frontier, no butter, or poultry frontier.

Women made a mess of masculine resource frontiers. We found them gardening in mining towns, raising poultry on ranches, making butter for the fur trade in the Fort Vancouver dairy.[51] Ojibwe and Hidatsa women farmed; Pueblo women raised turkeys; ranch women used the money from their chickens, eggs, and butter to buy livestock, windmills, flour, and gasoline.[52] Around Devils Lake, women farmed, raised poultry, manufactured butter and pemmican, processed hides, gardened, canned, and supported their homesteads washing dishes in hotels, or, like Mary Rushton, when she "would help a neighbor occasionally."

Women's paid and unpaid labor was similar in each resource economy—they cooked, cleaned, raised and processed fruits and vegetables, made clothing, kept poultry, made butter, hauled fuel and water, engaged in sex, did laundry, and washed dishes. As they gathered, raised, preserved, and prepared food, women created the human energy that enabled hunters, trappers, miners, lumberjacks, ranch hands, and threshing crews to harvest western resources. When the state provided resources, like land for homesteads and railroad construction, those contributions were called infrastructure. Women's labor produced the social and economic infrastructure of western mines, farms, ranches, fur trades, lumber mills, and communities.

Women on the egg and butter frontiers of settler colonialism organized through the Grange and Farmers' Alliance in the U.S. and the Women Grain Growers and United Farm Women of Alberta (UFWA) in Canada to protect their cash-producing butter. Women helped win the Federal Oleomargarine Act of 1886 that decreased the manufacture of U.S. oleomargarine for almost a decade, and the more successful 1886

Act of Parliament that outlawed margarine until 1917, and again from 1924-1948.[53] The Women Grain Growers and the UFWA campaigned for woman suffrage, farm women's property rights, reproductive rights, rural childcare, affordable medical care, and more. Despite their activism, histories chronicle the wheat pools that the male Grain Growers and United Farmers of Alberta established, but histories seldom mention that the UFWA created the first Egg and Poultry Pool in Canada.[54] Their activism fell at one end of a spectrum that ranged from individual resistance, like refusing to wash the dishes or asking a man to change a diaper, to organized collective action.

Dishwashing, in other words, was neither ahistorical nor separate from the public arenas of men's labor or of state and community formation. It got erased through social convention and public policies that privileged male sources that recorded women's homestead claims only because they were unmarried, or that prevented married women from incorporating the schools, libraries, hospitals, and churches they organized, so that their husbands' names appeared on the legal documents historians consulted to identify community leaders.

Class and race erased other women's activism. Maternal concerns inspired May McConaghy Wing (1890-1980), who lived most of her nine decades in hardrock mining towns. She started the hot school lunch program in Victor, Colorado, run by women volunteers who, she said, "washed dishes and they helped make sandwiches and they helped cook."[55] The building that hosted high school basketball games had no bathrooms, so that the boys relieved themselves outside in a cold alley and her son, James, "every year, had one cold right after the other." So, May Wing organized a mothers' "executive meeting" that "brought it to the PTA," which got the school system to install indoor plumbing and provide an apartment for a custodian to keep the pipes from freezing.[56]

Half a century later, Latina environmental justice activists organized the Mothers of East Los Angeles, using skills *they* learned in church work and the PTA to keep a prison, a hazardous waste incinerator, a waste treatment plant, and an above-ground oil pipeline out of their neighborhood. Then they distributed free low-flush toilets, fought against classroom overcrowding, opened a non-profit meat market to fund scholarships, and more.[57] Such social activism made a critical difference in under-served working-class and racial ethnic communities. The women who organized egg and poultry pools, cooked hot school lunches, and learned their organizing skills at the PTA were not mere "social dishwashers." They were activists: community organizers, civic leaders, and institution builders. Rethinking the labels and categories of women's community and domestic labor opens categories of inclusion in histories of western economic development and community formation.

As we hear women's stories on their own terms, the arenas and subjects of history expand. I went to Cripple Creek long ago to learn about unions and strikes and found women whose lives centered on family, who led me to private arenas of reproduction, sexuality, and abuse even more hidden from history than women's work and activism. Though much current U.S. political discourse concerns the public regulation of marriage, sexuality, and reproduction, those topics remain largely disconnected from U.S. history and western history.

In 1979, I sat with 85-year-old Beulah Pryor in her Colorado Springs living room, as she taught me to make rag rugs, fed me homemade ginger cookies and lemonade, and remembered running for help the night her stepfather threatened to shoot her mother. Neighboring miners called the police and persuaded Beulah Pryor's mother to leave her abusive husband by promising to board with her so she could feed her children.[58] That personal local approach to domestic violence is not yet connected to the more recent history of battered women's shelters, nor is domestic violence linked to the violence of vigilantes, gunslingers, and wars. Although Canadian historians have contrasted the Canadian West of "peace, order, and good government" to a violent U.S. West, that debatable distinction excludes domestic violence and the abuse Indigenous children suffered in the residential schools that so pained Buffalo Bird Woman.[59]

"Winners Get the Bragging Rights. . ."

Historical silences and erasures matter. Almost every woman I've interviewed began by saying "Why do you want to talk to me? I didn't do anything." They couldn't locate themselves in the histories they knew. And yet, like May Wing, they knew what they had done—they just didn't think a historian would care. Three years after we met, May Wing voiced the challenge that still animates my work. "I lived the history that I can tell," she said. "And of course, the history today, in books that's written a lot, is not really the true thing, as it was lived."[60]

Histories "in books" stopped short of the domestic threshold. In the formative narrative of the American West, Frederick Jackson Turner wrote that "Complex society" was "precipitated by the wilderness into a kind of primitive organization based on the family." History progressed as "primitive peoples" became "new nations" and moved from "families into states."[61] Among the constraints on women's narratives that Carolyn Heilbrun identified were the "limited plots and conventions of romance," like the Cinderella narrative in which a long foreground waiting for Prince Charming led quickly to "and they lived happily ever after."[62] In Cinderella's plot, women disappeared when Prince Charming arrived. In Turner's, they disappeared with complex society, with the state. These narrative conventions help explain why it has been easier to focus on women and families before the nation states of North American solidified their borders and authority.

A number of assumptions wall women, and most men, out of history: that the subject of history is the nation state; that kinship and family are more primitive social forms than governments; that private life is less important, historically, than battles and elections. These assumptions are reinforced by the teleologies of progress, demanding that "civilization" overtake "savagery," and that homesteaders spend the rest of their lives happily farming their hard-won acres.

Those assumptions and conventions pushed Buffalo Bird Woman to the margins of history, because Gilbert Wilson either couldn't hear the stories she told, or could not fit them into the stories he knew or wanted to tell. Wilson also interviewed her brother, Henry Wolf Chief, and her son, Edward Goodbird. Mahidiweash spoke Hidatsa; Goodbird and Wolf Chief learned English. Goodbird became a minister, Wolf Chief a storekeeper. Wilson published *Goodbird: The Indian* and *Waheenee* to introduce Christian children to Indigenous people.[63] Differences of gender and generation separated Goodbird and his mother on the historical trajectory that Wilson assumed was civilizing and progressive.

The narrative Wilson wrote did not fit Mahidiweash's experience, her concept of history, or her interpretations of progress. It corseted her life into a combined Turnerian and Cinderella narrative—a long tale of girlhood that ended with her first marriage to Magpie, his death, and her second marriage to Son-of-a-Star, followed by a hunting trip and Goodbird's birth, and then a fast flyover to the voice of a dying tradition. That narrative implicitly supported a Turnerian trajectory from "a primitive social organization based on the family" to assimilation, to the nation.

In the process it deleted much rich detail in Wilson's field notes. In the story of Buffalo Bird Woman's first marriage, he accurately reported that her younger sister Cold Medicine accompanied her in the ritual of taking gifts to Magpie's family, but he never explained that they were both marrying Magpie, as was the custom.[64] Mahidiweash told Wilson:

> ... I lived with my husband, for two years, when my father gave my sister also to my husband. ...
>
> Tho my sister and I had both gone to call Magpie to his lodge, yet he did not take my younger sister until my father said, "Take this one also as your wife."
>
> My sister however had been given to him only about a month, when she ran away with a man named Bush. They did not try to escape to another village, just went to another lodge in our village. My younger sister just left us one night, that was all.[65]

"In old times," she said, "we thought that a wife had a right to divorce herself from her husband just as the husband had the right to separate from her if he chose."[66]

Wilson's story most differed from Buffalo Bird Woman's regarding the trajectories of change. Mahidiweash did not think education and Christianity brought unqualified progress. She told Wilson, "In old days, mothers watched their daughters very carefully, and girls did not give birth to babies before marriage. But after schools were started on this reservation, then our daughters began to have babies before marriage, for they now learned English ways."[67]

Wilson concluded Buffalo Bird Woman's story with words that I have not found in his field notes:

> I am an old woman now. The buffaloes and black-tail deer are gone, and our Indian ways are almost gone ...
>
> My little son grew up in the white man's school. He can read books, and he owns cattle and has a farm. He is a leader among our Hidatsa people, helping teach them to follow the white man's road.
>
> ... Our Indian life, I know, is gone forever.[68]

Through Wilson's filters, Buffalo Bird Woman became the voice of a dying tradition. Goodbird learned English, converted to Christianity, owned cattle and a farm. He could join a mainstream history; his mother was a prelude to national progress. The imperatives of "civilization" moved Mahidiweash from collective gardens and lodges that women owned, from a matrilineal household to an isolated nuclear family on a farm to which her son held title.

Buffalo Bird Woman was marginalized on the same terms as many immigrant women, who stayed home while their children and husbands learned English in schools, jobs, and marketplaces. Preserving family histories, food, rituals, holidays, languages, and customs, they were denigrated as ignorant and unacculturated. Other women who built schools, churches, and libraries became too civilized, unfit for the rigors of an untamed land, or drags who wanted men to bathe, shave, stop drinking and philandering, go to church, and settle down.[69] Their stories became private family tales, not history.

Mary Rushton, Margaret Belgarde, Marguerite Azure, Rose Sheridan, Mahidiweash, May Wing, and Beulah Pryor are just a few of the diverse western women whose histories we've recovered. Some of their stories belonged to specific times and particular Wests; some experiences crossed the lines of nation, class, and race. Their complex variety can help us discern what has been particular about place and gender in the North American Wests, and what histories might bridge social, spatial, and national divides.

The impediments to those histories are significant. It is not easy to find narrative forms for separate but connected stories. It is hard to confront histories in which differences of gender, race, and nationality were forged through power and domination. To bridge these human and conceptual divides demands unsettling the categories and terrains of the histories we know. It also entails practical issues of power. States, after all, fund history programs, adopt the textbooks, and rarely want cherished histories unsettled.

Returning once more to *Lone Star*, a scene at a PTA meeting captured these struggles over content, as angry parents confronted school personnel about what their children learned in Texas history classes.

An impassioned Anglo mother exclaims, "You're just tearin' everything down! Tearin' down our heritage, tearin' down the memory of people that fought and died for this land." A Chicano father responds, "We fought and died for this land, too! We fought the U.S. Army, the Texas Rangers." An Anglo father interrupts: "Yeah, but you lost, buddy! Winners get the bragging rights, that's how it goes."

Histories of winners and losers establish power, but they don't explain the Wests we inhabit, told from all sides of the history. It is those alternate stories that the Anglo father in *Lone Star* wants to silence: "You may call it history," he says, "but I call it propaganda. I'm sure they got their own account of the Alamo on the other side, but we're not on the other side, so we're not about to have it taught in our schools!"[70]

This is not a new debate. The high school edition of *Out of Many* drew fire in Texas for two paragraphs on sex workers that stated that "perhaps 50,000 women engaged in prostitution west of the Mississippi during the second half of the nineteenth century."[71] The debate is not new, it is not settled, and it matters. In September 2015 over five million Texas school children opened new social studies textbooks that barely mentioned segregation and that treated slavery as a "side issue to the Civil War."[72]

It is hard enough to adopt textbooks that don't erase legacies of racism, and harder still to address gender. The casts of western histories have expanded since my childhood to include more people of color, more grassroots activists, more women, a few identified LGBTQ2S+ individuals. Those expanded casts stretch the histories I learned, and the power they encode, but they have not dissolved the categories, assumptions, and narratives that marginalize women. I grew up in a racist and sexist culture and still wrestle with its assumptions. From an uncertain threshold, somewhere between dishwashing and the West, I interrogate the values I assign to wheat or butter, to mining gold or hot school lunches, to battles, dates, and dirty dishes.

Hope animates these challenges—the hope that history can be a bridge, that histories that cross the lines of nations, of social boundaries, and households can help us see humanity on the other sides of those borders, and history beyond the thresholds of domesticity. Within that primitive social organization based on the family, people sometimes made choices to build schools or start social movements or changed behaviors that began to transform social relationships, as Beulah Pryor's mother did when she walked away from abuse.

Halfway across the lines of gender, race, class, or other borders of difference lie the thresholds to histories that are more accurate, more truthful, and that hold the hope of reconciliation. Truth comes before reconciliation, and the truth is that the histories that marginalize and erase women and relationships of gender are inaccurate and incomplete; they deny interdependence and connection. The problem is not simply histories in which winners claim the bragging rights. It is histories intended to buttress relationships of power—that insist that slavery was a side issue in the Civil War or that patriarchy is civilizing.

The histories of the past half century bring us to an uncertain threshold. Imagining new histories of the people and social relationships that have made the West is not easy work, and once imagined, such histories can be hard to teach because they don't fit narratives that most of our students or fellow citizens recognize. It is necessarily an incremental journey, imaginatively and practically.

The historical threshold at which I always stand is the present moment, halfway across the line from the past that shaped my world to the future I want my grandchildren to inherit. History—truthful history—can serve that intention. I want to write women into western history because people who don't see themselves in history don't know that they make history. I want those histories, not to be politically correct, but to be historically accurate and humanly compassionate. I want my grandchildren to inherit a world in which history is not about winners and losers, where history is made not only on the battlefields of San Jacinto, Wounded Knee, and Batoche, but also at the PTA—where the goal is not the right to tell the winners' story but the ability to hear all the stories. There are no roadmaps to those histories or those futures. They begin when women and men meet each other halfway across the lines of the histories that have separated us. Histories that map social divides can begin to bridge them. Gloria Anzaldúa voiced the challenge eloquently: "To bridge is to attempt community, and for that we must risk."

NOTES

Thanks to Gretchen Albers, Amy McKinney, Erin Millions, Andrew Varsanyi, Shawn Brackett, Stuart White, and Celeste Sharp for research assistance over the years; to Sarah Carter, Heather Devine, and Michel Hogue for generous advice; to David Rich Lewis for editorial support and patience as I prepared the longer version of this essay for publication in the *Western Historical Quarterly*, and to Diane Bush and Jessica Nelson for valiant copy-editing. My 2016 lecture was also my presidential address to the 2015 Western History Association conference in Portland, Oregon. I am grateful to former WHA Executive Secretary John Heaton for support organizing and administering that conference, to Dean Richard Sigurdson for support during my presidential year and for generous conference support, and to the *Western Historical Quarterly* and Oxford University Press for not requiring permission to publish this slightly shorter version of my article that appeared in the spring 2016 volume of that journal.

1 *Lone Star*, written and directed by John Sayles (Burbank, CA: Warner Brothers, 1996); Dennis West and Joan M. West, "Borders and Boundaries: An Interview with John Sayles," *Cineaste* 22:3 (Summer 1996): 14.

2 *Lone Star*. *Un jefe muy respetado*: a very respected leader. *Ay, que milagro!*: Ay, what a miracle! *Mi amigo*: my friend. *Camion*: truck.

3   Cherríe Moraga and Gloria Anzaldúa, eds., *This Bridge Called My Back: Writings by Radical Women of Color* (New York: Kitchen Table/Women of Color Press, 1981).
4   Gloria E. Anzaldúa, "Preface: (Un)natural bridges, (Un)safe spaces," in *This Bridge We Call Home: Radical Visions for Transformation*, eds. Gloria E. Anzaldúa and Analouise Keating (New York: Routledge, 2002), 3.
5   Carolyn G. Heilbrun, *Writing a Woman's Life* (New York: Ballantine Books, 1988), 13.
6   Carolyn G. Heilbrun, *Women's Lives: The View from the Threshold* (Toronto: University of Toronto Press, 1999), 3.
7   Miriam Amanda (Ma) Ferguson was elected Governor in 1924 after her husband, James Ferguson, was impeached and convicted of misapplication of public funds. She served two terms as Governor, from 1925-1927 and 1933-1935. See Ouida Ferguson Nalle, *The Fergusons of Texas, or "Two Governors for the Price of One": A Biography of James Edward Ferguson and His Wife* (San Antonio: Naylor, 1946).
8   Race, like gender and class, is a historical and cultural construct. In the contexts of 1950s Galveston, "White" generally excluded Mexican Americans.
9   Sarah Carter, "Categories and Terrains of Exclusion: Constructing the 'Indian Woman' in the Early Settlement Era in Western Canada," *Great Plains Quarterly* 13 (1993): 147-61.
10 Sylvia Van Kirk, *Many Tender Ties: Women in Fur Trade Society, 1670-1870* (Norman: University of Oklahoma Press and Winnipeg: Watson and Dwyer, 1980); Jennifer S. H. Brown, *Strangers in Blood: Fur Trade Company Families in Indian Country* (Vancouver: University of British Columbia Press, 1980); Jacqueline Peterson and Jennifer S.H. Brown, eds., *The New Peoples: Being and Becoming Métis in North America* (Winnipeg: University of Manitoba Press, 1985); William R. Swagerty, "Marriage and Settlement Patterns of Rocky Mountain Trappers and Traders," *Western Historical Quarterly* 11:2 (April 1980): 159-80; and Anne F. Hyde, *Empires, Nations, and Families: A New History of the North American West, 1800-1860* (Lincoln: University of Nebraska Press, 2011).
11 I distinguish women, as subjects, from gender as a category of analysis and as a mutable array of identities and roles. For an assessment and critique of the progress incorporating women and gender in western history, see Elizabeth Jameson, Margaret D. Jacobs, Susan Lee Johnson, and Karen J. Leong, "If Not Now, When?: Gender, Power, and the Decolonization of Western History," *Pacific Historical Review* 79:4 (November 2010): 573-628, a forum including Elizabeth Jameson, "Looking Back to the Road Ahead," 574-84; Margaret D. Jacobs, "Getting Out of a Rut: Decolonizing Western Women's History," 585-604; Susan Lee Johnson, "Nail This To Your Door: A Disputation on the Power, Efficacy, and Indulgent Delusion of Western Scholarship That Neglects the Challenge of Gender and Women's History," 605-17; and Karen J. Leong, "Still Walking, Still Brave: Mapping Gender, Race, and Power in U.S. Western History," 618-28.
12 The phrase as caricature was taken out of context from Gerda Lerner's serious discussion of the process of reconceiving history from gendered inclusion. Gerda Lerner, "The Challenge of Women's History," in Gerda Lerner, *The Majority Finds Its Past* (New York: Oxford University Press, 1979), 169.
13 Elliott West, "A Longer, Grimmer, But More Interesting Story," in *Trails: Toward a New Western History*, eds., Patricia Nelson Limerick, Clyde A. Milner II, and Charles E. Rankin (Lawrence: University Press of Kansas, 1991), 107.
14 For surveys of some of the extensive scholarship on western women, see Joan M. Jensen and Darlis A. Miller, "The Gentle Tamers Revisited: New Approaches to the History of Women in the American West," *Pacific Historical Review* 49:2 (May 1980): 173-213; Elizabeth Jameson, "Toward a Multicultural History of Women in the Western United States," *Signs* 13:4 (1988): 761-91; Marian Perales, "Empowering 'The Welder': A Historical Survey of Women of Color in the West," in *Writing the Range: Race, Class and Culture*

in the Women's West, eds. Elizabeth Jameson and Susan Armitage (Norman: University of Oklahoma Press, 1997), 21–41; and Elizabeth Jameson, "Bringing It All Back Home: Rethinking Women and the Nineteenth-Century West," in *A Companion to the American West*, ed. William Deverell (Malden, MA: Blackwell Publishing, 2004), 179–99. For Indigenous and settler women in colonial contexts, see Van Kirk, *Many Tender Ties*; Brown, *Strangers in Blood*; Adele Perry, *On The Edge of Empire: Gender, Race, and the Making of British Columbia, 1849–1871* (Toronto: University of Toronto Press, 2001) and *Colonial Relations: The Douglas-Connolly Family and the Nineteenth-Century Imperial World* (Cambridge: Cambridge University Press, 2015); and Margaret D. Jacobs, *White Mothers to a Dark Race: Settler Colonialism, Maternalism, and the Removal of Indigenous Children in the American West and Australia, 1880–1940* (Lincoln: University of Nebraska Press, 2009).

15 R. Douglas Francis, Richard Jones, and Donald B. Smith, *Journeys: A History of Canada* (Toronto: Thompson Nelson, 2006); Margaret Conrad and Alvin Finkel, *Canada: A National History*, 2nd ed.(Toronto: Pearson Longman, 2007); John Mack Faragher, Mari Jo Buhle, Daniel Czitrom, and Susan Armitage, *Out of Many: A History of the American People*, Combined Volume, 4th ed. (Upper Saddle River, NJ: Prentice Hall, 2006); Jacqueline Jones, Peter H. Wood, Thomas Borstelmann, Elaine Tyler May, and Vicki L. Ruiz, *Created Equal: A Social and Political History of the United States*, Brief Edition (New York: Pearson Longman, 2005); Richard White, *"It's Your Misfortune and None of My Own": A New History of the American West* (Norman: University of Oklahoma Press, 1991); Robert V. Hine and John Mack Faragher, *The American West: A New Interpretive History* (New Haven: Yale University Press, 2000). For more detail, see Elizabeth Jameson, "This Bridge Called Women's Stories: Private Lore and Public History," *Journal of the Canadian Historical Association/Revue de la Société historique du Canada* 18:2 (2007): 255–75.

16 The 6 percent was from Hine and Faragher, *The American West;* the high end of the six texts came from White, *It's Your Misfortune*. Thanks to Amy McKinney and Erin Millions who counted 30 women among 368 names in the index of White, *It's Your Misfortune*, and 35 of 478 in Hine and Faragher, *The American West*.

17 Mary J. Rushton Homestead Claim File, National Archives and Records Administration, Record Group 49, Washington, D.C. (Hereinafter cited as Homestead Files). See chapter 9 for a more complete treatment of the women who had won title to their homesteads by 1893. By 2015 the study had expanded to cover the first two decades the Devils Lake Land Office operated, 1883–1903, and included 773 women rather than the 121 discussed in chapter 9.

18 Rushton Homestead File. The Timber Culture Act of 1873 required forty acres of trees; as amended in 1878, it required ten acres.

19 Rushton Homestead File.

20 Originally called the Creelsburg Land Office, it became the Devils Lake office November 7, 1884, when the town of Creelsburg was renamed Devils Lake. North Dakota became a state in 1889; before that it was part of Dakota Territory. I use North Dakota for simplicity.

21 Despite increasing numbers of claimants from the first decade to the second, the proportions of women remained fairly constant: 107 women, 9.7 percent of 1100, filed their final claims during the first decade, August 21, 1883–August 20, 1893; another 666 women, 10.3 percent of the total, filed final proofs between August 21, 1893 and August 20, 1903. All figures were calculated from the Homestead Files of 773 women who filed final proof statements at the Devils Lake Land Office by August 20, 1903. Histories of women homesteaders began with Sheryll Patterson-Black's pathbreaking article, "Women Homesteaders on the Great Plains Frontier," *Frontiers: A Journal of Women Studies* 1:2 (Spring 1976): 67–88. For an excellent study of North Dakota women homesteaders,

see H. Elaine Lindgren, *Land in her Own Name: Women as Homesteaders in North Dakota* (1991; repr., Norman: University of Oklahoma Press, 1996). See also Katherine Benton-Cohen, "Common Purposes, Worlds Apart: Mexican-American, Mormon and Midwestern Women Homesteaders in Cochise County, Arizona," *Western Historical Quarterly* 36:4 (2005): 429–52; Dee Garceau, "Single Women Homesteaders and the Meaning of Independence: Places on the Map, Places in the Mind," *Frontiers: A Journal of Women Studies* 15:3 (1995): 1–26; and Sherry L. Smith, "Single Women Homesteaders: The Perplexing Case of Elinore Pruitt Stewart," *Western Historical Quarterly* 22:2 (May 1991): 163–83.

22 These figures are necessarily imprecise, but these three nationalities predominated. The nativity of 66 women is unknown. If all were native born, that total would rise to 44 percent. Fourteen women renounced their allegiance to the Queen of England without disclosing their countries of birth. If all were Canadian, that figure would rise to 137, or almost 18 percent. And twenty women renounced allegiance to the King of Norway and Sweden, but did not identify themselves as either Norwegian or Swedish. If all were Norwegian, that total would be 165, or 21 percent. Calculated from Homestead Files. Lindgren, *Land in Her Own Name*, 20–22, found that 24 percent of the women in her case studies were Norwegian, but only 5 percent were Canadian, and 65 percent were native-born Americans. Only two of her counties were along the 49th Parallel where the Canadian women clustered, and neither was in the Devils Lake Land Office Territory. My figures are based on all the women who filed final proof statements in one land office; Lindgren's sample of 306 women, which was spread throughout the state, was gathered by advertising for information about women homesteaders, and yielded richly detailed information about some women.

23 Sarah Carter, "'Daughters of British Blood' Or 'Hordes of Men of Alien Race': The Homesteads-For-Women Campaign In Western Canada," *Great Plains Quarterly* 29 (Fall 2009): 269–70.

24 For other examples, see Sarah Carter, "Transnational Perspectives on the History of Great Plains Women: Gender, Race, Nations and the Forty-ninth Parallel," *American Review of Canadian Studies* 33:4 (Winter 2003): 565–96 and *Imperial Plots: Women, Land, and the Spadework of British Colonialism on the Canadian Prairies* (Winnipeg: University of Manitoba Press, 2016), esp. 147–244.

25 Tonia M. Compton, "'They Have as Much Right There as Bachelors': Provisions for Female Landowners in Nineteenth-Century Homestead Legislation," paper presented to the Western History Association, Oklahoma City, October 2007; Sarah Carter, *The Importance of Being Monogamous: Marriage and Nation Building* in *Western Canada to 1915* (Edmonton: Athabasca University Press and University of Alberta Press, 2008). Until 1985 the Canadian Indian Act stipulated that Indigenous women lost Indian status if they married a non-status man.

26 See for instance Norma J. Wilson, "Essential Servants: Immigrant Domestics on the Canadian Prairies, 1885–1930," in Armitage and Jameson, *The Women's West*, 207–18; Linda Rasmussen, Lorna Rasmussen, Candace Savage, and Anne Wheeler, *A Harvest Yet To Reap: A History of Prairie Women* (Toronto: The Women's Press, 1976), 12–13, 18–21.

27 Twelve were deserted, four were divorced, one was a nun, and the marital status of twenty-nine was unknown. Most of the widows filed for their homesteads as widows; some inherited their husbands' claims when the men died after filing their homestead claims but before making final proof.

28 Belgarde's given name on her Homestead Claim File was Margaret; it appears as Margaret or Marguerite on different documents, and I have used both names.

29 "North Dakota: Turtle Mountain," https://www.ndstudies.gov/curriculum/high-school/turtle-mountain, accessed May 15, 2021.

30 Michel Hogue, *Metis and the Medicine Line: Creating a Border and Dividing a People* (Chapel Hill: University of North Carolina Press and Regina: University of Regina Press, 2015), 22–23, 29–30. Chippewa, Ojibwe, Ojibwa, and Ojibway refer to the same people. I use Ojibwe, and also Chippewa because it was the name the U.S. government used for bands and reservations.

31 Hogue, *Metis and the Medicine Line*, 42. Kittson, who was born in Lower Canada, was a business partner of future Minnesota Governor Henry Sibley.

32 Belgarde Homestead File; *Minnesota Territorial Census Schedules, 1849–1855* (St. Paul: Minnesota Historical Society, 2000); 1880 U.S. Federal Census, Pembina County, Dakota Territory. Margaret Belgarde died February 12, 1893, and was buried in Pembina.

33 Forty-three of 123 Canadians (35 percent) settled in Bottineau County and 29 (24 percent) in Rolette County. Calculated from Homestead Files.

34 Hogue, *Metis and the Medicine Line*, 198–99.

35 Hogue, *Metis and the Medicine Line*, 199.

36 This is a brief summary of the much more complex issues surrounding who, over time, "belonged" to which communities, and who could settle on the Turtle Mountain Reservation or claim Chippewa status. For more on this issue see Nicholas Vrooman, *"The Whole Country was... 'One Robe'": The Little Shell Tribe's America* (Helena: Drumlummon Institute, 2012); George T. Skibine, Acting Principal Deputy Assistant Secretary – Indian Affairs, *Summary under the Criteria and Evidence for Final Determination Against the Federal Acknowledgment of the Little Shell Tribe of Chippewa Indians of Montana Prepared in Response to a Petition Submitted to the Assistant Secretary - Indian Affairs for Federal Acknowledgment that this Group Exists as an Indian Tribe* (Washington, D.C.: October 27, 2009), hereinafter called *Montana Little Shell Final Government Report*; Gregory S. Camp, "Working out Their Own Salvation: The Allotment of Land in Severalty and the Turtle Mountain Chippewa Band, 1870–1920," *American Indian Culture and Research Journal* 14:2 (1990): 19–38; Gerhard J. Ens, "After the Buffalo: The Reformation of the Turtle Mountain Métis Community, 1879–1905," in *New Faces of the Fur Trade: Selected Papers of the Seventh North American Fur Trade Conference, Halifax, Nova Scotia, 1995*, eds. Jo-Anne Fiske, Susan Sleeper-Smith, and William Wicken (East Lansing: Michigan State University Press, 1998), 139–52. I am grateful to Heather Devine and Michel Hogue for advice on this section.

37 See Rhoda R. Gilman, Carolyn Gilman, and Deborah M. Stultz, *The Red River Trails: Oxcart Routes Between St. Paul and the Selkirk Settlements, 1820–1870* (St. Paul: Minnesota Historical Society Press, 1979).

38 Quoted in *Montana Little Shell Final Government Report*, 23.

39 *Montana Little Shell Final Government Report*, 133–34.

40 Marguerite Azure Homestead Claim File, Testimony of Claimant, July 4, 1891.

41 Canadian scrip commissions determining eligibility for Métis scrip also tried to determine whether a person was north or south of the 49th Parallel on July 15, 1870, the day the Manitoba Act went into effect, bringing Manitoba into the Canadian Confederation.

42 Testimony of Claimant, Azure Homestead File. The racial ethnic patterns of homestead settlement varied throughout the West, and within the Devils Lake Land Office territory. For a different pattern of ethnic homesteading around the Devils Lake Sioux Reservation (now the Spirit Lake Sioux Reservation) during the implementation of the Dawes Act,

see Karen V. Hansen, *Encounter on the Great Plains: Scandinavian Settlers and the Dispossession of Dakota Indians, 1890–1930* (New York: Oxford University Press, 2013).

43 Rose M. Sheridan Homestead Claim File. The two witnesses who supported her final proof statement, Phidoleme (or Phidolenne) Robarge and Napoleon Robarge, confirmed that she was absent as teacher and superintendent of the mission school. Both stated that the value of her homestead was $1000. Their testimonies were unusual in that they were not identical and did not simply repeat Sheridan's testimony. Testimony of Witnesses, Sheridan Homestead File.

44 Brenda J. Child, *Holding Our World Together: Ojibwe Women and the Survival of Community* (New York: Penguin Books, 2012), 22–27. Child discussed Cherokee and Iroquois women in this passage, but went on to discuss Ojibwe agriculture, and her observation fits the Hidatsa as well. On third gender roles among Indigenous tribes, see Evelyn Blackwood, "Sexuality and Gender in Certain Native American Tribes," *Signs* 10:1 (1984): 27–42; and Beatrice Medicine, "Warrior Women–Sex Role Alternatives for Plains Indian Women," in *The Hidden Half: Studies of Plains Indian Women*, eds. Patricia Albers and Beatrice Medicine (Latham, MD: University Press of America, 1983), 267–80.

45 Gilbert L. Wilson in *Buffalo Bird Woman's Garden* (1917; repr., St. Paul: Minnesota Historical Society Press, 1987), 6–7. Originally published as Gilbert Livingstone Wilson, *Agriculture of the Hidatsa Indians: An Indian Interpretation* (PhD diss., University of Minnesota, 1917). Buffalo Bird Woman's Hidatsa name is often spelled Maxidiwiac, but Michael W. Stevens, *Biographical Dictionary of the Mandan, Hidatsa, and Arikara* (New Town, ND: Fort Berthold Library, 2003) gives Mahidiweash as the first spelling; it more closely approximates the Hidatsa pronunciation. http://lib.fortbertholdcc.edu/FortBerthold/TATBIO.htm, accessed July 24, 2015.

46 Gilbert L. Wilson, *Waheenee: An Indian Girl's Story* (1921; repr., Lincoln: University of Nebraska Press, 1981), 7; Wilson, *Buffalo Bird Woman's Garden*, 7–8.

47 Wilson, *Buffalo Bird Woman's Garden* and *Waheenee*.

48 Hidatsa-Mandan Report, Fort Berthold Reservation 1912, Gilbert L. and Frederick N. Wilson Papers, Minnesota Historical Society, vol. 11, 36 (hereinafter cited as Wilson Papers, MHS); Wilson, *Buffalo Bird Woman's Garden*, 119.

49 "'INDIAN LIFE IN FORMER DAYS COMPARED WITH THE PRESENT LIFE' Related on Aug. 1918 by Buffalobird-woman, Hidatsa, born about 1841," Hidatsa-Mandan Report, Fort Berthold Reservation, 1918, vol., 22, 375, Wilson Papers, MHS. Wilson changed Mahidiweash's presumed birth year at times, dating it between 1839–1841.

50 William Cronon, Howard R. Lamar, Katherine G. Morrissey, and Jay Gitlin, "Women and the West: Rethinking the Western History Survey Course," *Western Historical Quarterly* 17: 3 (July 1986): 269–90.

51 Elizabeth Jameson, *All That Glitters: Class, Culture, and Community in Cripple Creek* (Urbana: University of Illinois Press, 1998), 132; Susan Armitage, "Making Connections: Gender, Race, and Place in Oregon Country," in *One Step over the Line: Toward a History of Women in the North American Wests*, eds. Elizabeth Jameson and Sheila McManus (Edmonton: University of Alberta Press and Athabasca University Press, 2008), 62. See also "Guns to Butter: Reconceiving the American West," chapter 2 in this volume.

52 Wilson, *Buffalo Bird Woman's Garden;* Child, *Holding Our World Together,* 22–27; Cheryl J. Foote and Sandra K. Schackel, "Indian Women of New Mexico, 1535–1696," in *New Mexico Women: Intercultural Perspectives*, eds. Joan M. Jensen and Darlis A. Miller (Albuquerque, University of New Mexico Press, 1986), 17–40; 18–21; Joan M. Jensen, "Cloth, Butter, and Boarders," in *Promise to the Land: Essays on Rural Women* (Albuquerque: University of New Mexico Press, 1991), 193–94; Jensen, *With These Hands: Women Working on the Land* (Old Westbury, NY: The Feminist Press, 1981), 107–8, 112,

145. For a dairy that financed a ranch herd, see Teresa Jordon, *Cowgirls: Women of the American West* (Lincoln: University of Nebraska Press, 1982; 1992 ed.), 120.

53   Jensen, "Cloth, Butter, and Boarders," 94; "Margarine," *The Canadian Encyclopedia*, http://www.thecanadianencyclopedia.ca/en/article/margarine/, accessed July 28, 2015.

54   "United Farm Women of Alberta," *The Canadian Encyclopedia*, http://www.thecanadianencyclopedia.ca/en/article/united-farm-women-of-alberta/, accessed July 28, 2015; Nanci Langford, *Politics, Pitchforks and Pickle Jars: 75 Years of Organized Farm Women in Alberta* (Calgary: Detselig Enterprises, 1997).

55   May Wing interview, Victor, Colorado, October 21, 1978.

56   May Wing interview, Boulder, Colorado, March 6, 1976.

57   Mary Pardo, "Mexican American Women Grassroots Community Activists: 'Mothers of East Los Angeles'," in Jameson and Armitage, *Writing the Range*, 553–68. Pardo's article first appeared in *Frontiers: A Journal of Women Studies* 11:1 (1990): 1–7. Hugh Dellios, "Group Preaches Gospel of Water Conservation," *Chicago Tribune*, March 20, 1995; Marilyn Martinez, "Legacy of a Mother's Dedication," *Los Angeles Times*, September 7, 1995; "Mother's Group Fights Back in Los Angeles," *New York Times*, December 5, 1989; Michael Quintanilla, "The Earth Mother," *Los Angeles Times*, April 24, 1995; Louis Sahagun, "The Mothers of East L.A. Transform Themselves and Their Community," *Los Angeles Times*, August 13, 1989; Nina Schuyler, "LA Moms Fight Back," *Progressive* 56:8 (August 1992): 13; "'Mothers of East LA' Takes On Air Quality at Boyle Heights Schools," EGP News.com, Eastman Group Publications, Inc., August 4, 2011; "Mothers Open Meat Market to Fund Scholarships," *Los Angeles Times*, October 7, 1999; Connie Koenenn, "To Protect the Children of East L.A.," *Los Angeles Times*, December 23, 1991.

58   Beulah Pryor interview, Colorado Springs, Colorado, May 6, 1979.

59   For this distinction between the U.S. and Canadian Wests, see for instance George F. G. Stanley, "Western Canada and the Frontier Thesis," Canadian Historical Association, *Report of the Annual Meeting, 1940*, 105–14. On the legacy of Canada's residential schools for Indigenous children, see Truth and Reconciliation Commission of Canada, *Final Report of the Truth and Reconciliation Commission of Canada, Volume One: Summary: Honouring the Truth, Reconciling for the Future* (Toronto: James Lorimer & Company Ltd., Publishers, 2015).

60   May Wing interview, Colorado Springs, February 16, 1979.

61   Frederick Jackson Turner, "The Significance of the Frontier in American History," in *History, Frontier, and Section*, ed. Martin Ridge (Albuquerque: University of New Mexico Press, 1993), 82; Frederick Jackson Turner, "The Significance of History," in Ridge *History, Frontier, and Section*, 49. This essay was originally published in the *Wisconsin Journal of Education* in 1891.

62   Heilbrun, *Writing a Woman's Life*, 13.

63   Wilson, *Waheenee*; Edward Goodbird as told to Gilbert L. Wilson, *Goodbird the Indian: His Story* (1914; repr., St. Paul: Minnesota Historical Society Press, 1965); Carolyn Gilman and Mary Jane Schneider, *The Way to Independence: Memories of A Hidatsa Indian Family, 1840–1920* (St. Paul: Minnesota Historical Society Press, 1987), Museum Exhibit Series No. 3.

64   Wilson, *Waheenee*, 121–27. Wilson gave more detailed attention to Mahidiweash's first brief marriage to Magpie. He ended chapter 13, about her first marriage to Magpie, with Waheenee saying simply "And so I was wed." He began chapter 14, "A Buffalo Hunt" with: "My young husband and I lived together but a few years. He died of lung sickness, and, after I had mourned a year, I married Son-of-a-Star, a Mandan," *Waheenee*, 126–27.

Hidatsa-Mandan Report – Fort Berthold Reservation, 1915 (part 1.), vol., 17, 318, 323–24, Wilson Papers, MHS.

65 Hidatsa-Mandan Report – Fort Berthold Reservation, 1915 (part 1.), vol. 17, 329, Wilson Papers, MHS.

66 Hidatsa-Mandan Report – Fort Berthold Reservation, 1915 (part 2.), vol., 18, 450, Wilson Papers, MHS.

67 Told in the summer of 1914, by Buffalobird-woman, an Hidatsa born about 1839," Notebook – Hidatsa-Mandan Indians, 1910–1916, 1918, vol., 30, 84, Wilson Papers, MHS.

68 Wilson, *Waheenee,* 175–76.

69 See Beverly Stoeltje, "A Helpmate for Man Indeed: The Image of the Frontier Woman," *Journal of American Folklore* 88:347 (January–March 1975): 27–31; Rayna Green, "The Pocahantas Perplex: The Image of Indian Women in American Culture," *Massachusetts Review* 16:4 (1976): 698–714.

70 *Lone Star.* The ethnic labels (Anglo, Chicano) are the ones Sayles used in the screenplay.

71 Faragher, Buhle, Czitrom, and Armitage, *Out of Many,* 481. For the controversy, see "Religious Right Groups Join Forces to Select Texas Textbooks," *Church and State,* October 2002; "Textbook Publishers Learn to Avoid Messing with Texas," *New York Times,* June 29, 2002; Dr. Ricky Dobbs, Assistant Professor of History, Texas A&M University at Commerce, "High School American History (After Reconstruction) Textbook Review," Texas Public Policy Foundation, State Board of Education Textbook Hearing, August 23, 2002.

72 "Texas officials: Schools should teach that slavery was 'side issue' to Civil War," *Washington Post,* July 6, 2015.

14

Torches Passed and Present

June 20, 2017

I retired from the University of Calgary July 1, 2017. My year as president of the Western History Association had seemed like a professional culmination; my presidential address, which I offered as my 2016 Chair's Lecture, wove together many threads of my research, much of it undertaken during my years in Calgary. My 2016 lecture felt like a summation. It seemed both egocentric and anticlimactic to deliver a final Chair's Lecture in 2017.

I had spent over forty years in higher education, eighteen of them at the University of Calgary as the Imperial Oil-Lincoln McKay Chair in American Studies. During those years, my greatest professional pleasures had included graduate teaching, my Chair's Lectures, and helping organize conferences that launched the field of western women's history and that promoted inclusive, comparative, and transnational histories. Combining these passions into a thank-you and farewell, I hosted a conference to celebrate and feature some of the graduate students with whom I had been privileged to work at the University of Calgary and the University of New Mexico.

I called the conference "Torches Passed and Present," taking the theme from a line in President John F. Kennedy's 1961 Inaugural Address: "the torch has been passed to a new generation. . . ." During my years of teaching, the torch-passing had felt less like a one-way hand-off and more like a continuous relay, in which students passed their ideas to me as much as I to them. Those exchanges and the ideas they sparked were part of what I loved about graduate teaching.

The talented speakers at the "Torches Passed" conference didn't really need me to pass any torches to them—they had already taken their own torches some distance down their own paths. The concept of a generation is problematic as well. The speakers had belonged to different academic cohorts, covered a wide age span, and one former student is older than I am.

Susan Armitage, my longtime friend and writing partner, simply announced that she was coming and wanted to speak. We had been friends since 1974, had worked together to organize the first conferences in western women's history, to edit two anthologies—*The Women's West* and *Writing the Range: Race, Class and History in the Women's West*—and to establish the Coalition for Western Women's History.[1] So multiple overlapping generations were represented on the conference program. I stuck with the "Torches Passed" theme because I'm a metaphor junkie, and it felt good to recognize that I was pulling back, and the next generations of historians were coming into professional maturity.

Part of my impetus to host "Torches Passed and Present" was my continuing mission to promote historians' cross-border exchanges. I wanted to introduce some of my former students to one another. Even people who had studied at the same university did not necessarily know one another, given the different times when they were enrolled. In my invitations to participants, I billed the conference as a family reunion for cousins who had never met.

Most of all, I wanted to showcase these colleagues, in all their diversity. Every student with whom I've worked brought personal interests, questions, goals, and career aspirations. The conference program reflected the range of subjects that engaged them and the uses to which they had put their graduate educations. Their multiple career paths offered an array of answers to the question "What can you do with a history degree?" I introduce them here in the approximate sequence of our association, basing these brief sketches on the biographies they submitted for the conference program.

Susan Armitage (PhD, London School of Economics) was, in 2017, an Emerita Professor of History and Women's Studies at Washington State University in Pullman, where she taught and wrote about women in the U.S. West for thirty years. In addition to our two co-edited volumes, she also co-edited *So Much to be Done* with Ruth Moynihan and Christiane Duchamps, and *Speaking History* with Laurie Mercier, and is the author of *Shaping the Public Good: Women Making History in the Pacific Northwest*.

Evelyn Schlatter (MA, University of Denver, PhD, University of New Mexico) was a senior analyst with the Intelligence Project at the Southern Poverty Law Center in 2017, where she specialized in anti-LGBTQ movements and White nationalist movements. Her expertise in right-wing political and social movements, gender, and sexuality could be traced, in part, to her UNM dissertation, "Aryan Cowboys: White Supremacist Ideology and the Search for a New Frontier, 1960–1995."[2] Some of her dissertation research had terrified me, like the times she stuffed her short hair into a baseball cap and visited gun shows, passing as an adolescent boy. Since 2021 she has been a research consultant for progressive organizations.

Dedra McDonald Birzer (MA, University of Wisconsin, PhD, University of New Mexico) worked as an Adjunct Professor at the University of Texas at San Antonio during 1998–1999, while completing her dissertation, "Negotiated Conquests: Domestic Servants and Gender in the Spanish and Mexican Borderlands, 1598–1860." From 2000–2020 she worked as a Lecturer in History and Rhetoric at Hillsdale College, Hillsdale, Michigan, while managing a six-child household and continuing to publish. In 2020 she was appointed director and editor-in-chief of the South Dakota Historical Society Press.

Benny Andrés, Jr. (MA, PhD, University of New Mexico) was an associate professor of history and Latin American Studies at the University of North Carolina, Charlotte, where he taught Latino history, the history of the American West, the U.S.-Mexico borderlands, U.S. immigration history, U.S. food history, and a graduate seminar in modern U.S. history. His research and publications examine transmigration, labor, race relations, and environmental issues along the California borderlands during the twentieth century. In 2015, Dr. Andrés published *Power and Control in the Imperial Valley: Nature, Agribusiness, and Workers on the California Borderland, 1900–1940*, based on his award-winning dissertation. Choice selected it as an Outstanding Academic Title.

Susan Kwiatkowski (MA, University of Calgary) was a student in my first undergraduate class at the University of Calgary, History of Women in the U.S. West, fall semester, 1999. She combined her pursuit of academic education with a full-time job with Information Technologies at the University of Calgary, taking one class each semester. Having worked for the University of Calgary since 1981 and having completed a BA in English from Mount Allison University in 1996, she earned a BA in History at the University of Calgary in 2004. In 2009 she completed her MA, with a thesis, "Creating Young Citizens: Education in the Borderlands of Alberta and Montana, 1895–1914." I was at a bit of a loss after she completed her MA—she had been a constant in my life for a decade, and it was weird to face a semester without Sue. In 2017 she was a senior analyst with Change and Release Management in IT Governance and Administration at the University of Calgary. She has since joined me in the ranks of the happily retired.

Sean Marchetto (MA, University of Calgary) was the first MA student I supervised at the University of Calgary, beginning in the fall of 1999. His thesis, "Tune In, Turn On, Go Punk: American Punk Counterculture, 1968–1985," introduced me to a history I would never otherwise have explored, and it's fair to say he taught me at least as much as I taught him. In 2017 he was an elementary school principal and a former high school chemistry and philosophy teacher. He was also a writer, a sometimes journalist, a former late-night radio host, and occasional art auctioneer. He was once honored as the Calgary Exhibition & Stampede Parking Lot Attendant of the Year.

Cynthia Loch-Drake (MA, University of Calgary, PhD, York University) is a historian of gender and labor. She and Sean Marchetto were both enrolled in the first graduate seminar I taught at the University of Calgary, on U.S. social history. Sarah Carter and I jointly supervised her MA thesis, "Jailed Heroes and Kitchen Heroines: Class, Gender, and the Medalta Potteries Strike in Postwar Alberta." Since earning her doctorate in history at York University, Dr. Loch-Drake has worked as an adjunct professor in the Toronto area teaching courses in the history of women, work, economics, and business.

Michel Hogue (MA, University of Calgary, PhD, University of Wisconsin) was, in 2017, an associate professor in the department of history at Carleton University in Ottawa, with teaching specialties in Indigenous, Canadian, and U.S. histories. His research to that point had focused on the experiences of Métis and First Nations on the transborder Great Plains and their encounters with the agents of the Canadian and U.S. governments. That research began at the University of Calgary, where Sarah Carter and I supervised his MA thesis, "Crossing the Line: The Plains Cree in the Canada-United States Borderlands, 1870–1900." He is the author of *Metis and the Medicine Line Creating a Border and Dividing a People* (Chapel Hill: University of North Carolina Press; Regina: University of Regina Press, 2015), which won the Stubbendieck Great Plains Distinguished Book Prize from the Centre for Great Plains Studies, University of Nebraska, and the Prairie Clio Award from the Canadian Historical Association.

Carol Archer (MA, PhD, University of Calgary) earned a BA in English and History at the University of Victoria. She later entered the Faculty of Education at the University of Calgary and received a Diploma in Curriculum and Instruction in the Library Program. After a career as a teacher-librarian and administrator with the Calgary Board of Education, she returned to the University of Calgary where she completed her MA and PhD in History with an MA thesis, "Surviving the Transition: Women's Property Rights and Inheritance in New Mexico, 1848–1912," and her dissertation, "'El Amparo de la Ley': Hispanas' Use of Spanish Mexican and Anglo American Law in Northern New Mexico and Southern Colorado, 1848–1912."

Gretchen Albers (MA University of Nebraska, PhD, University of Calgary) came to Canada in 2005 to pursue doctoral work. Her dissertation, "Boundaries of the Heart: White Women, Indigenous People, and the Christian Missions to the Dakotas, 1862–1910," focused on missionaries on the upper U.S. Plains and Manitoba. In 2017 she worked as a freelance editor of academic books and journals, and as a historical consultant, mainly in the area of First Nations land claims and treaty rights.

Amy McKinney (MA, Montana State University, PhD, University of Calgary) completed her doctorate in 2011. Her dissertation, "'How I Cook, Keep House, Help with Farm Work Too': Rural Women in Post-World War II Montana," examined how and to what degree the 1950s suburban housewife ideal translated to rural areas. In 2017 she was an associate professor of history at Northwest College in Powell, Wyoming, had published articles on rural women, and was researching Harriette Cushman, the first woman poultry specialist for the U.S. Extension Service, and her role as a professional woman in agriculture.

Andrew Varsanyi (MA, University of Calgary) was a student in my class, "Wild West/Mild West?: Comparative History of the Canadian and U.S. Wests" in 2007. He earned undergraduate degrees in History, Political Science, and Education at the University of Calgary, and taught before returning to graduate school to complete his MA in history in 2015. His thesis, "Principle vs. Pragmatism: Henry Loucks and South Dakota Populism 1884–1900," focused on Henry Langford Loucks, the South Dakota Populist leader who emigrated to South Dakota from Canada. In 2017 Andrew was the Director of Business Development at Critical Control Energy Services, a Calgary-based oil and gas software and service company. He was also the co-founder of Evolved Metrics, a software company. He has since continued his graduate studies as a doctoral student at the University of Nebraska, Lincoln.

These diverse academic interests and career paths represent only a sample of the twenty-two graduate students I supervised or co-supervised, whose work spanned two universities in two countries, two North American borderlands and some five centuries.

The conference presentations reflected the speakers' diverse academic interests and career paths. Susan Kwiatkowski, Carol Archer, and Andrew Varsanyi presented personal reflections in a session titled "Lifelong Learning." Benny Andrés and Michel Hogue presented research on two North American Borderlands, speaking on "Border Jumpers: A Forgotten Story of Americans Illegally Entering the U.S. from Mexico, 1924–1933," (Andrés) and "Wild West/Mild West: Writing Histories Across the Forty-Ninth Parallel" (Hogue). Susan Armitage spoke about "Collaborations," an incisive talk from a stellar collaborator and writing partner. Three speakers presented their recent research in women's histories. Dedra McDonald Birzer spoke on "'Militant Generosity': Dorothy Thompson's and Rose Wilder Lane's Practical Activism during the Great Depression and World War II." Cynthia Loch-Drake presented "'Standing up for ourselves': Connecting Women and Production and Reproduction in Edmonton's Postwar Packing Industry." Amy McKinney spoke on "Harriette Cushman: Building a Place for Poultry in Montana." The final session explored three distinct careers. Evelyn Schlatter's title demonstrated her characteristic way with words: "The Accidental Expert: How I Learned to Stop Worrying and Love the Qualm." Sean Marchetto traced his career "From Punk to Principal." And Gretchen Albers spoke as a public historian on "Historic Research in the Context of Land Development: Paskapoo Slopes and Indigenous Story-Telling." The program abundantly showcased the wide range of history graduate students' interests, talents, and achievements.

In the days leading up to the conference I had been packing up my university office. Like most historians, I'm a pack rat. I sorted decades of research notes, lecture notes, articles, class lists, and student's folders that evoked memories of research trips, conferences, and all the students at all stages of their educations. As I sorted, packed, and discarded mounds of documents, what I thought about most and what I treasure most are the relationships. I could continue to research and write after retirement if I wished; I could continue to visit with colleagues at conferences. My teaching would continue for a few years with the graduate students I was still supervising or on whose committees I served, but eventually it became the part of my work that ended.

As I prepared to celebrate the people I had once supervised, I thought about teaching relationships, and especially about the teachers who had inspired me and whose teaching I had tried to emulate. I was fortunate to learn from some extraordinary teachers. Mrs. Charlotte Matthews, my grade eight and nine English teacher, turned me into something of a grammar fanatic. My high school English teacher, Dr. William H. Hall, met each of his students where we were and pushed us. He made me cut everything I wrote in half. Three women I discussed in my 2012 lecture—Hannah Goldberg at Antioch College, Kathryn Kish Sklar, and Marilyn Blatt Young at the University of Michigan—encouraged me and inspired me with their intellects and with their abilities to manage whole lives that included families and careers.

I thought particularly about Robert S. Fogarty, my mentor at Antioch College, who unknowingly drew me into the profession because I thought everyone would be as smart and kind as he was. Antioch had a work-study program; every other quarter for five years we left campus to work somewhere. Bob found me my last job, organizing the archive of the Western Federation of Miners, at the Western History Collections at the University of Colorado. That job led to my BA thesis, and ultimately to my dissertation and subsequent book, *All That Glitters*. He also hired me as his teaching assistant and gave me my first course to teach on my own, the summer after I graduated. Bob Fogarty taught me two essentials about history and about teaching. First, history matters because people matter. And second, teaching is an act of faith.

In the first class I assisted for him, a young woman who was really caught up in historic preservation went on at some length about a building she had worked to save. Bob listened respectfully, commented on the significance of the structure, and complimented her on her work to save it. Then he said something like, "You know, we must always remember that the buildings are not what is most important; it's the people who lived and worked in them. The buildings are important because that's where people lived, worked, and made history." That simple statement clicked for me. History matters because it is about people. Bob introduced me to social history, and opened historical territory far removed from what my classmate Bob Berard called "battles, dates, and kings." That simple shift later helped me think about histories of work, family, and households.

Maybe the most important thing Bob told me about teaching was that it is an act of faith—that often the things you teach cannot connect for students until much later when they have the experience to connect with the history. You offer what you can and hope it is useful when it clicks with their experience. That insight was helpful when I discovered, as we all do, how quickly I no longer shared my students' frames of reference. Before I got my first full-time job in 1976, a student reminded me that for him

Vietnam was junior high, not a personally life-altering chapter in national history. And by the early 1980s I faced students in women's history classes who thought they were learning the ancient history of a movement that was no longer necessary, a movement that had, by then, occupied a lot of my life. It worried me that they might not be prepared for some of the realities they faced after they graduated, for which their experience had not yet prepared them. On the last day of class, which is an invitation to try to say something inspirational, I began to conclude by saying something like this:

> I hope that everything you learned this semester represents chapters in women's histories that remain in the past. I hope you never encounter the kinds of inequities that prompted women in the past to organize for change. I hope that you achieve everything you hope for, that you can reach what you want personally and professionally without regard to gender or race or any other socially constructed category of difference. I hope that you exceed all your professional goals. I hope that you find relationships that sustain you. But I also hope that if, someday, you are unjustly passed up for a promotion, or if Prince Charming hits you, or other things happen that I hope you never face—if that happens, I hope you know you are not to blame, you are not alone, you are not crazy, and you have resources.

I could only pitch it out there, hope they never needed to remember my words, but that the history I'd tried to teach might inform them as citizens and that it would be there when it mattered.

History matters because people matter. Teaching is an act of faith. It is also, in my experience, a relationship, a two-way exchange. Graduate teaching pushed me intellectually; students often gave me the sparks of ideas at just the right moment. "Torches Passed" was about those relationships, with the friends and colleagues who attended that day, and those with whom I have shared teaching relationships. It was a day, selfishly, to celebrate the folks who helped make my working years most rewarding.

History, too, has been a relationship for me—it connects my present with the past and future. More personally, it has been a relationship with the people who made the history I studied and taught. I got to know some of those people and their families personally, as I recorded their oral histories. I remain deeply grateful and honored by their trust. I got to "know" other historical actors in the archives, and in my colleagues' books, and tried to introduce them to students in my classes and to my readers. I have sought to tell their stories respectfully, clearly, and accessibly.

While I wanted "Torches Passed" to be about my former students, retirement was inescapably a time to reflect on what I valued in my career, the changes I'd seen in some four decades in higher education, and what I most valued. I concluded the "Torches Passed and Present" conference with a few reflections on the academic worlds in which I had worked, and those the next generations would inherit.

I entered graduate school as the social movements of the 1950s and 1960s inspired new approaches to history. Nothing in the textbook histories that focused on nation states, wars, and public politics could explain or illuminate the African American Civil Rights Movement, the Anti-Vietnam-War Movement, the Women's Liberation Movement, or any other grass-roots social movements that had made change. Struggles for racial justice, women's rights, workers' rights, and peace movements did not begin in the 20th century, but they had not gotten much attention in K–12 classrooms or university survey courses. Nor had histories of work, gender, or race relations that could explain why and how people had organized public movements for change. Those histories were never divorced from political and economic histories, from the histories of battles, dates, and elections. Many women were admitted to graduate and professional schools during World War II, like my mother who entered medical school in 1945, the last medical school class before returning soldiers took women's industrial jobs and used their veterans' benefits to enter higher education and professional schools. Many of those returning veterans became the first members of their families to attend universities, increasing the numbers of racial, ethnic, and religious minorities with post-secondary degrees. The confluence of post-World War II social movements just as increasing numbers of women, people of color, and ethnic minorities entered the university ultimately nourished the questions that led to the new social history, women's history, African American, Mexican American/Chicanx/Latinx, Indigenous, working-class, and LGBTQ2S+ histories. These in turn nourished the new western histories that sought to incorporate their topics into the regional narrative and that interrogated the triumphal national projects that celebrated European settlement of the U.S. and Canadian Wests.

I became part of a fortunate generation that got to develop women's history and women studies and establish women studies programs. The histories of previously silenced or marginalized people of color and "ordinary" working people informed my approaches to women's and labor histories. I tried always to be conscious of how race, class, and gender intersected in people's lives, shaping the challenges they faced, and the changes they sought.

There are now more women in our classrooms, curricula, and tenure streams than when I started. When I began teaching, I thought that women's presence would change academic culture, the knowledge we produced, and the ways we framed our inquiries. That process moves slowly, unevenly, and incrementally. The academic fields in which women have had the greatest impact have often also lost status within the university and in public perceptions. In my 2012 lecture (chapter 10) I told a story about the eminent historian and former president of the American Historical Association, Louise Tilly, who counseled me not to worry about the pressures I felt as a department chair with a demanding teaching load and a toddler. She told me I was measuring myself against a professional model based on a male work-cycle. "Men do their best work in their 30s and 40s," she told me. "We do our best work in our 50s and 60s." It is easier for many parents to be productive after our children are grown, or at least after the intense years of parenting infants and toddlers are past. Many professional expectations are projected from a now largely outdated normative male breadwinner career path rooted in gender, sexual, racial, and class privilege, with a female helpmate at home to do the primary childcare, cooking, cleaning, and laundry, freeing the scholar to focus on research and teaching. That model never applied to most people and no longer applies to most academics, including many male colleagues who share household and parental responsibilities.

The differences are starker in the U.S. than in Canada, which has a more flexible tenure clock. In the United States, one must come up for tenure by the sixth year after entering a tenure-stream position. For many women, this has meant that the pressures to publish and apply for tenure coincides with their last good childbearing years. Our professional expectations and timelines still do not adequately address how gender affects the ways we can combine career and family. As I compiled the presenters' biographies for this essay, I noticed that family commitments had affected the career options and choices of every partnered woman. Each of them had made choices to delay their educations, or to work or study in a specific locality, based on the needs of partners or children.

Those intertwined commitments still adversely affect women's pay and promotions. It is difficult to combine careers when both partners are academics, and particularly when both are in the same field. Finding two academic jobs in the same community is not easy. This has often led to the privileging of a man's career over a woman's, with women doing more sessional/adjunct teaching so they can live in the same community with their fully employed partners.[3] Women earn less in part because sessional/adjunct teaching doesn't pay well, and because if they are hired into a permanent position, their part-time teaching experience and previous publications rarely influence their starting pay or count toward promotion or tenure.

I discussed many of the obstacles to valuing women's academic work in chapter 10: the devaluing of work about women and gender, the assumption that women address "second rate" subjects and publish in "second rate" journals, and that we do too much service work.[4] We have not significantly expanded professional expectations of what constitutes valuable scholarship, or the multiple ways to contribute to scholarship and education. Historians still value monographs over articles, and single-authored work over collaboration. Those expectations made me think of Margaret Fuller, the subject of my first published article, an American transcendentalist and feminist, one of the leading U.S. intellectuals of the 19th century.[5] Fuller judged her own intellect as inferior to many of her male contemporaries, like Ralph Waldo Emerson and Henry David Thoreau. She thought she had "a second-rate mind" because, she said, "Conversation is my natural element. I need to be called out, and never think alone, without imagining a companion."[6] The insistence on the isolated intellectual and lone author undervalues the importance and richness of collaborative work, of conversations and relationships, of multiple perspectives on a collective and connected past.

The "Torches Passed" conference theme connoted legacies and inheritance. Although those metaphors were overly simple, they expressed my faith in those who continue this work after I retired, and I regretted that they would not inherit an easier academic world. It has seemed to me that teaching, history, and professors have all been increasingly devalued throughout North America during my years in higher education. When I started teaching at the University of Calgary, the faculty was featured prominently on the university web page as part of what made ours a great university. Over the years, the typeface about the faculty got smaller, and then moved to the bottom of the page, and then disappeared. When I started teaching, faculty determined the university mission and curriculum. Administrators would not attend a meeting of the Faculty Senate without an invitation but would focus on raising money and generating support for the programs the faculty generated and approved. In recent years I've become a little dizzy keeping up with the newest iterations of our mission as determined by an increasingly large body of administrators.

When I was an undergraduate, and when I started teaching, we had distribution requirements that ensured that students had some exposure to the social sciences, humanities, and sciences. In the United States, education majors had to take a U.S. history course. When I taught at the University of Wisconsin-La Crosse, all social work students were required to take a women's studies or African American studies course. The broad liberal arts base is no longer required in many universities.

Contrary to some popular concepts of a university education, we don't educate people for jobs—or not solely for jobs—but for the capacity to learn, to think critically, to change and adapt to changing circumstances. We know, if we are honest, that the specific jobs for which we can train students today will change radically or become obsolete during their working years. We educate not just for the job market, but also for democratic citizenship. We need look no further than south of the border to see how important it is that our citizens and our leaders know our core governing documents, the values they inscribe, and our history.

As I write this, the histories I have worked to recover and to include in history texts are under attack in the United States. The achievements of the social movements that inspired those histories are also under attack. The connection is not a coincidence. Much of what I have written can not be taught today in Florida classrooms, the result of a right-wing political agenda to erase the histories of race, women, LGBTQ2S+ persons, and social inequalities and to silence histories of resistance and dissent. Transgender children have become political targets, compounding the difficulty of already vulnerable young lives and using them as another way to attack public education. The history of slavery cannot be taught in some U.S. classrooms because it might make White children "feel bad." The result of all this will be another generation of children ill-prepared for the world they will inherit. The attacks on inclusive histories and "DEI (diversity, equity and inclusion) hires" reflect the challenge those histories pose to unearned power and privilege. They underscore how powerfully history informs citizenship.

Which brings me back to Bob Fogarty's basic maxim: History matters because it's about people, and people matter.

As I've noted, my move to the University of Calgary prompted me to change my teaching mission from making U.S. students' own histories accessible to making humanity visible across borders—social, economic, and national. Part of that re-visioning process was about me as well. Over time I stopped being startled by Canadian flags over schools and government buildings. I gradually stopped feeling I needed to apologize for being an American and began discerning what about my very American character I valued.

My new position gained me invitations to serve community institutions ranging from the Glenbow Museum and Archives Acquisitions Committee to the Mustard Seed Ministry's Storefront 101 Program that introduced college education to unhoused Calgarians. My community service helped integrate me into my new community. As I gradually felt more and more at home in Calgary, I began to view Canada, Canadian culture, and Canadian politics more fondly and with greater complexity. And I gradually developed different but equally strong loyalties to two nations.

My border-crossing experience is mine alone. I would guess that the process differs individually and is impacted by the age at which one emigrates, and the reasons that propel or draw each immigrant. I was not fleeing a pogrom, genocide, or similar upheaval, but was drawn by an opportunity. I didn't have to learn a new language, though I still wish I spoke French. I could still practice my profession. It was a relatively easy transplantation process—far easier for me than for my ill-fated irises. The move to Canada has been enormously enriching, not just for what I've learned about Canada, and borders and borderlands, but also for what I've learned about myself.

The hardest enduring change, as for many immigrants, remains distance from my family. I have developed even more respect for my grandmother, who left her parents and twelve siblings to emigrate to North America, and who returned to her native London only once before she died. I still miss living in the same city with my brother and sister-in-law, but except during the COVID-19 pandemic I traveled regularly to the United States. Since the COVID-19 pandemic introduced us all to Zoom, I enjoy regular Zoom visits with family and friends.

While I found ways to remain connected to family and friends in the United States, I gradually developed new close friendships and an adoptive family in Calgary. Some of those friends are other transplanted Americans with whom I still celebrate American Thanksgiving, though we have Thanksgiving dinner in the evening because people work, and American Thanksgiving is not a Canadian holiday. This was problematic for my Thanksgiving preparations because the monthly history department meetings were scheduled for noon the fourth Thursday of the month and American Thanksgiving is the fourth Thursday in November. For years, during the November department meeting my colleagues endured my anxiety about the turkey I had left to cook slowly, unbasted, in my oven. Finally, our department administrator, Marion McSheffrey, got tired of watching me squirm and look at my watch, and began scheduling the November department meeting for the third Thursday. The adaptations have sometimes been a two-way street, or maybe a two-way bridge, like the re-scheduled department meetings that became a place to accommodate American Thanksgiving.

When I arrived in 1999, I didn't know whether I would eventually return to the United States. By the time he was in university, my son Daniel told me he was staying in Canada. "What did you expect?" he said. "You brought me here when I was thirteen." I was surprised and gratified when he returned to Calgary after his university years in Ontario. Eventually our family grew, as Daniel blessed me with my treasured Calgary native daughter-in-law Barbara, and then with two grandsons, Stanley and Spencer. Now if someone asks me if I am going to return to the States, I smile and tell them "I have two anchor babies." Here, too, I think of my grandmother. When I was born, she retired from her long social work career in Newark and moved to Galveston. She took care of me while my mother went to medical school, and she shared treasured family stories and her often irreverent and salty humour. She also told me that when she retired at age sixty-nine, she was replaced by a man at three times her salary. She told me never to learn to type well, or if I did not to let my boss know, or I would only ever get to type. I forgot that advice until I was in graduate school and then realized she had taken her own leap of faith, sharing stories with which I couldn't connect personally until experience triggered my memories.

My cross-border journey progressed through stages of feeling uprooted to establishing new work relationships, friendships, and finally watching my family grow in now-familiar soil. My Siberian irises are thriving in my Calgary garden.

My younger colleagues will each continue to find their own paths, their own missions, guided by their own highest ethics and intentions. I do not prescribe my own values, ethics, and intentions for anyone else, but I do think it is important consciously to ground our work in our highest values and to be transparent about our place in our own work. And then we commit to that act of faith. The freedom to do that, trusting our students and our readers to take what they need and leave the rest, lies at the heart of academic freedom, the heart of what I most value about higher education.

In the years before I retired, it seemed to me that teaching began to be subject to something that resembled a factory speed-up. The value of our work was increasingly measured by how many people we could process through the university faster, training them for jobs we know will be obsolete sometime in the future. It's like substituting mass production for fine craftsmanship. I resisted these pressures in the interests of good teaching. Students are neither consumers nor products constructed on assembly lines. The best teaching does not happen in huge classes, and people learn in different ways at different speeds. The humanities, social sciences, and arts remain central for an educated citizenry. I fear that these values are threatened and that the universities that have upheld them are becoming history. Those of us who have security in the academy need to use it to protect those who don't, and to advocate for what we value in a university education.

These cautions and curmudgeonly complaints notwithstanding, I would not choose a different career. I treasure my years in higher education, and I've seen much positive change in those years. My cautions are about safeguarding the gains made in more accurate and inclusive histories and more representative faculty. Our classrooms can be places to build bridges over old divides, to see and value humanity across the boundaries of time, space, social inequality, and national borders. They can become thresholds to not-yet-imagined possibilities. That faith has for centuries maintained oral traditions and long-silenced histories.

When I was growing up in Galveston, each summer I noticed a large gathering of African Americans in Menard Park, on the Seawall along the Gulf of Mexico, down the block from the house at 2823 Ave. Q1/2 where I lived until I was four. It looked to me like a celebration and perhaps a ceremony—a barbecue with speeches, and sometimes with folks simply looking solemnly across the Seawall into the Gulf. It wasn't until I had been teaching U.S. history for some years that a colleague mentioned an African American holiday called Juneteenth. I began to learn its history and to realize that those annual gatherings might have been Juneteenth commemorations recognizing the events of June 19, 1865, when Major General Gordon Granger announced to the enslaved people of Galveston that they were free and ordered the final enforcement of the Emancipation Proclamation in Texas following the end of the Civil War. Although President Lincoln had signed the Proclamation freeing all slaves on September 22, 1862, the slaves of Galveston did not receive the news until General Granger's proclamation. African Americans celebrated Juneteenth in multiple ways over the years, and it became a practice for some African Americans to make a pilgrimage to Galveston on Juneteenth to celebrate African American independence from slavery. Juneteenth finally became a federal holiday in 2021.

I knew none of this growing up on Galveston Island, but my African American neighbors did. They preserved that history through oral tradition, and I suspect that African America teachers taught African American history as best they could in their segregated K–12 classes, just as local memory keepers built precious archives for the future. Teaching inclusive history has often been a private and subversive act. It may need to be yet again. But the histories we have worked so hard to write into our textbooks can never be entirely erased or forgotten.

Whatever I had learned in the seventy years before my retirement, much of it from talented students and colleagues, it has sometimes seemed that I am voicing variations on themes that have engaged me for decades. I made my first public speech in 1964. I was a senior in high school and was invited to speak at my old junior high, at the induction of new members into the Stephen F. Austin Junior High School Honor Society. I ended "Torches Passed and Present" as I ended that first public speech, with words from Carl Sandburg, a wish for those who carry their own torches and forge their own paths.

For You
By Carl Sandburg

The peace of great doors be for you.
Wait at the knobs, at the panel oblongs.
Wait for the great hinges.
. . .
The peace of great books be for you,
Stains of pressed clover leaves on pages,
Bleach of the light of years held in leather.
. . .
The peace of great hearts be for you,
Valves of the blood of the sun,
Pumps of the strongest wants we cry.

The peace of great silhouettes be for you,
Shadow dancers alive in your blood now,
Alive and crying, "Let us out, let us out."

The peace of great changes be for you.
Whisper, Oh beginners in the hills.
Tumble, Oh cubs—to-morrow belongs to you.

NOTES

I am grateful to Dean Richard Sigurdson, the University of Calgary Faculty of Arts, and the Imperial Oil-Lincoln McKay Chair in American Studies for their support over the years and for making the "Torches Passed and Present" conference possible. Thanks as well to Sarah Stevenson, Lori Sommers, Ginger Rodgers, and Shauna Selezinka, whose support made it all happen. Special thanks to Kayla Grabia and Shawn Brackett, conference assistants. Thanks most of all to the talented folks who agreed to come share their work with us, and to the friends who joined us.

1   Susan Armitage and Elizabeth Jameson, eds., *The Women's West* (Norman: University of Oklahoma Press, 1987); Elizabeth Jameson and Susan Armitage, eds. *Writing the Range: Race, Class and Culture in the Women's West* (Norman, University of Oklahoma Press, 1997).

2   The participants' theses and dissertations: Evelyn Schlatter, "Aryan Cowboys: White Supremacist Ideology and the Search for a New Frontier, 1960–1995" (PhD diss., University of New Mexico, 2000); Dedra McDonald Birzer, "Negotiated Conquests: Domestic Servants and Gender in the Spanish and Mexican Borderlands, 1598–1860" (PhD diss., University of New Mexico, 2000); Benny Andrés, Jr., "Power and Control in Imperial Valley, California: Nature, Agribusiness, Labor, and Race Relations, 1900–1940" (PhD diss., University of New Mexico, 2003); Amy McKinney, "'How I Cook, Keep House, Help with Farm Work Too': Rural Women in Post-World War II Montana" (PhD diss., University of Calgary, 2011); Gretchen Albers, "Boundaries of the Heart: White Women, Indigenous People, and the Christian Missions to the Dakotas, 1862–1910" (PhD diss., University of Calgary, 2011); Carol Archer, "Surviving the Transition: Women's Property Rights and Inheritance in New Mexico, 1848–1912" (master's thesis, University of Calgary, 2006) and "'El Amparo de la Ley': Hispanas' Use of Spanish Mexican and Anglo American Law in Northern New Mexico and Southern Colorado, 1848–1912" (PhD diss., University of Calgary, 2015); Sean Marchetto, "Tune in, Turn on, Go Punk: American Punk Counterculture, 1968–1985" (master's thesis, University of Calgary, 2001); Cynthia Loch-Drake, "Jailed Heroes and Kitchen Heroines: Class, Gender, and the Medalta Potteries Strike in Postwar Alberta" (master's thesis, University of Calgary 2001); Michel Hogue, "Crossing the Line: The Plains Cree in the Canada-United States Borderlands, 1870–1900" (master's thesis, University of Calgary, 2002); Susan Kwiatkowski, "Creating Young Citizens: Education in the Borderlands of Alberta and Montana, 1895–1914" (master's thesis, University of Calgary, 2009); and Andrew Varsanyi, "Principle vs. Pragmatism: Henry Loucks and South Dakota Populism 1884–1900" (master's thesis, University of Calgary, 2015).

3   The terms "sessional" and "adjunct" refer to part-time university teaching, in which teachers are hired by the course. The work is generally temporary, insecure, and massively underpaid.

4   I cannot think about these "second rate" categories without also remembering a course that Bob Fogarty taught and I assisted called "Second Rate Literature." He advertised it as a class taught by a second-rate professor with a second-rate assistant in which we would study second-rate novels. The novels mostly responded to social issues and violated the standards for "first rate" literature that required a single protagonist who matured or progressed. We interrogated those standards for "first rate" literature and voted at the end of the course to see if we considered any of our readings first rate. It was a great introduction to how standards are established to maintain power and authority in a field.

5   Elizabeth Jameson, "To Be All Human: Sex Role and Transcendence in Margaret Fuller's Life and Thought," *University of Michigan Papers in Women's Studies* 1:1 (February 1974): 91–126.

6   Ralph Waldo Emerson, William Henry Channing, and James Freeman Clarke, eds. *Memoirs of Margaret Fuller Ossoli, Volume 1* (New York: The Tribune Association, 1869), 107.

Coda

2024

In August 2024 I went on a road trip from Calgary to Albuquerque with my son Daniel, daughter-in-law Barbara, grandsons Stanley and Spencer, and many stuffed animals. Our trek south reversed the route Daniel and I had driven to Calgary a quarter century earlier. Along the way we stopped at the Ludlow Massacre site, and I got to tell my grandsons what had happened there and show my family the plaque designating Ludlow as a National Historic Landmark. In Albuquerque, we showed the boys their dad's elementary and junior high schools, and the houses where he'd lived. We had a wonderful visit with my brother Phil and sister-in-law Marjorie, who provided major support during our years in Albuquerque.

Then, on August 17, 2024, another hot Albuquerque summer morning, I hugged Phil and Marjorie goodbye, climbed into an overloaded SUV with Daniel, Barbara, Stanley, and Spencer (but thankfully no cats), and drove north toward home.

Epilogue: The Times They Are a-Changin'[1]

I have used section introductions to provide the contexts in which I wrote my lectures. I offer this final chapter to provide a sense of the contexts in which I finished this book. If I were still giving annual Chair's Lectures, this is what I would have said in May 2025. I would have begun by saying that I was in the final stages of publishing a book of my Chair's Lectures, which would wind up my years as the Imperial Oil-Lincoln McKay Chair at the University of Calgary. In a broader sense, I would say, *Thresholds, Walls, and Bridges* caps my years of teaching and scholarship, and this final lecture is about the contexts in which that book, and the career it represents, will be published.

It's a challenging time for historians, for teaching and writing the kinds of history in these pages. I used to conclude my women's history classes by saying that I hoped that what we had studied would remain history—that my students would not face the same inequalities as previous generations of women. Events are changing quickly, and I can only hope that by the time a reader sees this Epilogue, that it, too, will be history.

***

The American Historical Association proclaims on its website and publications that "Everything Has a History."[2] "Everything" includes this book. It originated as annual public lectures I presented at the University of Calgary as the Imperial Oil-Lincoln McKay Chair in American Studies. I added the footnotes and introductions during the COVID-19 pandemic, when research libraries were closed, which slowed my progress. It was hard to find peer reviewers for the manuscript during COVID, as historians faced illness and loss, learned to teach on-line, and struggled to conduct research without access to libraries or archives. Those pressures further slowed publication.

The COVID pandemic was only one of the contexts that influenced this volume. Contemporary events influenced my perspective and choice of subject for each lecture. So did the more personal contexts of my journey from the United States to Canada, as I adjusted to living and working in a new country.

This Epilogue locates *Thresholds, Walls, and Bridges* in some disturbing contexts in which it nears completion. The subtitle, "Journeys Through the Borderlands of History," refers most literally to my personal journey across national borders and through their borderlands. It also refers to the essays, which, in various ways, traverse the boundaries of national histories. Some compare how the United States and Canada have addressed common issues or have imagined our respective pasts. Some challenge the belief that the nation itself is the only important subject of history, focusing instead on daily acts and grass roots social movements. Some cross disciplinary boundaries, reflecting my graduate training in the University of Michigan interdisciplinary Program in American Culture. Its actors go beyond the "battles, dates, and politicians" of my childhood history classes to include women, workers, and people historically marginalized by virtue of race or sexuality. These boundary crossings have all faced official attacks in the United States from the second Trump presidential administration.

When I arrived in Calgary, I was unsure how American history might speak to Canadians. I probed what linked and separated our histories and sought in my teaching and public lectures to make humanity visible across national and social boundaries. Crossing national borders challenged my assumptions about national loyalties as well. I remain an engaged American citizen; I became a Canadian citizen in 2017. I never imagined that I could be caught in a conflict between my two countries. When I moved to Canada in 1999, the U.S.-Canada border was celebrated as the longest unpoliced border in the world. Canada and the United States were longstanding allies and trading partners, with linked economies and national security interests. I've lived in Canada for twenty-six years and regularly crossed the border to visit friends and family, do research, and attend professional conferences. Those border crossings were largely uneventful. The Immigration Officers of both countries generally welcomed me "home." I was at home on both sides of the border.

This work nears completion in less welcoming contexts. Since Donald Trump regained the presidency on January 20, 2025, his administration has challenged the Canada-U.S. relationship, the historical profession, academic freedom, education, and the significance of the border itself. This book has become uncomfortably timely and its content surprisingly controversial.

Even before re-gaining office, President Trump discredited the international boundary treaties between the two nations, threatened to "get rid of that artificially drawn line" (the border), discounted Canadian sovereignty, and asserted his intention to annex Canada as the 51st state through economic force.[3] There has been no similar border threat since the 1840s, when the boundary between British North American and United States territory remained undetermined from the crest of the Rocky Mountains to the Pacific Ocean. In 1819 Britain and the United States agreed to a "joint occupation" of Oregon Territory from the northern boundary of California to the southern boundary of Russian America, 54°40' north latitude. During the 1844 presidential campaign, American expansionists supported James K. Polk for president and chanted "54-40 or fight," threatening war unless Britain ceded all claims to the territory. Instead, the victorious Polk provoked a war with Mexico and claimed all or part of the present states of Texas, New Mexico, Arizona, California, Nevada, Utah, and Colorado. Polk couldn't fight two wars at once, so in 1846 he negotiated the Oregon Treaty with Britain, establishing the 49th Parallel as the boundary between British North America and U.S. territory from the Rockies westward, with a slight jog south to keep Vancouver Island in British North America. Which is how that "artificially drawn" portion of the border was established.

Trump's threats became concrete on February 1, 2025, when he announced 25 percent tariffs on all Canadian and Mexican goods, blaming both countries for an alleged "major threat of illegal aliens and deadly drugs killing our Citizens, including fentanyl." Since then, the details of the tariffs imposed on Canada have changed frequently, as the President exempted some goods and increased tariffs on others and then announced 10 percent tariffs on goods imported from many more countries. Some Americans believe Trump's depiction of the Canadian threats; most Canadians are united against Trump's tariffs and annexation plans.

Trump's chaotic tariff wars threaten to destabilize international economies in ways unparalleled since the U.S. Smoot-Hawley Tariff of 1930 destroyed two-thirds of international trade and helped escalate precipitous economic decline into a worldwide depression. The "major threat" of the fentanyl crisis is real in Canada and Mexico as well as the United States, but in 2024 only one percent of the fentanyl entering the United States came from Canada. Nonetheless, Canada appointed a "fentanyl czar" to coordinate increased border security; deployed sixty additional U.S.-made drones, two Black Hawk helicopters, and extra canine teams to the border; promised an increase of 10,000 "frontline" border personnel at a cost of $1.3 billion Canadian; and invested $200 million Canadian in new intelligence gathering.[4]

These facts don't matter. The President manufactured the crisis because he needed a loophole to circumvent Article 1, Section 8 of the U.S. Constitution, which gives Congress the power to "lay and collect Taxes, Duties, Imposts and Excises," and to regulate commerce with foreign countries. Congress delegated that power to the President in emergencies through the 1977 International Emergency Economic Powers Act, which grants the president broad authority over economic transactions when faced with an "unusual and extraordinary threat" from foreign sources, generally presumed to refer to an armed invasion or threat of similar magnitude. Fentanyl deaths are a public health tragedy, but no extraordinary threat from Canada caused U.S. fentanyl overdoses.

If the international trade crisis was artificial, the threats to the U.S. historical profession are alarmingly real. The conditions in which historians work have shifted radically since I wrote my lectures, changing in ways that would have impeded or prevented my work and that may affect its reception.

In the early months of his second administration, Donald Trump attacked archives, libraries, universities, and government institutions essential to historical scholarship. The President fired the National Archivist, decimated the staffs of the National Archives and Records Administration (NARA) and the National Endowment for the Humanities (NEH), and threatened to destroy the U.S. Department of Education. His administration arrested foreign students for exercising free speech, cancelled the government loans that enabled countless U.S. students to attend university, and withheld federal support from universities deemed hostile to his ideology.

Barely two months into the second Trump presidency, on March 24, 2025, the American Historical Association (AHA) condemned "the dismantling of federal departments and agencies through the indiscriminate termination of federal employees and elimination of programs, including historical offices."[5] The AHA is the largest historical association in the world, with over 10,400 members in May 2025. Nineteen other historical organizations co-signed its statement, protesting executive orders and acts of the Department of Government Efficiency (DOGE) that threatened the National Archives and Records Administration, the Institute of Museum and Library Services, and the National Park Service. They opposed the President's plan to dismantle the U.S. Department of Education and "many other vital agencies [that] employ and support the work of historians and interpret history for the public."[6]

The AHA focused particular attention on staff terminations at the National Archives, which preserves and accesses the records of the federal government and its agencies. On February 7, 2025, Trump fired Colleen J. Shogan, Archivist of the United States. Other senior NARA staff and dozens of recently hired employees were also fired or forced to resign, leaving the National Archives without experienced professional leadership. In the interim, Trump named Secretary of State Marco Rubio the acting NARA director. "Closing federal history offices, rolling back protections granted by the Freedom of Information Act, firing archivists, and dismantling departments responsible for education, the humanities, arts, and sciences will render it impossible for Americans to learn about and from the past," the AHA warned, cautioning that a "scorched-earth approach to the federal bureaucracy," would rob the nation of "the records and accumulated knowledge to make well-informed decisions."[7]

Eleven days later, the AHA and the same co-signers condemned "the evisceration" of the National Endowment for the Humanities, after DOGE notified some 75 percent of NEH staff that they had been placed on administrative leave and informed hundreds of NEH grant recipients that their funding had been terminated. The DOGE grant termination letters said NEH funds were being reallocated to "a new direction in furtherance of the President's agenda."[8]

Established in 1965 by an Act of Congress, the National Endowment for the Humanities provides grants that support humanities research, professional development workshops for teachers, preservation of historic sites, and a wide variety of public programs. DOGE declared that the termination of these programs was "an urgent priority for the administration." In response, the AHA denounced DOGE's "frontal attack on the nation's public culture" as "unpatriotic, anti-American, and unjustified." "Under the guise of 'safeguarding' the federal government," it continued, "DOGE has terminated grants and diminished staffing to a level that renders it impossible for the agency to perform its mission responsibly and with integrity. These actions imperil both the education of the American public and the preservation of our history."[9]

The "urgent priority for the administration" became clearer on April 24, 2025, when an NEH press release announced that future awards would "be merit-based, awarded to projects that do not promote extreme ideologies based upon race or gender." NEH had therefore "cancelled awards that are at variance with agency priorities, including but not limited to those on diversity, equity, and inclusion (or DEI) and environmental justice, as well as awards that may not inspire public confidence in the use of taxpayer funds." The grant terminations complied with Trump's Executive Orders, including "Ending Radical and Wasteful Government DEI Programs and Preferencing," "Defending Women from Gender Ideology Extremism and Restoring Biological Truth to the Federal Government," and "Ending Radical Indoctrination in K-12 Schooling."[10]

In response, the American Historical Association, the American Council of Learned Societies, and the Modern Language Association filed suit against NEH and DOGE, challenging the dismantling of NEH as unconstitutional. "Most fundamentally, the Constitution grants Congress—not the President—the power to create and prescribe the duties of Federal agencies, and Congress maintains the exclusive power of the purse in directing how Federal funds must be spent," the suit argued. "The President cannot unilaterally shut down an agency that Congress has created, nor may an agency refuse to spend funds that Congress has appropriated." Such Executive action, it charged, violates the constitutional separation of powers, the Impoundment Control Act of 1974, and the Administrative Procedure Act. The suit further argued that DOGE was not a legal federal agency, because Congress did not create it or grant it authority to do anything. DOGE's actions and DOGE itself were therefore unconstitutional. The three organizations sought "to enjoin and set aside Defendants' unlawful actions, and to require the Trump Administration to operate NEH as Congress intended, unless and until Congress says otherwise."[11]

If these constitutional arguments prevail, they could apply to other Trump administration executive orders and actions as well.

These events directly touch me and my work. I belong to the American Historical Association and to four organizations that co-signed the AHA statements: the Organization of American Historians, Western History Association, Labor and Working Class History Association, and the Alliance for Texas History.[12] I conducted research for two chapters of this book at the National Archives, with the help of professional archivists and of staff who fetched countless boxes of Homestead Proof Statements and patiently removed straight pins and paper clips that had been rusting in brittle files for over a century. An NEH summer stipend supported some of the background research for chapter 3. An NEH affiliate, the Colorado Humanities Program (CHP), funded my first work in public history.[13] CHP grants sent Women's Studies scholars to present our work in eleven Colorado communities from 1981–1983. Another CHP project, "With These Hands," took me to three small towns in 1982 to discuss Colorado labor history. The CHP funded three annual Colorado Women's History Week celebrations that I chaired. Another CHP grant allowed me to co-produce a slide-tape and video, "We Were Never Supposed to Be Rich," based on my oral history interviews with descendants of Cripple Creek miners. Some of their stories appear in chapter 3.

The Colorado Humanities Program and the Association for the Humanities in Idaho provided grant support for the first Women's West Conference in 1983, a catalytic meeting of scholars who established the field of western women's history, represented here in chapters 2, 3, 9, and 13. The Women's West conference generated a book, *The Women's West*, which I co-edited with Susan Armitage; a professional organization, the Coalition for Western Women's History; and professional networks that continue to nourish scholarship on women, gender, and sexuality in the North American Wests.[14] The opening plenary of the conference introduced me to Canadian historian Sylvia Van Kirk, whose pathbreaking *Many Tender Ties* placed Indigenous women at the center of the western Canadian fur trade.[15] Van Kirk's participation helped generate cross-border networks and exchanges among women's historians that continued through my years at the University of Calgary.

My work is the kind of history the Trump administration wants to suppress—work that addresses class, race, and gender; work "including but not limited to . . . diversity, equity, and inclusion (or DEI)." This administration seeks to erase histories that include people of color, women, workers and LGBTQ2S+ people, or topics like slavery and colonialism that might cause feelings of discomfort. I have worked to achieve a more diverse, equitable, and inclusive history, focusing on the histories of labor, women, gender, and social change movements devoted to justice and equity. I include these actors and topics not to indoctrinate or promote an ideology, but to be historically accurate.

Efforts to censor history predated recent political campaigns and animated many who voted for President Trump. In recent years, attacks on DEI content have banned histories of racial and gender discrimination from school libraries and classrooms in many states, led by Florida and my home state of Texas. *Newsweek* magazine reported in October 2024 that over 3,000 books had been banned across various states, "primarily driven by debates over race, gender identity, and LGBTQ+ rights."[16] PEN America documented nearly 16,000 book bans in public schools nationwide since 2021, more than at any time since the Red Scares of the 1950s. It counted over 10,000 public school book bans during the 2023–2024 school year, finding that "everywhere, it is the books that have long fought for a place on the shelf that are being targeted. Books by authors of color, by LGBTQ+ authors, by women. Books about racism, sexuality, gender, history."[17] *Books about history.*

I love historical research. I love to read. I have spent countless happy hours in archives and libraries. As I wrote this Epilogue, President Trump fired the Librarian of Congress, Dr. Carla Hayden, the first African American and the first woman to hold the position. I learned of her firing shortly after it happened on May 8, 2025, in a Facebook post from New Mexico Senator Martin Heinrich:

> President Trump fired our nation's Librarian, Dr. Carla Hayden, by email at 6:56 pm tonight, taking his assault on America's libraries to a new level.
>
> Over the course of her tenure, Dr. Hayden brought the Library of Congress to the people, with initiatives that reached into rural communities and made the Library accessible to all Americans, in person and online.
>
> While President Trump wants to ban books and tell Americans what to read—or not to read at all, Dr. Hayden has devoted her career to making reading and the pursuit of knowledge available to everyone.
>
> Be like Dr. Hayden.[18]

White House Press Secretary Karoline Leavitt said that Dr. Hayden was fired because the administration decided she "did not fit the needs of the American people" and because of "quite concerning things that she had done at the Library of Congress in the pursuit of D.E.I." including allowing "inappropriate books in the library for children." Leavitt did not specify the alleged "D.E.I." pursuits or offensive books.

The Library of Congress is the world's largest library, housing over 34 million books and printed materials. It houses the Congressional Research Office and the U.S. Copyright Office and receives several copies of most books published in the United States. It is a research library and does not lend books to anyone, including children. Dr. Hayden pioneered digitizing many of the documents in the Library, including maps and material essential to some historical research.[19]

The attacks on "DEI" implicitly encompass much of the content of this book, which includes histories of women, work, race, and movements for women's rights, African American rights, and LGBTQ2S+ rights. These subjects and the focus on "ordinary" people as historical change makers are at odds with the Trump administration's attacks on DEI programs as "Woke" (and therefore bad). The attack rhetoric pits diversity and inclusion against merit. It presumes that women, workers, LGBTQ2S+ people, and people of color are, by definition, less meritorious than straight White elite men, who constitute the appropriate subjects of history and whose work is, by definition, of superior merit.

People who hold these assumptions would never open this book. But people who might want to read it may be prevented from doing so by policies that would ban it in schools and libraries.

The second Trump administration is censoring the history that can be shared in federal libraries, museums, and public sites, and the words that can be used on federal websites and in federal documents. Under orders from Secretary of Defense Pete Hegseth, the U.S. Naval Academy library removed 381 books about race, racism, and gender from its shelves but kept books defending White power. The purged books include Maya Angelou, *I Know Why the Caged Bird Sings*; Bryan Massingale, *Racial Justice and the Catholic Church*; and Matthew F. Delmont, *Half American: the Epic Story of African Americans Fighting World War II at Home and Abroad*. Jane Jacobs, *Memorializing the Holocaust: Gender, Genocide, and Collective Memory* is gone but *Mein Kampf* remains. And Robert Shellow, *The Harvest of American Racism: The Political Meaning of Violence in the Summer of 1967* was removed from the library. I worked for Dr. Shellow in 1967 as a Research Assistant at the National Advisory Commission on Civil Disorders. *Harvest of American Racism* includes work I helped research. Dr. Shellow kindly mentioned me and acknowledged my work in the banned volume. I cite his book in chapter 7, which addresses *Harvest of American Racism*'s contested history.[20]

On Friday May 9, 2025, the Pentagon instructed all U.S. military educational institutions, including the War Colleges and Military Service Academies, to review their libraries, eliminate "divisive concepts" and "gender ideology," and to identify and "sequester" all "potentially incompatible" materials by May 21. Twenty keyword search terms were provided to identify the "incompatible" materials—among them "affirmative action," "anti-racism," "diversity, equity, and inclusion," "critical race theory," "transgender people," and "white privilege."[21]

The Trump administration banned or discouraged the use of many of the proscribed terms at government agencies and on federal websites. On March 7, 2025, the *New York Times* published a list of words its reporters found on federal documents that ordered the words expunged from public websites or on documents that ordered the elimination of other materials (including school curricula) in which the words might be found. The *Times* compared federal websites before and after Trump took office, revealing 250 websites that had amended their content to comply. The italics in the examples below denote deletions; bold type denotes new text:

> **Federal Aviation Administration's job page**
> Working at FAA offers a unique opportunity to experience a career where your impact not only reaches throughout the aviation industry but around the world as well. You'll be a part of a *diverse* workforce utilizing the latest technology and systems dedicated to maintaining the safety and integrity of our civil airspace.
>
> **National Park Service's Stonewall National Monument web page**
> Before the 1960s, almost everything about living openly as a lesbian, gay, bisexual **(LGB)** *transgender, or queer (LGBTQ+)* person was illegal. The Stonewall Uprising on June 28, 1969 is a milestone in the quest for LGB*T*Q+ civil rights and provided momentum for a movement.[22]

Some of the banned or discouraged words appear in this book, including—but not limited to—race, gender, women, Black, Latinx, LGBTQ+, diverse, inclusive, Native American, marginalized, feminism, social justice, Gulf of Mexico, and historically.

Articles and images containing the banned words disappeared from Department of Defense websites after Secretary Hegseth ordered content removed that highlighted diversity.[23] The Associated Press reported on March 7, 2025, that it had obtained a database flagging over 26,000 photos and online posts for removal. The purged materials included videos of the Tuskegee Airmen, the first African American U.S. military pilots, who served in a segregated unit during World War II; articles and images about the Navajo Code Talkers; the historic photo of six Marines hoisting a U.S. flag on Iwo Jima in 1945 because it was on a page celebrating Army Pfc. Ira Hayes, a Pima Indian; and articles and images of baseball legend Jackie Robinson, who served in a segregated Army unit during World War II and was court martialed for refusing to move to the back of a bus. A photo of the airplane that dropped the first atomic bomb on Hiroshima was deleted because the pilot named it for his mother, Enola Gay—so it contained the word "gay." A biography of World War II veteran and slain civil rights leader Medgar Evers disappeared from the Arlington National Cemetery website. Some of the material was restored in the wake of widespread public protests, including the tributes to Robinson and the Code Talkers. The Pentagon acknowledged that it had made mistakes and that it would be reviewing purged material, but some of it is still missing.[24]

Words matter. The proscribed words were part of a larger project to censor history, as the missing references to transexuals on the Stonewall National Monument web page demonstrated. Led by the American Historical Association and the Organization of American Historians, forty-two organizations signed an AHA–OAH Joint Statement on Federal Censorship of American History that condemned:

> ... recent efforts to censor historical content on federal government websites, at many public museums, and across a wide swath of government resources that include essential data. New policies that purge words, phrases, and content that some officials deem suspect on ideological grounds constitute a systemic campaign to distort, manipulate, and erase significant parts of the historical record. Recent directives insidiously prioritize narrow ideology over historical research, historical accuracy, and the actual experiences of Americans.[25]

Two weeks later, the President signed an executive order "Restoring Truth and Sanity to American History," charging that:

Over the past decade, Americans have witnessed a concerted and widespread effort to rewrite our Nation's history, replacing objective facts with a distorted narrative driven by ideology rather than truth. This revisionist movement seeks to undermine the remarkable achievements of the United States by casting its founding principles and historical milestones in a negative light. Under this historical revision, our Nation's unparalleled legacy of advancing liberty, individual rights, and human happiness is reconstructed as inherently racist, sexist, oppressive, or otherwise irredeemably flawed. Rather than fostering unity and a deeper understanding of our shared past, the widespread effort to rewrite history deepens societal divides and fosters a sense of national shame, disregarding the progress America has made and the ideals that continue to inspire millions around the globe.[26]

The President focused much of his attack on the Smithsonian Institution. Founded in 1846 "for the increase and diffusion of knowledge," the Smithsonian is a group of twenty-one museums, twenty-one libraries, fourteen education and research centers, the National Zoo, and historical and architectural landmarks, most of them in Washington D.C. It operates as a trust and is not formally part of the federal government. Its museums include the Museum of American History, Air and Space Museum, American Art Museum, National Museum of the American Indian, and the National Museum of African American History and Culture. In 2020, Congress voted to create the Smithsonian American Women's History Museum, which is still in the planning stages. Asserting that the Smithsonian "has, in recent years, come under the influence of a divisive, race-centered ideology," Trump critiqued depictions of race at the National Museum of African American History and Culture and in a Museum of American Art exhibit, "The Shape of Power: Stories of Race and American Sculpture." He was particularly concerned that the forthcoming Smithsonian American Women's History Museum would celebrate transexual women athletes. Accordingly, the President ordered Vice President J.D. Vance, through his role on the Smithsonian Board of Regents, to seek "to remove improper ideology" from Smithsonian properties and "recommend to the President any additional actions necessary to fully effectuate such policies." He directed Vance and the Director of the Office of Management and Budget to "work with the Congress" to guarantee that the American Women's History Museum would "not recognize men as women in any respect in the Museum," and to ensure that future Smithsonian appropriations would "prohibit expenditure on exhibits or programs that degrade shared American values, divide Americans based on race, or promote programs or ideologies inconsistent with Federal law and policy." Trump instructed the Secretary of the Interior to "ensure that all public monuments, memorials, statues, markers, or similar properties within the Department of the Interior's jurisdiction do not contain descriptions, depictions, or other content that inappropriately disparage Americans past or living (including persons living in colonial times), and instead focus on the greatness of the achievements and progress of the American people."[27]

The American Historical Association replied that Trump egregiously misrepresented the Smithsonian's work and that it was "among the premier research institutions in the world, widely known for the integrity of its scholarship, which is careful and based on historical and scientific evidence." The AHA contested Trumps's assertion that Smithsonian museums displayed "improper, divisive, or anti-American ideology."

> This is simply untrue; it misrepresents the work of those museums and the public's engagement with their collections and exhibits. It also completely misconstrues the nature of historical work.
>
> Historians explore the past to understand how our nation has evolved. We draw on a wide range of sources, which helps us to understand history from different angles of vision. Our goal is neither criticism nor celebration; it is to understand—to increase our knowledge of—the past in ways that can help Americans to shape the future.
>
> The stories that have shaped our past include not only elements that make us proud but also aspects that make us acutely aware of tragedies in our nation's history. No person, no nation, is perfect, and we should all—as individuals and as nations—learn from our imperfections.

. . . .

> Patriotic history celebrates our nation's many great achievements. It also helps us grapple with the less grand and more painful parts of our history. Both are part of a shared past that is fundamentally American. We learn from the past to inform how we can best shape our future. By providing a history with the integrity necessary to enable all Americans to be all they can possibly be, the Smithsonian is fulfilling its duty to all of us.[28]

The AHA statement expresses much of what I value about inclusive national histories. It also captures the understanding of patriotism my parents taught me as they resisted segregation to make the United States, the country they loved, more fair, just, and humane. It's part of why I studied movements for social justice.

The Trump administration's anti-DEI agenda erased diverse actors and perspectives from history, distorting the past and creating a false celebratory narrative. Policies that ban books, sequester national records, and censor historical narratives are intended to block access to knowledge and to deny power and authority to historically marginalized people.

These policies have affected public and private educational institutions, which have lost federal funds if they refuse to dismantle DEI programs or otherwise resist Trump administration demands, including federal control of curricula. The president threatened to cancel hundreds of millions in federal funding at prominent universities, sometimes because they maintained DEI programs and policies, sometimes because they did not prevent campus protests following the Hamas terrorist attacks on Israel of October 7, 2023, and because he charged that they had not protected Jewish students from antisemitism in the wake of October 7.[29]

These last justifications require a brief contextual digression. On October 7, 2023, Hamas launched the deadliest single attack on Jews since the Holocaust, killing some 1200 people and taking another 240 hostages in Gaza. In response, Israel cut off humanitarian aid to Gaza and launched a military campaign that by April 2025 had claimed over 50,000 lives.[30] Hamas cynically jeopardized civilians by placing its headquarters in schools and hospitals, and probably confiscated some humanitarian aid destined for innocent Palestinians. Those facts did not erase the widespread devastation of the Israeli campaign.

The devastation of Gaza and of innocent Palestinians generated international protests, including on U.S. and Canadian university campuses, and including some Jewish individuals and organizations that support Israel. A prominent dissent from Israel's Gaza campaign appeared in a May 12, 2025, *Washington Post* opinion column by Rabbi Rick Jacobs, President of the Union for Reform Judaism, the largest Jewish denomination in North America. Beneath the headline: "I'm a rabbi. Starving Gaza is immoral," Jacobs began, "Among the terrible lessons of Oct. 7, 2023, was that it became perfectly clear Hamas is willing to sacrifice the Palestinian people in its war to destroy Israel and the Jewish people. Israel must not help Hamas by sacrificing its own morality." Rabbi Jacobs opposed the complete ban of food and supplies Israel had imposed for the preceding two months, arguing that "Starving Gazan civilians neither will bring Israel the 'total victory' over Hamas it seeks nor can [it] be justified by Jewish values or humanitarian law. . . . Hamas is willing to sacrifice thousands of Palestinians by hoarding humanitarian aid; Israel must not."[31]

The heated rhetoric surrounding October 7 and Israel's response often failed to recognize differing opinions among Jews. On and off campuses there was a rise in antisemitic and Islamophobic rhetoric. Antisemitic attacks escalated in the United States and Canada. Some Jewish students were attacked either verbally or physically. University administrations struggled to balance the rights to free speech and protest while preventing hate speech and violence.

Tensions on campuses heightened as the Trump administration targeted foreign students and faculty for pro-Palestinian views. In March it deported Dr. Rasha Alawieh, an assistant professor at the Brown University Medical School, as she returned from visiting family in Lebanon. According to court documents, Dr. Alawieh was held for thirty-six hours at Boston's Logan Airport before being sent back to Lebanon in violation of a federal court order and despite her H-1B visa for her employment in the Brown Medicine Nephrology Department. Her deportation raised alarms for the treatment of foreign faculty on other campuses.[32]

Tensions continued to rise as the Trump administration cancelled foreign students' visas without notifying them or their universities and arrested and detained some for alleged antisemitism or terrorism. Two of the most prominent cases concerned the arrests of graduate students Mahmoud Khalil and Rumeysa Öztürk, who had voiced support for Palestinians. Khalil, a Columbia University graduate student and a legal permanent resident married to an American citizen, was taken from his student apartment on March 8, 2025, by U.S. Immigration and Customs Enforcement (ICE) agents without an arrest warrant. His student visa was revoked, and he was detained in the federal LaSalle Detention Center in Jena, Louisiana. Born in a Syrian refugee enclave to Palestinian parents, Khalil had helped lead pro-Palestinian protests on the Columbia campus. He was denied bail while contesting his arrest on the grounds that his rights of free speech and due process had been violated, rights guaranteed to all persons residing in the United States, regardless of citizenship.[33]

Tufts University doctoral student Rumeysa Öztürk was taken into custody on the street outside her Summerville, Massachusetts home on March 25, 2025, by six masked plainclothes agents of the Department of Homeland Security. Öztürk, a Turkish citizen and a Fulbright Scholar, was apparently targeted because she co-authored a pro-Palestinian opinion column in the Tufts student newspaper. Despite a U.S. District Court order, she, too, was sent to the Louisiana prison. Secretary of State Marco Rubio confirmed that he had revoked Öztürk's student visa, but did not disclose that he revoked it on March 21, four days before her arrest, without notifying either Öztürk or Tufts. Other universities discovered that the visas of more than 1200 foreign students had been revoked without notifying them or their educational institutions. Rumeysa Öztürk was freed from detention on May 9 after a Vermont federal court ordered her release and returned to Massachusetts pending a court hearing.[34]

In a similar case, on April 30, 2025, a judge ordered the release of Columbia University student Mohsen Mahdawi, a Palestinian arrested on April 14 at an interview to finalize his U.S. citizenship. Mahdawi, a U.S. permanent resident who also participated in pro-Palestinian student protests at Columbia, was among the first students successfully to challenge his arrest. He graduated from Columbia on May 19 amidst the cheers of his fellow graduates.[35]

The Trump administration had cancelled nearly 2,000 students' visas by mid-May 2025, often for minor traffic violations. Louisiana immigration attorney David Rozas, who represented students held in the LaSalle detention facility, reported that increasingly clients "with strong cases for release, some of whom had lived in the United States for years, were giving up, as hearings were delayed for weeks and as they got the feeling that the country simply did not want them."[36]

These actions further increased tensions on U.S. campuses already torn by protests. Students protested on Canadian campuses as well; antisemitic acts escalated in both countries in the wake of Israel's Gaza offensive. But the situation was never as simple as Trump's rhetoric suggested. Canada was also divided about responses to the student protests, but it did not revoke student visas or threaten to deport student protesters or foreign faculty.

The Trump administration began directly targeting some universities, using various charges related to campus antisemitism and university DEI programs to justify its attacks. It accused Columbia University of not protecting Jewish students from antisemitism. To avoid losing $400 million in federal funding, Columbia accepted some administration demands in March, including outside supervision of its Middle East studies department. Cornell, Brown, Northwestern, and Princeton were also charged with failing to combat antisemitism and threatened with loss of federal dollars. The University of Pennsylvania was attacked for allowing a transexual athlete on its swim team. In March, the Department of Education Office for Civil Rights threatened to penalize sixty educational institutions for failing to protect Jewish students. The University of Michigan, my graduate school alma mater, was among them, threatened with the loss of federal funding if it didn't scrap its DEI policies.[37]

Long recognized as a leader in DEI initiatives, Michigan adopted its first DEI strategic plan in 2016, and had since achieved a 46 percent increase in students whose parents hadn't attended university and a 32 percent increase in admissions from low-income families. DEI programs can provide financial aid, tutoring, and mentorship to help students from underrepresented groups adjust to the university. As Michigan's successes suggest, the programs are not limited to increasing representation by race or gender but can also help students with disabilities or who are the first in their family to attend university. Rather than lose federal funds, the University of Michigan closed its DEI office in March 2025.[38]

After Columbia capitulated, it appeared that other schools would follow suit. Then, in two letters to Harvard University on April 3 and 11, 2025, the Trump administration demanded that Harvard abandon all DEI considerations in admissions and hiring, deny admission to international students "hostile to the American values and institutions," that Harvard commission an external party "to audit the student body, faculty, staff, and leadership for viewpoint diversity, such that each department, field, or teaching unit must be individually viewpoint diverse." And the administration mandated an independent audit of programs, schools, and centers suspected of fostering antisemitism, including:

> the Divinity School, Graduate School of Education, School of Public Health, Medical School, Religion and Public Life

Program, FXB Center for Health & Human Rights, Center for Middle Eastern Studies, Carr Center for Human Rights at the Harvard Kennedy School, Department of Near Eastern Languages and Cultures, and the Harvard Law School International Human Rights Clinic.

Harvard was ordered to "immediately shutter all diversity, equity, and inclusion (DEI) programs, offices, committees, positions, and initiatives"; ban masks on campus; and refuse to support and recognize student organizations that engaged in alleged antisemitism, including the Harvard Palestine Solidarity Committee, Harvard Graduates Students 4 Palestine, Law Students 4 Palestine, Students for Justice in Palestine, and the National Lawyers Guild.[39]

Harvard President Alan Garber rejected the administration's demands and filed suit to oppose their implementation. Garber, who is Jewish, said it was clear that the government did not want to work with the university "to address antisemitism in a cooperative and constructive manner. Although some of the demands outlined by the government are aimed at combating antisemitism, the majority represent direct governmental regulation of the 'intellectual conditions' at Harvard." The university's legal response outlined changes in university policies and accountability procedures during the preceding fifteen months. "It is unfortunate, then, that your letter disregards Harvard's efforts and instead presents demands that, in contravention of the First Amendment, invade university freedoms long recognized by the Supreme Court." Whereupon the government froze $2.2 billion in research funds and threatened to withhold the university's tax-exempt status. The administration's Joint Task Force on Anti-Semitism accused Harvard of "the troubling entitlement mindset that is endemic in our nation's most prestigious universities and colleges— that federal investment does not come with the responsibility to uphold civil rights laws"—a particularly disingenuous charge given the demand that Harvard cease all DEI programs and initiatives.[40]

The Harvard chapter of the American Association of University Professors sued the Trump administration for withholding research funds, charging that this "was an illegal exploitation of the Civil Rights Act and an effort to impose political views upon the institution." It also joined other faculty groups in a lawsuit challenging the Trump administration's efforts to arrest and deport pro-Palestinian student activists.[41]

Harvard's resistance inspired other universities. Hundreds of college presidents signed a letter generated by the American Association of Colleges and Universities and the American Academy of Arts and Sciences on April 22, 2025 opposing "unprecedented government overreach and political interference" that threatened U.S. higher education. "We will always seek effective and fair financial practices, but we must reject the coercive use of public research funding," they wrote. By May 16, 2025, 652 college and university presidents had signed the statement.[42]

A leading U.S. Jewish Advocacy organization, the American Jewish Committee (AJC), urged the Trump administration to change the tactics it chose to combat campus antisemitism. A coalition of prominent educational organizations joined the call, including the Association of American Universities and the American Council on Education. "The proper and essential role for the U.S. government in addressing antisemitism is through the nation's powerful anti-discrimination laws," they stated. Asserting that federal law provided the framework for "vigorous enforcement" without endangering vital research or unfairly targeting individuals or schools, they cautioned that "overly broad" cuts to research funding "imperil science and innovation, and ultimately detract from the necessary fight against antisemitism while threatening the global pre-eminence of America's research universities."[43]

Despite growing resistance to pressure from the Trump administration, the situation on many campuses remained tense and unsettled. In late April 2025, as it negotiated its legal challenge to the administration's demands, Harvard renamed its office of diversity, equity, and inclusion the Office of Community and Campus Life in an apparent attempt to placate Trump. Other universities made similar adjustments to calm conservative critics who considered DEI programs left-wing indoctrination projects.[44] At the same time, two Harvard taskforces released highly critical reports about antisemitism and anti-Arab, anti-Muslim and anti-Palestinian bias on campus. They conducted a survey of some 2,300 students, faculty, and staff which found that 15 percent of Jewish respondents and 47 percent of Muslim respondents felt threatened on campus. They reported widespread fear to express personal views among 92 percent of Muslims, 51 percent of Christians, and 61 percent of Jews. These included Jews critical of Israel who were afraid to voice their opinions at Jewish campus organizations. Harvard president Alan Garber responded that the October 7, 2023, Hamas attack and ensuing war had brought long simmering tensions to the surface and promised to address issues raised in the taskforce reports. "Harvard cannot—and will not—abide bigotry," Garber insisted.[45]

The Trump administration's attacks on universities' controls of hiring, admissions, and free speech are deeply troubling to me as an educator. I have taught students of color admitted through DEI initiatives and poor students who received federal education loans. I attended graduate school with the support of a National Defense Education Act fellowship. This book would likely not exist without that financial support. The foreign students in my classrooms have enriched the educational experience for everyone. As a scholar, the cancellation of federal research funds to enforce the administration's ideological agenda is cause for profound concern. And as a Jew, I am heartsick that the administration uses antisemitism as an excuse to stifle free speech and threaten universities.

In the unsettled circumstances at United States borders and in U.S. higher education, the Canadian Association of University Teachers advised its members on April 15, 2025, that, "Given the rapidly evolving political landscape in the United States and reports of individuals encountering difficulties crossing the border, CAUT strongly recommends that academic staff travel to the U.S. only if essential and necessary."[46] It warned that travellers from Canada to the United States were "increasingly vulnerable to preclearance zones and border searches that may compromise research confidentiality and academic freedom." It cited the deportation of Brown University professor Dr. Rasha Alawieh and a March 2025 report from France's interior minister that a French researcher had been denied entry by U.S. border agents after they found messages on his phone criticizing the Trump administration's policies on academic research. CAUT therefore cautioned that "[a]cademics should carefully consider what information they have, or need to have, on their electronic devices when crossing borders and take actions to protect sensitive information where necessary."[47]

The CAUT travel advisory recommended that six categories of academics "exercise particular caution when considering travel to the U.S.":

- Citizens or residents of a country identified in media reports as likely to be subject to a travel ban

- Citizens or residents of a country where there are diplomatic tensions with the U.S.

- Travellers with passport stamps evidencing recent travel to countries that may be subject to a travel ban or where there are diplomatic tensions with the U.S.

- Those who have expressed negative opinions about the current U.S. administration or its policies

- Those whose research could be seen as being at odds with the position of the current U.S. administration

- Travellers who identify as transgender or whose travel documents indicate a sex other than their sex assigned at birth[48]

I fit three of these categories. I am a citizen of a country with diplomatic tensions with the United States. I have expressed negative opinions about the current U.S. administration and its policies, including in this essay. My research can be seen as being at odds with the position of the Trump administration. I have reluctantly decided that until these situations change, I will not be able to cross the border to help launch my book in the United States, and the University of Calgary Press has worked to adjust its marketing plan to reach American readers.

It might seem in these circumstances that my determination to make humanity visible across national and social boundaries is hopelessly naïve. I think it's more urgently needed. I taught Canadian and American students that though the United States has not always lived up to its values of democracy and equal opportunity, that American citizens have resisted injustice and fought for those values throughout American history. I taught the histories of movements for workers' rights, civil rights, women's rights, and LGBTQ2S+ rights out of great admiration for those who struggled to make the American promise a reality for everyone. Today, I am heartened by widespread citizen protests in the U.S. and by the organizations fighting to preserve academic integrity, access to knowledge, and inclusive histories. Former Prime Minister Justin Trudeau recognized humanity across national borders in his remarks on February 1, 2025, after President Trump signed an executive order imposing 25 percent tariffs on imports from Canada and Mexico. Trudeau first spoke directly to the American people:

> As I have consistently said, tariffs against Canada will put your jobs at risk, potentially shutting down American auto

> assembly plants and other manufacturing facilities. They will raise costs for you, including food at the grocery stores and gas at the pump. They will impede your access to an affordable supply of vital goods crucial for U.S. security such as nickel, potash, uranium, steel and aluminum. They will violate the free trade agreement that the president and I, along with our Mexican partner, negotiated and signed a few years ago.
>
> But it doesn't have to be this way. As President John F. Kennedy said many years ago, "Geography has made us neighbours, history has made us friends, economics has made us partners and necessity has made us allies." That rang true for many decades prior to President Kennedy's time in office and the decades since. From the beaches of Normandy to the mountains of the Korean Peninsula, from the fields of Flanders to the streets of Kandahar, we have fought and died alongside you during your darkest hours.
>
> During the Iranian hostage crisis, those 444 days, we worked around the clock from our embassy to get your innocent compatriots home. During the summer of 2005, when Hurricane Katrina ravaged your great city of New Orleans, or mere weeks ago, when we sent water bombers to tackle the wildfires in California, during the day the world stood still—Sept. 11, 2001—when we provided refuge to stranded passengers and planes, we were always there, standing with you, grieving with you, the American people.
>
> Together, we've built the most successful economic, military and security partnership the world has ever seen; a relationship that has been the envy of the world. Yes, we've had our differences in the past, but we've always found a way to get past them.[49]

Trudeau's rhetoric employed real historic ties to link the American people with Canada against the threat of Trump's divisive policies. It was part politics, but a politics that recognized mutual human experiences and interests. Many Americans appeared to see Canadian humanity in return. Canadians returning home from the U.S. have reported receiving frequent apologies from Americans for Trump's tariffs, and numerous expressions of support. I've gotten the same caring messages from American friends, along with heartbroken messages from colleagues who have lost research funding and who fear for their students. Looking across our borders I can separate Trump and his policies from the Americans they hurt and who are resisting.

I have written this to locate *Thresholds, Walls, and Bridges* in the difficult contexts in which it will be published. I am grieved by policies that hurt people in both my countries, that hurt refugees and foreign students, that threaten my profession and the people it serves. But I maintain the faith, expressed in these essays, that people make history—that ordinary people joining together can make positive change. We always stand on the threshold of history. We may need at times to erect protective walls around the values and institutions we cherish, but we can also build bridges of compassion across boundaries that divide us. I write with that hope.

NOTES

1 Bob Dylan, "The Times They Are a-Changin'," title track, album of the same name, 1964.
2 American Historical Association website, https://www.historians.org/, accessed April 30, 2025.
3 See for instance Mike Crawley "Trump has threatened Canada in all sorts of ways. What does he really want?," Analysis, CBC News, posted January 9, 2025, https://www.cbc.ca/lite/story/1.7426281, accessed April 24, 2025; The Politics Desk, "Canada, Greenland and the Panama Canal: Trump keeps up talk of U.S. expansion," NBC News, January 7, 2025, https://www.nbcnews.com/politics/trump-us-expansion-talk-canada-greenland-politics-desk-rcna18671, accessed April 24, 2025.
4 Vjosa Isai, "What to Know about Canada's Role in the Fentanyl Crisis," *New York Times*, February 6, 2025.
5 "American Historical Association Condemns Indiscriminate Cuts to the Federal Government," Statement Approved by the AHA Council, March 24, 2025, and endorsed by the Alliance for Texas History; American Society for Environmental History; Association for Slavic, East European, and Eurasian Studies; French Colonial Historical Society; Historians for Peace and Democracy; Immigration and Ethnic History Society; Labor and Working Class History Association; LGBTQ+ History Association; National Council on Public History; North American Conference on British Studies; Organization of American Historians; PEN America; Reacting Consortium; Society for Historians of American Foreign Relations; Society for Historians of the Gilded Age & Progressive Era; Society for the History of Children and Youth; Society for US Intellectual History; Southern Association for Women Historians; and Western History Association. American Historical Association website, https://www.historians.org/news/american-historical-association-condemns-indiscriminate-cuts-to-the-federal-government/, accessed April 30, 2025. For AHA membership, see American Council of Learned Societies, American Historical Association, and Modern Languages Association v. Michael McDonald, National Endowment for the Humanities, United States DOGE

Service, et al, Case 1:25-cv-03657, Document 1, Filed May 1, 2025, 6 (hereinafter cited as ACLS, AHA, and MLA v. NEH). The Department of Government Efficiency, or DOGE, was created by President Trump without Congressional approval or authority. Under the leadership of Elon Musk, it summarily fired employes of many government agencies and raided their data bases.

6 "American Historical Association Condemns Indiscriminate Cuts to the Federal Government."

7 "American Historical Association Condemns Indiscriminate Cuts to the Federal Government."

8 "Historians Defend the National Endowment for the Humanities and American Public Culture," Statement of the American Historical Association, April 4, 2025, American Historical Association website, accessed April 30, 2025.

9 "Historians Defend the National Endowment for the Humanities and American Public Culture."

10 "An Update on NEH Funding Priorities and the Agency's Recent Implementation of Trump Administration Executive Orders," Press Release, National Endowment for the Humanities, April 24, 2025, Washington, D.C., https://www.neh.gov/news/update-neh-funding-priorities-and-agencys-recent-implementation-trump-administration-executiveBottom, accessed May 6, 2025. The Executive Orders are available on the White House web page under Presidential Actions: https://www.whitehouse.gov/presidential-actions/executive-orders/. of Form

11 ACLS, AHA, and MLA v. NEH, 4–5. In conjunction with the lawsuit, on May 14, 2025 the ACLS, AHA and MLA filed a motion for a preliminary injunction to prevent the unlawful dismantling of NEH. Email from AHA Executive Director Jim Grossman, May 15, 2025.

12 I have held elective office in most of these organizations. I served on the Councils of the Labor and Working Class History Association (LAWCHA), Western History Association (WHA), and the Pacific Coast Branch – American History Association (PCB -AHA); on the Nominating Committees of the Organization of American Historians and WHA; and as President of the PCB – AHA and the WHA.

13 The Colorado Humanities Program has gone through several name changes and has also been called the Colorado Endowment for the Humanities and Colorado Humanities.

14 Susan Armitage and Elizabeth Jameson, eds., *The Women's West* (Norman: University of Oklahoma Press, 1987).

15 Sylvia Van Kirk, *"Many Tender Ties": Women in Fur-Trade Society, 1670–1870* (Norman & Winnipeg: University of Oklahoma Press and Watson & Dwyer, 1980).

16 Billal Rahman, "Map Shows State with Most Banned Books," *Newsweek*, October 3, 2024.

17 "Book Bans: PEN America tracks book bans and fights censorship in public schools and libraries across the country," PEN America website, https://pen.org/book-bans. PEN America, founded in 1922, is a non-profit organization of writers devoted to the advancement of literature, and the protection of freedom of expression and human rights. PEN stands for poets, essayists, novelists. PEN America is the largest of over 100 PEN centers worldwide that together comprise PEN International. For more on educational book bans and censorship, including state laws and policies that paved the way for Trump administration policies, see PEN America, "America's Censored Classrooms 2024," report issued October 8, 2024, https://pen.org/report/americas-censored-classrooms-2024/#heading-5, PEN America website, accessed May 12, 2025.

18 Senator Martin Heinrich, "BREAKING: President Trump just fired our nation's Librarian," Facebook, posted Friday night, May 8, 2025. See also Tim Balk, "Trump Administration Fires Librarian of Congress," *New York Times,* May 8, 2025.

19 Erica L. Green, "Trump Fired Librarian of Congress Over D.E.I.," *New York Times,* May 9, 2025. For more information see the Library of Congress website, https://www.loc.gov/.

20 John Ismay, "Who's In and Who's Out at the Naval Academy's Library?: An order by Defense Secretary Pete Hegseth's office resulted in a purge of books critical of racism but preserved volumes defending white power," *New York Times,* April 11, 2025; List of Removed Books from Nimitz Library Released: April 4, 2025, published in "Read the Naval Academy's List of Removed Books," *New York Times,* April 4, 2025.

21 The full list of search terms is: Affirmative Action Programs — Law and Legislation — United States; Affirmative Action Programs — United States; Affirmative Action; Allyship; Anti-Racism — United States; Critical Race Theory; Discrimination — Law and Legislation — United States; Diversity in the Workplace — United States; Diversity, Equity, and Inclusion; Gender Affirming Care – United States; Gender Dysphoria; Gender Expression; Gender Identity — United States; Gender Nonconformity; Gender Transition; Transgender Military Personnel — United States; Transgender People — United States; Transsexualism — United States; Transsexuals — United States; White privilege (Social structure). PEN America, "Pentagon Review of Military Libraries Poses Grave Threat to Intellectual Freedom," Press Release, May 10, 2025, https://pen.org/press-release/pentagon-review-of-military-libraries-poses-grave-threat-to-intellectual-freedom/, accessed May 12, 2025.

22 Karen Yourish, Annie Daniel, Saurabh Datar, Isaac White, and Lazaro Gamio, "These Words Are Disappearing in the New Trump Administration," *New York Times,* March 7, 2025. The *Times* list of banned or discouraged terms was on at least one agency's list and may not apply to all agencies. Some of the banned terms listed with a plus sign represent combinations of words that, "when used together, acknowledge transgender people, which is not in keeping with the current federal government's position that there are only two, immutable sexes." The full list of terms, which the *Times* acknowledged was probably incomplete, was: accessible, activism, activists, advocacy, advocate, advocates, affirming care, all-inclusive, allyship, anti-racism, antiracist, assigned at birth, assigned female at birth, assigned male at birth, at risk, barrier, barriers, belong, bias, biased, biased toward, biases, biases towards, biologically female, biologically male, BIPOC, Black, breastfeed + people, breastfeed + person, chestfeed + people, chestfeed + person, clean energy, climate crisis, climate science, commercial sex worker, community diversity, community equity, confirmation bias, cultural competence, cultural differences, cultural heritage, cultural sensitivity, culturally appropriate, culturally responsive, DEI, DEIA, DEIAB, DEIJ, disabilities, disability, discriminated, discrimination, discriminatory, disparity, diverse, diverse backgrounds, diverse communities, diverse community, diverse group, diverse groups, diversified, diversify, diversifying, diversity, enhance the diversity, enhancing diversity, environmental quality, equal opportunity, equality, equitable, equitableness, equity, ethnicity, excluded, exclusion, expression, female, females, feminism, fostering inclusivity, GBV, gender, gender based, gender based violence, gender diversity, gender identity, gender ideology, gender-affirming care, genders, Gulf of Mexico, hate speech, health disparity, health equity, hispanic minority, historically, identity, immigrants, implicit bias, implicit biases, inclusion, inclusive, inclusive leadership, inclusiveness, inclusivity, increase diversity, increase the diversity, indigenous community, inequalities, inequality, inequitable, inequities, inequity, injustice, institutional, intersectional, intersectionality, key groups, key people, key populations, Latinx, LGBT, LGBTQ, marginalize, marginalized, men who have sex with men, mental health, minorities, minority. most risk, MSM, multicultural, Mx, Native American, non-binary, nonbinary,

oppression, oppressive, orientation, people + uterus, people-centered care, person-centered, person-centered care, polarization, political, pollution, pregnant people, pregnant person, pregnant persons, prejudice, privilege, privileges, promote diversity, promoting diversity, pronoun, pronouns, prostitute, race, race and ethnicity, racial, racial diversity, racial identity, racial inequality, racial justice, racially, racism, segregation, sense of belonging, sex, sexual preferences, sexuality, social justice, sociocultural, socioeconomic, status, stereotype, stereotypes, systemic, systemically, they/them, trans, transgender, transsexual, trauma, traumatic, tribal, unconscious bias, underappreciated, underprivileged, underrepresentation, underrepresented, underserved, undervalued, victim, victims, vulnerable populations, women, women and underrepresented.

23   Hegseth said he ordered the material removed in compliance with Trump's executive order ending DEI programs throughout the federal government. Tara Copp, Lolita C. Baldor, and Kevin Vineys, "War heroes and military firsts are among 26,000 images flagged for removal in Pentagon's DEI purge," Associated Press, March 7, 2025.

24   Copp, Baldor, and Vineys, "War heroes and military firsts"; Seb Starcevic, "Pentagon admits to mistakes in campaign against 'DEI' content," *Politico,* March 21, 2025.

25   AHA-OAH Joint Statement on Federal Censorship of American History, March 13, 2025. The following organizations signed on to the statement: African Studies Association, Alliance for Texas History, American Academy of Religion, American Association for State and Local History, American Federation of Teachers, American Journalism Historians Association, American Society for Environmental History, American Studies Association, Asian & Pacific Islander Americans in Historic Preservation, Association for Spanish and Portuguese Historical Studies, Association for the Study of African American Life and History, Association of University Presses, College Art Association, Conference on Asian History, Education for All, French Colonial Historical Society, Historians for Peace and Democracy, H-Net Executive Council, Immigration and Ethnic History Society, Labor and Working Class History Association, LGBTQ+ Historians Association, National Council for the Social Studies, National Council on Public History, Network of Concerned Historians, North American Conference on British Studies, North American Society for Oceanic History, North American Society for Sport History, Norwegian Historical Association, Oral History Association, PEN America, Polish American Historical Association, Royal Netherlands Historical Society, Social Welfare History Group, Society for Historians of American Foreign Relations, Society for Historians of the Gilded Age and Progressive Era, Society for US Intellectual History, Society of Architectural Historians, Southern Association for Women Historians, Urban History Association, Western History Association, Western Society for French History, World History Association. American Historical Association website, accessed April 30, 2025.

26   "Restoring Truth and Sanity to American History," Executive Order, March 27, 2025, available on the White House website under Presidential Actions: https://www.whitehouse.gov/presidential-actions/executive-orders/.

27   "Restoring Truth and Sanity to American History."

28   American Historical Association, "Historians Defend the Smithsonian," Statement released March 31, 2025, American Historical Association website, accessed April 30, 2025.

29   These events were reported in numerous news sources and are effectively summarized in Joe Friesen, "'For what's next, look to Michigan': Fear and anxiety engulf the University of Michigan as Trump targets higher education," *Globe and Mail,* May 11, 2025.

30   "Death toll in Gaza rises to 52,000, territory's health ministry says, as Israel continues offensive," CBS News, April 27, 2025, https://www.cbsnews.com/news/war-gaza-israel-death-toll-april-2025/, accessed May 15, 2025; Ahmed Yussuf, Brianna Morris-Grant, Eric

Tlozek, and wires, "A closer look at the human toll in Gaza as deaths pass 50,000," ABC News, March 24, 2025, https://www.abc.net.au/news/2025-03-24/gaza-death-toll-50000-explained/105088110, accessed May 15, 2025; Nidal Al-Mughrabi and Emma Farge, "Gaza death toll: how many Palestinians has Israel's offensive killed?," Reuters, March 24, 2025, https://www.reuters.com/world/middle-east/how-many-palestinians-has-israels-gaza-offensive-killed-2025-01-15/, accessed May 15, 2025.

31 Rick Jacobs, Opinion, "I'm a rabbi. Starving Gaza is immoral: A just war must be fought by just means," *Washington Post*, May 12, 2025. Jewish organizations voicing opposition to the Netanyahu government's conduct in Gaza and desire to establish settlements there include the progressive advocacy groups J Street and Bend the Arc and the more centrist American Jewish Committee. Other groups that support a two-state solution or oppose Jewish settlement in Gaza include Jewish Federations of North America, the Anti-Defamation League, the Rabbinical Assembly, which represents clergy of the Conservative Jewish Movement, and the Union for Reform Judaism. See Andrew Lapin, "Bucking Israel's far right, several large American Jewish groups say they oppose resettling Gaza," *Jewish News*, December 10, 2024.

32 Yasmeen Persaud and Angela Yang, "Brown Medicine professor and doctor deported to Lebanon despite having valid visa, court filings claim," NBC News, March 16, 2025, https://www.nbcnews.com/news/us-news/brown-medicine-professor-doctor-deported-lebanon-valid-visa-court-fili-rcna196638, accessed May 15, 2025.

33 Friesen "'For what's next, look to Michigan'"; Annie Ma, "More than 1,000 international students have had visas or legal status revoked," Associated Press, April 17, 2025; Nina Pullano, "Judge rules Columbia activist Mahmoud Khalil's case belongs in federal, not immigration court," Courtroom News Service, April 29, 2025, https://www.courthousenews.com/judge-rules-columbia-activist-mahmoud-khalils-case-belongs-in-federal-not-immigration-court/, accessed May 15, 2025; "Mahmoud Khalil's Lawsuit Can Move Forward in Federal Court, Judge Finds," Center for Constitutional Rights, April 29, 2025, https://ccrjustice.org/home/press-center/press-releases/mahmoud-khalil-s-lawsuit-can-move-forward-federal-court-judge-finds, accessed May 15, 2025.

34 Friesen "'For what's next, look to Michigan'"; Jesús Marrero Suárez, "Judge rules Tufts student's detention case to be heard in Vermont, not Louisiana," WBUR Public Radio Station, Boston, April 4, 2025, https://www.wbur.org/news/2025/04/04/judge-tufts-students-deportation-hearing-vermont, accessed May 15, 2025.

35 "Judge releases Palestinian student at Columbia who was arrested at citizenship interview," PBS News, April 30, 2025, https://www.pbs.org/newshour/politics/judge-releases-palestinian-student-at-columbia-who-was-arrested-at-citizenship-interview, accessed May 15, 2025; Jake Offenhartz, "Freed from ICE custody, Palestinian activist Mohsen Mahdawi graduates from Columbia to cheers," Associate Press, May 19, 2025.

36 Campbell Robertson, "An Iranian Student in U.S. Detention Makes a Hard Choice: Stay or Go Home," *New York Times*, May 15, 2025.

37 Friesen "'For what's next, look to Michigan'."

38 Friesen "'For what's next, look to Michigan'"; Sharon Otterman and Wesley Parnell, "Columbia Faculty Protests as Trump Officials Hail University Concessions: While some professors rallied to criticize the changes, federal officials called the university's actions a 'positive first step' in maintaining a financial relationship," *New York Times*, published March 24, 2025, updated March 25, 2025.

39 Letter of April 11, 2025, superseding letter of April 3, 2025, to Harvard President Alan Garber and Penny Pritzker, Lead Member, Harvard Corporation, from Josh Gruenbaum, Commissioner of the Federal Acquisitions Service, General Services Administration; Sean R. Keveney, Acting General Counsel, U.S. Department of Health and Human

Services; and Thomas E. Wheeler, Acting General Counsel, U.S. Department of Education. This summary of demands is incomplete but captures some of the most disturbing requirements and suggests the range of demands placed on other institutions. https://www.harvard.edu/research-funding/wp-content/uploads/sites/16/2025/04/Letter-Sent-to-Harvard-2025-04-11.pdf, accessed May 14, 2025.

40   Josh Moody, "Harvard Resists Trump's Demands," *Inside Higher Ed*, April 14, 2025. Harvard's legal challenge holds huge implications for institutions facing similar demands and losses of funds, including Cornell University (more than $1 billion), Northwestern University ($790 million), Brown University ($510 million), Princeton University ($210 million), and the University of Pennsylvania ($175 million). Josh Moody, "Harvard Resists Trump's Demands."

41   Josh Moody, "Harvard Resists Trump's Demands."

42   Public Statement, "A Call for Constructive Engagement," April 22, 2025. This statement was developed in collaboration with university and college presidents and other educational leaders across the country, after national meetings convened by the American Association of Colleges and Universities (AAC&U) and the American Academy of Arts & Sciences. The statement remained open for endorsements and had 652 signatures as of May 16, 2025. https://www.aacu.org/newsroom/a-call-for-constructive-engagement, last accessed May 19, 2025. See also Tracey Tully, "This State University Has a Plan to Take on Trump: "Two professors from Rutgers University in New Jersey went out on a limb to write a 'mutual defense compact' for Big Ten schools. Their effort is gaining steam," *New York Times*, April 30, 2025. The mutual defense compact had been approved by faculty at more than a dozen universities by April 30, 2025, but did not have administrations' approval, nor any enforcement mechanism.

43   Alan Blinder, "Trump Is Fighting Antisemitism the Wrong Way, a Jewish Group Argues: The American Jewish Committee joined university groups in urging the White House to combat antisemitism with a careful, lawful process, not hasty, ill-advised actions," *New York Times*, May 6, 2025. The educational signatories pledged "continuing consequential reform and transparent action to root out antisemitism and all other forms of hate and prejudice from our campuses."

44   Stephanie Saul, "Harvard, Under Pressure, Revamps D.E.I. Office," *New York Times,* April 28, 2025.

45   Anemona Hartocollis and Vimal Patel, "Harvard Promises Changes After Reports on Antisemitism and Islamophobia," *New York Times*, April 29, 2025.

46   News Article, "CAUT advises academics against non-essential travel to the U.S.," CAUT website, April 15, 2025, https://www.caut.ca/latest/2025/04/caut-advises-academics-against-non-essential-travel-us.

47   "CAUT advises academics against non-essential travel to the U.S."

48   "CAUT advises academics against non-essential travel to the U.S."

49   CBC, "Read Justin Trudeau's speech in response to Trump's tariffs," February 2, 2025, yahoo!news, https://ca.news.yahoo.com/read-justin-trudeaus-speech-response-195815180.html, accessed April 26, 2025.

Index

9/11. *See* September 11, 2001
49th Parallel: crossing of, 125, 127, 132, 230, 236, 244, 338, 350, 351; meaning of, 98–120, 134, 174, 245, 393; perceived sameness along, 130, 352, 365n22; perspective from north of, 2, 4, 91, 92, 232, 366n41

Abbot, Edith, 274
Addonizio, Hugh, 188
Adelman, Jeremy, 113, 120n65, 133–4
Administrative Procedure Act (U.S., 1946), 396
African Americans: as voters, 251–2, 288, 289–90, 295; in Texas, 4, 139n22, 177, 345, 385–6; naming conventions for, 7–8; obstacles to voting, 295, 298–9, 303; post-secondary degree statistics for, 266; violence against, 175–6, 177–8, 179n4, 183–4, 252–3, 254–5, 256–8. *See also* gun violence (U.S.), against African Americans; Black Lives Matter Movement (U.S.); racial segregation (U.S.)
Alabama National Guard, mobilized against civil rights protestors, 295
Alaska, 145–69; American purchase of, 100, 145; author's time in, 94–95; Indigenous dialects in, 146–8, 150; Indigenous social status in, 149; land claims strategy in, 96n5; men's houses in, 150, 166n18; natural resources of, 148–9; Norwegians in, 151, 153–4, 158, 163; oomaliks in, 149, 159, 160, 161, 164; reindeer industry in, 146, 150–69
Alawieh, Rasha, 405, 410
Albers, Gretchen, 375, 376
Alliance for Texas History, 396, 413n5, 416n25
All That Glitters: Class, Conflict and Community in Cripple Creek (Jameson), 13, 377
Anthony, Susan B., 292, 293, 300, 307n18
Antioch College (OH), 18, 184–5, 200–201n20, 265, 272, 275, 377
Antisarlook family, 160–1. *See also* Alaska

American Historical Association (AHA), 63n5, 96n1, 115n7, 263, 270, 391; and Louise Tilly, 279, 380; statements on policies of second Trump administration, 394–6, 401, 403–4
American whiskey traders, 105–6, 113, 130
Ammons, Elias, 205, 314
Anderson, Benedict, 122–3
Andrés, Benny, Jr., 373, 376
Anzaldúa, Gloria, 113, 133, 344, 362
Archer, Carol, 374–5, 376
Armitage, Susan, 13, 24–25, 39, 128, 372, 376, 397
Aron, Stephen, 113, 120n65, 133–4
Associated Press, 401
Austen, Jane, 278
Azure, Marguerite, 352, 354, 355, 360

Bardwick, Judith, 274
Barnes, James, 26, 32, 33
Beaudoin, Azilda, 241, 244, 245–6, 248n32
Beck, Glenn, 322–3
Belgarde, Margaret (Marquerite) Dufort: biographical detail and homestead of, 237, 238, 244–5, 247n17, 248n32, 366n32; move from Red River to Pembina, 350–2, 354, 355, 360; name of, 365n28
Belknap, Kit, 55
Bell, Sherman, 69, 70, 83n9
Berard, Bob, 377
Biden, Joe, 259fn3, 303
Bierce, Ambrose, 45
Billington, Ray Allen, 105
Bingaman, Jeff, 287
Bingham, George Caleb, 46–47
Birzer, Dedra, 373, 376
Blackfoot Confederacy, 9, 132, 134
Black Lives Matter Movement (U.S.), 176, 179n4, 204n64. *See also* African Americans
Bloor, Ella Reeve, 320
Blow, Charles, 324
Bodnar, John, 214

419

Bolton, Herbert Eugene, 103–4, 116n21, 125
Boone, Daniel, 46, 47fig2.1, 62
Bordeaux, James, 49
borders and borderlands, definition of each, 113–4, 123–4, 126–7, 132, 133–34, 135, 337. *See also* Canada–U.S. border and borderlands; Mexico–U.S. border and borderlands
Boundary Commission (CAN–U.S.), 98–99, 115n5, 393. *See also* 49th Parallel
Boyd, Mary, 238–9, 242, 245
Boyd, Sarah, 239, 246
Boynton, Amelia, 294, 298
Bozeman, John and Catherine, 35
Brevig, Tollef, 153–4, 155, 156, 158, 161, 162
British Columbia (CAN): extension of border, 99, 131, 393; as a geographical region, 100–101, 104; historians, 103, 264; fur trade in, 355
Bromfield, Tiffany L., 254–255
Brooke, Edward, 183, 195–6
Brown, H. Rap, 182, 193. *See also* Civil Rights Movement (U.S.)
Brown, Jennifer, 133
Brown University, 405, 407, 410, 418n40
Buffalo Bird Woman. *See* Mahidiweash; Wilson, Gilbert L.
Bulger, Eddie, 80. *See also* Doran/Welch/Chapman family
Burns, James, 69, 70
Bush, Abigail, 292
Bush, George W., 2, 216, 220–1
butter: American legislation protecting women's markets for, 59; butter churns, 45, 46, 63n1; Canadian legislation protecting women's markets for, 355–6; frontier, 45–46, 54, 55, 60–61, 62, 355, 361; Indigenous women's sale of, 59, 355; men during the Gold Rush, made by, 33, 59; production of on the Oregon Trail, 55; women's domestic and commercialized production of, 32, 35, 55–56, 57–58, 62, 355

Cabeza de Vaca, Álvar Núñez, 125
Calgary, city of: social landscape of, 15–16, 45, 95, 127, 128, 131, 383–5; during and after September 11, 2001, 91–93. *See also* University of Calgary
Calgary Herald, The (CAN), 17, 130, 131, 263, 281
California Gold Rush, 5, 13, 18, 23–43; background of miners, 25–8, 53; women in, 30–31, 32, 34, 35–37; Chinese men in, 27–28, 30–31, 38, 59, 41n17: Cornish men in, 28–30, 37–38; food in, 33–35; masculinity in, 31–34; sex ratios in, 24–25, 30, 32; separation of couples, 35–37; social life in, 32, 34–35
Calof, Rachel, 16, 57–8, 60, 62, 65n51, 65n52, 127. *See also* women homesteaders in North Dakota
Calumet and Hecla Mining Company, 315, 317, 318. *See also* Calumet miners' strike (MI, 1913-1914)
Calumet copper miners' strike (MI, 1913–1914): Citizens' Alliance in, 315, 317, 318; comparisons to striking coal miners, 315–6; demands of miners, 315; ethnic backgrounds of miners in, 315–6; general violence of, 316–7; outcome of, 318; Western Federation of Miners (WFM) in, 315, 317. *See also* Italian Hall tragedy
Campbell, Edgar Omer, 155–6
Canada–U.S. border and borderlands, 3, 91–2, 93, 100, 103, 110, 124, 128, 130, 131, 174; fentanyl traffic across, 393–4; Milk River, 98–99; tariffs, 393, 411–2. *See also* 49th Parallel; Métis; women homesteaders in North Dakota
Canada and U.S. comparisons: dollars, distance, temperature, and measures of volume, 339; in hockey, 339; in knowledge of general North American history, 126; in outcomes for Indigenous peoples during and after newcomer settlement, 112; in spelling, 8, 339; numbers of women homesteaders, 235–6; of newcomer settlement land policy, 348–50; perception of violence in the historic Canada and U.S. Wests by George F. G. Stanley, 105–6; Thanksgiving celebrations, 384
Canadian Association of University Teachers (CAUT), travel advisory issued by, 410–1
Canadian Charter of Rights and Freedoms (1982), 15, 19–20n5, 251, 261–2
Canadian Historical Association, 5, 105
Canadian Pacific Railway, 106, 110
Cannon, Elizabeth, 267. *See also* University of Calgary
Capehart, Jonathan, 323–4
Careless, J. M. S., 101, 104
Carleton University, 374
Carkin, Theona, 56
Carter, Sarah, 91, 93–94, 112, 113, 122–3, 129, 133, 246, 346
Case, Clifford, P., 186

Cavanaugh, Catherine, 13, 128
CBC (Canadian Broadcasting Corporation), 17, 139–40n28, 263
Celucci, Paul, 131
Centers for Disease Control and Prevention (CDC), 325, 333n64
Chapman, Kathleen Welch, 54–5, 64n33, 74–6, 77, 79, 80, 81, 82–3. *See also* Doran/Welch/Chapman family
Chapman, Tracey, 124
Chase, John, 207. *See also* Colorado National Guard
Chicago Women's Trade Union League, 316
Chinese Exclusion Act (U.S., 1882), 28, 31, 41n31, 59, 77, 137n11
Chippewa: "full-blood Chippewa," 351; Pembina Chippewa, 232, 244, 355, 351–2, 367n44; Turtle Mountain Reservation (ND), 244, 348, 351, 353, 366n36; naming of, 366n30
Chopin, Kate, 273, 345
Cinco de Mayo, 126
Cinderella narrative, 16–17, 358. *See also* Turner, Frederick Jackson; Wilder, Laura Ingalls; Wilson, Gilbert L.
Civil Rights Movement (U.S.), 177, 178, 181, 184–5, 195, 204n72, 256–7; after Selma, 293–5, 298–9; erosion of gains from, 253–4; *Loving v. Virginia* (U.S., 1967), 298; Selma protests, 252, 259n11, 287. *See also* King, Martin Luther, Jr.; Selma voting rights campaign (U.S., 1965); Voting Rights Act (U.S., 1965)
Clark, Jim, 293–4, 305. *See also* Selma voting rights campaign (U.S., 1965)
class formation, 27, 29, 30–31, 37–38, 216, 276
Cleveland, Marion Beaton, 240, 241, 245–6
Clifford, James, 304
Clinton, Hillary, 199n2, 299, 301–2
CNN (Cable News Network), 92, 128, 130
Coalition for Western Women's History, 337, 372, 397
Colorado Fuel and Iron Company (CF&I), 206, 209, 223, 313, 316. *See also* Rockefeller, John D., Jr.
Colorado Humanities Program, 320, 397, 414n13. *See also* National Endowment for the Humanities (NEH) (U.S., 1965)
Colorado Labor Wars (1903–1904), 18, 67, 72–3, 82–3, 251. *See also* Cripple Creek district miners' strike (CO, 1893–1894); Cripple Creek district miners' strike (CO, 1903–1904)

Colorado National Guard, mobilized in miners' strikes, 68, 69, 83, 173, 205, 205–6, 207, 314, 320
Columbia University, 405, 406, 407
Comparative Studies in Society and History (journal), 264
Conklin, Nancy Faires, 274
Cook, Ramsay, 108–9
Cornell University, 262, 407, 418n40
Costa family, 205–6, 210, 212, 221, 223, 224n1, 314, 323. *See also* Ludlow Massacre (CO, 1914)
COVID-19, 92, 142n51, 340, 383, 391–2
Cree, 113, 120n65, 244, 350
Creighton, Donald, 107
Cripple Creek district miners' strike (CO, 1893–1894): achievements of, 67–8; Bull Hill, 54, 74–5, 86n37; labor's power following, 68, 77–78; start of gold mining in region, 67. *See also* Western Federation of Miners (WFM)
Cripple Creek district miners' strike (CO, 1903–1904): Citizens' Alliance in, 69, 70, 82; demands of, 68, 207; duration of, 69, 78; impact of defeat, 81; miners' defeat in, 54–5; Mine Owners' Association (MOA) in, 69, 70, 72, 80, 82; outcome of, 68, 70–1, 73; remembering, 13, 71–4, 81, 82–3; scabs in, 54; start and spread of, 68–9; strategies of miners in, 68–9; violence in, 68–71, 82. *See also* Western Federation of Miners (WFM)
Cronon, William, 355
Cumberland Gap, 46, 47fig2.1, 48, 62

Dakota Incident (film), 107–8
Darwinism, 156
Daughters of Bilitis, 296–7, 301, 304
Davis, Jordan, murder of 252–3, 312, 318, 323, 328n4; remembering, 256, 257–8, 321, 322, 327. *See also* McBath, Lucia (Lucy)
Dawes Act (U.S., 1887), 233, 348, 350, 366–7n42
Declaration of Independence (U.S.), 7, 288, 291
Denver Post (CO), 213
Detroit riot (1967), 182; demographics of rioters in, 193; Detroit riot (1943), 184; studied by National Advisory Commission on Civil Disorders (U.S., 1967–1968), 186, 201n22. *See also* National Advisory Commission on Civil Disorders (U.S., 1967–1968)
Deutsch, Sarah, 113, 133

Devils Lake Land Office: claims area of, 233–4, 348, 350–1, 365n22, 366–7n42; early operation, 174–5, 231, 236, 238, 242–3, 246n4, 247n10, 337, 364n17, 364–5n21; naming of 364n20. *See* Devils Lake region; women homesteaders in North Dakota

Devils Lake region (ND), 50–51, 57, 60, 240, 243, 246n4, 350, 353, 355; Devils Lake (now Spirit Lake) Sioux Reservation, 233–4, 348, 366–7n42. *See also* Devils Lake Land Office; women homesteaders in North Dakota

Devine, Heather, 248n32, 337

Diamond, Norma, 274

Dickie, Charles, 129

Diefenbaker, John, 16, 108

Directions West Conference (2012), 5. *See also* University of Calgary

dishwashing, women's history as history of, 273–4, 277, 346, 356–7, 361

Diversity, Equity and Inclusion (DEI): second Trump Administration opposition to, 382–3, 396–404, 404–9; within the professoriate, 277–9, 280–1; within historical scholarship, 27, 108, 354–7, 397, 404

Dobbs v. Jackson (U.S., 2022), 253

DOGE (U.S., Department of Government Efficiency), 394–6, 413–4n5. *See also* Trump Administration, Second

domesticity: among Chinese men during the California Gold Rush, 30–31, 59; during California Gold Rush, 32–34; of women in the home, 8, 9–10n3, 50, 54, 59

domestic wage work (service work), 33–5, 53–54, 57, 355; prostitution, 31, 54

Dominion Lands Act (CAN, 1872), 235, 348–9, 350; comparison to Homestead Act (U.S., 1862), 233–6; Manitoba Act (CAN, 1870) and scrip, 366n41

Doran/Welch/Chapman family, 18, 64n33, 74–77, 78–81, 82–3, 86n39, 87n59. *See also* Bulger, Eddie; Chapman, Kathleen Welch; Pryor, Beulah; Wing, May McConaghy

Douglass, Frederick, 292

Dream Defenders, 324–5

Dunn, Michael, 312, 328n4

Earle, Alice Morse, 274

Edwards, John, 198

Eisenhower Foundation, 175, 196, 204n67

Ellis, Anne, 54, 55–56, 57

Ellison, Keith, 177–8

Emerson, Ralph Waldo, 381

Equal Pay Act (U.S., 1963), 266

Erlenbach, Julius, 276

Esteban, 125

Farmers' Alliance (U.S.), 59, 355

Fazekas, Margaret, 316

FBI (U.S., Federal Bureau of Investigation), 132, 185–6, 187, 325

Ferguson, Miriam (Ma), 345, 363n7

Ferris, Woodbridge, 315

Fisher, Robin, 112

Flexner, Eleanor, 300

Floyd, George, 176, 177, 179n6, 257. *See also* African Americans, violence against

Fluke, Sandra, 263, 275, 281, 283n3

Fogarty, Robert S. (Bob), 377–8, 383, 388n4

Fort Berthold Indian Reservation (ND), 50, 51, 353. *See also* Hidatsa; Mandan

Fort Vancouver, 355

Foster, James C., 85–86n35, 319

Francis, R. Douglas, 91

Frazier, Darnella, 177, 179n6. *See also* Floyd, George

Frideres, Jim, 268. *See also* University of Calgary

First Organic Act (AK, 1884), 96n5, 145, 165n3

Frontier Thesis. *See* Turner, Frederick Jackson

Fuller, Margaret, 273, 345, 381

Fulton, Sybrina, 256–8, 311–3, 314, 319, 322, 325, 326–7, 329n8. *See also* Martin, Trayvon; African Americans, violence against

Gadsden Purchase (U.S., 1853–1854), 99–100

Gage, Mathilda Joslyn, 300, 309n49

Gailfus, Elizabeth Winkler, 242–3, 245–6

Galveston (TX): author's childhood in, 2–3, 3–4, 19n2, 125–6, 137n6, 139n22, 184, 363n8, 384, 385–6; Jews in, 16, 132, 138–9n21. *See also* Texas

Garber, Alan, 408, 409–10

Garcia, Matt, 135

Garver, Jennie Draper, 239, 240, 245

Gauthier, Eulalie and Arcade, 238–9, 244–5

Gay Liberation/Rights Movement (U.S.), 261, 288, 289, 296–8, 299, 300. *See also* Stonewall riot (U.S., 1969); same sex marriage; *Obergefell v. Hodges* (U.S., 2015)

Gaza campus protests. *See* Israel–Palestine conflict

gendered labor roles in U.S. West, 31–32, 38, 59, 353; separate gendered spheres, 34, 38, 53, 346, 355. *See also* domesticity

Ginsberg, David, 187, 194
Gitlin, Jay, 355
Goldberg, Hannah, 272, 273, 377
Granger, Gordon, 139n22, 386
Grew, Raymond, 264
Guangdong Province (CN), 27-28, 36, 39
Gulf of Mexico, 3, 385-6, 400, 415
Guthrie, Woody, 212-3, 319-20
Grange, The, 59, 355
Grass Valley (CA), 27, 28, 29, 30
Green, James (Jim), 174, 214, 216, 272
Greene, Julie, 213
Gregory, James, 184
gun violence (U.S.): against African Americans, 175-6, 254-7, 311-3, 325-6, 328-9n5, 329n6, 333n64; involving children, 254-5, 311-2, 322, 328-9n5, 329n6, 333n64

Haecker, Charles, 218, 220
Hall, Linda, 281
Hall, William H., 377
Handlin, Oscar, 121
Harper, Ida Husted, 309n49
Harris, Fred, 183, 187, 194, 195-6, 201n27, 203n60. *See also* National Advisory Commission on Civil Disorders (U.S., 1967-1968)
Harvard University, 103; conflict with second Trump Administration, 407-09, 418n40; perception of antisemitism on campus, 409-10
Hayden, Carla, 398-9
Hayes, Frank, 209, 211, 212-3
Haywood, W. D. (Big Bill), 70, 87n64
Heaton, Herbert, 109
Hegseth, Pete, 399, 401, 416n23. *See also* Trump Administration, Second
Heilbrun, Carolyn, 46, 47, 48, 63n3, 198, 338, 344, 347, 358
Heinrich, Martin, 398
Henry, Alexander, 350
Hickenlooper, John, 320
Hidatsa, 50-2, 64n16, 353-4, 355, 358, 359, 367n44, 367n45. *See also* Mahidiweash; Fort Berthold Reservation
High Noon (film), 107-8, 118n41
Hiller, Abiah Warren, 36-37
Hillsdale College (MI), 373
Hirsch, Susan E., 276
Hockney, Ann, 241-2, 245-6
Hogue, Michel, 113, 120n65, 248n32, 337, 374, 376

Holmes, Oliver Wendell, 319
Homestead Act (U.S., 1862), 56, 229, 233, 234-5, 235, 348, 350; comparison to Dominion Lands Act (CAN, 1872), 233-6
Hoover, J. Edgar, 187
Howard University, 324
How to Have Intercourse Without Getting Screwed (pamphlet), 275
Hudson's Bay Company, 155
Huffaker, Lucy, 222
Hunt, Jane, 290-1, 300-301
Huntkahitawin, 49-50
Hurricane Katrina, 197, 412
Hurtado, Albert, 133

Immigration Act (U.S., 1917), 122, 136n7
Imperial Oil-Lincoln McKay Chair in American Studies, 1, 3, 4-5, 13, 17, 18-19, 125, 371, 383, 391; Chair's Lectures, 5-7, 13, 18, 93-94, 173-4, 177, 251-3, 337, 340, 371, 380, 391. *See also* University of Calgary
Impoundment Control Act (U.S., 1974), 396
Indian Act (CAN, 1876), 365n25
Indigenous Peoples: diseases among, 38, 51, 152-3, 158, 163, 353, 354; graves of children, 255; in Alaska, 5, 94-95, 145-69 (*See also* Alaska); in the Calgary area, 9, 95; in the Frontier Thesis, 48; Miwok women, 38; naming conventions for, 7-8, 64n16, 119n55, 146, 165n1, 165n4, 165n6, 168n72, 366n30, 367n45; women's commercial production, 58-59; women in the fur trade, 49, 53, 55, 113, 245, 346, 355, 397. *See also* Mahidiweash; Métis
Industrial Workers of the World (IWW), 67, 316
Innis, Harold, 61, 102-4, 105, 106, 107, 110-1, 116n18, 130
International Emergency Economic Powers Act (U.S., 1977), 394
Italian Hall tragedy, 208, 316-23; aftermath, 317-9; death of children and death count, 317, 321, 331n31; remembering, 319, 320, 321-2, 323 *See also* Calumet copper miners' strike (MI, 1913)
Irish immigrants, 15-16, 18, 25, 27, 38, 56, 60, 74, 127, 139n26, 352-3
Ise, Rosa (Rosie), 57, 60
Israel-Palestine conflict: Hamas attack (October 7, 2023), 404; protests on campuses, 404-10, commentary from Jewish organizations, 417n31. *See also* Jews

Index   *423*

Jackson, Jimmie Lee, 252, 294. *See also* Civil Rights Movement (U.S.)
Jackson, Sheldon, 145–6, 149–52, 154, 155, 157, 163. *See also* Alaska
Jacobs, Jane, 399
Jacobs, Rick, 405. *See also* Jews
Jacoby, Robin, 275
Jews: American Jewish Committee (AJC) and antisemitism on campus, 409, 418n43; as settlers, 16, 106, 125–6, 235; author's family, 4, 114, 121, 122, 124, 133, 136n1, 137n5, 137n6, 271; impact of Israel–Palestine conflict on American universities, 404–10; racial ethnic label of, 9n2; in Texas and the South, 138–9n21, 184; opinions on Israel–Palestine conflict, 417n31. *See also* Calof, Rachel; Israel–Palestine conflict
Johnson, Lyndon B., 173, 181, 182–3, 195, 201n27, 203n60, 252, 257, 259–60n11, 294–5
Johnson, Susan Lee, 40, 135
Joldersma, Hermina, 268, 269
Jones, Mary Harris (Mother Jones), 211–2, 221, 316, 322
Journal of American History, 124
Juneteenth, 126, 139n22, 385–6

Kanipe, Mildred, 56
Kaunonen, Gary, 320
Kelly, Jerry, 78, 87n56
Kelly, Wayne, 268
Kennedy, John F., 266, 290, 371, 412
Kennedy, Robert, 197, 290
Kerner, Otto, 173, 183, 186–7. *See also* National Advisory Commission on Civil Disorders (U.S., 1967–1968)
Kerner Commission. *See* National Advisory Commission on Civil Disorders (U.S., 1967–1968)
Kerner Report. *See* National Advisory Commission on Civil Disorders (U.S., 1967–1968)
Khalil, Mahmoud, 405–6
Kilbuck, John Henry, 153, 156
King, Martin Luther, Jr., 181, 195, 197, 203n60, 256, 290, 293–4, 301
King, William Lyon Mackenzie, 127, 139n27, 209, 210, 221, 318
Kittredge, Ellen, 154
Kittson, Norman, 350, 366n31
Knights of Labor, 73, 207
Knights of St. John, 76
Kwiatkowski, Susan, 373, 376

Labor and Working Class History Association (LAWCHA), 5, 174, 213, 214–5, 216, 220, 321, 396, 413–4n5, 414n12, 416n25
La Jornada (MX), 132
Lamar, Howard, 112, 355
Langdon, Emma, 71, 72
Lantis, Margaret, 146
Lavallee, Frizine, Sayer, 238–9, 240–1, 244, 245–6
Leavitt, Karoline, 398. *See also* Trump Administration, Second
Lee, Bob, 206
Lee, Ivy, 209, 318
Lee-Ashley, Matt, 218–9
Lenfest-Jameson, Barbara (and Stanley and Spencer), 389
Lenfest-Jameson, Daniel, 1, 384, 389
Lerner, Gerda, 47, 49, 59, 346, 359, 46, 363n12
Lewis, John, 252, 257, 259–60n11, 294, 295, 299, 303, 305
Lewis, Meriwhether and Clark, William, 127, 139n27, 346
Lightfoot, Gordon, 182, 195
Lilly Ledbetter Fair Pay Act (U.S., 2009), 289, 305–6n5
Limbaugh, Rush, 263, 281, 283n3
Lincoln, Abraham, 386. *See also* United States Civil War and slavery
Lindgren, H. Elaine, 56, 232, 234, 242, 365n22
Lippiati, Gerald, 206, 316
Liuzzo, Viola, 295, 301
Loch-Drake, Cynthia, 374, 376
Lomen, Carl (and Lomen family), 158, 163
London School of Economics, 372
Lone Star (film), 98, 338, 343–4, 345, 360–1, 362n2, 369n70
Lopp, Thomas, 154–5, 157, 158, 167–8n45
Loretto Heights College (CO), 276
Louisiana Purchase (U.S., 1803), 99–100
Lower, Arthur R. M., 104
Ludlow Massacre (CO, 1914): annual memorial, 205, 209, 210, 221; blame for, 209, 213, 216, 323; details of, 205–6, 313–4; campaign for National Historic Landmark status, 173, 213–21, 327; remembering, 173, 210, 211–3, 217, 222–3, 319–22, 389; deaths of children in, 205–6, 208, 210, 313, 314, 321–2, 323, 325, 327; legacy of, 208, 221–3; monument, 205, 210–1, 213, 215, 216, 221, 224n1, 226n25, 319; spelling of victims' names, 224n1. *See also* Ludlow mining strike (CO, 1913–1914)

Ludlow mining strike (CO, 1913–1914): death rate of workers in Colorado coal mines, 208; ethnicity of miners, 207–8, 315; miners' demands, 206–7, 313; reasons for strike, 208, 217, 313; start of strike, 206. *See also* Ludlow Massacre (CO, 1914)

Mahdawi, Mohsen, 406
Mahidiweash (Buffalo Bird Woman), 50–53, 57, 58, 60, 62, 337, 353–4, 357, 358–60, 367n45, 368n64; Goodbird, son of, 52, 358, 359–60; Henry Wolf Chief, brother of, 358; Magpie, husband of, 358–9, 368–9n64; naming conventions for, 52, 64n16, 367n45
Making Western Canada: Essays on European Colonization and Settlement (Cavanaugh/ Mouat), 13, 111
Malintzin, 127, 139n27
Mandan, 51, 353, 368–9n64. *See also* Fort Berthold Reservation
Manifest Destiny, 16, 25, 100, 101
Marchetto, Sean, 374, 376
Marquette, Frye, 177, 295. *See also* Watts riot (1965)
Martin, Chester, 264
Martin, Tracy, 256, 312–3, 325, 329n8
Martin, Trayvon, 252–3, 256–8, 311–3, 318, 321–8, 329n8. *See also* African Americans, violence against
Marx, Gary, 185, 193, 194
Mattachine Society, 296–7, 299, 304
Matthews, Charlotte, 376–7
McBath, Lucia (Lucy), 256–8, 259n10, 259–60n11, 312, 314, 329n7. *See also* Davis, Jordan
McClelland, Thomas, 70
McClintock, Mary Ann, 290–1, 300–301
McGill University (CAN), 264
McGuire, Randall, 214, 215, 217
McIntyre, C. W., 351–2
McKinney, May, 375, 376
McManus, Sheila, 93–94
McSheffrey, Marion, 384
Meek, Joe, 50, 62, 63n15
Métis: 1885 Rebellion (CAN), 113, 248n32, 351, 362; in the fur trade, 49, 102, 113, 244; in North Dakota, 232, 244, 351–2; Red River settlement of, 232, 237, 245, 350; scrip in Canada, 366n41. *See also* women homesteaders in North Dakota
Mexico–U.S. border and borderlands, 3, 92, 98, 103, 123, 125, 127, 128, 130, 343; John Sayles' definition of, 343; Mexican–American War (1848), 99–100, 140n30;

tariffs, 393, 411; labor unions across, 139n26
Michigan National Guard, mobilized during miners' strike, 315
Mines and Collieries Act (UK, 1842), 38
miners: children as, 28–9; in California, 23–43; in Cripple Creek (CO), 67–87; in Ludlow (CO), 173–4, 205–27, 313–23, 327; in Keweenaw Peninsula (MI), 208, 314–21, 322; women as, 28–29, 38, 43n61. *See also* mining
mining: accidents in, 53–54, 69, 80, 86n43, 329–30n10; child labor in, 28–29, 319; child participation in strikes, 321–2; "dead work," 206–7, 313; diseases, 28, 322; domestic violence, 357, 361; gold/placer and quartz mining in California, 23–43; hard rock compared to coal, unions in, 207, 319; tools for, 29; types of, 25. *See also* miners
Mining History Association, 97, 214,
Minutemen (U.S., 21st century), 132, 134
missionaries, 51, 353, 354, 355; in Alaska, 95, 146, 151–2, 153–7, 159, 160, 162, 164, 168n72
Mitchell, Juliet, 277–8
Mitchell, Yolanda T., 254–5
Montana State University, 375
Montreal, QC (CAN), 3, 114, 122, 124, 137n6
Moraga, Cherríe, 344
Morgan, William Ives, 26–27
Morrissey, Katherine, 355
Morton, W. L., 107
Mothers of East Los Angeles, 356
Mott, Lucretia, 290–1, 292, 302. *See also* Seneca Falls Convention (U.S., 1848)
Mouat, Jeremy, 2, 13, 93, 97–120
Mount Allison University, 373
Moyer, Charles, 70, 76, 317. *See also* Western Federation of Miners (WFM)
Murray, Patty, 132
My Brother's Keeper initiative, 327

NAACP (National Association for the Advancement of Colored People), 183, 189, 256,
Nash, Gerald D., 108
National Advisory Commission on Civil Disorders (U.S., 1967–1968), 173, 181, 399; context of civil disorders, 183–4; establishment and work of, 182–3, 185–7; production and outcome of report, 175, 177–8, 183, 192–4, 195–6, 198–9, 200n10, 202n49, 203n56, 203n60, 204n64, 251; research sample for, 201n22; use of "ghetto" in documents of, 199n4

National Archives and Records Administration (NARA) (U.S.), 219, 230-1, 396-7; second Trump Administration threats to, 394-5, 398
National Endowment for the Humanities (NEH) (U.S., 1965), 394-7; fellowships, 397; staff firings and funding terminations under second Trump Administration, 394, 395; response to DOGE's personnel cuts, 396
U.S. National Guard: mobilized against gun violence protestors, 255; patrols along Canada–U.S. border, 132. *See also* Alabama National Guard, mobilized against civil rights protestors; Colorado National Guard, mobilized in miners' strikes; Michigan National Guard, mobilized during miners' strike; New Jersey National Guard, mobilized during 1967 riots
National Labor Relations Act (U.S., 1935), 217
NBC (National Broadcasting Company), 128, 294, 298
New Brunswick riot (NJ, 1967), 191-2, 198. *See also* New Jersey "chain" riots (1967)
New Western History, 17, 20n12, 61, 112-4, 119-20n60, 137-38n13, 362, 379
Nettel, John and Fred, 30
Nevada City (CA), 27, 28, 29, 34
Newark riot (NJ, 1967), 177, 182, 188-9, 192-3, 196-7, 201n24
New Jersey "chain" riots (1967), studied by National Advisory Commission on Civil Disorders (U.S., 1967-1968), 186, 187-188, 201n22. *See also* National Advisory Commission on Civil Disorders (U.S., 1967-1968); Newark riot; New Brunswick riot; Plainfield riot
New Jersey National Guard, mobilized during 1967 riots, 188, 189-90
New Mexico, 1, 3, 14, 15, 70, 132, 199n1, 208, 283n8, 393, 398; Pueblos, 95, 96n6. *See also* University of New Mexico
Newsweek (U.S.), 398
New York Times, 323, 324, 400
New York Tribune, 222
Nixon, Richard, 195
Nochlin, Linda, 274
Northwest College (WY), 375
North West Company, 350
Northwestern University, 407, 418n40
North West Mounted Police (NWMP), 105-6, 130. *See also* Royal Canadian Mounted Police

Obama, Barack, 173, 1175, 181, 197-8, 199n2, 200n16, 220, 251, 287-288, 302, 304, 305, 325-6, 327, 340
Obergefell v. Hodges (U.S., 2015), 252, 303, 306n6. *See also* same sex marriage
O'Connor, Maggie, 56
Odall, Rodney, 33
Ohio State University, 272-3
Ojibwe. *See* Chippewa
Oleomargarine Act (U.S., 1886), 59, 355-6. *See also* butter
Olsdatter, Guri, 56
Olsen, Wallace, 153
One Step Over the Line: Toward a History of Women in the North American Wests (Jameson/McManus), 94
Open Range (film), 108
oral history, 18, 21n14, 57, 71, 72, 73, 86n37, 137n4, 211, 277-8, 327, 338, 357, 358, 378-9, 385, 386, 397
Orchard, Harry, 70-71, 82, 87n64
Oregon Treaty, 99-100, 393. *See also* 49th Parallel; Boundary Commission (CAN–U.S.)
Organization of American Historians (OAH), 5, 93, 301, 396, 401, 413n5, 414n12
Owyhee Avalanche (ID), 29, 31, 37
Öztürk, Rumeysa, 405-6

Pacific Coast Branch – American Historical Association (PCB–AHA), 5-6, 94
Palmer, Alice Freeman, 264, 265
Palmer, Rhoda, 293
Palmieri, Victor, 185, 194, 203n55. *See also* National Advisory Commission on Civil Disorders (U.S., 1967-1968)
Parent-Teacher Associations (PTA), 356-7, 360, 362
Parks, Rosa, 195
Patterson-Black, Sheryll, 232, 246n5
Peabody, James H., 67, 68, 69, 76, 84n9, 207
Pedrogon family, 205-6, 221-2, 223, 314, 323. *See also* Ludlow Massacre (CO, 1914)
PEN America, 398, 413n5, 414n17, 416n25
Petrucci, Frank, 327. *See also* Ludlow Massacre (CO, 1914)
Petrucci, Mary, 221-3, 313-4, 319, 322, 327; deaths of children, 205-6, 221-3, 224n1, 313-4, 323, 327. *See also* Ludlow Massacre (CO, 1914)
Pettibone, George, 70
Pierson, George, 104

Plainfield riot (NJ, 1967), 189–91, 198. *See also* New Jersey "chain" riots (1967)
Polk, James K., 393
Pomeroy, Earl, 108, 117n27
populism, 59, 68, 73, 77, 110, 111, 375
Princeton University, 176, 407, 418n40
private detective agencies, use of in mining strikes, 68, 82, 206, 315, 316, 318
Pryor, Beulah, 54, 357, 360, 361. *See also* Doran/Welch/Chapman family
Putrich, Steve, 316

Quillan, Kevin, 198, 199n3

racial ethnic, use of term, 7–8, 9n2, 19n2, 363n8, 369n70
racial segregation (U.S.), 4, 125, 175, 183, 184, 190, 195, 196, 198, 199n4, 275, 287, 293, 304, 345, 361, 386, 401, 404
Randall, Stephen, 198
Rapp, Rayna, 274
Rasmussen, Lorna, 13
Rastall, Benjamin McKie, 72
Reeb, James, 294
Reindeer Act (U.S., 1937), 164
Ressam, Ahmed, 130
Riel, Louis, 125. *See also* Métis
Rio Grande River, 3, 134
Robbins, William G., 111
Roberts, John (Chief Justice), 254
Roberts, John (miner), 29
Robertson, Henry, 83
Robeson, Paul, 113
Robin, Martin, 112
Robinson, Eugene, 324
Rubio, Marco, 395, 406
Rockefeller, Jay, 219, 220
Rockefeller, John D., Jr., 139n27, 206, 209–10, 213, 216, 221, 223, 313, 318, 319
Rocky Mountain News, The (CO), 206
Roe v. Wade (U.S., 1972), 252, 253
Rogers, Stan, 129
Rossland, BC (CAN), 18, 127
Royal Canadian Mounted Police (RCMP), 108–9, 130–1. *See also* North West Mounted Police
Rozas, David, 406
Rubin, Gayle, 274
Rushton, Mary J., 229–32, 234, 237, 241, 244, 245–6, 347–8, 350, 354, 355, 360

Sacagawea, 127, 139n27, 346
Sage, Walter, 104, 107, 117n24, 238, 247n19, 264
Salazar, Ken, 216, 218–20
Sam, Ah, 59, 60
Samek, Hana, 112
same sex marriage, 123–4, 125, 138n16, 252, 265, 283n8, 303–4; Proposition 8 (CA), 289; Defense of Marriage Act (U.S., 1996), 289. *See also Obergefell v. Hodges* (U.S., 2015); Gay Liberation/Rights Movement (U.S.)
Sandburg, Carl, 386–7
Schenck v. United States (1919), 310
Schiller, Lee Chambers, 274
Schlatter, Evelyn, 372–3, 376
Scott, Rick, 324–5
Selma voting rights campaign (U.S., 1965), 252, 259–6n11, 293–5, 303, 304; in relation to Seneca Falls and Stonewall, 251, 288–90, 298–9, 302–3, 304, 305. *See also* Civil Rights Movement (U.S.); Voting Rights Act (U.S., 1965)
Seneca County Courier (NY), 291
Seneca Falls Convention (U.S., 1848), 251, 290–3, 297–8, 300–302, 303; Declaration of Sentiments, 291–2, 293, 303; key abolitionist figures in, 290; in relation to Selma and Stonewall, 251, 288–90, 302–3, 304, 305. *See also* Women's Rights Movement
September 11, 2001 (9/11), 91–93, 94, 129–32, 140n34, 199n2, 213, 290, 340–1
Shannon, Fred A., 104–5, 246–7n7
Sharp, Paul, 109–10, 111, 113, 114
Sheehan, Patricia, 191
Shelby County v. Holder (U.S., 2013), 253–4, 303, 306n6
Shellow, Robert, 185, 186, 194, 200n19, 200–201n20, 203n55, 399
Sheridan, Rose M., 352–3, 354, 355, 360, 367n43
Shields, Walter, 158
Shoemaker, Pauline, 58
Shogan, Colleen J., 395. *See also* National Archives and Records Administration (U.S.)
Sibley, Henry, 366n31
Sigurdson, Richard, 362, 388
Simmons, Tom and Laurie, 218, 227n43
Sinclair, Upton, 209, 217, 221, 319, 331n41
Sioux, 113, 352. *See also* Devils Lake region (ND), Devils Lake (now Spirit Lake) Sioux Reservation; Huntkahitawin; Sitting Bull
Sitting Bull, 104–5, 125. *See also* Sioux

Skinner, Constance Lindsay, 103
Sklar, Kathryn (Kitty), 273, 274, 277, 285n33, 377
Slotkin, Richard, 109
Small Legs, Edwin, 132
Smith, Donald, 117n27
Smith, Henry Nash, 107–8
Smith, John, 177, 188
Smithsonian Institution, 402–4; Ludlow monument in Save Outdoor Sculpture inventory of, 224n1; second Trump Administration criticism of, 402–4; professional historians' defense of, 403–4
Smoot-Hawley Tariff (U.S., 1930), 393
Snyder, Frank, 205, 223, 224n1, 314, 321. *See also* Ludlow Massacre (CO, 1914)
Spangler, Jewel, 91
Stand Your Ground Law (FL, 2005), 311, 312, 324–5
Stanley, George F. G., 92, 105–7, 108, 109, 111, 117n27, 130
Stanton, Elizabeth Cady, 290–3, 300–301, 302, 307n18, 309n49. *See also* Seneca Falls Convention (U.S., 1848)
Stanton, Henry, 290, 292, 305
Staples Thesis. *See* Innis, Harold
Stearns, Almira Fay, 37. *See also* California Gold Rush
Steunenberg, Frank, 70–71, 87n64
Stewart, Pruitt Elinore, 56
Stewart, Thomas, 69
St. Lawrence Island (AK), 145, 146–7, 148, 149, 151, 155, 161–3, 165, 166n18
St. Lawrence River, 122, 124, 128
Stockton Independent, The (CA), 59
Stonewall riot (U.S., 1969), 252, 296–7, 299–300, 303–4, 400, 401; in relation to Seneca Falls and Selma, 251, 288–90, 297–8, 302–3, 304, 305. *See also* Gay Liberation/Rights Movement (U.S.)
South Dakota Historical Society Press, 373
Supreme Court (U.S.). *See* United States Supreme Court

Takpuk, 160–2. *See also* Alaska; oomalik
teaching: university, 267, 269, 380–1, 385, 388n3; as women's wage work during newcomers' settlement of the West, 35, 36, 37, 240, 353; author's at University of Calgary, 2, 6, 13–14, 18, 129, 177, 338, 371 (*See also* University of Calgary); author's at University of Michigan, 262; author's career in, 276, 278, 376–8, 380, 381–3, 386,

391, 392; in Alaska, 145, 150, 154–5, 156 (*See also* Jackson, Sheldon); under second Trump Administration, 282–3, 391, 396–9, 410–1 (*See also* Trump Administration, Second); women university professors, 263–70, 272–4
Texas, 4, 125, 259n5, 306n6, 338, 343, 360–1, 393: annexation of, 99–100; War for Independence from Mexico, 126, 139n23, 345, 362. *See also* Jews; African Americans
Texas A&M University, 325
The Women's West (Armitage/Jameson), 111, 372, 397
Thingvold, Anna, 56
Thompson, Charlotte Small, 127, 139n27, 346
Thompson, David, 127, 139n27, 346
Thompson, Leonard, 112
Thoreau, Henry David, 381
Thornton, Harrison R., 154, 155
Thrupp, Sylvia, 264–5, 273, 278, 280
Tijan, Alois, 316
Tikas, Louis, 205, 211–2, 215, 221, 223, 224n1, 314. *See also* Ludlow Massacre (CO, 1914)
Till, Emmett, 177, 195, 322–3, 326, 327, 328, 332n55
Till-Mobley, Mamie, 322–3, 326, 327. *See also* Till, Emmett
Tilly, Louise A., 279, 282, 380
Timber Culture Act (U.S., 1873), 230, 246n2, 347–8, 364n18
Title IX of the U.S. Educational Amendments of 1972, 251, 261, 262–3, 282. *See also* women's representation: in higher education
Torches Passed and Present Conference (2017), 9n1, 338, 371–6, 378, 379, 381, 386–7. *See also* University of Calgary
Townsend, Emery, 26, 34, 53
Townsend, Susanna, 26, 34–35, 53, 59
Trudeau, Justin, 411–2
Trump Administration, Second, 253, 258–9n3, 340, 382–3, 392–6, 397–410, 411–3; resistance from AHA and 42 other professional organizations, 394–6, 403–4, 413–4n5, 414n11, 416n25, 418n42 (*See also* Harvard University); banned words/phrases, 399, 400–401, 415n21, 415–6n22, 416n23; books banned from U.S. Naval Academy library by, 397–400; detention of foreign university students, 394, 405–7; firing Librarian of Congress, 398; firing National Archivist, 394, 395; firing staff of and cancelling funding for the National

Endowment for the Humanities, 394, 395; opposition to Diversity, Equity and Inclusion (DEI) programs, 382-3, 396-404, 404-9; tariffs against Canadian goods, 393-4, 411-3 (*See also* Canada-U.S. border and borderlands); images removed from government websites by, 401, 416n23; concerns about Smithsonian American Women's History Museum, 402-3
Truth and Reconciliation Commission (CAN), 340; Ludlow Centennial Commemoration Commission, compared to, 320
Tufts University, 406
Turner, Frederick Jackson, 45-66; Canadian border's ill-fit to the theories of, 100-101; challenges to and reasons why, 17-18, 48, 61-2, 104-5, 111 (*See also* New Western History); comparison to Harold Innis, 102-3, 130; explanation of theories and assumptions of, 46-47, 48-49, 52, 53, 55, 56, 60-1, 101-2, 110, 121, 123, 357-8; George F. G. Stanley's views of, 105-7; how Laura Ingalls Wilder's narrative fits theories of, 16-17
Turtle Mountain Reservation. *See* Chippewa
Twain, Mark, 23-24, 25, 27, 30, 32, 38, 39

United Farm Women of Alberta (UFWA), 355-6
United Mine Workers of America (UMWA): Ludlow strike, 78-79, 80-81, 173, 205-6, 210, 211-3, 215, 216, 217, 223-4, 226n26, 313-5, 318-9, 323; Western Federation of Miners (WFM), comparison to, 207, 315, 319; founded, 207; Women's Auxiliary, 212-3
United States Civil War, 125-6, 177, 253, 261, 276, 292-3, 361, 386
United States Commission on Industrial Relations (1912), 209, 212, 217, 323
United States Constitution, 15, 69-70, 289, 394, 396; 1st Amendment, 295, 319, 408; 11th Amendment, 293; 13th Amendment, 253; 14th Amendment, 251, 252, 253, 293; 15th Amendment, 251-2, 253, 293, 307n21; 19th Amendment, 15, 251, 293, 306n7
United States Educational Amendments (1972), 251, 261, 262-3, 282. *See also* Title IX
United States Land Ordinance (1785), 234
United States Park Service, 174, 214-6, 218-9, 220, 221, 227n43, 300-301, 320, 321, 394-5, 400

United States Revolution, 99, 100. *See also* Declaration of Independence
United States Supreme Court, 138n16, 195, 252, 253-4, 258-9n3, 265, 287, 289, 293, 298, 303, 306n6, 319, 408
University of Calgary (CAN), 373, 374, 375: author's community service via, 383; author's invited lecture for English Department, 16-17, 20n9; author's professional affiliations while at, 5-6, 414n12; author's retirement from, 337, 338, 386, 371, 376; author's colleagues at, 93-94, 97, 109, 263, 381-2, 397 (*See also* Carter, Sarah; Francis, R. Douglas; Smith, Donald; Spangler, Jewel); concentration of women in the Humanities, Arts and Education, at, 268-9; graduate programs and students at, 2, 13-14, 113, 266-70, 278, 281, 338, 371, 372-6; gender pay equity at, 263, 268-70, 388n3; maternity and parental leaves at, 269
University of Calgary Press, 8, 411
University of Chicago, 200n16, 264
University of Colorado, 18, 213, 272, 377
University of Denver, 372
University of Michigan, 94, 164, 185, 262, 264, 273-5, 277, 279, 300, 346, 377, 392, 407
University of Minnesota, 270
University of Nebraska, 374, 375
University of Nebraska, Lincoln, 375
University of New Mexico, 1, 196, 276-7, 281; students at, 9n1, 13-14, 95, 338, 371, 372-6
University of North Carolina, Charlotte, 373
University of Pennsylvania, 276, 407, 418
University of Texas, San Antonio, 373
University of Toronto (CAN), 264, 275, 279
University of Victoria (CAN), 374
University of Virginia, 275-6, 282
University of Wisconsin, 72, 373, 374
University of Wisconsin, La Crosse, 276, 382
Unsettled Pasts Conference (2002), 5, 94. *See also* University of Calgary

Valdez family, 205-6, 222-3, 224n1, 314. *See also* Ludlow Massacre (CO, 1914)
Valeriani, Richard, 294, 298
Vance, J. D., 402-3
Van Kirk, Sylvia, 49, 113, 133, 397
Vargas, Zaragosa, 214
Varney, Jotham, 26, 33, 35
Varsanyi, Andrew, 242, 375, 376
Victor and Cripple Creek Daily Press, The (CO), 68, 71, 77-78
Victor Record, The (CO), 71

Vietnam War, 111, 195, 203n60, 377–8; anti-Vietnam War movement, 125, 204n72, 297, 379; Ludlow Massacre monument compared to Vietnam Veterans' Memorial, 213
Voting Rights Act (U.S., 1965), 181, 252, 253–4, 259n4, 259–60n11, 288, 289, 294, 295, 298, 299, 303, 306n6, 306n8, 307n21. *See also* Selma voting rights campaign (U.S., 1965); Civil Rights Movement (U.S.)

Wallace, Jean, 268–9, 284n27
War of 1812, 99
Washington Post (DC), 196, 323, 324, 405
Washington State University, Pullman, 372
Watts riot (1965), 177–8, 182, 295. *See also* Civil Rights Movement (U.S.)
Wayne, John, 108
Weatherford, Will, 324–5
Webb, Walter Prescott, 104, 108, 117n27
Wegman-French, Lysa, 214–5, 218
Welke, Barbara Young 270–1
West, Elliott, 346
Western Federation of Miners (WFM) (later International Union of Mine, Mill and Smelter Workers), 84n4, 85–86n35, 87n64, 377; archives of, 18, 71, 377; Cripple Creek district strikes, 67–69, 70, 72, 73, 74, 78, 83, 127, 207; crossing borders, 139n26; in the Calumet copper miners' strike (MI, 1913-1914), 314–5, 316, 317, 318–9; compared to the United Mine Workers of America, 207, 315, 319; Women's Auxiliary of, 76, 82, 316–7
Western History Association (WHA), 5, 6, 7, 109, 337, 344, 371, 396, 414n12
western homestead colonies, ethnic and religious, 16, 110, 232, 235
"Where Have All the Flowers Gone?" (song), 23, 40n1
White, Richard, 111, 134
Wilder, Laura Ingalls, 16–17, 20n10
Williams, Ida, 238–9, 241
Wilson, Gilbert L., 50–53, 57, 337, 353–4, 357, 358–60. *See also* Mahidiweash
Wilson, Luzena Stanley, 34, 35
Wilson, Woodrow, 206, 272–3
Winfrey, Oprah, 322–3
Wing, May McConaghy, 18, 64n35, 71, 72, 74, 79, 81, 83, 127, 338, 356, 357, 360. *See also* Doran/Welch/Chapman family
Wisconsin State Historical Society, 72
Women Grain Growers (CAN), 355–6

women homesteaders in Canada, 235, 348–50. *See also* Carter, Sarah
women homesteaders in Colorado, Kansas and Wyoming, 56, 57, 232. *See also* Patterson-Black, Sheryll
women homesteaders in North Dakota, 229–48: ages of, 239, 350–1; background of Norwegian, 236, 237, 239; Canadians as, 229–48; ethnicity and citizenship of, 56, 230, 232, 234, 244, 245, 348, 351–2, 365n22, 366n33; H. Elaine Lindgren's research on, 56, 232, 242; marital status of, 232, 239–40, 349–50, 354, 365n27; Métis, 236–8, 243–5, 248n32, 337, 350–2; number of final proof statements, 234, 246–7n7; portion of women's claims in Devils Lake Service Area, 364–5n21; naming convention for territory, 178n1. *See also* Devils Lake region (ND)
Women's Bureau of the Department of Labor (U.S.), 274
Women's Liberation Movement (U.S.), 8, 138n16, 181, 297–8, 300–301, 303, 379
women's representation: in higher education, 261–85 (*See also* Title IX); in history faculties, 267; in history textbooks, 47–48, 270, 345, 346, 347, 361, 364n16, 379, 382, 386
Women's Rights Movement (U.S.): suffrage, 15, 59, 251, 258n2, 292–3, 300–301, 306n7, 346. *See also* Seneca Falls Convention (U.S., 1848)
Woods Investment Company (CO), 76, 77
Wright, Jeremiah, 181, 197–8, 199n2
Wright, Martha Coffin, 290–1
Writing the Range: Race, Class, and Culture in the Women's West (Jameson/Armitage), 13, 372
Woodward, Charlotte, 301, 302

York University (CAN), 374
Young, Marilyn Blatt, 273, 285n33, 377
Young, Mary, 272–3, 285n33

Zimmerman, George, 311, 321, 323, 324, 325, 327. *See also* Martin, Trayvon

www.ingramcontent.com/pod-product-compliance
Lightning Source LLC
Chambersburg PA
CBHW041310240426
43661CB00065B/2889